**urseMate** **Engaging. Trackable. Aff**

Course Mate brings course concepts to life with interactive learning, study, and exam preparation tools that support *Survey of ECON*.

INCLUDES:

Integrated eBook, Interactive teaching and learning tools, and Engagement Tracker, a first-of-its-kind tool that monitors student engagement in the course.

ON THE
WEB

SURVEY OF
ECON
Are you in?

ON LINE RESOURCES INCLUDED!

FOR INSTRUCTORS:
- First Day of Class Instructions
- Custom Options through 4LTR+ Program
- Instructor's Manual
- Test Bank
- PowerPoint® Slides
- Instructor Prep Cards
- Student Review Cards
- Engagement Tracker

FOR STUDENTS:
- Interactive eBook
- Interactive Quizzes
- Flashcards
- Videos
- Global Economic Watch
- Graphing Workshop
- Economic Applications

Students sign in at **login.cengagebrain.com**

SOUTH-WESTERN
CENGAGE Learning

Survey of ECON, 2011–2012 Edition
Robert L. Sexton

Vice President of Editorial, Business:
 Jack W. Calhoun

Publisher: Joe Sabatino

Senior Acquisitions Editor: Steven Scoble

Supervising Developmental Editor:
 Katie Yanos

Developmental Editor: David Ferrell,
 B-books, Ltd.

Product Development Manager,
 4LTR Press: Steven E. Joos

Executive Brand Marketing Manager,
 4LTR Press: Robin Lucas

Senior Marketing Manager: John Carey

Associate Marketing Manager: Betty Jung

Marketing Communications Manager:
 Sarah Greber

Production Director: Amy McGuire,
 B-books, Ltd.

Content Project Manager: Corey Geissler

Media Editor: Deepak Kumar

Senior Print Buyer: Sandee Milewski

Production Service: B-books, Ltd.

Senior Art Director: Michelle Kunkler

Cover and Internal Design: Ke Design

Cover Image: © Kamalova/images.com

Photo Researcher: Sam Marshall

For product information and technology assistance, contact us at
Cengage Learning Academic Resource Center, 1-800-423-0563

For permission to use material from this text or product,
submit all requests online at **www.cengage.com/permissions**
Further permissions questions can be emailed to
permissionrequest@cengage.com

Library of Congress Control Number: 2010934321

ISBN-13: 978-0-53847-809-0
ISBN-10: 0-538-47809-8

South-Western Cengage Learning
5191 Natorp Boulevard
Mason, OH 45040
USA

Cengage Learning products are represented in Canada by
Nelson Education, Ltd.

For your course and learning solutions, visit **www.cengage.com**
Purchase any of our products at your local college store or at our
preferred online store **www.cengagebrain.com**

Printed in the United States of America
1 2 3 4 5 6 7 13 12 11 10

BRIEF CONTENTS

CONTENTS

PART TWO
MICROECONOMICS 110

6 Production and Costs 110

7 Firms in Competitive Markets 128

8 Monopoly 148

9 Monopolistic Competition and Oligopoly 168

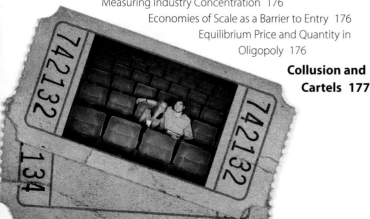

10 Labor Markets, Income Distribution, and Poverty 190

PART THREE
MACROECONOMICS 212

11 Introduction to Macroeconomics: Unemployment, Inflation, and Economic Fluctuations 212

12 Economic Growth 236

13 Aggregate Demand and Aggregate Supply 260

14 Fiscal Policy 282

15 Monetary Institutions 306

16 The Federal Reserve and Monetary Policy 326

17 Issues in Macroeconomic Theory and Policy 348

18 International Economics 370

Index 401

There's nothing like a global

financial crisis to bring economists out of the woodwork. If you followed the news, you probably heard many experts try to give explanations of what happened and what should be done about it. And even if you didn't, it would be difficult to ignore the changes going on around you: maybe you had a harder time getting student loans this year, or maybe you had a harder time getting a job last summer. Seem confusing? A study of economics can help.

I

The Role and Method of Economics

as you begin your first course in economics, you may be asking yourself why you're here. What does economics have to do with your life?

Although we can list many good reasons to study economics, perhaps the best reason is that many issues in our lives are at least partly economic in character. A good understanding of economics would allow you to answer such questions as: Why do 10 A.M. classes fill up more quickly than 8 A.M. classes during registration? Why is it so hard to find an apartment in cities such as San Francisco, Berkeley, and New York? Why is teenage unemployment higher than adult unemployment? Why is the price of your prescription drugs so high? How does inflation impact you and your family? Will higher taxes on cigarettes reduce the number of teenagers smoking? If so, by how much? Why do female models make more than male models? Why is it easier for college graduates to find jobs in some years rather than others? Why do U.S. auto producers like tariffs (taxes) on imported cars? Is outsourcing jobs to India a good idea? Is globalization good for the economy? The study of economics improves your understanding of these and many other concerns.

Economics is a unique way of analyzing many areas of human behavior. Indeed, the range of topics to which economic analysis can be applied is broad. Many researchers discover that the economic approach to human behavior sheds light on social problems that have been with us for a long time: discrimination, education, crime, divorce, political favoritism, and more. In fact, your daily newspaper is filled with economics. You can find economics on the domestic page, the international page, the business page, the sports page, the entertainment page, and even the weather page—economics is all around us.

However, before we delve into the details and models of economics, it is important that we present an overview of how economists approach problems—their methodology. How does an economist apply the logic of science to approach a problem? And what are the pitfalls that economists should avoid in economic thinking? We also discuss why economists disagree.

Ⓢ1 Economics: A Brief Introduction

Keep the following questions in mind as you read through this section. You'll find the answers in **Section Check 1**.

1.1 What is economics?

1.2 What is scarcity?

1.3 What are goods and services?

The study of economics is concerned with the choices we make when confronted with resource scarcity.

ECONOMICS—A WORD WITH MANY DIFFERENT MEANINGS

Some individuals think economics involves the study of the stock market and corporate finance, and it does—in part. Others think that economics is concerned with the wise use of money and other matters of personal finance, and it is—in part. Still others think that economics involves forecasting or predicting what business conditions will be like in the future, and again, it does—in part. The word *economics* is, after all, derived from the Greek word *oikonomicos*, which referred to the management of household affairs.

Precisely defined, **economics** is the study of the choices we make among our many wants and desires given our limited resources. What are resources? **Resources** are inputs—land, human effort and skills, and machines and factories, for instance—used to produce goods and services. The problem is that our unlimited wants exceed our limited resources, a fact that we call **scarcity**. Scarcity forces us to decide how to best use our limited resources. This is **the economic problem**: Scarcity forces us to choose, and choices are costly because we must give up other opportunities that we value. Consumers must make choices on what to buy, how much to save, and how much to invest of their limited incomes. Workers must decide what types of jobs they want, when to enter the workforce, where they will work, and the number of hours they wish to work. Firms must decide what kinds of products to produce, how much to produce, and how to produce those goods and services at the lowest cost. Local governments may have to decide between building a new park or a school. That is, consumers, workers, firms, and the government all face choices because of scarcity.

SCARCITY AND UNLIMITED HUMAN WANTS

We may want "essential" items such as food, clothing, schooling, and health care. We may want many other items, such as vacations, cars, computers, and concert tickets. We may want more friendship, love, knowledge, and so on. We also may have many goals—perhaps an A in this class, a college education, and a great job. Unfortunately, people are not able to fulfill all their wants and desires, material and nonmaterial. And as long as human wants exceed available resources, scarcity will exist.

SCARCITY AND LIMITED RESOURCES

The scarce resources used in the production of goods and services can be grouped into four categories: labor, land, capital, and entrepreneurship.

Labor is the total of both physical and mental effort expended by people in the production of goods and services. The services of a teacher, nurse, cosmetic surgeon, professional golfer, and electrician all fall under the general category of labor.

Land includes the "gifts of nature," or the natural resources, used in the production of goods and services. Economists consider land to include trees, animals, water, minerals, and so on, along with the physical space we normally think of as land.

Capital is the equipment and structures used to produce goods and services. Office buildings, tools, machines, and factories are all considered capital goods. When we invest in factories, machines, research and development, or education, we increase the potential to create more goods and services in the future. Capital also includes **human capital**—the productive

economics the study of choices we make among our many wants and desires given our limited resources

resources inputs used to produce goods and services

scarcity exists when human wants (material and nonmaterial) exceed available resources

the economic problem scarcity forces us to choose, and choices are costly because we must give up other opportunities that we value

labor the physical and human effort used in the production of goods and services

land the natural resources used in the production of goods and services

capital the equipment and structures used to produce goods and services

human capital the productive knowledge and skill people receive from education, on-the-job training, health, and other factors that increase productivity

knowledge and skill people receive from education and on-the-job training.

Entrepreneurship is the process of combining labor, land, and capital to produce goods and services. Entrepreneurs make the tough and risky decisions about what and how to produce goods and services. Entrepreneurs are always looking for new ways to improve production techniques or to create new products. They are lured by the chance of making a profit. It is this opportunity to make a profit that leads entrepreneurs to take risks.

However, not every entrepreneur is a Bill Gates (Microsoft) or a Henry Ford (Ford Motor Company). In some sense, we are all entrepreneurs when we try new products or when we find better ways to manage our households or our study time. Rather than money, then, our profits might take the form of greater enjoyment, additional time for recreation, or better grades.

WHAT ARE GOODS AND SERVICES?

Goods are the items that we value or desire. Goods tend to be **tangible**—objects that can be seen, held, tasted, or smelled like shirts, pizzas, and perfume. But other goods that we cannot reach out and touch are called **intangible goods**. Intangible goods include fairness for all, friendship, leisure, knowledge, security, prestige, respect, and health.

Services are intangible acts for which people are willing to pay, such as haircuts, dental cleanings, legal counsel, medical care, and education. Services are intangible because they are less overtly visible, but they are certainly no less valuable than goods.

All goods and services, whether tangible or intangible, are produced from scarce resources and can be subjected to economic analysis. Scarce goods created from scarce resources are called **economic goods**. These goods are *desirable but limited* in supply. Without enough economic goods for all of us, we are forced to compete. That is, scarcity

entrepreneurship the process of combining labor, land, and capital to produce goods and services

goods items we value or desire

tangible goods items we value or desire that we can reach out and touch

intangible goods goods that we cannot reach out and touch, such as friendship and knowledge

services intangible items of value provided to consumers, such as education

economic goods scarce goods created from scarce resources—goods that are desirable but limited in supply

Capital

Land

Labor

Entrepreneurship

bads items that we do not desire or want, where less is preferred to more, such as terrorism, smog, or poison oak

ultimately leads to competition for the available goods and services, a subject we will return to often in this text.

What Are Bads?

In contrast to goods, **bads** are those items that we do not desire or want. For most people, garbage, pollution, weeds, and crime are bads. People tend to eliminate or minimize bads, so they will often pay to have bads, such as garbage, removed. The elimination of the bad—garbage removal, for example—is a good.

DOES EVERYONE FACE SCARCITY?

We all face scarcity because we cannot have all the goods and services we desire. However, because we all have different wants and desires, scarcity affects everyone differently. For example, a child in a developing country may face a scarcity of food and clean drinking water, while a rich man in Beverly Hills may face a scarcity of garage space for his growing antique car collection. Likewise, a harried middle-class working mother may find time for exercise particularly

scarce, while a pharmaceutical company may be concerned with the scarcity of the natural resources it uses in its production process. Its effects may vary, but no one can escape scarcity.

We often hear it said of rich people that "he has everything" or "she can buy anything she wants." Actually, even the richest person must live with scarcity and must, at some point, choose one want or desire over another. And of course, we all have only 24 hours in a day! The problem is that as we become more affluent, we learn of new luxuries to provide us with satisfaction. Wealth, then, creates a new set of wants to be satisfied. No evidence indicates that people would not find a valuable use for additional income, no matter how rich they became. Even the wealthy individual who decides to donate all her money to charity faces the constraints of scarcity. If she had greater resources, she could do still more for others.

WILL SCARCITY EVER BE ERADICATED?

It is probably clear by now that scarcity never has and never will be eradicated. The same creativity that develops new methods to produce goods and services in greater quantities also reveals new wants. Fashions are always changing. Clothes and shoes that are "in" one year will likely be "out" the next. New wants quickly replace old ones. It is also quite possible that over a period of time, a rising quantity of goods and services will not increase human happiness. Why? Because our wants may grow as fast as—if not faster than—our ability to meet those wants.

"I think I'll give all my money to the Gates Foundation.

With a net worth of $37 billion, even Warren Buffett must contend with scarcity. He may wish he could do even more for others, if he only had more resources. He, like everyone else, only has 24 hours in a day, so when he chooses to do something with his time, he presumably gives up something else he could have done that has value.

SECTION CHECK 1

1.1 Economics is the study of the choices we make among our many wants and desires, given our limited resources. It is a problem-solving science that concerns itself with the choices we make in the face of scarcity.

1.2 Scarcity is the fact that our unlimited wants exceed our limited resources, so we must make choices.

1.3 Goods and services are things we value. They can be tangible (e.g., food, shelter) or intangible (e.g., love, compassion, intelligence).

ⓢ2 Economic Behavior

Keep the following questions in mind as you read through this section. You'll find the answers in **Section Check 2**.

2.1 How is self-interest relevant to economics?

2.2 What is rational behavior?

2.3 Can we predict how people will respond to changes in incentives?

Economic behavior is usually determined by self-interest and rational behavior, which can help in predicting how people will react to changes in incentives.

SELF-INTEREST

Economists assume that individuals act *as if* they are motivated by self-interest and respond in predictable ways to changing circumstances. In other words, self-interest is a good predictor of human behavior in most situations. For example, to a worker, self-interest means pursuing a higher-paying job and/ or better working conditions. To a consumer, it means gaining a higher level of satisfaction from limited income and time.

We seldom observe employees asking employers to cut their wages and increase their workload to increase a company's profits. Or how often do you think customers walk into a supermarket demanding to pay more for their groceries? In short, a great deal of human behavior can be explained and predicted by assuming people act as if they are motivated by their own self-interest.

There is no question that self-interest is a powerful force that motivates people to produce goods and services. But self-interest can include benevolence. Think of the late Mother Teresa, who spent her life caring for others. One could say that her work was in her self-

interest, but who would consider her actions selfish? Similarly, workers may be acting in self-interest when they choose to work harder and longer to increase their charitable giving or saving for their children's education. That is, self-interest to an economist is not a narrow monetary self-interest. A person acting in self-interest might pursue personal gain, but that does not necessarily exclude helping others.

In the United States, people typically give more than $250 billion annually to charities. They also pay more money for environmentally friendly goods. Consumers can derive utility or satisfaction from these choices. It is clearly not selfish—it is in their best interest to care about the environment and those who are less fortunate than themselves.

> **rational behavior** people do the best they can, based on their values and information, under current and anticipated future circumstances

WHAT IS RATIONAL BEHAVIOR?

Economists assume that people, for the most part, engage in rational behavior. Now, you might think that could not possibly apply to your brother, sister, or roommates. But the key is in the definition. To an economist, **rational behavior** merely means that people do

Enormous amounts of resources (time and money) were donated to the Hurricane Katrina victims. If individuals are acting to promote the things that interest them, are these self-interested acts necessarily selfish? Acting in one's own self-interest is only selfish if one's interests are selfish.

© LEE CELANO/REUTERS/LANDOV

market the process of buyers and sellers exchanging goods and services

the best they can, based on their values and information, under current and anticipated future circumstances. It is even rational when people make choices they later regret, because they have limited information. Rational behavior applies to the actions people take to pursue their own goals—whatever those goals may be—and they need not be materialistic or widely shared. Therefore, rational behavior applies to criminals and people who dedicate their lives to caring for others. In addition, rational behavior does not mean that people do not make mistakes, but it does mean that people learn from past mistakes and that their decisions in the future reflect that information. That is, they do not keep making the same mistake.

In short, rational individuals weigh the benefits and costs of their actions, and they only pursue actions if they perceive the benefits to be greater than the costs. We will discuss this concept more thoroughly in the next chapter.

PEOPLE RESPOND TO CHANGES IN INCENTIVES

Because most people are seeking opportunities to make themselves better off, they respond to changes in incentives. That is, they are reacting to changes in benefits and costs. In fact, much of human behavior can be explained and predicted as a response to incentives. In the words of Levitt and Dubner, the authors of *SuperFreakonomics*, "People are people and they respond to incentives. They can nearly always be manipulated for good or ill, if only you find the right levers."

For example, a tax on cars that emit lots of pollution (an increase in costs) would be a negative incentive that would lead to a reduction in emitted pollution. On the other hand, a subsidy (the opposite of a tax) on hybrid cars—part electric, part internal combustion—would be a positive incentive that would encourage greater production and consumption of hybrid cars. Human behavior is influenced in predictable ways by such changes in economic incentives, and economists use this information to predict what will happen when the benefits and costs of any choice are changed.

Because most people seek opportunities that make them better off, we can predict what will happen when incentives are changed. If salaries increase for engineers and decrease for MBAs, we would predict fewer people would go to graduate school in business and more would go into engineering. A permanent change to a

much higher price of gasoline would lead us to expect fewer gas-guzzling SUVs on the highway. People who work on commission tend to work harder. If the price of downtown parking increased, we would predict that commuters would look for alternative methods to get to work that would save money. If households were taxed for water consumption in an attempt to conserve water, economists would expect people to use less water, and to use substantially less water than if they were simply asked to conserve water. Incentives matter.

SECTION CHECK 2

2.1 Economists assume that people act as if they are motivated by self-interest and respond predictably to changing circumstances.

2.2 Rational behavior means that people do the best they can based on their values and information, under current and future anticipated consequences.

2.3 People respond to incentives in predictable ways.

Ⓢ3 Markets

Keep the following questions in mind as you read through this section. You'll find the answers in **Section Check 3**.

3.1 How does a market economy allocate scarce resources?

3.2 What is a market failure?

3.3 What are product and factor markets?

3.4 What is the circular flow model?

Let's look at markets, how they allocate resources, and what happens when they fail. We'll then examine a model that illustrates market activities.

Although we usually think of a market as a place where some sort of exchange occurs, a market is not really a place at all. A **market** is the process of buyers and sellers exchanging goods and services. Supermarkets, the New York Stock Exchange, drug stores, roadside stands, garage sales, Internet stores, and restaurants are all markets.

Every market is different. That is, the conditions under which the exchange between buyers and sellers takes place can vary. These differences make it difficult to precisely define a market.

HOW DOES THE MARKET WORK TO ALLOCATE SCARCE RESOURCES?

Collectively, our wants far exceed what can be produced from nature's scarce resources. So how should we allocate those scarce resources? Some methods of resource allocation might seem bad and counterproductive—for example, the "survival of the fittest" competition that takes place on the floor of the jungle. Physical violence has been used since the beginning of time, as people, regions, and countries attacked one another to gain control over resources. We could argue that government should allocate scarce resources on the basis of equal shares or according to need. However, this approach poses problems because of diverse individual preferences, the difficulty of ascertaining needs, and the negative work and investment incentives involved. In reality, society is made up of many approaches to resource allocation. For now, we will focus on one form of allocating goods and services found in most countries—the market economy.

The market economy provides a way for millions of producers and consumers to allocate scarce resources. For the most part, markets are efficient. To an economist, **efficiency** is achieved when the economy gets the most out of its scarce resources. In short, efficiency makes the economic pie as large as possible.

efficiency when an economy gets the most out of its scarce resources

Competitive markets are powerful—they can make existing products better and/or less expensive, they can improve production processes, and they can create new products, from video games to life-saving drugs. Buyers and sellers indicate their wants through their action and inaction in the marketplace, and it is this collective "voice" that determines how resources are allocated. But how is this information communicated? Market prices serve as the language of the market system. By understanding what these market prices mean, you can get a better understanding of the vital function that the market economy performs.

Markets may not always lead to your desired tastes and preferences. You may think that markets produce too many pet rocks, chia pets, breast enhancements, and face lifts. Some markets are illegal, such as the market for cocaine, the market for stolen body parts, the market for child pornography, and the market for pirated music. Markets do not come with a moral compass; they simply provide what buyers are willing and able to pay for and what sellers are willing and able to produce.

> Competitive markets are powerful, helping to make existing products better, improve production processes, and even create new products.

MARKET PRICES PROVIDE IMPORTANT INFORMATION

Market prices communicate important information to both buyers and sellers. These prices communicate information about the relative availability of products to buyers, and they provide sellers with critical information about the relative value that consumers place on those products. In short, buyers look at the price and decide how much they are willing and able to demand and sellers look at the price and decide how much they are able and willing to supply. The market price reflects the value a buyer places on a good and the cost to society of producing that good. Thus, market prices provide a way for both buyers and sellers to communicate about the relative value of resources. To paraphrase Adam Smith, prices adjust like an "invisible hand" to direct buyers and sellers to an outcome that is socially desirable. We will see how this works beginning in Chapter 3.

The basis of a market economy is voluntary exchange and the price system that guides people's choices and produces solutions to the questions of what goods to produce and how to produce and distribute them.

Take something as simple as the production of a pencil. Where did the wood come from? Perhaps the Northwest or Georgia. The graphite may have come from the mines in Michigan and the rubber may be from Malaysia. The paint, the glue, the metal piece that holds the eraser—who knows? The point is that market forces coordinated this production activity among literally thousands of people, some of whom live in different countries and speak different languages. The market brought these people together to make a pencil that sells for 25

Wood—Georgia

cents at your bookstore. It all happened because the market economy provided the incentive for people to pursue activities that benefit others. This same process produces millions of goods and services around the world, from automobiles and computers to pencils and paper clips.

The same is true of the iPod and iPhone. The entrepreneurs of Apple have learned how to combine almost 500 generic parts to make something of much greater value. The whole is greater than the sum of the parts.

COUNTRIES THAT DO NOT RELY ON A MARKET SYSTEM

Countries that do not rely on the market system have no clear communication between buyers and sellers. The former Soviet Union, where quality was virtually nonexistent, experienced many shortages of quality goods and surpluses of low-quality goods. For example, thousands of tractors had no spare parts and millions of pairs of shoes were left on shelves because the sizes did not match those of the population. Before the breakup of the Soviet Union, one of President Reagan's favorite stories was about a man who goes to the Soviet Bureau of Transportation to order an automobile. He is informed that he will have to put down his

market failure when the economy fails to allocate resources efficiently on its own

Graphite—Michigan

money now, but there is a 10-year wait. The man fills out all the various forms, has them processed through the various agencies, and finally he gets to the last agency. He pays them his money and they say, "Come back in 10 years and get your car." He asks, "Morning or afternoon?" The man from the agency says, "We're talking 10 years from now. What is the difference?" He replies, "The plumber is coming in the morning."

MARKET FAILURE

The market mechanism is a simple but effective and efficient general means of allocating resources among alternative uses. When the economy fails to allocate resources efficiently on its own, however, it is known as **market failure**. For example, a steel mill might put soot and other forms of "crud" into the air as a by-product of making steel. When it does, it imposes costs on others not connected with using or producing steel from the steel mill. The soot may require homeowners to paint their homes more often, entailing a cost. And studies show that respiratory diseases are greater in areas with more severe air pollution, imposing costs that may even include life itself. In addition, the steel mill might

Rubber—Malaysia

discharge chemicals into a stream, thus killing wildlife and spoiling recreational activities for the local population. In this case, the steel factory does not bear the costs of its polluting actions, and it continues to emit too much pollution. In other words, by transferring the pollution costs onto society, the firm lowers its costs of production and so produces more than the ideal output—which is inefficient because it is an overallocation of resources.

Markets sometimes produce too little of a good—research, for example. Therefore, the government might decide to subsidize promising scientific research that could benefit many people—such as cancer research. When one party prevents other parties from participating in mutually beneficial exchange, it also causes a market failure. This situation occurs in a monopoly, with its single seller of goods. Because the monopolist can raise its end price above the competitive price, some potential consumers are kept from buying the goods they would have bought at the lower price, and inefficiency occurs. Whether the market economy has produced too little (underallocation) or too much (overallocation), the government can improve society's well-being by intervening. The case of market failure will be taken up in more detail in Chapter 5.

We cannot depend on the market economy to always communicate accurately. Some firms may have market power to distort prices in their favor. For example, the only regional cement company in the area has the ability to charge a higher price and provide lower-quality services than if the company were in a highly competitive market. In this case, the lack of competition can lead to higher prices and reduced product quality. And without adequate information, unscrupulous producers may be able to misrepresent their products to the disadvantage of unwary consumers.

In sum, government can help promote efficiency when there is a market failure—making the economic pie larger.

Does the Market Distribute Income Fairly?

Sometimes a painful trade-off exists between how much an economy can produce efficiently and how that output is distributed—the degree of equality. An efficient market rewards those that produce goods and services that others are willing and able to buy. But this does not guarantee a "fair" or equal distribution of income. That is, how the economic pie is divided up. A market economy cannot guarantee everyone adequate amounts of food, shelter, and health care. In other words, not only does the market determine what goods are going to be produced and in what quantities, but it also determines the distribution of output among members of society.

As with other aspects of government intervention, the degree-of-equity argument can generate some sharp disagreements. What is "fair" for one person may seem highly "unfair" to someone else. One person may find it terribly unfair for some individuals to earn many times the amount earned by other individuals who work equally hard, and another person may find it highly unfair to ask one group, the relatively rich, to pay a much higher proportion of their income in taxes than another group pays.

Government Is Not Always the Solution

However, just because the government could improve the situation does not mean it will. After all, the political process has its own set of problems, such as special interests, shortsightedness, and imperfect information. For example, government may reduce competition through tariffs and quotas, or it may impose inefficient regulations that restrict entry. That is, there is government failure as well as market failure.

THE CIRCULAR FLOW MODEL

How do we explain how the millions of people in an economy interact when it comes to buying, selling, producing, working, hiring, and so on? A continuous flow of goods and services is bought and sold between the producers of goods and services (which we call firms) and the buyers of goods and services (which we call households). A continuous flow of income also moves from firms to households as firms buy inputs to produce the goods and services they sell. In our simple economy, these exchanges take place in product markets and factor markets.

PRODUCT MARKETS

Product markets are the markets for consumer goods and services. In the product market, households are buyers and firms are sellers. Households buy the goods and services that firms produce and sell. The payments from the households to the firms for the purchases of goods and services flow to the firms at the same time as goods and services flow to the households.

FACTOR MARKETS

Factor or **input markets** are markets in which households sell the use of their inputs (capital, land, labor, and entrepreneurship) to firms. In the factor market, households are the sellers and firms are the buyers. Households receive money payments from firms as compensation for the labor, land, capital, and entrepreneurship needed to produce goods and services. These payments take the form of wages (salaries), rent, interest payments, and profit.

EXHIBIT 1.1 The Circular Flow Diagram

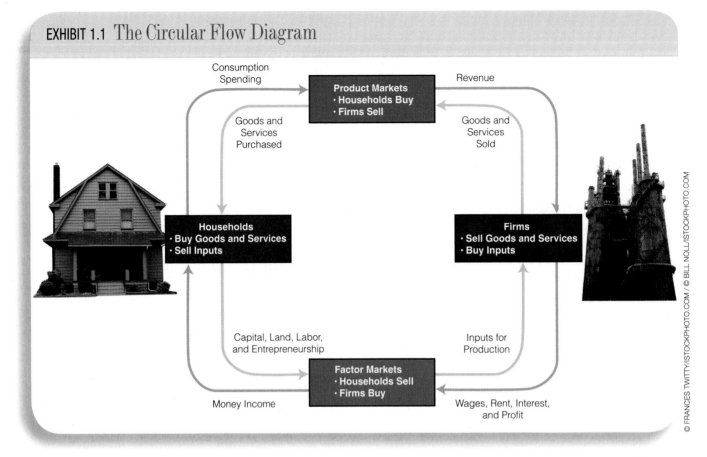

The Circular Flow Diagram. Consumption Spending → Product Markets (Households Buy, Firms Sell) → Revenue. Goods and Services Purchased; Goods and Services Sold. Households (Buy Goods and Services, Sell Inputs); Firms (Sell Goods and Services, Buy Inputs). Capital, Land, Labor, and Entrepreneurship; Inputs for Production. Factor Markets (Households Sell, Firms Buy). Money Income; Wages, Rent, Interest, and Profit.

© FRANCES TWITTY/ISTOCKPHOTO.COM / © BILL NOLL/ISTOCKPHOTO.COM

THE SIMPLE CIRCULAR FLOW MODEL

The **simple circular flow model** is illustrated in Exhibit 1.1. In the top half of the exhibit, the product markets, households purchase goods and services that firms have produced. In the lower half of the exhibit, the factor (or input) markets, households sell the inputs that firms use to produce goods and services. Households receive income (wages, rent, interest, and profit) from firms for the inputs used in production (capital, land, labor, and entrepreneurship).

Let's take a simple example to see how the circular flow model works. Suppose a teacher's supply of labor generates personal income in the form of wages (the factor market), which she can use to buy automobiles, vacations, food, and other goods (the product market). Suppose she buys an automobile (product market); the automobile dealer now has revenue to pay for his inputs (factor market)—wages to workers, purchase of new cars to replenish his inventory, rent for his building, and so on. So we see that in the simple

simple circular flow model an illustration of the continuous flow of goods, services, inputs, and payments between firms and households

circular flow model, income flows from firms to households (factor markets), and spending flows from households to firms (product markets). The simple circular flow model shows how households and firms interact in product markets and factor markets and how the two markets are interrelated.

SECTION CHECK 3

3.1 Markets provide what buyers are willing and able to pay for and what sellers are willing and able to produce.

3.2 A market failure is said to occur when the economy is unable to allocate resources efficiently on its own.

3.3 In the product market, households are buyers and firms are sellers. In the factor market, households are sellers and firms are buyers.

3.4 The circular flow model illustrates the flow of goods, services, and payments among firms and households.

Ⓢ4 Economic Theory

Keep the following questions in mind as you read through this section. You'll find the answers in **Section Check 4**.

4.1 What are economic theories?

4.2 Why do we need to abstract?

4.3 What is a hypothesis?

4.4 What are microeconomics and macroeconomics?

Here we'll examine economic theories, what they are, how they're developed, and how they're used.

ECONOMIC THEORIES

A **theory** is an established explanation that accounts for known facts or phenomena. Specifically, economic theories are statements or propositions about patterns of human behavior that occur expectedly under certain circumstances. These theories help us sort out and understand the complexities of economic behavior and guide our analysis. We expect a good theory to explain and predict well. A good economic theory, then, should help us better understand and, ideally, predict human economic behavior.

ABSTRACTION IS IMPORTANT

Economic theories cannot realistically include every event that has ever occurred. A theory weeds out the irrelevant facts from the relevant ones. We must abstract. A road map of the United States may not include every creek, ridge, and gully between Los Angeles and Chicago; indeed, such an all-inclusive map would be too large and too detailed to be of value. A road map designating major interstate highways will provide enough information to travel by car from Los Angeles to Chicago. Likewise, an economic theory is

more useful when it ignores the details that are not relevant to the questions that are being investigated.

Without abstraction or simplification, the world is too complex to analyze. For the same reason, economists make a number of simplifying assumptions in their models. Sometimes economists make very strong assumptions, such as that all people seek self-betterment or all firms attempt to maximize profits. Of course, this may not hold for every single person or firm. Only when we test our models using these assumptions do we find out if they were too simplified or too limiting.

> **theory** a statement or proposition used to explain and predict behavior in the real world
>
> **hypothesis** a testable proposition

DEVELOPING A TESTABLE PROPOSITION

The beginning of any theory is a **hypothesis**, a testable proposition that makes some type of prediction about behavior in response to certain changes in conditions based on our assumptions. In economic theory, a hypothesis is a testable prediction about how people will behave or react to a change in economic circumstances.

MUCH LIKE A ROAD MAP OF THE U.S., AN ECONOMIC THEORY IGNORES DETAILS THAT ARE NOT RELEVANT TO THE QUESTION AT HAND.

For example, if we notice an increase in the price of DVDs, we might hypothesize that sales of DVDs will drop, or if the price of DVDs decreases, our hypothesis might be that DVD sales will rise. Once we state our hypothesis, we test it by comparing what it predicts will happen to what actually happens.

Using Empirical Analysis

To determine whether our hypothesis is valid, we must engage in **empirical analysis**. That is, we must examine the data to see whether our hypothesis fits well with the facts. If the hypothesis is consistent with real-world observations, we can accept it; if it does not fit well with the facts, we must "go back to the drawing board."

Determining whether a hypothesis is acceptable is more difficult in economics than it is in the natural or physical sciences. Chemists, for example, can observe chemical reactions under laboratory conditions. They can alter the environment to meet the assumptions of the hypothesis and can readily manipulate the variables (chemicals, temperatures, and so on) crucial to the proposed relationship. Such controlled experimentation is seldom possible in economics. The laboratory of economists is usually the real world. Unlike chemists in their labs, economists cannot easily control all the variables that might influence human behavior.

Economists are reluctant to use survey data because of the huge variance between how people say they behave and how they actually behave. Economists prefer to measure actual behavior, or revealed preference, not declared preference.

From Hypothesis to Theory

After gathering their data, economic researchers must evaluate the results to determine whether their hypothesis is supported or refuted. If supported, the hypothesis can be tentatively accepted as an economic theory.

Every economic theory is on life-long probation; the hypothesis underlying an economic theory is constantly being tested against empirical findings. Do the observed findings support the prediction? When a hypothesis survives a number of tests, it is accepted until it no longer predicts well.

SCIENCE AND STORIES

Much of scientific discovery is expressed in terms of stories, not unlike the stories told by writers of novels. This similarity is not accidental. The novelist tries to persuade us that a story could be true; the scientist tries to persuade us that certain events fall into a certain meaningful pattern. The scientist does not (or is not supposed to) invent the underlying "facts" of the story, whereas the novelist is not so constrained. However, a scientist does select *certain* facts from among many facts that could have been chosen, just as the novelist chooses from an infinite number of possible characters and situations to make the story most persuasive. In both cases, the author "invents" the story. Therefore, we should not be surprised to find order in economic theory any more than we are surprised to find order in a good novel. Scientists would not bother to write about "life" if they were not convinced that they had stories worth telling.

What makes a story "worth telling?" When we look for order in nature, we cannot suppose that the "facts" are a sufficient basis for understanding observed events. The basic problem is that the facts of a complex world simply do not organize themselves. Understanding requires that a *conceptual order* be imposed on these "facts" to counteract the confusion that would otherwise result. For example, to interpret the impact of rising housing prices on the amount of housing desired, economists must separate out the impact of increasing wealth, population, and other contributing factors. Failing to do so would obscure the central insight that people tend to buy less housing at higher prices. Without a story—a theory of causation—scientists could not sort out and understand the complex reality that surrounds us. In short, theory is how we attempt to make order out of a nearly infinite number of events.

THE *CETERIS PARIBUS* ASSUMPTION

Virtually all economic theories share a condition usually expressed by the Latin phrase **ceteris paribus**. A rough translation of the phrase is "letting everything else be equal" or "holding everything else constant." When economists try to assess the effect of one variable on another, they must keep the relationship between the two variables isolated from other events that might also influence the situation that the theory tries to explain or predict. The following example should make this concept clearer.

Suppose you develop your own theory describing the relationship between studying and exam performance: If I study harder, I will perform better on the test. That sounds logical, right? Holding other things constant (*ceteris paribus*), your theory is likely to be true. However, what if you studied harder but inadvertently overslept the day of the exam? What if you were so sleepy during the test that you could not think clearly? Or what if you studied the wrong material? Although it might look like additional studying did not improve your performance, the real problem could lie in the impact of other variables, such as sleep deficiency or how you studied.

WHY DO ECONOMISTS PREDICT ON A GROUP LEVEL?

Economists' predictions usually refer to the collective behavior of large groups rather than to that of specific individuals. Why is this? Looking at the behaviors of a large group allows economists to discern general patterns of actions. For example, consider what would happen if the price of air travel from the United States to Europe was reduced drastically, say from $1,000 to $400, because of the invention of a more fuel-efficient jet. What type of predictions could we make about the effect of this price reduction on the buying habits of typical consumers?

What Does Individual Behavior Tell Us?

Let's look first at the responses of individuals. As a result of the price drop, some people will greatly increase their intercontinental travel, taking theater weekends in London or week-long trips to France to indulge in French food. Some people, however, are terribly afraid to fly, and the price reduction will not influence their behavior in the slightest. Others might detest Europe and, despite the lowered airfares, prefer to spend a few days in Aspen, Colorado, instead. A few people might respond to the airfare reduction in precisely the opposite way from ours: At the lower fare, they might make fewer trips to Europe, because they might believe (rightly or wrongly) that the price drop would be accompanied by a reduction in the quality of service, greater crowding, or reduced safety. In short, we cannot predict with any level of certainty how a given individual will respond to this airfare reduction.

What Does Group Behavior Tell Us?

Group behavior is often more predictable than individual behavior. When the weather gets colder, more firewood will be sold. Some individuals may not buy firewood, but we can predict with great accuracy that a group of individuals will establish a pattern of buying more firewood. Similarly, while we cannot say what each individual will do, within a group of persons, we can predict with great accuracy that more flights to Europe from Los Angeles will be sold at lower prices than at higher prices, holding other things such as income and preferences constant. We cannot predict exactly how many more airline tickets will be sold at $400 than at $1,000, but we can predict the direction of the impact and approximate the extent of the impact. By observing the relationship between the price of goods and services and the quantities people purchase in different places and during different time periods, it is possible to make some reliable generalizations about how much people will react to changes in the prices of goods and services. Economists use this larger picture of the group for most of their theoretical analysis.

microeconomics the study of household and firm behavior and how they interact in the marketplace

THE TWO BRANCHES OF ECONOMICS: MICROECONOMICS AND MACROECONOMICS

Conventionally, we distinguish two main branches of economics: microeconomics and macroeconomics. **Microeconomics** deals with the smaller units within the

MICROECONOMICS

© ISTOCKPHOTO.COM / JAY SPOONER/ISTOCKPHOTO.COM

macroeconomics the study of the whole economy, including the topics of inflation, unemployment, and economic growth

aggregate the total amount—such as the aggregate level of output

correlation when two events occur together

causation when one event brings about another event

MACROECONOMICS

economy, attempting to understand the decision-making behavior of firms and households and their interaction in markets for particular goods or services. Microeconomic topics include discussions of health care, agricultural subsidies, the price of everyday items such as running shoes, the distribution of income, and the impact of labor unions on wages. **Macroeconomics**, in contrast, deals with the **aggregate**, or total economy; it looks at economic problems as they influence the whole of society. Topics covered in macroeconomics include inflation, unemployment, business cycles, and economic growth. To put it simply, microeconomics looks at the trees while macroeconomics looks at the forest.

SECTION CHECK 4

4.1 Economic theories are statements used to explain and predict patterns of human behavior.

4.2 The world is too complex to analyze, so we must abstract to focus on the most important components of a particular problem.

4.3 A hypothesis makes a prediction about human behavior and is then tested.

4.4 Microeconomics focuses on smaller units within the economy—firms and households—and how they interact in the marketplace. Macroeconomics deals with the aggregate, or total, economy.

⑤5 Pitfalls to Avoid in Scientific Thinking

© STACEY PUTMAN / ISTOCKPHOTO.COM

Think about the following questions as you read through this section. You'll find the answers in Section Check 5.

5.1 If two events usually occur together, does it mean one event caused the other to happen?

5.2 What is the fallacy of composition?

In our discussion of economic theory we have not yet mentioned that there are certain pitfalls to avoid that may hinder scientific and logical thinking: confusing correlation and causation, and the fallacy of composition.

CONFUSING CORRELATION AND CAUSATION

Without a theory of causation, no scientist could sort out and understand the enormous complexity of the real world. But one must always be careful not to confuse correlation with causation. In other words, the fact that two events usually occur together (**correlation**) does not necessarily mean that one caused the other to occur (**causation**). For example, say a groundhog awakes after a long winter of hibernation, climbs out of his hole, and sees his shadow—then six weeks of bad weather ensue. Did the groundhog cause the bad weather? In Europe, the stork population has fallen and so have birth rates. Does this mean that the one event caused the other to occur? It is highly unlikely.

It is also important to consider in which direction causality runs. A rooster may always crow before the sun rises, but it does not cause the sunrise; rather, the early light from the sunrise causes the rooster to crow.

Why Is the Correlation between Ice Cream Sales and Property Crime Positive?

Did you know that when ice cream sales rise, so do property crime rates? What do you think causes the two events

© BILL NOLL/ISTOCKPHOTO.COM / © ISTOCKPHOTO.COM

to occur together? The explanation is that property crime peaks in the summer because of warmer weather, more people on vacations (leaving their homes vacant), teen-agers out of school, and so on. It just happens that ice cream sales also peak in those months because of the weather. It is the case of a third variable causing both to occur. Or what if there were a positive correlation between sales of cigarette lighters and the incidence of cancer? The suspect might well turn out to be the omitted variable (the so-called "smoking gun"): the cigarette.

THE FALLACY OF COMPOSITION

Economic thinking requires us to be aware of the prob-lems associated with aggregation (adding up all the parts). One of the biggest problems is the **fallacy of composition**. This fallacy states that even if something is true for an individual, it is not necessarily true for many individuals as a group. For example, say you are at a football game and you decide to stand up to get a better view of the playing field. This works as long as the people seated around you don't stand up. But what happens if everyone stands up at the same time? Then your standing up does nothing to improve your view. Thus, what is true for an individual does not always hold true in the aggregate. The same can be said of get-ting to school early to get a better parking place—what if everyone arrived early? Or studying harder to get a better grade in a class that is graded on a curve—what if everyone studied harder? These are all examples of the fallacy of composition.

SECTION CHECK 5

5.1 The fact that two events are related does not mean that one caused the other to occur.

5.2 What is true for the individual is not necessarily true for the group.

Ⓢ6 Positive and Normative Economics

Keep the following questions in mind as you read through this section. You'll find the answers in **Section Check 6**.

6.1 What is a positive statement?
6.2 What is a normative statement?
6.3 Why do economists disagree?

Economists are asked to explain the world as scientists and improve the world as policy advisers. Positive anal-ysis deals with factual statements trying to explain the world. Normative analysis deals with value judgments trying to improve the world.

POSITIVE STATEMENT

Most economists view themselves as scientists seek-ing the truth about the way people behave. They make speculations about economic behavior, and then, ide-ally, they assess the validity of those predictions based on human experience. Their work emphasizes how peo-ple do behave, rather than how people should behave. In the role of scientist, an economist tries to observe patterns of behavior objectively, without reference to the appropriateness or inappropriateness of that behav-ior. This objective, value-free approach, based on the scientific method, is called positive analysis. In positive analysis, we want to know the impact of variable A on variable B. We want to be able to test a hypothesis. For example, the following is a **positive statement**: If rent controls are imposed, vacancy rates will fall. This state-ment is testable. A positive statement does not have to be a true statement, but it does have to be a testable statement.

Keep in mind, however, that it is doubtful that even the most objective scientist can be totally value free in his or her analysis. An economist may well emphasize data or evidence that supports a hypothesis, putting less weight on other evidence that might be contradic-tory. This tendency, alas, is human nature. But a good economist/scientist strives to be as fair and objective as possible in evaluating evidence and in stating conclu-sions based on the evidence. In some sense, economists are like engineers; they try to figure out how things work and then describe what would happen if you changed something.

NORMATIVE STATEMENT

Economists, like anyone else, have opinions and make value judgments. And when economists, or anyone else for that

fallacy of composition the incorrect view that what is true for the individual is always true for the group

positive statement an objective, testable statement that describes what happens and why it happens

matter, express opinions about an economic policy or statement, they are indicating in part how they believe things should be, not stating facts about the way things are. In other words, they are performing normative analysis. **Normative statements** involve judgments about what should be or what ought to happen. For example, normative questions might include: Should the government raise the minimum wage? Should the government increase spending in the space program? Should the government give "free" prescription drugs to senior citizens?

Positive versus Normative Analysis

The distinction between positive and normative analysis is important. It is one thing to say that everyone should have universal health care, an untestable normative statement, and quite another to say that universal health care would lead to greater worker productivity, a testable positive statement. It is important to distinguish between positive and normative analysis because many controversies in economics revolve around policy considerations that contain both. For example, what impact would a 3 percent reduction in income taxes across the board have on the economy? This question requires positive analysis. Whether we should have a 3 percent reduction in income taxes requires normative analysis as

well. When economists are trying to explain the way the world works, they are scientists. When economists start talking about how the economy should work rather than how it does work, they have entered the normative world of the policymaker. In short, positive statements are attempts to *describe* what happens and why it happens, while normative statements are attempts to *prescribe* what should be done.

DISAGREEMENT IS COMMON IN MOST DISCIPLINES

Although economists do frequently have opposing views on economic policy questions, they probably disagree less than the media would have you believe. Disagreement is common in most disciplines: Seismologists differ over predictions of earthquakes or volcanic eruption; historians can be at odds over the interpretation of historical events; psychologists disagree on proper ways to raise children; and nutritionists debate the merits of large doses of vitamin C.

The majority of disagreements in economics stem from normative issues; differences in values or policy beliefs result in conflict. For example, a policy might increase efficiency at the expense of a sense of fairness or equity, or it might help a current generation at the expense of a future generation. Because policy decisions involve trade-offs, they will always involve the potential for conflict.

How should the government distribute its funds? The space program? Higher minimum wage? Prescription drugs? This kind of decision requires normative analysis.

Often Economists Do Agree

According to a survey among members of the American Economic Association, most economists agree on a wide range of issues, including rent control, import tariffs, export restrictions, the use of wage and price controls to curb inflation, and the minimum wage. In fact, most economists would agree that the following statements are correct:

ECONOMISTS DO AGREE

1. A ceiling on rents (rent control) reduces the quantity and quality of rental housing available (93 percent agree).
2. Tariffs and import quotas usually reduce general economic welfare (93 percent agree).
3. The United States should not restrict employers from outsourcing work to foreign countries (90.1 percent agree).
4. Fiscal policy (e.g., tax cuts and/or increases in government expenditure) has significant stimulative impact on an economy that is less than fully employed (90 percent agree).
5. Flexible and floating exchange rates offer an effective international monetary arrangement (90 percent).
6. The gap between Social Security funds and expenditures will become unsustainably large within the next 50 years if the current policies remain unchanged (85 percent agree).
7. The United States should eliminate agricultural subsidies (85 percent agree).
8. Local and state governments in the United States should eliminate subsidies to professional sport franchises (85 percent agree).
9. A large budget deficit has an adverse effect on the economy (83 percent agree).
10. A minimum wage increases unemployment among young and unskilled workers (79 percent agree).
11. Effluent taxes and marketable pollution permits represent a better approach to pollution control than imposition of pollution ceilings (78 percent agree).
12. Economists favor expanding competition and market forces in education (67.1 percent agree).

SOURCE: Richard M. Alston, J.R. Kearl and Michael B. Vaughn, "Is there Consensus among Economists in the 1990s?" American Economic Review (May 1992): 203-09; Robert Whaples, Do Economists Agree on Anything? Yes!" Economists' Voice (November 2006):1-6.

SECTION CHECK 6

6.1 Positive analysis is objective and free. They are testable statements. It describes what happens and why it happens.

6.2 Normative analysis involves value judgments and opinions about the desirability of various actions. It is not testable. These statements prescribe what should be done.

6.3 Disagreement is common in most disciplines. Most disagreement among economists stems from normative issues.

Ⓢ7 Why Study Economics?

Among the many good reasons to study economics, perhaps the best reason is that so many of the things of concern in the world around us are at least partly economic in character. A quick look at newspaper headlines reveals the vast range of problems that are related to economics—global warming, health care, education, and Social Security. The study of economics improves your understanding of these concerns. A student of economics becomes aware that, at a basic level, much of economic life involves choosing among alternative possible courses of action—making choices between our conflicting wants and desires in a world of scarcity. Economics provides some clues as to how to intelligently evaluate these options and determine the most appropriate choices in given situations.

The problem-solving tools you will develop by studying economics will prove valuable to you both in your personal and professional life, regardless of your career choice. In short, the study of economics provides a systematic, disciplined way of thinking.

ECONOMICS IS ALL AROUND US

The tools of economics are far reaching. In fact, other social scientists have accused economists of being imperialistic because their tools have been used in so many fields outside the formal area of economics, such as crime, education, marriage, divorce, addiction, finance, health, law, politics, and religion.

So while you might think that much of what you desire in life is "non-economic," economics concerns everything an individual might consider worthwhile, including things that you might consider "priceless." For instance, although we may long for love, sexual fulfillment, or spiritual enlightenment, few of us would be able to set a price for them. But even these matters have an economic dimension. Consider spirituality, for example. Concern for spiritual matters has led to the development of institutions such as churches, synagogues, and temples that conduct religious and spiritual services. In economic terms, these services are goods that many people desire. Love and sex likewise have received economists' scrutiny. One product of love, the institution of the family, is an important economic decision-making unit.

Even time has an economic dimension. In fact, in modern culture, time has become perhaps the single most precious resource we have. Everyone has the same limited amount of time per day, and how we divide our time between work and leisure (including study, sleep, exercise, and so on) is a distinctly economic matter. If we choose more work, we must sacrifice leisure. If we choose to study, we must sacrifice time with friends or time spent sleeping or watching TV. Virtually everything we decide to do, then, has an economic dimension.

Living in a world of scarcity involves trade-offs. As you are reading this text, you are giving up other things you value, such as shopping, spending time on Facebook or texting your friends, going to the movies, sleeping, or working out. When we know what the trade-offs are, we can make better choices from the options all around us, every day. As George Bernard Shaw once said, "Economy is the art of making the most of life."

Who Studies Economics?

The study of economics is useful in many career paths. Here is a short list of some relatively well-known people who studied economics in college.

POLITICIANS, POLICY MAKERS, AND SUPREME COURT JUSTICES

George H. W. Bush, former U.S. President (Yale)

Ronald Reagan, former U.S. President (Eureka College)

Gerald Ford, former U.S. President (University of Michigan)

Arnold Schwarzenegger, Body Builder/Actor/Governor (University of Wisconsin)

Sandra Day-O'Connor, retired U.S. Supreme Court Justice (Stanford)

Stephen Breyer, U.S. Supreme Court Justice (Stanford)

Anthony Kennedy, U.S. Supreme Court Justice (Stanford and London School of Economics)

Kofi Annan, former Secretary General of the United Nations (Macalester College)

BILLIONAIRES

Sam Walton, founder of Wal-Mart (University of Missouri)

Warren Buffett, financier (Columbia School of Business, Masters in Economics)

Meg Whitman, former President and CEO of eBay, Inc. (Princeton)

Ted Turner, media tycoon (Brown)

Steve Ballmer, CEO of Microsoft (Harvard)

Donald Trump, real-estate/television mogul (University of Pennsylvania—Wharton)

Paul Otellini, President and CEO of Intel (University of San Francisco)

CELEBRITIES

John Elway, former NFL quarterback (Stanford University)

Mick Jagger, lead singer of The Rolling Stones (London School of Economics)

Cate Blanchett, actress (Melbourne University)

Scott Adams, cartoonist, creator of *Dilbert* (Hartwick College)

Tiger Woods, golfer (Stanford)

Bill Belichick, NFL head coach, New England Patriots (Wesleyan University)

According to Bob McTeer, former president and CEO of the Federal Reserve Bank of Dallas, "My take on training in economics is that it becomes increasingly valuable as you move up the career ladder. I can't think of a better major for corporate CEOs, congressmen (and women), or presidents of the United States. You've learned a systematic, disciplined way of thinking that will serve you well.

Chapter 1: Self-Review

Now that you're finished reading the chapter, review the questions below. You can write your answers in the space provided, then go online to see the answers at www.cengagebrain.com.

S1–ECONOMICS: A BRIEF INTRODUCTION

1. What is the definition of economics?

2. Which of the following goods are scarce?
   a. garbage
   b. salt water in the ocean
   c. clothes
   d. clean air in a big city
   e. dirty air in a big city
   f. a public library

S2–ECONOMIC BEHAVIOR

3. What does rational self-interest involve?

4. What is rational behavior?

S3–MARKETS

5. What do market prices communicate to others in society?

6. Why does the circular flow of money move in the opposite direction from the flow of goods and services?

S4–ECONOMIC THEORY

7. Why do economic predictions refer to the behavior of groups of people rather than individuals?

8. Are the following topics ones that would be covered in microeconomics or macroeconomics?
   a. the effects of an increase in the supply of lumber on the home-building industry
   b. changes in the national unemployment rate
   c. changes in the inflation rate
   d. changes in the country's economic growth rate
   e. the price of concert tickets

S5–PITFALLS TO AVOID IN SCIENTIFIC THINKING

9. What types of misinterpretation result from confusing correlation and causation?

10. Do any of the following statements involve fallacies? If so, which ones?
    a. Because sitting in the back of the classroom is correlated with getting lower grades in the class, students should always sit closer to the front of the classroom.
    b. Historically, the stock market rises in years the NFC team wins the Super Bowl and falls when the AFC wins the Super Bowl; I am rooting for the NFC team to win for the sake of my investment portfolio.
    c. Gasoline prices were higher last year than in 1970, yet people purchased more gas, which contradicts the law of demand.

S6–POSITIVE AND NORMATIVE ECONOMICS

11. Why is the positive/normative distinction important?

S7–WHY STUDY ECONOMICS?

12. Why is economics worth studying?

Appendix—Working with Graphs

Sometimes the use of visual aids, such as graphs, greatly enhances our understanding of a theory. It is much the same as finding your way to a friend's house with the aid of a map rather than with detailed verbal or written instructions. In this section we'll go over the basics of creating graphs and how graphs are used in economics.

GRAPHS ARE AN IMPORTANT ECONOMIC TOOL

Graphs are important tools for economists. They allow us to understand better the workings of the economy. To economists, a graph can be worth a thousand words. This textbook will use graphs throughout to enhance the understanding of important economic relationships. This appendix provides a guide on how to read and create your own graphs.

The most useful graph for our purposes is one that merely connects a vertical line (the **Y-axis**) with a horizontal line (the **X-axis**), as seen in Exhibit 1.2. The intersection of the two lines occurs at the *origin*, which is where the value of both variables is equal to zero. In Exhibit 1.2, the graph has four quadrants, or boxes. In this textbook, we will be primarily concerned with the shaded box in the upper-right corner. This portion of the graph deals exclusively with positive numbers. Always keep in mind that moving to the right on the horizontal axis and moving up along the vertical axis both lead to higher values.

Y-axis the vertical axis on a graph

X-axis the horizontal axis on a graph

pie chart visual display showing the relative size of various quantities that add up to 100 percent

bar graph visual display showing the comparison of quantities

time-series graph visual tool to show changes in a variable's value over time

scatter diagram a graph showing the relationship of one variable to another

variable something that is measured by a number, such as your height

Using Graphs and Charts

Exhibit 1.3 presents four common types of graphs. The **pie chart** in Exhibit 1.3(a) shows the revenues received from various taxes levied on households and corporations. Each slice in the pie chart represents the percentage of finances that are derived from different sources—for example, personal income taxes account for 43 percent

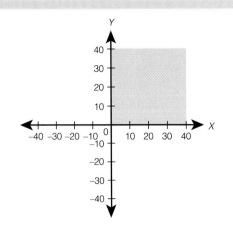

EXHIBIT 1.2 Plotting a Graph

of the federal government's tax revenues. Therefore, pie charts are used to show the relative size of various quantities that add up to 100 percent.

Exhibit 1.3(b) is a **bar graph** that shows the unemployment rate by age and sex in the United States. The height of the line represents the unemployment rate. Bar graphs are used to show a comparison of quantities.

Exhibit 1.3(c) is a **time-series graph**. This type of graph shows changes in the value of a variable over time. This visual tool allows us to observe important trends over a certain time period. In Exhibit 1.3(c), we see a graph that shows trends in the inflation rate over time. The horizontal axis shows us the passage of time, and the vertical axis shows us the inflation rate (annual percent change). From the graph, we can see the trends in the inflation rate from 1913–2009.

Exhibit 1.3(d) is a **scatter diagram**. Each point on this graph represents a point that corresponds to an actual observation along the X-axis and Y-axis. It shows the relationship of one variable to another. A linear curve is usually fitted to the scatter of points—it represents the best fit for the observations. In this case, the graph shows that rates of economic growth are positively associated with saving rates. Higher saving rates lead to greater economic growth rates, and lower saving rates are associated with lower economic growth rates.

USING GRAPHS TO SHOW THE RELATIONSHIP BETWEEN TWO VARIABLES

Even though the graphs and chart in Exhibit 1.3 are important, they do not allow us to show the relationship between two variables (a **variable** is something that

EXHIBIT 1.3 Pie Chart, Bar Graph, Time-Series Graph, and Scatter Diagram

a. Pie Chart—Tax Revenues—Federal Government, 2009

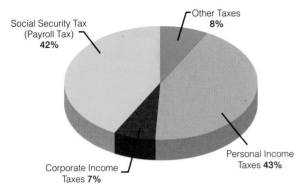

SOURCE: *Economic Report of the President, 2010*. Statistical Tables. Table B-80. Washington, D.C., February 2010. Available at http://www.gpoaccess.gov/eop/tables10.html (accessed March 25, 2010).

b. Bar Graph—U.S. Unemployment, by Sex and Age

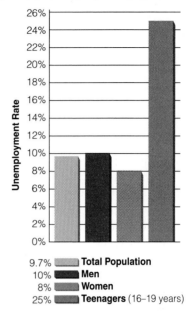

9.7% ▢ **Total Population**
10% ▢ **Men**
8% ▢ **Women**
25% ▢ **Teenagers** (16–19 years)

SOURCE: Bureau of Labor Statistics, Current Population Survey, Employment Situation Summary Table A. Washington, D.C., March 5, 2010. Available at http://www.bls.gov/news.release/empsit.a.htm (accessed March 25, 2010).

c. Time-Series Graph—Inflation in the United States, 1913–2009

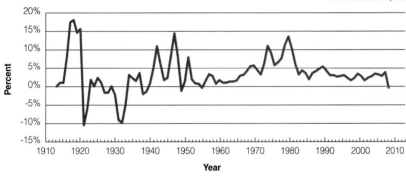

SOURCE: Bureau of Labor Statistics, Consumer Price Index, Table Containing History of CPI-U U.S. All Items Indexes and Annual Percent Changes from 1913 to Present. Washington, D.C., March 18, 2010. Available at ftp://ftp.bls.gov/pub/special.requests/cpi/cpiai.txt (accessed March 25, 2010).

d. Scatter Diagram—Saving Rates and GDP Growth

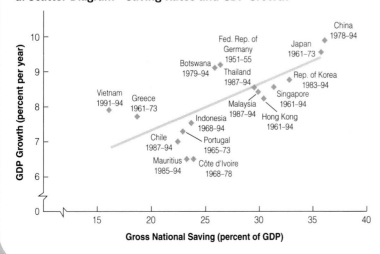

SOURCE: *World Bank, World Development Report, 1996*, Oxford University Press, 1996. Republished with permission of the World Bank; permission conveyed through Copyright Clearance Center, Inc.

is measured by a number, such as your height). To more closely examine the structures and functions of graphs, let's consider the story of Josh, an avid skateboarder who has aspirations of winning the Z Games next year. He knows that to get there, he'll need to put in many hours of practice. But how many hours? In search of information about the practice habits of other skateboarders, he logs onto the Internet, where he pulls up the results of a study that looked at the score of each Z Games competitor in relation to the amount of practice time per week spent by each skateboarder. As Exhibit 1.4 shows, the results of the study indicate that skateboarders had to practice 10 hours per week to receive a score of 4, 20 hours per week to receive a score of 6, 30 hours per week to get a score of 8, and 40 hours per week to get a perfect score of 10. How does this information help Josh? By using a graph, he can more clearly understand the relationship between practice time and overall score.

A Positive Relationship

The study on scores and practice times reveals what is called a direct relationship, also called a **positive relationship**. A positive relationship means that the variables change in the same direction. That is, an increase in one variable (practice time) is accompanied by an increase in the other variable (overall score), or a decrease in one variable (practice time) is accompanied by a decrease in the other variable (overall score). In short, the variables change in the same direction.

A Negative Relationship

When two variables change in opposite directions, they have an inverse relationship, also called a **negative relationship**. That is, when one variable rises, the other variable falls, or when one variable decreases, the other variable increases.

THE GRAPH OF A DEMAND CURVE

Let's now examine one of the most important graphs in economics—the demand curve. In Exhibit 1.5, we see Emily's individual demand curve for DVDs. It shows the price of DVDs on the vertical axis and the quantity of DVDs purchased per month on the horizontal axis. Every point in the space shown represents a price and quantity combination. The downward-sloping line, labeled "Demand curve," shows the different combinations of price and quantity purchased. Note that the higher the price of the DVDs (as shown on the vertical axis), the smaller the quantity purchased (as shown on the horizontal axis), and the lower the price (shown on the vertical axis), the greater the quantity purchased (shown on the horizontal axis).

In Exhibit 1.5, we see that moving up the vertical price axis from the origin, the price of DVDs increases from $5 to $25 in increments of $5. Moving out along the horizontal quantity axis, the quantity purchased increases from zero to five DVDs per month. Point A represents a price of $25 and a quantity of one DVD, point B represents a price of $20 and a quantity of two DVDs, point C a price of $15 and a quantity of three DVDs, and so on. When we connect all the points, we have what economists call a curve. As you can see, curves are sometimes drawn as straight lines for ease of illustration. Moving down along the curve, we see that

EXHIBIT 1.4 A Positive Relationship

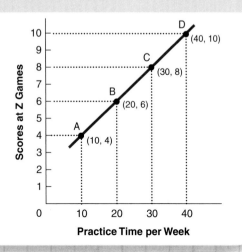

EXHIBIT 1.5 A Negative Relationship

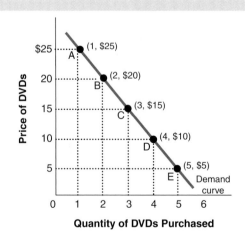

as the price falls, a greater quantity is demanded; moving up the curve to higher prices, a smaller quantity is demanded. That is, when DVDs become less expensive, Emily buys more DVDs. When DVDs become more expensive, Emily buys fewer DVDs, perhaps choosing to go to the movies or buy a pizza instead.

USING GRAPHS TO SHOW THE RELATIONSHIP AMONG THREE VARIABLES

Although only two variables are shown on the axes, graphs can be used to show the relationship among three variables. For example, say we add a third variable—income—to our earlier example. Our three variables are now income, price, and quantity purchased. If Emily's income rises—say she gets a raise at work—she is now able and willing to buy more DVDs than before at each possible price. As a result, the whole demand curve shifts outward (to the right) compared with the old curve. That is, the new income gives her more money to buy more DVDs. This shift is seen in the graph in Exhibit 1.6(a).

EXHIBIT 1.6 Shifting a Curve

a. Demand Curve with Higher Income

b. Demand Curve with Lower Income

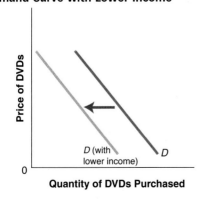

On the other hand, if her income falls—say she quits her job to go back to school—she would have less income to buy DVDs. A decrease in this variable causes the whole demand curve to shift inward (to the left) compared with the old curve. This shift is seen in the graph in Exhibit 1.6(b).

> **slope** the ratio of rise (change in the *Y* variable) over run (change in the *X* variable)

The Difference between a Movement Along and a Shift in the Curve

It is important to remember the difference between a movement between one point and another along a curve and a shift in the whole curve. A change in one of the variables on the graph, such as price or quantity purchased, will cause a movement along the curve, say from point A to point B, as shown in Exhibit 1.7. A change in one of the variables not shown (held constant in order to show only the relationship between price and quantity), such as income in our example, will cause the whole curve to shift. The change from D_1 to D_2 in Exhibit 1.7 shows such a shift.

SLOPE

In economics, we sometimes refer to the steepness of a line or curve on a graph as the **slope**. A slope can be either positive (upward-sloping) or negative (downward-sloping). A curve that is downward-sloping represents an inverse, or negative, relationship between the two variables and slants downward from left to right, as seen in Exhibit 1.8(a). A curve that is upward-sloping represents a direct, or positive, relationship between the two variables and slants upward from left to right, as seen in Exhibit 1.8(b). The numeric value of the slope shows the number of units of change of the *Y*-axis variable for each unit of change in the *X*-axis

EXHIBIT 1.7 Shifts versus Movements

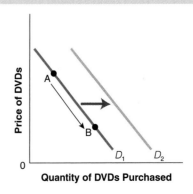

EXHIBIT 1.8 Downward- and Upward-Sloping Linear Curve

a. Downward-Sloping Linear Curve

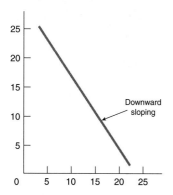

Downward sloping

b. Upward-Sloping Linear Curve

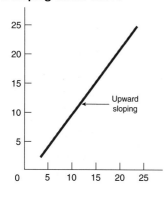

Upward sloping

EXHIBIT 1.9 Slopes of Positive and Negative Curves

a. Positive Slope

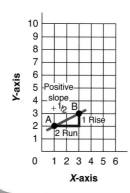

b. Negative Slope

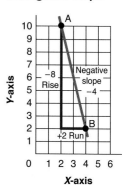

variable. Slope provides the direction (positive or negative) as well as the magnitude of the relationship between the two variables.

Measuring the Slope of a Linear Curve

A straight-line curve is called a linear curve. The slope of a linear curve between two points measures the relative rates of change of two variables. Specifically, the slope of a linear curve can be defined as the ratio of the change in the Y value to the change in the X value. The slope can also be expressed as the ratio of the rise over the run, where the rise is the vertical change and the run is the horizontal change.

Exhibit 1.9 shows two linear curves, one with a positive slope and one with a negative slope. In Exhibit 1.9(a), the slope of the positively sloped linear curve from point A to B is 1/2, because the rise is 1 (from 2 to 3) and the run is 2 (from 1 to 3). In Exhibit 1.9(b), the negatively sloped linear curve has a slope of –4: A rise of –8 (a fall of 8, from 10 to 2) and a run of 2 (from 2 to 4) gives us a slope of –8/2, or –4. Notice the appropriate

signs on the slopes: The negatively sloped line carries a minus sign and the positively sloped line, a plus sign.

Finding the Slope of a Nonlinear Curve

In Exhibit 1.10, we show the slope of a nonlinear curve. A nonlinear curve is a line that actually curves. Here the slope varies from point to point along the curve. However, we can find the slope of this curve at any given point by drawing a straight line tangent to that point on the curve. A tangency is when a straight line just touches the curve without actually crossing it. At point A, we see that the positively sloped line that is tangent to the curve has a slope of 1: the line rises 1 and runs 1. At point B, the line is horizontal, so it has zero slope. At point C, we see a slope of –2, because the negatively sloped line has a rise of –2 (a fall of 2) for every run of 1.

Remember, many students have problems with economics simply because they fail to understand graphs, so make sure that you understand this material before going on to Chapter 2.

EXHIBIT 1.10 Slopes of a Nonlinear Curve

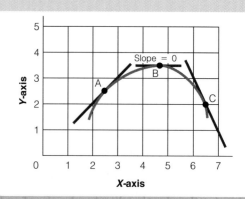

GET ONLINE

HE DID

Discover your **Survey of ECON** online experience at **www.cengagebrain.com**.

You'll find everything you need to succeed in your class.

- Interactive Quizzes
- PowerPoint® Slides
- Printable Flash Cards
- Videos
- Animated Flash Games
- And more

www.cengagebrain.com

Economic questions

are all around you. Take for instance the people who lined up to buy the Apple iPhone when it was released in 2007. Not only did it cost them money to purchase the item, but it also cost them time waiting in line—time that they might have spent doing other things. Choices like this one are all around us, and by studying economics we can better understand these choices and hopefully make better ones in the future.

2

The Economic Way of Thinking

Studying economics may teach you how to "think better," because economics helps develop a disciplined method of thinking about problems.

A student of economics becomes aware that, at a basic level, much of economic life involves choosing one course of action rather than another—making choices among our conflicting wants and desires in a world of scarcity. Economics provides insights about how to intelligently evaluate these options and determine the most appropriate choices in given situations. *Most of economics really involves knowing certain principles well and knowing when and how to apply them.*

This chapter presents some important tools that will help you understand the economic way of thinking. The economic way of thinking provides a logical framework for organizing and analyzing your understanding of a broad set of issues, many of which do not even seem directly related to economics as you now know it.

The basic ideas that you learn in this chapter will occur repeatedly throughout the text. If you develop a good understanding of these principles and master the problem-solving skills inherent in them, they will serve you well for the rest of your life. Learning to think like an economist takes time. Like most disciplines, economics has its own specialized vocabulary, including such terms as *elasticity*, *comparative advantage*, *supply and demand*, *deadweight loss*, and *consumer surplus*. Learning economics requires more than picking up this new terminology; however, it also involves using its powerful tools to improve your understanding of a whole host of issues in the world around you.

Sections in Chapter 2

S1 Choices, Costs, and Trade-Offs

Consider the following questions as you read through this section. You'll find the answers in **Section Check 1.**

1.1 Why do we have to make choices?

1.2 What do we give up when we have to choose?

1.3 Why are "free" lunches not free?

In this section, we'll discuss the costs, both monetary and nonmonetary, and the trade-offs that we must make when presented with choices.

SCARCITY FORCES US TO CHOOSE

Each of us may want a nice home, two luxury cars, wholesome and good-tasting food, a personal trainer, and a therapist, all enjoyed in a pristine environment with zero pollution. If we had unlimited resources, and thus an ability to produce all the goods and services everyone wants, we would not have to choose among those desires. However, we all face scarcity, and as a consequence, we must make choices. If we did not have to make meaningful economic choices, the study of economics would not be necessary. The essence of economics is to understand fully the implications that scarcity has for wise decision making.

TRADE-OFFS

In a world of scarcity, we all face trade-offs. If you spend more time at work, you might give up an opportunity to go shopping at the mall or watch your favorite TV show. Or when you decide how to spend your income, buying a new car may mean you have to forgo a summer vacation. Businesses have trade-

offs, too. If a farmer chooses to plant cotton on his land this year, he gives up the opportunity to plant wheat. If a firm decides to produce only cars, it gives up the opportunity to use those resources to produce refrigerators or something else that people value. Society, too, must make trade-offs. For example, the federal government faces trade-offs when it comes to spending tax revenues; additional resources used to enhance the environment may come at the expense of additional resources to provide health care, education, or national defense.

TO CHOOSE IS TO LOSE

Every choice involves a cost. The highest or best forgone opportunity resulting from a decision is called the **opportunity cost**. Another way to put it is that "to choose is to lose" or "an opportunity cost is an opportunity lost." To get more of anything that is desirable, you must accept less of something else that you also value.

For example, time spent exercising costs time that could be spent doing something else that is valuable—perhaps relaxing with friends or studying for an upcoming exam. One of the reasons drivers talk so much on their cell phones is because they have little else to do with their time while driving—a low opportunity cost. However, drivers using cell phones should pay attention; otherwise, they are giving up safety. Trade-offs are everywhere. The famous poet Robert Frost understood that to live is to choose. In his poem, "The Road Not Taken," he writes, "two roads diverged in a yellow wood, and sorry I could not travel both."

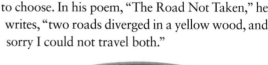

Money Prices and Costs

If you go to the store to buy groceries, you have to pay for the items you bought. This amount is called the *money price*. It is an opportunity cost, because you could have used that money to purchase other goods or services. However, additional opportunity costs include the nonprice costs incurred to acquire the groceries—time spent getting to the grocery store, finding a parking place, shopping for groceries, and waiting in the checkout line. The nonprice costs are measured by assessing the sacrifice involved—the value you place on what you would have done with that time if you had not gone shopping. So the cost of grocery shopping is the price paid for the goods, plus the nonprice costs incurred. Consider another example: Your concert ticket may have only been $50, but what if you had to wait in line for six hours in the freezing cold? Waiting and enduring the cold are costs, too. Seldom are costs just dollars and cents. Shopping at a large discount store may save you money on the price but cost you time waiting in long checkout lines. Also, buying food in bulk quantities may be less expensive per ounce but cost inventory space in your pantry, or the food may spoil before it is eaten.

Remember that many costs do not involve money but are still costs. Do I major in economics or engineering? Do I go to Billy Madison University or Tech State University? Should I get an MBA now or work and wait a few years to go back to school?

Policy makers, too, are unavoidably faced with opportunity costs. Consider airline safety. Both money costs and time costs affect airline safety. New airline safety devices cost money (for luggage inspection devices, smoke detectors, fuel tank safeguards, new radar equipment, and so on), and time costs are quite evident with the new security checks. Waiting in line costs time that could be used to do something else that is valuable. New airline safety requirements could also actually cost lives. If the new safety equipment costs are passed on in the form of higher airline ticket prices, people may choose to travel by car, which is far more dangerous per mile traveled than by air. Opportunity costs are everywhere!

The Opportunity Cost of Going to College

The average person often does not correctly calculate opportunity costs. For example, the (opportunity) cost of going to college includes not just the direct expenses of tuition and books. Of course, those expenses do involve an opportunity cost because the money used for books and tuition could be used to buy other things that you value. But what about the nonmoney costs? That is, going to college also includes the opportunity cost of your time. Specifically, the time spent going to school is time that could have been spent on a job earning, say, $30,000 over the course of an academic year. Bill Gates, Tiger Woods, and Oprah Winfrey all quit college to pursue their dreams. Tiger Woods dropped out of Stanford (where he was pursuing an economics major) to join the PGA golf tour. Bill Gates dropped out of Harvard to start a software company. Oprah Winfrey dropped out of Tennessee State to pursue a career in broadcasting. At the early age of 19, she became the co-anchor of the evening news. Staying in school would have cost each of them millions of dollars. We cannot say it would have been the wrong decision to stay in school, but it would have been costly.

Consider some other costs. What about room and board? That aspect is a little tricky because you would presumably have to pay room and board whether you went to college or not. The relevant question may be how much more it costs you to live at school rather than at home (and living at home may have substantial nonmoney costs). Even if you stayed at home, your parents would sacrifice something; they could rent your room out or use the room for some other purpose such as storage, a guest room, a home office, a sibling's room, and so on.

IS THAT REALLY A FREE LUNCH, A FREEWAY, OR A FREE BEACH?

The expression "there's no such thing as a free lunch" clarifies the relationship between scarcity and opportunity cost. Suppose the school cafeteria is offering "free" lunches today. Although the lunch is free to you, is it really free from society's perspective? The answer is no, because some of society's scarce resources will

© TERRANCE EMERSON/SHUTTERSTOCK

have been used in the preparation of the lunch. The issue is whether the resources that went into creating that lunch could have been used to produce something else of value. Clearly, the scarce resources that went into the production of the lunch—the labor and materials (foodservice workers, lettuce, meat, plows, tractors, fertilizer, and so forth)—could have been used in other ways. They had an opportunity cost and thus were not free.

Do not confuse free with a zero monetary price. A number of goods—freeways, free beaches, and free libraries, for instance—do not cost consumers money, but they are still scarce. Few things are free in the sense that they use none of society's scarce resources. So what does a free lunch really mean? It is, technically speaking, a "subsidized" lunch—a lunch using society's scarce resources, but one that the person receiving does not have to pay for personally.

SECTION CHECK 1

1.1 Scarcity means we all have to make choices.

1.2 When we are forced to choose, we give up the next highest-valued alternative.

1.3 Few things are free in the sense that they don't use any of society's scarce resources. A thing may still be scarce even though it costs consumers no money.

Ⓢ2 Marginal Thinking

Keep the following questions in mind as you read through this section, and review the answers in **Section Check 2**.

2.1 What do we mean by marginal thinking?

2.2 What is the rule of rational choice?

2.3 Why do we use the word "expected" with marginal benefits and costs?

Now let's consider how marginal thinking influences our decision making.

MANY CHOICES WE FACE INVOLVE MARGINAL THINKING

Some decisions are "all or nothing," like whether to start a new business or go to work for someone else, or whether to attend graduate school or take a job. But many choices we face involve *how much* of something to do rather than *whether* to do something. It is not *whether* you eat but *how much* you eat. Or, how many caffe lattes will I buy this week? Or, how often do I change the oil in my car? Or how much of my paycheck do I spend, and how much do I save? Your instructors hope that the question is not *whether* you study this semester but *how much* you study. You might think to yourself, "If I studied a little more, I might be able to improve my grade," or "If I had a little better concentration when I was studying, I could improve my grade." That is, spending more time has an additional expected benefit (a higher grade) and an additional expected cost (giving up time to do something else that is valuable, such as watching TV or sleeping). These examples reflect what economists call **marginal thinking** because the focus is on the additional, or marginal, choices available to you. Or think of marginal as the edge—marginal decisions are made around the edge of what you are currently doing. Marginal choices involve the effects of adding or subtracting from the current situation. In short, they are the small (or large) incremental changes to a plan of action.

The question may not be whether you'll have coffee today, but rather how much coffee you will have.

© DORON GILD/GETTY IMAGES

Businesses are constantly engaged in marginal thinking. For example, firms have to decide whether the additional (marginal) revenue received from increasing production is greater than the marginal cost of that production.

Always watch out for the difference between average and marginal costs. Suppose an airline had 10 unoccupied seats on a flight from Los Angeles to New York, and the average cost was $400 per seat (the total cost divided by the number of seats—$100,000/250). If 10 people are waiting on standby, each willing to pay $300, should the airline sell them the tickets? Yes! The unoccupied seats earn nothing for the airline. What are the additional (marginal) costs of a few more passengers? The marginal costs are minimal—slight wear and tear on the airplane, handling some extra baggage, and 10 extra in-flight meals. In this case, thinking at the margin can increase total profits, even if it means selling at less than the average cost of production.

Another good example of marginal thinking is an auction. Prices are bid up marginally as the auctioneer calls out one price after another. When bidders view the new price (the marginal cost) to be greater than the value they place on the good (the marginal benefit), they withdraw from further bidding.

In trying to make themselves better off, people alter their behavior if the expected marginal benefits from doing so outweigh the expected marginal costs, which is the **rule of rational choice**. Economic theory is often called marginal analysis because it assumes that people are always weighing the expected marginal benefits against the expected marginal costs. The term *expected* is used with *marginal benefits* and *marginal costs* because the world is uncertain in many important respects, so the actual result of changing behavior may not always make people better off—but on average it will. However, as a matter of rationality, people are assumed to engage only in behavior that they think will make them better off. That is, individuals will only pursue an activity if their expected marginal benefits are greater than their expected marginal costs of pursuing that activity one step further, $E(MB) > E(MC)$.

This fairly unrestrictive and realistic view of individuals seeking self-betterment can be used to analyze a variety of social phenomena.

Suppose that you have to get up for an 8 A.M. class but have been up very late. When the alarm goes off at 7 A.M., you weigh the marginal benefits and marginal costs of an extra 15 minutes of sleep. If you perceive the marginal benefits of 15 additional minutes of sleep to be greater than the marginal costs of those extra minutes, you may choose to hit the snooze button. Or perhaps you may decide to blow off class completely. But it's unlikely that you will choose that action if it's the day of the final exam—because it is now likely that the **net benefits** (the difference between the expected marginal benefits and the expected marginal costs) of skipping class have changed. When people have opportunities to make themselves better off, they usually take them. And they will continue to seek those opportunities as long as they expect a net benefit from doing so.

The rule of rational choice is simply the rule of being sensible, and most economists believe that individuals act *as if* they are sensible and apply the rule of rational choice to their daily lives. It is a rule that can help us understand our decisions to study, walk, shop, exercise, clean house, cook, and perform just about every other action.

It is also a rule that we will continue to use throughout the text. Because whether it is consumers, producers, or policy makers making decisions, they all must compare the expected marginal benefits and the expected marginal cost to determine the best level to consume, produce, or provide public programs.

Zero Pollution Would Be Too Costly

Let's use the concept of marginal thinking to evaluate pollution levels. We all know the benefits of a cleaner environment, but what would we have to give up—that is, what marginal costs would we have to incur—to achieve zero pollution? A

How might the net benefits of waking up on time change between a normal day of class and the day of your semester exam?

rule of rational choice individuals will pursue an activity if the expected marginal benefits are greater than the expected marginal costs

net benefit the difference between the expected marginal benefits and the expected marginal costs

lot! You could not drive a car, fly in a plane, or even ride a bicycle, especially if everybody else were riding bikes, too (because traffic congestion is a form of pollution). How would you get to school or work, or go to the movies or the grocery store? Everyone would have to grow their own food because transporting, storing, and producing food uses machinery and equipment that pollute. And even growing your own food would be a problem because many plants emit natural pollutants. We could go on and on. The point is not that we shouldn't be concerned about the environment, but rather that we have to weigh the expected marginal benefits of a cleaner environment against the expected marginal costs of a cleaner environment. This discussion is not meant to say the environment should not be cleaner, only that zero pollution levels would be far too costly in terms of what we would have to give up.

Optimal (Best) Levels of Safety

Like pollution, crime and safety can have optimal (or best) levels that are greater than zero. Take crime. What would it cost society to have zero crime? It would be prohibitively costly to divert a tremendous amount of our valuable resources toward the complete elimination of crime. In fact, it would be impossible to eliminate crime totally. Even reducing crime significantly would be costly. Because lower crime rates are costly, society must decide how much it is willing to give up. The additional resources for crime prevention can only come from limited supplies, which could be used to produce something else the people may value even more.

The same is true for safer products. Nobody wants defective tires on their car or cars that are unsafe and roll over at low speeds. However, optimal amounts of safety that are greater than zero are available. The issue is not safe versus unsafe products but rather *how much* safety we want. It is not risk versus no risk but rather *how much* risk we are willing to take. Additional safety can only come at higher costs. To make all products perfectly safe would be impossible, so we must weigh the benefits and costs of safer products. In fact, according to one study by Sam Peltzman, a University of Chicago economist, additional safety regulations in cars (mandatory safety belts and padded dashboards) in the late 1960s may have had little impact on highway fatalities. Peltzman found that making cars safer led to more reckless driving and more accidents. The safety regulations did result in fewer deaths per automobile accident, but the total number of deaths remained unchanged because more accidents occurred.

Reckless driving has a benefit in the form of getting somewhere more quickly, but it can also have a cost—an accident or even a fatality. Most people will compare the marginal benefits and marginal costs of safer driving and make the choices that they believe will get them to their destination safely.

⑤3 Specialization and Trade

Consider the following questions as you read through this section. You'll find the answers in **Section Check 3.**

3.1 What is the relationship between opportunity cost and specialization?

3.2 What are the advantages of specialization in production?

As we go through this section, we'll discuss specialization, the comparative advantage gained through specialization, and how trade allows us to take advantage of specialization.

WHY DO PEOPLE SPECIALIZE?

As you look around, you can see that people specialize in what they produce. They tend to dedicate their resources to one primary activity, whether it be child rearing, driving a cab, or making bagels. Why? The answer, short and simple, is opportunity costs. By concentrating their energies on only one, or a few, activities, individuals are **specializing**. This focus allows them to make the best use of (and thus gain the most benefit from) their limited resources. A person, a region, or a country can gain by specializing in the production of the good in which they have a comparative advantage. That is, if they can produce a good or service at a lower opportunity cost than others, we say that they have a **comparative advantage** in the production of that good or service.

WE ALL SPECIALIZE

We all specialize to some extent and rely on others to produce most of the goods and services we want. The work that we choose to do reflects our specialization. For example, we may specialize in selling or fixing automobiles. The wages from that work can then be used to buy goods from a farmer who has chosen to specialize in the production of food. Likewise, the farmer can use the money earned from selling his produce to get his tractor fixed by someone who specializes in that activity.

Specialization is evident not only among individuals but among regions and countries as well. In fact, the story of the economic development of the United States and the rest of the world involves specialization.

Specialization allows this farmer to earn more money producing food, which he can then use to hire someone to fix his tractor, who is better than him at that kind of work.

Within the United States, the Midwest with its wheat, the coastal waters of the Northeast with its fishing fleets, and the Northwest with its timber are each examples of regional specialization.

> **specializing** concentrating on the production of one or a few goods
>
> **comparative advantage** occurs when a person or country can produce a good or service at a lower opportunity cost than others

THE ADVANTAGES OF SPECIALIZATION

In a small business, every employee usually performs a wide variety of tasks—from hiring to word processing to marketing. As the size of the company increases, each employee can perform a more specialized job, with a consequent increase in output per worker. The primary advantages of specialization are that employees acquire greater skill from repetition, they avoid wasted time in shifting from one task to another, and they do the types of work for which they are best suited. Furthermore, specialization promotes the use of specialized equipment for specialized tasks.

The advantages of specialization are seen throughout the workplace. For example, in larger firms, specialists conduct personnel relations, and accounting is in the hands of full-time accountants instead of someone with half a dozen other tasks. Owners of small retail stores select the locations for their stores primarily through guesswork, placing them where they believe sales will be high or where low-rent buildings are available. In contrast, larger chains have store sites selected by experts who have experience in analyzing the factors that make different locations relatively more desirable, such as traffic patterns, income levels, demographics, and so on.

SPECIALIZATION AND TRADE LEAD TO GREATER WEALTH AND PROSPERITY

Trade, or voluntary exchange, directly increases wealth by making both parties better off (or they wouldn't trade). It is the prospect of wealth-increasing exchange that leads to productive specialization. That is, trade increases wealth by allowing a person, a region, or a nation to specialize in those products that it produces at a lower opportunity cost and to trade them for products that others produce at a lower opportunity cost. That is, we trade with others because it frees up time and resources to do other things that we do better.

In short, if we divide tasks and produce what we do *relatively* best and trade for the rest, we will be better off than if we were self-sufficient—that is, without trade. Imagine life without trade, where you were completely self-sufficient—growing your own food, making your own clothes, working on your own car, building your own house—do you think you would be better off? For example, say the United States is better at producing wheat than is Brazil, and Brazil is better at producing coffee than is the United States. The United States and Brazil would each benefit if the United States produces wheat and trades some of it to Brazil for coffee. Coffee growers in the United States could grow coffee in expensive greenhouses, but it would result in higher coffee costs and prices, while leaving fewer resources available for employment in more beneficial jobs, such as wheat production.

In the words of growth theorist Paul Romer, "There are huge potential gains from trade. Poor countries can supply their natural and human resources. Rich countries can supply their know-how. When these are combined, everyone can be better off. The challenge is for a country to arrange its laws and institutions so that both sides can profitably engage in trade." Standards of living can be increased through trade and exchange. In fact, the economy as a whole can create more wealth when each person specializes in a task that he or she does best. And through specialization and trade, a country can gain a greater variety of goods and services at a lower cost. So while countries may be competitors in the global market, they are also partners.

SECTION CHECK 3

3.1 The person, region, or country that can produce a good or service at a lower opportunity cost than other producers has a comparative advantage in the production of that good or service.

3.2 The primary advantages of specialization are that employees acquire greater skill from repetition, they avoid wasted time in shifting from one task to another, and they do the types of work for which they are best suited.

⑤4 The Production Possibilities of an Economy

Keep the following questions in mind as you read through this section. You'll find the answers in **Section Check 4.**

4.1 What is a production possibilities curve?

4.2 What is efficiency?

4.3 What is the law of increasing opportunity costs?

4.4 How do we show economic growth on the production possibilities curve?

In this section, we'll examine the production possibilities curve, the law of increasing opportunity cost, and how economic growth is generated.

THE PRODUCTION POSSIBILITIES CURVE

The economic concepts of scarcity, choice, and trade-offs can be illustrated visually by means of a simple graph called a production possibilities curve. The **production possibilities curve** represents the potential total output combinations of any two goods for an economy, given the inputs and technology available to the economy. That is, it illustrates an economy's potential for allocating its limited resources in producing various combinations of goods in a given time period.

The Production Possibilities Curve for Food and Shelter

To illustrate the production possibilities curve, imagine living in an economy that produces just two goods, food and shelter. The fact that we have many goods in the real world makes actual decision making more complicated, but it does not alter the basic principles being illustrated. Each point on the production possibilities curve shown in Exhibit 2.1 represents the potential amounts of food and shelter that we can produce in a given period with a given quantity and quality of resources in the economy available for production.

Notice in Exhibit 2.1 that if we devote all our resources to making shelters, we can produce 10 units of shelter but no food (point A). If,

EXHIBIT 2.1 Production Possibilities Curve: The Trade-Off between Food and Shelter

Combinations	Shelter (units)	Food (units)
A	10	0
B	9	20
C	7	40
D	4	60
E	0	80

on the other hand, we choose to devote all our resources to producing food, we end up with 80 units of food but no shelters (point E).

In reality, nations rarely opt for production possibility A or E, preferring instead to produce a mixture of goods. For example, our fictional economy might produce 9 units of shelter and 20 units of food (point B) or perhaps 7 units of shelter and 40 units of food (point C). Still other combinations along the curve, such as point D, are possible.

Off the Production Possibilities Curve

The economy cannot operate at point N (not attainable) during the given period because not enough resources are currently available to produce that level of output. However, it is possible the economy can operate inside the production possibilities curve, at point I (inefficient). If the economy is operating at point I, or any other point inside the production possibilities curve, it is not at full capacity and is operating inefficiently. In short, the economy is not using all its scarce resources efficiently; as a result, actual output is less than potential output.

USING RESOURCES EFFICIENTLY

Most modern economies have resources that are idle at least some of the time—during periods of high unemployment, for instance. If those resources were not idle, people would have more scarce goods and services available for their use. Unemployed resources create a serious problem. For example, consider an unemployed coal miner who is unable to find work at a "reasonable" wage, or those unemployed in depressed times when factories are already operating below capacity. Clearly, the resources of these individuals are not being used efficiently.

The fact that factories can operate below capacity suggests that it is not just labor resources that should be most effectively used. Rather, all resources entering into production should be used effectively. However, social concern focuses on labor, for several reasons. A primary reason is that labor costs are the largest share of production costs. Another major reason is that unemployed or underemployed laborers (whose resources are not being used to their full potential) may have mouths to feed at home, while an unemployed machine does not (although the owner of the unemployed machine may).

INEFFICIENCY AND EFFICIENCY

Suppose for some reason employment is widespread or resources are not being put to their best uses. The economy would then be operating at a point inside the production possibilities curve, such as I in Exhibit 2.1, where the economy is operating inefficiently. At point I, 4 units of shelter and 40 units of food are being produced. By putting unemployed resources to work or by putting already employed resources to better uses, we could expand the output of shelter by 3 units (moving to point C) without giving up any units of food. Alternatively, we could boost food output by 20 units (moving to point D) without reducing shelter output. We could even get more of both food and shelter by moving to a point on the curve between C and D. Increasing or improving the utilization of resources, then, can lead to greater output of all goods. As you may recall from Chapter 1, an efficient use of our resources means that more of everything we want can be available for our use. Thus, *efficiency* requires society to use its resources to the fullest extent—getting the most from our scarce resources and wasting none. If resources are being used efficiently—that is, at some point along a production possibilities curve—then more of one good or service requires the sacrifice of another good or service. Efficiency does not tell us which point along the production possibilities curve is *best*, but it does tell us that points inside the curve cannot be best, because some resources are wasted.

THE LAW OF INCREASING OPPORTUNITY COST

As in Exhibit 2.1, the production possibilities curve in Exhibit 2.2 is not a straight line. It is concave from below (that is, bowed outward from the origin). Looking at Exhibit 2.2, you can see that at low food output, an increase in the amount of food produced will lead to only a small reduction in the number of units of shelter produced. For example, increasing food output from 0 to 20 (moving from point A to point B on the curve) requires the use of resources capable of producing 1 unit of shelter. In other words, for the first 20 units of food, 1 unit of shelter must be given up. When food output is higher, however, more units of shelter must be given up when switching additional resources from the production of shelter to food. Moving from point D to point E, for example, an increase in food output of 20 (from 60 to 80) reduces the production of shelters from

4 to 0. At this point, then, the cost of those 20 additional units of food is 4 units of shelter, considerably more than the 1 unit of shelter required in the earlier scenario. This difference shows us that opportunity costs do not remain constant but rise because more units of food and fewer units of shelter are produced. It is this **increasing opportunity cost**, then, that is represented by the bowed production possibilities curve.

What Is the Reason for the Law of Increasing Opportunity Cost?

The basic reason for the increasing opportunity cost is that some resources and skills cannot be easily adapted from their current uses to alternative uses. And the more you produce of one good, the more you are forced to employ inputs that are relatively more suitable for producing other goods. For example, at low levels of food output, additional increases in food output can be obtained easily by switching relatively low-skilled carpenters from making shelters to producing food. However, to get even more food output, workers who are less well suited or appropriate for producing food (i.e., they are better adapted to making shelters) must be released from shelter making to increase food output. For example, a skilled carpenter may be an expert at making shelters but a very bad farmer because he lacks the training and skills necessary in that occupation. So using the skilled carpenter to farm results in a relatively greater opportunity cost than using the unskilled carpenter to farm. The production of additional units of food becomes increasingly costly as progressively lower-skilled farmers (but good carpenters) convert to farming.

In short, resources tend to be specialized. As a result, we lose some of their productivity when we transfer those resources from producing what they are relatively good at to producing something they are relatively bad at.

GENERATING ECONOMIC GROWTH

How have some nations been able to rapidly expand their outputs of goods and services over time, while others have been unable to increase their standards of living at all?

The economy can only grow with qualitative or quantitative changes in the factors of production—land, labor, capital, and entrepreneurship. Advancement in technology, improvements in labor productivity, or new sources of natural

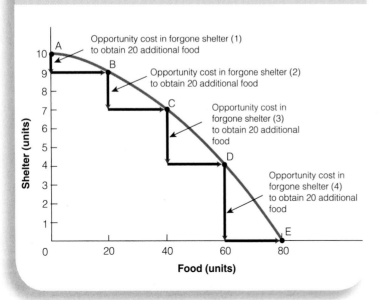

EXHIBIT 2.2 Increasing Opportunity Cost and the Production Possibilities Curve

resources (such as previously undiscovered oil) could lead to outward shifts of the production possibilities curve.

In terms of the production possibilities curve, an outward shift in the possible combinations of goods and services produced indicates economic growth, as seen in Exhibit 2.3. With growth comes the possibility of having more of both goods than was previously available. Suppose we were producing at point C (7 units of shelter, 40 units of food) on our original production possibilities curve. Additional resources and/or new methods of using them (technological progress) can lead to new production possibilities, creating the potential for more of all goods (or more of some with no less of others). These increases will push the production possibilities curve outward. For example, if we invest in human capital by training the workers making the shelters, it will increase the productivity of those workers. As a result, they will produce more units of shelter. Ultimately, then, we will use fewer resources to make shelters, freeing the resources to be used for farming, which will result in more units of food. Notice that at point F (future) on the new curve, we can produce 9 units of shelter and 70 units of food, more of both goods than we previously could produce, at point C.

GROWTH DOES NOT ELIMINATE SCARCITY

With all of this discussion of growth, it is important to remember that growth, or increases in a society's output, does not make scarcity disappear. When output grows more rapidly than population, people are better off. But they still face trade-offs; at any point along the production possibilities curve, to get more of one thing, you must give up something else. There are no free lunches on the production possibilities curve.

Capital Goods versus Consumer Goods

Economies that choose to invest more of their resources for the future will grow faster than those that don't. To generate economic growth, a society must produce fewer consumer goods (video games, DVD players, cell phones, cars, vacations, and so on) in the present and produce more capital goods (machines, factories, tools, education, and the like). The society that devotes a larger share of its productive capacity to capital goods than to consumer goods will experience greater economic growth. It must sacrifice some present consumption of consumer goods and services to experience growth

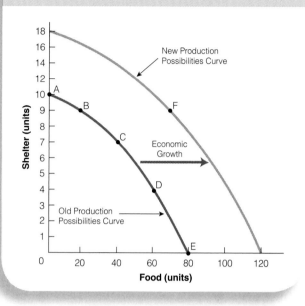

EXHIBIT 2.3 Economic Growth and Production Possibilities

in the future. Why? Investing in capital goods, such as computers and other new technological equipment, as well as upgrading skills and knowledge, expands the ability to produce in the future. It shifts the economy's production possibilities curve outward, increasing the future production capacity of the economy. That is, the economy that invests more (consumes less) now will be able to produce (and therefore consume) more in the future. In Exhibit 2.4 on the next page, we see that Economy A invests more in capital goods than does Economy B. Consequently, Economy A's production possibilities curve shifts outward further than does Economy B's over time.

THE EFFECTS OF A TECHNOLOGICAL CHANGE ON THE PRODUCTION POSSIBILITIES CURVE

In Exhibit 2.5 on page 41, we see that a technological advance does not have to impact all sectors of the economy equally. There is a technological advance in food production but not in housing production. The technological advance in agriculture causes the production possibilities curve to extend out further on the horizontal axis, which measures food production. We can move to any point on the new production possibilities curve. For example, we could move from point A on the original production possibilities curve to point B

EXHIBIT 2.4 Economic Growth and the Production Possibilities Curve

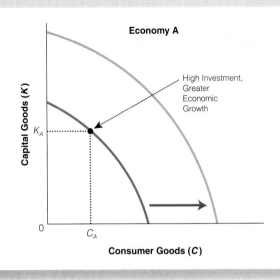

Economy A

High Investment, Greater Economic Growth

K_A

Capital Goods (K)

0   C_A

Consumer Goods (C)

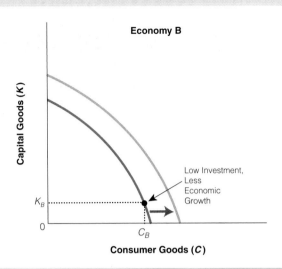

Economy B

Low Investment, Less Economic Growth

K_B

Capital Goods (K)

0   C_B

Consumer Goods (C)

on the new production possibilities curve. This would lead to 150 more units of food and the same amount of housing—200 units. Or we could move from point A to point C, which would allow us to produce more units of both food and housing. How do we produce more housing if the technological advance occurred in agriculture? The answer is that the technological advance in agriculture allows us to produce more from a given quantity of resources. That is, it allows us to shift some of our resources out of agriculture into housing. This is actually an ongoing story in U.S. economic history. In colonial days, about 90 percent of the population made a living in agriculture. Today it is less than 3 percent.

SUMMING UP THE PRODUCTION POSSIBILITIES CURVE

The production possibilities curve shown in Exhibit 2.6 illustrates the choices faced by an economy that makes military goods and consumer goods.

How are the economic concepts of scarcity, choice, opportunity costs, efficiency, and economic growth illustrated in the framework of this production possibilities curve? In Exhibit 2.6, we can show scarcity because resource combinations outside the initial production possibilities

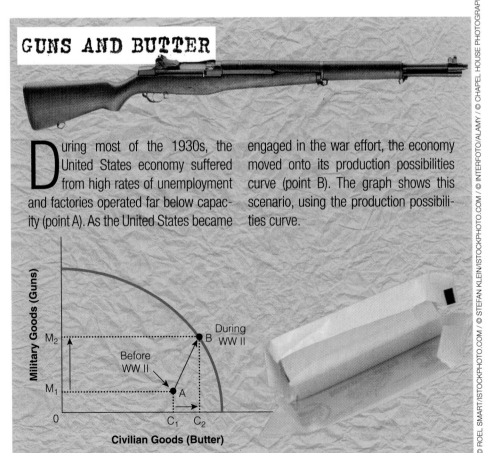

GUNS AND BUTTER

During most of the 1930s, the United States economy suffered from high rates of unemployment and factories operated far below capacity (point A). As the United States became engaged in the war effort, the economy moved onto its production possibilities curve (point B). The graph shows this scenario, using the production possibilities curve.

Military Goods (Guns)

M_2 B During WW II

Before WW II

M_1 A

0   C_1 C_2

Civilian Goods (Butter)

EXHIBIT 2.5 The Effects of a
Technological Change on the
Production Possibilities Curve

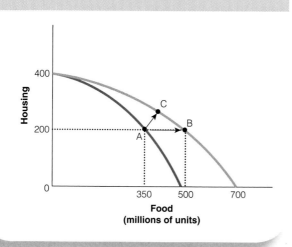

Food
(millions of units)

famine in the 1990s and was again on the brink of famine in 2008. The 1990s famine was estimated to have killed roughly 4 percent of their population. Finally, we see that over time, with economic growth, the whole production possibilities curve can shift outward, making point D attainable.

SECTION CHECK 4

4.1 The production possibilities curve represents the potential total output combinations of two goods available to a society given its resources and existing technology.

4.2 Efficiency means that society uses its resources to the fullest extent—no wasted resources.

4.3 The law of increasing opportunity costs says that the opportunity costs of producing additional units of a good rise as society produces more of that good. This is indicated by a bowed production possibilities curve.

4.4 Economic growth is represented by an outward shift of the production possibilities curve.

curve, such as point D, are unattainable without economic growth. If the economy is operating efficiently, we are somewhere on that production possibilities curve, perhaps at point B or point C. However, if the economy is operating inefficiently, we are operating inside that production possibilities curve, at point A, for example. We can also see in this graph that to get more military goods, you must give up consumer goods, which represents the opportunity cost. The trade-offs between military goods and consumer goods are very real. When North Korea's leaders decided to build up their military, it came at the expense of consumer goods. North Korea experienced a devastating

Ⓢ5 Economic Systems

Think about the following questions as you read through this section, then check for the answers in Section Check 5.

5.1 What goods and services will be produced?

5.2 How will the goods and services be produced?

5.3 Who will get the goods and services?

In this section, we'll address the three economic questions every society must answer.

SCARCITY AND THE ALLOCATION OF RESOURCES

In the last section, we noted that each point on the production possibilities curve is efficient. But each economic system might answer certain economic questions

EXHIBIT 2.6 Production Possibilities
Curve

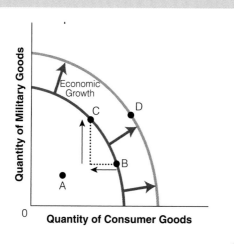

Quantity of Consumer Goods

consumer sovereignty consumers vote with their dollars in a market economy; this accounts for what is produced

command economy economy in which the government uses central planning to coordinate most economic activities

market economy an economy that allocates goods and services through the private decisions of consumers, input suppliers, and firms

mixed economy an economy in which government and the private sector determine the allocation of resources

regardless of the level of affluence of the society or its political structure. We will consider three fundamental questions that every society inevitably faces: (1) What goods and services will be produced? (2) How will the goods and services be produced? (3) Who will get the goods and services produced? These questions are unavoidable in a world of scarcity.

WHAT GOODS AND SERVICES WILL BE PRODUCED?

How do individuals control production decisions in market-oriented economies? Questions arise such as should society produce more baseball stadiums or more schools? Should Apple produce more iPhones or laptops? The government has a limited budget, too, and must make choices on how much to spend on defense, health care, highways, and education. In short, consumers, firms, and governments must all make choices about what goods and services will be produced and each one of those decisions has an opportunity cost—the highest valued alternative forgone. In the marketplace, the answer to these and other similar questions is that people "vote" in economic affairs with their dollars (or pounds or yen). This concept is called **consumer sovereignty**. Consumer sovereignty explains how individual consumers in market economies determine what is to be produced.

Televisions, DVD players, cell phones, iPods, camcorders, and laptops, for example, became part of our lives because consumers "voted" hundreds of dollars apiece on these goods. As TVs became more advanced, consumers "voted" fewer dollars on regular color TVs and more on high-definition TVs. Similarly, vinyl record albums gave way to

What are you "voting" for with your dollars?

tapes, and CDs to downloadable music as consumers voted for these items with their dollars. If consumers vote for more fuel-efficient cars and healthier foods, then firms that wish to remain profitable must listen and respond.

How Different Types of Economic Systems Answer the Question "What Goods and Services Will Be Produced?"

Economies are organized in different ways to answer the question of what is to be produced. The dispute over the best way to answer this question has inflamed passions for centuries. Should a central planning board make the decisions, as in North Korea and Cuba? Sometimes this highly centralized economic system is referred to as a **command economy**. Under this type of regime, decisions about how many tractors or automobiles to produce are largely determined by a government official or committee associated with the central planning organization. That same group decides on the number and size of school buildings, refrigerators, shoes, and so on. Other countries, including the United States, much of Europe, and, increasingly, Asia and elsewhere, have largely adopted a decentralized decision-making process where literally millions of individual producers and consumers of goods and services determine what goods, and how many of them, will be produced. A country that uses such a decentralized decision-making process is often said to have a **market economy**. Actually, no nation has a pure market economy. The United States, along with most countries, is said to have a **mixed economy**. In such an economy, the government and the private sector together determine the allocation of resources.

HOW WILL THE GOODS AND SERVICES BE PRODUCED?

Because of scarcity, all economies, regardless of their political structure, must decide how to produce the goods and services that they want. Goods and services can generally be produced in several ways. Firms may face a trade-off between using more machines or more workers. For example, a company might decide to move its production to a plant in another country that uses more workers and fewer machines.

A ditch can be dug by many workers using their hands, by a few workers with shovels, or by one person with a backhoe. Someone must decide which method is most appropriate. From this example, you might be tempted to conclude that it is desirable to use the biggest, most elaborate form of capital. But would you really want to plant your spring flowers with huge earth-moving machinery? That is, the most capital-intensive method of production may not always be the best. The best method is the least-cost method.

What Is the Best Form of Production?

The best or "optimal" form of production will usually vary from one economy to the next. For example, earthmoving machinery is used in digging large ditches in the United States and Europe, while in developing countries, shovels are often used. Why do these optimal forms of production vary? Compared with capital, labor is relatively cheap and plentiful in developing countries but relatively scarce and expensive in the United States. In contrast, capital (machines and tools, mainly) is comparatively plentiful and cheap in the United States but scarcer and more costly in developing countries. That is, in developing countries, production tends to be more **labor intensive**, or labor driven. In the United States, production tends to be more **capital intensive**, or capital driven. Each nation tends to use the production processes that conserve its relatively scarce (and thus relatively more expensive) resources and use more of its relatively abundant resources.

WHO WILL GET THE GOODS AND SERVICES PRODUCED?

> **labor intensive** production that uses a large amount of labor
>
> **capital intensive** production that uses a large amount of capital

In every society, some mechanism must exist to determine how goods and services are to be distributed among the population. Who gets what? Why do some people get to consume or use far more goods and services than others? This question of distribution is so important that wars and revolutions have been fought over it. Both the French and Russian revolutions were concerned fundamentally with the distribution of goods and services. Even in societies where political questions are usually settled peacefully, the question of the distribution of income is an issue that always arouses strong emotional responses. As we will see, in a market economy with private ownership and control of the means of production, the amounts of goods and services an individual can obtain depend on her or his income. Income, in turn, will depend on the quantity and quality of the scarce resources the individual controls. Income is also determined by the price others are willing and able to pay for what you have to sell. If you are a medical doctor and make $300,000 a year, that is income you will have available to buy goods and services. If you also own a condominium you rent out in Aspen, Colorado, you will have an even greater amount of income to spend on goods and services. For instance, markets reward education, hard

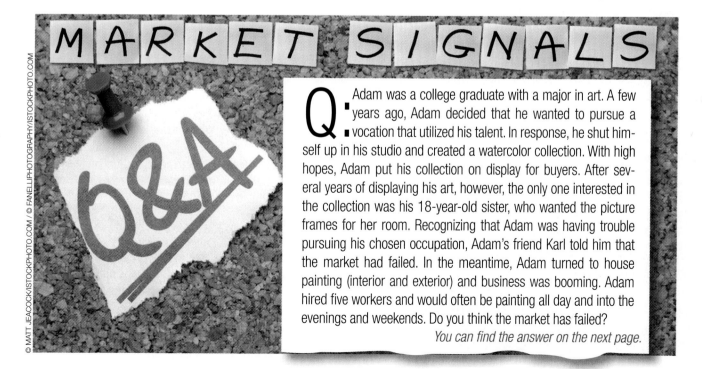

MARKET SIGNALS

Q: Adam was a college graduate with a major in art. A few years ago, Adam decided that he wanted to pursue a vocation that utilized his talent. In response, he shut himself up in his studio and created a watercolor collection. With high hopes, Adam put his collection on display for buyers. After several years of displaying his art, however, the only one interested in the collection was his 18-year-old sister, who wanted the picture frames for her room. Recognizing that Adam was having trouble pursuing his chosen occupation, Adam's friend Karl told him that the market had failed. In the meantime, Adam turned to house painting (interior and exterior) and business was booming. Adam hired five workers and would often be painting all day and into the evenings and weekends. Do you think the market has failed?

You can find the answer on the next page.

MARKET SIGNALS

A: No. Markets provide important signals, and the signal being sent in this situation is that Adam should look for some other means of support—something that society values. Remember the function of consumer sovereignty in the marketplace. Clearly, consumers were not voting for Adam's art. The market seems to be telling Adam, "less painting on canvas and more painting on walls, doors, and trim."

work, and training. Education (years of schooling) and earnings are highly (positively) correlated. Also, people with unique and marketable skills, like talk show host Oprah Winfrey, can make lots of money. This basis for distribution may or may not be viewed as "fair," an issue we will look at in detail later in this book.

Castaway and Resource Allocation

In the movie *Castaway*, Chuck Noland's (played by Tom Hanks) plane crashes, leaving him stranded on a deserted island, and he has to find a way to survive. On the island, he must find answers to the *what*, *how*, and *for whom* questions. The *for whom* question is pretty easy: He is the only one on the island—he gets what is produced. The *what* question is pretty easy, too: He is trying to survive, so he is looking to produce food, shelter, and clothing. The *how* question is where this scene becomes interesting. Noland salvages several boxes from the plane crash. After a failed attempt to leave the island, he decides to open the boxes to see whether they contain anything useful. He first finds a pair of ice skates. He uses the blades of the ice skates as a knife to

open coconuts, to cut a dress to convert into a fishing net, and to sharpen a stick to use as a spear for catching fish. He uses the laces from the skate and the bubble wrap in the package to dress an injury. He uses the raft as a lean-to for his shelter. He builds a fire and even "makes" a friend out of a volleyball. In short, Noland must use his entrepreneurial talents to make the best use of the scarce resources to survive on the island.

SECTION CHECK 5

5.1 In a decentralized market economy, independent buyers and sellers decide what goods and services will be produced. In a mixed economy, government and the private sector make these decisions.

5.2 The best form of production is the one that conserves the relatively scarce (more costly) resources and uses more of the abundant (less costly) resources. When capital is relatively scarce and labor plentiful, production tends to be labor intensive. When capital is abundant and labor scarce, production tends to be capital intensive.

5.3 In a market economy, the amount of goods and services one is able to obtain depends on one's income. The amount of an individual's income depends on the quantity and quality of the scarce resources that he or she controls.

Chuck Noland (Tom Hanks) had to make the best use of his scarce resources to survive on the island.

Chapter 2: Self-Review

Now that you're finished reading the chapter, review the questions below. You can write your answers in the space provided, then go online to see the answers at www.cengagebrain.com.

S1—CHOICES, COSTS, AND TRADE-OFFS

1. Why does scarcity force us to make choices?

2. The price of a one-way bus trip from Los Angeles to New York City is $150.00. Sarah, a school teacher, pays the same price in February (during the school year) as in July (during her vacation), so the cost is the same in February as in July. Do you agree?

3. McDonald's once ran a promotion that whenever St. Louis Cardinals slugger Mark McGwire hit a home run into the upper deck at Busch Stadium, McDonald's gave anyone with a ticket to that day's game a free Big Mac. If holders of ticket stubs have to stand in line for 10 minutes, is the Big Mac really "free"?

S2—MARGINAL THINKING

4. Which of the following activities require marginal thinking? Why?
   a. studying
   b. eating
   c. driving
   d. shopping
   e. getting ready for a night out

5. How could the rule of rational choice be expressed in terms of net benefits?

S3—SPECIALIZATION AND TRADE

6. Farmer Fran can grow soybeans and corn. She can grow 50 bushels of soybeans or 100 bushels of corn on an acre of her land for the same cost. The price of soybeans is $1.50 per bushel and the price of corn is $0.60 per bushel. Show the benefits to Fran of specialization. What should she specialize in?

7. True or False: Autarky, a government policy under which countries choose not to trade with other countries, is the best way for an emerging nation to grow.

S4—THE PRODUCTION POSSIBILITIES OF AN ECONOMY

8. True or False: Economy A produces more capital goods and fewer consumer goods than Economy B; therefore, Economy A will grow more rapidly than Economy B.

9. How does the production possibilities curve illustrate increasing opportunity costs?

10. If people reduced their savings (thus reducing the funds available for investment), what would that change do to the society's production possibilities curve over time?

S5—ECONOMIC SYSTEMS

11. What are the three basic economic questions?

12. Why do consumers have to "vote" for a product with their dollars for it to be a success?

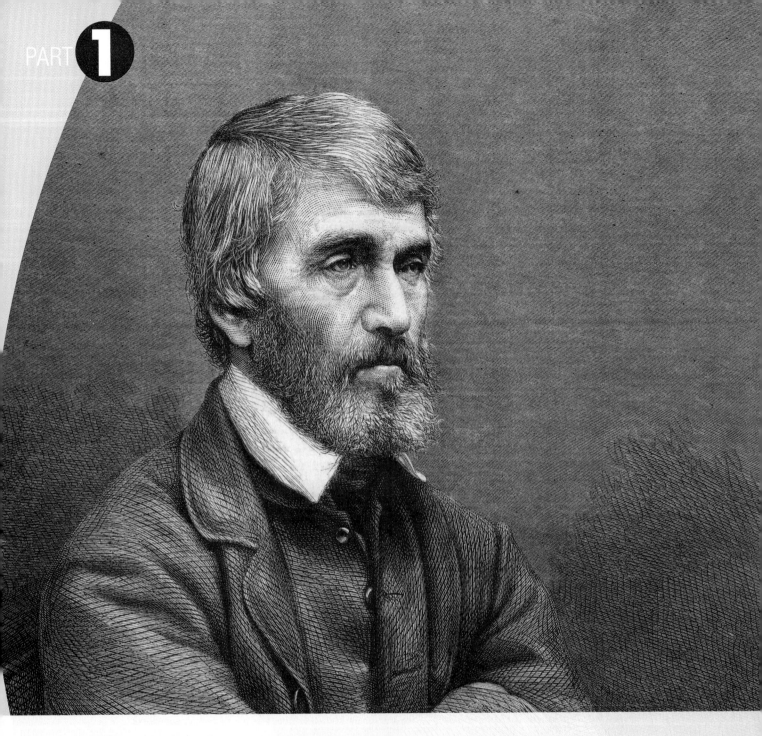

According to Thomas Carlyle,

a nineteenth-century philosopher, "Teach a parrot the term 'supply and demand' and you've got an economist." Unfortunately, economics is more complicated than that.

3

Supply and Demand

i f Carlyle was hinting at the importance of supply and demand, he was right on target. Supply and demand is without a doubt the most powerful tool in the economist's toolbox. It can help explain much of what goes on in the world and help predict what will happen tomorrow. In this chapter, we begin with an introduction to markets. Every market has a demand side and a supply side. Buyers represent the demand side of the market and sellers represent the supply side. In this chapter, we will learn about the law of demand and the law of supply and the factors that can change supply and demand. We will also learn how markets with many buyers and sellers adjust to temporary shortages and surpluses, as prices move back to equilibrium. In addition, we will study the impact of a change in one or more of the determinants of supply and demand and see how it impacts the market price and quantity exchanged. That is, if you want to know how an event or policy may affect the economy, you must know supply and demand.

Ⓢ1 Competitive Markets

Consider the question below as you read this section. You'll find the answer in Section Check 1.

1.1 **Who determines the demand and supply sides of the market?**

The roles of buyers and sellers in markets are important. Buyers, as a group, determine the demand side of the market. Buyers include the consumers who purchase the goods and services and the firms that buy inputs—labor, capital, and raw materials. Sellers, as a group, determine the supply side of the market. Sellers include the firms that produce and sell goods and services and the resource owners who sell their inputs to firms—workers who "sell" their labor and resource owners who sell raw materials and capital. Through the forces of supply and demand, the interaction of buyers and sellers determines market prices and output.

competitive market a market in which the many buyers and sellers have little market power—each buyer's or seller's effect on market price is negligible

law of demand the quantity of a good or service demanded varies inversely (negatively) with its price, *ceteris paribus*

individual demand schedule a schedule that shows the relationship between price and quantity demanded

In the next few sections, we focus on how supply and demand work in a **competitive market**. A competitive market is one in which a number of buyers and sellers are offering similar products, and no single buyer or seller can influence the market price. That is, buyers and sellers have little market power. Because many markets contain a large degree of competitiveness, the lessons of supply and demand can be applied to many different types of problems.

The supply and demand model is particularly useful in markets such as agriculture, finance, labor, construction, services, wholesale, and retail. In short, a model is only as good as its ability to provide accurate explanations and predictions. The model of supply and demand is very good at predicting changes in prices and quantities in many markets large and small.

SECTION CHECK 1

1.1 Buyers determine the demand side of the market and sellers determine the supply side of the market.

Ⓢ2 Demand

Keep the following questions in mind as you read through this section. You'll find the answers in **Section Check 2**.

2.1 What is the law of demand?

2.2 What is an individual demand curve?

2.3 What is a market demand curve?

2.4 What is the difference between a change in demand and a change in quantity demanded?

2.5 What are the determinants of demand?

Sometimes observed behavior is so pervasive it is called a law; the law of demand is an example. According to

EXHIBIT 3.1 Elizabeth's Demand Schedule for Coffee

Price of Coffee (per pound)	Quantity of Coffee Demanded (pounds per year)
$5	5
4	10
3	15
2	20
1	25

the **law of demand**, the quantity of a good or service demanded varies inversely (negatively) with its price, *ceteris paribus*. More directly, the law of demand says that, other things being equal, when the price (P) of a good or service falls, the quantity demanded (Q_D) increases. Conversely, if the price of a good or service rises, the quantity demanded decreases.

For example, a lower price may encourage consumers who were already buying the good to buy a larger quantity. Or the lower price may encourage people who could not afford to buy the product at the higher price to buy it now.

INDIVIDUAL DEMAND: AN INDIVIDUAL DEMAND SCHEDULE

The **individual demand schedule** shows the relationship between the price of the good and the quantity demanded. For example, suppose Elizabeth enjoys drinking coffee. How many pounds of coffee would Elizabeth be willing and able to buy at various prices during the year? At a price of $3 per pound, Elizabeth buys 15 pounds of coffee over the course of a year. If the price is higher, at $4 per pound, she might buy only 10 pounds; if it is lower, say $1 per pound, she might buy 25 pounds of coffee during the year. Elizabeth's demand for coffee for the year is summarized in the demand schedule in Exhibit 3.1. Elizabeth might not be consciously aware of the amounts that she would purchase at prices other than the prevailing one, but that does not alter the fact that she has a schedule in the sense that she would have bought various other amounts had other prices prevailed. It must be emphasized that the schedule is a list of alternative possibilities. At any one time, only one of the prices will prevail, and thus a certain quantity will be purchased.

EXHIBIT 3.2 Elizabeth's Demand Curve for Coffee

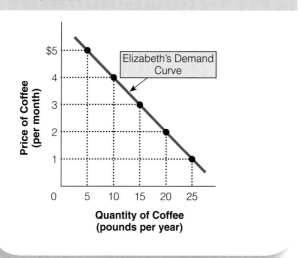

Price of Coffee (per month) vs **Quantity of Coffee (pounds per year)**

Elizabeth's Demand Curve

An Individual Demand Curve

By plotting the different prices and corresponding quantities demanded in Elizabeth's demand schedule in Exhibit 3.1 and then connecting them, we can create the **individual demand curve** for Elizabeth, as shown in Exhibit 3.2. From the curve, we can see that when the price is higher, the quantity demanded is lower, and when the price is lower, the quantity demanded

is higher. The demand curve shows how the quantity demanded of the good changes as its price varies.

WHAT IS A MARKET DEMAND CURVE?

Economists usually speak of the demand curve in terms of large groups of people—a whole nation, a community, or a trading area. That is, to analyze how the market works, we will need to use market demand. As you know, every individual has his or her demand curve for every product. The horizontal summing of the demand curves of many individuals is called the **market demand curve**.

Suppose the consumer group is composed of Homer, Marge, and the rest of their small community of Springfield, and that the product is still coffee. The effect of price on the quantity of coffee demanded by Marge, Homer, and the rest of Springfield is given in the demand schedule and demand curves shown in Exhibit 3.3. At $4 per pound, Homer would be willing and able to buy 20 pounds of coffee per year, Marge would be willing and able to buy 10 pounds, and the rest of Springfield would be willing and able to buy 2,970

individual demand curve a graphical representation that shows the inverse relationship between price and quantity demanded

market demand curve the horizontal summation of individual demand curves

EXHIBIT 3.3 Creating a Market Demand Curve

a. Creating a Market Demand Schedule for Coffee

	Quantity of Coffee Demanded (pounds per year)						
Price (per pound)	Homer	+	Marge	+	Rest of Springfield	=	Market Demand
$4	20	+	10	+	2,970	=	3,000
$3	25	+	15	+	4,960	=	5,000

b. Creating a Market Demand Curve for Coffee

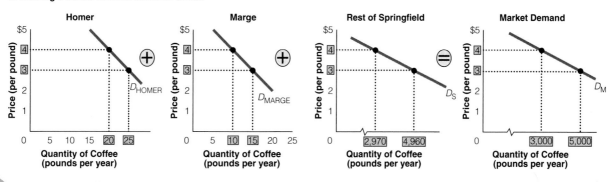

change in quantity
demanded a change in a
good's own price leads to a
change in quantity demanded,
a move along a given demand
curve

change in demand the
prices of related goods,
income, number of buyers,
tastes, and expectations can
change the demand for a
good; that is, a change in one
of these factors shifts the
entire demand curve

EXHIBIT 3.4 A Market Demand Curve

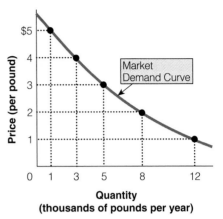

a. Market Demand Schedule for Coffee

Price (per pound)	Quantity Demanded (pounds per year)
$5	1,000
4	3,000
3	5,000
2	8,000
1	12,000

b. Market Demand Curve for Coffee

pounds. At $3 per pound, Homer would be willing and able to buy 25 pounds of coffee per year, Marge would be willing and able to buy 15 pounds, and the rest of Springfield would be willing and able to buy 4,960 pounds. The market demand curve is simply the (horizontal) sum of the quantities Homer, Marge, and the rest of Springfield demand at each price. That is, at $4, the quantity demanded in the market would be 3,000 pounds of coffee (20 + 10 + 2,970 = 3,000), and at $3, the quantity demanded in the market would be 5,000 pounds of coffee (25 + 15 + 4,960 = 5,000).

In Exhibit 3.4, we offer a more complete set of prices and quantities from the market demand for coffee during the year. The market demand curve shows the amounts that all the buyers in the market would be willing and able to buy at various prices. For example, when the price of coffee is $2 per pound, consumers in the market collectively would be willing and able to buy 8,000 pounds per year. At $1 per pound, the amount collectively demanded would be 12,000 pounds per year. The market demand curve is the negative (inverse) relationship between price and the quantity demanded, while holding constant all other factors that affect how much consumers are able and willing to buy *ceteris paribus*.

A CHANGE IN DEMAND VERSUS A CHANGE IN QUANTITY DEMANDED

Consumers are influenced by the prices of goods when they make their purchasing decisions. People prefer to buy more of a good at lower prices than they do at higher prices, holding other factors constant. Why? Primarily, it is because many goods are substitutes for one another. For example, an increase in the price of

coffee might tempt some buyers to switch from buying coffee to buying tea or soft drinks.

Understanding this relationship between price and quantity demanded is so important that economists make a clear distinction between it and the various other factors that can influence consumer behavior. A change in a good's own price is said to lead to a **change in quantity demanded**. That is, it "moves you along" a given demand curve. The demand curve is drawn under the assumption that all things except the price of the good are held constant. However, economists know that price is not the only thing that affects the quantity of a good that people buy. The other factors that influence the demand curve are called *determinants of demand*, and a change in these other factors *shifts the entire demand curve*. These determinants of demand are called demand shifters, and they lead to **changes in demand**.

SHIFTS IN DEMAND

An increase in demand shifts the demand curve to the right; a decrease in demand shifts the demand curve to the left, as shown in Exhibit 3.5. Some possible demand shifters are the prices of related goods, income, number of buyers, tastes, and expectations. We will now look more closely at each of these variables.

THE PRICES OF RELATED GOODS

In deciding how much of a good or service to buy, consumers are influenced by the price of that good

EXHIBIT 3.5 Demand Shifts

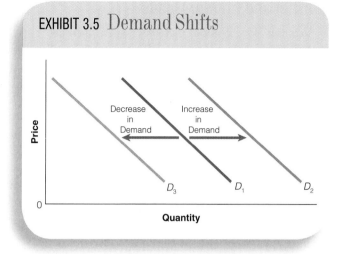

or service, a relationship summarized by the law of demand. However, sometimes consumers are also influenced by the prices of *related* goods and services—substitutes and complements.

Substitutes

Substitutes are generally goods for which one could be used in place of the other. To many, substitutes would include butter and margarine, domestic and foreign cars, movie tickets and video rentals, jackets and sweaters, Exxon and Shell gasoline, and Nike and Reebok shoes.

Suppose you go into a store to buy a couple of six-packs of Coca-Cola and you see that Pepsi is on sale for half its usual price. Is it possible that you might decide to buy Pepsi instead of Coca-Cola? Economists argue that many people would. Empirical tests have confirmed that consumers are responsive to both the price of the good in question and the prices of related goods. When two goods are substitutes, the more people buy of one good, the less they will buy of the other. Suppose there is a fall in the price of Pepsi; this would cause an increase in the quantity demanded for Pepsi (a movement down along the demand curve). Many Coke drinkers may switch to the relatively lower-priced Pepsi, causing a reduction in demand for Coca-Cola, which will shift the demand curve for Coca-Cola to the left. Alternatively, if there is an increase in the price of Pepsi, this causes a decrease in the quantity demanded of Pepsi (a movement up along the demand curve). At the new higher price for Pepsi, many Pepsi drinkers will switch to the relatively lower-priced Coca-Cola, shifting the demand curve for Coca-Cola to the right.

In this example, Pepsi and Coca-Cola are said to be substitutes.

Two goods are **substitutes** if an increase (a decrease) in the price of one good causes the demand curve for another good to shift to the right (left)—a direct (or positive) relationship.

Complements

Complements are goods that "go together," or are often consumed and used simultaneously, such as skis and bindings, peanut butter and jelly, hot dogs and buns, digital music players and downloadable music, and printers and ink cartridges. For example, if the price of motorcycles falls, the quantity of motorcycles demanded will rise—a movement down along the demand curve for motorcycles. As more people buy motorcycles, they will demand more motorcycle helmets—the demand curve for motorcycle helmets shifts to the right. In short, when two goods are **complements**, the more people buy of one good, the more they

Normal and Inferior Goods

If demand for a good increases when incomes rise and decreases when incomes fall, the good is called a **normal good**. Most goods are normal goods. Consumers will typically buy more CDs, clothes, pizzas, and trips to the movies as their incomes rise. However, if demand for a good decreases when incomes rise or if demand increases when incomes fall, the good is called an **inferior good**. These goods include inexpensive cuts of meat, second-hand clothing, and retread tires, which customers generally buy only because they cannot afford more expensive substitutes. As incomes rise, buyers shift to preferred substitutes and decrease their demand for the inferior goods. Suppose most individuals prefer hamburger to beans, but low-income families buy beans because they are less expensive. As incomes rise, many consumers may switch from buying beans to buying hamburgers. Hamburgers may be inferior, too; as incomes rise still further, consumers may substitute steak or chicken for hamburger. The term *inferior* in this sense does not refer to the quality of the good in question but shows that demand decreases when income increases and demand increases when income decreases. So beans are inferior not because they are low quality but because you buy less of them as your income increases.

COMPLEMENTS

will buy of the other. That is, if a decrease in the price of good A leads to an increase in the demand for good B, the two goods are complements. Alternatively, if an increase in the price of good A leads to a decrease in the demand for good B, the two goods are complements.

INCOME

Economists have observed that generally the consumption of goods and services is positively related to the income available to consumers. Empirical studies support the notion that as individuals receive more income, they tend to increase their purchases of most goods and services. Other things held equal, rising income usually leads to an increase in the demand for goods (a rightward shift of the demand curve), and decreasing income usually leads to a decrease in the demand for goods (a leftward shift of the demand curve).

normal good a good for which demand increases if income increases and demand decreases if income decreases

inferior good a good for which demand decreases if income decreases and demand increases if income decreases

NUMBER OF BUYERS

The demand for a good or service will vary with the size of the potential consumer population. The demand for wheat, for example, rises as population increases because the added population wants to consume wheat products, such as bread or cereal. Marketing experts, who closely follow the patterns of consumer behavior regarding a particular good or service, are usually very concerned with the *demographics* of the product—the vital statistics of the potential consumer population, including size, race, income, and age. For example, market researchers for baby food companies keep a close watch on the birth rate.

CONSUMERS' PREFERENCES AND INFORMATION

The demand for a good or service may increase or decrease suddenly with changes in people's tastes or preferences. Changes in taste may be triggered by advertising or promotion, a news story, the behavior of some popular public figure, and so on. Changes in taste are particularly noticeable in apparel. Skirt lengths, coat lapels, shoe styles, and tie sizes change frequently.

Changes in preferences naturally lead to changes in demand. A person may grow tired of one type of recreation or food and try another type. People may decide they want more organic food; consequently, we will see more stores and restaurants catering to this change in taste. Changes in occupation, number of dependents, state of health, and age also tend to alter preferences. The birth of a baby might cause a family to spend less on recreation and more on food and clothing. Illness increases the demand for medicine and lessens purchases of other goods. A cold winter increases the demand for heating oil. Changes in customs and traditions also affect preferences, and the development of new products draws consumer preferences away from other goods. Compact discs replaced record albums, just as DVD players replaced VCRs. A change in information can also impact consumers' demand. For example, a breakout of *E. coli* or new information about a defective and/or dangerous product, such as a baby's crib, can reduce demand.

EXPECTATIONS

Sometimes the demand for a good or service in a given period will dramatically increase or decrease because consumers expect the good to change in price or availability at some future date. If people expect the future price to be higher, they will purchase more of the good now before the price increase. If people expect the future price to be lower, they will purchase less of the good now and wait for the price decrease. For example, if you expect the price of computers to fall soon, you may be less willing to buy one today. Or, if you expect to earn additional income next month, you may be more willing to dip into your current savings to buy something this month.

CHANGES IN DEMAND VERSUS CHANGES IN QUANTITY DEMANDED—REVISITED

Economists put particular emphasis on the impact on consumer behavior of a change in the price of a good. We are interested in distinguishing between consumer behavior related to the price of a good itself (movement *along* a demand curve) and behavior related to changes in other factors (shifts of the demand curve).

As indicated earlier, if the price of a good changes, it causes a *change in quantity demanded*. If one of the other factors (determinants) influencing consumer behavior changes, it results in a *change in demand*. For example, there are two different ways to curb teenage smoking: raise the price of cigarettes (a reduction in the quantity of cigarettes demanded) or decrease the demand for cigarettes (a leftward shift in the demand curve for cigarettes). Both would reduce the amount of smoking. Specifically, to increase the price of cigarettes, the government could impose a higher tax on manufacturers. Most of this would be passed on to consumers in the form of higher prices (more on this in Chapter 4). Or to shift the demand curve leftward, the government could adopt policies to discourage smoking, such as advertising bans and increasing consumer awareness of the harmful side effects of smoking—disease and death.

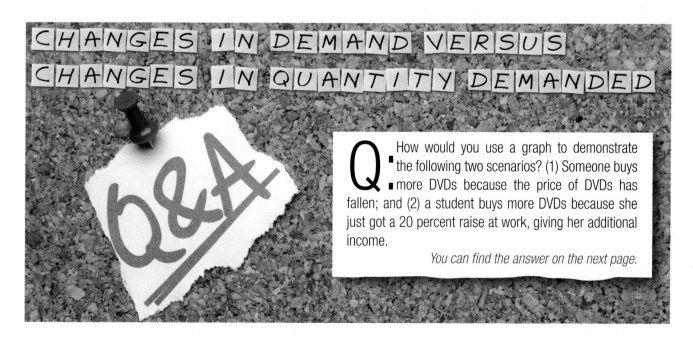

CHANGES IN DEMAND VERSUS CHANGES IN QUANTITY DEMANDED

Q: How would you use a graph to demonstrate the following two scenarios? (1) Someone buys more DVDs because the price of DVDs has fallen; and (2) a student buys more DVDs because she just got a 20 percent raise at work, giving her additional income.

You can find the answer on the next page.

decrease in demand" is reserved for a shift in the whole curve. So if an individual buys more DVDs because the price fell, we call it an increase in quantity demanded. However, if she buys more DVDs even at the current price, say $10, we say it is an increase in demand. In this case, an increase in income was responsible for the increase in demand, because she chose to spend some of her new income on DVDs.

Change in Demand versus Change in Quantity Demanded

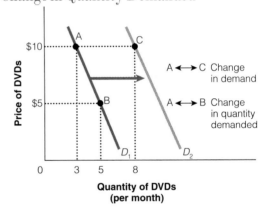

A: In the accompanying exhibit, the movement from A to B is called an increase in quantity demanded, and the movement from B to A is called a decrease in quantity demanded. Economists use the phrase "increase or decrease in quantity demanded" to describe movements along a given demand curve. However, the change from A to C is called an increase in demand, and the change from C to A is called a decrease in demand. The phrase "increase or

---

SECTION CHECK 2

2.1 The law of demand states that when the price of a good falls (rises), the quantity demanded rises (falls), *ceteris paribus*.

2.2 An individual demand curve is a graphical representation of the relationship between the price and the quantity demanded.

2.3 The market demand curve is the amount of a good that all buyers in the market would be willing and able to buy at various prices.

2.4 A change in demand shifts the entire demand curve. An increase in demand shifts the demand curve to the right; a decrease shifts it to the left.

2.5 The determinants of demand are the prices of related goods, income, number of buyers, tastes, and expectations. These factors can create a change in demand for a good—that is, a change in one of these factors shifts the entire demand curve.

ⓢ3 Supply

Keep the following questions in mind as you read through this section. You can find the answers in **Section Check 3.**

3.1 What is the law of supply?

3.2 What is an individual supply curve?

3.3 What is a market supply curve?

3.4 What is the difference between a change in supply and a change in quantity supplied?

3.5 What are the determinants of supply?

In a market, the answer to the fundamental question, "What do we produce, and in what quantities?" depends on the interaction of both buyers and sellers. Demand is only half the story. The willingness and ability of suppliers to provide goods are equally important factors that must be weighed by decision makers in all societies. As with demand, the price of the good is an important factor. Factors other than the price of the good are also important to suppliers, such as the cost of inputs or advances in technology. While behavior will vary among individual suppliers, economists expect that, *ceteris paribus*, the quantity supplied will vary directly with the price of the good, a relationship called the **law of supply**. According to the law of supply, the higher the price of the good (P), the greater the quantity supplied (Q_S), and the lower the price of the good, the smaller the quantity supplied.

The relationship described by the law of supply is a direct, or positive, relationship, because the variables move in the same direction.

A POSITIVE RELATIONSHIP BETWEEN PRICE AND QUANTITY SUPPLIED

Firms supplying goods and services want to increase their profits, and the higher the price per unit, the greater the profitability generated by supplying more of that good.

© IMAGE SOURCE/PHOTOLIBRARY

For example, if you were a coffee grower, wouldn't you much rather be paid $5 a pound than $1 a pound, *ceteris paribus*? When the price of coffee is low, the coffee business is less profitable and less of the good will be produced. Some suppliers may even shut down, reducing their quantity supplied to zero.

AN INDIVIDUAL SUPPLY CURVE

To illustrate the concept of an **individual supply curve**, consider the amount of coffee that an individual supplier, Juan Valdes, is willing and able to supply in one year. The law of supply can be illustrated, like the law of demand, by a table or graph. Juan's **individual supply schedule** for coffee is shown in Exhibit 3.6(a) on the next page. The combinations of price and quantity supplied were then plotted and joined to create the individual supply curve shown in Exhibit 3.6(b). Note that the individual supply curve slopes upward as you move from left to right. At higher prices, it will be more attractive to increase production. Existing firms or growers will produce more at higher prices than at lower prices.

THE MARKET SUPPLY CURVE

The **market supply curve** may be thought of as the horizontal summation of the supply curves for individual firms. The market supply curve shows how the total quantity supplied varies positively with the price of a good, while holding constant all other factors that affect how much producers are able and willing to supply. The market supply schedule, which reflects the total quantity supplied at each price by all of the coffee producers, is shown in Exhibit 3.7(a) on the next page. Exhibit 3.7(b) illustrates the resulting market supply curve for this group of coffee producers.

A CHANGE IN QUANTITY SUPPLIED VERSUS A CHANGE IN SUPPLY

Changes in the price of a good lead to changes in the quantity supplied by suppliers, just as changes in

law of supply the quantity of a good or service supplied varies directly (positively) with its price, *ceteris paribus*

individual supply curve a graphical representation that shows the positive relationship between the price and quantity supplied

individual supply schedule a schedule that shows the relationship between price and quantity supplied

market supply curve a graphical representation of the amount of goods and services that suppliers are willing and able to supply at various prices

EXHIBIT 3.6 An Individual Supply Curve

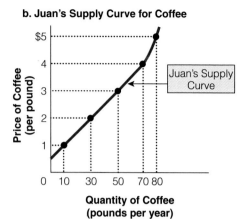

a. Juan's Supply Schedule for Coffee

Price (per pound)	Quantity Supplied (pounds per year)
$5	80
4	70
3	50
2	30
1	10

b. Juan's Supply Curve for Coffee

the price of a good lead to changes in the quantity demanded by buyers. Similarly, a change in supply, whether an increase or a decrease, can occur for reasons other than changes in the price of the product itself, just as changes in demand may be due to factors (determinants) other than the price of the good. In other words, a change in the price of the good in question is shown as a movement along a given supply curve, leading to a **change in quantity supplied**. A change in any other factor that can affect supplier behavior (input prices, prices of related products, expectations, number of suppliers, technology, regulation, taxes and subsidies, and weather) results in *a shift in the entire supply curve*, leading to a **change in supply**.

SHIFTS IN SUPPLY

An increase in supply shifts the supply curve to the right; a decrease in supply shifts the supply curve to the left, as shown in Exhibit 3.8. Anything that affects the costs of production will influence supply and the position of the supply curve. We will now look at some of the possible determinants of supply—factors that determine the position of the supply curve—in greater depth.

Input Prices

Suppliers are strongly influenced by the costs of inputs used in the production process, such as steel used for

EXHIBIT 3.7 A Market Supply Curve

a. Market Supply Schedule for Coffee

Price (per pound)	Quantity Supplied (pounds per year)				
	Juan	+	Other Producers	=	Market Supply
$5	80	+	7,920	=	8,000
4	70	+	6,930	=	7,000
3	50	+	4,950	=	5,000
2	30	+	2,970	=	3,000
1	10	+	990	=	1,000

b. Market Supply Curve for Coffee

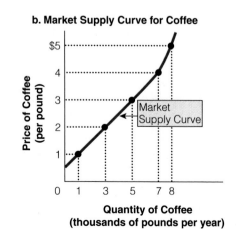

EXHIBIT 3.8 Supply Shifts

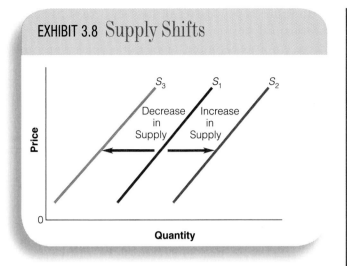

automobiles or microchips used in computers. For example, higher labor, materials, energy, or other input costs increase the costs of production, causing the supply curve to shift to the left at each and every price. If input prices fall, the costs of production decrease, causing the supply curve to shift to the right—more will be supplied at each and every price.

Prices of Related Goods

The supply of a good increases if the price of one of its substitutes in production falls, and the supply of a good decreases if the price of one of its substitutes in production rises. Suppose you own your own farm on which you plant cotton and wheat. One year, the price of wheat falls, and farmers reduce the quantity of wheat supplied, as shown in Exhibit 3.9(a). What effect does the lower price of wheat have on your cotton production? It increases the supply of cotton. You want to produce relatively less of the crop that has fallen in price (wheat) and relatively more of the now more attractive other crop (cotton). Cotton and wheat are *substitutes in production* because both goods can be produced using the same resources. Producers tend to substitute the production of more profitable products for that of less profitable products. So the decrease in the price in the wheat market has caused an increase in supply (a rightward shift) in the cotton market, as seen in Exhibit 3.9(b).

If the price of wheat—a substitute in production—increases, then that crop becomes more profitable. This leads to an increase in the quantity supplied of wheat. Consequently,

farmers will shift their resources out of the relatively lower-priced crop (cotton); the result is a decrease in supply of cotton.

Other examples of substitutes in production include automobile producers that have to decide between producing sedans and pick-ups or construction companies that have to choose between building single residential houses or commercial buildings.

Some goods are *complements in production*. This means that producing one good does not prevent the production of the other, but actually enables production of the other. For example, leather and beef are complements in production. Suppose the price of beef rises and as a result cattle ranchers increase the quantity supplied of beef, moving up the supply curve for beef, as seen in Exhibit 3.9(c). When cattle ranchers produce more beef, they automatically produce more leather. Thus, when the price of beef increases, the supply of the related good (leather) shifts to the right, as seen in Exhibit 3.9(d). Suppose the price of beef falls, and as a result, the quantity supplied of beef falls; this leads to a decrease (a leftward shift) in the supply of leather.

EXHIBIT 3.9 Substitutes and Complements in Production

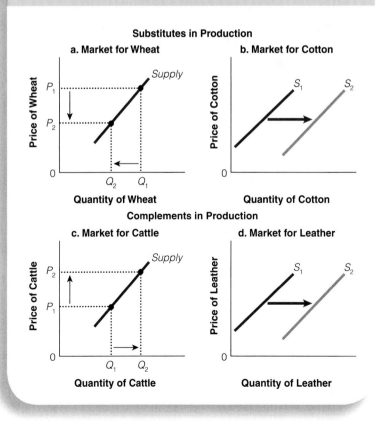

Expectations

Another factor that shifts supply is suppliers' expectations. If producers expect a higher price in the future, they will supply less now than they otherwise would have, preferring to wait to sell when their goods will be more valuable. For example, if a cotton producer expected the price of cotton to be higher next year, he might decide to store some of his current production of cotton and sell it next year when the price will be higher. Similarly, if producers expect now that the price will be lower later, they will supply more now. Oil refiners will often store some of their spring supply of gasoline for summer because gasoline prices typically peak in summer. In addition, some of the heating oil for the fall is stored to supply it in the winter when heating oil prices peak.

Number of Suppliers

We are normally interested in market demand and supply (because together they determine prices and quantities) rather than in the behavior of individual consumers and firms. As we discussed earlier in the chapter, the supply curves of individual suppliers can be summed horizontally to create a market supply curve. An increase in the number of suppliers leads to an increase in supply, denoted by a rightward shift in the supply curve. For example, think of the number of gourmet coffee shops that have sprung up over the last 15 to 20 years, shifting the supply curve of gourmet coffee to the right. An exodus of suppliers has the opposite impact, a decrease in supply, which is indicated by a leftward shift in the supply curve.

Technology

Technological change can lower the firm's costs of production through productivity advances. Human creativity works to find new ways to produce goods and services using fewer or less costly inputs of labor, natural resources, or capital. In recent years, despite generally rising prices, the prices of electronic equipment such as computers, cellular telephones, and high-definition (HD) televisions have fallen dramatically. These technological changes allow the firm to spend less on inputs and produce the same level of output. Human creativity works to find new ways to produce goods and services using fewer or less costly inputs of labor, natural resources, or capital. Because the firm can now produce the good at a lower cost, it will supply more of the good at each and every price, and the supply curve shifts to the right.

Government (Regulation, Taxes, and Subsidies)

Supply may also change because of changes in the legal and regulatory environment in which firms operate. Government regulations can influence the costs of production to a firm, leading to cost-induced supply changes similar to those just discussed. For example, if new safety or clean air requirements increase labor and capital costs, the increased cost will result, *ceteris paribus*, in a decrease in supply, shifting the supply curve to the left, or up. However, deregulation can shift the supply curve to the right.

Certain types of taxes can also alter the costs of production borne

During the global recession of 2007–2009, oil demand dropped substantially. Early in 2009, as oil prices bottomed out, a situation known as contango developed, in which a large gap developed between oil prices trading on the daily spot market and future dated oil contracts. Traders bought oil on the spot market and parked it in tankers until the prices went back up. Floating storage worldwide peaked in April with nearly 90 million barrels sitting in oil tankers waiting to be sold.

by the supplier, causing the supply curve to shift to the left at each price. A subsidy, the opposite of a tax, can lower a firm's costs and shift the supply curve to the right. For example, the government sometimes provides farmers with subsidies to encourage the production of certain agricultural products.

Weather

In addition, weather can sometimes dramatically affect the supply of certain commodities, particularly agricultural products and transportation services. A drought or freezing temperatures will almost certainly cause the supply curves for many crops to shift to the left, while exceptionally good weather can shift a supply curve to the right. For example, unusually cold weather in California during the winter of 2006 destroyed billions of dollars worth of citrus fruit. Hurricane Rita disrupted oil and refining processes. Both events shifted the supply curve for those products to the left.

CHANGE IN SUPPLY VERSUS CHANGE IN QUANTITY SUPPLIED—REVISITED

If the price of a good changes, it leads to a change in the quantity supplied. If one of the other factors influences sellers' behavior, we say it results in a change in supply. For example, if production costs rise because of a wage increase or higher fuel costs, *ceteris paribus*, we would expect a decrease in supply—that is, a leftward shift in the supply curve. Alternatively, if some variable, such as lower input prices, causes the costs of production to fall, the supply curve will shift to the right.

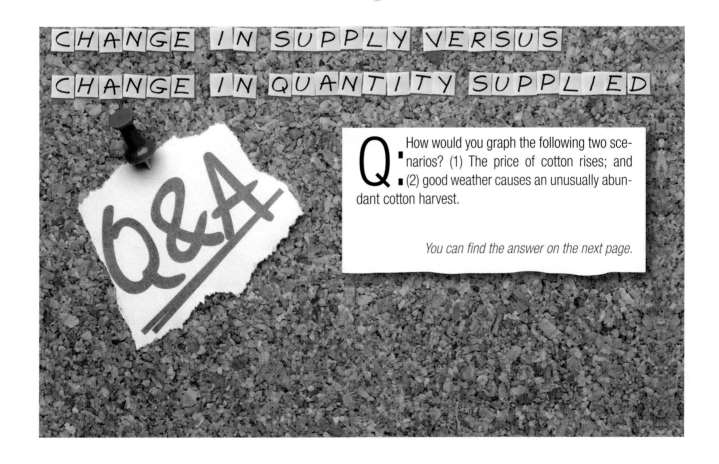

CHANGE IN SUPPLY VERSUS CHANGE IN QUANTITY SUPPLIED

Q: How would you graph the following two scenarios? (1) The price of cotton rises; and (2) good weather causes an unusually abundant cotton harvest.

You can find the answer on the next page.

CHANGE IN SUPPLY VERSUS CHANGE IN QUANTITY SUPPLIED

quantity supplied, and the movement from B to A is called a decrease in quantity supplied. However, the change from B to C is called an increase in supply, and the movement from C to B is called a decrease in supply.

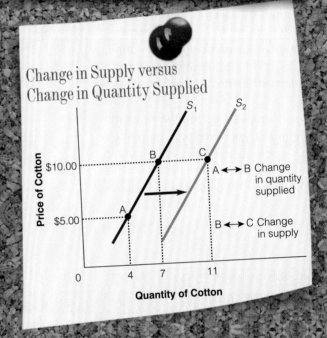

Change in Supply versus Change in Quantity Supplied

© HANIBARAM/ISTOCKPHOTO.COM

A: In the first scenario, the price of cotton increases, so the quantity supplied changes (i.e., a movement along the supply curve). In the second scenario, the good weather causes the supply curve for cotton to shift to the right, which is called a change in supply (not quantity supplied). A shift in the whole supply curve is caused by one of the other variables, not by a change in the price of the good in question.

As shown in the accompanying exhibit, the movement from A to B is called an increase in

---

SECTION CHECK 3

3.1 The law of supply states that the higher (lower) the price of a good, the greater (smaller) the quantity supplied.

3.2 An individual supply curve is a graphical representation that shows the positive relationship between the price and quantity supplied.

3.3 The market supply curve is a graphical representation of the amount of goods and services that suppliers are willing and able to supply at various prices.

3.4 A change in quantity supplied describes movement along a given supply curve in response to a change

in the price of the good in question. A change in supply shifts the entire supply curve. An increase in supply shifts the supply curve to the right; a decrease shifts it to the left.

3.5 The determinants of supply are the input prices, the prices of related products, expectations, number of suppliers, technology, regulation, taxes and subsidies, and weather. These factors can create a change in supply for a good—that is, a change in one of these factors shifts the entire supply curve.

S4 Market Equilibrium Price and Quantity

Keep the following questions in mind as you read through this section. You'll find the answers in **Section Check 4**.

4.1 What is market equilibrium?

4.2 What are surpluses and shortages?

4.3 What happens to equilibrium price and quantity when the demand curve shifts? What happens when the supply curve shifts?

4.4 What happens when both supply and demand shift in the same time period?

4.5 What is an indeterminate solution?

Enough has been said for now about supply and demand separately. We now bring the market supply and demand together.

EQUILIBRIUM PRICE AND QUANTITY

The **market equilibrium** is found at the point at which the market supply and market demand curves intersect. The price at the intersection of the market supply curve and the market demand curve is called the **equilibrium price**, and the quantity is called the **equilibrium quantity**. *At the equilibrium price, the amount that buyers are willing and able to buy is exactly equal to the amount that sellers are willing and able to produce.* The equilibrium market solution is best understood with the help of a simple graph. Let's return to the coffee example we used in our earlier discussions of supply and demand. Exhibit 3.10 combines the market demand curve for coffee with the market supply curve. At $3 per pound, buyers are willing to buy 5,000 pounds of coffee and sellers are willing to supply 5,000 pounds of coffee. Neither may be "happy" about the price; the buyers would probably like a lower price and the sellers would probably like a higher price. But both buyers and sellers are able to carry out their purchase and sales plans at the $3 price. At any other price, either suppliers or demanders would be unable to trade as much as they would like.

Equilibrium is not some mythical notion. It is very real. Every morning fishermen bring in their fresh catch. Along the pier, they negotiate with fish brokers—sellers find buyers and buyers find sellers. Equilibrium is reached when the quantity demanded equals the quantity supplied. Only at the equilibrium price is the amount that sellers want to sell equal to the amount that buyers want to buy.

Shortages and Surpluses

What happens when the market price is not equal to the equilibrium price? If the price is not at the equilibrium level, buyers and sellers have an incentive to drive the price to equilibrium. Suppose the market price is above the equilibrium price, as seen in Exhibit 3.11(a) on the next page. At $4 per pound, the quantity of coffee demanded would be 3,000 pounds, but the quantity supplied would be 7,000 pounds. At this price, a **surplus**, or excess quantity supplied, would exist. That is, at this price, growers would be willing to sell more coffee than consumers would be willing to buy. To get rid of the unwanted surplus, frustrated suppliers would have an incentive to cut their price to increase sales and rid themselves of storage costs and cut back on production. And as price falls, the quantity consumers would be willing to buy increases, ultimately eliminating the unsold surplus and returning the market to the equilibrium level. As long as the price is above the equilibrium

market equilibrium the point at which the market supply and market demand curves intersect

equilibrium price the price at the intersection of the market supply and demand curves; at this price, the quantity demanded equals the quantity supplied

equilibrium quantity the quantity at the intersection of the market supply and demand curves; at the equilibrium quantity, the quantity demanded equals the quantity supplied

surplus a situation in which quantity supplied exceeds quantity demanded

shortage a situation in which quantity demanded exceeds quantity supplied

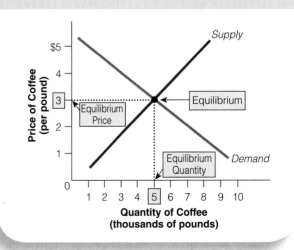

EXHIBIT 3.10 Market Equilibrium

EXHIBIT 3.11 Markets in Temporary Disequilibrium

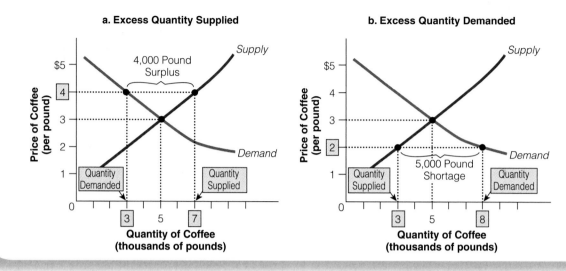

a. Excess Quantity Supplied

b. Excess Quantity Demanded

level, some sellers will have unsold coffee and want to lower the price until it reaches equilibrium.

What would happen if the market price of coffee were below the equilibrium price? As seen in Exhibit 3.11(b), at $2 per pound, the yearly quantity demanded of 8,000 pounds would be greater than the 3,000 pounds that producers would be willing to supply at that low price. So at $2 per pound, a **shortage** or excess quantity demanded of 5,000 pounds would exist. Some consumers are lucky enough to find coffee, but others are not able to find any sellers who are willing to sell them coffee at $2 per pound. Some frustrated consumers may offer to pay sellers more than $2. In addition, sellers noticing that there are disappointed consumers raise their prices. These actions by buyers and sellers cause the market price to rise. As the market price rises, the amount that sellers want to supply increases and the amount that buyers want to buy decreases. The upward pressure on price continues until equilibrium is reached at $3.

Scarcity and Shortages

People often confuse scarcity with shortages. Remember, most goods are scarce—desirable but limited. A shortage occurs when the quantity demanded is greater than the quantity supplied at the current price. We can eliminate shortages by increasing the price, but we cannot eliminate scarcity.

CHANGES IN EQUILIBRIUM PRICE AND QUANTITY

When one of the many determinants of demand or supply (input prices, prices of related products, number of

suppliers, expectations, technology, and so on) changes, the demand and/or supply curves will shift, leading to changes in the equilibrium price and equilibrium quantity. We first consider a change in demand.

A CHANGE IN DEMAND

A shift in the demand curve—caused by a change in the price of a related good (substitutes or complements), income, the number of buyers, tastes, or expectations—results in a change in both equilibrium price and equilibrium quantity, assuming the supply curve has not changed. But how and why does this relationship happen? The answer can be most clearly explained by means of an example. Suppose a new study claimed that two cups of coffee per day had significant health benefits. We would expect an increase in the demand for coffee. That is, at any given price, buyers want more coffee than before. At the original equilibrium, E_1, consumers want to buy Q_3 but sellers only want to sell Q_1, as seen in Exhibit 3.12. Market pressure drives the price up to a new equilibrium, E_2 at P_2. Both the equilibrium price and quantity rise because of the increase in demand. Notice that the *rightward shift in the demand curve causes a movement up along the supply curve*, causing an increase in quantity supplied.

A CHANGE IN SUPPLY

Like a shift in demand, a shift in the supply curve will also influence both equilibrium price and equilibrium quantity, assuming that demand for the product has not changed. For example, what impact would unfavorable weather conditions have in coffee-producing countries?

Such conditions could cause a reduction in the supply of coffee. At any given price, sellers now want to sell less coffee. At the original equilibrium price of P_1, consumers still want to buy Q_1, but sellers are now only willing to supply Q_3. Thus, a shortage develops. Market pressure forces the price of coffee up until it reaches the new equilibrium at E_2, where the equilibrium price is P_2 and the equilibrium quantity is Q_2. A decrease in supply, *ceteris paribus*, will lead to a higher equilibrium price and a lower equilibrium quantity, as shown in Exhibit 3.13. Notice that the decrease in supply causes a *leftward shift in the supply curve resulting in a movement up along the demand curve*; a decrease in quantity demanded.

CHANGES IN BOTH SUPPLY AND DEMAND

We have discussed that, as part of the continual process of adjustment that occurs in the marketplace, supply and demand can each shift in response to many different factors, with the market then adjusting toward the new equilibrium. So far, we have considered only what happens when just one such change occurs at a time. In these cases, we learned that the results of the adjustments in supply and demand on the equilibrium price and quantity are predictable. However, both supply and demand will often shift in the same time period. Can

EXHIBIT 3.12 An Increase in Demand

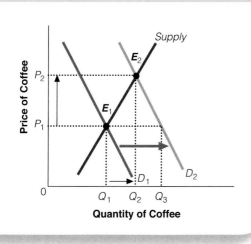

EXHIBIT 3.13 A Decrease in Supply

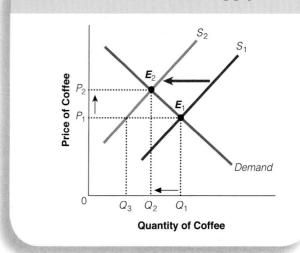

EXHIBIT 3.14 Shifts in Supply and Demand

a. A Small Increase in Supply and a Large Decrease in Demand

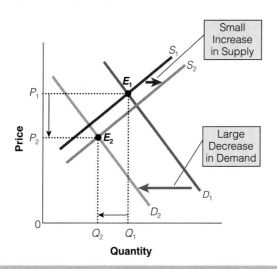

b. A Large Increase in Supply and a Small Decrease in Demand

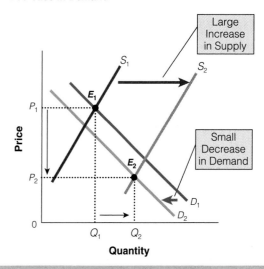

we predict what will happen to equilibrium prices and equilibrium quantities in these situations?

As you will see, when supply and demand move at the same time, we can predict the change in one variable (price or quantity), but we are unable to predict the direction of the effect on the other variable with any certainty. The change in the second variable, then, is said to be *indeterminate*, because it cannot be determined without additional information about the size of the relative shifts in supply and demand. This concept will become clearer to you as we work through the following example.

An Increase in Supply and a Decrease in Demand

In Exhibit 3.14 we have an increase in supply and a decrease in demand. These changes will clearly result in a decrease in the equilibrium price, because both the increase in supply and the decrease in demand work to push this price down. This drop in equilibrium price (from P_1 to P_2) is shown in the movement from E_1 to E_2 in Exhibit 3.14.

The effect of these changes on equilibrium price is clear, but how does the equilibrium quantity change? The impact on equilibrium quantity is indeterminate because the increase in supply increases the equilibrium quantity and the decrease in demand decreases it. In this scenario, the change in the equilibrium quantity will vary depending on the relative changes in supply and demand. If, as shown in Exhibit 3.14(a), the decrease in demand is greater than the increase in supply, the equilibrium quantity will decrease. If, however, as shown in Exhibit 3.14(b), the increase in supply is greater than the decrease in demand, the equilibrium quantity will increase.

An Increase in Demand and Supply

It is also possible that both supply and demand will increase (or decrease). This situation, for example, has happened with HD televisions (and with DVDs, laptops, cell phones, digital cameras, and other electronic equipment, too). As a result of technological breakthroughs and new factories manufacturing HD televisions, the supply curve for HD televisions shifted to the right. That is, at any given price, more HD televisions were offered than before. But with rising income and an increasing number of buyers in the market, the demand for HD televisions increased as well. As shown in Exhibit 3.15, both the increased demand and the increased supply caused an increase in the equilibrium quantity—more HD televisions were sold. The equilibrium price could have gone either up (because of increased demand) or down (because of increased supply), depending on the relative sizes of the demand and supply shifts. In this case, price is the indeterminate

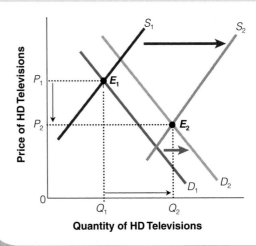

EXHIBIT 3.15 An Increase in the Demand and Supply of HD Televisions

variable. However, in the case of HD televisions, we know that the supply curve shifted more than the demand curve, so that the effect of increased supply pushing prices down outweighed the effect of increased demand pushing prices up. As a result, the equilibrium price of HD televisions has fallen (from P_1 to P_2) over time.

THE COMBINATIONS OF SUPPLY AND DEMAND

The possible changes in demand and/or supply shifts are presented in Exhibit 3.16, along with the resulting changes in equilibrium quantity and equilibrium price. While you could memorize the impact of the various possible changes in demand and supply, it would be better to draw a graph, whenever a situation of changing demand and/or supply arises. Give it a try.

EXHIBIT 3.16 The Impact of Supply and Demand Shifts on Price and Quantity

	Supply Unchanged	An Increase in Supply	A Decrease in Supply
Demand unchanged	P unchanged Q unchanged	$P \downarrow$ $Q \uparrow$	$P \uparrow$ $Q \downarrow$
An increase in demand	$P \uparrow$ $Q \uparrow$	P indeterminate* $Q \uparrow$	$P \uparrow$ Q indeterminate*
A decrease in demand	$P \downarrow$ $Q \downarrow$	$P \downarrow$ Q indeterminate*	P indeterminate* $Q \downarrow$

*Indeterminate means it may increase, decrease, or remain the same, depending on the size of the change in demand relative to the change in supply.

SUPPLY, DEMAND, AND THE MARKET ECONOMY

Supply and demand are at the very foundation of the market system. They determine the prices of goods and services and how our scarce resources are allocated. What is truly amazing is how producers respond to the complex wants of the population without having tremendous shortages or surpluses, despite the fact that in a "free market," no single individual or agency makes decisions about what to produce. The market system provides a way for millions of producers and consumers to allocate scarce resources. Buyers and sellers indicate their wants through their actions and inactions in the marketplace, and this collective "voice" determines how resources are allocated. But how is this information communicated? Market prices serve as the language of the market system.

We often say the decision is made by "the market" or "market forces," but this is of little help in pinpointing the name and the place of the decision maker. In fact, no single person makes decisions about the quantity and quality of television, cars, beds, or any other goods or services consumed in the economy. Literally millions of people, both producers and consumers, participate in the decision-making process. To paraphrase a statement made popular by the first great modern economist, Adam Smith, it is as if an invisible hand works to coordinate the efforts of millions of diverse participants in the complex process of producing and distributing goods and services.

Market prices communicate important information to both buyers and sellers. They reveal information about the relative availability of products to buyers and they provide sellers with critical information about the relative value that consumers place on those products. In effect, market prices provide a way for both buyers and sellers to communicate about the relative value of resources. This communication results in a shifting of resources from those uses that are less valued to those that are more valued.

SECTION CHECK 4

4.1 The intersection of the supply and demand curves shows the equilibrium price and equilibrium quantity in a market. This point is the market equilibrium point.

4.2 A surplus occurs when quantity supplied exceeds quantity demanded; a shortage occurs when quantity demanded exceeds quantity supplied.

4.3 Shifts in the demand or the supply curve will cause a corresponding change in the equilibrium price and/or quantity, *ceteris paribus*.

4.4 Supply and demand curves can shift simultaneously in response to changes in both supply and demand determinants.

4.5 When simultaneous shifts occur in both supply and demand curves, either the equilibrium price or the equilibrium quantity will be indeterminate without more information.

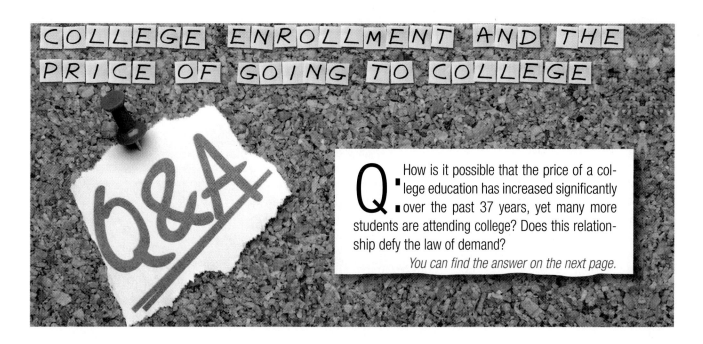

COLLEGE ENROLLMENT AND THE PRICE OF GOING TO COLLEGE

Q: How is it possible that the price of a college education has increased significantly over the past 37 years, yet many more students are attending college? Does this relationship defy the law of demand?

You can find the answer on the next page.

COLLEGE ENROLLMENT AND THE PRICE OF GOING TO COLLEGE

A: If we know the price of a college education (adjusted for inflation) and the number of students enrolled in college for the two years 1970 and 2010, we can tell a plausible story using the analysis of supply and demand. In exhibit (a) below suppose that we have data for points A and B, the price of a college education and the quantity (the number of college students enrolled in the respective years, 1970 and 2010). In exhibit (b), we connect the two points with supply and demand curves and see a decrease in supply and an increase in demand. Demand increased between 1970 and 2010 for at least two reasons: First, on the demand side, as population grows, a greater number of buyers want a college education. Second, a college education is a normal good; as income increases, buyers increase their demand for a college education. On the supply side, several factors caused the supply curve for education to shift to the left: the cost of maintenance (hiring additional staff and increasing faculty salaries), new equipment (computers, lab equipment, and library supplies), and buildings (additional classrooms, labs, cafeteria expansions, and dormitory space).

This situation does not defy the law of demand that states that there is an inverse relationship between price and quantity demanded, *ceteris paribus*. The truth is that supply and demand curves are shifting constantly. In this case, the demand (increasing) and supply (decreasing) caused price and quantity to rise.

Market for College Education

a. Price of College Education and Quantity of College Students

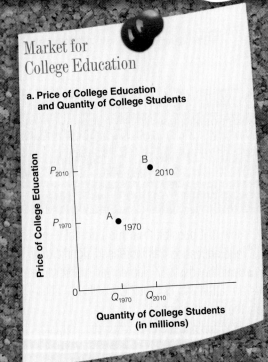

b. Simultaneous Increase in Demand and Decrease in Supply

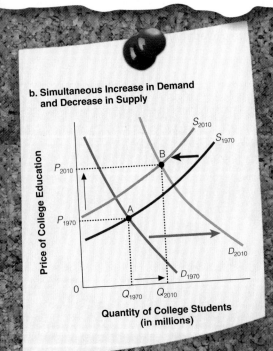

Chapter 3: Self-Review

Now that you're finished reading the chapter, review the questions below. You can write your answers in the space provided, then go online to see the answers at www.cengagebrain.com.

S1–COMPETITIVE MARKETS

1. True or False: In a competitive market, buyers and sellers have significant market power.

S2–DEMAND

2. What is the difference between an individual demand curve and a market demand curve?

3. If the price of zucchini increases, causing the demand for yellow squash to rise, what do we call the relationship between zucchini and yellow squash?

4. If plane travel is a normal good and bus travel is an inferior good, what will happen to the demand curves for plane and bus travel if people's incomes increase?

5. What would be the effects of each of the following on the demand for hamburger in Hilo, Hawaii? In each case, identify the responsible determinant of demand.
   a. The price of chicken falls.
   b. The price of hamburger buns doubles.
   c. Scientists find that eating hamburger prolongs life.
   d. The population of Hilo doubles.

S3–SUPPLY

6. What are the two reasons that a supply curve is positively sloped?

7. If the price of corn rose,
   a. what would be the effect on the supply of corn?
   b. what would be the effect on the supply of wheat?

8. The following table shows the supply schedule for Rolling Rock Oil Co. Plot Rolling Rock's supply curve on a graph.

Price (dollars per barrel)	Quantity Supplied (barrels per month)
$5	10,000
10	15,000
15	20,000
20	25,000
25	30,000

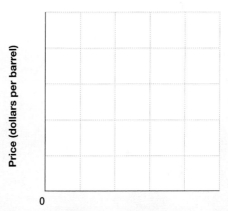

S4–MARKET EQUILIBRIUM PRICE AND QUANTITY

9. True or False: If the price charged is less than the equilibrium price, resulting in buyers wanting to buy more at that price than sellers are willing to sell, a shortage will occur.

10. When both supply and demand shift, what added information do we need to know in order to determine in which direction the indeterminate variable changes?

The National Football League

posted attendance of roughly 74,000 for Super Bowl XLIV in Miami. Just weeks before the game, however, tickets were selling on secondary ticket exchange sites such as StubHub and TicketMaster for anywhere from $1,200 to $3,500—well above face value. What does this tell us about the prices that fans are willing to pay and the number of tickets they are willing to buy? Why does the NFL set its ticket prices so low? Do scalpers "rip off" innocent buyers? A further look at supply and demand will help us answer these and many other questions.

4

Using Supply and Demand

if a rock group increased the price it charges for concert tickets, what impact would that have on ticket sales? More precisely, would ticket sales fall a little or a lot? Would the group make more money by lowering the price or by raising the price? This chapter will allow you to answer these types of questions and more.

Some of the results in this chapter may surprise you. A huge flood in the Midwest that destroyed much of this year's wheat crop would leave some wheat farmers better off. Ideal weather that led to a bountiful crop of wheat everywhere might leave most wheat farmers worse off. As you will soon find out, these issues hinge on the tools of elasticity.

Recall from Chapter 1 that the economist wears two hats—as the scientist that explains the world around him and as the policy maker who uses his theories to make the world a better place. In this chapter, we look at various government policies using supply and demand. But beware—policies often have unintended effects that the policy maker may not have anticipated. We will also see the importance of elasticity in determining the effects of taxes. If a tax is levied on the seller, will the seller pay all of the taxes? If the tax were levied on the buyer, will the buyer pay all of the taxes? We will see that elasticity, not who is legally required to pay the tax, is critical in the determination of tax burden. Elasticities will also help us to more fully understand many policy issues, such as luxury taxes. If Congress were to impose a large tax on yachts, what do you think would happen to yacht sales? What would happen to employment in the boat industry?

Finally, we'll consider whether the price and output that result from the equilibrium of supply and demand are right from society's standpoint. Using the tools of consumer and producer surplus, we can demonstrate the efficiency of a competitive market. In other words, we can show that the equilibrium price and quantity in a competitive market maximize the economic welfare of consumers and producers. Maximizing total surplus (the sum of consumer and producer surplus) leads to an efficient allocation of resources. Efficiency makes the size of the economic pie as large as possible. How we distribute that economic pie (equity) is the subject of future chapters. Efficiency can be measured on objective, positive grounds, whereas equity involves normative analysis.

Sections in Chapter 4

⑤1 Price Elasticity of Demand

Consider the following questions as you read through this section. You'll find the answers in **Section Check 1**.

1.1 What is price elasticity of demand?

1.2 How do we measure consumers' responses to price changes?

1.3 What determines the price elasticity of demand?

In learning and applying the law of demand, we have established the basic fact that quantity demanded changes inversely with change in price, *ceteris paribus*. But how much does quantity demanded change? The extent to which a change in price affects quantity demanded may vary considerably from product to product and over the various price ranges for the same product. The **price elasticity of demand** measures the responsiveness of quantity demanded to a change in price. Specifically, price elasticity is defined as the percentage change in quantity demanded divided by the percentage change in price, or

$$\text{Price elasticity of demand } (E_D) = \frac{\text{Percentage change in quantity demand}}{\text{Percentage change in price}}$$

Note that, following the law of demand, price and quantity demanded show an inverse relationship. For this reason, the price elasticity of demand is, in theory, always negative. But in practice and for simplicity, this quantity is always expressed in absolute value terms—that is, as a positive number.

IS THE DEMAND CURVE ELASTIC OR INELASTIC?

It is important to understand the basic concepts behind elasticities. To do this, we must focus on the percentage changes in quantity demanded and price.

If the quantity demanded is responsive to even a small change in price, we call it elastic. On the other hand, if a huge change in price results in only a small

change in quantity demanded, then the demand is said to be inelastic. For example, if a 10 percent increase in the price leads to a 50 percent reduction in the quantity demanded, we say that demand is elastic because the quantity demanded is sensitive to the price change.

$$E_D = \frac{\%\Delta Q_D}{\%\Delta P} = \frac{50\%}{10\%} = 5$$

Demand is elastic in this case because a 10 percent change in price led to a larger (50 percent) change in quantity demanded.

Alternatively, if a 10 percent increase in the price leads to a 1 percent reduction in quantity demanded, we say that demand is *inelastic* because the quantity demanded did not respond much to the price reduction.

$$E_D = \frac{\%\Delta Q_D}{\%\Delta P} = \frac{1\%}{10\%} = 0.10$$

Demand is inelastic in this case because a 10 percent change in price led to a smaller (1 percent) change in quantity demanded.

TYPES OF DEMAND CURVES

Economists refer to a variety of demand curves based on the magnitude of their elasticity. A demand curve, or

© BLUE JEAN IMAGES/ALAMY

Think of price elasticity like an elastic rubber band. When small price changes greatly affect, or "stretch," quantity demanded, the demand is elastic, much like a very stretchy rubber band. When large price changes can't "stretch" demand, however, then demand is inelastic, more like a very stiff rubber band.

EXHIBIT 4.1 Elastic Demand

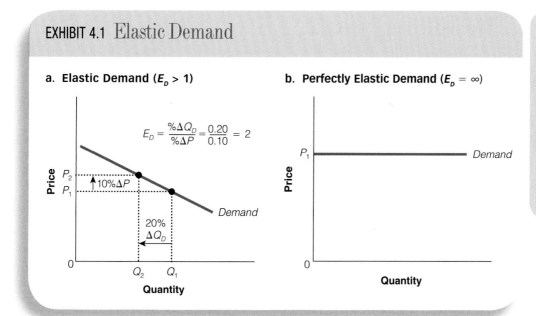

a. Elastic Demand ($E_D > 1$)

$$E_D = \frac{\%\Delta Q_D}{\%\Delta P} = \frac{0.20}{0.10} = 2$$

10%ΔP

20% ΔQ_D

Price: P_2, P_1

Quantity: Q_2, Q_1

Demand

b. Perfectly Elastic Demand ($E_D = \infty$)

P_1

Demand

Price

Quantity

elastic when the quantity demanded is greater than the percentage change in price ($E_D > 1$)

inelastic when the quantity demanded is less than the percentage change in price ($E_D < 1$)

unit elastic demand demand with a price elasticity of 1; the percentage change in quantity demanded is equal to the percentage change in price

a portion of a demand curve, can be elastic, inelastic, or unit elastic.

Demand is **elastic** when the elasticity is greater than 1 ($E_D > 1$)—the quantity demanded changes proportionally more than the price changes. In this case, a given percentage increase in price, say 10 percent, leads to a larger percentage change in quantity demanded, say 20 percent, as seen in Exhibit 4.1(a). If the curve is *perfectly elastic*, the demand curve is horizontal. The elasticity coefficient is infinity because even the slightest change in price will lead to a huge change in quantity demanded—for example, a tiny increase in price will cause the quantity demanded to fall to zero. In Exhibit 4.1(b), a *perfectly elastic* demand curve (horizontal) is illustrated.

Demand is **inelastic** when the elasticity is less than 1; the quantity demanded changes proportionally less than the price changes. In this case, a given percentage change in price (for example, 10 percent) is accompanied by a smaller reduction in quantity demanded (for example, 5 percent), as seen in Exhibit 4.2(a) on the next page. If the demand curve is *perfectly inelastic*, the quantity demanded is the same regardless of the price. The elasticity coefficient is zero because the quantity demanded does not respond to a change in price. This relationship is illustrated in Exhibit 4.2(b).

Goods for which E_D equals one ($E_D = 1$) are said to have **unit elastic demand**. In this case, the quantity demanded changes proportionately to price changes. For example, a 10 percent increase in price will lead to a 10 percent reduction in quantity demanded. This relationship is illustrated in Exhibit 4.3 on the next page.

The price elasticity of demand is closely related to the slope of the demand curve. Generally speaking, the flatter the demand curve passing through a given point, the more elastic the demand. The steeper the demand curve passing through a given point, the less elastic the demand.

THE DETERMINANTS OF THE PRICE ELASTICITY OF DEMAND

As you have learned, the elasticity of demand for a specific good refers to movements along its demand curve as its price changes. A lower price will increase quantity demanded, and a higher price will reduce quantity demanded. But what factors will influence the magnitude of the change in quantity demanded in response to a price change? That is, what will make the demand curve relatively more elastic (where Q_D is responsive to price changes), and what will make the demand curve relatively less elastic (where Q_D is less responsive to price changes)?

For the most part, the price elasticity of demand depends on three factors: (1) the availability of close substitutes, (2) the proportion of income spent on the good, and (3) the amount of time that has elapsed since the price change.

PED depends on 3 factors:
1) available substitutes
2) income spent on good
3) time since price change

Availability of Close Substitutes

Goods *with* close substitutes tend to have more elastic demands. Why? Because if the price of such a good increases, consumers can easily switch to other now relatively lower priced substitutes. In many examples, such as different brands of root beer or gasoline, the ease of substitution will make demand quite elastic for most individuals. Goods *without* close substitutes, such as insulin for diabetics, cigarettes for chain smokers, heroin for addicts, or emergency medical care for those with appendicitis or broken legs, tend to have inelastic demands. The demand for an antivenom shot after a

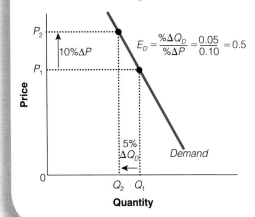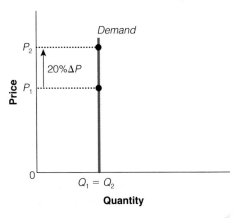

EXHIBIT 4.2 Inelastic Demand

a. Inelastic Demand ($E_D < 1$)

$$E_D = \frac{\%\Delta Q_D}{\%\Delta P} = \frac{0.05}{0.10} = 0.5$$

b. Perfectly Inelastic Demand ($E_D = 0$)

rattle snake bite is another example. Once a person is bitten, that demand curve becomes extremely inelastic.

The degree of substitutability can also depend on whether the good is a necessity or a luxury. Goods that are necessities, such as food, have no ready substitutes and thus tend to have lower elasticities than do luxury items, such as jewelry.

When the good is broadly defined, it tends to be less elastic than when it is narrowly defined. For example, the elasticity of demand for food (a broad category) tends to be inelastic because few substitutes are available for food. But for a certain type of food, such as pizza (narrowly defined good) it is much easier to find a substitute—perhaps tacos, burgers, salads, burritos, or

chili fries. That is, the demand for a particular type of food is more elastic because more and better substitutes are available than for food as an entire category.

Proportion of Income Spent on the Good

The smaller the proportion of income spent on a good, the lower its elasticity of demand. If the amount spent on a good relative to income is small, then the impact of a change in its price on one's budget will also be small. As a result, consumers will respond less to price changes for small-ticket items than for similar percentage changes in large-ticket items, where a price change could potentially have a large impact on the consumer's budget. For example, a 50 percent increase in the price of salt will have a much smaller impact on consumers' behavior than a similar percentage increase in the price of a new automobile. Similarly, a 50 percent increase in the cost of private university tuition will have a greater impact on students' (and sometimes parents') budgets than a 50 percent increase in textbook prices.

Time

For many goods, the more time that people have to adapt to a new price change, the greater the elasticity of demand. Immediately after a price change, consumers may be unable to locate good alternatives or easily change their consumption patterns. But as time passes, consumers have more time to find or develop suitable substitutes and to plan and implement changes in their patterns of consumption. For example, drivers may not respond immediately to an increase in gas prices,

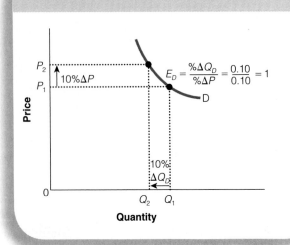

EXHIBIT 4.3 Unit Elastic Demand

$$E_D = \frac{\%\Delta Q_D}{\%\Delta P} = \frac{0.10}{0.10} = 1$$

perhaps believing it to be temporary. However, if the price persists over a longer period, we would expect people to drive less, buy more fuel-efficient cars, move closer to work, carpool, take the bus, or even bike to work. So for many goods, especially nondurable goods (goods that do not last a long time), the short-run demand curve is generally less elastic than the long-run demand curve, as illustrated in Exhibit 4.4.

Estimated Price Elasticities of Demand

Because of shifts in supply and demand curves, researchers have a difficult task when trying to estimate empirically the price elasticity of demand for a particular good or service. Despite this difficulty, Exhibit 4.5 presents some estimates for the price elasticity of demand for certain goods. As you would expect, certain goods such as medical care, air travel, and gasoline are all relatively price inelastic in the short run because buyers have fewer substitutes. On the other hand, air travel in the long run is much more sensitive to price (elastic) because the available substitutes are much more plentiful. Exhibit 4.5 shows that the price elasticity of demand for air travel is 2.4, which means that a 1 percent increase in price will lead to a 2.4 percent reduction in quantity demanded. Notice, in each case where the data are available, the estimates of the long-run price elasticities of demand are greater than the short-run price elasticities of demand. In short, the price elasticity of demand is greater when the price change persists over a longer time period.

EXHIBIT 4.5 Price Elasticities of Demand for Selected Goods

Good	Short Run	Long Run
Salt	—	0.1
Air travel	0.1	2.4
Gasoline	0.2	0.7
Medical care and hospitalization	0.3	0.9
Jewelry and watches	0.4	0.7
Physician services	0.6	—
Alcohol	0.9	3.6
Movies	0.9	3.7
China, glassware	1.5	2.6
Automobiles	1.9	2.2
Chevrolets	—	4.0

SOURCES: Adapted from Robert Archibald and Robert Gillingham, "An Analysis of the Short-Run Consumer Demand for Gasoline Using Household Survey Data," *Review of Economics and Statistics* 62 (November 1980): 622–628; Hendrik S. Houthakker and Lester D. Taylor, Consumer Demand in the United States: Analyses and Projections (Cambridge, Mass.: Harvard University Press, 1970), pp. 56–149; Richard Voith, "The Long-Run Elasticity of Demand for Commuter Rail Transportation," *Journal of Urban Economics* 30 (November 1991): 360–372.

EXHIBIT 4.4 Short-Run and Long-Run Demand Curves

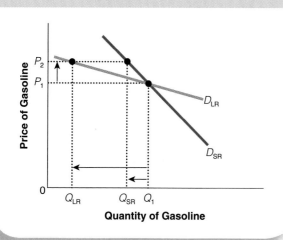

SECTION CHECK 1

1.1 Price elasticity of demand measures the percentage change in quantity demanded divided by the percentage change in price that caused it, moving along a demand curve.

1.2 If the demand for a good is price elastic in the relevant range, quantity demanded is very responsive to a price change. If the demand for a good is relatively price inelastic, quantity demanded is not very responsive to a price change.

1.3 The price elasticity of demand depends on: (1) the availability of close substitutes, (2) the proportion of income spent on the good, and (3) the amount of time that buyers have to respond to a price change.

total revenue (*TR*) the amount sellers receive for a good or service, calculated as the product price times the quantity sold

⑤2 Total Revenue and the Price Elasticity of Demand

Keep the following questions in mind as you read through this section, and review the answers in **Section Check 2.**

2.1 What is total revenue?

2.2 What is the relationship between total revenue and the price elasticity of demand?

2.3 Does the price elasticity of demand vary along a linear demand curve?

Now that we understand what price elasticity is, let's examine the relationship between it and total revenue.

HOW DOES THE PRICE ELASTICITY OF DEMAND IMPACT TOTAL REVENUE?

The price elasticity of demand for a good also has implications for total revenue. **Total revenue (*TR*)** is the amount sellers receive for a good or service. Total revenue is simply the price of the good (*P*) times the quantity of the good sold (*Q*): $TR = P \times Q$. The elasticity of demand will help to predict how changes in the price will impact total revenue earned by the producer for selling the good. Let's see how this works.

$$TR = P \times Q$$

In Exhibit 4.6, we see that when the demand is price elastic ($E_D > 1$), total revenues will rise as the price declines, because the percentage increase in the quantity demanded is greater than the percentage reduction in price. For example, if the price of a good is cut in half (say from \$10 to \$5) and the quantity demanded more

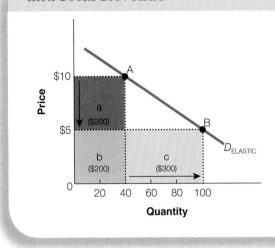

EXHIBIT 4.6 Elastic Demand and Total Revenue

than doubles (say from 40 to 100), total revenue will rise from \$400 (\$10 × 40 = \$400) to \$500 (\$5 × 100 = \$500). Equivalently, if the price rises from \$5 to \$10 and the quantity demanded falls from 100 to 40 units, then total revenue will fall from \$500 to \$400. As this example illustrates, if the demand curve is relatively elastic, total revenue will vary inversely with a price change.

You can see from the following what happens to total revenue when demand is price elastic. (*Note*: The size of the price and quantity arrows represents the size of the percentage changes.)

When Demand Is Price Elastic

$$\downarrow TR = \uparrow P \times \downarrow Q$$

or

$$\uparrow TR = \downarrow P \times \uparrow Q$$

On the other hand, if demand for a good is relatively inelastic ($E_D < 1$), the total revenue will be lower at lower prices than at higher prices because a given price reduction will be accompanied by a proportionately smaller increase in quantity demanded. For example, as shown in Exhibit 4.7, if the price of a good is cut (say from \$10 to \$5) and the quantity demanded less than doubles (say it increases from 30 to 40), then total revenue will fall from \$300 (\$10 × 30 = \$300) to \$200 (\$5 × 40 = \$200). Equivalently, if the price increases from \$5 to \$10 and the quantity demanded falls from 40 to 30, total revenue will increase from \$200 to \$300. To summarize, then: If the demand curve is inelastic, total revenue will vary directly with a price change.

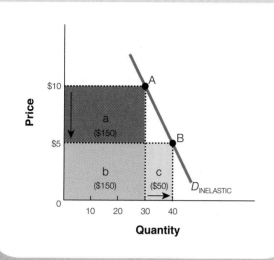

EXHIBIT 4.7 Inelastic Demand and Total Revenue

When Demand Is Price Inelastic

$$\downarrow TR = \uparrow P \times \downarrow Q$$

or

$$\uparrow TR = \downarrow P \times \uparrow Q$$

In this case, the "net" effect on total revenue is reversed but easy to see. (Again, the size of the price and quantity arrows represents the size of the percentage changes.)

PRICE ELASTICITY CHANGES ALONG A LINEAR DEMAND CURVE

As we have just seen, the slopes of demand curves can be used to estimate their *relative* elasticities of demand: The steeper one demand curve is relative to another, the more inelastic it is relative to the other. However, except for the extreme cases of perfectly elastic and perfectly inelastic curves, great care must be taken when trying to estimate the degree of elasticity of one demand curve from its slope. In fact, as we will soon see, a straight-line demand curve with a constant slope will change elasticity continuously as you move up or down it. This is because the slope is the ratio of changes in the two variables (price and quantity), while the elasticity is the ratio of percentage changes in the two variables.

We can easily demonstrate that the elasticity of demand varies along a linear demand curve by using what we already know about the interrelationship between price and total revenue. Exhibit 4.8 shows a linear (constant slope) demand curve. In Exhibit 4.8(a), we see that when the price falls on the upper half of the demand curve from P_1 to P_2, and quantity demanded increases from Q_1 to Q_2, total revenue increases. That is, the new area of total revenue (area b + c) is larger than the old area of total revenue (area a + b). It is also true that if price increased in this region (from P_2 to P_1), total revenue would fall, because b + c is greater than a + b. In this region of the demand curve, then, there is a negative relationship between price and total revenue. As we discussed earlier, this is characteristic of an elastic demand curve ($E_D > 1$).

EXHIBIT 4.8 Price Elasticity along a Linear Demand Curve

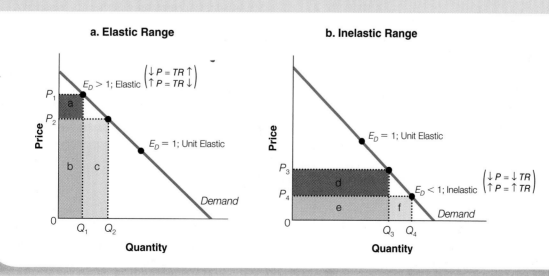

Exhibit 4.8(b) illustrates what happens to total revenue on the lower half of the same demand curve. When the price falls from P_3 to P_4 and the quantity demanded increases from Q_3 to Q_4, total revenue actually decreases, because the new area of total revenue (area e + f) is less than the old area of total revenue (area d + e). Likewise, it is clear that an increase in price from P_4 to P_3 would increase total revenue. In this case, there is a positive relationship between price and total revenue, which, as we discussed, is characteristic of an inelastic demand curve ($E_D < 1$). Together, parts (a) and (b) of Exhibit 4.8 illustrate that, although the slope remains constant, the elasticity of a linear demand curve changes along the length of the curve—from relatively elastic at higher price ranges to relatively inelastic at lower price ranges.

SECTION CHECK 2

2.1 Total revenue is the price of the good times the quantity sold ($TR = P \times Q$).

2.2 If demand is price elastic ($E_D > 1$), total revenue will vary inversely with a change in price. If demand is price inelastic ($E_D < 1$), total revenue will vary in the same direction as a change in price.

2.3 A linear demand curve is more price elastic at higher price ranges and more price inelastic at lower price ranges, and it is unit elastic at the midpoint: $E_D = 1$.

⑤3 Price Elasticity of Supply

Consider the following questions as you read through this section. You will find the answers in **Section Check 3**.

3.1 What is the price elasticity of supply?

3.2 How does time affect the supply elasticity?

Now let's discuss price elasticity of supply.

WHAT IS THE PRICE ELASTICITY OF SUPPLY?

According to the law of supply, there is a positive relationship between price and quantity supplied, *ceteris paribus*. But by how much does quantity supplied change as price changes? It is often helpful to know the degree to which a change in price changes the quantity supplied. The **price elasticity of supply** measures how responsive the quantity sellers are willing and able to sell is to changes in price. In other words, it measures the relative change in the quantity supplied that results from a change in price. Specifically, the price elasticity of supply (E_S) is defined as the percentage change in the quantity supplied divided by the percentage change in price, or

$$E_S = \frac{\%\Delta \text{ in the quantity supplied}}{\%\Delta \text{ in price}}$$

Calculating the Price Elasticity of Supply

The price elasticity of supply is calculated in much the same manner as the price elasticity of demand. Consider, for example, the case in which it is determined that a 10 percent increase in the price of artichokes results in a 25 percent increase in the quantity of artichokes supplied after, say, a few harvest seasons. In this case, the price elasticity is +2.5 (+25 percent ÷ +10 percent = +2.5). This coefficient indicates that each 1 percent increase in the price of artichokes induces a 2.5 percent increase in the quantity of artichokes supplied.

Types of Supply Curves

As with the elasticity of demand, the ranges of the price elasticity of supply center on whether the elasticity

coefficient is greater than or less than 1. Goods with a supply elasticity that is greater than 1 ($E_S > 1$) are said to be relatively elastic in supply. With that, a 1 percent change in price will result in a greater than 1 percent change in quantity supplied. In our example, artichokes were elastic in supply because a 1 percent price increase resulted in a 2.5 percent increase in quantity supplied. An example of an *elastic supply curve* is shown in Exhibit 4.9(a).

Goods with a supply elasticity that is less than 1 ($E_S < 1$) are said to be inelastic in supply. In other words, a 1 percent change in the price of these goods will induce a proportionately smaller change in the quantity supplied. An example of an *inelastic supply curve* is shown in Exhibit 4.9(b).

Finally, two extreme cases of price elasticity of supply are perfectly inelastic supply and perfectly elastic

supply. In a condition of *perfectly inelastic supply*, an increase in price will not change the quantity supplied. In this case, the elasticity of supply is zero. For example, in a sports arena in the short run (that is, in a period too brief to adjust the structure), the number of seats available will be almost fixed, say at 20,000 seats. Additional portable seats might be available, but for the most part, even if a higher price is charged, only 20,000 seats will be available. We say that the elasticity of supply is zero, which describes a perfectly inelastic supply curve. Famous paintings, such as Van Gogh's *Starry Night*, provide another example: Only one original exists; therefore, only one can be supplied, regardless of price. An example of this condition is shown in Exhibit 4.9(c).

At the other extreme is a perfectly elastic supply curve, where the elasticity equals infinity, as shown in

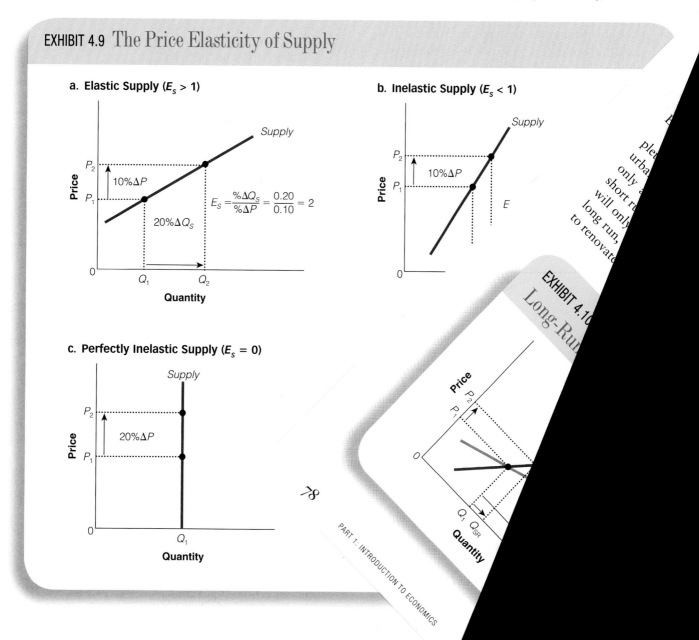

EXHIBIT 4.9 The Price Elasticity of Supply

a. Elastic Supply ($E_s > 1$)

$$E_S = \frac{\%\Delta Q_S}{\%\Delta P} = \frac{0.20}{0.10} = 2$$

b. Inelastic Supply ($E_s < 1$)

c. Perfectly Inelastic Supply ($E_s = 0$)

EXHIBIT 4.10
Long-Run

Exhibit 4.9(d). In a condition of *perfectly elastic supply*, the price does not change at all. It is the same regardless of the quantity supplied, and the elasticity of supply is infinite. Firms would supply as much as the market wants at the market price (P_1) or above. However, firms would supply nothing below the market price because they would not be able to cover their costs of production. Most cases fall somewhere between the two extremes of perfectly elastic and perfectly inelastic.

How Does Time Affect Supply Elasticities?

Time is usually critical in supply elasticities (as well as in demand elasticities), because it is more costly for sellers to bring forth and release products in a shorter period. For example, higher wheat prices may cause farmers to grow more wheat, but big changes cannot occur until the next growing season. That is, immediately after harvest season, the supply of wheat is relatively inelastic, but over a longer time extending over the next growing period, the supply curve becomes much more elastic. Thus, supply tends to be more elastic in the long run than in the short run, as shown in Exhibit 4.10.

Another example of a good whose supply is completely inelastic in the short run is rental units in most urban areas without rent controls. There is generally a fixed number of rental units available in the short run. Thus, in the short run, an increase in demand may lead to higher prices (rents). However, in the long run, the higher prices (rents) provide an incentive to renovate and build new rental units.

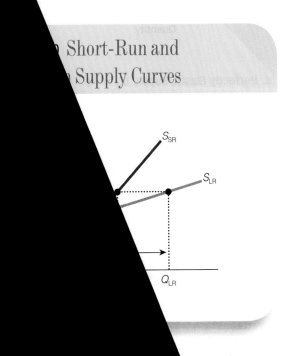

Short-Run and
Supply Curves

S_{SR}

S_{LR}

Q_{LR}

In the short run, firms can increase output by using their existing facilities to a greater capacity, paying workers to work overtime, and hiring additional workers. However, firms will be able to change output much more in the long run when firms can build new factories or close existing ones. In addition, some firms can enter as others exit. In other words, the quantity supplied will be much more elastic in the long run than in the short run.

SECTION CHECK 3

3.1 The price elasticity of supply measures the relative change in the quantity supplied that results from a change in price. If the supply price elasticity is greater than 1, it is elastic; if it is less than 1, it is inelastic.

3.2 Supply tends to be more elastic in the long run than in the short run.

Ⓢ4 Supply, Demand, and Policies of Government

Here are some important questions to think about as you read through this section. You will find the answers in **Section Check 4**.

4.1 What are price controls?

4.2 What are price ceilings?

4.3 What are price floors?

4.4 What is the law of unintended consequences?

4.5 How does the relative elasticity of supply and demand determine the tax burden?

In this section, we use the tools of supply and demand to analyze government policies such as rent control and minimum wages. We also consider the impact of taxes and see how the burden of tax is split between buyers and sellers and how government can use taxes to raise revenue and influence market outcomes.

PRICE CONTROLS

Although nonequilibrium prices can occur naturally in the private sector, reflecting uncertainty, they seldom last for long. Governments, however, may impose non-equilibrium prices for significant periods. Price controls involve the use of the power of the state to establish prices different from the equilibrium prices that would otherwise prevail. The motivations for price controls vary with the market under consideration. For example, a **price ceiling**, a legal maximum price, is often set for goods deemed important to low-income households, such as housing. Or a **price floor**, a legal minimum price, may be set on wages because wages are the primary source of income for most people.

Price controls are not always implemented by the federal government. Local governments (and more rarely, private companies) can and do impose local price controls. One fairly well-known example is rent control. The inflation of the late 1970s meant rapidly rising rents, and some communities, such as Santa Monica, California, decided to do something about it. In response, they limited how much landlords could charge for rental housing.

price ceiling a legally established maximum price

price floor a legally established minimum price

PRICE CEILINGS: RENT CONTROLS

Rent control experiences can be found in many cities across the country. San Francisco, Berkeley, and New York City all have had some form of rent control. Although the rules may vary from city to city and over time, generally the price (or rent) of an apartment remains fixed over the tenure of an occupant, except for allowable annual increases tied to the cost of living or some other price index. When an occupant moves out, the owners can usually, but not always, raise the rent to a near-market level for the next occupant. The controlled rents for existing occupants, however, are generally well below market rental rates.

Results of Rent Controls

Most people living in rent-controlled apartments are getting a good deal, one that they would lose by moving as their family circumstances or income changes.

© MAURITIUS/PHOTOLIBRARY

When faced with rent controls, some landlords might be less inclined to maintain their apartments. As a result, the value of the property may drop until it more closely matches the controlled price.

Tenants thus are reluctant to give up their governmentally granted right to a below-market-rent apartment. In addition, because the rents received by landlords are constrained and below market levels, the rate of return (roughly, the profit) on housing investments falls compared with that on other forms of real estate not subject to rent controls, such as office rents or mortgage payments on condominiums. Hence, the incentive to construct new housing is reduced.

Further, when landlords are limited in the rents they can charge, they have little incentive to improve or upgrade apartments—by putting in new kitchen appliances or new carpeting, for instance. In fact, rent controls give landlords some incentive to avoid routine maintenance, thereby lowering the cost of apartment ownership to a figure approximating the controlled rental price, although the quality of the housing stock will deteriorate over time.

Another impact of rent controls is that they promote housing discrimination. Where rent controls do not exist, prejudiced landlords might willingly rent to people they believe are undesirable simply because the undesirables are the only ones willing to pay the requested rents (and the landlords are not willing to lower their rents substantially to get desirable renters because of the possible loss of thousands of dollars in income). With rent controls, each rent-controlled apartment is likely to attract many possible renters, some desirable and some undesirable as judged by the landlord, simply because the rent is at a below-equilibrium price. Landlords can indulge in their "taste" for discrimination without any additional financial loss beyond that required by the controls. Consequently, they will be more likely to choose to rent to desirable people, perhaps a couple without children or pets, rather than to undesirable ones, perhaps a family with lower income and so a greater risk of nonpayment.

Exhibit 4.11 shows the impact of rent controls. If the price ceiling (P_{RC}) is set below the equilibrium price (P_E), consumers are willing to buy Q_D, but producers are only willing to supply Q_S. The rent control policy will therefore create a persistent shortage, the difference between Q_D and Q_S.

PRICE FLOORS: THE MINIMUM WAGE

The argument for a minimum wage is simple: Existing wages for workers in some types of labor markets do not allow for a very high standard of living, and a minimum wage allows those workers to live better than before. Since the first minimum wage was established in 1938 (at 25 cents per hour), the federal government

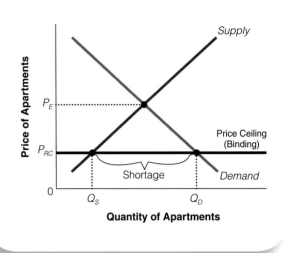

EXHIBIT 4.11 Rent Controls

has, by legislation, made it illegal to pay most workers an amount below the current legislated minimum wage. As of July of 2009, the federal minimum wage was set at $7.25. A number of states also have minimum wage laws. In cases where an employee is subject to both state and federal minimum wage laws, the employee is entitled to the higher minimum wage.

Let's examine graphically the impact of a minimum wage on low-skilled workers. In Exhibit 4.12 on the next page, suppose the government sets the minimum wage, W_{MIN}, above the market equilibrium wage, W_E. In Exhibit 4.12, we see that the price floor is binding. That is, there is a surplus of low-skilled workers at W_{MIN}, because the quantity of labor supplied is greater than the quantity of labor demanded. The reason for the surplus of low-skilled workers (unemployment) at W_{MIN} is that more people are willing to work than employers are willing and able to hire.

Notice that not everyone loses from a minimum wage. Workers who continue to hold jobs have higher incomes—those between 0 and Q_D in Exhibit 4.12. However, many low-skilled workers suffer from a minimum wage—those between Q_D and Q_S in Exhibit 4.12—because they either lose their jobs or are unable to get them in the first place. Although studies disagree somewhat on the precise magnitudes, they largely agree that minimum wage laws do create some unemployment and that the unemployment is concentrated among teenagers—the least-experienced and least-skilled members of the labor force.

Most U.S. workers are not affected by the minimum wage because in the market for their skills, they earn

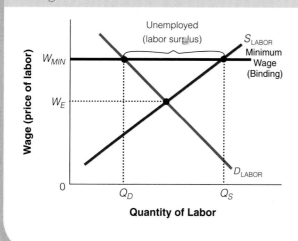

EXHIBIT 4.13 Unemployment Effects of a Minimum Wage on Skilled Workers

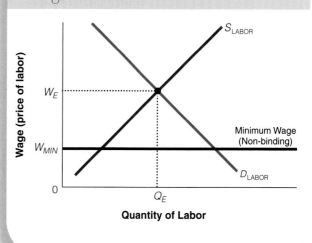

wages that exceed the minimum wage. For example, a minimum wage will not affect the unemployment rate for physicians. In Exhibit 4.13, we see the labor market for skilled and experienced workers. In this market, the minimum wage (the price floor) is not binding because these workers are earning wages that far exceed the minimum wage—W_E is much higher than W_{MIN}.

This analysis does not "prove" that minimum wage laws are "bad" and should be abolished. First, consider the empirical question of how much unemployment is caused by minimum wages. Economists David Card and Alan Kreuger published a controversial study on the increase in minimum wage in the fast food industry in New Jersey and Pennsylvania. They found the effect on employment to be quite small. However, other researchers using similar data have found the effect on employment to be much larger. In fact, most empirical studies indicate that a 10 percent increase in the minimum wage would reduce employment of teenagers between 1 and 3 percent. Second, some might believe that the cost of unemployment resulting from a minimum wage is a reasonable price to pay for ensuring that those with jobs get a "decent" wage. However, opponents of minimum wage argue that it might induce teenagers to drop out of school.

Did you know that less than one-third of minimum wage earners are from families with incomes below the poverty line? In fact, many recipients of the minimum wage are part-time teenage workers from middle income families. There may be more efficient methods to transfer income to low-wage workers like a wage subsidy, such as an earned income tax credit. This is a government program that supplements low-wage workers. Of course, there are no free lunches, so subsidies in the form of wages, income, or rent ultimately cost taxpayers. We will revisit this topic in upcoming chapters.

However, the analysis does point out there is a cost to having a minimum wage: The burden of the minimum wage falls not only on low-skilled workers and employers but also on consumers of products made more costly by the minimum wage.

PRICE CEILINGS: PRICE CONTROLS ON GASOLINE

Another example of price ceilings leading to shortages is the price controls imposed on gasoline in 1974. In 1973, the Organization of Petroleum Exporting Nations (OPEC) reduced the supply of oil. Because crude oil is the most important input in the production of gasoline, this reduction in the supply of oil caused a shift in the supply curve for gasoline leftward from S_1 to S_2 in Exhibit 4.14. In an effort to prevent sharply rising prices, the government imposed price controls on gasoline in 1974. The government told gasoline stations they could not charge more than P_C for gasoline. But people wanted to buy more gasoline than was available at the controlled price, P_C. That is, a shortage developed at P_C, as you can see in Exhibit 4.14. Some customers were lucky enough to get their gasoline at P_C (0 to Q_S), but others were left wanting (Q_S to Q_D). The price ceiling was binding. Consequently, people wasted hours waiting in line for gasoline. Some gas stations sold their gas on a first-come, first-served basis. Some states implemented an even/odd license plate system. If your license plate ended in an odd number, you could buy gas on only odd-numbered days. In addition, quantity restrictions meant that some stations would only allow you to buy a few gallons a day; when they ran out of gas, they closed for the day. Many gas stations were closed in the evenings and on weekends.

A number of government officials wanted to put the blame on OPEC, but if prices were allowed to rise to their equilibrium at E_2, shortages would have been avoided. Instead, it would have meant higher prices at P_2 and a greater quantity sold, Q_2 rather than Q_S. Of course, not everybody was unhappy with the price ceiling. Recall our discussion of opportunity cost in

EXHIBIT 4.14 Gasoline Price Ceiling

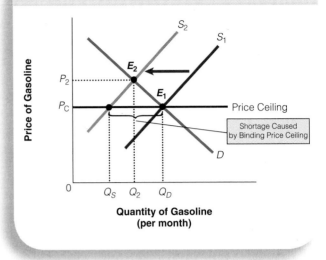

Chapter 2. People place different values on their time. People with a low opportunity cost of time but who cannot as easily afford the higher price per gallon (e.g., poor retired senior citizens) would be more likely to favor the controls. Surgeons, lawyers, and others who have high hourly wages and salaries would view the controls less favorably, because the time spent waiting in line would likely be worth more to them than paying the higher price for gasoline.

UNINTENDED CONSEQUENCES

When markets are altered for policy reasons, it is wise to remember that actions do not always have the results that were initially intended—in other words, actions can have **unintended consequences**. As economists, we must always look for the secondary effects of an action, which may occur along with the initial effects. For example, the government often has good intentions when it adopts price controls to help low-skilled workers or tenants in search of affordable housing, but such policies may also cause unintended consequences that could completely undermine the intended effects. Rent controls may have the immediate effect of lowering rents, but secondary effects may well include low vacancy rates, discrimination against low-income and large families, deterioration of the quality of rental units, and black markets. Similarly, a sizable increase in the minimum wage may help many low-skilled workers or apprentices but may also result in higher unemployment and/or a reduction in fringe benefits, such as vacations and discounts to employees. Society has to

In 1974, the government imposed price ceilings on gasoline. The result was shortages. In some cities, such as Chicago, Portland, and New York, drivers waited over an hour to fill up their tanks. As you know, the value of your time has an opportunity cost.

make tough decisions, and if the government subsidizes some programs or groups of people in one area, then something must always be given up somewhere else. The "law of scarcity" cannot be repealed!

ELASTICITIES AND TAXES: COMBINING SUPPLY AND DEMAND ELASTICITIES

Who pays the tax? Someone may be legally required to send the check to the government but that party is not necessarily the one who bears the burden of the tax.

The relative elasticity of supply and demand determines the distribution of the tax burden for a good. As we will see, if demand is relatively less elastic than supply in the relevant tax region, the largest portion of the tax is paid by the consumer. However, if demand is relatively more elastic than supply in the relevant

As economists, we must always look for the secondary effects of an action, which may occur along with the initial effects.

tax region, the largest portion of the tax is paid by the producer.

In Exhibit 4.15(a), the pre-tax equilibrium price is \$1.00 and the pre-tax equilibrium quantity is Q_{BT}—the quantity before tax. If the government imposes a \$0.50 tax on the seller, the supply curve shifts vertically by the amount of the tax (just as if an input price rose \$0.50).

RENT CONTROL: NEW YORK'S SELF-DESTRUCTION

"Rent control appears to be the most efficient technique presently known to destroy a city—except for bombing," Swedish economist Assar Lindbeck observed in a 1972 book. Rent control is a big cause of New York City's chronic financial mess, a huge cause of its notorious housing scarcity and a neat illustration of its political unreality. Ending it would be a big step toward unleashing a construction boom and boosting its economy to offset destructive tax increases.

New York has maintained price controls on rent since World War II. . . . William Tucker, the writer who has studied the costs most closely, estimates the direct costs of rent control at \$2 billion a year, exclusive of the effect of shrinking the property tax base.

Rent control . . . has inhibited construction in the city. During the recession of 1990–91, the city actually lost more housing units than it gained. . . .

The Manhattan Institute chartered an elaborate study by Henry O. Pollakowski, an MIT housing expert. He concluded, "tenants in low- and moderate-income areas receive little or no benefit from rent stabilization, while tenants in more affluent locations are effectively subsidized for a substantial portion of their rent."

Do tenants in low- and moderate-income areas reap the benefits of rent control?

SOURCE: Robert L. Bartley, "Rent Control: New York's Self-Destruction," *Wall Street Journal*, May 19, 2003, p. A17.

When demand is relatively less elastic than supply in the relevant region, the consumer bears more of the burden of the tax. For example, in Exhibit 4.15(a), the demand curve is relatively less elastic than the supply curve. In response to the tax, the consumer pays $1.40 per unit, $0.40 more than the consumer paid before the tax increase. The producer, however, receives $0.90 per unit, which is $0.10 less than the producer received before the tax.

In Exhibit 4.15(b), demand is relatively more elastic than the supply in the relevant region. Here we see that the greater burden of the same $0.50 tax falls on the producer. That is, the producer is now responsible for $0.40 of the tax, while the consumer only pays $0.10. In general, then, the tax burden falls on the side of the market that is relatively less elastic.

ELASTICITY APPLICATIONS: YACHTS, TAXES, AND ELASTICITIES

In 1991, Congress levied a 10 percent luxury tax. The tax applied to the "first retail sale" of luxury goods with sales prices above the following thresholds: automobiles, $30,000; boats, $100,000; private planes, $250,000; and furs and jewelry, $10,000. The Congressional Budget Office forecasted that the luxury tax would raise about $1.5 billion over five years. However, in 1991, the luxury tax raised less than $30 million in tax revenues. Why? People stopped buying items subject to the luxury tax.

Let's focus our attention on the luxury tax on yachts. Congress passed this tax thinking that the demand for yachts was relatively inelastic and that the tax would have only a small impact on the sale of new yachts. However, the people in the market for new boats had plenty of substitutes—used boats, boats from other countries, new houses, vacations, and so on. In short, the demand for new yachts was more elastic than Congress thought. Remember, when demand is relatively more elastic than supply, most of the tax is passed on to the seller—in this case, the boat industry (workers and retailers). And supply was relatively inelastic because boat factories are not easy to change in the short run. So sellers received a lower price for their boats, and sales fell. In the first year after the tax, yacht retailers reported a 77 percent drop in sales, and approximately 25,000 workers were laid off. The point is that incorrectly predicting elasticities can lead to huge social, political, and economic problems. After intense lobbying by industry groups, Congress repealed the luxury tax on boats in 1993, and on January 1, 2003, the tax on cars finally expired.

EXHIBIT 4.15 Elasticity and the Burden of Taxation

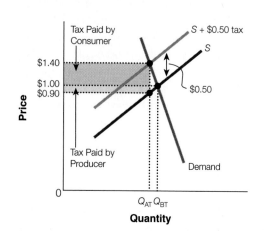

a. Demand Is Relatively Less Elastic Than Supply

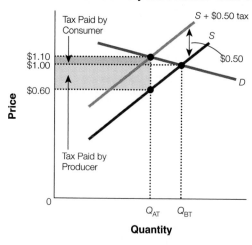

b. Demand Is Relatively More Elastic Than Supply

4.1 Price controls involve government mandates to keep prices above or below the market-determined equilibrium price.

4.2 Price ceilings are government-imposed maximum prices. If price ceilings are set below the equilibrium price, shortages will result.

4.3 Price floors are government-imposed minimum prices. If price floors are set above the equilibrium price, surpluses will result.

4.4 The law of unintended consequences states that the results of certain actions may not always be as clear as they initially appear.

4.5 The relative elasticity of supply and demand determines the distribution of the tax burden for a good. If demand is more elastic than supply, producers bear the greater burden of the tax; if the supply is more elastic than the demand, consumers bear the greater burden.

Ⓢ5 Consumer Surplus, Producer Surplus, and the Efficiency of Markets

Consider the following questions as you read through this section. You will find the answers in **Section Check 5**.

5.1 What is consumer surplus?

5.2 What is producer surplus?

5.3 How do we measure the total gains from trade?

While we've seen how market forces allocate society's scarce resources, we have not determined whether this is desirable. Let's consider how consumer and producer surplus demonstrate the *efficiency* of a competitive market.

consumer surplus the difference between the price a consumer is willing and able to pay for an additional unit of a good and the price the consumer actually pays; for the whole market, it is the sum of all the individual consumer surpluses

CONSUMER SURPLUS

In a competitive market, consumers and producers buy and sell at the market equilibrium price. However, some consumers will be willing and able to pay more for the good than they have to. But they would never knowingly buy something that is worth less to them. That is, what a consumer actually pays for a unit of a good is usually less than the amount she is *willing* to pay. For example, you would be willing and able to pay far more than the market price for a rope ladder to get out of a burning building. You would be willing to pay more than the market price for a tank of gasoline if you had run out of gas on a desolate highway in the desert. **Consumer surplus** is the monetary difference between the amount a consumer is willing and able to pay for an additional unit of a good and what the consumer actually pays—the market price. Consumer surplus for the whole market is the sum of all the individual consumer surpluses for those consumers who have purchased the good.

MARGINAL WILLINGNESS TO PAY FALLS AS MORE IS CONSUMED

Suppose it is a hot day and iced tea is going for $1 per glass, but Julie is willing to pay $4 for the first glass (point a), $2 for the second glass (point b), and $0.50 for the third glass (point c), reflecting the law of demand. How much consumer surplus will Julie receive? First, it is important to note the general fact that if the consumer is a buyer of several units of a good, the earlier units will have greater marginal value and therefore create more consumer surplus, because *marginal willingness to pay* falls as greater quantities are consumed in any period. In fact, you can think of the demand curve as a marginal benefit curve—the additional benefit derived from consuming one more unit. Notice in Exhibit 4.16 that Julie's demand curve for iced tea has a step-like shape. This is demonstrated by Julie's willingness to pay $4 and $2 successively for the first two glasses of iced tea. Thus, Julie will receive $3 of consumer surplus for

EXHIBIT 4.16 Julie's Consumer Surplus for Iced Tea

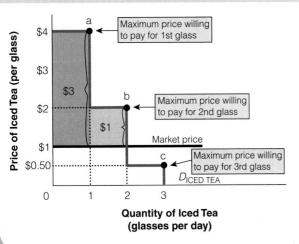

Maximum price willing to pay for 1st glass — a

Maximum price willing to pay for 2nd glass — b

Market price

Maximum price willing to pay for 3rd glass — c

$D_{ICED\ TEA}$

Quantity of Iced Tea (glasses per day)

EXHIBIT 4.17 Consumer Surplus

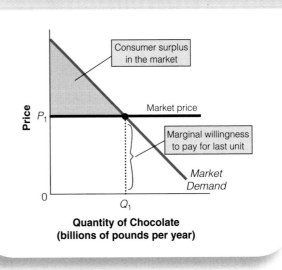

Consumer surplus in the market

Market price

Marginal willingness to pay for last unit

Market Demand

Quantity of Chocolate (billions of pounds per year)

the first glass ($4 – $1) and $1 of consumer surplus for the second glass ($2 – $1), for a total consumer surplus of $4, as seen in Exhibit 4.16. Julie will not be willing to purchase the third glass, because her willingness to pay is less than its price ($0.50 versus $1.00).

In Exhibit 4.17, we can easily measure the consumer surplus in the market by using a market demand curve rather than an individual demand curve. In short, the market consumer surplus is the area under the market demand curve and above the market price (the shaded area in Exhibit 4.17). The market for chocolate contains millions of potential buyers, so we will get a smooth demand curve. Because the demand curve represents the *marginal benefits* consumers receive from consuming an additional unit, we can conclude that all buyers of chocolate receive at least some consumer surplus in the market because the marginal benefit is greater than the market price—the shaded area in Exhibit 4.17.

Julie will receive $3 in consumer surplus for the first glass and $1 of consumer surplus for the second. She won't purchase a third, however, because the market price is higher than what she is willing to pay.

PRICE CHANGES AND CHANGES IN CONSUMER SURPLUS

Imagine that the price of your favorite beverage fell because of an increase in supply. Wouldn't you feel better off? An increase in supply and a lower price will increase your consumer surplus for each unit you were already consuming and will also increase your consumer surplus from additional purchases at the lower price. Conversely, a decrease in supply and an increase in price will lower your consumer surplus.

Exhibit 4.18 shows the gain in consumer surplus associated with, say, a technological advance that shifts the supply curve to the right. As a result, equilibrium price falls (from P_1 to P_2) and quantity rises (from Q_1 to Q_2). Consumer surplus then increases from area P_1AB to area P_2AC, or a gain in consumer surplus of P_1BCP_2. The increase in consumer surplus has two parts. First, there is an increase in consumer surplus, because Q_1 can now be purchased at a lower price; this amount of additional consumer surplus is illustrated by area P_1BDP_2 in Exhibit 4.18. Second, the lower price makes it advantageous for buyers to expand their purchases from Q_1 to Q_2. The net benefit to buyers from expanding their consumption from Q_1 to Q_2 is illustrated by area BCD.

PRODUCER SURPLUS

As we have just seen, the difference between what a consumer would be willing and able to pay for a given quantity of a good and what a consumer actually has to pay is called consumer surplus. The parallel concept for producers is called producer surplus. **Producer surplus** is the difference between what a producer is paid for a good and the cost of producing one unit of that good. Producers would never knowingly sell a good that is worth more to them than the asking price. Imagine selling coffee for half of what it cost to produce—you won't be in business very long with that pricing strategy. The supply curve shows the minimum amount that sellers must receive to be willing to supply any given quantity; that is, the supply curve reflects the marginal cost to sellers. The **marginal cost (MC)** is the cost of producing one more unit of a good. In other words, the supply curve is the marginal cost curve, just like the demand curve is the marginal benefit curve. Because some units can be produced at a cost that is lower than the market price, the seller receives a surplus, or a net benefit, from producing those units. For example, in Exhibit 4.19, the market price is $5. Say the firm's marginal cost is $2 for the first unit, $3 for the second unit, $4 for the third unit, and $5 for the fourth unit. Because producer surplus for a particular unit is the difference between the market price and the seller's cost of producing that unit, producer surplus would be as follows: The first unit would yield $3; the second unit would yield $2; the third unit would yield $1; and the fourth unit would

> **producer surplus** the difference between what a producer is paid for a good and the cost of producing that unit of the good; for the market, it is the sum of all the individual sellers' producer surpluses—the area above the market supply curve and below the market price
>
> **marginal cost (MC)** the change in total costs resulting from a one-unit change in output

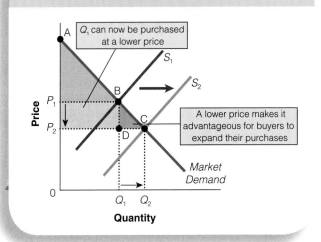

EXHIBIT 4.18 Impact of an Increase in Supply on Consumer Surplus

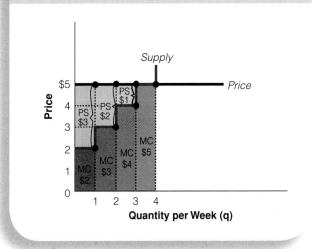

EXHIBIT 4.19 A Firm's Producer Surplus

add no more to producer surplus, because the market price equals the seller's cost.

When there are a lot of producers, the supply curve is more or less smooth, like in Exhibit 4.20. Total producer surplus for the market is obtained by summing all the producer surpluses of all the sellers—the area above the market supply curve and below the market price up to the quantity actually produced—the shaded area in Exhibit 4.20. Producer surplus is a measurement of how much sellers gain from trading in the market.

Suppose an increase in market demand causes the market price to rise, say from P_1 to P_2; the seller now receives a higher price per unit, so additional producer surplus is generated. In Exhibit 4.21, we see the additions to producer surplus. Part of the added surplus (area P_2DBP_1) is due to a higher price for the quantity already being produced (up to Q_1) and part (area DCB) is due to the expansion of output made profitable by the higher price (from Q_1 to Q_2).

MARKET EFFICIENCY AND PRODUCER AND CONSUMER SURPLUS

With the tools of consumer and producer surplus, we can better analyze the total gains from exchange. The demand curve represents a collection of maximum prices that consumers are willing and able to pay for additional quantities of a good or service. It also shows the marginal benefits derived by consumers. The supply curve represents a collection of minimum prices that suppliers require to be willing and able to supply each

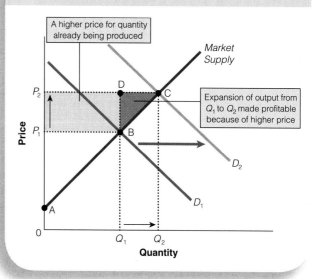

EXHIBIT 4.21 Impact of an Increase in Demand on Producer Surplus

additional unit of a good or service. It also shows the marginal cost of production. Both are shown in Exhibit 4.22. For example, for the first unit of output, the buyer is willing to pay up to $7, while the seller would have to receive at least $1 to produce that unit. However, the equilibrium price is $4, as indicated by the intersection of the supply and demand curves. It is clear that the two would gain from getting together and trading that unit, because the consumer would receive $3 of consumer

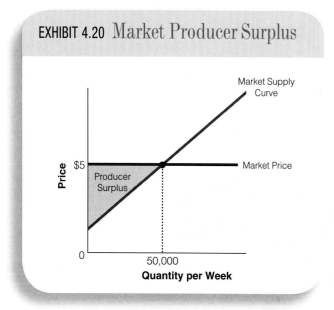

EXHIBIT 4.20 Market Producer Surplus

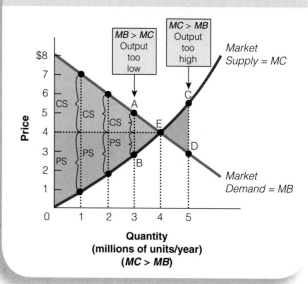

EXHIBIT 4.22 Consumer and Producer Surplus

surplus ($7 – $4), and the producer would receive $3 of producer surplus ($4 – $1). Both would also benefit from trading the second and third units of output—in fact, both would benefit from trading every unit up to the market equilibrium output. That is, the buyer purchases the good, except for the very last unit, for less than the maximum amount she would have been willing to pay; the seller receives for the good, except for the last unit, more than the minimum amount for which he would have been willing to supply the good. Once the equilibrium output is reached at the equilibrium price, all the mutually beneficial trade opportunities between the demander and supplier will have taken place, and the sum of consumer surplus and producer surplus is maximized. This is where the marginal benefit to buyers is equal to the marginal cost to producers. Both buyer and seller are better off from each of the units traded than they would have been if they had not exchanged them.

It is important to recognize that, in this case, the **total welfare gains** to the economy from trade in this good is the sum of the consumer and producer surpluses created. That is, consumers benefit from additional amounts of consumer surplus, and producers benefit from additional amounts of producer surplus. Improvements in welfare come from additions to both consumer and producer surpluses. In competitive markets with large numbers of buyers and sellers, at the market equilibrium price and quantity, the net gains to society are as large as possible.

Why would it be inefficient to produce only 3 million units? The demand curve in Exhibit 4.22 indicates that the buyer is willing to pay $5 for the 3 millionth unit. The supply curve shows that it only costs the seller $3 to produce that unit. That is, as long as the buyer values the extra output by more than it costs to produce that unit, total welfare would increase by expanding output. In fact, if output is expanded from 3 million units to 4 million units, total welfare (the sum of consumer and producer surpluses) will increase by area AEB in Exhibit 4.22.

What if 5 million units are produced? The demand curve shows that the buyer is only willing to pay $3 for the 5 millionth unit. However, the supply curve shows that it would cost about $5.50 to produce that 5 millionth unit. Thus, increasing output beyond equilibrium decreases total welfare, because the cost of producing this extra output is greater than the value the buyer places on it. If output is reduced from 5 million units to 4 million units, total welfare will increase by area ECD in Exhibit 4.22.

Not producing the efficient level of output, in this case 4 million units, leads to what economists call a **deadweight loss**. A deadweight loss is the reduction in both consumer and producer surpluses—it is the net loss of total surplus that results from the misallocation of resources.

In a competitive equilibrium, supply equals demand at the equilibrium. This means that the buyers value the last unit of output consumed by exactly the same amount that it cost to produce. If consumers valued the last unit by more than it cost to produce, welfare could be increased by expanding output. If consumers valued the last unit by less than it cost to produce, then welfare could be increased by producing less output.

In sum, *market efficiency* occurs when we have maximized the sum of consumer and producer surplus, when the margin of benefits of the last unit consumed is equal to the marginal cost of productivity, *MB = MC*.

total welfare gains the sum of consumer and producer surpluses

deadweight loss net loss of total surplus that results from an action that alters a market equilibrium

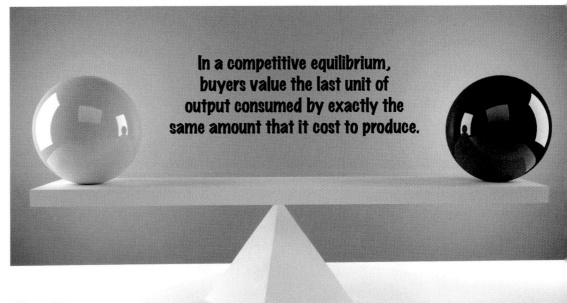

In a competitive equilibrium, buyers value the last unit of output consumed by exactly the same amount that it cost to produce.

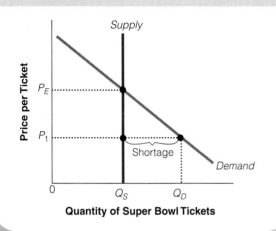

EXHIBIT 4.23 The Market for Super Bowl Tickets

Quantity of Super Bowl Tickets

(Axis labels: Price per Ticket, P_E, P_1, Supply, Demand, Shortage, Q_S, Q_D, 0)

EFFICIENCY AND TICKET SCALPING

The Super Bowl is a high-demand, limited-supply sports event. The face value on most Super Bowl tickets is in the $700 to $900 range. Many of the recipients of the tickets are corporate sponsors or are affiliated with the teams playing in the game. There are also some tickets that are allocated through a lottery. However, at the face value for the tickets at P_1, the quantity demanded far exceeds the quantity supplied as seen in Exhibit 4.23. In other words, the National Football League (NFL) has not priced their tickets equal to what the market will bear. Consequently, some fans are willing to pay much more, sometimes $6,000 to $7,000, for these tickets from scalpers, who buy the tickets at face value and try to sell them for a higher price. While ticket scalping is illegal in many states, scalpers will still descend on the host city to make a profit, even though the probability of arrest and conviction are substantial.

But is ticket scalping for athletic events and concerts really so objectionable? Could scalpers be transferring tickets into the hands of those who value them the most? The buyer must value attending the event more than the scalped price of the ticket or he would not buy the ticket. The seller would not sell her ticket unless she valued the money from the ticket more than attending the event. That is, scalpers may help markets achieve efficient outcomes by transferring tickets from those placing lower values on them to those placing higher values on them. Scalping is a voluntary activity that benefits both sellers and buyers.

The sponsors of the event are the losers, in the form of lost profits, for failing to charge the higher equilibrium market price. Why would the NFL not charge the higher price? Perhaps it sends a sign of goodwill to NFL fans, even if they have no appreciable chance of getting a ticket. That is, maybe the NFL is willing to take a hit on short-run profits to make sure they keep their base of fans (long-run profits).

SECTION CHECK 5

5.1 The price elasticity of supply measures the relative change in the quantity supplied that results from a change in price. If the supply price elasticity is greater than 1, it is elastic; if it is less than 1, it is inelastic.

5.2 Supply tends to be more elastic in the long run than in the short run.

5.3 The relative elasticity of supply and demand determines the distribution of the tax burden for a good. If demand is more elastic than supply, producers bear the greater burden of the tax; if the supply is more elastic than the demand, consumers bear the greater burden.

Chapter 4: Self-Review

Now that you're finished reading the chapter, review the questions below. You can write your answers in the space provided, then go online to see the answers at www.cengagebrain.com.

S1–PRICE ELASTICITY OF DEMAND

1. How is the price elasticity of demand calculated?

2. Why is the price elasticity of demand for products at a 24-hour convenience store likely to be lower at 2 A.M. than at 2 P.M.?

3. In each of the following cases, indicate which good you think has a relatively more price elastic demand and identify the most likely reason, in terms of the determinants of the elasticity of demand (more substitutes, greater share of budget, or more time to adjust).
   a. cars or Chevrolets
   b. salt or housing
   c. going to a New York Mets game or a Cleveland Indians game
   d. natural gas this month or over the course of a year

S2–TOTAL REVENUE AND THE PRICE ELASTICITY OF DEMAND

4. If taxi fares in a city rise, what will happen to the total revenue received by taxi operators? If the fares charged for subway rides, a substitute for taxi rides, do not change, what will happen to the total revenue earned by the subway as a result?

5. Why is a linear demand curve more price elastic at higher price ranges and more price inelastic at lower price ranges?

S3–PRICE ELASTICITY OF SUPPLY

6. What does it mean to say the elasticity of supply for one good is greater than that for another?

7. True or False: Supply tends to be more elastic in the long run than in the short run.

S4–SUPPLY, DEMAND, AND POLICIES OF GOVERNMENT

8. What predictable effects result from price ceilings such as rent control?

9. What predictable effects result from price floors such as the minimum wage?

10. True or False: The consumer bears more of the tax burden when demand is relatively more elastic than supply.

S5–CONSUMER SURPLUS, PRODUCER SURPLUS, AND THE EFFICIENCY OF MARKETS

11. Why do the earlier units consumed at a given price add more consumer surplus than the later units consumed?

12. Why does a reduction in output below the efficient level create a deadweight loss?

13. Why is the efficient level of output in an industry defined as the output where the sum of consumer and producer surplus is maximized?

Historically, space exploration

has been dominated by the public sphere—until recently governments have been the only organizations able to afford it. In the President's budget for 2011, however, plans have been outlined to open the door to new opportunities for partnership, investment, and competition in space exploration for the private sector. Do you think the private sector can provide better services and take better advantages of the opportunities in this field than the public sector has?

5

Market Failure and Public Choice

i n the previous chapter, we concluded that markets are efficient. But we made some assumptions about how markets work. If these assumptions do not hold, our conclusion about efficiency may be flawed. So, what are the assumptions?

First, in our model of supply and demand, we assumed that markets are perfectly competitive—many buyers and sellers exchanging similar goods in an environment where buyers and sellers can easily enter and exit the market. This is not always true. In some markets, few firms may have control over the market price. When firms can control the market price, we say that they have market power. This market power can cause inefficiency because it will lead to higher prices and lower quantities than the competitive solution.

Sometimes the market system fails to produce efficient outcomes because of side effects economists call *externalities*. With *positive externalities*, the private market supplies too little of the good in question (such as education). In the case of *negative externalities* (such as pollution), the market supplies too much.

Another possible source of market failure is that competitive markets provide less than the efficient quantity of public goods. A public good is a good or service that someone can consume simultaneously with everyone else even if he or she doesn't pay for it. For example, everyone enjoys the benefits of national defense and yet it would be difficult to exclude anyone from receiving these benefits. The problem is that if consumers know it is too difficult to exclude them, then they could avoid paying their share of the public good (take a free ride), and producers would find it unprofitable to provide the good. Therefore, the government provides important public goods such as national defense.

Many economists believe that asymmetric information can cause market failures. *Asymmetric information* is a situation in which some people know what other people don't know. This can lead to adverse selection, which occurs when an informed party benefits in an exchange by taking advantage of knowing more than the other party.

In the last section of this chapter, we will discuss public choice economics, the application of economic principles to politics.

⑤1 Externalities

Keep the following questions in mind as you read through this section. You'll find the answers in **Section Check 1**.

1.1 What is a negative externality?

1.2 How are negative externalities internalized?

1.3 What is a positive externality?

1.4 How are positive externalities internalized?

Even if the economy is competitive, it is still possible that the market system fails to produce the efficient level of output because of side effects economists call **externalities**. With **positive externalities**, the private market supplies too little of the good in question (such as education). In the case of **negative externalities** (such as pollution), the market supplies too much. Both types of externalities are caused by economic agents—producers and consumers—receiving the wrong signals. That is, the free market works well in providing most goods but does less well without regulations, taxes, and subsidies in providing others.

NEGATIVE EXTERNALITIES IN PRODUCTION

The classic example of a negative externality in production is air pollution from a factory, such as a steel mill. If the firm uses clean air in production and returns dirty air to the atmosphere, it creates a negative externality. The polluted air "spills over" to outside parties. Now people in the neighboring communities may experience higher incidences of disease, dirtier houses, and other property damage. Such damages are real costs; but because no one owns the air, the firm does not have to pay for its use, unlike the other resources the firm uses in production. A steel mill pays for labor, capital, energy, and raw materials because it must compensate the owners of those inputs for their use. If a firm can avoid paying the costs it imposes on others—the external costs—it has lowered its own costs of production, but not the true costs to society.

Examples of negative externalities are numerous: the roommate who plays his stereo too loud at 2:00 A.M., the neighbor's dog that barks all night long or leaves "messages" on your front lawn, or the gardener who runs her leaf blower on full power at 7:00 A.M. on a Saturday. Driving our cars may be another area in which people don't bear the full costs of their choices. We pay the price to purchase cars, as well as to maintain, insure, and fuel them—those are the private costs. But do we pay for all of our external costs such as emissions, congestion, wear and tear on our highways, and the possible harm to those driving in cars smaller than ours?

Graphing Negative External Costs in Production

Let's take a look at the steel industry. In Exhibit 5.1, we see the market for steel. Notice that at each level of output, the first supply curve, S_{PRIVATE}, is lower than the second, S_{SOCIAL}. The reason is simple: S_{PRIVATE} only includes the private costs to the firm—the capital, entrepreneurship, land, and labor for which it must pay. However, S_{SOCIAL} includes all of these costs plus the external costs that production imposes on others. If the firm could somehow be required to compensate society for the damage it causes, the cost of production for the firm would increase and would shift the supply curve to the left. That is, the true social cost of producing steel is represented by S_{SOCIAL} in

externality a benefit or cost from consumption or production that spills over onto those who are not consuming or producing the good

positive externality occurs when benefits spill over to an outside party who is not involved in producing or consuming the good

negative externality occurs when costs spill over to an outside party who is not involved in producing or consuming the good

© KIMBERLY DEPREY/ISTOCKPHOTO.COM

Exhibit 5.1. The equilibrium at P_2 and Q_2 is efficient. The market equilibrium is not efficient because the true supply curve is above the demand curve at Q_1. At $Q1$, the marginal benefits (point a) are less than the marginal cost (point b) and society would be better off if the firm produced less steel. The deadweight loss from overproduction is measured by the shaded area in Exhibit 5.1. From society's standpoint, Q_2 is the efficient level of output because it represents all the costs (private plus external costs) associated with the production of this good. If the suppliers of steel are not aware of or not responsible for the external costs, they will tend to produce too much. From society's standpoint, Q_1 and efficiency would be improved if less were produced.

WHAT CAN THE GOVERNMENT DO TO CORRECT FOR NEGATIVE EXTERNALITIES?

The government can intervene in market decisions in an attempt to take account of these negative externalities. It may do this by estimating the amount of those external costs and then taxing the manufacturer by that amount, forcing the manufacturer to internalize (bear) the costs.

Pollution Taxes

Pollution taxes are designed to internalize negative externalities. If government could impose a pollution tax equal to the exact size of the external cost, then the firm would produce the efficient level of output, Q_2. That is, the tax would shift the supply curve for steel leftward to S_{SOCIAL} and would provide an incentive for the firm to produce at the socially optimum level of output. Additionally, tax revenues would be generated that could be used to compensate those who had suffered damage from the pollution or in some other productive way.

Regulation

Alternatively, the government could use regulation. The government might simply prohibit certain types of activities that cause pollution, or it might force firms to adopt a specific technology to reduce their emissions. However, regulators would have to know the best available technology for each and every industry. The purchase and use of new pollution-control devices would increase the cost of production and shift the supply curve to the left, from $S_{PRIVATE}$ to S_{SOCIAL}.

Which Is Better—Pollution Tax or Regulation?

Most economists agree that a pollution tax, or a corrective tax, is more efficient than regulation. The pollution

© ISTOCKPHOTO.COM

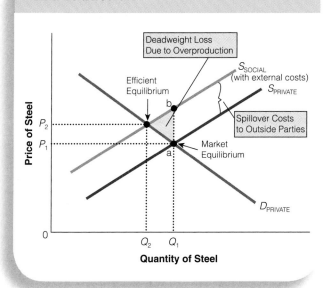

EXHIBIT 5.1 Negative Externalities in Production

Many would consider that texting while driving creates a negative externality, as the dangers of multitasking behind the wheel are well documented. Of course, if you pull over to the side of the road and use your cell phone to report a crime or an accident, the use of the phone may provide a positive externality.

tax is good because it gets rid of the externality and moves society closer to the efficient level of output. The tax also gives firms an incentive to find and apply new technology to further reduce pollution levels in their plant and consequently lower the tax they would have to pay. Under regulation, a firm has little incentive to further reduce emissions once it reaches the predetermined level set by the regulated standard.

For example, a gas tax is a form of pollution tax: It helps reduce the externalities of pollution and congestion. The higher the tax, the fewer the vehicles on the road, the fewer miles driven, and the more fuel efficient vehicles purchased, each of which leads to less congestion and pollution. Therefore, the pollution tax, unlike other taxes, can enhance economic efficiency while generating revenue for the government.

POSITIVE EXTERNALITIES IN CONSUMPTION

Unlike negative externalities, positive externalities benefit others. For some goods, the individual consumer receives all the benefits. If you buy a hamburger, for example, you get all its benefits. On the other hand, consider education. This is a positive externality in consumption whose benefits extend beyond the individual consumer of education. Certainly, when you "buy" an education, you receive many of its benefits: greater future income, more choice of future occupations, and the consumption value of knowing more about life as a result of classroom (and extracurricular) learning. However, these benefits, great as they may be, are not all the benefits associated with your education. You may be less likely to be unemployed or commit crimes; you may end up curing cancer or solving some other social problem. These nontrivial benefits are the positive external benefits of education.

Many economists like the gas tax because it is easy to collect, difficult for users to avoid, and encourages fuel economy. It puts the tax on highway users. But completely internalizing the externality may cost an additional $2 a gallon; the national average gas tax is $0.50. In England, the gas tax is over $3 per gallon. It is much more efficient to pay for transportation improvements by using a gas tax than a sales tax because it associates the tax with those who are creating the externality.

The government frequently subsidizes education. Why? Presumably because the private market does not provide enough. It is argued that the education of a person benefits not only that person but all society,

because a more informed citizenry can make more intelligent collective decisions, which benefits everyone. Public health departments sometimes offer "free" inoculations against certain communicable diseases, such as influenza, because by protecting one group of citizens, everyone gets some protection; if one citizen is prevented from getting the disease, that person cannot pass it on to others. Many governmental efforts in the field of health and education are justified on the basis of positive externalities. Of course, because positive externalities are often difficult to measure, it is hard to demonstrate empirically whether many governmental education and health programs achieve their intended purposes.

In short, the presence of positive externalities interferes with reaching economic efficiency because of the tendency for the market to underallocate (produce too little) of this good.

Graphing Positive External Benefits of Consumption

Let's take the case of a new vaccine against the common cold. The market for the vaccine is shown in Exhibit 5.2. The demand curve, $D_{PRIVATE}$, represents the prices and quantities that buyers would be willing to pay in the private market to reduce their probability of catching the common cold. The supply curve shows the amounts that suppliers would offer for sale at different prices. However, at the equilibrium market output, Q_1, the output of vaccinations falls far short of the efficient level, Q_2. Why? Many people benefit from the vaccines, including those who do not have to pay for them; they are now less likely to be infected because others took the vaccine. If we could add the benefits derived by nonpaying consumers, the demand curve would shift to the right, from $D_{PRIVATE}$ to D_{SOCIAL}. The greater level of output, Q_2, that would result if D_{SOCIAL} were the observed demand reflects the efficient output level.

The market equilibrium at P_1 and Q_1 is not efficient because D_{SOCIAL} is above $D_{PRIVATE}$ for all levels of output between Q_1 and Q_2. That is, at Q_1 the marginal benefits (D_{SOCIAL}) at point b are greater than the marginal cost (S_{SOCIAL}) at point a. Consequently, a deadweight loss is associated with underproduction. In short, too little of the good is produced. Because producers are unable to collect payments from all those who benefit from the good or service, the market has a tendency to underproduce. In this case, the market is not producing enough vaccinations from society's standpoint and an *underallocation* of resources occurs.

EXHIBIT 5.2 Positive Externalities in Consumption

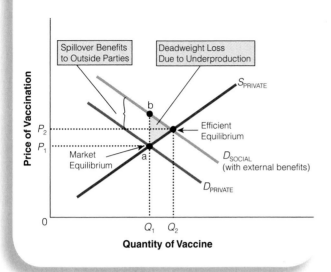

Spillover Benefits to Outside Parties

Deadweight Loss Due to Underproduction

Price of Vaccination (vertical axis)

Quantity of Vaccine (horizontal axis)

$S_{PRIVATE}$

b

P_2

P_1

Efficient Equilibrium

Market Equilibrium

a

D_{SOCIAL} (with external benefits)

$D_{PRIVATE}$

0   Q_1 Q_2

WHAT CAN THE GOVERNMENT DO TO CORRECT FOR POSITIVE EXTERNALITIES?

How could society correct for this market failure? Two particular methods of achieving the higher preferred output are subsidies and regulation.

Subsidies

Government could provide a subsidy—either give refunds to individuals who receive an inoculation or provide an incentive for businesses to give their employees "free" inoculations at the office. If the subsidy was exactly equal to the external benefit of inoculation, the demand curve would shift from $D_{PRIVATE}$ to D_{SOCIAL}, resulting in an efficient level of output, Q_2.

Regulation

The government could also pass a regulation requiring each person to get an inoculation. This approach would also shift the demand curve rightward toward the efficient level of output.

In summary, with positive externalities, the private market supplies too little of the good in question (such as education or inoculations for communicable diseases). In the case of negative externalities, the market supplies too much. In either case, buyers and sellers are receiving the wrong signals. The producers and consumers are not doing what they do because they are evil; rather, whether well-intentioned or ill-intentioned, they are behaving according to the incentives they face. The free market, then, works fine in providing most goods, but it functions less well without regulations, taxes, and subsidies in providing others.

NONGOVERNMENTAL SOLUTIONS TO EXTERNALITIES

Sometimes the externality problems can be handled by individuals without the intervention of government, and people may decide to take steps on their own to minimize negative externalities. Moral and social codes may prevent some people from littering, driving gas-guzzling cars,

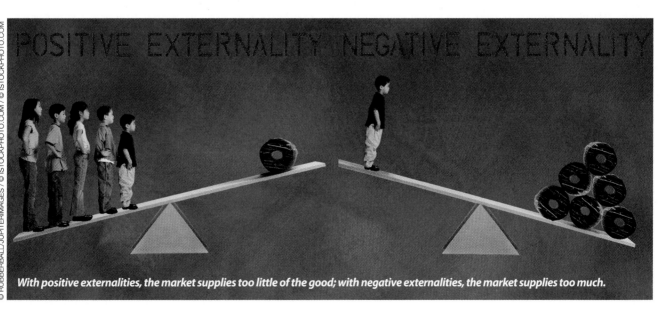

With positive externalities, the market supplies too little of the good; with negative externalities, the market supplies too much.

or using gas-powered mowers and log-burning fireplaces. The same self-regulation also applies to positive externalities. Philanthropists, for example, frequently donate money to public and private schools. In part, this must be because they view the positive externalities from education as a good buy for their charitable dollars.

SECTION CHECK 1

1.1 When the action of one party poses a cost on another party, it is called a negative externality.

1.2 The government can use taxes or other forms of regulation to correct the overallocation problem brought about by negative externalities.

1.3 When the action of one party benefits another party, it is called a positive externality.

1.4 The government can provide subsidies or other forms of regulation to correct the underallocation problem associated with positive externalities.

Ⓢ2 Public Goods

Keep the following questions in mind as you read through this section. You'll find the answers in **Section Check 2.**

2.1 What is a public good?

2.2 What is the free-rider problem?

2.3 What is a common resource good?

Now let's consider how public goods can cause market failure through resource misallocation.

PRIVATE GOODS VERSUS PUBLIC GOODS

Externalities are not the only culprit behind resource misallocation. A **public good** is another source of market failure. As used by economists, this term refers not to how these particular goods are purchased (i.e., by a government agency rather than some private economic agent) but to the properties that characterize them. In this section, we learn the difference between private goods, public goods, and common resources.

Private Goods

A **private good** such as a cheeseburger has two critical properties in this context: it is rival and excludable. First, a cheeseburger is rival in consumption because if one person eats a particular cheeseburger, nobody else can eat the same cheeseburger. Second, a cheeseburger is excludable. It is easy to keep someone from eating your cheeseburger by not giving it to him. Most goods in the economy, such as food, clothing, cars, and houses, are private goods that are rival and excludable.

Public Goods

The consumption of public goods, unlike private goods, is neither rival nor excludable. A public good is not rival because everyone can consume the good simultaneously; that is, one person's use of it does not diminish another's ability to use it. A public good is likewise *not excludable* because once the good is produced, it is prohibitively costly to exclude anyone from consuming the good. Consider national defense. Everyone enjoys the benefits of national defense (not rival) and it would be too costly to exclude anyone from those benefits (not excludable). That is, once the military has its defense in place, everyone is protected simultaneously (not rival) and it would be prohibitively costly to exclude anyone from consuming national defense (not excludable).

Another example of a public good is a flood control project. A flood control project would allow all the people who live in the flood plain area to enjoy the protection of the new program simultaneously. It would also be very difficult to exclude someone who lived in the middle of the project area who said she did not want to pay. Like national defense, the good is nonrival in consumption—everyone within the flood project enjoys the protection simultaneously. Other examples of public goods include outdoor fireworks (not stadium) displays and tornado sirens in small towns. You cannot easily keep someone from seeing the fireworks or hearing the siren (not excludable). Also, when one person gets the benefits of the fireworks display or the siren warning, it does not reduce the benefits to anyone else (not rival). Clean air is also a public good. Everyone will benefit from cleaner air (nonrival). In addition, if we clean up the air we cannot prevent others from benefitting (non-excludable). Remember, a positive externality can be a public good.

PUBLIC GOODS AND THE FREE-RIDER PROBLEM

The fact that a public good is not rival and not exclud-able makes the good difficult to produce privately. Some would know they could derive the benefits from the good without paying for it, because once it is produced, it is too difficult to exclude them. Some would try to take a *free ride*—derive benefits from something they did not pay for. Let's return to the example of national defense. Suppose the private protection of national defense is actually worth $100 to you. Assume that 100 million households in the United States are willing to make a $100 contribution for national defense. These contributions would add up to $10 billion. You might write a check for $100, or you might reason as follows: "If I don't give $100 and everybody else does, I will be equally well protected plus derive the benefits of $100 in my pocket." Taking the latter course represents a rational attempt to be a **free rider**. The rub is that if everyone attempts to take a free ride, the ride will not exist.

> If everyone attempts to take a free ride, the ride will not exist.

The free-rider problem prevents the private market from supplying the efficient amounts of pub-lic goods. That is, no private firm would be willing to supply national defense because people can con-sume it without paying for it—the free-rider problem. Therefore, the government provides important public goods such as national defense.

THE GOVERNMENT AND BENEFIT-COST ANALYSIS

Everything the government provides has an opportu-nity cost. What is the best level of national defense? More national defense means less of something else that society may value more, such as health care or Social Security. To be efficient, additional goods from the public sector must also follow the rule of rational choice: pursue additional government activities if and only if the expected marginal benefits exceed the expected marginal costs. It all comes back to the adage "there are no free lunches."

In addition, there is the problem of assessing the value of these goods. Consider the case of a new high-way. Before it builds the highway, the appropriate gov-ernment agency will undertake a benefit-cost analysis of the situation. In this case, it must evaluate consum-ers' willingness to pay for the highway against the costs that will be incurred for construction and maintenance. However, those individuals who want the highway have an incentive to exaggerate their desire for it. At the same time, individuals who will be displaced or other-wise harmed by the highway have an incentive to exag-gerate the harm that will be done to them. Together, these elements make it difficult for the government to accurately assess need. Ultimately, their evaluations are reduced to educated guesses about the net impact, weighing both positive and negative effects, of the highway on all parties concerned.

COMMON RESOURCES AND THE TRAGEDY OF THE COMMONS

In many cases, we do not have exclusive private property rights to things such as the air around us or the fish in the sea. They are common resources—goods that are owned by every-one and therefore not owned by anyone. When a good is not owned by anyone, individuals feel little incentive

REMEMBER... No free lunch

to conserve or use the resource efficiently.

A **common resource** is a rival good that is nonexcludable; that is, nonpayers cannot be easily excluded from consuming the good, and when one unit is consumed by one person, it means that it cannot be consumed by another. Fish in the vast ocean waters are a good example of a common resource. They are rival because fish are limited—a fish taken by one person is not available for others. They are nonexcludable because it is prohibitively costly to keep anyone from catching them—almost anyone with a boat and a fishing rod could catch one. Common resources can lead to tragedy—the tragedy of the commons. This is the case of private incentives failing to provide adequate maintenance of public resources.

Other examples of common resources to which individuals have relatively free access and that can be easily exploited are congested roads and the Internet.

"Free"way is a misnomer. No one owns the space on the freeway. Because there are no property rights to the freeway you cannot exclude others from driving on and sharing the freeway. When you occupy a part of the freeway you are keeping others from using that portion. So, all drivers compete for limited space causing a negative externality in the form of congestion.

The Internet poses a similar problem. If everyone attempts to access the same web site at the same time, overcrowding occurs and congestion can cause the site to slow down.

There are two possible solutions to the common property rights problem. First, the government, through taxes and fees, can attempt to internalize the externality. To prevent road congestion the government could charge drivers a toll—a corrective tax on congestion—or they could charge higher tolls on bridges during rush hour. A gasoline tax would be an inferior policy solution because although it would reduce driving, it would not necessarily reduce driving during peak periods. Similarly, the government can charge fees to reduce congestion in National Parks during peak periods. They can have restrictions through licensing on hunting and fishing to control animal populations.

Second, the government could assign private property rights to common resources. For example, private fish farms have become more profitable as overfishing depletes the stock of fish in open waters.

SECTION CHECK 2

2.1 A public good is both nonrival in consumption (one person's usage of it does not diminish another's ability to use it) and nonexclusive (no one can be excluded from using it).

2.2 A free rider is someone who attempts to enjoy the benefits of a good without paying for it. The free-rider problem prevents the private market from supplying the efficient amount of public goods.

2.3 A common resource good is rival in consumption but nonexcludable.

⑤3 Asymmetric Information

Keep the following questions in mind as you read through this section. You'll find the answers in Section Check 3.

3.1 What is asymmetric information?

3.2 What is adverse selection?

3.3 What is moral hazard?

In this section, we'll discuss the third potential cause of market failure—asymmetric information.

WHAT IS ASYMMETRIC INFORMATION?

When the available information is initially distributed in favor of one party relative to another, **asymmetric information** is said to exist. Suppose you bought a new car for $25,000 and about a month later you decide that you would be much happier with your old car and the money. So you call your salesperson and ask what your car is worth—perfect condition and less than 1,000 miles on the odometer. The salesperson tells you about $20,000. Why did your "new" car depreciate $5,000 in just one month? The problem is that a potential buyer

is going to be skeptical. Why is that new car being sold? Is it a lemon?

Sellers are at an information advantage over potential buyers when selling a car because they have more information about the car than does the potential buyer. However, potential buyers know that sellers are more likely to sell a lemon. As a result, potential buyers will offer a lower price than they would if they could be certain of the quality. This is known as the lemon problem. Without incurring significant quality detection costs, such as having it inspected by a mechanic, the potential buyer is at an informational disadvantage relative to the seller. It is rational for the seller to claim that the car is in good shape and has no known defects, but the potential buyer cannot detect whether the car is a lemon or not without incurring costs. If the quality detection costs are sufficiently high, a solution is to price all used cars as if they are average quality. That is, used cars of the same year, make, and model generally will be offered at the same price, regardless of their known conditions. The seller of a lemon will then receive a payment that is more than the car is worth, and the seller of a relatively high-quality car will receive less than the car is worth. However, if a seller of a high-quality car does *not* receive what the car would sell for if the potential buyer knew its quality, the seller will rationally withdraw the offer to sell the car. Given the logical response of sellers of higher-than-average quality cars, the average quality of used cars on the market will fall, and consequently, many people will avoid buying in the used car market. In other words, the bad cars will drive the good cars out of the market. Thus, fewer used cars are bought and sold because fewer good cars are offered for sale. That is, information problems reduce economic efficiency. A situation where an informed party benefits in an exchange by taking advantage of knowing more than the other party is called **adverse selection**.

This distortion in the used car market resulting from adverse selection can be reduced by the buyer acquiring more information so that the buyer and seller have equal information. In the used car example, it might mean that an individual buyer would demand that an independent mechanic do a detailed inspection of the used car or that the dealership provide an extended warranty. A warranty provides a credible signal that this dealer is not selling lemons. In addition, new services such as carfax.com allow you to pay to find the history of a used car before you buy it. These services help in eliminating the adverse selection problem because buyers would have more information about the product they are buying.

The least-cost solution would have sellers reveal their superior information to potential buyers. The problem is that it is not individually rational for the seller to provide a truthful and complete disclosure, a point that is known by a potential buyer. Only if the seller is punished for not truthfully revealing exchange-relevant information will a potential buyer perceive the seller's disclosure as truthful.

Adverse selection also occurs in the insurance market. Imagine an auto insurance company that has a one-size-fits-all policy for their insurance premiums. Careful drivers would be charged the same premium as careless drivers. The company would assess the average risk of accidents for all drivers and then set the premium. Of course, this would be very appealing to careless drivers who are more likely to get in an accident, but not very appealing to careful drivers who have a much lower probability of getting in an accident. Under this pricing scheme, the bad drivers would drive the good drivers out of the market. Good drivers would be less likely to buy a policy, thinking that they are paying too much, since they are less likely to get in an accident than a careless driver. Many good drivers would exit the market, leaving a disproportionate share of bad drivers—exactly what the insurance companies do not want—people with a higher risk of getting in accidents. So what do they do?

Insurance companies set premiums according to the risk associated with particular groups of drivers, so good drivers do not exit the market. One strategy they use for dealing with adverse selection is called *screening*, where they use observable information about people to reveal private information. For example, a 17-year-old male driving a sports car will be charged a much higher premium than a 40-year-old female driving a minivan,

adverse selection a situation in which an informed party benefits in an exchange by taking advantage of knowing more than the other party

even if he is a careful driver. Or someone with a good driving record or good grades gets a discount on his insurance. Insurance companies have data on different types of drivers and the probability of those drivers being in accidents, and they use this data to set insurance premiums. They may be wrong on an individual case (the teenager may be accident-free for years), but they are likely to be correct on average.

Reputation and Standardization

Asymmetric information is also present in other markets, such as rare stamps, coins, paintings, and sports memorabilia, in which the dealer (seller) knows more about the product than does the potential buyer. Potential buyers want to be assured that these items are authentic, not counterfeits. Unless the seller can successfully provide evidence of the quality of the product, bad products will tend to drive good products out of the market, resulting in a market failure.

One method that sellers can use to convince potential buyers that their products are high quality is *reputation*. For example, if a supermarket has a reputation of selling fresh produce, you will be more likely to shop there. The same is true when you choose an electrician, plumber, or physician. In the used car market, the dealer might advertise how long he has been in business. This provides a signal that he has many satisfied customers. Therefore, he is likely to sell more used cars at a higher price. In short, if there is a reputation of high quality, it will minimize the market failure problem.

However, there may be cases in which it is difficult to develop a reputation. For example, take a restaurant or a motel on a desolate highway. These establishments may not receive repeat customers. Customers have little idea of the quality of food, the probability of bedbugs, and so on. In this case, *standardization* is important. A national restaurant or a motel chain provides standardization. While you may not frequent McDonald's when you are at home, when confronted with the choice between a little known restaurant and McDonald's, you may pick the McDonald's because of the standardized products backed by a large corporation.

Asymmetric Information and Job Market Signaling

Why does non–job-related schooling raise your income? Why would salaried workers work longer hours, putting in 60 to 70 hours a week? The reason is this behavior provides a useful signal to the employer about the person's intelligence and work ethic.

Signaling is important because it reduces information costs associated with asymmetric information; the seller of labor (potential employee) has more information about her work ethic and reliability than the buyer of labor (potential employer). Imagine how costly it would be to try out 150 potential employees for a job. In short, signals provide a measure that can help reduce asymmetric information and lower hiring costs.

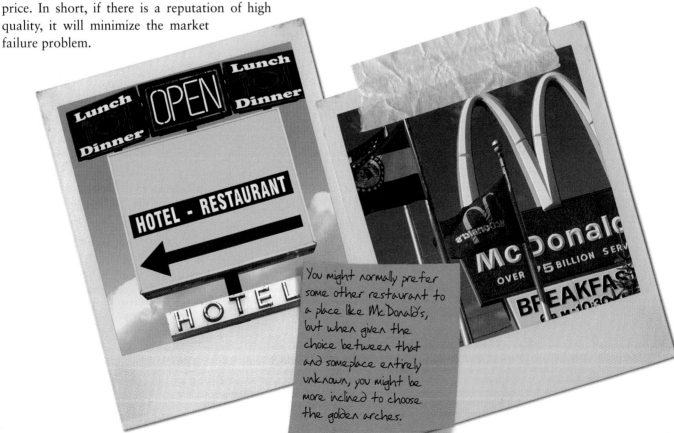

You might normally prefer some other restaurant to a place like McDonald's, but when given the choice between that and someplace entirely unknown, you might be more inclined to choose the golden arches.

There are strong signals and weak signals. Wearing a nice suit to work would be a weak signal because it does not necessarily distinguish a high-productivity worker from a low-productivity worker—a lazy worker can dress well, too. To provide a strong signal, it must be harder for a low-productivity worker to give the signal than it is for a high-productivity worker. Education is a strong signal in labor markets because it requires effort that many low-productivity workers may find too difficult to obtain. The education signal is also relatively easy to measure via years of education, grade-point average, highest degree attained, reputation of the university or college, rigor of courses attempted, and so on. Education can clearly improve a person's productivity; even if it did not, however, it would be a useful signal because more productive people find it easier to obtain education than lazy people. Furthermore, productive people are more likely to attain more education in order to signal to their employer that they are productive. So it may not just be the knowledge obtained from a college education, it may be the effort that you are signaling—something you presumably already had before you entered college. So according to the signaling model, workers go to college not for the knowledge gained, but to send the important signal that they are highly productive.

Education sends an important signal, but it also provides knowledge, enhancing productivity. For example, many firms will not hire managers without an MBA because of the knowledge potential employees gained in courses such as finance and economics, but also because an MBA sends a powerful signal that the worker is disciplined and hard working.

Durable Goods, Signals, and Warranties

Why are people reluctant to buy durable goods such as televisions, refrigerators, and cameras without a warranty? Warranties are a signal. Honest and reliable firms find it less expensive to provide a warranty than do dishonest firms. The dilemma for consumers is that they are trying to distinguish the good brands from the bad brands. One way to do this is to see what kind of warranty the producer offers. Low-quality items would require more frequent and expensive servicing than high-quality items. Thus, producers of low-quality items will tend to not offer extensive warranties. In short, extensive warranties signal high quality, while items without extensive warranties signal poor quality. With this knowledge, consumers will pay more for high-quality products with good warranties.

WHAT IS MORAL HAZARD?

Another information problem is associated with the insurance market and is called moral hazard. If an individual is fully insured for fire, theft, auto, life, and so on, what incentives will this individual have to take additional precautions from risk? For example, a person with auto insurance may drive less cautiously than would a person without auto insurance.

Health insurance companies do, however, try to remedy the adverse selection problem by requiring regular checkups, offering discounts for nonsmokers, charging different deductibles and different rates for different age and occupational groups, and so on.

Additionally, those with health insurance may devote less effort and resources to staying healthy than those who are not covered. The problem, of course, is that if the insured are behaving more recklessly than they would if they were not insured, the result might be much higher insurance rates. The **moral hazard** arises from the fact that it is costly for the insurer to monitor the behaviors of the insured party. Suppose an individual knew that his car was protected with a "bumper to bumper" warranty. He might have less incentive to take care of the car, despite the manufacturer's contract specifying that the warranty was only valid under "normal wear and tear." It would be too costly for the manufacturer to detect if a product failure was the consequence of a manufacturing defect or abuse by the owner.

Adverse Selection versus Moral Hazard

Don't confuse adverse selection and moral hazard. Adverse selection is the phenomenon that occurs when one party in the exchange takes advantage of knowing more than the other party. Moral hazard involves the action taken *after* the exchange, such as if you were a nonsmoker who had just bought a life insurance policy and then started smoking heavily.

Winner's Curse

Suppose you and five other classmates were asked to bid on a jar of pennies. Nobody knows how many pennies are in the jar and you are not allowed to open the jar. The winner gets the jar of pennies. Let's say there are 500 pennies ($5) in the jar and you win by bidding $7. You are happy you won the bid until they count the pennies and you realize you just paid $7 for $5 worth of pennies. A common-value auction is where

> **moral hazard** taking additional risks because you are insured

the auctioned item has the same value than its worth for all buyers but the value is unknown prior to the bidding. We call this a **winner's curse** because in this case the "winner" is overly optimistic and bids more for an item than it is worth. Therefore, the winner could end up being worse off (cursed) than the loser.

The problem also occurs because value is subjective. In some cases, bidders have a difficult time establishing an item's value. Without complete information, participants with limited skill in establishing valuation may overpay for an item. Historically, we have seen this when speculative bubbles in the stock or real estate markets occur. Then, investors with little skill in valuation and incomplete information tend to push prices beyond their true value.

However, an actual overpayment will generally occur only if the winner fails to account for the winner's curse when bidding. So despite its dire-sounding name, the winner's curse does not necessarily have ill effects.

The severity of the winner's curse tends to increase with the number of bidders. This is because the more bidders there are, the more likely it is that some of them have overestimated the auctioned item's value. The more serious your error of overbidding, the more likely you are to win. However, if you win, you probably made a serious error. The best strategy may be to underbid. If the winner normally overestimates the true value by 20 percent, then you might offer 80 percent of what you think the item is worth. That way, if you happen to win by overbidding you won't "get taken to the cleaners." You might also choose not to participate in auctions likely to generate a winner's curse.

© JEFFERY STONE/SHUTTERSTOCK

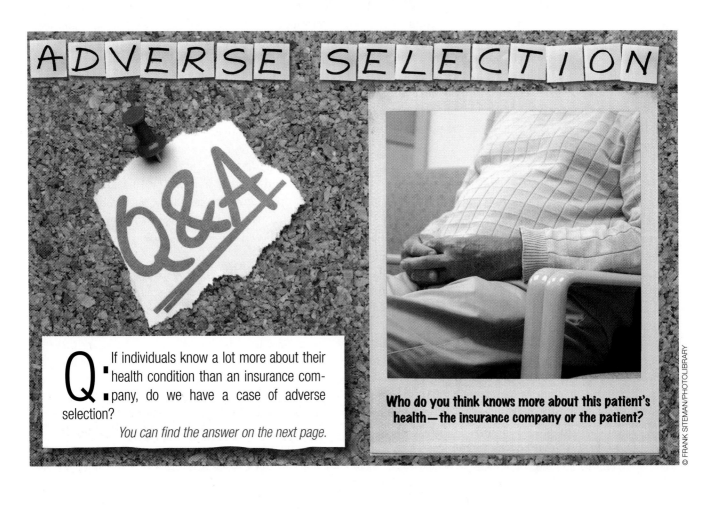

ADVERSE SELECTION

Q&A

Q: If individuals know a lot more about their health condition than an insurance company, do we have a case of adverse selection?

You can find the answer on the next page.

Who do you think knows more about this patient's health—the insurance company or the patient?

© FRANK SITEMAN/PHOTOLIBRARY

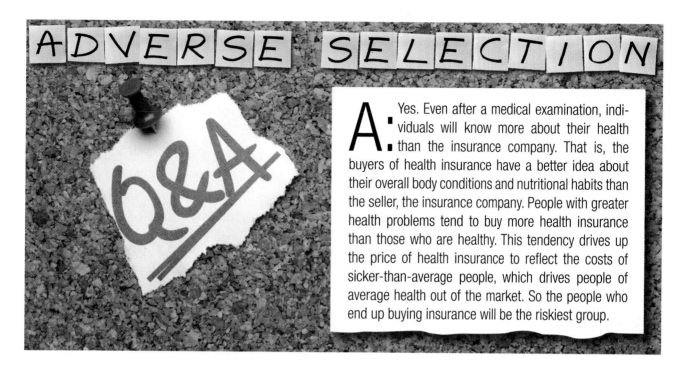

ADVERSE SELECTION

Q&A

A: Yes. Even after a medical examination, individuals will know more about their health than the insurance company. That is, the buyers of health insurance have a better idea about their overall body conditions and nutritional habits than the seller, the insurance company. People with greater health problems tend to buy more health insurance than those who are healthy. This tendency drives up the price of health insurance to reflect the costs of sicker-than-average people, which drives people of average health out of the market. So the people who end up buying insurance will be the riskiest group.

There is often confusion that the winner's curse applies to the winners of all auctions. However, it is worth repeating here that for auctions based on the private value someone places on a good (i.e., when the item is desired independent of its value in the market), the winner's curse does not arise.

The winner's curse can also occur with underbidding, where people offer to do a job for less than other bidders. Imagine you need to hire a landscaper, so you get estimates from various landscapers. Who is likely to win? Probably the landscaper with the lowest estimate. However, he may not think he won if he underestimated the amount of work required in your yard.

SECTION CHECK 3

3.1 Asymmetric information occurs when the available information is initially distributed in favor of one party relative to another in an exchange.

3.2 Adverse selection is a situation in which an informed party benefits in an exchange by taking advantage of knowing more about the good than the other party does.

3.3 Moral hazard occurs when one party to a contract passes on the cost of its behavior to the other party.

⑤4 Public Choice

Keep the following questions in mind as you read through this section. You'll find the answers in **Section Check 4**.

4.1 What is public choice theory?

4.2 What is rational ignorance?

4.3 Why do special-interest groups arise?

When the market fails, as in the case of an externality or public good, it may be necessary for the government to intervene and make public choices. However, it is possible for government actions in response to externalities to make matters worse. That is, just because markets have failed to generate efficient results does not necessarily mean that government can do a better job—see Exhibit 5.3 on the next page. One explanation for this outcome is presented by public choice theory.

WHAT IS PUBLIC CHOICE THEORY?

Public choice theory is the application of economic principles to politics. Public choice economists believe that government actions are an outgrowth of individual behavior. Specifically, they assume that the behavior of individuals in politics, as in the marketplace, will

EXHIBIT 5.3 Do People in Government Waste Tax Money? 1970–2004 (percent of population agreeing)

	'70	'72	'74	'76	'78	'80	'82	'84	'86	'88	'90	'92	'94	'96	'98	'00	'02	'04
A Lot	69	66	74	74	77	78	66	65	**	63	67	67	70	59	61	59	48	61
Some	26	30	22	20	19	18	29	29	**	33	30	30	27	39	34	38	49	37
Not Very Much	4	2	1	3	2	2	2	4	**	2	2	2	2	1	4	3	3	2
Don't Know	1	2	2	3	2	2	3	2	**	2	1	1	1	0	1	1	0	1

**No data available for 1986.

Source: The American National Election Studies (www.electionstudies.org). THE ANES GUIDE TO PUBLIC OPINION AND ELECTORAL BEHAVIOR. Ann Arbor, MI: University of Michigan, Center for Political Studies [producer and distributor]. Table 5A.3. Available at http://www.electionstudies.org/nesguide/gd-index.htm#4, (accessed April, 16, 2010).

be influenced by self-interest. Bureaucrats, politicians, and voters make choices that they believe will yield them expected marginal benefits that will be greater than their expected marginal costs. Of course, the private sector and the public sector differ when it comes to the "rules of the game" that they must follow. The self-interest assumption is, however, central to the analysis of behavior in both arenas.

SCARCITY AND THE PUBLIC SECTOR

The self-interest assumption is not the only similarity between the market and public sectors. For example, scarcity is present in the public sector as well as in the private sector. Public schools and public libraries come at the expense of something else. Competition is also present in the public sector, as different government agencies compete for government funds and lobbyists compete with each other to get favored legislation through Congress.

THE INDIVIDUAL CONSUMPTION-PAYMENT LINK

In private markets, when a shopper goes to the supermarket to purchase groceries, the shopping cart is filled with many different goods that the consumer presumably wants and is willing to pay for; the shopping cart reflects the individual consumption-payment link. The link breaks down when an assortment of political goods is decided on by majority rule. These political goods might include such items as additional national defense, additional money for the space program, new museums, new public schools, increased foreign aid, and so on. Even though an individual may be willing to pay for some of these goods, it is unlikely that she will want to consume or pay for everything placed in the

When you go shopping, you put the goods that you are willing to pay for in your cart. But what about political goods that people vote for like schools, parks, museums, foreign aid, and space programs? How much are you willing to pay for these goods?

political shopping cart. However, if the majority decides that these political goods are important, the individual will have to purchase the goods through higher taxes, whether she values the goods or not.

MAJORITY RULE AND THE MEDIAN VOTERS

In a two-party system, the candidate with the most votes wins the election. Because voters are likely to vote for the candidate who holds views similar to their own candidates must pay close attention to the preferences of the majority of voters.

For example, in Exhibit 5.4, we assume a normal distribution, with a continuum of voter preferences from the liberal left to the conservative right. We can see from the figure that only a few are extremely liberal or extremely conservative. A successful campaign would have to address the concerns of the median voters (those in the middle of the distribution in Exhibit 5.4), resulting in moderate policies. For example, if one candidate ran a fairly conservative campaign, attracting voters at and to the right of V_1, an opponent could win by a landslide by taking a fairly conservative position just to the left of this candidate. Alternatively, if the candidate takes a liberal position, say V_2, then the opponent can win by campaigning just to the right of that position. In this case, it is easy to see that the candidate who takes the median position, V_M, is least likely to be defeated. Of course, the distribution does not have to be normal or symmetrical; it could be skewed to the right or left. Regardless of the distribution, however, the successful candidate will still seek out the median voters.

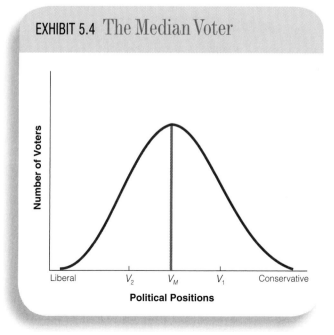

EXHIBIT 5.4 The Median Voter

y-axis: Number of Voters
x-axis: Political Positions — Liberal, V_2, V_M, V_1, Conservative

In fact, the **median voter model** predicts a strong tendency for both candidates to choose a position in the middle of the distribution, and therefore the election will be close.

> **median voter model** a model that predicts candidates will choose a position in the middle of the distribution

Of course, this model does not mean that all politicians will find or even attempt to find the median. For example, politicians may take different positions because they have arrived at different predictions of voter preferences or have merely misread public sentiment; or they may think they have the charisma to change voter preferences.

VOTERS AND RATIONAL IGNORANCE

Representative democracy provides a successful mechanism for making social choices in many countries. But some important differences are evident in the way democracy is ideally supposed to work and how it actually works.

One of the keys to an efficiently working democracy is a concerned and informed electorate. Everyone is supposed to take time to study the issues and candidates and then carefully weigh the relevant information before deciding how to vote. Although an informed citizenry is desirable from a social point of view, it is not clear that individuals will find it personally desirable to become politically informed.

Obtaining detailed information about issues and candidates is costly. Many issues are complicated, and a great deal of technical knowledge and information is necessary to make an informed judgment on them. To find out what candidates are really going to do requires a lot more than listening to their campaign slogans. It requires studying their past voting records, reading a great deal that has been written either by or about them, and asking them questions at public meetings. Taking the time and trouble to do these things—and more—is the cost that each eligible voter has to pay personally for the benefits of being politically informed. These costs may help to explain why the majority of Americans cannot identify their congressional representatives and are unlikely to be acquainted with their representatives' views on Social Security, health care, tariffs, and agricultural policies.

For many people the costs of becoming politically informed are high, whereas the benefits are low. As a result, they limit their quest for political information to listening to the radio on the way to work, talking with friends, casual reading, and other things they would do anyway. Even though most people in society might be

Some people perceive that the benefits they derive from being well-informed about political issues do not outweigh the costs.

SPECIAL-INTEREST GROUPS

Even though many voters may be uninformed about specific issues, others may feel a strong need to be politically informed. Such individuals may be motivated to organize a **special-interest group**. These groups may have intense feelings about and a degree of interest in particular issues that is at variance with the general public. However, as a group these individuals are more likely to influence decision makers and have a far greater impact on the outcome of a political decision than they would with their individual votes.

If a special-interest group is successful in getting everyone else to pay for a project that benefits them, the cost will be spread over so large a number of taxpayers that the amount any one person will have to pay is negligible. Hence, the motivation for an individual citizen to spend the necessary time and effort to resist an interest group is minimal, even if she had a guarantee that this resistance would be effective.

For example, many taxpayers and consumers are unaware of the federal subsidy to sugar growers. The subsidy is estimated to cost consumers more than $1 billion a year, which is less than $5 per person. However, the gain from the subsidy is estimated to be over $100,000 per sugar grower. At that price, few customers are going to invest the time and money to fight this issue. However, the effort to keep the subsidy is surely enough to get sugar growers to make trips to Washington, D.C., and help in political campaigns.

better off if everyone became more informed, it isn't worth the cost for most individuals to make the requisite effort to become informed themselves. Public choice economists refer to this lack of incentive to become informed as **rational ignorance**. People will generally make much more informed decisions as buyers than as voters. For example, you are likely to gather more information when making a decision on a car purchase than when you are deciding between candidates in an upcoming election. An uninformed decision on a car purchase will most likely affect your life much more than an uninformed decision on a candidate, especially when your vote will most likely not alter the outcome of the election.

The fact that one vote, especially in a state or national election, is highly unlikely to affect the outcome of the election may explain why some citizens choose not to vote. Many factors may determine the net benefits for voting, including candidates and issues on the ballot, weather, and distance to the polling booths. For example, we would certainly expect fewer voters to turn out at the polls on the day of a blizzard; the blizzard would change the net benefits. We would also expect more voters at the polls if the election were predicted to be a close one, with emotions running higher and voter perception that their individual vote is more significant.

If the cost of being an informed voter is high and the benefits low, why do people vote? Many people vote for reasons other than to affect the outcome of the election. They vote because they believe in the democratic process and because of civic pride. In other words, they perceive that the benefits they derive from being involved in the political process outweigh the costs.

Furthermore, rational ignorance does not imply that people should not vote; it is merely one explanation for why some people do not vote. The point that public choice economists are making is that some people will vote only if they think that their vote will make a difference; otherwise, they will not vote.

SECTION CHECK 4

4.1 Public choice theory holds that the behavior of individuals in politics, as in the marketplace, is influenced by self-interest.

4.2 Rational ignorance is the condition in which voters tend to be relatively uninformed about political issues because of the high information costs and low benefits of being politically informed.

4.3 A special-interest group is a political pressure group formed by individuals with a common political objective.

Chapter 5: Self-Review

Now that you're finished reading the chapter, review the questions below. You can write your answers in the space provided, then go online to see the answers at www.cengagebrain.com.

S1–EXTERNALITIES

1. Why are externalities also called spillover effects?

2. Indicate which of the following activities create a positive externality, a negative externality, or no externality at all:
   a. During a live theater performance, an audience member's cell phone loudly rings.
   b. You are given a flu shot.
   c. You purchase and drink a soda during a break from class.
   d. A college fraternity and sorority clean up trash along a two-mile stretch of the highway.
   e. A firm dumps chemical waste into a local water reservoir.
   f. The person down the hall in your dorm plays loud music while you are trying to sleep.

S2–PUBLIC GOODS

3. Is a lighthouse a public good if it benefits many ship owners? What if it primarily benefits ships going to a port nearby?

4. In what way can government provision of public goods solve the free-rider problem?

5. True or False: Public goods are rival in consumption and nonexclusive.

6. For each of the following goods, indicate whether they are nonrival and/or nonexclusive. Indicate whether they are private or public goods.
   a. hot dogs
   b. cable TV
   c. broadcast TV
   d. automobiles
   e. national defense
   f. pollution control
   g. parking in a parking structure
   h. a sunset
   i. admission to a theme park

S3–ASYMMETRIC INFORMATION

7. Why might withdrawals in several classes send a poor signal to potential employers?

8. Why is the winner's curse less likely for repeat-purchase items?

9. How would the adverse selection problem arise in the insurance market? How is it like the "lemon" used-car problem?

S4–PUBLIC CHOICE

10. What principles does the public choice analysis of government behavior share with the economic analysis of market behavior?

11. Why is the tendency strong for candidates to choose positions in the middle of the distribution of voter preferences?

12. Why do you think news reporters are more informed than average citizens about public policy issues?

13. Fill-in-the-Blank: The _____ predicts that a candidate will choose a position in the middle of the distribution.

What questions

do you think Toyota had to ask when it decided to build this auto plant? Maybe how long it would take to get it up and running. What about the other possible uses of the building funds? Perhaps those could have been diverted to researching new engine technology. What if the economy slows down and Toyota finds it doesn't need the extra capacity anymore? Should it shut the plant down? What about all the money it already invested in the plant?

© ISIFA/GETTY IMAGES

6

Production and Costs

osts exist because resources are scarce and have competing uses—to produce more of one good means foregoing the production of another good. The cost of producing a good is measured by the worth of the most valuable alternative that was given up to obtain the resource, which is called the *opportunity cost*.

In Chapter 2, the production possibilities curve highlighted this trade-off. Recall that the opportunity cost of producing additional shelter was the units of food that had to be sacrificed. Other examples of opportunity costs abound: Paper used in this book could have been used in newspapers or magazines; the steel used in the construction of a new building could have been used in the production of an automobile or a washing machine.

In this chapter, we examine the firm's costs in more detail—what really lies behind the firm's supply curve? A firm's costs are a key determinant in pricing and production decisions. As we'll discover, the discussions in this chapter will prove to be very important building blocks for the theory of the firm.

⑤1 Firms and Profits: Total Revenues Minus Total Costs

Keep the following questions in mind as you read through this section. You'll find the answers in **Section Check 1**.

1.1 What are explicit and implicit costs?
1.2 What are accounting profits?
1.3 What are economic profits?
1.4 What are sunk costs?

What exactly makes up a firm's cost of production? Let's begin by looking at the two distinct components of a firm's total cost: explicit costs and implicit costs.

Sections in Chapter 6

Explicit Cost
Explicit costs are the opportunity costs that are visible, requiring an outlay of money.

Implicit Cost
Implicit costs are the non-monetary opportunity costs that are less visible, such as foregone salaries or interest.

© ERLEND KVALSVIK/ISTOCKPHOTO.COM

EXPLICIT COSTS

Explicit costs are the input costs that require monetary payment—the out-of-pocket expenses that pay for labor services, raw materials, fuel, transportation, utilities, advertising, and so on. It is important to note that the explicit costs are opportunity costs to the firm. For example, money spent on electricity cannot be used for advertising. Remember that in a world of scarcity we are always giving up something to get something else. Trade-offs are pervasive. The costs discussed so far are relatively easy to measure, and an economist and an accountant would most likely arrive at the same figures. However, that will not always be the case.

IMPLICIT COSTS

Some of the firm's (opportunity) costs of production are implicit. **Implicit costs** do not require an outlay of money. Here is where the economist's and accountant's ideas of costs diverge, because accountants do not include implicit costs. For example, whenever an investment is made, opportunities to invest elsewhere are forgone. This lost opportunity is an implicit cost that economists include in the firm's total cost even though no money is expended. A typical farmer or small business owner may perform work without receiving formal wages, but the value of the alternative earnings forgone represents an implicit opportunity cost to the individual. Because other firms could have used the resources, what the resources could have earned elsewhere is an implicit cost to the firm. It is important to emphasize that whenever we are talking about costs—explicit or implicit—we are talking about opportunity costs.

PROFITS

Economists generally assume that the ultimate goal of every firm is to maximize its **profits**. In other words, firms try to maximize the difference between what they give up for their inputs—their total costs (explicit and implicit)—and the amount they receive for their goods and services—their total revenues. Like revenues and costs, profits refer to flows over time. When we say that a firm earned $5 million in profit, we must specify the period in which the profit was earned—a week, month, year, and so on.

ARE ACCOUNTING PROFITS THE SAME AS ECONOMIC PROFITS?

A firm can make profits in the sense that the total revenues it receives exceed the explicit costs it incurs in the process of doing business. We call these profits **accounting profits**. Profits as accountants record them are based on total revenues and explicit costs and do not include implicit costs.

Economists prefer an alternative way of measuring profits; they are interested in total revenues minus total costs (both explicit and implicit). Economists include the implicit costs as well as the explicit costs when calculating the total costs of the firm.

Summing up, measured in terms of accounting profits such as those reported in real-world financial statements, a firm has a profit if its total revenues exceed its explicit costs. In terms of **economic profits**, a firm has profits if its total revenues exceed its total opportunity costs—both its explicit costs and implicit costs. Exhibit 6.1 illustrates the difference between accounting profits and economic profits.

A ZERO ECONOMIC PROFIT IS A NORMAL PROFIT

As we just discussed, an economic profit is less than an accounting profit because an economic profit includes implicit as well as explicit costs. In fact, an economist considers a zero economic profit a normal profit. A zero economic profit means that the firm is covering both explicit and implicit costs—the total opportunity costs of its resources. In other words, the firm's total revenues are sufficient to compensate for the time and money that owners put in the business. This view is clearly different from making a zero accounting profit, when

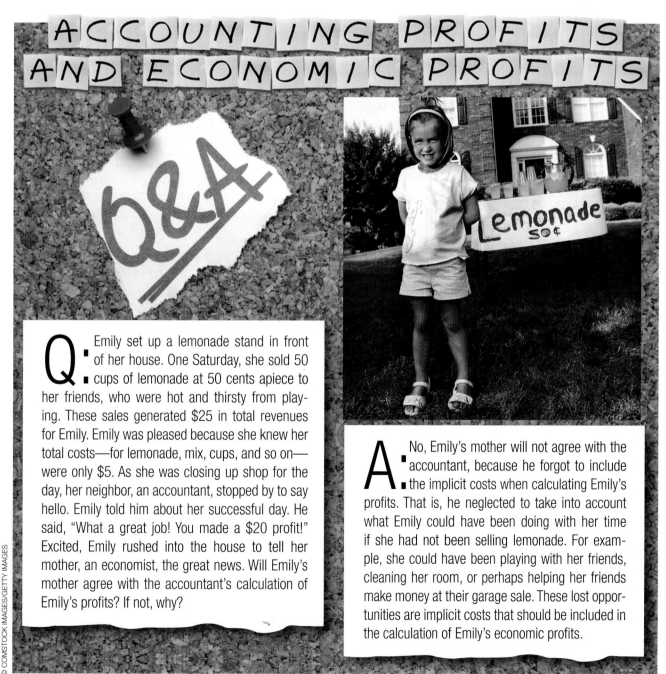

economic profits total revenues minus explicit and implicit costs

Q: Emily set up a lemonade stand in front of her house. One Saturday, she sold 50 cups of lemonade at 50 cents apiece to her friends, who were hot and thirsty from playing. These sales generated $25 in total revenues for Emily. Emily was pleased because she knew her total costs—for lemonade, mix, cups, and so on— were only $5. As she was closing up shop for the day, her neighbor, an accountant, stopped by to say hello. Emily told him about her successful day. He said, "What a great job! You made a $20 profit!" Excited, Emily rushed into the house to tell her mother, an economist, the great news. Will Emily's mother agree with the accountant's calculation of Emily's profits? If not, why?

A: No, Emily's mother will not agree with the accountant, because he forgot to include the implicit costs when calculating Emily's profits. That is, he neglected to take into account what Emily could have been doing with her time if she had not been selling lemonade. For example, she could have been playing with her friends, cleaning her room, or perhaps helping her friends make money at their garage sale. These lost opportunities are implicit costs that should be included in the calculation of Emily's economic profits.

sunk costs costs that have been incurred and cannot be recovered

revenues would not cover the implicit costs.

SUNK COSTS

We just saw how opportunity costs are often hidden, as in the case of implicit costs, and that economists believe they should be taken into account when making economic decisions. Another type of cost should also be discussed: sunk costs. **Sunk costs** have already been incurred and cannot be recovered. These costs are visible but should be ignored when making economic decisions. Suppose, for example, that you buy a DVD that sounds interesting but when you get home and play it, you regret your purchase. Now your friend comes over and says he likes that DVD and will buy it from you for $5. You say "no way" because you paid $15 for the DVD. Are you acting rationally? Economists believe that what you paid for the DVD is now irrelevant. Now you must simply decide whether you would rather have the $5 or the DVD. If you decide to keep the DVD, the cost is the $5 you could have received from your friend, and the rest is sunk.

Or suppose a donut shop has a one-year lease, but after three months the owner decides that the shop would do much better by relocating to a new mall that just opened. Should the donut shop just stay put until the end of the year because it is legally obligated to pay the 12-month lease? No, the nonrefundable lease payment is sunk and irrelevant to the decision to relocate. The decision to relocate should be based on the prospects of future profits, regardless of the length of the current lease.

In short, sunk costs are irrelevant for any future action because they have already been incurred and cannot be recovered.

SECTION CHECK 1

1.1 Explicit costs are the opportunity costs of production that require a monetary payment. Firms also have some implicit opportunity costs, which do not represent an outlay of money or a contractual obligation.

1.2 Accounting profits are total revenues minus explicit costs.

1.3 Economic profits are total revenues minus total opportunity costs—both explicit and implicit costs.

1.4 Sunk costs have already been incurred and cannot be recovered.

EXHIBIT 6.1 Accounting Profits versus Economic Profits

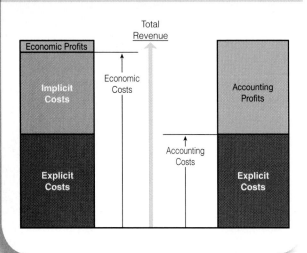

⑤2 Production in the Short Run

Keep the following questions in mind as you read through this section. You'll find the answers in **Section Check 2.**

2.1 What is the difference between the short run and the long run?

2.2 What is a production function?

2.3 What is diminishing marginal product?

The short run and the long run are the time periods in which the firm operates. Here we'll discuss the distinction between the two and then examine the firm's production in the short run.

THE SHORT RUN VERSUS THE LONG RUN

The extent to which a firm is able to adjust inputs as it varies output is of fundamental importance for cost and production behavior. Because it takes more time to vary some inputs than others, we must distinguish between the short run and the long run. The **short run** is defined as a period too brief for some inputs to be varied. For example, a firm cannot alter the current size of its plant in a day, and it cannot obtain new equipment overnight. If demand increases for the firm's product and the firm chooses to produce more output in the short run, it must do so with its existing equipment and factory. Inputs such as buildings and equipment that do not change with output are called *fixed* inputs.

The **long run** is a period in which a firm can adjust all inputs. That is, in the long run, all inputs to the firm are *variable*, changing as output changes. The long run can vary considerably from industry to industry. For a chain of coffeehouses that wants to add a few more stores, the long run may only be a few months. In other industries, such as automobiles or steel, the long run might be a couple of years, as a new plant or factory in this type of industry takes much longer to build.

PRODUCTION IN THE SHORT RUN

Exhibit 6.2 shows how the quantity of bagels produced by Moe's Bagel Shop per hour varies with the number of workers. This relationship between the quantity of inputs (workers) and the quantity of outputs (bagels) is called the **production function**. Suppose that Moe's has just one input that is variable (labor) and the size of the bagel shop is fixed in the short run. What will happen to the **total output (Q)** (bagels) generated by Moe's as the level of the variable input (labor) rises? Common sense suggests that total output will start at a low level and increase—perhaps rapidly at first and

short run a period too brief for some production inputs to be varied

long run a period over which all production inputs are variable

production function the relationship between the quantity of inputs and the quantity of outputs

total output (Q) the total amount of output of a good produced by the firm

EXHIBIT 6.2 Moe's Production Function with One Variable, Labor

Variable Input Labor (workers)	Total Output (bagels per hour), Q	Marginal Product of Labor (bagels per hour), $\Delta Q/\Delta V$
0	0	
1	10	10
2	24	14
3	36	12
4	46	10
5	50	4
6	51	1

marginal product (MP) the change in total output of a good that results from a one-unit change in input

diminishing marginal product as a variable input increases, with other inputs fixed, a point will be reached at which the additions to output will eventually decline

then more slowly—as the amount of the variable input increases. It will continue to increase until the quantity of the variable input (labor) becomes so large in relation to the quantity of other inputs—the size of the bagel shop, for example—that further increases in output become more and more difficult or even impossible. In the second column of Exhibit 6.2, we see that as Moe increases the number of workers in his bagel shop, the number of bagels Moe is able to produce increases. The addition of the first worker results in a total output of 10 bagels per hour. When Moe adds a second worker, bagel output climbs to 24, an increase of 14 bagels per hour. Total output continues to increase even with the sixth worker hired; but you can see that it has slowed considerably, with the sixth worker only increasing total output by 1 bagel per hour. Beyond this point, additional workers may even result in a decline in total bagel output as workers bump into each other in the small bagel shop. This outcome is evident both in Exhibit 6.2 and in the total output curve shown in Exhibit 6.3(a).

DIMINISHING MARGINAL PRODUCT

The **marginal product (MP)** of any single input is defined as the change in total output resulting from a small change in the amount of input used. This concept is shown in the

final column in Exhibit 6.2 and is illustrated by the *MP* curve in Exhibit 6.3(b). As you can see in Exhibit 6.3(b), the *MP* curve first rises and then falls.

The Rise in Marginal Product

The initial rise in the marginal product is the result of more effective use of fixed inputs as the number of workers increases. For example, certain types of capital equipment may require a minimum number of workers for efficient operation, or perhaps any operation at all. With a small number of workers (the variable input), some machines cannot operate at all, or only at a low level of efficiency. As additional workers are added, machines are brought into efficient operation and thus the marginal product of the workers rises. Similarly, if one person tried to operate a large department store alone—doing all the types of work necessary in the store—her energies would be spread so thin in so many directions that total output (sales) might be less than if she were operating a smaller store (working with less capital). As successive workers are added, up to a certain number, each worker adds more to total output than the previous one, and the marginal product rises. This relationship is seen in the shaded area of Exhibit 6.3(b) labeled "Increasing Marginal Product."

The Fall in Marginal Product

Too many workers in a store make it more difficult for customers to shop; too many workers in a factory get in each other's way. Adding more and more of a variable input to a fixed input will eventually lead to **diminishing marginal product**. Specifically, as the amount of a variable input is increased, with the amount of other (fixed)

EXHIBIT 6.3 Total Output and Marginal Product

a. Total Output

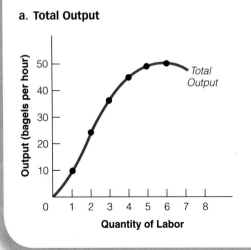

b. Marginal Product

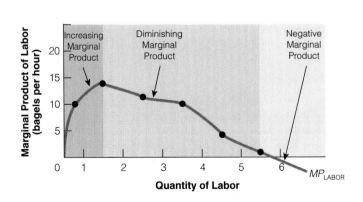

What do you think the marginal product would be for additional workers at this factory?

inputs held constant, a point will ultimately be reached beyond which marginal product will decline. Beyond this point, output increases but at a decreasing rate. It is the crowding of the fixed input with more and more workers that causes the decline in the marginal product.

The point of this discussion is that production functions conform to the same general pattern as that shown by Moe's Bagel Shop in the third column of Exhibit 6.2 and illustrated in Exhibit 6.3(b). In the third column of Exhibit 6.2, we see that as the number of workers in Moe's Bagel Shop increases, Moe is able to produce more bagels. The first worker is able to produce 10 bagels per hour. When Moe adds a second worker, total bagel output climbs to 24, an increase of 14 bagels per hour. When Moe hires a third worker, bagel output still increases. However, a third worker's marginal production (12 bagels per hour) is less than that of the second worker. In fact, the marginal product continues to drop as more and more workers are added to the bagel shop. This example shows diminishing marginal product at work. Note that it is not because the third worker is not as "good" as the second worker that marginal product falls. Even with identical workers, the increased "crowding" of the fixed input eventually causes marginal output to fall.

A firm never *knowingly* allows itself to reach the point at which the marginal product becomes negative—the situation in which the use of additional variable input units actually reduces total output. In such a situation, having so many units of the variable input (inputs with positive opportunity costs) actually impairs

efficient use of the fixed input units; therefore, *reducing* the number of workers would actually *increase* total output.

SECTION CHECK 2

2.1 The short run is defined as a period too brief for some inputs to be varied. Inputs such as buildings and equipment that do not change with output are called fixed inputs. The long run is a period of time long enough to allow the firm to adjust all inputs. That is, in the long run, all costs are variable and will change as output changes.

2.2 The production function is the relationship between the quantity of inputs and the quantity of outputs.

2.3 A diminishing marginal product occurs when the amount of a variable input keeps increasing while the amount of fixed inputs holds constant; eventually, the marginal product declines.

Ⓢ3 Costs in the Short Run

Keep the following questions in mind as you read through this section. You'll find the answers in **Section Check 3**.

3.1 What are fixed costs?

3.2 What are variable costs?

3.3 What are marginal costs?

3.4 What are average fixed, average variable, and average total costs?

In the preceding section, we discussed the relationship between a firm's inputs and its level of output. But that relationship is only one part of the discussion; we must also consider how much it will cost the firm to use each of these inputs in production. In this section, we examine the short-run costs of the firm—what they are and how they vary with the output levels that are produced.

© ALANDJ/ISTOCKPHOTO.COM

fixed costs costs that do not vary with the level of output

total fixed cost (TFC) the sum of the firm's fixed costs

variable costs costs that change with the level of output

total variable cost (TVC) the sum of the firm's variable costs

total cost (TC) the sum of the firm's total fixed costs and total variable costs

average total cost (ATC) a per-unit cost of operation; total cost divided by output

average fixed cost (AFC) a per-unit measure of fixed costs; fixed costs divided by output

average variable cost (AVC) a per-unit measure of variable costs; variable costs divided by output

marginal cost (MC) the change in total costs resulting from a one-unit change in output

The short-run total costs of a business fall into two distinct categories: fixed costs and variable costs.

FIXED COSTS, VARIABLE COSTS, AND TOTAL COSTS

Fixed costs are those costs that do not vary with the level of output. For example, the rent on buildings or equipment is usually fixed, at least for some period; whether the firm produces lots of output or little output, the rent stays the same. Insurance premiums, property taxes, and interest payments on debt used to finance capital equipment are other examples of fixed costs; they have to be paid even if no output is produced. In the short run, fixed costs cannot be avoided. The sum of the firm's fixed costs is called the **total fixed cost (TFC)**.

Variable costs change with the level of output. As more variable inputs such as labor and raw materials are added, output increases. The variable cost (expenditures for wages and raw materials) increases as output increases. The sum of the firm's variable costs is called the **total variable cost (TVC)**. The sum of the total fixed costs and total variable costs is called the firm's **total cost (TC)**.

AVERAGE TOTAL COSTS

Although we are often interested in the total amount of costs incurred by the firm, sometimes we find it convenient to discuss these costs on a per-unit-of-output, or an average, basis. For example, if Pizza Shack Company has a total fixed cost of $1,600 and a total variable cost of $2,400, its total cost is $4,000. If it produces 800 pizzas in the period in question, its total cost per unit of output equals $5 ($4,000 total cost ÷ 800 units of output = $5). We call this per-unit cost the **average total cost**

(**ATC**). Likewise, we might talk about the fixed cost per unit of output, or **average fixed cost (AFC)**. In the case of Pizza Shack, the average fixed cost, or *AFC*, would equal $2 ($1,600 fixed cost ÷ 800 units of output = $2). Similarly, we can speak of the per-unit variable cost, or **average variable cost (AVC)**. In this example, the average variable cost would equal $3 ($2,400 variable cost ÷ 800 units of output = $3).

MARGINAL COSTS

Up to this point, six different short-run cost concepts have been introduced: total cost, total fixed cost, total variable cost, average total cost, average fixed cost, and average variable cost. All these concepts are relevant to a discussion of firm behavior and profitability. However, the most important single cost concept has yet to be mentioned: marginal (or additional) cost. You may recall this concept from Chapter 2, where we highlighted the importance of using marginal analysis—that is, analysis that focuses on *additional* or marginal choices. Specifically, **marginal cost (MC)**

Six fundamental short-run cost concepts
1) total cost
2) total fixed cost
3) total variable cost
4) average total cost
5) average fixed cost
6) average variable cost

Marginal Cost

$$MC = \Delta TC/\Delta Q$$

Pizza Shack Company's total cost per unit

shows the change in total cost (TC) associated with a change in output (Q) by one unit ($\Delta TC/\Delta Q$). Put a bit differently, marginal cost is the cost of producing one more unit of output. As such, looking at marginal cost is a useful way to view variable cost (cost that varies as output varies). Marginal cost represents the added labor, raw materials, and miscellaneous expenses incurred in making an additional unit of output. Marginal cost is the additional, or incremental, cost associated with the "last" unit of output produced.

HOW ARE THESE COSTS RELATED?

Exhibit 6.4 summarizes the definitions of the seven different short-run cost concepts introduced in this chapter. To further clarify these concepts and to illustrate the relationships between them, let's return to our discussion of the costs faced by Pizza Shack.

Exhibit 6.5 on the next page presents the costs incurred by Pizza Shack at various levels of output. Notice that the total fixed cost is the same at all output

EXHIBIT 6.4 A Summary of the Short-Run Cost Concept

Concept	Abbreviation	Definition
Total fixed cost	TFC	Costs that are the same at all output levels (e.g., insurance, rent)
Total variable cost	TVC	Costs that vary with the level of output (e.g., hourly labor, raw materials)
Total cost	TC	Sum of the firm's total fixed costs and total variable costs at a level of output ($TC = TFC + TVC$)
Marginal cost	MC	Added cost of producing one more unit of output; change in TC associated with one more unit of output ($\Delta TC/\Delta Q$)
Average total cost	ATC	TC per unit of output; TC divided by output (TC/Q)
Average fixed cost	AFC	TFC per unit of output; TFC divided by output (TFC/Q)
Average variable cost	AVC	TVC per unit of output; TVC divided by output (TVC/Q)

TRUE OR FALSE

Q: If a baseball team signs a superstar free agent, they will have to increase their ticket prices to cover the costs. Is this true or false?

You can find the answer on the next page.

© RICH PILLING/GETTY IMAGES

TRUE OR FALSE

A: False. Whether the team sells 1,000 tickets or 1,000,000 tickets during the season, their fixed cost (which includes the superstar and other players' salaries) remains the same. However, they might be able to charge more because people want to see this superstar play. But in that case the shifting demand curve, not a changing supply curve, is causing the price to rise.

EXHIBIT 6.5 Cost Calculations for Pizza Shack Company

(1) Hourly Output (Q)	(2) Total Fixed Cost (TFC)	(3) Total Variable Cost (TVC)	(4) Total Cost ($TC = TVC + TFC$)	(5) Average Fixed Cost ($AFC = TFC/Q$)	(6) Average Variable Cost ($AVC = TVC/Q$)	(7) Average Total Cost ($ATC = TC/Q$ or $AFC + AVC$)	(8) Marginal Cost ($MC = \Delta TC/\Delta Q$)
0	$40	$ 0	$40	—	—	—	—
1	40	10	50	$40.00	$10.00	$50.00	$10
2	40	18	58	20.00	9.00	29.00	8
3	40	25	65	13.33	8.33	21.66	7
4	40	33	73	10.00	8.25	18.25	8
5	40	43	83	8.00	8.60	16.60	10
6	40	56	96	6.67	9.33	16.00	13
7	40	73	113	5.71	10.43	16.14	17
8	40	94	134	5.00	11.75	16.75	21
9	40	120	160	4.44	13.33	17.77	26
10	40	152	192	4.00	15.20	19.20	32

levels and that at low output levels (four or fewer units in the example), total fixed cost is the dominant portion of total costs. At high output levels (eight or more units in the example), total fixed cost becomes quite small relative to total variable cost. As the firm increases its output, it spreads its total fixed cost across more units; as a result, the average fixed cost declines continuously.

It is often easier to understand these cost concepts by examining graphs that show the levels of the various costs at different output levels. The graph in Exhibit 6.6

shows the first three cost concepts: fixed, variable, and total costs. The total fixed cost (TFC) curve is always a horizontal line because, by definition, fixed costs are the same at all output levels—even at zero level of output. In Exhibit 6.6, notice that $TVC = 0$ when $Q = 0$; if no output is being produced, no variable costs are incurred.

The total cost (TC) curve is the summation of the total variable cost (TVC) and total fixed cost (TFC) curves. Because the total fixed cost curve is horizontal,

EXHIBIT 6.6 Total and Fixed Costs

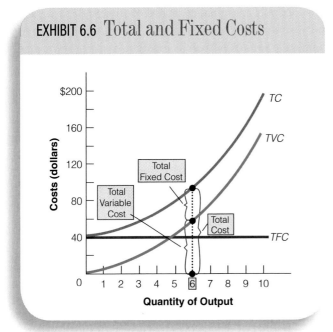

the total cost curve lies above the total variable cost curve by a fixed (vertical) amount.

Exhibit 6.7 shows the average fixed cost curve, the average variable cost curve, the average total cost curve, and the associated marginal cost curve. In this exhibit, notice how the average fixed cost (AFC) curve constantly declines, approaching but never reaching zero. Remember, AFC is simply TFC/Q, so as output expands, AFC declines, because the total fixed cost is being spread over successively larger volumes of output. Also observe how the marginal

cost (MC) curve crosses the average variable cost (AVC) and average total cost (ATC) curves at their lowest points. At higher output levels, high marginal costs pull up the average variable cost and average total cost curves, while at low output levels, low marginal costs pull the curves down. In the next section, we will explain why the marginal cost curve intersects the average variable cost curve and the average total cost curve at their minimum points.

SECTION CHECK 3

3.1 Fixed costs are costs that do not change with the level of output.

3.2 Variable costs are not fixed. Variable costs change as the level of output changes.

3.3 Marginal cost (MC) is the added cost of producing one more unit of output; it is the change in total associated with one more unit of output. Marginal cost is the cost relevant to decisions to produce more or less.

3.4 Average fixed cost (AFC) is fixed cost divided by output. Average variable cost (AVC) is variable cost divided by output. Average total cost (ATC) is total cost divided by output.

EXHIBIT 6.7 Average and Marginal Costs

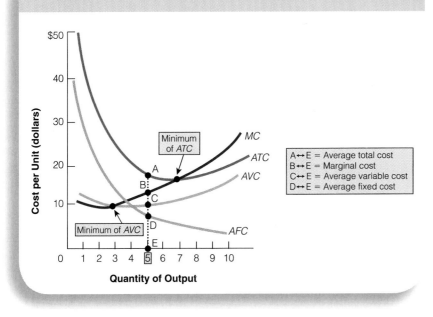

⑤4 The Shape of the Short-Run Cost Curves

Consider the following questions as you read through this section. You'll find the answers in Section Check 4.

4.1 What is the relationship between marginal costs and marginal product?

4.2 Why is the average total cost curve U-shaped?

4.3 When marginal cost is greater than average cost, what happens to the average?

As we continue our discussion of costs in the short run, let's take a closer look at the various short-run cost curves.

THE RELATIONSHIP BETWEEN MARGINAL COSTS AND MARGINAL PRODUCT

The behavior of marginal costs bears a definite relationship to marginal product (*MP*). Say, for example, that the variable input is labor. Initially, as the firm adds more workers, the marginal product of labor tends to rise. When the marginal product of labor is rising, marginal costs are falling, because each additional worker adds more to the total output than the previous worker. Thus, the increase in total cost resulting from the production of another unit of output—marginal cost—falls. However, when marginal product of labor is declining, marginal costs are rising, because additional workers are adding less to total output. In sum, if an additional worker's marginal product is lower (higher) than that of previous workers, marginal costs increase (decrease), as seen in Exhibit 6.8. In area a of the two graphs in Exhibit 6.8, we see that as marginal product rises, marginal costs fall; in area b, we see that as marginal

product falls, marginal costs rise. For example, if we are only producing a few bagels in our bagel shop, we have some idle resources such as toasters, cash registers, and so on. At this point, the marginal product of an extra worker is large and the marginal cost of producing one more bagel is small. However, when the bagel shop is crowded, producing many bagels with many workers using the equipment to capacity, the marginal product of hiring another worker is low. Why? Because the new worker has to work in crowded conditions where she may be bumping into other workers as she waits to use the toasters and cash register. In short, when the number of bagels produced is high, the marginal product of another worker is low and the marginal cost of an additional bagel is large.

THE RELATIONSHIP BETWEEN MARGINAL AND AVERAGE AMOUNTS

The relationship between the marginal and the average is simply a matter of arithmetic; when a number (the marginal cost) being added into a series is smaller than the previous average of the series, the new average will be lower than the previous one. Likewise, when the marginal number is larger than the average, the average

When the bagel shop is crowded, producing many bagels with many workers using the equipment to capacity, the marginal product of hiring another worker is low.

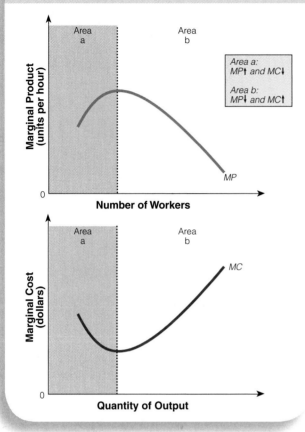

EXHIBIT 6.8 Marginal Product and Marginal Costs

Area a
Area b

Area a:
MP↑ and MC↓

Area b:
MP↓ and MC↑

Marginal Product (units per hour)

0
Number of Workers

MP

Marginal Cost (dollars)

0
Quantity of Output

MC

will rise. For example, if you have taken two economics exams and received a 90 percent on your first exam and an 80 percent on your second exam, you have an 85 percent average. If, after some serious studying, you get a 100 percent on the third exam (the marginal exam), what happens to your average? It rises to 90 percent. Because the marginal is greater than the average, it "pulls" the average up. However, if the score on your third (marginal) exam is lower—a 70 percent—your average will fall to 80 percent, because the marginal is below the average. Similarly, a baseball or softball player will improve on his batting average if the next trip to the plate is a hit, and the player's average will fall if the player strikes out.

WHY IS THE AVERAGE TOTAL COST CURVE U-SHAPED?

Why is the average total cost curve usually U-shaped, as seen in Exhibit 6.9? At very small and very large levels of output, average total cost is very high. The reason for

The **average total cost rises at high levels of output because of diminishing marginal product.**

the high average total cost when the firm is producing a very small amount of output is the high average fixed cost—when the output rate of the plant is small relative to its capacity, the plant is being underutilized. But as the firm expands output beyond this point, the average total cost falls. Why? Remember that $ATC = AFC + AVC$, and average fixed cost always falls when output expands because the fixed costs are being spread over more units of output. Thus, it is the declining AFC that is primarily responsible for the falling ATC.

The average total cost rises at high levels of output because of diminishing marginal product. For example, as more and more workers are put to work using a fixed quantity of machines, the result may be crowded working conditions and/or increasing maintenance costs as equipment is used more intensively or as older, less-efficient machinery is called on to handle the greater output. In fact, diminishing marginal product sets in at the bottom of the marginal cost curve, as seen in Exhibit 6.9. That is, it is diminishing marginal product that causes marginal costs to increase, eventually causing the average variable cost and average total cost curves to rise. At large levels of output, where the plant

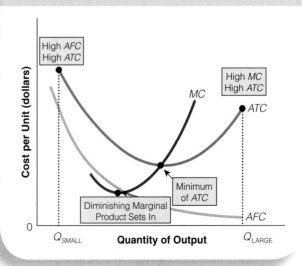

EXHIBIT 6.9 U-Shaped Average Total Cost Curve

High AFC
High ATC

High MC
High ATC

MC

ATC

Minimum of ATC

Diminishing Marginal Product Sets In

AFC

Cost per Unit (dollars)

0
Q_{SMALL} **Quantity of Output** Q_{LARGE}

approaches full capacity, the fixed plant is overutilized, leading to high marginal costs that cause a high average total cost.

THE RELATIONSHIP BETWEEN MARGINAL COSTS AND AVERAGE VARIABLE AND AVERAGE TOTAL COSTS

Certain relationships exist between marginal costs and average variable and average total costs. For example, when the average variable cost is falling, marginal costs must be less than the average variable cost; and when the average variable cost is rising, marginal costs are greater than the average variable cost. Marginal costs are equal to the average variable cost at the lowest point of the average variable cost curve, as seen in Exhibit 6.10. In the left-hand (shaded) portion of Exhibit 6.10, marginal costs are less than the average variable cost, and the average is falling. On the right side, marginal costs are greater than the average variable cost, and the average is rising. The same relationship holds for the marginal cost curve and the average total cost curve. In the left-hand (shaded) portion of Exhibit 6.11, marginal costs are less than the average total cost, and the average is falling. On the right side, marginal costs are greater than the average total cost, and the average is rising. So it is the marginal cost curve that determines the U shape of the *AVC* and *ATC* curves.

EXHIBIT 6.10 Marginal Cost and Average Variable Cost

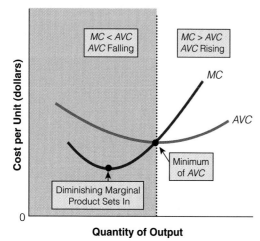

EXHIBIT 6.11 Marginal Cost and Average Total Cost

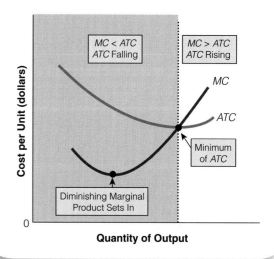

SECTION CHECK 4

4.1 As marginal product rises, marginal cost falls. As marginal product falls, marginal cost rises.

4.2 Average total cost declines as output expands but then increases again as output expands still further beyond a certain point. Declining *AFC* is primarily responsible for the *ATC*. The *ATC* rises at high levels of output because of the diminishing marginal product.

4.3 When marginal costs are greater than the average variable cost, the average variable cost must be rising; when marginal costs are greater than the average total cost, the average total cost must be rising.

⑤5 Cost Curves: Short-Run versus Long-Run

Think about the following questions as you read through this section, then check for the answers in Section Check 5.

In this section we will compare short-run cost curves to long-run cost curves.

WHY ARE LONG-RUN COST CURVES DIFFERENT FROM SHORT-RUN COST CURVES?

Over long enough periods, firms can vary all of their productive inputs. That is, time provides an opportunity to substitute lower-cost capital, such as larger plants or newer, more sophisticated equipment, for more expensive labor inputs. However, in the short run a firm cannot alter its plant size and equipment. These inputs are fixed in the short run, so the firm can only expand output by employing more variable inputs (e.g., workers

A factory, exterior view

Factory worker

and raw materials) in order to get extra output from the existing factory. If a company has to pay many workers overtime wages to expand output in the short run, over the long run firms may opt to invest in new equipment to conserve on expensive labor. That is, in the long run, the firm can expand its factories, build new ones, or shut down unproductive ones. Of course, the time it takes for a firm to get to the long run varies from firm to firm. For example, it may take only a couple of months to build a new coffee shop, while it may take a few years to build a new automobile plant.

In Exhibit 6.12 on the next page, we see that the long-run average total cost ($LRATC$) curve lies equal to or below the short-run average total cost ($SRATC$) curves. The reason for the difference between the firm's long-run total cost curve and its short-run total cost curve is that in the long run, costs are lower because firms have greater flexibility in changing inputs that are fixed in the short run. Exhibit 6.12 presents three short-run average total cost curves, representing small, medium, and large plant sizes.

It also shows the long-run average total cost curve. In the *short run*, the firm is restricted to the current plant size, but in the long run it can choose the short-run cost curve for the level of production it is planning on producing. As the firm moves along the long-run average total cost curve, it is adjusting the size of the factory to the quantity of production.

For example, in Exhibit 6.12, if Apple computer wanted to expand output in the medium plant size from 1,000 computers per day to 1,200 computers per day, it would have no choice but to hire more workers in the short run, moving from point A to point B. Because of diminishing marginal product (adding more workers to fixed plant size), the short-run average total cost rises from $400 to $500. However, in the long run, Apple can expand its factory size and workforce and the average total cost returns to $400, moving from point A to point C.

WHAT ARE ECONOMIES OF SCALE?

By examining the long-run average total cost curve for a firm, we can see three possible production patterns. In Exhibit 6.12 on the next page, we see that extremely small firms experience **economies of scale**, falling per-unit costs as output expands. These firms, then, are functioning inefficiently from a long-run perspective. The **minimum efficient scale** is the output

EXHIBIT 6.12 Short- and Long-Run Average Total Costs

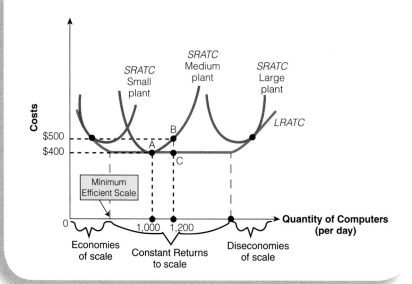

level in which the economies of scale are exhausted and the long-run average total costs are minimized. Similarly, firms that expand beyond a certain point encounter **diseconomies of scale**; that is, they incur rising per-unit costs as their output grows. In more intermediate output ranges, firms of varying sizes can compete on a roughly equal basis as far as costs are concerned because they all exhibit approximately **constant returns to scale**. That is, their per-unit costs remain stable as output grows. In this example, Apple computers have economies of scale at low levels of output, constant returns to scale at intermediate levels of output, and diseconomies of very high levels of output.

WHY DO ECONOMIES AND DISECONOMIES OF SCALE OCCUR?

As we have just seen, economies of scale exist when there is a reduction in the firm's long-run average costs as output expands. This may occur because the firm can capture gains from specialization that might not be possible if the firm were producing at lower levels of output. For example, workers might experience greater proficiency gains if they concentrated on a few specific tasks rather than on many different tasks. That is, people who try to do everything may end up doing nothing very well.

Recall that diseconomies of scale exist when there is an increase in the firm's long-run average costs as output expands. This may occur as the firm finds it increasingly difficult to handle the complexities of large-scale management. For example, information and coordination problems tend to increase when a firm becomes very large. This is why the *LRATC* is usually U-shaped. At low levels of output, firms generally benefit from increased size because they can take advantage of specialization. However, at high levels of output, the gains from specialization have already occurred, but coordination and bureaucratic problems increase.

SECTION CHECK 5

5.1 Over longer time periods, firms can alter their production inputs in ways that are impossible in shorter periods. For instance, given enough time, a firm might be able to build new factories or purchase and install new equipment to improve their output. In the short run, however, a firm might have to pay workers overtime to improve output, resulting in higher costs.

5.2 At low output levels, when all inputs can be varied, some firms will experience economies of scale, where their per-unit costs decrease as output increases.

5.3 Firms that expand all inputs beyond a certain point will encounter diseconomies of scale, incurring rising per-unit costs as output grows in the long run.

5.4 In intermediate output ranges, firms may exhibit roughly constant returns to scale; in this range, their per-unit costs remain stable as output increases.

Chapter 6: Self-Review

Now that you're finished reading the chapter, review the questions below. You can write your answers in the space provided, then go online to see the answers at www.cengagebrain.com.

S1—FIRMS AND PROFITS: TOTAL REVENUES MINUS TOTAL COSTS

1. If you turn down a job offer of $45,000 per year to work for yourself, what is the opportunity cost of working for yourself?

S2—PRODUCTION IN THE SHORT RUN

2. True or False: All inputs vary in the long run.

3. What relationship does a production function represent?

4. Draw a typically shaped total output curve.

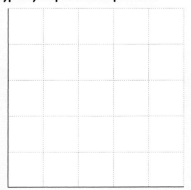

S3—COSTS IN THE SHORT RUN

5. True or False: Average variable cost is the relevant cost to consider when a producer is deciding whether to produce more or less of a product.

6. If your season batting average going into a game was .300 (three hits per ten at bats) and you got two hits in five at bats during the game, would your season batting average rise or fall as a result?

7. A one-day ticket to visit the Screaming Coasters theme park costs $36, but you can also get a two-consecutive-day ticket for $40. What is the average cost per day for the two-day ticket? What is the marginal cost of the second consecutive day?

8. If your university pays lecture note takers $20 per hour to take notes in your economics class and then sells subscriptions for $15 per student, is the cost of the lecture note taker a fixed or variable cost of selling an additional subscription?

S4 - THE SHAPE OF THE SHORT-RUN COST CURVES

9. True or False: Average total cost rises as output expands over low-output ranges.

10. Why does the average total cost rise at some point as output expands further?

S5—COST CURVES: SHORT-RUN VERSUS LONG-RUN

11. True or False: The *LRATC* curve has a shallower U shape than the *SRATC* because some inputs are fixed in the long run.

12. What may cause economies or diseconomies of scale?

At the Chicago Board of Trade (CBOT),

prices are set by thousands of buyers interacting with thousands of sellers. The goods in question are typically standardized, and information is readily available. Every buyer and seller knows the price, the quantity, and the quality of the goods. Transaction costs are negligible. Here we can see a pretty close approximation of a perfectly competitive market.

7

Firms in Competitive Markets

a firm must answer two critical questions: What price should we charge for the goods and services we sell, and how much should we produce? The answers to these two questions will depend on the market structure.

The behavior of firms will depend on the number of firms in the market, the ease with which firms can enter and exit the market, and the ability of firms to differentiate their products from those of other firms. There is no typical industry. An industry might include one firm that dominates the market, or it might consist of thousands of smaller firms that each produce a small fraction of the market supply. Between these two end points are many other industries. However, because we cannot examine each industry individually, we break them into four main categories: perfect competition, monopoly, monopolistic competition, and oligopoly.

In a perfectly competitive market, the market price is the critical piece of information that a firm needs to know. A firm in a perfectly competitive market can sell all it wants at the market price. A firm in a perfectly competitive market is said to be a price taker, because it cannot appreciably affect the market price for its output or the market price for its inputs. For example, suppose a Washington apple grower decides that he wants to get out of the family business and go to work for Microsoft. Because he may be one of 50,000 apple growers in the United States, his decision will not appreciably change the price of the apples, the production of apples, or the price of inputs.

Sections in Chapter 7

Ⓢ1 A Perfectly Competitive Market

Keep the following questions in mind as you read through this section. You'll find the answers in Section Check 1.

1.1 What are the characteristics of a firm in a perfectly competitive market?

1.2 What is a price taker?

This chapter examines **perfect competition**, a market structure characterized by (1) many buyers and sellers, (2) identical (homogeneous) products, and (3) easy market entry and exit. Let's examine these characteristics in greater detail.

3 Characteristics of Perfect Competition
- many buyers and sellers
- identical products
- easy entry and exit

MANY BUYERS AND SELLERS

In a perfectly competitive market, there are *many buyers and sellers*—perhaps thousands or conceivably millions. Because each firm is so small in relation to the industry, its production decisions have no impact on the market; each regards price as something over which it has little control. For this reason, perfectly competitive firms are called price takers: They must take the price given by the market because their influence on price is insignificant. If the price of apples in the apple market is $2 a pound, then individual apple farmers will receive $2 a pound for their apples. Similarly, no single buyer of apples can influence the price of apples, because each buyer purchases only a small amount of the apples traded. We will see how this relationship works in more detail in the next section.

IDENTICAL (HOMOGENEOUS) PRODUCTS

Consumers believe that all firms in perfectly competitive markets *sell identical (or homogeneous) products*. For example, in the wheat market, it is not possible to determine any significant and consistent qualitative differences in the wheat produced by different farmers. Wheat produced by Farmer Jones looks, feels, smells, and tastes like that produced by Farmer Smith. In short, a bushel of wheat is a bushel of wheat. The products of all the firms are considered to be perfect substitutes.

EASY ENTRY AND EXIT

Product markets characterized by perfect competition *have no significant barriers to entry or exit*. Therefore it is fairly easy for entrepreneurs to become suppliers of the product or, if they are already producers, to stop supplying the product. "Fairly easy" does not mean that any person on the street can instantly enter the business but rather that the financial, legal, educational, and other barriers to entering the business are modest, enabling large numbers of people to overcome the barriers and enter the business if they so desire in any given period. If buyers can easily switch from one seller to another and sellers can easily enter or exit the industry, then they have met the perfectly competitive condition of easy entry and exit. Because of this easy market entry, perfectly competitive markets generally consist of a large number of small suppliers.

A perfectly competitive market is approximated most closely in highly organized markets for securities and agricultural commodities, such as the New York Stock Exchange or the Chicago Board of Trade. Wheat, corn, soybeans, cotton, and many other agricultural products are sold in perfectly competitive markets. Although all the criteria for a perfectly competitive market are rarely met, a number of markets come close to satisfying them. Even when all the assumptions don't hold, it is important to note that studying the model of perfect competition is useful because many markets resemble perfect competition—that is, markets in which firms face highly elastic (flat) demand curves and relatively easy entry and exit. The model also gives us a standard of comparison. In other words, we can make comparisons with the perfectly competitive model to help us evaluate what is going on in the real world.

1.1 A perfectly competitive market is characterized by many buyers and sellers, an identical (homogeneous) product, and easy market entry and exit.

1.2 In markets with so many buyers and so many sellers, neither buyers nor sellers have any control over price in perfect competition. They must take the going price and hence are called price takers.

⑤2 An Individual Price Taker's Demand Curve

Keep the following questions in mind as you read through this section. You'll find the answers in **Section Check 2.**

2.1 Why won't individual price takers raise or lower their prices?

2.2 Will the position of individual price takers' demand curves change when market price changes?

In this section, we'll discuss how perfectly competitive firms are price takers and how a change in the market price affects the perfectly competitive firm's demand curve.

> **price taker** a perfectly competitive firm that takes the price it is given by the intersection of the market demand and market supply curves

AN INDIVIDUAL FIRM'S DEMAND CURVE

Perfectly competitive firms are **price takers**; that is, they must sell at the market-determined price, where the market price and output are determined by the intersection of the market supply and demand curves, as seen in Exhibit 7.1(b). Individual wheat farmers know that they cannot dispose of their wheat at any figure higher than the current market price; if they attempt to charge a higher price, potential buyers will simply make their purchases from other wheat farmers. Further, the farmers certainly would not knowingly charge a lower price, because they could sell all they want at the market price.

Likewise, in a perfectly competitive market, individual sellers can change their outputs, and it will not alter the market price. The large number of sellers who are selling identical products make this situation possible. Each producer provides such a small fraction of the total supply that a change in the amount he offers does *not* have a noticeable effect on market equilibrium price. In a perfectly competitive market, then, an individual firm can sell as much as it wishes to place on the market at the prevailing price; the demand, as seen by the seller, is perfectly elastic.

It is easy to construct the demand curve for an individual seller in a perfectly competitive market. Remember,

EXHIBIT 7.1 Market and Individual Firm Demand Curves in a Perfectly Competitive Market

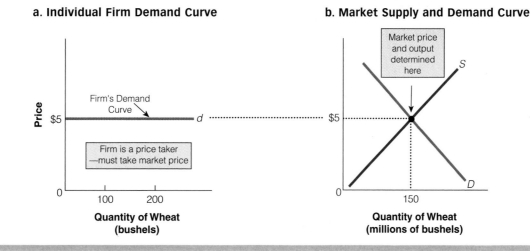

a. Individual Firm Demand Curve

Firm's Demand Curve

Firm is a price taker —must take market price

Price

$5 ⋯⋯⋯ d

0   100   200

Quantity of Wheat (bushels)

b. Market Supply and Demand Curve

Market price and output determined here

S

$5 ⋯⋯⋯

D

0   150

Quantity of Wheat (millions of bushels)

she won't charge more than the market price because no one will buy it, and she won't charge less because she can sell all she wants at the market price. Thus, the farmer's demand curve is horizontal over the entire range of output that she could possibly produce. If the prevailing market price of the product is $5, the farmer's demand curve will be represented graphically by a horizontal line at the market price of $5, as shown in Exhibit 7.1(a).

A CHANGE IN MARKET PRICE AND THE FIRM'S DEMAND CURVE

To say that producers under perfect competition regard price as a given is not to say that price is constant. The *position* of the firm's demand curve varies with every change in the market price. In Exhibit 7.2, we see that when the market price for wheat increases, say as a result of an increase in market demand, the price-taking firm will receive a higher price for all its output. Or when the market price decreases, say as a result of a decrease in market demand, the price-taking firm will receive a lower price for all its output.

In effect, sellers are provided with current information about market demand and supply conditions as a result of price changes. It is an essential aspect of the perfectly competitive model that sellers respond to the signals provided by such price movements, so they must alter their behavior over time in the light of actual experience, revising their production decisions to reflect changes in market price. In this respect, the perfectly competitive model is straightforward; it does not assume any knowledge on the part of individual buyers and sellers about market demand and supply—they only have to know the price of the good they sell.

SECTION CHECK 2

2.1 An individual seller won't sell at a higher price than the going price, because buyers can purchase the same good from someone else at the going price. They would not knowingly sell below the going price, because they are so small relative to the market that they can sell all they want at the going price.

2.2 The position of the individual firm's demand curve varies directly with the market price.

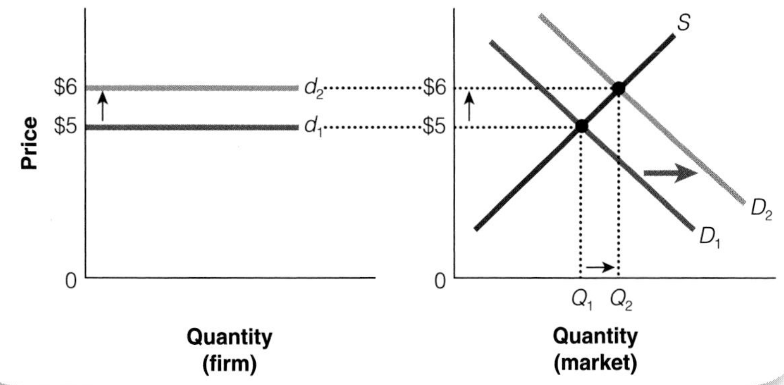

Ⓢ3 Profit Maximization

Keep the following questions in mind as you read through this section. You'll find the answers in **Section Check 3**.

3.1 What is total revenue?

3.2 What is average revenue?

3.3 What is marginal revenue?

3.4 Why does the firm maximize profits where marginal revenue equals marginal costs?

The objective of the firm is to maximize profits. To maximize profits, the firm wants to produce the amount that maximizes the difference between its total revenues and total costs. In this section, we will examine the different ways to look at revenue in a perfectly competitive market: total revenue, average revenue, and marginal revenue.

TOTAL REVENUE

Total revenue (TR) is the revenue that the firm receives from the sale of its products. Total revenue from a product

EXHIBIT 7.2 Market Prices and the Position of a Firm's Demand Curve

Total Revenue (TR)

$$TR = P \times q$$

Average Revenue (AR)

$$AR = TR \div q = (P \times q) \div q$$

Marginal Revenue (MR)

$$MR = \Delta TR \div \Delta q$$

average revenue (AR) the total revenue divided by the number of units sold

marginal revenue (MR) the increase in total revenue resulting from a one-unit increase in sales

equals the price of the good (P) times the quantity (q) of units sold ($TR = P \times q$). For example, if a farmer sells 10 bushels of wheat a day for $5 a bushel, his total revenue is $50 ($5 × 10 bushels). (*Note*: We will use the lowercase letter q to denote the single firm's output and reserve the uppercase letter Q for the output of the entire market. For example, q would be used to represent the output of one lettuce grower, while Q would be used to represent the output of all lettuce growers in the lettuce market.)

AVERAGE REVENUE AND MARGINAL REVENUE

Average revenue (AR) equals total revenue divided by the number of units sold of the product ($TR \div q$, or $[P \times q] \div q$). For example, if the farmer sells 10 bushels at $5 a bushel, total revenue is $50 and average revenue is $5 per bushel ($50 ÷ 10 bushels). Thus, in perfect competition, average revenue is equal to the price of the good.

Marginal revenue (MR) is the additional revenue derived from the production of one more unit of the good. In other words, marginal revenue represents the increase in total revenue that results from the sale of one more unit ($MR = \Delta TR \div \Delta q$). In a perfectly competitive market, because additional units of output can be sold without reducing the price of the product, marginal revenue is constant at all outputs and equal to average revenue. For example, if the price of wheat per bushel is $5, the marginal revenue is $5. Because total revenue is equal to price multiplied by quantity ($TR = P \times q$), as we add one additional unit of output, total revenue will always increase by the amount of the product price, $5. Marginal revenue facing a perfectly competitive firm is equal to the price of the good.

In perfect competition, then, we know that marginal revenue, average revenue, and price are all equal: $P = MR = AR$. These relationships are clearly illustrated in the calculations presented in Exhibit 7.3.

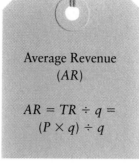

If the price of wheat per bushel is $5, the marginal revenue is $5.

EXHIBIT 7.3 Revenues for a Perfectly Competitive Firm

Quantity (q)	Price (P)	Total Revenue (TR = P × q)	Average Revenue (AR = TR ÷ q)	Marginal Revenue (MR = ΔTR ÷ Δq)
1	$5	$5	$5	
2	5	10	5	$5
3	5	15	5	5
4	5	20	5	5
5	5	25	5	5

HOW DO FIRMS MAXIMIZE PROFITS?

Now that we have discussed the firm's cost curves (in Chapter 6) and its revenues, we are ready to see how a firm maximizes its profits. A firm's profits equal its total revenues minus its total costs. However, at what output level must a firm produce and sell to maximize profits? In all types of market environments, the firm will maximize its profits at the level of output that maximizes the difference between total revenue and total cost, which is at the same output level at which marginal revenue equals marginal cost.

EQUATING MARGINAL REVENUE AND MARGINAL COST

The importance of equating marginal revenue and marginal cost is seen in Exhibit 7.4. As output expands beyond zero up to q^*, the marginal revenue derived from each unit of the expanded output exceeds the marginal cost of that unit of output; so the expansion of output creates additional profits. This addition to profit is shown as the leftmost shaded section in Exhibit 7.4. As long as marginal revenue exceeds marginal cost, profits continue to grow. For example, if the firm decides to produce q_1, the firm sacrifices potential profits, because the marginal revenue from producing more output is greater than the marginal cost. Only at q^*, where $MR = MC$, is the output level just right (not too large, not too small). Further expansion of output beyond q^* will lead to losses on the additional output (i.e., decrease the firm's overall profits), because $MC > MR$. For example, if the firm produces q_2, the firm incurs losses on the output produced beyond q^*; the firm should reduce its output. Only at output q^*, where $MR = MC$, can we find the **profit-maximizing level of output**.

Be careful to avoid making the mistake of focusing on profit per unit rather than total profit. That is, you might think that at q_1, if MR is much greater than MC, the firm should not produce more because the profit

Be careful to avoid making the mistake of focusing on profit per unit rather than total profit.

Be careful to avoid making the mistake of focusing on profit per unit rather than total profit.

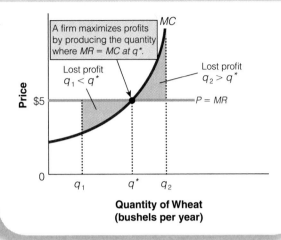

EXHIBIT 7.4 Finding the Profit-Maximizing Level of Output

A firm maximizes profits by producing the quantity where $MR = MC$ at q^*.

Lost profit $q_1 < q^*$

Lost profit $q_2 > q^*$

$P = MR$

MC

Price

$5

0   q_1 q^* q_2

Quantity of Wheat (bushels per year)

per unit is high at this point. However, that would be a mistake because a firm can add to its total profits as long as $MR > MC$—that is, all the way to q^*.

The Marginal Approach

We can use the data from the table in Exhibit 7.5 to find Farmer Jones's profit-maximizing position. Columns 5 and 6 show the marginal revenue and marginal cost, respectively. We see that output levels of 1 and 2 bushels produce outputs that have marginal revenues that exceed marginal costs—Farmer Jones wants to produce those units and more. That is, as long as marginal revenue exceeds marginal cost, producing and selling those units add more to revenues than to costs; in other words, they add to profits. However, once he expands production beyond four units of output, Farmer Jones's costs are less than his marginal revenues, and his profits begin to fall. Clearly, Farmer Jones should not produce beyond 4 bushels of wheat.

Let's take another look at profit maximization using the table in Exhibit 7.5. Comparing columns 2 and 3—the calculations of total revenue and total cost, respectively—we see that Farmer Jones maximizes his profits at output levels of 3 or 4 bushels, where he will make profits of $4. In column 4—profit—you can see that there is no higher level of profit at any of the other output levels. Producing 5 bushels would reduce profits by $1, because marginal revenue, $5, is less than the marginal cost, $6. Consequently, Farmer Jones would not produce this bushel of output. If $MR > MC$, Farmer Jones should increase production; if $MR < MC$, he should decrease production.

Quantity (1)	Total Revenue (2)	Total Cost (3)	Profit (TR − TC) (4)	Marginal Revenue ($\Delta TR \div \Delta q$) (5)	Marginal Cost ($\Delta TC \div \Delta q$) (6)	Change in Profit (MR − MC) (7)
0	$0	$2	$−2			
				$5	$2	$3
1	5	4	1			
				5	3	2
2	10	7	3			
				5	4	1
3	15	11	4			
				5	5	0
4	20	16	4			
				5	6	−1
5	25	22	3			

In the next section, we will use the profit-maximizing output rule to see what happens when changes in the market cause the price to fall below average total cost and even below average variable cost. We will introduce the three-step method to determine whether the firm is making an economic profit, is minimizing its losses, or should be temporarily shut down.

SECTION CHECK 3

3.1 Total revenue is price times the quantity sold ($TR = P \times q$).

3.2 Average revenue is total revenue divided by the quantity sold ($AR = TR \div q = P$, or $[P \times q] \div q$).

3.3 Marginal revenue is the change in total revenue from the sale of an additional unit of output ($MR = \Delta TR \div \Delta q$). In a competitive industry, the price of the good equals both the average revenue and the marginal revenue.

3.4 As long as the marginal revenue exceeds marginal cost, the seller should expand production, because producing and selling those units adds more to revenues than to costs; that is, it increases profits. However, if the marginal revenue is less than the marginal cost, the seller should decrease production.

S4 Short-Run Profits and Losses

Keep the following questions in mind as you read through this section. You'll find the answers in **Section Check 4**.

4.1 How do we determine whether a firm is generating an economic profit?

4.2 How do we determine whether a firm is experiencing an economic loss?

4.3 How do we determine whether a firm is making zero economic profits?

4.4 Why doesn't a firm produce when price is below average variable cost?

In the previous section, we discussed how to determine the profit-maximizing output level for a perfectly competitive firm. So how do we know whether a firm is actually making economic profits or losses?

THE THREE-STEP METHOD

Determining whether a firm is generating economic profits, economic losses, or zero economic profits at the profit-maximizing level of output, q^*, can be done in three easy steps. First, we will walk through these steps, and then we will apply the method to three situations for a hypothetical firm in the short run in Exhibit 7.6.

1. Find where marginal revenue equals marginal cost and proceed straight down to the horizontal quantity axis to find q^*, the profit-maximizing output level.

2. At q^*, go straight up to the demand curve and then to the left to find the market price, P^*. Once you have identified P^* and q^*, you can find total revenue at the profit-maximizing output level, because $TR = P \times q$.

3. The last step is to find the total cost. Again, go straight up from q^* to the average total cost (ATC) curve and then left to the vertical axis to compute the average total cost *per unit*. If we multiply average total cost by the output level, we can find the total cost ($TC = ATC \times q$).

If total revenue is greater than total cost at q^*, the firm is generating economic profits. If total revenue is less than total cost at q^*, the firm is generating economic losses. If total revenue is equal to total cost at q^*, there are zero economic profits (or a normal rate of return).

Alternatively, to find total economic profits, we can take the product price at P^* and subtract the average total cost at q^*. This will give us per-unit profit. If we multiply this by output, we will arrive at total economic profit. Or $(P^* - ATC) \times q^* =$ total economic profit.

Remember, the cost curves include implicit and explicit costs—that is, we are covering the opportunity costs of our resources. Therefore, even with zero economic profits, no tears should be shed, because the firm is covering both its implicit and explicit costs. Because firms are also covering their implicit costs, or what they could be producing with these resources in another endeavor, economists sometimes call this zero economic profit a *normal rate of return*. That is, the owners are doing as well as they could elsewhere, in that they are getting the normal rate of return on the resources they invested in the firm.

Total Economic Profit = $(P^* - ATC) \times q^*$

The Three-Step Method in Action

Exhibit 7.6 shows three different short-run equilibrium positions; in each case, the firm is producing at a level where marginal revenue equals marginal cost. Each of these alternatives shows that the firm is maximizing profits or minimizing losses in the short run.

Assume that three alternative prices—$6, $5, and $4—are available for a firm with given costs. In Exhibit 7.6(a), the firm receives $6 per unit at an equilibrium level of output ($MR = MC$) of 120 units. Total revenue ($P \times q^*$) is $6 $\times$ 120, or $720. The average total cost at 120 units of output is $5, and the total cost ($ATC \times q^*$) is $600. Following the three-step method, we can calculate that this firm is earning a total economic profit of $120. Or we can calculate total economic profit by using the following equation: $(P^* - ATC) \times q^* = (\$6 - \$5) \times 120 = \$120$.

In Exhibit 7.6(b), the market price has fallen to $4 per unit. At the equilibrium level of output, the firm is now producing 80 units of output at an average total cost of $5 per unit. The total revenue is now $320 ($4 $\times$ 80), and the total cost is $400 ($5 $\times$ 80). We can see that the firm is now incurring a total economic loss of $80. Or we can calculate total economic profit by using the following equation: $(P^* - ATC) \times q^* = (\$4 - \$5) \times 80 = -\$80$.

EXHIBIT 7.6 Short-Run Profits, Losses, and Zero Economic Profits

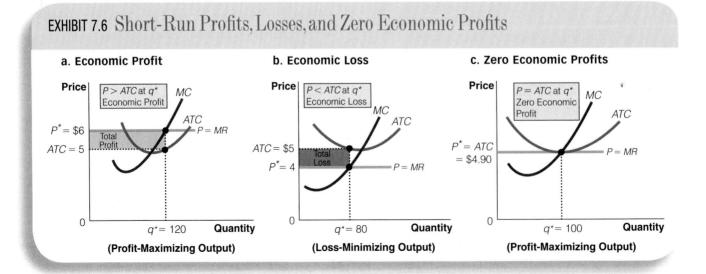

a. Economic Profit

Price

$P > ATC$ at q^*
Economic Profit

MC

ATC

$P = MR$

$P^* = \$6$
$ATC = 5$

Total Profit

0    $q^* = 120$ Quantity
(Profit-Maximizing Output)

b. Economic Loss

Price

$P < ATC$ at q^*
Economic Loss

MC

ATC

$ATC = \$5$
$P^* = 4$

Total Loss

$P = MR$

0    $q^* = 80$ Quantity
(Loss-Minimizing Output)

c. Zero Economic Profits

Price

$P = ATC$ at q^*
Zero Economic Profit

MC

ATC

$P^* = ATC$
$= \$4.90$

$P = MR$

0    $q^* = 100$ Quantity
(Profit-Maximizing Output)

In Exhibit 7.6(c), the firm is earning zero economic profits, or a normal rate of return. The market price is $4.90, and the average total cost is $4.90 per unit for 100 units of output. In this case, economic profits are zero, because total revenue, $490, minus total cost, $490, is equal to zero. This firm is just covering all its costs, both implicit and explicit. Or we can calculate total economic profit by using the following equation: $(P^* - ATC) \times q^* = (\$4.90 - \$4.90) \times 100 = \$0$.

EVALUATING ECONOMIC LOSSES IN THE SHORT RUN

A firm generating an economic loss faces a tough choice: Should it continue to produce or should it shut down its operation? To make this decision, we need to add another variable to our discussion of economic profits and losses: average variable cost. Variable costs are costs that vary with output—for example, wages, raw material, transportation, and electricity. If a firm cannot generate enough revenues to cover its variable costs, it will have larger losses if it operates than if it shuts down (when losses are equal to fixed costs). That is, the firm will shut down if its total revenue $(P \times q)$ is less than its variable costs (VC). If we divide $P \times q$ by q we get P, and if we divide VC by q we get AVC, so if $P < AVC$, a profit-maximizing firm will shut down. Thus, a firm will not produce at all unless the price is greater than its average variable cost.

Why might a restaurant stay open at lunch even though there are only a few customers?

Operating at a Loss

At price levels greater than or equal to the average variable cost, a firm may continue to operate in the short run even if its average total cost—variable and fixed costs—is not completely covered. That is, the firm may continue to operate even though it is experiencing an economic loss. Why? Because fixed costs continue whether the firm produces or not; it is better to earn enough to cover a portion of fixed costs than to earn nothing at all. For example, a restaurant may decide to stay open for lunch if its revenues can cover variable costs. Many of a restaurant's costs are fixed—rent, insurance, kitchen appliances, pots, pans, tableware, and so on. These are sunk costs in the short run and shutting down for lunch would not reduce these costs. The restaurant's lunch decision hinges on whether or not the revenue from the few lunchtime customers can cover the variable costs like staff and extra food. If the restaurant owner cannot cover the variable costs at lunchtime, she shuts it down for lunch.

Similarly, a grocery store may stay open all night even if it anticipates only a few customers. To the person on the street, this may look unprofitable. However, the relevant question to the store owner is not whether all the cost can be covered, but whether the additional sales from staying open all night cover the variable costs of electricity, staff, and extra food. Many businesses that are "failing" may continue to operate so they can at least cover part of their fixed costs, like rent.

In Exhibit 7.7, price is less than average total cost but more than average variable cost. In this case, the firm produces in the short run, but at a loss. To shut

EXHIBIT 7.7 Short-Run Losses: Price above *AVC* but below *ATC*

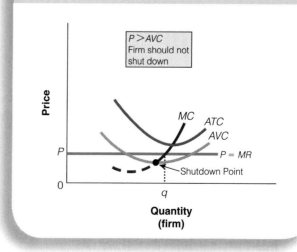

down would make this firm worse off, because it can cover at least some of its fixed costs with the excess of revenue over its variable costs.

The Decision to Shut Down

Exhibit 7.8 illustrates a situation in which the price a firm is able to obtain for its product is below its average variable cost at all ranges of output. In this case, the firm is unable to cover even its variable costs in the short run. Because the firm is losing even more than the fixed costs it would lose if it shut down, it is more logical for the firm to cease operations. Hence, if $P < AVC$, the firm can cut its losses by shutting down. For example, because the demand for a summer camp will be lower during the off season, it is likely that revenues may be too low for the camp to cover its variable costs and the owner will choose to shut down. And by shutting down during the off season the owner will at least not have to pay the variable costs like salaries for the camp staff, food, and electricity. Similarly, an auto plant may respond to a reduction in demand for their automobiles by temporarily shutting down one of their plants. However, remember these firms cannot escape their fixed costs by shutting down. When demand picks up, and the firm can cover its variable costs, production will resume.

The Short-Run Supply Curve

As we have just seen, at all prices above the minimum *AVC*, a firm produces in the short run even if average total cost (*ATC*) is not completely covered; and at all prices below the minimum *AVC*, the firm shuts down. The firm produces above the minimum *AVC* even if it is incurring economic losses because it can still earn enough in total revenues to cover all its average variable cost and a portion of its fixed costs, which is better than not producing and earning nothing at all.

In graphical terms, the **short-run supply curve** of an individual competitive seller is identical to the portion of the *MC* curve that lies above the minimum of the *AVC* curve. As a cost relation, this curve shows the marginal cost of producing any given output; as a supply curve, it shows the equilibrium output that the firm will supply at various prices in the short run. The solid red line in Exhibit 7.9 is the firm's supply curve—the portion of *MC* above its intersection with *AVC*. The declining portion of the *MC* curve has no significance for supply, because if the price falls below the average variable cost, the firm

EXHIBIT 7.8 Short-Run Losses: Price below *AVC*

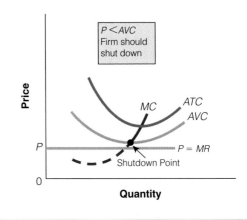

is better off shutting down—producing no output. The shutdown point is at the minimum point on the average variable cost curve where the output level is $q_{\text{SHUT DOWN}}$. Beyond the point of lowest *AVC*, the marginal costs of successively larger amounts of output are progressively greater, so the firm will supply larger and larger amounts only at higher prices. The absolute maximum that the firm can supply, regardless of price, is the maximum quantity that it can produce with the existing plant.

DERIVING THE SHORT-RUN MARKET SUPPLY CURVE

The **short-run market supply curve** is the summation of all the individual firms' supply curves (that

EXHIBIT 7.9 The Firm's Short-Run Supply Curve

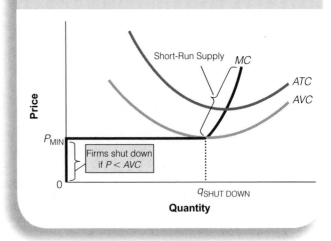

is, the portion of the firms' *MC* above *AVC*) in the market. Because the short run is too brief for new firms to enter the market, the market supply curve is the summation of *existing* firms. For example, in Exhibit 7.10 on the next page, at P_1, each of the 1,000 identical firms in the industry produces 500 bushels of wheat per day at point a in Exhibit 7.10(a); and the quantity supplied in the market is 500,000 bushels of wheat, point A, in Exhibit 7.10(b). We can again sum horizontally at P_2; the quantity supplied for each of the 1,000 identical firms is 800 bushels of wheat per day at point b in Exhibit 7.10(a), so the quantity supplied for the industry is 800,000 bushels of wheat per day, point B in Exhibit 7.10(b). Continuing this process gives us the market supply curve for the wheat market. In a market of 1,000 identical wheat farmers, the market supply curve is 1,000 times the quantity supplied by each firm, as long as the price is above *AVC*.

EVALUATING SHORT-RUN ECONOMIC LOSSES

Q: Lei-ann is one of many florists in a medium-size urban area. That is, we assume that she works in a market similar to a perfectly competitive market and operates, of course, in the short run. Lei-ann's cost and revenue information is shown in the accompanying table. Based on this information, what should Lei-ann do in the short run and why?

A: Fixed costs are unavoidable unless the firm goes out of business. Lei-ann really has two choices in the short run—either to operate or to shut down temporarily. In the table of Lei-ann's daily revenue and cost schedule, we saw that Lei-ann makes $2,000 a day in total revenue, but her daily costs (fixed and variable) are $2,500. She has to pay her workers, pay for fresh flowers, and pay for the fuel used by her drivers in picking up and delivering flowers. She must also pay the electricity bill to heat her shop and keep her refrigerators going to protect her flowers. That is, every day, poor Lei-ann is losing $500; but she still might want to operate the shop despite the loss. Why? Lei-ann's average variable cost (comprised of flowers, transportation, fuel, daily wage earners, and so on) amounts to $1,500 a day; her fixed costs (insurance, property taxes, rent for the building, and refrigerator payments) are $1,000 a day. Now, if Lei-ann does not operate, she will save on her variable cost—$1,500 a day—but she will be out the $2,000 a day she makes in revenue from selling her flowers. Thus, every day she operates, she is better off than if she had not operated at all. That is, if the firm can cover the average variable cost, it is better off operating than not operating. But suppose Lei-ann's *VC* were $2,100 a day. Then Lei-ann should not operate, because every day she does, she is $100 worse off than if she shut down altogether. In short, a firm will shut down if $TR < VC$ or $(P \times q) < VC$. If we divide both sides by q, the firm will shut down if $P < AVC$ or $(P \times q) \div q < VC \div q$.

Why does Lei-ann even bother operating if she is making a loss? Perhaps the economy is in a recession and the demand for flowers is temporarily down, but Lei-ann thinks things will pick up again in the next few months. If Lei-ann is right and demand picks up, her prices and marginal revenue will rise, and she may have a chance to make short-run economic profits.

EXHIBIT 7.10 Deriving the Short-Run Market Supply Curve

a. Individual Firm Supply Curve for Wheat

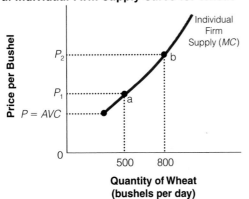

b. Market Supply Curve for Wheat

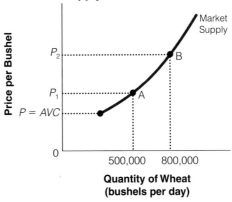

SECTION CHECK 4

4.1 The profit-maximizing output level is found by equating MR to MC at q^*. If at that output the firm's price is greater than its average total costs, it is making an economic profit.

4.2 If at the profit-maximizing output level, q^*, the price is less than the average total cost, the firm is incurring an economic loss.

4.3 If at the profit-maximizing output level, q^*, the price is equal to average total cost, the firm is making zero economic profits; that is, the firm is covering both its implicit and explicit costs (making a normal rate of return).

4.4 If the price falls below average variable cost, the firm is better off shutting down than operating in the short run, because it would incur greater losses from operating than from shutting down.

⑤5 Long-Run Equilibrium

Keep the following questions in mind as you read through this section. You'll find the answers in **Section Check 5**.

5.1 When an industry is earning profits, will it encourage the entry of new firms?

5.2 What happens when an industry experiences economic loss?

5.3 Why do perfectly competitive firms make zero economic profits in the long run?

Now let's consider how firms will behave in the long run.

ECONOMIC PROFITS AND LOSSES DISAPPEAR IN THE LONG RUN

If farmers are able to make economic profits producing wheat, what will their response be in the long run? Farmers will increase the resources that they devote to the lucrative business of producing wheat. Suppose Farmer Jones is making an economic profit (he is earning an above-normal rate of return) producing wheat. To make even more profits, he may take land away from other crops to plant more wheat. Other farmers or people who are holding land for speculative purposes may also decide to plant wheat on their land.

As word gets out that wheat production is proving profitable, it will cause a supply response—the market supply curve will shift to the right as more firms enter the industry and existing firms expand as shown in Exhibit 7.11(b). With this shift, the quantity of wheat supplied at any given price is greater than before. It may take a year or even longer, of course, for the complete supply response to take place, simply because it takes some time for information on profit opportunities to spread and

still more time to plant, grow, and harvest the wheat. Note that the effect of increasing supply, *ceteris paribus,* is a reduction in the equilibrium price of wheat.

Suppose that, as a result of the supply response, the price of wheat falls from P_1 to P_2. The impact of the change in the market price of wheat, over which Farmer Jones has absolutely no control, is simple. If his costs don't change, he moves from making a profit ($P_1 > ATC$) to zero economic profits ($P_2 = ATC$), as shown in Exhibit 7.11(a). In long-run equilibrium, perfectly competitive firms make zero economic profits. Remember, a zero economic profit means that the firm actually earns a normal return on the use of its capital. A zero economic profit is an equilibrium or stable situation because any positive economic (above-normal) profit signals resources into the industry, beating down prices and therefore revenues to the firm.

Any economic losses signal resources to leave the industry, causing supply reductions that lead to increased prices and higher firm revenues for the remaining firms. For example, in Exhibit 7.12 on the next page we see a firm that continues to operate despite its losses—*ATC* is greater than P_1 at q_1. With losses, however, some firms

will exit the industry, causing the market supply curve to shift from S_1 to S_2 and driving up the market price to P_2. This price increase reduces the losses for the firms remaining in the industry, until the losses are completely eliminated at P_2. The remaining firms will maximize profits by producing at q_2 units of output, where profits and losses are zero. Only at zero economic profits is there no tendency for firms to either enter or leave the industry.

THE LONG-RUN EQUILIBRIUM FOR THE COMPETITIVE FIRM

The long-run competitive equilibrium for a perfectly competitive firm is illustrated graphically in Exhibit 7.13. At the equilibrium point, e (where $MC = MR$), short-run and long-run average total costs are also equal. The average total cost curves touch the marginal cost and marginal revenue (demand) curves at the equilibrium output point. Because the marginal revenue curve is also the average revenue curve, average revenue and average total cost are equal at the equilibrium point. The

---

EXHIBIT 7.11 Profits Disappear with Entry

a. Individual Firm

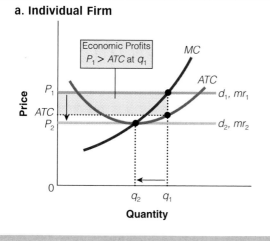

b. Market

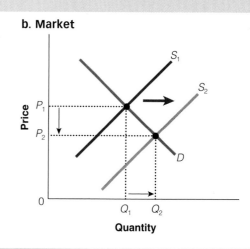

EXHIBIT 7.12 Losses Disappear with Exit

a. Individual Firm

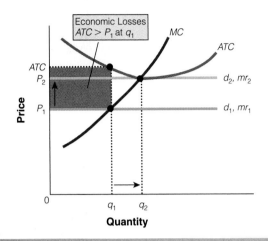

b. Market

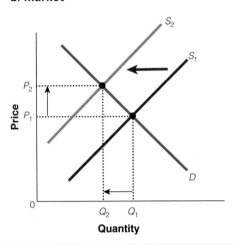

long-run equilibrium in perfect competition depicted in Exhibit 7.13 has an interesting feature. Note that the equilibrium output occurs at the lowest point on the average total cost curve. As you may recall, this occurs because the marginal cost curve must intersect the average total cost curve at the latter curve's lowest point. Hence, the equilibrium condition in the long run in perfect competition is for each firm to produce at the output that minimizes average total cost—that is, the firm is operating at its minimum efficient scale. At this long-run equilibrium, all firms in the industry earn zero economic profits consequently, new firms have no incentive to enter the market and existing firms have no incentive to exit the market.

EXHIBIT 7.13 The Long-Run Competitive Equilibrium

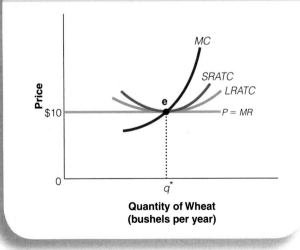

Quantity of Wheat
(bushels per year)

SECTION CHECK 5

5.1 Economic profits encourage the entry of new firms, which shift the market supply curve to the right. Any positive economic profits signal resources into the industry, driving down prices and revenues to the firm.

5.2 Any economic losses signal resources to leave the industry, leading to supply reduction, higher prices, and increased revenues.

5.3 Only at zero economic profits is there no tendency for firms to either enter or exit the industry.

Ⓢ6 Long-Run Supply

Keep the following questions in mind as you read through this section. You'll find the answers in **Section Check 6.**

6.1 What are constant-cost industries?

6.2 What are increasing-cost industries?

6.3 What are decreasing-cost industries?

6.4 What is productive efficiency?

6.5 What is allocative efficiency?

The preceding sections considered the costs for an individual, perfectly competitive firm as it varies output, on the assumption that the prices it pays for inputs (costs) are given. However, when the output of an entire industry changes, the likelihood is greater that changes in costs will occur. How will the changes in the number of firms in an industry affect the input costs of individual firms? In this section, we develop the long-run supply (*LRS*) curve. As we will see, the shape of the long-run supply curve depends on the extent to which input costs change with the entry or exit of firms in the industry. We will look at three possible types of industries when considering long-run supply: constant-cost industries, increasing-cost industries, and decreasing-cost industries.

A CONSTANT-COST INDUSTRY

In a **constant-cost industry**, the prices of inputs do not change as output is expanded. The industry may not use inputs in sufficient quantities to affect input prices. For example, say the firms in the industry use a lot of unskilled labor but the industry is small. In such a case, as output expands, the increase in demand for unskilled labor will not cause the market wage for unskilled labor to rise. Similarly, suppose a paper clip maker decides to double its output. It is highly unlikely that its demand for steel will have an impact on steel prices, because its demand for the input is so small.

Once long-run adjustments are complete, by necessity each firm operates at the point of lowest long-run average total cost, because supply shifts with entry and exit, eliminating profits. Therefore, each firm supplies the market with the quantity of output that it can produce at the lowest possible long-run average total cost.

In Exhibit 7.14 on the next page, we can see the impact of an unexpected increase in market demand. Suppose that recent reports show that blueberries can lower cholesterol, lower blood pressure, and significantly reduce the risk of all cancers. The increase in market demand for blueberries leads to a price increase from P_1 to P_2 as the firm increases output from q_1 to q_2, and blueberry industry output increases from Q_1 to Q_2, as seen in Exhibit 7.14(b). The increase in market demand generates a higher price and positive profits for existing firms in the short run. The existence of economic profits

will attract new firms into the industry, causing the short-run supply curve to shift from S_1 to S_2 and lowering price until excess profits are zero. This shift results in a new equilibrium, point C in Exhibit 7.14(c). Because the industry is one with constant costs, industry expansion does not alter firms' cost curves, and the industry long-run supply curve is horizontal. That is, the long-run equilibrium price is at the same level that prevailed before demand increased; the only long-run effect of the increase in demand is an increase in industry output, as more firms enter that are just like existing firms (shown in Exhibit 7.14[c]). The long-run supply curve is horizontal when the market has free entry and exit, there is a large number of firms with identical costs, and input prices are constant. Because these strong assumptions do not generally hold, we will now discuss when the long-run supply curve has a positive or negative slope.

<table>
<tr><td>**constant-cost industry** an industry in which input prices (and cost curves) do not change as industry output changes</td></tr>
<tr><td>**increasing-cost industry** an industry in which input prices rise (and cost curves rise) as industry output rises</td></tr>
</table>

AN INCREASING-COST INDUSTRY

In an **increasing-cost industry**, a more likely scenario, the cost curves of individual firms rise as the total output of the industry increases. Increases in input prices (upward shifts in cost curves) occur as larger quantities of factors are employed in the industry. When an industry utilizes a large portion of an input whose total supply is not huge, input prices will rise when the industry uses more of the input.

Increasing cost conditions are typical of *extractive* industries, such as agriculture, fishing, mining, and lumber, which utilize large portions of the total supply of specialized natural resources such as land or mineral deposits. As the output of such an industry expands, the increased demand for the resources raises the prices that must be paid for their use. Because additional resources of giving quality cannot be produced, greater supplies can be obtained (if at all) only by luring them away from other industries, or by using lower-quality (and less-productive, thus higher-cost) resources.

Wheat production is a typical example of an increasing-cost industry. As the output of wheat increases, the demand for land suitable for the production of wheat rises, and thus the price paid for the use of land of any given quality increases.

If there were a construction boom in a fully employed economy, would it be more costly to get additional resources such as skilled workers and raw materials? Yes;

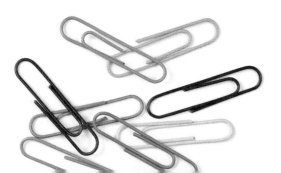

EXHIBIT 7.14 Demand Increase in a Constant-Cost Industry

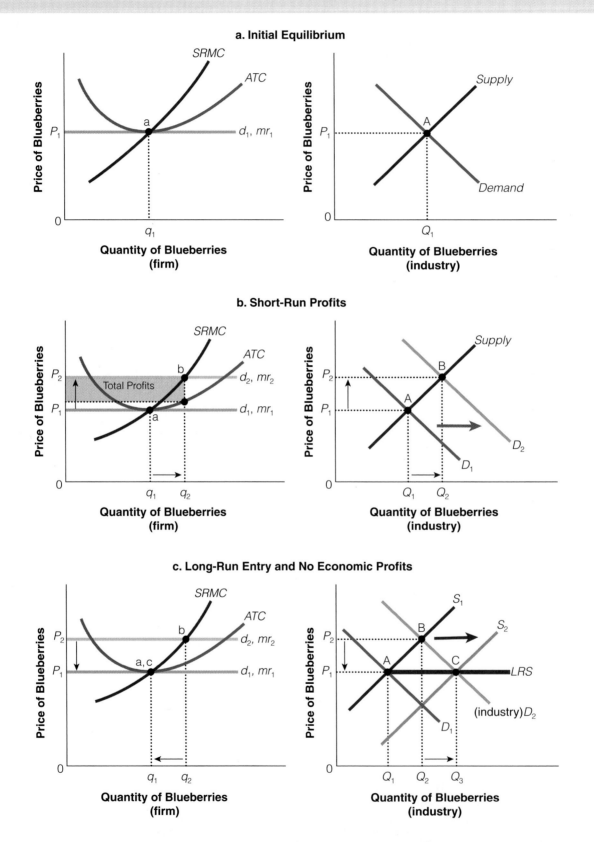

a. Initial Equilibrium

b. Short-Run Profits

c. Long-Run Entry and No Economic Profits

if this is an increasing-cost industry, the industry can only produce more output if it gets a higher price because the firm's costs of production rise as output expands. As new firms enter and output expands, the increase in demand for inputs causes the price of inputs to rise—the cost curves of all construction firms shift upward as the industry expands. Or consider a downtown building boom in which the supply of workers who are willing to work on tall skyscrapers is very small (a very steep supply of labor curve). The high demand for these few workers causes their wages to rise sharply and the cost of skyscrapers to rise. The industry can produce more output but only at a price increased enough to compensate the firm for the higher input costs. In an increasing-cost industry, the long-run supply curve is upward sloping.

Another example is provided by the airlines. Growth in the airline industry results in more congestion of airports and airspace. That is, as the output of the airline industry increases, the firm's cost increases, *ceteris paribus*. This situation of an upward sloping long-run industry supply curve is what economists call *external diseconomies of scale*—factors that are beyond the firm's control (that is, external) raise the firm's costs as industry output expands. In contrast, recall the discussion of diseconomies of scale in the previous chapter: the costs were internal to the firm—the costs were higher due to managing a larger firm.

Growth in the airline industry results in more congestion of airports and airspace— external diseconomies of scale.

A DECREASING-COST INDUSTRY

It is also possible that an expansion in the output of an industry can lead to a reduction in input costs and shift

As the output of an increasing cost industry expands, the increased demand for the resources raises the prices that must be paid for their use.

decreasing-cost industry
an industry in which input prices fall (and cost curves fall) as industry output rises

the *MC* and *ATC* curves downward, and the market price falls because of *external economies of scale*. We use the term *external* because the cost decreases are external to the firm; no one firm can gain by its own expansion. That is, the gain occurs when the total industry's output expands. The new long-run market equilibrium has more output at a lower price—that is, the long-run supply curve for a **decreasing-cost industry** is downward sloping (not shown).

Consider a new mining region developed in an area remote from railroad facilities back in the days before motor vehicles. So long as the total output of the mines was small, the ore was hauled by wagon, an extremely expensive form of transportation. But when the number of mines increased and the total output of the region rose substantially, it became feasible to construct a railroad to serve the area. The railroad lowered transportation costs and reduced the costs of all firms in the industry. As a practical matter, decreasing-cost industries are rarely encountered, at least over a large range of output. However, some industries may operate under decreasing-cost conditions in the short intervals of output expansion when continued growth makes possible the supply of materials or services at reduced cost. A larger industry might benefit from improved transportation or financial services, for example.

This situation might occur in the computer industry. The firms in the industry may be able to acquire computer chips at a lower price as the industry's demand for computer chips rises. Why? Perhaps it is because the computer chip industry can employ cost-saving techniques that become more economical at higher levels of output. That is, the marginal and average costs of the firm fall as input prices fall because of expanded output in the industry.

PERFECT COMPETITION AND ECONOMIC EFFICIENCY

In this chapter, we have seen that a firm in a perfectly competitive market produces at the minimum of the *ATC* curve in the long run and charges a price consistent with that cost. Because competitive firms are producing using the least-cost method, the minimum amount of resources is being used to produce a given level of output. This leads

EXHIBIT 7.15 Allocative Efficiency and Perfect Competition

<table>
<tr>
<td>

a. Producing Less Than the Competitive Level of Output Lowers Welfare

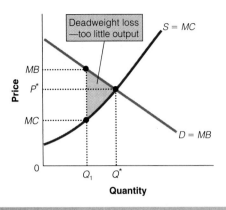

</td>
<td>

b. Producing More Than the Competitive Level of Output Lowers Welfare

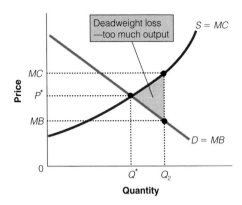

</td>
</tr>
</table>

to lower product prices for consumers. In short, **productive efficiency** requires that firms produce goods and services in the least costly way, where P = minimum ATC, as seen in Exhibit 7.13 on page 142. However, productive efficiency alone does not guarantee that markets are operating efficiently—society must also produce the goods and services that society wants most. This leads us to what economists call **allocative efficiency**.

We say that the output that results from equilibrium conditions of market demand and market supply in perfectly competitive markets achieve an efficient allocation of resources.

At the intersection of market supply and market demand, we find the competitive equilibrium price, P^*, and the competitive equilibrium output, Q^*. In competitive markets, market supply equals market demand, and $P = MC$. When $P = MC$, buyers value the last unit of output by the same amount that it cost sellers to produce it. If buyers value the last unit by more than the marginal cost of production, resources are not being allocated efficiently, as at Q_1 in Exhibit 7.15(a). Think of the demand curve as the marginal benefit curve ($D = MB$) and the supply curve as the marginal cost curve ($S = MC$). According to the rule of rational choice, we should pursue an activity as long as the expected marginal benefits are greater than the expected marginal costs. For example, in Exhibit 7.15(a), if Q_1 is produced, then the marginal benefits from producing additional units are greater than the marginal costs. The shaded area is deadweight loss. That is, at Q_1, resources are not being allocated efficiently, and output should be expanded.

We can also produce too much output. For

example, if output is expanded beyond Q^* in Exhibit 7.15(b), the cost to sellers for producing the good is greater than the marginal benefit to consumers. The shaded area is deadweight loss. Society would gain from a reduction in output back to Q^*. Once the competitive equilibrium is reached, the buyers' marginal benefit equals the sellers' marginal cost. That is, in a competitive market, producers efficiently use their scarce resources (labor, machinery, and other inputs) to produce what consumers want. In this sense, perfect competition achieves allocative efficiency.

productive efficiency
where a good or service is produced at the lowest possible cost

allocative efficiency
where $P = MC$ and production will be allocated to reflect consumer preferences

SECTION CHECK 6

6.1 In constant-cost industries, the cost curves of the firm are not affected by changes in the output of the entire industry. Such industries must be small demanders of resources in the market.

6.2 In an increasing-cost industry, the cost curves of the individual firms rise as total output increases. This case is the most typical.

6.3 A decreasing-cost industry has a downward-sloping long-run supply curve. Firms experience lower costs as the industry expands.

6.4 Productive efficiency occurs in perfect competition because the firm produces at the minimum of the ATC curve.

6.5 Allocative efficiency occurs when $P = MC$; production is allocated to reflect consumers' wants.

Chapter 7: Self-Review

Now that you're finished reading the chapter, review the questions below. You can write your answers in the space provided, then go online to see the answers at www.cengagebrain.com.

S1—A PERFECTLY COMPETITIVE MARKET

1. Why do firms in perfectly competitive markets involve homogeneous goods?

2. Which of the following are most likely to be perfectly competitive?
   a. Chicago Board of Trade
   b. fast-food industry
   c. computer software industry
   d. New York Stock Exchange
   e. clothing industry

S2—AN INDIVIDUAL PRICE TAKER'S DEMAND CURVE

3. True or False: The demand curve of a perfectly competitive firm can be represented as perfectly elastic (horizontal) at the market price.

4. How does an individual perfectly competitive firm's demand curve change when the market price changes?

S3—PROFIT MAXIMIZATION

5. True or False: For a perfectly competitive firm, marginal revenue is always greater than the price.

S4—SHORT-RUN PROFITS AND LOSSES

6. How is the profit-maximizing output quantity determined?

7. If a profit-maximizing perfectly competitive firm is earning a profit because total revenue exceeds total cost, why must the market price exceed average total cost?

8. Complete the following table and identify the profit-maximizing output.

Quantity	Price	Total Revenue	Marginal Revenue	Marginal Cost	Total Profit
10	$12	$120	$12	$8	$25
11	12			9	
12	12			11	
13	12			12	
14	12			14	

S5—LONG-RUN EQUILIBRIUM

9. Why does entry eliminate positive economic profits in a perfectly competitive industry?

10. True or False: A situation of zero economic profits is a stable long-run equilibrium situation for a perfectly competitive industry.

S6—LONG-RUN SUPPLY

11. What must be true about input costs as industry output expands for a constant-cost industry?

12. What must be true about input costs as industry output expands for an increasing-cost industry?

With the formation of

Standard Oil of Ohio in 1870, John D. Rockefeller Sr. embarked on a massive expansion of his oil firm, waging vicious price wars and buying up competing oil refiners while investing in tank cars and new pipelines to put pressure on freight haulers and gain control of distribution. In 1882, he created the Standard Oil Trust, a corporation designed to run the nearly 40 oil companies in Rockefeller's oil empire, spread all across the United States. By the 1880s, Standard Oil held almost complete control over oil refining in the United States. In 1911, Standard Oil was broken up under violation of the Sherman Antitrust Act.

8 Monopoly

monopoly is at the other end of the spectrum from perfect competition. Pure monopoly is a market with a single seller. Because it is the sole supplier, a monopoly faces the market demand curve for its product.

Consequently, the monopolist has control over the market price—it is a price maker. The monopolist can choose any combination of price and quantity along its market demand curve. But do not confuse ability with incentive. The monopolist, just like the perfectly competitive firm, will maximize profits (or minimize losses) by producing at the output level where $MR = MC$.

A pure monopoly, with literally one seller, is rare in the real world. But situations in which a few firms compete with each other are quite common. For example, Microsoft's Windows operating system, certain patented prescription drugs, and your cable company are all examples of near monopolies. All of these firms have some monopoly power—control over prices and output.

In this chapter, we will see how a monopolist determines the profit-maximizing price and output. We will also compare monopoly and perfect competition to see which is more efficient. Does the monopoly equilibrium solution lead to higher prices and lower output levels than does the perfectly competitive equilibrium solution? If so, what can the government do about it?

Sections in Chapter 8

Ⓢ1 Monopoly: The Price Maker

Keep the following questions in mind as you read through this section. You'll find the answers in Section Check 1.

1.1 What is a monopoly?

1.2 Why is pure monopoly rare?

1.3 What are the sources of monopoly power?

1.4 What is a natural monopoly?

monopoly the single supplier of a product that has no close substitute

natural monopoly a firm that can produce at a lower cost than a number of smaller firms can

What is a monopoly? A true or pure **monopoly** exists when a market consists of only one seller of a product with no close substitute and natural or legal barriers to prevent entry competition. The reason a monopoly is the only firm in the market is because other firms cannot enter—there are barriers to entry. In monopoly, "the firm" and "the industry" are one and the same. Consequently, the firm sets the price of the good, because the firm faces the industry demand curve and can pick the most profitable point on that demand curve. Monopolists are price makers (rather than price takers) that try to pick the price that will maximize their profits.

PURE MONOPOLY IS A RARITY

Few goods and services truly have only one producer. One might think of a small community with a single bank, a single newspaper, or even a single grocery store. Even in these situations, however, most people can bank out of town, use a substitute financial institution, buy out-of-town newspapers or read them on the Web, go to a nearby town to buy groceries, and so on. Near-monopoly conditions exist, but absolutely pure monopoly is unusual.

One market in which there is typically only one producer of goods and services within an area is public utilities. In any given market, usually only one company provides natural gas or supplies water. Moreover, governments themselves provide many services for which they are often the sole provider, such as sewer services, fire and police protection, and military protection. Most of these situations resemble a pure monopoly. However, for most of these goods and services, substitute goods and services are available. People heating their homes with natural gas can switch to electric heat (or vice versa). In some areas, residents can even substitute home-collected rainwater or well water for what the local water company provides.

Even though the purist may correctly deny the existence of monopoly, the number of situations where monopoly conditions are closely approximated is numerous enough to make the study of monopoly more than a theoretical abstraction; moreover, the study of monopoly is useful in clarifying certain desirable aspects of perfect competition.

BARRIERS TO ENTRY

A monopolist can use several ways to make it virtually impossible for other firms to overcome barriers to entry. For example, a monopolist might prevent potential rivals from entering the market by establishing legal barriers, taking advantage of economies of scale, or controlling important inputs.

Legal Barriers

In the case of legal barriers, the government might franchise only one firm to operate an industry, as is the case for postal services in most countries. The government can also provide licensing designed to ensure a certain level of quality and competence. Workers in many trade industries—hair stylists, bartenders, contractors, electricians, and plumbers, for instance—must obtain government licensing.

Also, the government could award patents that encourage inventive activity. It can cost millions of dollars to develop a new drug or computer chip, for example, and without a patent to recoup some of the costs, a company would certainly be less motivated to pursue inventive activity. As long as the patent is in effect, the company has the potential to enjoy monopoly profits for many years. After all, why would a firm engage in costly research if any company could take a free ride on their discovery and produce and sell the new drug or computer chip?

Economies of Scale

The situation in which one large firm can provide the output of the market at a lower cost than two or more smaller firms is called a **natural monopoly**. With a natural monopoly, it is more efficient to have one firm produce the good. The reason for the cost advantage is economies of scale; that is, *ATC* falls as output expands throughout the relevant output range, as seen in Exhibit 8.1. Public utilities, such as water, gas, and electricity, are examples of natural monopoly. It is less costly for one firm to lay down pipes and distribute water than for competing firms to lay down a maze of competing pipes. That is, a single water

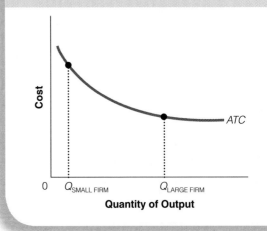

EXHIBIT 8.1 Economies of Scale

Stay out of my market!

Monopolists create almost insurmountable barriers to keep competitors from entering the market.

company can supply the town water more efficiently than a large number of competing firms.

Control Over an Important Input

Another barrier to entry could exist if a firm had control over an important input. For example, from the late nineteenth century to the early 1940s, the Aluminum Company of America (Alcoa) had a monopoly in the production of aluminum. Its monopoly power was guaranteed because of its control over an important ingredient in the production of aluminum—bauxite. Similarly, the De Beers diamond company of South Africa had monopoly power because it controlled roughly 80 percent of the world's output of diamonds.

However, today De Beers accounts for less than 40 percent of diamond production. Increased competition and the discovery of new diamond deposits has finally broken the monopoly in the diamond industry. A number of producers from countries such as Russia, Canada, and Australia chose to start distributing diamonds outside of the De Beers channel, thus effectively ending the monopoly. To keep their share of the market from falling further, De Beers differentiated their diamonds by branding them with a mark only visible under a microscope, and many other diamond firms have followed suit. By branding diamonds, sellers are assuring their customers of the quality of their diamonds and that the customers are not buying "blood" diamonds that have been exported from war-ravaged areas of Africa, where the revenues are used to fund military efforts. De Beers's new strategy has been effective; they are now more profitable today with a 40 percent market share than when they maintained an 80 percent market share.[1]

1. Cockburn, A., (2002) Diamonds: the real story. *National Geographic*, vol. 201, no. 3, March 2002, pp. 2–35.

A key resource for professional sports leagues in the United States is a stadium. The teams in Major League Baseball (MLB), the National Basketball Association (NBA) and the National Football League (NFL) have long term leases for the best stadiums and arenas in major cities. Control over this resource is an important barrier that deters new professional teams from forming.

However, the ownership of key resources is rarely the source of monopoly power. Many goods are traded internationally and resources are owned by many different people around the world. It is uncommon that a firm would control a resource where there was not a close substitute.

SECTION CHECK 1

1.1 A pure monopoly exists in a market with only one seller of a product for which no close substitute is available.

1.2 Pure monopolies are rare because few goods and services have only one existing producer.

1.3 Sources of monopoly power include legal barriers, economies of scale, and control over important inputs.

1.4 A natural monopoly occurs when one firm can provide the good or service at a lower cost than two or more smaller firms.

⑤2 Demand and Marginal Revenue in Monopoly

Keep the following questions in mind as you read through this section. You'll find the answers in Section Check 2.

2.1 How does the demand curve for a monopolist differ from that for a perfectly competitive firm?

2.2 Why is marginal revenue less than price in monopoly?

In monopoly, the market demand curve may be regarded as the demand curve for the firm's product because the

EXHIBIT 8.2 Comparing Demand Curves: Perfect Competition versus Monopoly

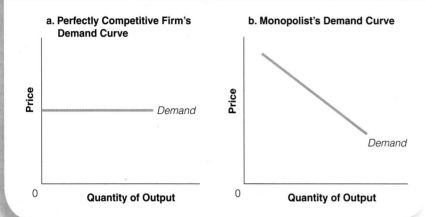

a. Perfectly Competitive Firm's Demand Curve

Price — Quantity of Output — Demand

b. Monopolist's Demand Curve

Price — Quantity of Output — Demand

monopoly firm is the market for that particular product. The demand curve indicates the quantities that the firm can sell at various possible prices. In monopoly, the demand curve for the firm's product declines as additional units are placed on the market—the demand curve is downward sloping. In monopoly, the firm cannot set both its price and the quantity it sells. That is, a monopolist would love to sell a larger quantity at a high price, but it can't. If the monopolist raises the price, the amount sold will fall; if the monopolist lowers the price, the amount sold will rise.

Recall that in perfect competition, many buyers and sellers of homogeneous goods (resulting in a perfectly elastic demand curve) mean that competitive firms can sell all they want at the market price. They face a horizontal demand curve. The firm takes the price of its output

as determined by the market forces of supply and demand. Monopolists, and all other firms that are price makers, face a downward-sloping demand curve. If the monopolist raises its price, it will lose some—but not all—of its customers. The two demand curves are displayed side by side in Exhibit 8.2.

In Exhibit 8.3 below, we see the price of the good, the quantity of the good, the *total revenue* (which is the quantity sold times the price [$TR = P \times Q$]), and the average revenue, that is, the amount of revenue the firm receives per unit sold ($AR = TR \div Q$). The average revenue is simply the price per unit sold, which is exactly equal to the market demand curve, and the *marginal revenue* (MR)—the amount of revenue the firm receives from selling an additional unit—is equal to $\Delta TR \div \Delta Q$.

Taking the information from Exhibit 8.3, we can create the demand and marginal revenue curves as seen in Exhibit 8.4. We see that the marginal revenue is always less than the price of the good. To understand why, suppose the firm cuts its price from $4 to $3.

To induce a third daily customer to purchase the good, the firm must cut its price to $3. In doing so, it gains $3 in revenue from the newest customer—the output effect. However, it loses $2 in revenue because each of the first two customers are now paying $1 less than previously—the price effect. The marginal revenue is $1 ($3 − $2), which is less than the price of the good ($3).

EXHIBIT 8.3 Total, Marginal, and Average Revenue

Total and Marginal Revenue				Average Revenue
Price	Quantity	Total Revenue ($TR = P \times Q$)	Marginal Revenue ($MR = \Delta TR/\Delta Q$)	Average Revenue ($AR = TR/Q$)
$6	0	—		—
5	1	$5	$5	$5
4	2	8	3	4
3	3	9	1	3
2	4	8	−1	2
1	5	5	−3	1

EXHIBIT 8.4 Demand and Marginal Revenue for the Monopolist

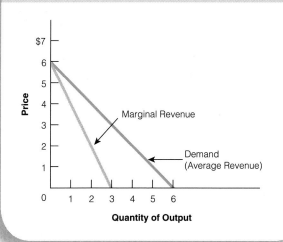

Exhibit 8.4 graphs the relationship between the demand curve and the marginal revenue curve for a monopolist. Because *a monopolist's marginal revenue is always less than the price*, the marginal revenue curve will always lie below the demand curve, as shown in Exhibit 8.4. Recall that in perfect competition, the firm could sell all it wanted at the market price, and the price was equal to marginal revenue. However, in monopoly, if the seller wants to expand output, it will have to lower the price on *all* units; the monopolist receives additional revenue from the new unit sold (the output

effect) but will receive less revenue on all the units it was previously selling (the price effect). Thus, when the monopolist cuts the price to attract new customers, the old customers benefit.

In Exhibit 8.5, we can compare marginal revenue for the competitive firm with marginal revenue for the monopolist. The firm in perfect competition can sell another unit of output without lowering its price; hence, the marginal revenue from selling its last unit of output is the market price. However, the monopolist has a downward-sloping demand curve. To sell an extra unit of output, the price falls from P_1 to P_2, and the monopolist loses area c in Exhibit 8.5(b).

It is important to note that even though a monopolist can set its price anywhere it wants, it will not set its price as high as possible—be careful not to confuse ability with incentive. As we will see in the next section, some prices along the demand curve will not be profitable for a firm. In other words, the monopolist can enhance profits by either lowering the price or raising it, depending on the circumstances.

THE MONOPOLIST'S PRICE IN THE ELASTIC PORTION OF THE DEMAND CURVE

The relationships between the elasticity of demand and the marginal and total revenue are shown in Exhibit 8.6 on the next page. In Exhibit 8.6(a), elasticity varies along a linear demand curve. Recall from Chapter 4 that above the midpoint, the demand curve is elastic ($E_D > 1$); below the midpoint, it is inelastic ($E_D < 1$); and at the midpoint, it is unit elastic ($E_D = 1$). How does elasticity relate to total and marginal revenue? In the elastic portion of the curve shown in Exhibit 8.6(b), when the price falls, total revenue rises and marginal revenue is positive. In the inelastic region of the demand curve, when the price falls, total revenue falls, and marginal revenue is

EXHIBIT 8.5 Marginal Revenue—Competitive Firm versus Monopolist

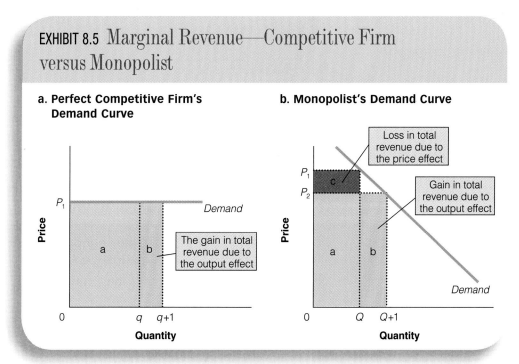

a. Perfect Competitive Firm's Demand Curve

b. Monopolist's Demand Curve

EXHIBIT 8.6 The Relationship between the Elasticity of Demand and Total and Marginal Revenue

a. Demand and Marginal Revenue

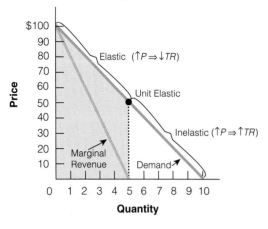

b. Total Revenue

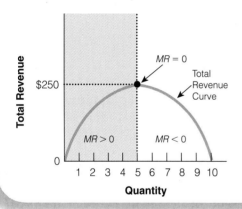

negative. At the midpoint of the linear demand curve in Exhibit 8.6(b), the total revenue curve reaches its highest point and $MR = 0$.

For example, suppose the price falls on the top half of the demand curve in Exhibit 8.6(a) from $90 to $80; total revenue increases from $90 ($90 × 1) to $160 ($80 × 2), and marginal revenue is positive at $70. Because a reduction in price leads to an increase in total revenue, the demand curve is elastic in this region. Now suppose the price falls from $20 to $10 on the lower portion of the demand curve; total revenue falls from $160 ($20 × 8) to $90 ($10 × 9), and marginal revenue is negative at −$70. Because a reduction in price leads to a decrease in total revenue, the demand curve is inelastic in this region.

A monopolist will never knowingly operate on the inelastic portion of its demand curve, because increased output will lead to lower total revenue in this region. Not only are total revenues falling, but total costs will rise as the monopolist produces more output. Similarly, if the monopolist were to lower its output, it could increase its total revenue and lower its total costs (because it costs less to produce fewer units), leading to greater economic profits.

SECTION CHECK 2

2.1 The monopolist's demand curve is downward sloping because it is the market demand curve. To produce and sell another unit of output, the firm must lower its price on all units sold. As a result, the marginal revenue curve lies below the demand curve.

2.2 The monopolist's marginal revenue will always be less than the price because of its downward-sloping demand curve. In order to sell more output, the monopolist must accept a lower price on all units sold; the monopolist will receive additional revenue from the new unit sold but will receive less revenue on all of the units it was previously selling.

⑤3 The Monopolist's Equilibrium

Keep the following questions in mind as you read through this section. You'll find the answers in **Section Check 3.**

3.1 How does the monopolist decide what output to produce?

3.2 How does the monopolist decide what price to charge?

3.3 How do we know whether the monopolist is making a profit or incurring a loss?

3.4 Can the monopolist's economic profits last into the long run?

So how does the monopolist determine the profit-maximizing output? In the preceding section, we saw

EXHIBIT 8.7 Equilibrium Output and Price for a Monopolist

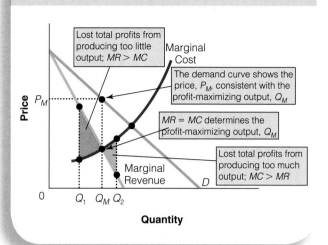

Lost total profits from producing too little output; $MR > MC$

Marginal Cost

The demand curve shows the price, P_M, consistent with the profit-maximizing output, Q_M

$MR = MC$ determines the profit-maximizing output, Q_M

Lost total profits from producing too much output; $MC > MR$

Marginal Revenue

D

P_M · Price

0 · Q_1 · Q_M · Q_2

Quantity

The monopolist's three-step method

—Find the profit-maximizing output level

—Find total revenue at the profit-maximizing output level

—Find total cost.

how a monopolist could choose any point along a demand curve. However, the monopolist's decision as to what level of output to produce depends on more than the marginal revenue derived at various outputs. The firm faces production costs; and the monopolist, like the perfect competitor, will maximize profits at that output where $MR = MC$. This point is demonstrated graphically in Exhibit 8.7.

As you can see in Exhibit 8.7, at output level Q_1, the marginal revenue exceeds the marginal cost of production, so it is profitable for the monopolist to expand output. Profits continue to grow until output Q_M is reached. Beyond that output, say at Q_2, the marginal cost of production exceeds the marginal revenue from production, so profits decline. The monopolist should cut production back to Q_M. Therefore, the equilibrium output is Q_M. At this output, marginal cost and marginal revenue are equal.

THE THREE-STEP METHOD FOR THE MONOPOLIST

Let's return to the three-step method we used in Chapter 7. Determining whether a firm is generating positive economic profits, economic losses, or zero economic profits at the profit-maximizing level of output, Q_M, can be done in three easy steps.

1. Find where marginal revenue equals marginal cost and proceed straight down to the horizontal (quantity) axis to find Q_M, the profit-maximizing output level for the monopolist.

2. At Q_M, go straight up to the demand curve and then to the left to find the market price, P_M. Once you have identified P_M and Q_M, you can find total revenue at the profit-maximizing output level, because $TR = P \times Q$.

3. The last step is to find total cost. Again, go straight up from Q_M to the average total cost (ATC) curve and then left to the vertical axis to compute the average total cost at Q_M. If we multiply average total cost by the output level, we can find the total cost ($TC = ATC \times Q$).

PROFITS FOR THE MONOPOLIST

Exhibit 8.7 does not show what profits, if any, the monopolist is actually making. This missing information is found in Exhibit 8.8, which shows the equilibrium position for a monopolist, this time adding an average total cost (ATC) curve. As we just discussed, the firm produces where $MC = MR$, at output Q_M. At output Q_M (100) and price P_M

EXHIBIT 8.8 A Monopolist's Profits

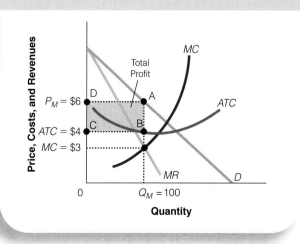

MC

Total Profit

$P_M = \$6$ · D · A · ATC

$ATC = \$4$ · C · B

$MC = \$3$

MR · D

0 · $Q_M = 100$

Quantity

Price, Costs, and Revenues

($6) the firm's total revenue is equal to DAQ_M0, which is $P_M \times Q_M$ ($600). At output Q_M, the firm's total cost is CBQ_M0, which is $ATC \times Q_M$ ($400). In Exhibit 8.8, we see that total revenue is greater than total cost, so the firm has a total profit of area DABC. Or, $P_M - ATC$ (price minus average total cost) is the per-unit profit, $2. The width of the box (segment CB) is the quantity sold (0 to Q_M), 100 units. Hence, the area of the box is the monopoly firm's total profit, $200 (per-unit profit × quantity sold).

In perfect competition, profits in an economic sense will persist only in the short run. In the long run, new firms will enter the industry and increase industry supply, thereby driving down the price of the good and eliminating profits. In monopoly, however, profits are not eliminated, because one of the conditions for monopoly is that barriers to entry exist. Other firms cannot enter, so economic profits persist in the long run.

LOSSES FOR THE MONOPOLIST

It is easy to imagine a monopolist ripping off consumers by charging prices that result in long-run economic profits. However, many companies with monopoly power have gone out of business. Imagine that you received a patent on a bad idea such as a roof ejection seat for a helicopter, or that you had the sole rights to turn an economics textbook into a screenplay for a motion picture. Although you may be the sole supplier of a product, you are not guaranteed that consumers will demand your product. Even without a close substitute for your product, you will always face competition for the consumer dollar, and other goods may provide greater satisfaction.

Exhibit 8.9 illustrates loss in a monopoly situation. In this graph, notice that the demand curve is below the average total cost curve. In this case, the monopolist will incur a loss because of insufficient demand to cover the average total cost at any price and output combination along the demand curve. At Q_M, total cost, CBQ_M0, is greater than total revenue, DAQ_M0, so the firm incurs a total loss of CBAD. Or, total revenue is $600 ($P_M \times Q_M$ = $6 × 100) and total cost is $700 ($ATC \times Q_M$ = $7 × 100), for an economic loss of $100. Notice that the total revenue is great enough to cover the variable costs of $400 ($TVC$ = $4 × 100). That is, the firm can reduce its losses by operating rather than shutting down in the short run. However, in monopoly as in perfect competition, a firm will go out of business in the long run if it cannot generate enough revenue to cover its total costs.

In summary, if total revenue is greater than total cost at Q_M, the firm generates a total economic profit; and if total revenue is less than total cost at Q_M, the firm generates a total economic loss. If total revenue is equal to total cost at Q_M, the firm earns zero economic profit. Remember, the cost curves include implicit and explicit costs, so in this case, the monopolist is covering the total opportunity costs of its resources and earning a normal profit or rate of return.

PATENTS

Governments confer one form of monopoly power through patents and copyrights. A patent puts the government's police power behind the patent-holder's exclusive right to make a product for a specified period (up to 20 years) without anyone else being able to make an identical product. As Exhibit 8.10 suggests, the patent gives the

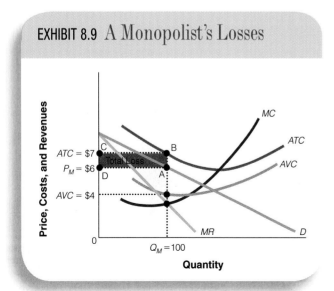

EXHIBIT 8.9 A Monopolist's Losses

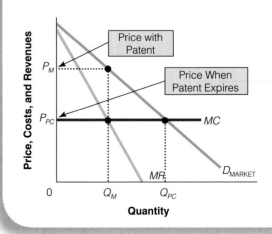

EXHIBIT 8.10 Impact of Patent Protection on Equilibrium Price and Quantity

supplier at least temporary monopoly power over that good or service. The firm with the patent can then price its product well above marginal costs, at P_M. Notice that the marginal cost curve is flat. The reason is that most of the cost of many products under patent, such as prescription drugs, is in the development stage. Once the drug is available for the market, the marginal costs are close to constant (flat). When the patent expires, the price of the patented good or service usually falls substantially with the entry of competing firms into the market. The price will fall toward the perfectly competitive price P_{PC}, and the output will increase toward Q_{PC}. However, if the company's patent expires, it does not lose all of its monopoly power. Some of its loyal customers will continue to pay slightly more than the competitive price because of their concern that the generic product is not a perfect substitute for the drug they had been taking for years.

Why does the government give inventors this limited monopoly power, raising the prices of pharmaceutical drugs and other "vital" goods? The rationale is simple. Without patents, inventors would have little incentive to incur millions of dollars in research and development expenses to create new products (e.g., lifesaving drugs), because others could immediately copy the idea and manufacture the products without incurring the research expenses. Similarly, copyrights stimulate creative activity of other kinds, giving writers the incentive to write books that earn royalties and are not merely copied for free. The enormous number of computer programs written for home computers reflects the fact that program writers receive royalties from the sale of each copy sold; that is why they and the firms they work for vehemently oppose unauthorized copying of their work.

— COPYRIGHTS

Without copyrights, writers would have much less incentive to write books, because they would not be able to profit from the effort put into creating them.

SECTION CHECK 3

3.1 The monopolist, like the perfect competitor, maximizes profits at that output where marginal revenue equals marginal cost.

3.2 The monopolist sets the price according to the demand for the product at the profit-maximizing output.

3.3 Monopoly profits can be found by comparing the price per unit and average total cost per unit at Q^*. If $P > ATC$, a firm realizes economic profits. If $P < ATC$, it has economic losses.

3.4 Monopolists' profits can last into the long run because of a monopoly's barriers to entry.

(S)4 Monopoly and Welfare Loss

Keep the following questions in mind as you read through this section. You'll find the answers in **Section Check 4**.

4.1 How does monopoly lead to inefficiencies?

4.2 What is the welfare loss in monopoly?

4.3 Does monopoly retard innovation?

Is monopoly a good or bad thing? In this section, we'll consider various arguments as to the effects a monopoly might have on the market.

DOES MONOPOLY PROMOTE INEFFICIENCY?

Monopoly is often considered to be bad. Two main objections form the basis for concerns about the establishment of monopoly power. First, on equity grounds, many people feel that it is not "fair" for monopoly owners to have persistent economic profits when they work no harder than other firms. However, to most economists, the more serious objection is that monopolies

result in market inefficiencies. That is, monopoly leads to a lower output and higher prices than would exist under perfect competition. Exhibit 8.11 demonstrates why. In monopoly, the firm produces output Q_M and charges price P_M. Suppose, however, that perfect competition exists and the industry is characterized by many small firms that could produce output with the same efficiency (at the same cost) as one large firm. Then the marginal cost curve shown in Exhibit 8.11 is the sum of all the individual marginal cost curves of the individual firms, which is the industry supply curve.

In the perfectly competitive market, the equilibrium price and quantity would be determined where the marginal cost (or supply) curve intersects with the demand curve, at output Q_{PC} and price P_{PC}. Thus, the competitive equilibrium solution provides for more output and lower prices than the solution prevailing in monopoly, which leads to the major efficiency objection to monopoly: Monopolists charge higher prices and produce less output. This situation may also be viewed as "unfair," in that consumers are burdened more than under the alternative competitive arrangement.

Welfare Loss in Monopoly

In addition to the monopolist producing lower levels of output at higher prices, notice that the monopolist produces at an output where the price (P_M) is greater than the marginal cost (MC_M). Because $P > MC$, the value

---

EXHIBIT 8.11 Perfect Competition versus Monopoly

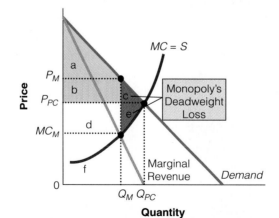

	Perfect Competition	Monopoly	Change
Consumer Surplus	a + b + c	a	− b − c
Producer Surplus	d + e + f	b + d + f	b − e
Welfare	a + b + c + d + e + f	a + b + d + f	− c − e

---

to society from the last unit produced is greater than its costs (MC_M). That is, the monopoly is not producing enough of the good from society's perspective. We call the area c + e in Exhibit 8.11 the welfare or deadweight loss due to monopoly. In perfect competition, the equilibrium is P_{PC} and the equilibrium quantity is Q_{PC}. Consumer surplus is area a + b + c, and the product surplus is area d + e + f. In monopoly, the equilibrium price is higher at P_M and the equilibrium quantity is lower at Q_M. Under monopoly, consumer surplus is area a, producer surplus is area b + d + f, and lost welfare or the deadweight loss of monopoly is c + e.

The actual amount of the welfare loss in monopoly is of considerable debate among economists. Estimates vary from between one-tenth of 1 percent to 6 percent of national income. The variation depends on the researchers' estimates of elasticity of demand, whether firm or industry data were used, whether adjustments for profits were made (for the inclusion of royalties and intangibles), and whether the researcher included some proxy for scarce resources used in attempting to create the monopoly.

DOES MONOPOLY RETARD INNOVATION?

Another argument against monopoly is that a lack of competition tends to retard technological advancement. Monopolists become comfortable reaping their monopolistic profits, so they do not work hard at product improvement, technical advances designed to promote efficiency, and so forth. The American railroad is sometimes cited as an example of this situation. Early in the last century, railroads had strong monopoly power, but they did not spend much on research or development; they did not aggressively try to improve rail transport. Consequently, technical advances in substitute modes of transportation—such as cars, trucks, and airplanes—led to a loss of monopoly power for the railroads.

However, the notion that monopoly retards all innovation can be disputed. Many near-monopolists are, in fact, important innovators. Companies such as Microsoft, International Business Machines (IBM), Polaroid, and Xerox have all, at one time or another, had strong market positions, in some instances approaching monopoly secured by patent protection, but they were also important innovators. Indeed, innovation helps firms initially obtain a degree of monopoly status, because patents can give a monopoly to new products and/or cost-saving technology. Even the monopolist wants more profits, and any innovation that lowers costs or expands revenues creates profits for the monopolist. In addition, because patents expire, a monopolist may be expected to innovate

Patent protections helped Xerox drive forward innovation in copier and printer technology. It also gave them a practical monopoly over the copier market until the Federal Trade Commision forced them to license their patent portfolio to competitors.

in order to obtain additional patents and preserve its monopoly power. Therefore, the incentive to innovate might well exist in monopolistic market structures.

SECTION CHECK 4

4.1 Monopoly results in smaller output and a higher price than would be the case under perfect competition.

4.2 The monopolist produces at level of output where $P > MC$ and the value to society of the last unit produced is greater than its cost. In other words, the monopoly is not producing enough output from society's standpoint.

4.3 Monopoly may lead to greater concentration of economic power and could retard innovation.

⑤5 Monopoly Policy

Keep the following questions in mind as you read through this section. You'll find the answers in Section Check 5.

5.1 What is the objective of antitrust policy?

5.2 What is regulation?

5.3 What is average cost pricing?

Because monopolies pose certain problems with respect to efficiency, equity, and power, the public, through its governments, must decide how to deal with the phenomenon. Two major approaches to dealing with such problems are commonly employed: antitrust policies and regulation. It should be pointed out that in these discussions, the word *monopoly* is sometimes used in a loose, general sense to refer to imperfectly competitive markets, not just to "pure" monopoly.

ANTITRUST POLICIES

Perhaps the most obvious way to deal with monopoly is to make it illegal. The government can bring civil lawsuits or even criminal actions against businesspeople or corporations engaged in monopolistic practices. By imposing costs on monopolists that can be either monetary or nonmonetary (such as the fear of lawsuits or even jail sentences), antitrust policies reduce the profitability of monopoly.

ANTITRUST LAWS

The first important law regulating monopoly was the Sherman Antitrust Act. The Sherman Act prohibited "restraint of trade"—price fixing and collusion—but narrow court interpretation of the legislation led to a number of large mergers, such as U.S. Steel. Some important near-monopolies were broken up, however. For example, in 1911, the Standard Oil Trust, which controlled most of the country's oil refining, and the American Tobacco Co., which had similar dominance in tobacco, were both forcibly divided up into smaller companies.

Antitrust Acts Strengthened

Antitrust efforts were strengthened by subsequent legislation, the most important of which was the Clayton Act in 1914. Additional legislation in the same year created the Federal Trade Commission (FTC), which became the second government agency concerned with antitrust actions. The Clayton Act made it illegal to engage in predatory pricing—setting prices to drive out competitors or deter potential entrants in order to ensure higher prices in the future. The Clayton Act also prohibited mergers if it led to weakened competition. Not all of the later legislation actually served to enhance competition. A case in point is the Robinson-Patman Act of 1936, which forbade most forms of price discrimination, and the Cellar-Kefauver Act in 1950, which toughened restrictions on mergers that reduced competition.

However, antitrust laws may have costs as well as benefits because mergers may lead to lower costs and greater efficiency. A number of banks recently merged, lowering costs. So, good antitrust policy must be able to recognize which mergers are desirable and which are not.

Promoting More Price Competition

Many professional associations restrict the promotion of price competition by prohibiting advertising among their members. Recently, both the FTC and the Justice Department successfully attacked these types of restrictions on the grounds that they violate the antitrust laws. They have been spurred on in their efforts by consumer groups who noticed that prices tend to be much lower when price competition is allowed to flourish. Thus, optometrists were prodded to advertise the price of

COLLUSION

In the early 1990s, Ivy League schools were charged with illegally colluding to fix the price of scholarships. Ivy League schools wanted to make sure they did not get into a "scholarship war," so the participating schools collectively met and fixed scholarship packages. Students would then pick their schools on the basis of academic quality, not the size of the scholarship package. These activities guaranteed that any student applying to more than one of these schools would be offered the same financial package. The Justice Department charged the eight Ivy League schools and MIT with an illegal conspiracy to set prices and required these schools to stop their collusion on tuition, salaries, and financial aid by signing a consent order.

SOURCE: Anthony DePalma, "Ivy universities deny price-fixing but agree to avoid it in the future," *The New York Times,* (May 23, 1991). Available at http://www.nytimes.com/1991/05/23/us/ivy-universities-deny-price-fixing-but-agree-to-avoid-it-in-the-future.html?pagewanted=all (accessed June 21, 2010).

eyeglasses; pharmacists, the price of commonly prescribed drugs; and even lawyers, the price of a divorce.

HAVE ANTITRUST POLICIES BEEN SUCCESSFUL?

The success of antitrust policies can be debated. It is true that few giant monopolies were disbanded as a consequence of antitrust policies. Studies showed little change in the degree of monopoly/oligopoly power in the first 100 years or so of U.S. antitrust legislation. Manufacturing, as a whole, actually became more concentrated; that is, fewer firms are now in the industry. However, it is likely that at least some anticompetitive practices were prevented simply by the existence of laws prohibiting monopoly-like practices. Although the laws were probably enforced in an imperfect fashion, on balance they impeded monopoly influences to at least some degree.

GOVERNMENT REGULATION

Government regulation is an alternative approach to dealing with monopolies. Under regulation, a company would not be allowed to charge any price it wants. Suppose the government does not want to break up a natural monopoly in the water or power industry. Remember that natural monopolies occur when one large firm can produce as much output as many smaller firms but at a lower average cost per unit. The government may decide to regulate the monopoly price; but what price does it let the firm charge? The goal is to achieve the efficiency of large-scale production without permitting the high monopoly prices and low output that can promote allocative inefficiency.

The basic policy dilemma that regulators often face in attempting to fix maximum prices can be illustrated rather easily. Consider Exhibit 8.12. Without regulation, say the profit-maximizing monopolist operates at point A—at output Q_M and price P_M. At this output, the price exceeds the average total cost, so economic profits exist, as seen in Exhibit 8.12. However, the monopolist is producing relatively little output and is charging a relatively high price; and it is producing at a point where price is above marginal cost. This point is not the best from society's perspective.

Allocative Efficiency

From society's point of view, what would be the best price and output position? As we discussed in Chapter 7, the best position is at the competitive equilibrium output, where $P = MC$, because the equilibrium price

For a natural monopolist, the "optimal" output from a welfare perspective is not really viable, because firms incur losses.

represents the marginal value of output. The marginal cost represents society's opportunity costs of making the good as opposed to something else. Where price equals marginal cost, society matches marginal value and marginal cost—that is, it achieves allocative efficiency, as seen at point C in Exhibit 8.12.

Can the Regulated Monopolist Operate at $P = MC$?

Unfortunately, the natural monopoly cannot operate profitably at the allocative efficiency point, where $P = MC$, indicated as point C in Exhibit 8.12. At point C, the intersection of the demand and marginal cost curves, average total cost is greater than price. The optimal output, then, is an output that results in losses for the producer. Any regulated business that produced for long at this "optimal" output would go bankrupt; it would be impossible to attract new capital to the industry.

Therefore, the "optimal" output from a welfare perspective is not really viable, because firms incur losses. The regulators cannot force firms to price their products at P_{MC} and to sell Q_{MC} output, because they would go out of business. Indeed, in the long run, the

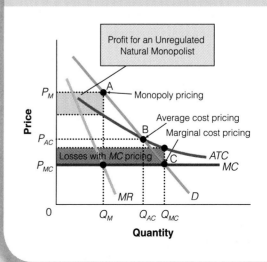

EXHIBIT 8.12 Marginal Cost Pricing versus Average Cost Pricing

industry's capital would deteriorate as investors failed to replace old capital as it became worn out or obsolete. If the monopolist's unregulated output at point A is not optimal from society's standpoint, and the short-run optimal output at point C is not feasible from the monopolist's standpoint, where should the regulated monopolist be allowed to operate?

One possible solution to the problem is for the government to subsidize the losses associated with marginal cost pricing. However, the burden of this solution would ultimately fall on the taxpayers, as the government would have to raise the money to pay for the losses.

The Compromise: Average Cost Pricing

A compromise between monopoly pricing and marginal cost pricing is found at point B in Exhibit 8.12, at output Q_{AC}, which is somewhere between the excessively low output and high prices of an unregulated monopoly and the excessively high output and low prices achieved when prices are equated with marginal cost pricing. At point B, price equals average total cost. The monopolist is permitted to price the product where economic profit is zero, earning a normal economic profit or rate of return, such as firms experience in perfect competition in the long run. This compromise is called **average cost pricing**.

In the real world, regulators often permit utilities to receive a "fair and reasonable" return that is a rough approximation to that suggested by average cost pricing, at point B. Point B would seem "fair" in that the monopolist is receiving rewards equal to those that a perfect competitor would ordinarily receive—no more, no less. Point B permits more output at a significantly lower price than is possible at point A, where the monopolist is unregulated, even though output is still somewhat less and price somewhat more than that suggested by point C, the socially optimum or best position.

DIFFICULTIES IN AVERAGE COST PRICING

Several difficulties arise in trying to implement an average cost pricing strategy. These include inaccuracies in cost calculations, a lack of incentives to keep costs down, and the influence of special interest groups.

Inaccurate Calculations of Costs

The actual implementation of a rate (price) that permits a "fair and reasonable" return is more difficult than the

analysis suggests. The calculations of costs and values are difficult. In reality, the firm may not know exactly what its demand and cost curves look like, which forces regulatory agencies to use profits, another somewhat ambiguous target, as a guide. If profits are "too high," lower the price; if profits are "too low," raise the price. In addition, what if the regulated firm has more information than the regulators about its firm, workers, and technology (asymmetric information)? If the firm can persuade regulators that its average cost is higher than it actually is, the regulated price could be set higher, closer to the monopoly price.

No Incentives to Keep Costs Down

Another problem is that average cost pricing offers the monopolist no incentive to reduce costs. That is, if the firm's costs rise from ATC_1 to ATC_2 in Exhibit 8.13, the price will rise from P_1 to P_2. If costs fall, the firm's price will fall. In either scenario, the firm will still be earning a normal rate of return. In other words, if the regulatory agency sets the price at any point where the ATC curve intersects the demand curve, the firm will earn a normal rate of return. Thus, if the agency is going to set the price wherever ATC intersects the demand curve, the firm might just think, "Why not let average costs rise? Why not let employees fly first class and dine in the finest restaurants? Why not buy concert tickets and season tickets to sporting events?" And if the regulated monopolist knows that the regulators will reduce prices if costs fall, the regulated monopolist does not benefit from lower costs. Regulators have tackled this problem by allowing the regulated firm to keep some of the profits that come from lower costs; that is, they do not adhere strictly to average cost pricing.

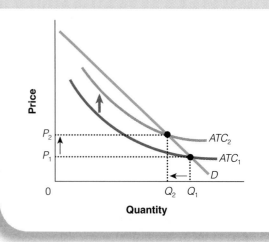

EXHIBIT 8.13 Changes in Average Costs

Special-Interest Groups

In the real world, consumer groups are constantly battling for lower utility rates, while the utility companies themselves are lobbying for higher rates so they can approach the monopoly profits indicated by point A in Exhibit 8.12. Decisions are not always made in a calm, objective, dispassionate atmosphere free from outside involvement. It is precisely the political economy of rate setting that disturbs some critics of this approach to dealing with the monopoly problem. For example, a rate-making commissioner could become friendly with a utility company, believing that he could obtain a nice job after his tenure as a regulator expires. The temptation would be great for the commissioner to be generous to the utility company. On the other hand, the tendency might be for regulators to bow to pressure from consumer groups. A politician who wants to win votes can almost always succeed by attacking utility rates and promising rate "reform" (lower rates). If zealous rate regulators listen too closely to consumer groups and push rates down to a level indicated by point C in Exhibit 8.12, the industry might be too unstable to attract capital for expansion.

In recent years, we have seen a trend away from regulation toward competition; for example, after AT&T was broken up by the courts in 1982, the long-distance market became very competitive, and local telephone service is much more competitive now than in the past. Technological advances now allow us to separate the production of electronic power or natural gas from the distributor, which will ultimately lead to greater competition in these markets. Some states have already started deregulation in the electricity market.

Regulators can come under pressure from both industry lobbyists and special-interest groups.

Consumer groups   **Utility companies**

© ISTOCKPHOTO.COM / © ROBNROLL/SHUTTERSTOCK

SECTION CHECK 5

5.1 Antitrust policies are government policies to reduce the profitability of a monopoly and push production closer to the social optimum.

5.2 Under government regulation, a monopolist might be allowed to continue operation but with certain price limits imposed on it.

5.3 Average cost pricing sets price equal to average total cost, where the demand curve intersects average total costs.

⑤6 Price Discrimination

Keep the following questions in mind as you read through this section. You'll find the answers in **Section Check 6**.

6.1 What is price discrimination?

6.2 Why does price discrimination exist?

6.3 Does price discrimination work when reselling is easy?

Sometimes sellers will charge different customers different prices for the same good or service when the cost of providing that good or service does not differ among customers. This practice is called **price discrimination**. Under certain conditions, the monopolist finds it profitable to discriminate among various buyers, charging higher prices to those who are more willing to pay and lower prices to those who are less willing to pay.

price discrimination the practice of charging different consumers different prices for the same good or service

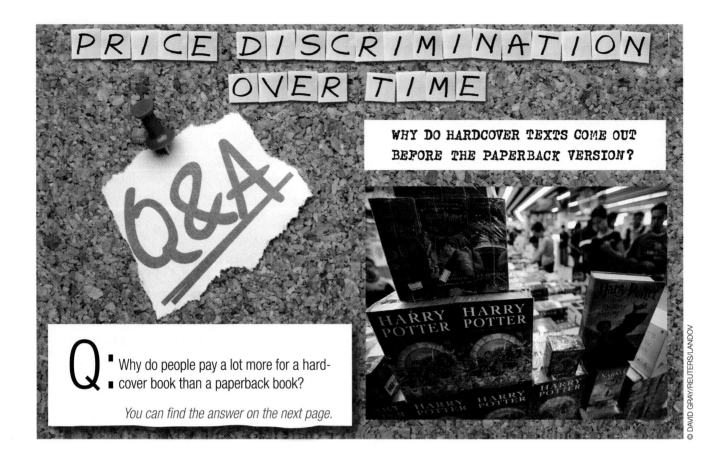

PRICE DISCRIMINATION OVER TIME

WHY DO HARDCOVER TEXTS COME OUT BEFORE THE PAPERBACK VERSION?

Q: Why do people pay a lot more for a hardcover book than a paperback book?

You can find the answer on the next page.

CONDITIONS FOR PRICE DISCRIMINATION

The ability to practice price discrimination is not available to all sellers. To practice price discrimination, the following three conditions must hold:

Monopoly Power

Price discrimination is possible only with monopoly or where members of a small group of firms (firms that are not price takers) follow identical pricing policies. In cases with a large number of competing firms, discrimination is less likely because competitors tend to undercut the high prices charged by the firms that are engaging in price discrimination.

Market Segregation

Price discrimination can only occur if the demand curves for markets, groups, or individuals are different. If the demand curves are not different, a profit-maximizing monopolist would charge the same price in both markets. In short, price discrimination requires the ability to separate customers according to their willingness to pay.

No Resale

For price discrimination to work, the person buying the product at a discount must have difficulty in reselling the product to customers being charged more. Otherwise, those getting the items cheaply would want to buy extra amounts of the product at the discounted price and sell it at a profit to others. Price differentials between groups erode if reselling is easy.

WHY DOES PRICE DISCRIMINATION EXIST?

Price discrimination results from the profit-maximization motive. Our graphical analysis of monopoly described the demand curve for the product and the corresponding marginal revenue curve. Sometimes, however, different groups of people have different demand curves and therefore react differently to price changes. A producer can make more money by charging these different buyers different prices. For example, if the price of a movie ticket is increased from $7 to $10, many kids who would attend at $7 may have to stay home at $10, as they (and perhaps their parents) balk at paying the higher price. The impact of raising prices on attendance may be less,

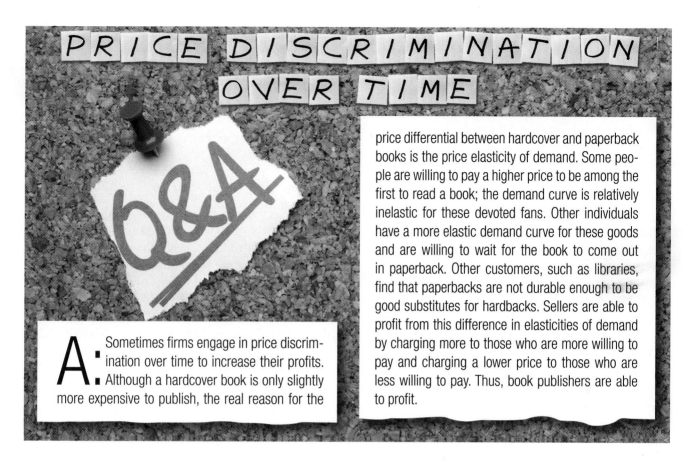

PRICE DISCRIMINATION OVER TIME

Q&A

A: Sometimes firms engage in price discrimination over time to increase their profits. Although a hardcover book is only slightly more expensive to publish, the real reason for the price differential between hardcover and paperback books is the price elasticity of demand. Some people are willing to pay a higher price to be among the first to read a book; the demand curve is relatively inelastic for these devoted fans. Other individuals have a more elastic demand curve for these goods and are willing to wait for the book to come out in paperback. Other customers, such as libraries, find that paperbacks are not durable enough to be good substitutes for hardbacks. Sellers are able to profit from this difference in elasticities of demand by charging more to those who are more willing to pay and charging a lower price to those who are less willing to pay. Thus, book publishers are able to profit.

however, for adults, who have higher incomes in the first place and for whom the ticket price may represent a smaller part of the expenses of an evening out.

Thus, a different demand curve applies for those, say, under 2, as opposed to those who are older. Specifically, the elasticity of demand with respect to price is greater for children than for adults, meaning that the demand and marginal revenue curves for children are different from the curves for adults. Assume, for simplicity, that the marginal cost is constant. The profit-maximizing movie theater owner will price where the constant marginal costs equal marginal revenue for each group. As you can see in Exhibit 8.14(a), the demand curve for children is relatively elastic—firms will charge these customers a lower price. The adult demand curve, shown in Exhibit 8.14(b), is less elastic; firms will charge adult customers a higher price. But in order for price discrimination to be feasible, the seller must be able to successfully distinguish members of targeted groups.

EXAMPLES OF PRICE DISCRIMINATION

Other examples of price discrimination in the United States are plentiful. Here are just a few.

EXHIBIT 8.14 Price Discrimination in Movie Ticket Prices

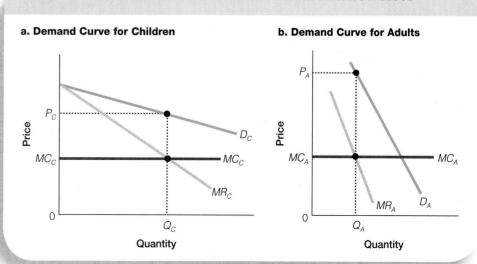

a. Demand Curve for Children

b. Demand Curve for Adults

Airline Tickets

Seats on airplanes usually go for different prices. Airlines sell high-priced, no-strings-attached fares, and they sell restricted fares—tickets that require Saturday night layovers or must be purchased weeks in advance. This airline pricing strategy allows the airlines to discriminate against business travelers, who usually have little advance warning, travel on the weekdays, and are not as willing to spend their weekends away from home and family. Because business travelers have a high willingness to pay (a relatively inelastic demand curve), the airlines can charge them higher prices. If the airlines were to cut prices for these clients, their revenues would fall. On the other hand, the personal traveler (perhaps a vacationer) can choose among many substitutes, such as other modes of transportation and different times. In short, the personal traveler has a lower willingness to pay (a relatively elastic demand curve). Thus, the airlines can clearly make more money by charging a higher price to those who have a higher willingness to pay (less elastic demand) and a lower price to those who have a lower willingness to pay (more elastic demand)—those who are willing to book in advance and stay over on Saturday nights. If the airlines charged a higher single price to everyone, those with a lower willingness to pay would not travel; if they charged a lower single price to everyone, they would lose profits by receiving less revenue from those who were willing to pay more.

Coupons

The key to price discrimination is observing the difference in demand curves for different customers. The coupon cutter, who spends an hour looking through the Sunday paper for coupons, will probably have a relatively more elastic demand curve than, say, a busy and wealthy physician or executive. Consequently, firms charge a lower price to customers with a lower willingness to pay (more elastic demand)—the coupon cutter—and a higher price to those who don't use coupons (less elastic demand).

College and University Tuition

Another example of price discrimination is the financial aid packages given by many colleges and universities. That is, even though colleges do not charge different tuitions to different students, they do offer different financial aid packages. Furthermore, to receive financial aid, parents must disclose their family income and wealth. In short, students who are well off financially tend to pay more for their education than do students who are less well off.

Quantity Discounts

Another form of price discrimination occurs when customers buy in large quantities, as with public utilities and wholesalers. But even stores will sell a six-pack of soda for less than six single cans. For example, the local bagel shop might sell you a baker's dozen, where you get 13 bagels for the price of 12. This type of price discrimination allows the producer to charge a higher price for the first unit than for, say, the 20th. This form of price discrimination is effective because a buyer's willingness to pay declines as additional units are purchased.

SECTION CHECK 6

6.1 When producers charge different prices for the same good or service when no cost difference exists, it is called price discrimination.

6.2 Price discrimination occurs if demand differs among buyers and the seller can successfully identify group members, because producers can make profits by charging different prices to each group.

6.3 Price discrimination would not work well if the person buying the product could easily resell the product to another customer at a higher profitable price.

Chapter 8: Self-Review

Now that you're finished reading the chapter, review the questions below. You can write your answers in the space provided, then go online to see the answers at www.cengagebrain.com.

S1—MONOPOLY: THE PRICE MAKER

1. Why does monopoly depend on the existence of barriers to entry?

2. Why is a pure monopoly a rarity?

3. Which of the following could be considered a monopoly?
   a. Kate Hudson (an actress)
   b. De Beers diamond company
   c. the only doctor in a small town
   d. Ford Motor Company

S2—DEMAND AND MARGINAL REVENUE IN MONOPOLY

4. Fill-in-the-Blank: The market and firm demand curves are _____ for a monopolist.

5. Why is a monopoly a price maker, but a perfectly competitive firm a price taker?

6. True or False: Marginal revenue is less than price for a profit-maximizing monopolist.

S3—THE MONOPOLIST'S EQUILIBRIUM

7. How do you find the profit-maximizing price for a monopolist?

8. True or False: A monopolist cannot earn positive economic profits in the long run.

S4—MONOPOLY AND WELFARE LOSS

9. How is the welfare cost of monopoly measured?

10. How can economies of scale lead to monopoly?

S5—MONOPOLY POLICY

11. True or False: Antitrust laws promote greater price competition.

12. What are some difficulties encountered when regulators try to implement average cost pricing for natural monopolies?

S6—PRICE DISCRIMINATION

13. Why is it generally easier to price discriminate for services than for goods?

14. How can offering quantity discounts increase a producer's profits?

What kind of market do you think

the coffee market is in which McDonald's and Starbucks compete? Obviously these firms aren't the only coffee sellers out there. And McDonald's had little difficulty getting into the market when it introduced its new McCafé coffee line. Sounds like a competitive market, right? But are they really selling the same product? Think about their prices. And what about the atmosphere of their stores? Do you associate the same ideas with their different brands? Perhaps this market doesn't quite fit the perfectly competitive mold.

© CLARO CORTES/REUTERS/LANDOV

9

Monopolistic Competition and Oligopoly

restaurants, clothing stores, beauty salons, video stores, hardware stores, and coffee houses have elements of both competitive and monopoly markets. Recall that the perfectly competitive model includes many buyers and sellers; coffee houses can be found in almost every town in the country. You can even find Starbucks in Barnes & Noble bookstores and in grocery stores. In addition, the barriers to entry of owning an individual coffee shop are relatively low. However, monopolistically competitive firms sell a differentiated product and thus each firm has an element of monopoly power. Each coffee store is different. It might be different because of its location or décor. It might be different because of its products. It might be different because of the service it provides. Monopolistically competitive markets are common in the real world. They are the topic of this chapter.

ⓢ1 Monopolistic Competition

Keep the following questions in mind as you read through this section. You'll find the answers in Section Check 1.

1.1 What are the distinguishing features of monopolistic competition?

1.2 How can a firm differentiate its product?

Monopolistic competition is a market structure in which many producers of somewhat different products compete with one another. For example, a restaurant is a monopoly in the sense that it has a unique name, menu, quality of service, location, and so on; but it also has many competitors—others selling prepared meals. That is, monopolistic competition has features in common with both monopoly and perfect competition, even though this explanation may sound like an oxymoron—like "jumbo shrimp" or "civil war." As with monopoly, individual sellers in monopolistic competition believe that they have some market power.

> **monopolistic competition** a market structure with many firms selling differentiated products

Sections in Chapter 9

But monopolistic competition is probably closer to competition than monopoly. Entry into and exit out of the industry is unrestricted, and consequently, the industry has many independent sellers. In virtue of the relatively free entry of new firms, the long-run price and output behavior, and zero long-run economic profits, monopolistic competition is similar to perfect competition. However, the monopolistically competitive firm produces a product that is different (that is, *differentiated* rather than identical or homogeneous) from others, which leads to some degree of monopoly power. In a sense, sellers in a monopolistically competitive market may be regarded as "monopolists" of their own particular brands; but unlike firms with a true monopoly, competition occurs among the many firms selling similar (but not identical) brands. For example, a buyer living in a city of moderate size and in the market for books, CDs, toothpaste, furniture, shampoo, video rentals, restaurants, eyeglasses, running shoes, movie theaters, super markets, and music lessons has many competing sellers from which to choose.

THE THREE BASIC CHARACTERISTICS OF MONOPOLISTIC COMPETITION

The theory of monopolistic competition is based on three characteristics: (1) product differentiation, (2) many sellers, and (3) free entry.

Product Differentiation

One characteristic of monopolistic competition is **product differentiation**—the accentuation of unique product qualities, real or perceived, to develop a specific product identity.

The significant feature of differentiation is the buyer's belief that various sellers' products are not the same, whether the products are actually different or not. Aspirin and some brands of over-the-counter cold medicines are examples of products that are similar or identical but have different brand names. Product differentiation leads to preferences among buyers dealing with or purchasing the products of particular sellers.

Physical Differences Physical differences constitute a primary source of product differentiation. For

example, brands of ice cream (such as Dreyer's and Breyers), running shoes (such as Nike and Asics), or fast-food Mexican restaurants (such as Taco Bell and Del Taco) differ significantly in taste to many buyers.

Prestige Prestige considerations also differentiate products to a significant degree. Many people prefer to be seen using the currently popular brand, while others prefer the "off" brand. Prestige considerations are particularly important with gifts—Cuban cigars, Montblanc pens, beluga caviar, Godiva chocolates, Dom Perignon champagne, Rolex watches, and so on.

Location Location is a major differentiating factor in retailing. Shoppers are not willing to travel long distances to purchase similar items, which is one reason for the large number of convenience stores and service station mini-marts. Most buyers realize brands of gasoline do not differ significantly, which means the location of a gas station might influence their choice of gasoline. Location is also important for restaurants. Some restaurants can differentiate their products with beautiful views of the city lights, ocean, or mountains.

Service Service considerations are likewise significant for product differentiation. Speedy and friendly service or lenient return policies are important to many people. Likewise, speed and quality of service may significantly influence a person's choice of restaurants.

The Impact of Many Sellers

When many firms compete for the same customers, any particular firm has little control over or interest in what other firms do. That is, a restaurant may change prices or improve service without a retaliatory move on the part of other competing restaurants, because the time and effort necessary to learn about such changes may have marginal costs that are greater than the marginal benefits.

The Significance of Free Entry

Entry in monopolistic competition is relatively unrestricted in the sense that new firms may easily start the production of close substitutes for existing products, as happens with restaurants, styling salons, barber shops, and many forms of retail activity. Because of relatively free entry, economic profits tend to be eliminated in the long run, as is the case with perfect competition.

Characteristics of Monopolistic Competition
1) product differentiation
2) many sellers
3) free entry

ⓢ2 Price and Output Determination in Monopolistic Competition

Keep the following questions in mind as you read through this section. You'll find the answers in Section Check 2.

2.1 How are short-run economic profits and losses determined?

2.2 How is long-run equilibrium determined?

In this section we'll discuss the factors that determine price and output in monopolistic competition. We'll begin by looking at short-run equilibrium.

DETERMINING SHORT-RUN EQUILIBRIUM

Because monopolistically competitive sellers are price makers rather than price takers, they do not regard price as a given by market conditions as perfectly competitive firms do.

The cost and revenue curves of a typical seller are shown in Exhibit 9.1; the intersection of the marginal revenue and marginal cost curves indicates that the short-run profit-maximizing output will be q^*. Now, by observing how much will be demanded at that output level, we find our profit-maximizing price, P^*. That is, at the equilibrium quantity, q^*, we go vertically to the demand curve and read the corresponding price on the vertical axis, P^*.

Three-Step Method for Monopolistic Competition

Let us return to the same three-step method we used in Chapters 7 and 8. Determining whether a firm is generating economic profits, economic losses, or zero economic profits at the profit-maximizing level of output, q^*, can be done in three easy steps.

1. Find where marginal revenues equal marginal costs and proceed straight down to the horizontal quantity axis to find q^*, the profit-maximizing output level.

EXHIBIT 9.1 Short-Run Equilibrium in Monopolistic Competition

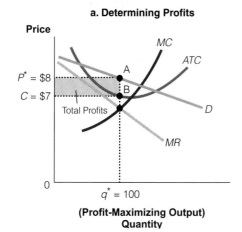

a. Determining Profits

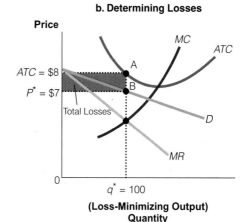

b. Determining Losses

2. At q^*, go straight up to the demand curve then to the left to find the market price, P^*. Once you have identified P^* and q^*, you can find total revenue at the profit-maximizing output level, because $TR = P \times q$.

3. The last step is to find total costs. Again, go straight up from q^* to the average total cost (ATC) curve then left to the vertical axis to compute the average total cost *per unit*. If we multiply average total costs by the output level, we can find the total costs ($TC = ATC \times q$).

If total revenue is greater than total costs at q^*, the firm is generating total economic profits. And if total revenue is less than total costs at q^*, the firm is generating total economic losses.

Or, if we take the product price at P^* and subtract the average cost at q^*, this will give us per-unit profit. If we multiply this by output, we will arrive at total economic profit, that is, $(P^* - ATC) \times q^* = $ total profit.

Remember, the cost curves include implicit and explicit costs—that is, even at zero economic profits the firm is covering the total opportunity costs of its resources and earning a normal profit or rate of return.

SHORT-RUN PROFITS AND LOSSES IN MONOPOLISTIC COMPETITION

Exhibit 9.1(a) shows the equilibrium position of a monopolistically competitive firm. As we just discussed, the firm produces where $MC = MR$, or output q^*. At output q^* and price P^*, the firm's total revenue is equal to $P^* \times q^*$, or \$800. At output q^*, the firm's total cost is $ATC \times q^*$, or \$700. In Exhibit 9.1(a), we see that total revenue is greater than total cost so the firm has a total economic profit. That is, $TR - TC$ (\$800 − \$700) or $P^* - ATC \times q^*$ ([\$8 − \$7] $\times$ 100) = total economic profit (\$100).

In Exhibit 9.1(b), at q^*, price is below average total cost, so the firm is minimizing its economic loss. At q^*, total cost (\$800) is greater than total revenue (\$700). So the firm incurs a total loss (\$100) or $(P^* - ATC) \times q^* = $ total economic losses ([\$7 − \$8] $\times$ 100 = −\$100).

DETERMINING LONG-RUN EQUILIBRIUM

The short-run equilibrium situation, whether involving profits or losses, will probably not last long, because entry and exit occur in the long run. If market entry and exit are sufficiently free, new firms will have an incentive to enter

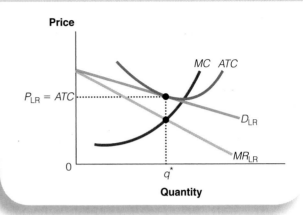

EXHIBIT 9.2 Long-Run Equilibrium for a Monopolistically Competitive Firm

the market when there are economic profits, and exit when there are economic losses.

ACHIEVING LONG-RUN EQUILIBRIUM

Long-run equilibrium will occur when demand is equal to average total costs for each firm at a level of output at which each firm's demand curve is just tangent to its ATC curve. The point of tangency will always occur at the same level of output as that at which marginal cost is equal to marginal revenue, as seen in Exhibit 9.2. At this equilibrium point, there are zero economic profits and there are no incentives for firms to either enter or exit the industry. Notice that the point of tangency and the point where $MR = MC$ is at the same quantity, q^*. This is not a coincidence. It occurs because at q^* the firm is maximizing profit and that maximum profit is equal to zero in the long run.

© MARCUS LINDSTROM/ISTOCKPHOTO.COM

If market entry and exit are sufficiently free, new firms have incentive to enter the market when there are economic profits.

ⓢ3 Monopolistic Competition versus Perfect Competition

Keep the following questions in mind as you read through this section. You'll find the answers in Section Check 3.

3.1 What are the differences and similarities between monopolistic competition and perfect competition?

3.2 Why does the monopolistically competitive firm fail to meet productive efficiency?

3.3 Why does the monopolistically competitive firm fail to meet allocative efficiency?

We have seen that both monopolistic competition and perfect competition have many buyers and sellers and relatively free entry. However, product differentiation enables a monopolistic competitor to have some influence over price. Consequently, a monopolistically competitive firm has a downward-sloping demand curve, but because of the large number of good substitutes for its product, the curve tends to be much more elastic than the demand curve for a monopolist.

THE SIGNIFICANCE OF EXCESS CAPACITY

Because the demand curve is downward sloping in monopolistic competition, its point of tangency with the *ATC* curve will not and cannot be at the lowest level of average cost. What does this statement mean? It means that even when long-run adjustments are complete, firms are not operating at a level that permits the lowest average cost of production—the efficient scale of the firm. The existing plant, even though optimal for the equilibrium volume of output, is not used to capacity; that is, **excess capacity** exists at that level of output. Excess capacity occurs when the firm produces below the level where average total cost is minimized.

Unlike a perfectly competitive firm, a monopolistically competitive firm could increase output and lower its average total cost, as shown in Exhibit 9.3(a) on the next page. However, any attempt to increase output to attain lower average cost would be unprofitable, because the price reduction necessary to sell the greater output would cause marginal revenue to fall below the marginal cost of the increased output. As we can see in Exhibit 9.3(a), to the right of q^*, marginal cost is greater than marginal revenue. Consequently, in monopolistic competition, the tendency is too many firms in the industry, each producing a volume of output less than what would allow lowest cost. Economists call this tendency a failure to reach productive efficiency. For example, the market may have too many grocery stores or too many service stations, in the sense that if the total volume of business were concentrated in a smaller number of sellers, average cost, and thus price, could in principle be less.

FAILING TO MEET ALLOCATIVE EFFICIENCY, TOO

Productive inefficiency is not the only problem with a monopolistically competitive firm. Exhibit 9.3(a) shows a firm that is not operating where price is equal to marginal costs. In the monopolistically competitive model, at the intersection of the *MC* and *MR* curves (q^*), we can clearly see that price is greater than marginal cost. Society is willing to pay more for the product (the price, P^*) than it costs society to produce it (*MC* at q^*). In this case, the firm is failing to reach allocative efficiency, where price equals marginal cost. Because the price is greater than the marginal cost, it would be profitable for the

excess capacity occurs when the firm produces below the level at which average total cost is minimized

EXHIBIT 9.3 Comparing Long-Run Perfect Competition and Monopolistic Competition

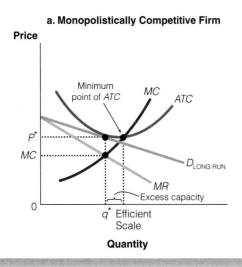

a. Monopolistically Competitive Firm

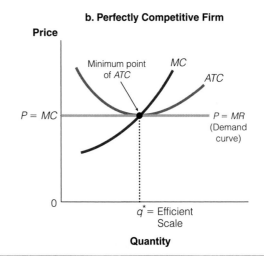

b. Perfectly Competitive Firm

monopolistically competitive firm to sell to another customer. If it were a perfectly competitive firm, it would not care because price is equal to marginal cost and the extra profit from another customer would be zero.

In short, firms are not producing at the minimum point of ATC, failing to meet productive efficiency; and they are not charging a price equal to marginal cost, failing to meet allocative efficiency. Note that in Exhibit 9.3(b), the perfectly competitive firm has reached both productive efficiency ($P = ATC$ at the minimum point on the ATC curve) and allocative efficiency ($P = MC$).

Critics of monopolistic competition state that there are too many firms producing too little output at inflated prices, therefore inefficiently using society's scarce resources. For example, there are often many restaurants with empty tables and idle cooks and servers. Their resources are underutilized. If there were fewer restaurants, each would produce a greater output at a lower price, but fewer restaurants would mean fewer choices in terms of location, ambience, quality, and so on. The same excess capacity is seen in retail gas stations—often gas station islands are unoccupied.

However, in defense of monopolistic competition, the higher average cost and the slightly higher price and lower output may simply be the price firms pay for differentiated products—variety. That is, just because monopolistically competitive firms have not met the conditions for productive and allocative efficiency, it is not obvious that society is not better off.

WHAT ARE THE REAL COSTS OF MONOPOLISTIC COMPETITION?

We just argued that perfect competition meets the tests of allocative and productive efficiency and that monopolistic competition does not. Can we "fix" a monopolistically competitive firm to look more like an efficient, perfectly competitive firm? One remedy might entail using government regulation, as in the case of a natural monopoly. However, this process would be costly because a monopolistically competitive firm makes no economic profits in the long run. Therefore, asking monopolistically competitive firms to equate price and marginal cost would lead to economic losses, because long-run average total cost would be greater than price at $P = MC$. Consequently, the government would have to subsidize the firm. Living with the inefficiencies in monopolistically competitive markets might be easier than coping with the difficulties entailed by regulations and the cost of the necessary subsidies.

We argued that the monopolistically competitive firm does not operate at the minimum point of the ATC curve, whereas the perfectly competitive firm does. However, is this comparison fair? A monopolistic competition involves differentiated goods and services, whereas a perfect competition does not. In other words, the excess capacity that exists in monopolistic competition is the price we pay for product differentiation. Have you ever thought about the many restaurants, movies, and gasoline stations that have "excess capacity"? Can you imagine a world where all firms were working at full capacity? After all, choice is a good, and most of us value some choice.

In short, the inefficiency of monopolistic competition is a result of product differentiation. Because consumers value variety—the ability to choose from competing products and brands—the loss in efficiency must be weighed against the gain in increased product variety. The gains from product diversity can be large and may easily outweigh the inefficiency associated with a downward-sloping demand curve. Remember, firms differentiate their products to meet consumers' demand.

SECTION CHECK 3

3.1 Both the competitive firm and the monopolistically competitive firm may earn short-run economic profits, but these profits will be eliminated in the long run.

3.2 Because monopolistically competitive firms face a downward-sloping demand curve, average total cost is not minimized in the long run, after entry and exit have eliminated profits. Monopolistically competitive firms fail to reach productive efficiency, producing at output levels less than the efficient output.

3.3 The monopolistically competitive firm does not achieve allocative efficiency, because it does not operate where the price is equal to marginal costs, which means that society is willing to pay more for additional output than it costs society to produce additional output.

Ⓢ4 Oligopoly

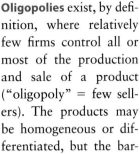

Keep the following questions in mind as you read through this section, and review the answers in **Section Check 4**.

4.1 What is oligopoly?

4.2 What is mutual interdependence?

4.3 Are economies of scale a major barrier to entry?

Oligopolies exist, by definition, where relatively few firms control all or most of the production and sale of a product ("oligopoly" = few sellers). The products may be homogeneous or differentiated, but the barriers to entry are often high, which makes it difficult for firms to enter into the industry. Consequently, long-run economic profits may be earned by firms in the industry.

> **oligopoly** a market structure in which relatively few firms control all or most of the production and sale of a product
>
> **mutual interdependence** when a firm shapes its policy with an eye to the policies of competing firms

Examples of oligopolistic markets include commercial airlines, oil, automobiles, steel, breakfast cereals, computers, cigarettes, tobacco, and sports drinks. In all of these instances, the market is dominated by anywhere from a few to several big companies, although they may have many different brands (e.g., General Motors, General Foods, and Apple Computers). In this chapter, we will learn about the unique characteristics of firms in this industry.

MUTUAL INTERDEPENDENCE

Oligopoly is characterized by **mutual interdependence** among firms; that is, each firm shapes its policy with an eye to the policies of competing firms. Oligopolists must strategize, much like good chess or bridge players who are constantly observing and anticipating the moves of their rivals. Oligopoly is likely to occur whenever the number of firms in an industry is so small that any change in output or price by one firm appreciably impacts the sales of competing firms. In this situation, it is almost inevitable that competitors will respond directly to these actions in determining their own policies.

WHY DO OLIGOPOLIES EXIST?

Primarily, oligopoly is a result of the relationship between the technological conditions of production and potential sales volume. For many products, a firm cannot obtain a reasonably low cost of production unless it is producing a large fraction of the market output. In other words, substantial economies of scale are present in oligopoly markets. Automobile and steel production are classic examples of this. Because of legal concerns such as patents, large start-up costs, and the presence of pronounced economies of scale, the barriers to entry are quite high in oligopoly.

MEASURING INDUSTRY CONCENTRATION

The extent of oligopoly power in various industries can be measured by means of concentration ratios. A concentration ratio indicates the proportion of total industry shipments (sales) of goods produced by a specified number of the largest firms in the industry, or the proportion of total industry assets held by these largest firms. We can use four-firm or eight-firm concentration ratios; most often, concentration ratios are for the four largest firms.

The extent of oligopoly power is indicated by the four-firm concentration ratio for the United States shown in Exhibit 9.4. Note that for breakfast cereals, to take an example, the four largest firms produce 87 percent of all breakfast cereals produced in the United States. Concentration ratios of 70 to 100 percent are common in oligopolies. That is, a high concentration ratio means that a few sellers dominate the market.

Concentration ratios, however, are not a perfect guide to industry concentration. One problem is that they do not take into consideration foreign competition. For example, the U.S. auto industry is highly concentrated but faces stiff competition from foreign automobile producers. The same is true for motorcycles and bicycles.

EXHIBIT 9.4 Four-Firm Concentration Ratios, U.S. Manufacturing

Industry	Share of Value of Shipments by the Top Four Firms (%)
Breweries	90.8
Electric light bulbs	89.6
Tobacco products	88.3
Refrigerators	84.5
Small arms ammunition	83.0
Motor vehicles	81.2
Aircraft	80.7
Breakfast cereals	78.4
Tires	72.9
Motorcycles and bicycles	67
Soaps, detergents	63.1
Lawn and garden equipment	61.6
Coffee and tea	51.6

SOURCE: U.S. Census Bureau, 2002 Economic Census, Concentration Ratios, 2002. Washington, D.C. (Issued May, 2006). Available at http://www.census.gov/epcd/www/concentration.html, (accessed April, 16, 2010).

ECONOMIES OF SCALE AS A BARRIER TO ENTRY

Economies of large-scale production make operation on a small scale during a new firm's early years extremely unprofitable. A firm cannot build up a large market overnight; in the interim, average total cost is so high that losses are heavy. Recognition of this fact discourages new firms from entering the market, as illustrated in Exhibit 9.5. We can see that if an automobile company produces quantity Q_{LARGE} rather than Q_{SMALL}, it will be able to produce cars at a significantly lower cost. If the average total cost to a potential entrant is equivalent to point A on the *ATC* curve and the price of automobiles is less than P_1, a new firm would be deterred from entering the industry.

EQUILIBRIUM PRICE AND QUANTITY IN OLIGOPOLY

It is difficult to predict how firms will react in situations of mutual interdependence. No firm knows what its

The barriers to entry in the auto industry are formidable. A new entrant would have to start out as a large producer investing billions of dollars in plants, equipment, and advertising to compete with existing firms.

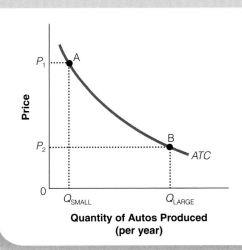

EXHIBIT 9.5 Economies of Scale as a Barrier to Entry

demand curve looks like with any degree of certainty, and therefore it has a limited knowledge of its marginal revenue curve. To know anything about its demand curve, the firm must know how other firms will react to its prices and other policies. In the absence of additional assumptions, then, equating marginal revenue and expected marginal cost is relegated to guesswork. Thus, it is difficult for an oligopolist to determine its profit-maximizing price and output.

SECTION CHECK 4

4.1 Oligopolies exist where relatively few firms control all or most of the production and sale of a product. The products may be homogeneous or differentiated, but the barriers to entry are often very high and, consequently, they may be able to realize long-run economic profits.

4.2 When firms are mutually interdependent, each firm shapes its policy with an eye to the policies of competing firms.

4.3 Economies of large-scale production make operation on a small scale extremely unprofitable. Recognition of this fact discourages new firms from entering the market.

ⓢ5 Collusion and Cartels

Consider the following questions as you read through this section. You'll find the answers in **Section Check 5**.

5.1 Why do firms collude?

5.2 Why does collusion break down?

5.3 How can existing firms deter potential entrants?

The uncertainties of pricing decisions are substantial in oligopoly. The implications of misjudging the behavior of competitors could prove to be disastrous. An executive who makes the wrong pricing move may force the firm to lose sales or, at a minimum, be forced himself to back down in an embarrassing fashion from an announced price increase. Because of this uncertainty, some believe that oligopolists change their prices less frequently than perfect competitors, whose prices may change almost continually. The empirical evidence, however, does not clearly indicate that prices are in fact always slow to change in oligopoly situations.

COLLUSION

Because the actions and profits of oligopolists are so dominated by mutual interdependence, the temptation is great for firms to **collude**—to get together and agree to act jointly in pricing and other matters. If firms believe they can increase their profits by coordinating their actions, they will be tempted to collude. Collusion reduces uncertainty and increases the potential for economic profits. From society's point of view, collusion creates a situation in which goods very likely become overpriced and underproduced, with consumers losing out as the result of a misallocation of resources.

JOINT PROFIT MAXIMIZATION

Agreements between or among firms on sales, pricing, and other decisions are usually referred to as cartel agreements. A **cartel** is a collection of firms making an agreement.

Cartels may lead to what economists call

collude when firms act together to restrict competition

cartel a collection of firms that agree on sales, pricing, and other decisions

joint profit maximization determination of price based on the marginal revenue derived from the market demand schedule and marginal cost schedule of the firms in the industry

joint profit maximization: Price is based on the marginal revenue function, which is derived from the product's total (or market) demand schedule and the various firms' marginal cost schedules, as shown in Exhibit 9.6. With outright agreements—necessarily secret because of antitrust laws (in the United States, at least)—firms that make up the market will attempt to estimate demand and cost schedules and then set optimum price and output levels accordingly.

Equilibrium price and quantity for a collusive oligopoly are determined according to the intersection of the marginal revenue curve (derived from the market demand curve) and the horizontal sum of the short-run marginal cost curves for the oligopolists. As shown in Exhibit 9.6, the resulting equilibrium quantity is Q^* and the equilibrium price is P^*. Collusion facilitates joint profit maximization for the oligopoly. If the oligopoly is maintained in the long run, it charges a higher price, produces less output, and fails to maximize social welfare, relative to perfect competition, because $P^* > MC$ at Q^*.

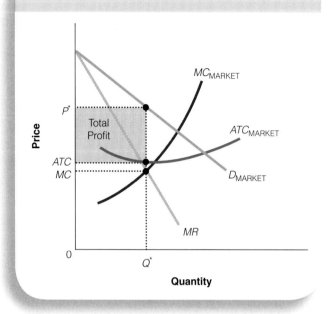

EXHIBIT 9.6 Collusion in Oligopoly

The manner in which total profits are shared among firms in the industry depends in part on the relative costs and sales of the various firms. Firms with low costs and large supply capabilities will obtain the largest profits, because they have greater bargaining power. Sales, in turn, may depend in large measure on consumer preferences for various brands if there is product differentiation. With outright collusion, firms may agree on market shares and the division of profits. The division of total profits will depend on the relative bargaining strength of each firm, influenced by its relative financial strength, ability to inflict damage (through price wars) on other firms if an agreement is not reached, ability to withstand similar actions on the part of other firms, relative costs, consumer preferences, and bargaining skills.

WHY ARE MOST COLLUSIVE OLIGOPOLIES SHORT LIVED?

Collusive oligopolies are potentially highly profitable for participants but detrimental to society. Fortunately, most strong collusive oligopolies are rather short lived for two reasons. First, in the United States and in some other nations, collusive oligopolies are strictly illegal under antitrust laws. Second, for collusion to work, firms must agree to restrict output to a level that will support the profit-maximizing price. At that price, firms can earn positive economic profits. Yet a great temptation is for firms to cheat on the agreement of the collusive oligopoly; and because collusive agreements are

Recent examples of collusion (price fixing) have occurred in a wide range of industries, from art auctions to tomatoes, paint to vitamins, and cars to LCD panels.

illegal, the other parties have no way to punish the offender. Why do they have a strong incentive to cheat? Because any individual firm could lower its price slightly and thereby increase sales and profits, as long as it goes undetected. Undetected price cuts could bring in new customers, including rivals' customers. In addition, non-price methods of defection include better credit terms, rebates, prompt delivery service, and so on.

PRICE LEADERSHIP

Over time, an implied understanding may develop in an oligopoly market that a large firm is the **price leader**, sending a signal to competitors, perhaps through a press release, that they have increased their prices. This approach is not outright collusion because no formal cartel arrangement or formal meetings are used to determine price and output, but this is what is called tacit collusion. Any competitor that goes along with the pricing decision of the price leader is called a **price follower**.

Price leadership is most likely to develop when one firm, the so-called dominant firm, produces a large portion of the total output. The dominant firm sets the price that maximizes its profits, and the smaller firms, which would have little influence over price anyway, act as if they are perfect competitors and sell all they want at that price. In the past, a number of firms have been price leaders: U.S. Steel and Bethlehem Steel, RJ Reynolds (tobacco), General Motors (automobiles), Kellogg's (breakfast cereals), and Goodyear (tires). In the banking industry, various dominant banks have taken turns being the dominant firm in announcing changes in the prime interest rate—the interest rate that banks charge large corporate clients. Because the prime rate is widely cited in newspapers, it makes it easy for other banks to follow the lead and avoid frequent changes and competitive warfare.

> **price leader** a large firm in an oligopoly that unilaterally makes changes in its product prices that competitors tend to follow
>
> **price follower** a competitor in an oligopoly that goes along with the pricing decision of the price leader
>
> **price leadership** when a dominant firm that produces a large portion of the industry's output sets a price that maximizes its profits, and other firms follow

WHAT HAPPENS IN THE LONG RUN IF ENTRY IS EASY?

Mutual interdependence is, in itself, no guarantee of economic profits, even if the firms in the industry succeed in maximizing joint profits. The extent to which economic profits disappear depends on the ease with which new firms can enter the industry. When entry is easy, excess profits attract newcomers. New firms may break down existing price agreements by undercutting prices in an attempt to establish themselves in the industry. In response, older firms may reduce prices to avoid excessive sales losses; as a result, the general level of prices will begin to approach average total cost.

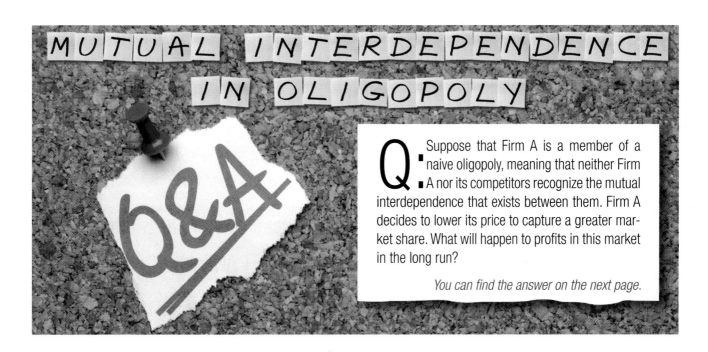

MUTUAL INTERDEPENDENCE IN OLIGOPOLY

Q: Suppose that Firm A is a member of a naive oligopoly, meaning that neither Firm A nor its competitors recognize the mutual interdependence that exists between them. Firm A decides to lower its price to capture a greater market share. What will happen to profits in this market in the long run?

You can find the answer on the next page.

MUTUAL INTERDEPENDENCE IN OLIGOPOLY

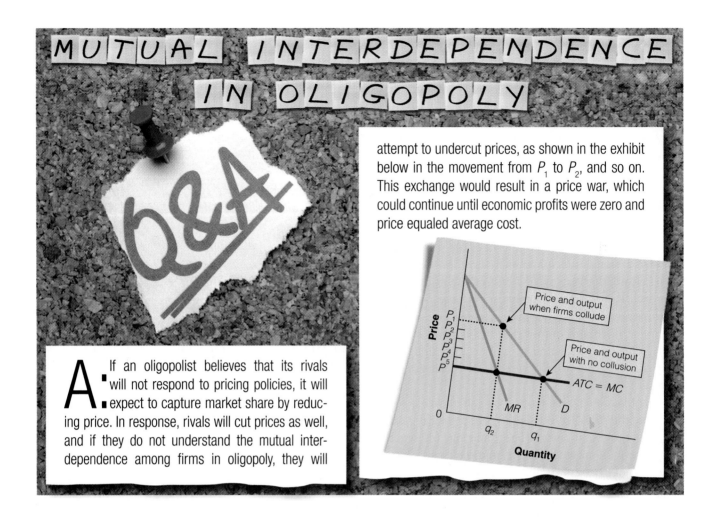

attempt to undercut prices, as shown in the exhibit below in the movement from P_1 to P_2, and so on. This exchange would result in a price war, which could continue until economic profits were zero and price equaled average cost.

A: If an oligopolist believes that its rivals will not respond to pricing policies, it will expect to capture market share by reducing price. In response, rivals will cut prices as well, and if they do not understand the mutual interdependence among firms in oligopoly, they will

HOW DO OLIGOPOLISTS DETER MARKET ENTRY?

If most firms reach a scale of plant and firm size great enough to allow lowest-cost operation, their long-run positions will be similar to that shown in Exhibit 9.7. To simplify, we have drawn MC and ATC constant. The equilibrium, or profit-maximizing, price in an established oligopoly is represented by P^*. Typically, the rate of profit in these industries is high, which would encourage entry. However, empirical research indicates that oligopolists often initiate pricing policies that reduce the entry incentive for new firms. Established firms may deliberately hold prices below the maximum profit point at P^*, charging a price of, say, P_1. This lower-than-profit-maximizing price may discourage newcomers from entering. Because new firms would likely have higher costs than existing firms, the lower price may not be high enough to cover their costs. However, once the threat of entry subsides, the market price may return to the profit-maximizing price, P^*.

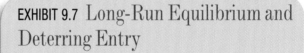

EXHIBIT 9.7 Long-Run Equilibrium and Deterring Entry

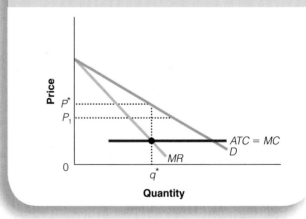

ANTITRUST AND MERGERS

In the beginning of this chapter, we introduced a method for determining an industry's market structure called a concentration ratio. However, the Justice Department and the Federal Trade Commission (FTC) both prefer to use a measure called the Herfindahl-Hirshman Index (HHI). The HHI is measured by taking the square for each firm's share of market sales summed over the firms in the industry. For example, if the industry has three firms and their market share is 50 percent, 30 percent, and 20 percent, respectively, the HHI would be:

$$HHI = 50^2 + 30^2 + 20^2 = 3,800$$

By squaring, the HHI produces a much larger number when the industry is dominated by a few firms. According to the Justice Department, an HHI below 1,000 is very competitive, an HHI between 1,000 and 1,800 is somewhat competitive, and an HHI over 1,800 indicates an oligopoly. The HHI takes into account the relative size and distribution of the firms in a market. The HHI is lowest when a market consists of a large number of firms of relatively equal size. The HHI increases both as the number of firms in the market decreases and as the disparity in size between those firms increases.

A potential merger resulting in an HHI over 1,000 will receive close scrutiny. In 2007, for example, Whole Foods made a takeover bid for Wild Oats. Both were organic grocery stores. The FTC argued that the takeover would increase prices and limit competition in the organic food market. Whole Foods argued that it competes with many grocery stores that carry healthy food and organic products. The merger was eventually completed in August 2007, when a federal appeals court refused to block the deal.

Three Types of Mergers

There are three different types of mergers.

1. A *horizontal merger* combines firms that sell similar products; for example, if Motel 6 merges with Holiday Inn or GM merges with Chrysler.
2. A *vertical merger* combines firms at different stages of production; for example, Pepsi merged with Pizza Hut and Taco Bell. Similarly, a hotel chain may merge with a mattress company.
3. A *conglomerate merger* combines firms in different industries. For example, an automobile company might merge with a pharmaceutical company.

Since vertical mergers are not often a threat to competition, they are not usually subject to antitrust probes. They do not reduce competition in other markets. This is also true of conglomerate mergers—when an auto company merges with a

> Three Types of Mergers
> 1) horizontal
> 2) vertical
> 3) conglomerate

pharmaceutical company, neither increases market share. Most of the antitrust issues occur with horizontal mergers. For example, an attempted merger between Office Depot and Staples was blocked.

predatory pricing setting a price deliberately low in order to drive out competitors

ANTITRUST AND PRICING STRATEGIES

Most economists agree that price fixing should be illegal. However, there are antitrust laws that forbid other types of activities of which the effects are not as obvious: predatory pricing, price discrimination, and tying.

Predatory Pricing

If the price is deliberately kept low (below average variable cost) to drive a competitor out of the market, it is called **predatory pricing**. However, both economists and the courts have a difficult time deciding whether or not a price is truly predatory. Even if the price is driven down below average variable cost (recall from Chapter 7 that when price is below *AVC*, it is the shutdown point of a firm), the courts still have to determine whether the low price destroyed the rival and kept it out of business and whether the firm raised its price to the monopoly level once the rival had been driven out of the industry. Microsoft, American Airlines, and other companies have been accused of predatory pricing, but none of them were convicted because it is so difficult to distinguish predatory pricing from vigorous competition.

Price Discrimination

Price discrimination, as we studied in Chapter 8, is a common pricing strategy for many businesses. It generally does not reduce competition unless it is part of a strategy to block entry or force a competitor out of the market; therefore, it is not normally challenged by antitrust authorities. However, it can be challenged under the Robinson-Patman Act, which places restrictions on allowable price discrimination.

Tying

Tie-in-sales *require* that a customer who buys one product (the tying good) must also buy another product (the tied good) that the customer needs in order to use the first product. Two companies that followed this practice were Xerox and IBM. When Xerox was the largest photocopier producer, they required companies that rented their

game theory firms attempt to maximize profits by acting in ways that minimize damage from competitors

cooperative game collusion by two firms in order to improve their profit maximizations

machines to also buy paper from them. Similarly, IBM required that users of its computers buy IBM computer cards. IBM charged more for the computer cards than other firms would have charged.

Antitrust authorities look for dominant firms that use these types of pricing discrimination policies. For example, the Supreme Court ruled that studios could not force theaters to buy an entire package of films in order to get the rights to show a blockbuster movie. That is, tying a blockbuster movie together with a package of not-so-good B movies could allow studios to expand their market power. To economists, the "jury" is still out on whether various forms of price discrimination really impede competition.

SECTION CHECK 5

5.1 The mutual interdependence of oligopolists tempts them to collude in order to reduce uncertainty and increase potential for economic profits.

5.2 Most strong collusive oligopolies are rather short lived for primarily two reasons: (1) Collusive oligopolies are strictly illegal under U.S. antitrust laws, and (2) there is a great temptation for firms to cheat on the agreement of the collusive oligopoly.

5.3 Firms in an oligopoly may deliberately hold prices below the short-run profit-maximizing point in order to discourage newcomers from entering the market.

Ⓢ6 Game Theory and Strategic Behavior

Consider the following questions as you read through this section. You'll find the answers in **Section Check 6**.

6.1 What is game theory?

6.2 What is a dominant strategy?

6.3 What is Nash equilibrium?

In some respects, noncollusive oligopoly resembles a military campaign or a poker game. Firms take certain actions not because they are necessarily advantageous in themselves but because they improve the position of the oligopolist relative to its competitors and may ultimately improve its financial position. For example, a firm may deliberately cut prices, sacrificing profits either to drive competitors out of business or to discourage them from undertaking actions contrary to the interests of other firms.

WHAT IS GAME THEORY?

Some economists have suggested that the entire approach to oligopoly equilibrium price and output should be recast. They replace the analysis that assumes that firms attempt to maximize profits with one that examines firm behavior in terms of a strategic game. This point of view, called **game theory**, stresses the tendency of various parties in such circumstances to act in a way that minimizes damage from opponents. This approach involves a set of alternative actions (with respect to price and output levels, for example); the action that would be taken in a particular case depends on the specific policies followed by each firm. The firm may try to figure out its competitors' most likely countermoves to its own policies and then formulate alternative defense measures.

Each firm will react to the price, quantity, and quality of rival firms. Because each firm is interdependent, each must observe the moves of its rivals.

Cooperative and Noncooperative Games

Games, in interactions between oligopolists, can either be cooperative or noncooperative. An example of a **cooperative game** would be two firms that decide to collude in order to improve their profit-maximization position. However, as we discussed earlier, enforcement costs are usually too high to keep all firms from cheating on collusive agreements. Consequently, most games are noncooperative **games,** in which each firm sets its own price without consulting other firms. The primary difference between cooperative and noncooperative games is the contract. For example, players in a cooperative game can talk and set binding contracts, while those in noncooperative games are assumed to act independently, with no communication and no binding contracts. Because antitrust laws forbid firms to collude, we will assume that most strategic behavior in the marketplace is noncooperative.

THE PRISONERS' DILEMMA

A firm's decision makers must map out a pricing strategy based on a wide range of information. They must also decide whether their strategy will be effective and whether it will be affected by competitors' actions. A strategy that will be optimal regardless of the opponents' actions is called a **dominant strategy.** A famous game that has a dominant strategy and demonstrates the basic problem confronting noncolluding oligopolists is known as the **prisoners' dilemma.**

Imagine that a bank robbery occurs and two suspects are caught. The suspects are placed in separate cells in the county jail and are not allowed to talk with each other. Four results are possible in this situation: both prisoners confess, neither confesses, Prisoner A confesses but Prisoner B doesn't, or Prisoner B confesses but

noncooperative game each firm sets its own price without consulting other firms

dominant strategy strategy that will be optimal regardless of opponents' actions

prisoners' dilemma the basic problem facing noncolluding oligopolists in maximizing their own profits

payoff matrix a summary of the possible outcomes of various strategies

Prisoner A doesn't. In Exhibit 9.8, we see the **payoff matrix,** which summarizes the possible outcomes from the various strategies. Looking at the payoff matrix, we can see that if both prisoners confess to the crime, each will serve six years in jail. However, if neither confesses, each prisoner may only get one year because of insufficient evidence. Now, if Prisoner A confesses and Prisoner B does not, Prisoner A will go free (because of his cooperation with the authorities and his evidence) and Prisoner B will get ten years. Alternatively, if Prisoner B confesses and Prisoner A does not, Prisoner B will go free and Prisoner A will get ten years. As you can see, then, the prisoners have a dilemma. What should each prisoner do?

Looking at the payoff matrix, we can see that if Prisoner A confesses, it is in the best interest of Prisoner B to confess. If Prisoner A confesses, Prisoner B will get either six years or go free, depending on what Prisoner B does. However, Prisoner B knows the temptation to confess facing Prisoner A, so confessing is also the best strategy for Prisoner B. A confession would mean a lighter sentence for Prisoner B—six years rather than ten years.

It is clear that both would be better off confessing *if* they knew for sure that the other was going to remain silent, because then they would go free. However, in each case, can the prisoner take the chance that

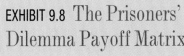

EXHIBIT 9.8 The Prisoners' Dilemma Payoff Matrix

		Prisoner B	
		Confesses	Doesn't Confess
Prisoner A	**Confesses**	6 years (A) / 6 years (B)	goes free (A) / 10 years (B)
	Doesn't Confess	10 years (A) / goes free (B)	1 year (A) / 1 year (B)

the co-conspirator will not talk? The dominant strategy is the best strategy regardless of the strategy of others. In this case, the dominant strategy for Prisoner A is to confess because he would spend less time in jail regardless of whether Prisoner B confesses or remains silent. Confessing is also the dominant strategy for Prisoner B. That is, regardless of what Prisoner A does, Prisoner B can reduce his jail time by confessing. So, the prisoners know that confessing is the way to make the best of a bad situation. No matter what their counterpart does, the maximum sentence will be six years for each, and each understands the possibility of getting out free. In summary, when the prisoners follow their dominant strategy and confess, both will be worse off than if each had remained silent—hence, the "prisoners' dilemma." The dilemma faced by the prisoners is that whatever the other does, each is better off confessing than remaining silent. However, the outcome obtained when both confess is worse for each than the outcome they would have obtained had they both remained silent. That is, we see a conflict between group and individual rationality. When each prisoner independently pursues his or her own self-interest, the two prisoners reach an outcome that is worse for both of them. Could they have avoided this problem if they had made an oath of silence before they were captured? Probably not. Once they are captured, if Prisoner A thinks Prisoner B will keep his promise and remain silent, he will in his own self-interest confess so he can go free. Cooperation is difficult in the prisoners' dilemma.

Firms in oligopoly often behave like the prisoners in the prisoners' dilemma, carefully anticipating the moves of their rivals in an uncertain environment. For example, should a firm cut its prices and try to gain more sales by luring customers away from its competitors? What if the firm keeps its price stable and competitors lower theirs? Or what if the firm and its competitors all lower their prices? What if all of the firms decide to raise their prices? Each of these situations will have vastly different implications for an oligopolist, so it must carefully watch and anticipate the moves of its competitors.

PROFITS UNDER DIFFERENT PRICING STRATEGIES

To demonstrate how the prisoners' dilemma can shed light on oligopoly theory, let us consider the pricing strategy of two firms. In Exhibit 9.9, we present the payoff matrix—the possible profits that each firm would earn under different pricing strategies. Assume that each firm has total production costs of $1 per unit. When both firms set their price at $10 and each sells 1,000 units per week, then each earns a profit of $9,000 a week. If each firm sets its price at $9, each sells 1,100 units per week for a profit of $8,800 [($9 − $1) × 1,100]. However, what if one firm charges $10 and the other firm charges $9? The low-price firm increases its profits through additional sales. It now sells, say, 1,500 units for a profit of $12,000, while the high-price firm sells only 600 units per week for a profit of $5,400.

When the two firms each charge $9 per unit, they are said to have reached a Nash equilibrium (named after Nobel Prize–winning economist and mathematician John Nash). At a Nash equilibrium, each firm is said to be doing as well as it can *given the actions of its competitor*. For example, if each firm believes the other is going to charge $9, then the best strategy for both firms is to charge $9. In this scenario, if Firm A charges $9, the worst possible outcome is a profit of $8,800. However, if Firm A prices at $10 and Firm B prices at $9, Firm A will have a profit of only $5,400. Hence, the price that minimizes the risk of the worst scenario is $9. The same is true for Firm B; it too minimizes the risk of the worst scenario by choosing to price at the Nash equilibrium, $9. In this case, the Nash equilibrium is also the dominant strategy. The Nash equilibrium takes on particular importance because it is a self-enforcing equilibrium. That is, once this equilibrium is established, neither firm has an incentive to move.

In sum, we see that if the two firms were to collude and set their price at $10, it would be in their best interest. However, each firm has a strong incentive to lower its price to $9 if this pricing strategy goes undetected by its competitor. However, if both firms defect by lowering their prices from the level of joint profit maximization, both will be worse off than if they

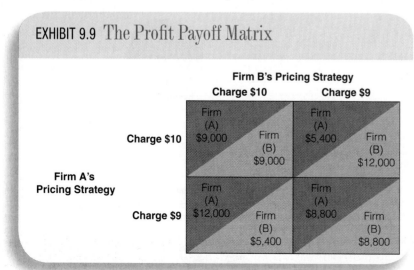

EXHIBIT 9.9 The Profit Payoff Matrix

		Firm B's Pricing Strategy	
		Charge $10	Charge $9
Firm A's Pricing Strategy	Charge $10	Firm (A) $9,000 / Firm (B) $9,000	Firm (A) $5,400 / Firm (B) $12,000
	Charge $9	Firm (A) $12,000 / Firm (B) $5,400	Firm (A) $8,800 / Firm (B) $8,800

THE GAME THEORY OF THE BAR SCENE PROBLEM FROM A BEAUTIFUL MIND

The Problem

You and three male friends are at a bar trying to pick up women. Suddenly one blonde and four brunettes enter in a group. What's the individual strategy?

Here are the rules. Each of you wants to talk to the blonde. If more than one of you tries to talk to her, however, she will be put off and talk to no one. At that point it will also be too late to talk to a brunette, as no one likes being second choice. Assume anyone who starts out talking to a brunette will succeed.

The Movie

Nash suggests the group should cooperate. If everyone goes for the blonde, they block each other and no one wins. The brunettes will feel hurt as a second choice and categorically reject advances. Everyone loses.

But what if everyone goes for a brunette? Then each person will succeed, and everyone ends up with a good option.

It's a good thought, except for one question: what about the blonde?

The Equilibrium

The movie is directed so well that it sounds persuasive. But it's sadly incomplete. It misses the essence of non-cooperative game theory.

A Nash equilibrium is a state where no one person can improve given what others are doing. This means you are picking the best possible action in response to others; the formal phrasing is *you are picking a best response.*

As an example, let's analyze whether everyone going for a brunette is a Nash equilibrium. You are given that three of your friends go for brunettes. What is your best response?

You can either go for the brunette or the blonde. With your friends already going for brunettes, you have no competition to go for the blonde. The answer is clear that you would talk to the blonde. That's your best response. Incidentally, this is a Nash equilibrium. You are happy, and your friends cannot do better. If your friends

try to talk to the blonde, they end up with nothing and give up talking to a brunette. So you see, when Nash told his friends to go for the brunettes in the movie, it really does sound like he was leaving the blonde for himself.

The Lesson

Advice that sounds good for you might really be better for someone else. Be skeptical of the strategic implications.

Now, in practical matters it will be hard to achieve the equilibrium that one person goes for a blonde. There is going to be competition and someone in the group will surely sabotage the mission. So there are two ways you might go about it using strategies outside the game. One is to ignore the current group and wait for another group of blondes (the classic "wait and see" strategy). The second is to let a random group member go for the blonde as the others distract the brunettes (also practiced as "wingman theory").

EXHIBIT 9.10 The Advertising Payoff Matrix

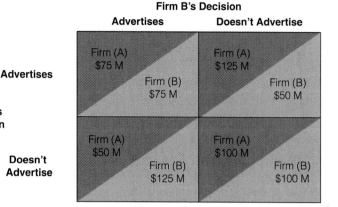

Firm B's Decision

		Advertises	Doesn't Advertise
Firm A's Decision	**Advertises**	Firm (A) $75 M / Firm (B) $75 M	Firm (A) $125 M / Firm (B) $50 M
	Doesn't Advertise	Firm (A) $50 M / Firm (B) $125 M	Firm (A) $100 M / Firm (B) $100 M

had colluded, but at least each will have minimized its potential loss if it cannot trust its competitor. This situation is the oligopolists' dilemma.

Advertising

Advertising can lead to a situation like the prisoners' dilemma. For example, perhaps the decision makers of a large firm are deciding whether to launch an advertising campaign against a rival firm. According to the payoff matrix in Exhibit 9.10, if neither company advertises, the two companies split the market, each making $100 million in profits. They also split the market if they both advertise, but their net profits are smaller, $75 million, because they would both incur advertising costs that are greater than any gains in additional revenues from advertising. However, if one advertises and the other does not, the company that advertises takes customers away from the rival. Profits for the company that advertises would be $125 million, and profits for the company that does not advertise would be $50 million.

The dominant strategy—the optimal strategy regardless of the rival's actions—is to advertise. In this game, both firms will choose to advertise, even though both would be better off if no one advertised. But one company can't take a chance and not advertise, because if its competitor then elects to advertise, the competitor could have a big year, primarily at the expense of the firm that doesn't advertise.

Arms Race

The arms race provides a classic example of the prisoners' dilemma. During the Cold War (mid-1940s to the early 1990s), the United States and the former Soviet Union were engaged in costly military expansion that hampered both economies. It exacted a greater toll on

the Soviets because their economy was not as productive as that of the United States and may have ultimately led to their decline. The United States' power was based on economic and military strength; the USSR's was based solely on military strength. Each country raced to produce more military goods than the other. Representatives from both sides would periodically meet to discuss arms reduction but to no avail. Neither party was willing to risk losing its military superiority.

The dilemma was that each country wanted to achieve military superiority, and building more arms could make that possible, for a given level of arms spending by the other. Each would prefer less spending on the military but each rationally chose to spend more to avoid the risk of becoming militarily inferior. They were trapped in a spending war. Of course, negotiations to spend less would be the preferred outcome for both, if they could be assured the other party would not cheat.

As you can see in the payoff matrix in Exhibit 9.11, if Country A spends more money on arms, then Country B must do the same or risk military inferiority. If Country A chooses to spend less on arms, then Country B gains military superiority by not following. For each country, the dominant strategy is to build arms, which leads to an inferior outcome—a less safe world. This is similar to the collusion game we examined earlier in which self-interest drives each participant to a noncooperative outcome that is worse for both parties.

REPEATED GAMES

In the one-shot prisoners' dilemma game in Exhibit 9.8, we saw that the best strategy is to confess regardless of what your opponent does—your behavior does not

EXHIBIT 9.11 The Arms Race Payoff Matrix

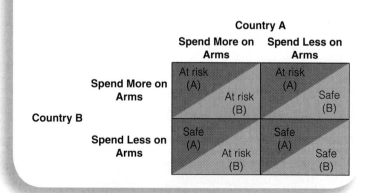

Country A

		Spend More on Arms	Spend Less on Arms
Country B	**Spend More on Arms**	At risk (A) / At risk (B)	At risk (A) / Safe (B)
	Spend Less on Arms	Safe (A) / At risk (B)	Safe (A) / Safe (B)

EXHIBIT 9.12 Characteristics of the Four Major Market Structures

Characteristic	Perfect Competition	Monopoly	Monopolistic Competition	Oligopoly
Number of firms	Very many	One	Many	A few
Firm role in determining price	No role; price taker	Major role; price maker	Some role	Some role
Close substitutes available	Perfect substitutes	No	Yes	Usually but not always
Barriers to entry or exit from industry	No substantial ones	Extremely great	Minor barriers	Considerable barriers
Type of product	Homogeneous	Homogeneous	Differentiated	Homogeneous or differentiated
Key characteristic	Firms are price takers	Only one firm	Product differentiation	Mutual interdependence

influence the other player's behavior. In one-shot prisoners' dilemma games, self-interest prevents cooperative behavior and leads to an inferior joint outcome for the participants.

However, cooperation is not impossible because most oligopolistic interactions are not one-shot games; rather, they are repeated games. Most firms assume that they will have repeat customers. For example, if a grocery store fails to provide fresh produce, customers can punish the store by shopping elsewhere in the future. These future consequences change the incentives from those in a one-shot game. All stores might have gained short-run profits from low-quality (and cost) produce, but all may offer high-quality produce because of the adverse future effects of offering lower-quality produce. In a repeated game, cooperation occurs as long as others continue to cooperate.

Suppose two firms are both going to be in business for many years. Several studies have shown that, in this type of situation, the best strategy is to do what your opponent did to you earlier. This type of response tends to elicit cooperation rather than competition. This form of strategic behavior is called a **tit-for-tat strategy**.

A repeated game allows the firm to establish a reputation of cooperation. Cooperation may mean maintaining a high price or a certain advertising budget, provided that the other firm did the same in the previous round. In short, a firm has an incentive to cooperate now so there is greater cooperation in the future. However, if your opponent cheats, you cheat in the next round to punish your opponent for a lack of cooperation. You do what your opponent did in the previous round. In the tit-for-tat game, both firms will be better off if they stick to the plan rather than cheat—that is, fail to cooperate. Many cartels appear to employ the tit-for-tat strategy. In short, the most effective strategy to promote cooperation is tit-for-tat.

THE FOUR MAJOR MARKET STRUCTURES REVISITED

You might legitimately ask the question: If perfectly competitive and monopolistic firms are rare and monopolistically competitive and oligopoly firms are common, why did we study the former first? What we learned from the perfectly competitive model about costs, entry, exit, and efficiency are still important concepts for imperfectly competitive firms. In addition, the applications of oligopoly and monopolistic competition theory are still somewhat controversial among economists—so we started with what we know best. Exhibit 9.12 provides an overview of the various types of market structures.

tit-for-tat strategy used in repeated games, the strategy in which one player follows the other player's move in the previous round; leads to greater cooperation

SECTION CHECK 6

6.1 Game theory stresses the tendency of various parties to minimize damage from opponents. A firm may try to figure out its competitors' most likely countermoves to its own policies and then formulate alternative defense measures.

6.2 A dominant strategy is optimal regardless of the opponents' actions.

6.3 At a Nash equilibrium, each player is said to be doing as well as it can, given the actions of its competitor.

Chapter 9: Self-Review

Now that you're finished reading the chapter, review the questions below. You can write your answers in the space provided, then go online to see the answers at www.cengagebrain.com.

S1—MONOPOLISTIC COMPETITION

1. How is monopolistic competition a mixture of monopoly and perfect competition?

2. Why is free entry necessary for monopolistic competition?

3. List three ways in which a grocery store might differentiate itself from its competitors.

S2—PRICE AND OUTPUT DETERMINATION IN MONOPOLISTIC COMPETITION

4. What is the short-run profit-maximizing policy of a monopolistically competitive firm?

5. How is the long-run equilibrium of monopolistic competition like that of perfect competition?

S3—MONOPOLISTIC COMPETITION VERSUS PERFECT COMPETITION

6. True or False: A monopolistic competitor's demand curve is downward sloping and relatively inelastic.

7. What is the price we pay for differentiated goods under monopolistic competition?

S4—OLIGOPOLY

8. True or False: Concentration ratios indicate the fraction of total industry labor supply accounted for by the largest firms in the industry.

9. How do economies of scale result in barriers to entry in oligopoly models?

S5—COLLUSION AND CARTELS

10. True or False: Barriers to entry are necessary for successful, ongoing collusion.

11. Why do horizontal mergers tend to concern antitrust authorities more than vertical or conglomerate mergers?

S6—GAME THEORY AND STRATEGIC BEHAVIOR

12. True or False: Noncooperative games are those in which actions are taken independently.

13. In the prisoners' dilemma, if each prisoner believed that the other prisoner would deny the crime, would each choose to deny the crime?

LISTEN UP!

SHE DID

Survey of ECON was designed for students just like you— busy people who want choices, flexibility, and multiple learning options.

Survey of ECON delivers concise, focused information in a fresh and contemporary format. And… **Survey of ECON** gives you a variety of online learning materials designed with you in mind.

At **www.cengagebrain.com,** you'll find electronic resources such as **videos,** and **interactive quizzes** for each chapter.

These resources will help supplement your understanding of core concepts in a format that fits your busy lifestyle. Visit **www.cengagebrain.com** to learn more about the multiple resources available to help you succeed!

After the Civil War,

as industrialization spread, union membership began to grow as well. This was partially in response to the horrible working conditions in factories—initially unions' demands were not just for higher wages but better working conditions. Though the percentage of union workers has dropped sharply over the last 60 years, still nearly 40 percent of public sector workers are union members. Only about 8 percent of workers in the private sector, however, are in unions. We'll talk more about unions in section 10.4.

10

Labor Markets, Income Distribution, and Poverty

pproximately 75 percent of national income goes to wages and salaries for labor services. So, how are salary levels among the individuals who supply those services determined? After laborers take their share, the remaining 25 percent of national income is compensation received by the owners of land and capital and the entrepreneurs who employ these resources to produce valued goods and services.

In labor markets, actor Johnny Depp can make more than $20 million acting in one film. Baseball player Alex Rodriguez of the New York Yankees makes $25 million a year. Singer Madonna's income is many times larger than that of the average college professor or medical doctor. Female models make more than male models, yet male basketball players make more than female basketball players. Why do these differences occur? To understand the reasons for the wide variation in compensation workers receive for their labors, we must focus on the workings of supply and demand in the labor market.

In this chapter, we will also study the relationship between productivity and wages, labor unions, income distribution, and poverty.

Ⓢ1 Input Markets

Keep the following questions in mind as you read through this section. You'll find the answers in Section Check 1.

1.1 How is income distributed among workers, landowners, and the owners of capital?

1.2 What is derived demand?

Let's begin by looking at derived demand and how it affects production in input markets.

DETERMINING THE PRICE OF A PRODUCTIVE FACTOR: DERIVED DEMAND

Input markets are the markets for the factors of production used to produce output. Output (goods and services)

derived demand the demand for an input derived from consumers' demand for the good or service produced with that input

marginal revenue product (MRP) marginal product times the price of the output

marginal resource cost (MRC) the amount that an extra input adds to the firm's total cost

markets and input markets have one major difference. In input or factor markets, the demand for an input derived from consumers' demand for the good or service produced with that input is called a **derived demand**. That is, the demand for an input such as labor is derived from the demand for the good or service. Thus, consumers do *not* demand the labor directly—it is the goods and services the labor produces that consumers demand. For example, the chef at a restaurant is paid and her skills are in demand because she produces what customers want—great-tasting meals. The "price" of any productive factor is directly related to consumer demand for the final good or service.

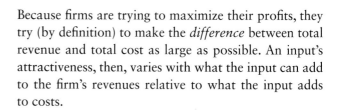

SECTION CHECK 1

1.1 Supply and demand determine the prices paid to workers, landowners, and capital owners.

1.2 In factor or input markets, demand is derived from consumers' demand for the final good or service that the input produces.

⑤2 Supply and Demand in the Labor Market

Keep the following questions in mind as you read through this section. You'll find the answers in **Section Check 2**.

2.1 What is the marginal revenue product for an input?

2.2 Why is the demand curve for labor downward sloping?

2.3 What is the relationship between the wage rate and the quantity of labor supplied?

Because firms are trying to maximize their profits, they try (by definition) to make the *difference* between total revenue and total cost as large as possible. An input's attractiveness, then, varies with what the input can add to the firm's revenues relative to what the input adds to costs.

WILL HIRING THAT INPUT ADD MORE TO REVENUE THAN COSTS?

In a competitive labor market, the demand for labor is determined by its **marginal revenue product (MRP)**, which is the additional revenue that a firm obtains from one more unit of input. Why? Suppose a worker adds $500 per week to a firm's sales by his productivity; he produces 100 units that add $5 each to firm revenue. To determine whether the worker adds to the firm's profits, we would need to calculate the marginal resource cost associated with the worker. The **marginal resource cost (MRC)** is the amount that an extra input adds to the firm's total costs. In this case, the marginal resource cost is the wage the employer has to pay to entice an extra worker. Assume that the marginal resource cost of the worker, the market wage, is $350 per worker per week. In our example, the firm would find its profits growing by adding one more worker, because the marginal benefit (*MRP*) associated with the worker, $500, would exceed the marginal cost (*MRC*) of the worker, $350. So we can see that just by adding another worker to its labor force, the firm would increase its weekly profits by $150 ($500 − $350). Even if the market wage was $490 per week, the firm could slightly increase its profits by hiring the employee, because the marginal revenue product, $500, is greater than the added labor cost, $490. At wage payments greater than $500, however, the firm would not be interested in the worker, because the marginal resource cost would exceed the marginal revenue product, making additional hiring unprofitable.

THE DEMAND CURVE FOR LABOR SLOPES DOWNWARD

The downward-sloping demand curve for labor indicates a negative relationship between wage and the quantity of labor demanded. Higher wages will decrease the quantity of labor demanded, whereas lower wages will increase the quantity of labor demanded. But why does this relationship exist?

The major reason for the downward-sloping demand curve for labor (illustrated in Exhibit 10.1) is

EXHIBIT 10.1 The Marginal Revenue Product of Labor

Marginal Revenue Product (demand curve for labor)

the law of diminishing marginal product. Remember that the law of diminishing marginal product states that as increasing quantities of some variable input (say, labor) are added to fixed quantities of another input (say, land or capital), output will rise, but at some point it will increase by diminishing amounts.

Consider a farmer who owns a given amount of land. Suppose the farmer is producing wheat, and the relationship between output and labor force requirements is that indicated in Exhibit 10.2. Output expands as more workers are hired to cultivate the land, but the growth in output steadily slows, meaning that the added output associated with one more worker declines as more workers are added. For example, in Exhibit 10.2, when a third worker is hired, total wheat output increases from 5,500 bushels to 7,000 bushels, an increase of 1,500 bushels in terms of marginal product. However, when a fourth worker is added, total wheat output only increases from 7,000 bushels to 8,000 bushels, or a marginal increase of 1,000 bushels. Note that the reason for the decline in marginal product is *not* that the workers being added are steadily inferior in terms of ability or quality relative to the first workers. Indeed, for simplicity, we assume that each worker has exactly the same skills and productive capacity. But as more workers are added, each additional worker has fewer of the fixed resources with which to work, and marginal product falls. For example, the fifth worker might merely cultivate the same land more intensively. The work of the fifth worker, then, might only slightly improve output. That is, the **marginal product (MP)**—the number of physical units of added output from the addition of one additional unit of input—falls.

As we discussed earlier, the marginal revenue product (MRP) is the change in total revenue associated with an additional unit of input. The marginal revenue product is equal to the marginal product (that is, the units of output added by a worker) multiplied by marginal revenue (MR) (that is, the price of the output):

$$MRP = MP \times MR$$

The MRP curve takes on different characteristics depending on whether the output market is competitive or imperfectly competitive. In this chapter, we assume the product, or output markets, are competitive. Recall from Chapter 7 that in perfectly competitive markets, the firm will sell all its output at the market price. Consequently, the marginal revenue from the sale of an additional unit is also equal to the market price. Therefore, when output markets are perfectly competitive, the marginal revenue product of a factor is equal to the marginal product times the price of the product the firm is selling:

$$MRP = MP \times P$$

For example, if an additional worker adds 10 bushels of wheat per day (marginal product) and each of these 10 bushels sells for $10 (price of the product), then the worker's marginal revenue product is $100 per day.

The marginal revenue product of labor declines because of the diminishing marginal product of labor when additional workers are added. This decline in MRP is illustrated in Exhibit 10.3 on the next page,

marginal product (MP)
the change in total output of a good that results from a one-unit change in input

EXHIBIT 10.2 Diminishing Marginal Productivity on a Hypothetical Farm

Units of Labor Input (workers)	Total Wheat Output (bushels per year)	Marginal Product of Labor (bushels per year)
0	—	
		3,000
1	3,000	
		2,500
2	5,500	
		1,500
3	7,000	
		1,000
4	8,000	
		500
5	8,500	
		300
6	8,800	
		200
7	9,000	

EXHIBIT 10.3 Marginal Revenue Product, Output, and Labor Inputs

Quantity of Labor	Total Output (bushels per week)	Marginal Product of Labor (bushels per week)	Product Price (dollars per bushel)	Marginal Revenue Product of Labor	Wage Rate (MRC) (dollars per week)	Marginal Profit (MRP − W)
0	0					
		100	$10	$1,000	$550	$450
1	100					
		90	10	900	550	350
2	190					
		80	10	800	550	250
3	270					
		70	10	700	550	150
4	340					
		60	10	600	550	50
5	400					
		50	10	500	550	−50
6	450					
		40	10	400	550	−150
7	490					
		30	10	300	550	−250
8	520					

which shows various output and revenue levels for a wheat farmer using different quantities of labor. We see in Exhibit 10.3 that the marginal product, or the added physical volume of output, declines as the number of workers grows, because of diminishing marginal product. Thus, the fifth worker adds only 60 bushels of wheat per week compared with 100 bushels for the first worker.

HOW MANY WORKERS WILL AN EMPLOYER HIRE?

Profits are maximized if the firm hires only to the point at which the wage equals the expected marginal revenue product; that is, the firm will hire up to the last unit of input for which the marginal revenue product

People attending the Long Island National Career Fairs event at the Mariott Hotel in Melville, N.Y., line up outside the door before the opening on January 21, 2010. Even six months into the economic recovery, jobs still remained scarce.

is expected to exceed the wage. Because the demand curve for labor and the value of the marginal revenue product show the quantity of labor that a firm demands at a given wage in a competitive market, we say that the marginal revenue product (MRP) is the same as the demand curve for labor for a competitive firm.

Using the data in Exhibit 10.3, if the market wage is $550 per week, it would pay for the wheat farmer to employ five workers. The fifth worker's marginal revenue product ($600) exceeds the wage, so profits are increased $50 by adding the worker. Adding a sixth worker would be unprofitable, however, as that worker's marginal revenue product of $500 is less than the wage of $550. Hiring the sixth worker would reduce profits by $50.

But what if the market wage increases from $550 to $650? In this case, hiring the fifth worker becomes unprofitable, because the marginal resource cost, $650, is now greater than the marginal revenue product of $600. That is, a higher wage rate, *ceteris paribus*, lowers the employment levels of individual firms.

In a competitive labor market, many firms are competing for workers, and no single firm is big enough by itself to have any significant effect on the level of wages. The intersection of the market supply of labor and the market demand for labor determines the competitive market wage, as shown in Exhibit 10.4(a). The firm's ability to hire all the workers it wishes at the prevailing wage is analogous to perfect competition in output markets, where a firm can sell all it wants at the going price.

In Exhibit 10.4(b), when the firm hires less than q^* workers, the marginal revenue product exceeds the market wage, so adding workers expands profits. With more than q^* workers, however, the "going wage" exceeds

EXHIBIT 10.4 The Competitive Firm's Hiring Decision

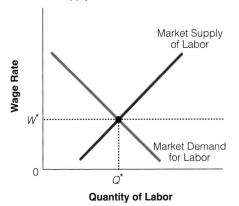

a. Market Supply and Demand for Labor

Market Supply of Labor

Wage Rate

W^*

Market Demand for Labor

0 Q^*

Quantity of Labor

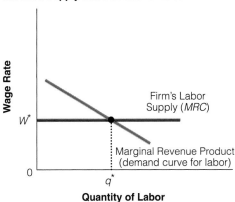

b. Firm's Supply and Demand for Labor

Wage Rate

W^*

Firm's Labor Supply (*MRC*)

Marginal Revenue Product (demand curve for labor)

0 q^*

Quantity of Labor

marginal revenue product, and hiring additional workers lowers profits. With q^* workers, profits are maximized.

In this chapter, we assume that labor markets are competitive, with many buyers and sellers of labor, and no individual worker having an impact on wages. It is generally a realistic assumption because in most labor markets firms compete with each other to attract workers, and workers can choose from many possible employers.

THE MARKET LABOR SUPPLY CURVE

How much work effort individuals are collectively willing and able to supply in the marketplace is the essence of the market supply curve. Just as was the case in our

earlier discussion of the law of supply, a positive relationship exists between the wage rate and the quantity of labor supplied. As the wage rate rises, the quantity of labor supplied increases, *ceteris paribus*; as the wage rate falls, the quantity of labor supplied falls, *ceteris paribus*. This positive relationship is consistent with the evidence that the total quantity of labor supplied by *all* workers increases as the wage rate increases, as shown in Exhibit 10.5.

EXHIBIT 10.5 The Market Supply Curve of Labor

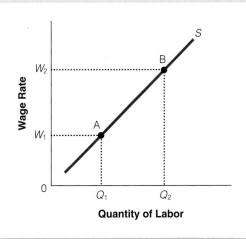

SECTION CHECK 2

2.1 Marginal revenue product (*MRP*) is the additional revenue that a firm obtains from one more unit of input. In other words, marginal revenue product equals marginal product times the price of the output.

2.2 The demand curve for labor is downward sloping because of diminishing marginal product. That is, if additional labor is added to a fixed quantity of land or capital equipment, output will increase, but eventually by smaller amounts.

2.3 The relationship between the wage rate and the quantity of labor supplied is positive. Along a market supply curve, a higher wage rate will increase the quantity supplied of labor and a lower wage rate will decrease the quantity of supplied labor.

⑤3 Labor Market Equilibrium

Keep the following questions in mind as you read through this section. You'll find the answers in Section Check 3.

3.1 How are the equilibrium wage and employment determined in labor markets?

3.2 What shifts the labor demand curve?

3.3 What shifts the labor supply curve?

The equilibrium wage and quantity in competitive markets for labor is determined by the intersection of labor demand and labor supply. As shown in Exhibit 10.6, the equilibrium wage, W^*, and equilibrium employment level, Q^*, are found at that point where the quantity of labor demanded equals the quantity of labor supplied. At any wage higher than W^*—at W_1, for example—the quantity of labor supplied exceeds the quantity of labor demanded, resulting in a surplus of labor. In this situation, unemployed workers are willing to undercut the established wage in order to get jobs, pushing the wage down and returning the market to equilibrium. At a wage below the equilibrium level—at W_2, for example—quantity demanded exceeds quantity supplied, resulting in a labor shortage. In this situation, employers are forced to offer higher wages in order to hire as many workers as they would like. Note that only at the equilibrium wage are both suppliers and demanders able to exchange the quantity of labor they desire.

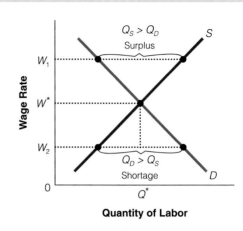

EXHIBIT 10.6 Supply and Demand in the Competitive Labor Market

SHIFTS IN THE LABOR DEMAND CURVE

In Chapter 3, we demonstrated that the determinants of demand can shift the demand curve for a good or service. In the case of an input such as labor, two important factors can shift the demand curve: increases in labor productivity—caused by technological advances, for instance—or changes in the output price of the good—caused by, say, an increased demand for the firm's product. Exhibit 10.7 highlights the impact of these changes.

EXHIBIT 10.7 Shifts in the Labor Demand Curve

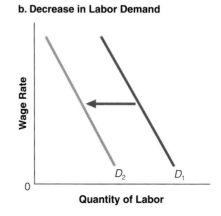

a. Increase in Labor Demand

b. Decrease in Labor Demand

Changes in Labor Productivity

Workers can increase productivity if they have more capital or land with which to work, if technological improvements occur, or if they acquire additional skills or experience (human capital). This increase in productivity will increase the marginal product of the labor and shift the demand curve for labor to the right from D_1 to D_2, as in Exhibit 10.7(a). However, if labor productivity falls, then marginal product will fall, and the demand curve for labor will shift to the left [see Exhibit 10.7(b)].

Changes in the Demand for the Firm's Product

The greater the demand for the firm's product, the greater the firm's demand for labor or any other variable input (the *derived demand* discussed earlier). The reason for this is that the higher demand for the firm's product increases the firm's marginal revenue, which increases marginal revenue product. That is, the greater demand for the product causes prices to rise, and the price of the product is part of the value of the labor to the firm ($MRP = MP \times P$). Therefore, the rising product price shifts the labor demand curve to the right. Of course, if demand for the firm's product falls, the labor demand curve will shift to the left as marginal revenue product falls.

SHIFTING THE LABOR SUPPLY CURVE

In Chapter 3, we learned that changes in the determinants of supply can shift the supply curve for goods and services to the right or left. Likewise, several factors can cause the labor supply curve to shift. These factors include immigration and population growth, the number of hours workers are willing to work at a given wage (worker tastes or preferences), nonwage income, and amenities. Exhibit 10.8 on the next page illustrates the impact of these factors on the labor supply curve.

Immigration and Population Growth

If new workers enter the labor force, the labor supply curve will shift to the right—from S_1 to S_2 in Exhibit 10.8(a). Of course, if workers leave the country—and thus the labor force—or the relevant population declines, the supply curve will shift to the left, as shown in Exhibit 10.8(b).

Number of Hours People Are Willing to Work (Worker Preferences)

If people become willing to work more hours at a given wage (due to changes in worker tastes or preferences), the labor supply curve will shift to the right, as shown in the movement from S_1 to S_2 in Exhibit 10.8(a). If they

Q: Why do teachers, who provide a valuable service to the community, make millions and millions of dollars less than star basketball players?

You can find the answer on the next page.

LABOR SUPPLY AND DEMAND

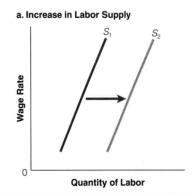

A: It is the marginal revenue product of additional teachers and the supply of teachers that determine the market wage (regardless of how important we consider the job). A teacher's marginal revenue product is likely to be well below $5 million a year. Most people probably think that teachers are more important than star basketball players, yet teachers make a lot less money. Of course, the reason for this is simple supply and demand. A lot of people enjoy watching star basketball players, but only a few individuals have the skill to perform at that level. Although demand for teachers is large, the number of potential suppliers is also relatively large. As shown in the accompanying exhibits, this relationship between supply and demand translates into a much lower wage for teachers than for star basketball players.

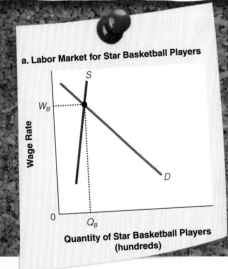

a. Labor Market for Star Basketball Players

b. Labor Market for Teachers

EXHIBIT 10.8 Shifts in the Labor Supply Curve

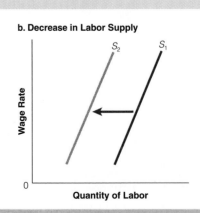

become willing to work fewer hours at a given wage, the labor supply curve will shift to the left, as shown in Exhibit 10.8(b).

Nonwage Income

Increases in income from other sources than employment can cause the labor supply curve to shift to the left. For example, if you just won $20 million in your state's Super Lotto, you might decide to take yourself out of the labor force. Likewise, a decrease in nonwage income might push a person back into the labor force, thus shifting the labor supply curve to the right.

Amenities

Amenities associated with a job or location—such as good fringe benefits, safe and friendly working conditions, a child-care center, and so on—will make for a more desirable work environment, *ceteris paribus*.

If the prize is significant enough, lottery winners might take themselves out of the labor force.

© BLEND IMAGES/GETTY IMAGES

These amenities will cause an increase in the supply of labor, resulting in a rightward shift of the labor supply curve—from S_1 to S_2 in Exhibit 10.8(a). If job conditions deteriorate, the labor supply will decrease, shifting the labor supply curve to the left, as shown in Exhibit 10.8(b).

SECTION CHECK 3

3.1 The intersection of the labor demand curve and the labor supply curve determines equilibrium wages and employment levels in the labor market.

3.2 The labor demand curve can shift when a change in productivity or a change in the demand for the final product occurs.

3.3 The labor supply curve can shift when changes in immigration or population growth, workers' preferences, nonwage income, or amenities occur.

Ⓢ4 Labor Unions

Consider the following questions as you read through this section. You'll find the answers in **Section Check 4**.

4.1 Why do labor unions exist?

4.2 What is the impact of unions on wages?

4.3 Can unions increase productivity?

While the percentage of workers in labor unions in the U.S. has fallen sharply over the last 60 years, unions can still exert a significant influence on markets. In this section we'll examine what labor unions are, why they exist, and their relationship to various markets.

WHY ARE THERE LABOR UNIONS?

The supply and demand curves for labor can help us better understand the impact of labor unions. Labor unions such as the United Auto Workers (UAW) and the United Farm Workers (UFW) were formed to increase their members' wages and to improve working conditions.

collective bargaining
negotiations between representatives of employers and unions

On behalf of its members, the union negotiates with firms through a process called **collective bargaining**—discussions between representatives of employers and unions focused on balancing what's best for workers and employers. Why is collective bargaining necessary? The argument is that when economies begin to industrialize and urbanize, firms become larger, and often the "boss" becomes more distant from the workers. In small shops or on farms, workers usually have a close relationship with an owner/employer; but in larger enterprises, the workers may only know a supervisor and have no direct contact with either the owner or upper management. Workers realize that acting together as a union of workers they have more power in the collective bargaining process than they would acting individually.

UNION IMPACT ON LABOR SUPPLY AND WAGES

Labor unions influence the quantity of union labor hired and the wages at which they are hired, primarily through their ability to alter the supply of labor services from what would exist if workers acted independently. One way of influencing supply, of course, is by raising barriers to entry into a given occupation. For example, by restricting membership, unions can reduce the quantity of labor supplied to industry employers from what it otherwise would be. As a result, wages in that occupation will increase, as shown in Exhibit 10.9(a), from W_1 to W_2. As you can see in the shift from Q_1 to Q_2, some union workers will consequently receive higher wages, but others will become unemployed.

Unions raise wages above what would prevail in a competitive labor market, causing (1) some workers to be unemployed and (2) lower wages in the non-union sector. Many economists believe that this relationship explains why wages are approximately 15 percent higher in union jobs, even when nonunion workers have comparable skills. Of course, the unions will appropriate some of these gains through dues, initiation fees, and the like, so the workers themselves will not receive the full benefit.

WAGE DIFFERENCES FOR SIMILARLY SKILLED WORKERS

Suppose you have two labor sectors: the union sector and the nonunion sector. If unions are successful in obtaining higher wages, either through bargaining or threatening to strike or by restricting membership, wages will rise and employment will fall in the union sector, as shown in Exhibit 10.9(a). With a downward-sloping demand curve for labor, higher wages mean that less labor will be demanded in the union sector. Workers who are equally skilled but unable to find union work will seek nonunion work, thus increasing supply and, in turn, lowering wages in the nonunion sector. This effect is shown in Exhibit 10.9(b). Thus, comparably skilled workers will experience higher wages in the union sector (W_1) than in the nonunion sector (W_2).

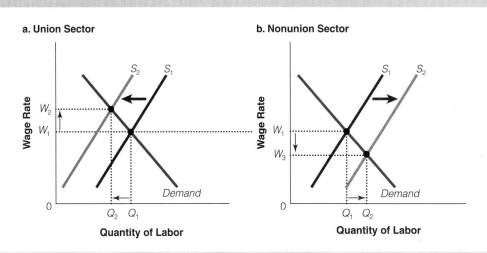

EXHIBIT 10.9 The Effect of Unions on Wages

a. Union Sector

b. Nonunion Sector

CAN UNIONS LEAD TO INCREASED PRODUCTIVITY?

Harvard economists Richard Freeman and James Medoff argue that unions might actually increase worker productivity by increasing marginal productivity. Their argument is that unions provide a collective voice that workers can use to communicate their discontents more effectively, thereby lowering the number of union workers who quit their jobs. Resignations can be particularly costly for firms that invest in training their employees in job-specific skills. In addition, by handling workers' grievances, unions may increase worker motivation and morale. The combined impact of fewer resignations and improved morale could boost productivity.

However, this improvement in worker productivity in the labor sector should show up on the bottom line—the profit statement of the firm. Although the evidence is still preliminary, it appears that unions tend to lower the profitability of firms, not raise it.

In sum, there is disagreement on the impact of unions on the economy. Like many other institutions, there are benefits and costs to unions.

SECTION CHECK 4

4.1 Workers form labor unions because they realize that acting together gives them collective bargaining power.

4.2 Labor unions try to increase their members' wages. Through restrictive membership, a union can reduce the labor supply in the market for union workers, thus reducing employment and raising wages. This union "restriction" increases the supply of workers in the nonunion sector and shifts supply to the right, lowering wages for nonunion workers.

4.3 Some argue that unions can help reduce job turnover, thus reducing the need for repeated investment in job-specific skills training, and improve morale by handling worker grievances. However, what evidence exists suggests that unions tend to lower the profitability of firms. Obviously there are both benefits and costs to unions.

⑤5 Income Distribution

Consider the following questions as you read through this section. You'll find the answers in **Section Check 5**.

5.1 What has happened to income distribution since 1935?

5.2 Are income distribution statistics accurate?

5.3 How significant is income mobility?

5.4 How much income inequality exists in other countries?

In many economies, some individuals will have high income and others will have low income. How unequal is the U.S. income distribution? And why do some individuals earn more than others? We will address these and other questions regarding income distribution and poverty in this section.

MEASURING INCOME INEQUALITY

Exhibit 10.10 shows a breakdown of average annual family income by groups of five (or quintiles): the bottom fifth, the second fifth, the third fifth, the fourth fifth, and the top fifth.

Exhibit 10.11 on the next page illustrates the changing distribution of measured income in the United States since 1935. As you can see in this table, the proportion of income received by the richest Americans (top 5 percent) declined sharply after 1935

EXHIBIT 10.10 Income Distribution of the United States, 2008

Group	Household Income (Average)
Bottom Fifth	$ 11,656
Second Fifth	$ 29,517
Third Fifth	$ 50,132
Fourth Fifth	$ 79,760
Top Fifth	$171,057

SOURCE: U.S. Census Bureau, Income, Poverty, and Health Insurance Coverage in the United States: 2008, Current Population Report: Consumer Income, Table A-3. Washington, D.C. (September 2009). Available at http://www.census.gov/prod/2009pubs/p60-236.pdf (accessed April 16, 2010).

EXHIBIT 10.11 Income Inequality in the United States

Year	Lowest Fifth	Second Fifth	Third Fifth	Fourth Fifth	Highest Fifth	Highest 5%
1935	4.1%	9.2%	14.1%	20.9%	51.7%	26.5%
1950	4.5	12.0	17.4	23.4	42.7	17.3
1960	4.8	12.2	17.8	24.0	41.3	15.9
1970	5.4	12.2	17.6	23.8	40.9	15.6
1980	5.3	11.6	17.6	24.4	41.1	14.6
1990	4.6	10.8	16.6	23.8	44.3	17.4
2000	4.3	9.8	15.5	22.8	47.4	20.8
2005	4.0	9.6	15.3	22.9	48.1	21.1
2008	4.0	9.6	15.5	23.1	47.8	20.5

SOURCE: U.S. Census Bureau, Current Population Survey, Annual Social and Economic Supplements. Historical Income Inequality Tables, Table F-2. Washington, D.C. (last updated March 23, 2010). Available at http://www.census.gov/hhes/www/income/histinc/ineqtoc.html (accessed April 26, 2010).

but has been edging back up since the 1980s. The proportion received by the poorest Americans (the lowest 20 percent) has remained virtually unchanged since 1935. Most of the observed changes occurred between 1935 and 1950, probably reflecting the impact of the Great Depression and new government programs in the 1930s, as well as World War II. From 1950 to 1980, there was little change in the overall distribution of income. Two significant changes have occurred since the 1980s: The lowest one-fifth of families have seen their share of measured income fall from 5.3 percent to 4.0 percent of all income, and the top one-fifth of families have seen their share of measured income rise from 41.1 to 47.8 percent of all income.

© PAUL PRESCOTT/ISTOCKPHOTO.COM

ARE WE OVERSTATING THE DISPARITY IN THE DISTRIBUTION OF INCOME?

Failing to take into consideration differences in age, certain demographic factors, institutional factors, and government redistributive activities have all been identified as elements that influence income distribution data and may suggest that we might be overstating inequality.

Differences in Age

At any moment in time, middle-age people tend to have higher incomes than both younger and older people. Middle age is when most people are at their peak in terms of productivity and participate in the labor force to a greater extent than do the very old or very young. Put differently, if every individual earned exactly the same total income over his or her lifetime, we would still observe some inequality at any given moment in time simply because people usually earn more in middle age.

Inequality resulting from this demographic difference overstates the true inequality in the lifetime earnings of people. A typical 50-year-old male earns nearly twice the income of a male in his early 20s and nearly one-third more than workers over 65. Since 1950, the proportion of individuals who are either very young or very old has grown, meaning that in a relative sense, more people are in lower-income age groups.

Other Demographic Trends

Other demographic trends, such as the increased number of divorced couples and the rise of two-income families,

> In short, high-income and low-income earners will always be with us, but more than likely they will be different people.

also cause the measured distribution of income (which is measured in terms of household income) to appear more unequal. For example, in the 1950s, the overwhelming majority of families had single incomes. Today, many households have two breadwinners instead of one. Suppose their incomes rise from $50,000 a year to roughly $100,000; thus, these households move into a higher-income quintile and create greater apparent income inequality. At the same time, divorces create two households instead of one, lowering income per household for divorced couples; thus, they move into lower-income quintiles, also creating greater apparent income inequality.

Government Activities

Some economists argue that the impact of increased government activity should be considered in evaluating the measured income distribution. Government-imposed taxes burden different income groups in different ways. Also, government programs benefit some groups of income recipients more than others. For example, state-subsidized higher education seems to benefit the high- and middle-income groups more than the poor (because far more students from the higher-income groups go to college), as have such things as government subsidies to airports and airlines, operas, and art museums. Some programs, though, clearly aid the poor more than the rich. Food stamps, school lunch programs, housing subsidies, Medicaid, and several other programs provide recipients with **in-kind transfers**. In-kind transfers are given in the form of goods and services rather than money. When in-kind transfers are included in income distribution data, many economists conclude that they have served to reduce levels of inequality significantly from the levels suggested by aggregate income statistics.

On balance, the evidence suggests that inequality of money income in the United States declined from 1935 to 1950 and then remained rather stable until 1980. Since then, the distribution of income has become less equal. However, if we consider age distribution, institutional factors, and in-kind transfer programs, it is safe to say that the income distribution is more equal than it appears in Exhibit 10.11.

in-kind transfers transfers in the form of goods and services instead of money, including food stamps, school lunch programs, housing subsidies, and Medicaid, among others

HOW MUCH MOVEMENT HAPPENS ON THE ECONOMIC LADDER?

A study of income mobility during the decade of 1985–1995 found that less than 50 percent of individuals who began in the poorest quintile ended up there a decade later, and almost 30 percent of those in the poorest quintile moved up to the top three quintiles. Although roughly 80 percent of individuals in the richest quintile were still there a decade later, the research does not show that people moving into the top quintile tended to stay there. The middle quintiles appear to experience considerable movement up and down the income ladder. Generational studies also suggest a considerable income mobility—that is, incomes of fathers and sons tend to be only slightly positively correlated. If a father had lifetime income earnings 20 percent above his generation, his son could expect to earn income about 8 percent above his generation. Virtually no positive correlation could be made between the earnings of grandchildren and grandparents. In short, high-income and low-income earners will always be with us, but more than likely they will be different people.

In sum, most Americans experience significant fluctuations in their economic well-being from one year to the next. According to a Census Bureau study in the mid-1990s, about three-fourths of the population see their economic well-being go either up or down by at least 5 percent from one year to the next. Economic well-being can be affected by changes in personal and family circumstances, such as work experience, marital status, and household composition, as well as changes in earnings.

WHY DO SOME EARN MORE THAN OTHERS?

Many reasons explain why some people earn more income than others. Some reasons for income differences include differences in age, skill, human capital (education and training), and preferences toward risk and leisure.

Age

The amount of income people earn varies over their lifetimes. Younger people with few skills tend to make little income when they begin their working careers. Income rises as workers gain experience and on-the-job training. As productivity increases, workers can command higher wages. These wage earnings generally increase up to the age of 50 and fall dramatically at retirement age, around 65.

Skills and Human Capital

Some workers are just more productive than others and therefore earn higher wages. Greater productivity can be a result of innate skills or of improvements in human capital, such as training and education. In Exhibit 10.12, we see that college graduates' average earnings are 81 percent greater than those of high school graduates. The financial rewards for attending college are higher than ever. Why is the gap widening between skilled and unskilled workers? One possibility is that increasing international trade over the last 30 years prompted an increase in domestic demand for skilled workers and a decrease in demand for

domestic unskilled workers (unskilled workers are relatively cheap and plentiful in developing countries). That is, the United States tends to import goods produced with unskilled workers and export goods produced with skilled workers. In addition, technological changes to more sophisticated equipment can lead to an increase in demand for skilled workers. Other workers, such as star athletes and rock stars, have specialized talents that are in huge demand, so they make more money than those with fewer skills or with skills that are in less demand.

Worker Preferences

Aside from differences in age, skills, education, and training, people have different attitudes about and preferences regarding their work. Because workaholics (by definition) work longer hours, they earn

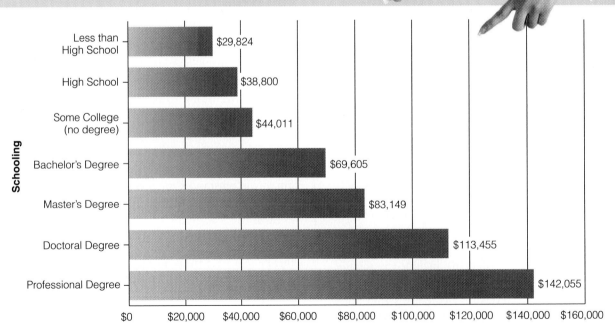

EXHIBIT 10.12 Education and Earnings, 2008

Schooling	Mean Earnings
Less than High School	$29,824
High School	$38,800
Some College (no degree)	$44,011
Bachelor's Degree	$69,605
Master's Degree	$83,149
Doctoral Degree	$113,455
Professional Degree	$142,055

Mean Earnings of Year-Round Full-Time Workers, 2008

SOURCE: U.S. Census Bureau, Current Population Survey, 2009 Annual Social and Economic Supplement. Table PINC-04. Washington, D.C. (last modified September 11, 2009). Available at http://www.census.gov/hhes/www/cpstables/032009/perinc/new04_001.htm (accessed April 17, 2010).

more than others with comparable skills. Some workers earn more because they work more intensely than others. Still others may choose jobs that pay less but have more amenities—flexible hours, favorable job locations, generous benefit programs, child care, and so on. Some people choose to work less and spend more time pursuing leisure activities, such as traveling, hobbies, or spending time with family and friends. It is not for us to say that one preference is better than another but simply to recognize that these choices lead to differences in earnings.

Job Preferences

Finally, some of the differences in income are the result of the risks or undesirable features of some occupations. Police officers and firefighters are paid higher wages because of the dangers associated with their jobs. The same would be true for window washers on skyscrapers and painters on the Golden Gate bridge. Coal miners and garbage collectors are paid more than other workers with comparable skill levels because of the unpleasantness of the jobs. In short, some workers have higher earnings because they are compensated for the difficult, risky, or unappealing nature of their jobs.

INCOME DISTRIBUTION IN OTHER COUNTRIES

Is the United States typical of advanced, industrial nations with respect to the distribution of income among its population? This question is difficult to answer with absolute certainty, given international differences in defining income, difficulties in measuring the impact of taxes, the problem of nonmonetary payments, and so on. Despite these hurdles, international comparisons of income distribution have been made.

Exhibit 10.13, constructed with data from the World Bank, shows that income inequality is greater in the United States and the United Kingdom than in Sweden and Japan. Japan's ratio of 4.5 means that the richest 10 percent of the population makes 4.5 times as much income as the bottom ten percent. In Brazil, the richest ten percent of the population makes 51.3 times as much income as the bottom 10 percent. The table shows that some of the greatest disparities in income are found in developing countries such as Mexico, South Africa, and Brazil.

EXHIBIT 10.13 Global Income Inequalities

Income Inequality	Country	Gap between Rich and Poor (Ratio)
Most Equal	Japan	4.5
	Sweden	6.2
	Germany	6.9
	India	8.6
	France	9.1
	Canada	9.4
	Russia	11.0
	China	13.2
	United Kingdom	13.8
	United States	15.9
	Nigeria	16.3
	Mexico	21.0
	Chile	26.2
	Argentina	31.6
	South Africa	35.1
Least Equal	Brazil	40.6

NOTE: The ratio of the richest 10% to the poorest 10% gives us the gap between rich and poor. The smaller the ratio the greater the equality.

SOURCE: World Bank (2009d). "World Development Indicators." Washington, D.C.: World Bank. Available at http://hdrstats.undp.org/en/indicators/160.html (accessed April 19, 2010).

poverty rate the percentage of the population who fall below the poverty line

poverty line a set of money income thresholds, established by the federal government, that vary by family size and are used to detect who is poor; if a family's total income is less than the established family threshold, then that family, and every individual in it, is considered poor

Although income inequality within nations is often substantial, it is far less than income inequality among nations. A majority of income inequality on Earth reflects differences in living standards among countries rather than disparities within nations. This conclusion is borne out by statistics.

SECTION CHECK 5

5.1 From 1935 to 1980, the distribution of income became more equal. However, since 1980, inequality has increased.

5.2 Nonmonetary income and privileges to the well-to-do may understate the disparity in income inequality, while demographics, institutional factors, measuring current income rather than permanent income, and government programs may overstate the disparity in income inequality.

5.3 High-income and low-income earners will always exist, but the individuals in these groups tends to change quite a bit. Most Americans experience significant fluctuations in their economic well-being even from one year to the next.

5.4 The level of income inequality differs from country to country.

ⓢ6 Poverty

Consider the following questions as you read through this section. You'll find the answers in **Section Check 6.**

6.1 How do we define poverty?

6.2 How many people live in poverty?

6.3 What is a negative income tax?

At several points in the previous discussion, the words *rich* and *poor* were used without being defined. Of particular interest is the question of poverty. Our concern over income distribution largely arises because most people believe that those with low incomes have lower satisfaction than those with higher incomes. Thus, the "poor" people are those who, in a material sense, suffer relative to other people. It is desirable, therefore, to define and measure the extent of poverty in the United States.

DEFINING POVERTY

The federal government measures poverty by using a set of money income thresholds that vary by family size. If the family's total income is less than the established family threshold, then that family, and every individual in it, is considered poor. The poverty thresholds are adjusted annually for inflation. The **poverty rate** is the percentage of the population that falls below this absolute level, called the **poverty line**. The official poverty rate for the United States is currently set at three times the cost of providing a nutritionally adequate diet—roughly $20,000 for a family of four. The official poverty definition may overstate the level of poverty because it does not include noncash benefits (such as public housing, Medicaid, and food stamps).

The amount of poverty fell steadily in the 1960s, was steady in the 1970s, and rose during the recession in the early 1980s. The poverty rate then fell slightly during the rest of the 1980s and rose again during the recessions of 1990–1991 and the recessions of 2001 and 2008–2009. As you would expect, when the economy is in a recession, unemployment rises and poverty tends to increase. Exhibit 10.14 provides some statistics on the U.S. poverty rate.

Poverty rates vary considerably among different races. Exhibit 10.15 shows that poverty rates for blacks and Hispanics were much higher than for whites. However, poverty rates fell markedly for blacks and Hispanics during the 1990s. Household status also influences poverty. A family headed by a female with no husband present is about five times more likely to experience poverty than a family headed by a married couple. Children are also more likely than average to be members of poor families—see Exhibit 10.15.

INCOME REDISTRIBUTION

A variety of programs are designed to reduce poverty and redistribute income. We examine several of them here.

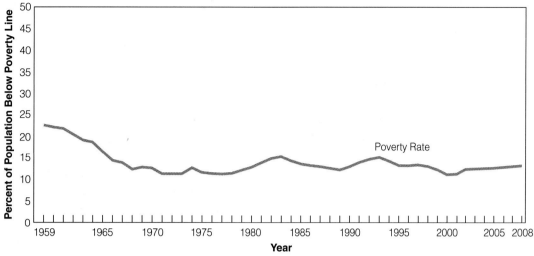

EXHIBIT 10.14 Poverty Rate: 1959 to 2008

SOURCE: U.S. Census Bureau, Income, Poverty, and Health Insurance Coverage in the United States: 2008, Current Population Report: Consumer Income, Figure 3. Washington, D.C. (September 2009). Available at http://www.census.gov/prod/2009pubs/p60-236.pdf (accessed April 19, 2010).

Taxes

One way to redistribute income to reduce disparities among individuals is through federal income tax. The federal income tax is designed to be a **progressive tax system**—one that imposes higher marginal tax rates on higher incomes. For example in 2006, if individuals made less than $30,650, their marginal tax rate was 15 percent. Income in excess of $30,650 but less than $74,200 was taxed at a marginal tax rate of 25 percent; income between $74,200 and $154,800 was taxed at a marginal tax rate of 28 percent; and income in the range of $154,800 to $336,500 was taxed at a marginal tax rate of 33 percent. Any income earned by an individual over $336,500 was taxed at a marginal tax rate of 35 percent.

Transfer Payments

A second means by which income redistribution can be carried out by the government is through direct transfer payments to the lower part of the income distribution. Transfer payments are payments made to individuals, for which goods or services are exchanged. They come in the form of in-kind transfers—direct transfers of goods or services such as food stamps, housing subsidies, and Medicaid—and **cash transfers** of direct cash payments such as welfare, Social Security, and unemployment compensation.

EXHIBIT 10.15 Poverty among Different Groups, 2008

Group	Below Poverty Rate
Female household, no husband present	28.7
Black	24.7
Hispanic	23.2
Children (under age 18)	19.0
Male household, no wife present	13.8
All persons	13.2
Asian	11.8
Elderly (over age 65)	9.7
White, not Hispanic	8.6
Married-couple families	5.5

SOURCE: U.S. Census Bureau, Income, Poverty, and Health Insurance Coverage in the United States: 2008, Current Population Report: Consumer Income. Washington, D.C. (September 2009) pp.14–16. Available at http://www.census.gov/prod/2009pubs/p60-236.pdf (accessed April 19, 2010).

progressive tax system tax system that imposes higher marginal tax rates on higher incomes; the federal income tax is designed to be a progressive tax system

cash transfers direct cash payments such as welfare, Social Security, and unemployment compensation

Social Security, Medicare, and Unemployment Compensation Social Security is a cash transfer program that provides income primarily to older persons. Social Security accounts for almost 45 percent of all federal transfer payments. Medicare is an in-kind transfer—a health insurance subsidy program that pays many of the doctor and hospital bills for those over the age of 65. Neither of these programs are considered welfare programs because one does not have to be poor to receive benefits. These two programs, Social Security and Medicare, account for almost 70 percent of all transfer payments. Benefits for unemployed in the form of unemployment compensation are also a social insurance form of transfer payments. All three of these social insurance programs are event based—they are received upon job loss, old age, or disability.

Welfare Programs

The social insurance programs (Social Security, Medicare, and unemployment compensation) are different from welfare programs, for which a person or a family must prove they have a low enough income to qualify. Medicaid, a program designed to give health care to the poor, and the food stamp program are examples. Other welfare programs include **Supplemental Security Income (SSI)**, a program designed for the most needy, elderly, disabled, and blind, and **Temporary Assistance for Needy Families (TANF)**, designed to help families that have few financial resources. The **Earned Income Tax Credit (EITC)** is a program that allows the working poor to receive income refunds that can be greater than the taxes they paid during the last year. It is a **means-tested income transfer program** (eligibility is dependent on low income) like food stamps, Medicaid, and housing subsidies.

Supplemental Security Income (SSI) a welfare program designed for the most needy, elderly, disabled, and blind

Temporary Assistance for Needy Families (TANF) a welfare program designed to help families that have few financial resources

Earned Income Tax Credit (EITC) a welfare program that allows the working poor to receive income refunds that can be greater than the taxes they paid during the last year

means-tested income transfer program program in which eligibility is dependent on low income; food stamps, Medicaid, and housing subsidies are examples of means-tested income transfer programs

Negative Income Tax

A negative income tax collects taxes from high-income families and gives subsidies to low-income families. Thus, it is a tax and a transfer program. It uses the personal income tax system to set up a series of payments to citizens and tax receipts by the U.S. Treasury according to a schedule based on family size and actual income earned. The plan would not require setting up a new system. It could be an extension of the fully computerized system that already exists.

How Does it Work? High-income families would pay a tax; low-income families would receive a subsidy. For example, suppose the government formula for a negative tax is Tax = (25 percent × income) − $10,000. So, if a family earned $100,000 a year, it would pay $15,000 in taxes (0.25 × $100,000 = $25,000 − $10,000 = $15,000). A family that earned $40,000 a year would pay $0.00 in taxes (0.25 × $40,000 = $10,000 − $10,000 = $0). And a family that earned $20,000 would owe −$5,000 (0.25 × $20,000 = $5,000 − $10,000 = −$5,000). That is, this family would get $5,000 in return.

The Case for a Negative Income Tax Many economists favor a negative income tax. They point out that it would not require the massive bureaucracy that now exists for administering public assistance, food stamps, and other programs. Hence, many of the resources now spent for this huge bureaucracy could be spent on other priorities, or used to provide the negative tax (the government payment) to needy families. No one would have to demonstrate need. It would not encourage illegitimate births, family break-ups, or many claims the current welfare system does.

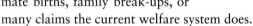

Negative income tax: Pros
- no bureaucracy

The Case Against a Negative Income Tax On the other hand, many economists oppose a negative income tax, pointing out that it might cost "too much." In particular, if for political reasons such current welfare programs as food stamps and subsidized housing cannot be dismantled, then the negative income tax would just be one more facet of the welfare system.

Negative income tax: Cons
- the work disincentive effect

They also contend that any effective negative income tax would have a *work disincentive effect*. That is, the payoff for returning to work would be smaller with an effective negative income tax program, so that many who could work might nevertheless decide not to do so. There

Not all government programs benefit the relatively poor at the expense of the rich. Government subsidies for public rail transportation generally benefit more affluent suburban commuters.

© RENÉ MANSI/ISTOCKPHOTO.COM

is also concern that cash assistance, rather than in-kind welfare (food stamps, housing subsidies, etc.) would lead to poor consumption choices—perhaps drugs and alcohol. However, recipients would substitute food stamps for cash purchases, allowing them to buy whatever they wanted. And some critics say while it subsidizes the unfortunate, it also subsidizes the lazy and undeserving.

Government Subsidies

A third way that governments can help the less affluent is by using government revenues to provide low-cost public services. Inexpensive public housing, subsidized public transport, and even public parks are services that probably serve the poor to a greater extent than the rich. "Free" public education is viewed by many as an equalizing force in that it opens opportunities for children of less prosperous members of society to obtain employment that could improve their economic status. Of course, not all government programs benefit the relatively poor at the expense of the rich. For example, federal government subsidies to commuter railroads primarily lower the cost to affluent suburbanites of getting to work in the central city. Support for public universities may help the middle- or even upper-income groups more than the poor. In addition, agricultural subsidies often provide large benefits to farmers who already have large incomes.

SECTION CHECK 6

6.1 One method of defining poverty is to determine an absolute income level that is necessary to provide the basic necessities of life in minimum quantities. The poverty rate, then, would be the proportion for persons who fail to earn the minimum income standard.

6.2 The poverty level fell steadily in the 1960s, remained steady during the 1970s, and rose during the early 1980s. After falling again in the late 1980s, the poverty rate rose during the recessions of 1990–1991, 2001, and 2008–2009. The poverty rate can vary widely between different segments of the population.

6.3 A negative income tax is a tax and transfer program the collects taxes from higher income families and gives subsidies to lower income families.

Chapter 10: Self-Review

Now that you're finished reading the chapter, review the questions below. You can write your answers in the space provided, then go online to see the answers at www.cengagebrain.com.

S1–INPUT MARKETS

1. Why is the demand for tractors and fertilizer derived from the demand for agricultural products?

S2–SUPPLY AND DEMAND IN THE LABOR MARKET

2. True or False: A firm will hire another worker if the marginal revenue product of labor exceeds the market wage rate.

3. Why does the marginal product of labor eventually fall?

S3–LABOR MARKET EQUILIBRIUM

4. True or False: If wages were above their equilibrium level, they would tend to fall toward the equilibrium level.

5. Why do increases in technology or increases in the amounts of capital or other complementary inputs increase the demand for labor?

S4–LABOR UNIONS

6. Why are service industries harder to unionize than are manufacturing industries?

7. How do union restrictions on membership or other barriers to entry affect the wages of members?

S5–INCOME DISTRIBUTION

8. How does the growth of both two-earner families and divorced couples increase measured income inequality?

9. How might each of the following affect the distribution of income in the near term?
   a. There is a massive influx of low-skilled immigrants.
   b. A new baby boom occurs.
   c. The new baby boomers enter their 20s.
   d. The new baby boomers reach age 65 or older.
   e. There is an increase in cash transfer payments, such as Supplemental Security Income.
   f. There is an increase in in-kind transfer payments, such as food stamps.

S6–POVERTY

10. What are some of the programs designed to reduce poverty and redistribute income?

REVIEW HE DID

Survey of ECON puts a multitude of study aids at your fingertips. After reading the chapters, check out these resources for further help:

• **Chapter in Review cards**, found in the back of your book, include all learning outcomes, definitions, and visual summaries for each chapter.

• **Online printable flash cards** give you three additional ways to check your comprehension of key concepts.

Other great ways to help you study include **interactive games** and **online tutorial quizzes with feedback**.

You can find it all at **www.cengagebrain.com**.

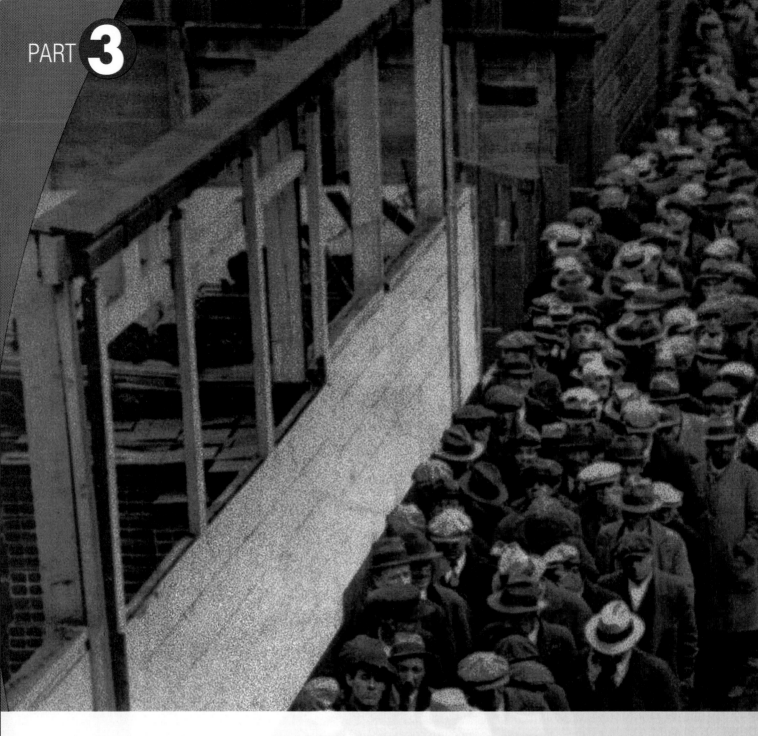

During the Great Depression,

U.S. unemployment levels reached historic highs—nearly 25%. Unemployment levels remained in the double-digits through 1941. Keeping high levels of employment, price stability, and high rates of economic growth are the major goals of macroeconomic policy. We'll discuss unemployment and other macroeconomic issues in this chapter.

II

Introduction to Macroeconomics: Unemployment, Inflation, and Economic Fluctuations

now we focus our attention on macroeconomics and, in particular, on two key concepts that are at the heart of macroeconomics and economic policy making: unemployment and inflation.

To those who have just lost a job, unemployment ranks high on the stress meter. To an elderly person who is living on a fixed income, inflation and the loss of purchasing power may be just as threatening.

In this chapter, we see how economists define unemployment and inflation and consider the problems associated with each. In the last section of this chapter, we examine the short-run fluctuations in the economy—the so-called business cycle.

Ⓢ1 Macroeconomic Goals

Keep the following questions in mind as you read through this section. You'll find the answers in Section Check 1.

1.1 What are the most important macroeconomic goals in the United States?

1.2 How has the United States shown its commitment to these goals?

Recall from Chapter 1 that macroeconomics is the study of the whole economy—the study of the forest, not the trees. Let's begin by looking at some of the major issues that ultimately drive macroeconomic decisions.

THREE MAJOR MACROECONOMIC GOALS

Nearly every society has been interested in three major macroeconomic goals: (1) maintaining employment of human resources at relatively high levels, meaning that jobs are relatively plentiful and financial suffering from lack of work and income is relatively uncommon; (2) maintaining prices at a relatively stable level so that consumers and producers can make better decisions; and (3) achieving a high rate of economic growth, meaning a

3 Major Macroeconomic Goals
1) High employment
2) Stable price levels
3) High economic growth levels

growth in output per person over time. We use the term **real gross domestic product (RGDP)** to measure output or production. The term *real* is used to indicate that the output is adjusted for the general increase in prices over time. Technically, gross domestic product (GDP) is defined as the total value of all final goods and services produced in a given period of time, such as a year or a quarter. Accomplishing smooth, rapid economic growth in an environment of stable prices and low unemployment is no easy task. Sometimes the cure for one problem comes at the expense of another. In the coming chapters we will discuss the causes and possible remedies for high inflation, high unemployment, and sluggish economic growth.

ACKNOWLEDGING OUR GOALS: THE EMPLOYMENT ACT OF 1946

Many economic problems—particularly those involving unemployment, price instability, and economic stagnation—are pressing concerns for the U.S. government. The **Employment Act of 1946** and the Full Employment and Balanced Growth Act of 1978 (the Humphrey–Hawkins Act) commit the U.S. government to pursuing unemployment policies that are also consistent with price stability. This legislation was the first formal acknowledgment of these primary macroeconomic goals.

SECTION CHECK 1

1.1 The most important U.S. macroeconomic goals are full employment, price stability, and economic growth.

1.2 The Employment Act of 1946 and the Full Employment and Balanced Growth Act of 1978 (the Humphrey–Hawkins Act) demonstrated the United States' commitment to the major macroeconomic goals.

S2 Employment and Unemployment

Keep the following questions in mind as you read through this section. You'll find the answers in **Section Check 2**.

2.1 What are the consequences of unemployment?

2.2 What is the unemployment rate?

2.3 Does unemployment affect everyone equally?

2.4 How long are people typically unemployed?

In this section, we'll discuss the issues surrounding unemployment and how it affects the economy.

THE CONSEQUENCES OF HIGH UNEMPLOYMENT

Unemployment figures are reported by the U.S. Department of Labor on a monthly basis. The news of lower unemployment usually sends stock prices higher; and the news of higher unemployment usually sends stock prices lower. Politicians are also concerned about the unemployment figures because elections often hinge precariously on whether unemployment has been rising or falling.

Nearly everyone agrees that it is unfortunate when a person who wants a job cannot find one. A loss of a job can mean financial insecurity and a great deal of anxiety. High rates of unemployment in a society can increase tensions and despair. A family without income from work undergoes great suffering; as a family's savings fade, family members wonder where they are going to obtain the means to survive. Society loses some potential output of goods when some of its productive

THE COSTS OF HIGH UNEMPLOYMENT

resources—human or nonhuman—remain idle, and potential consumption is reduced. Clearly, then, a loss in efficiency occurs when people willing to work and equipment able to produce remain idle. That is, other things being equal, relatively high rates of unemployment are viewed almost universally as undesirable.

WHAT IS THE UNEMPLOYMENT RATE?

When discussing unemployment, economists and politicians refer to the **unemployment rate**. To calculate the unemployment rate, you must first understand another important concept—the **labor force**. The labor force is the number of people aged 16 and older who are available for employment, as shown in Exhibit 11.1. The civilian labor force figure excludes people in the armed services and those in prisons or mental hospitals. Other people regarded as outside the labor force include homemakers, retirees, and full-time students. These groups are excluded from the labor force because they are not considered currently available for employment.

When we say that the unemployment rate is 5 percent, we mean that 5 percent of the population aged 16 and older who are willing and able to work are unable to get jobs. This 5 percent means that 5 out of 100 people in the total labor force are unemployed. To calculate the unemployment rate, we simply divide the number of unemployed by the number in the civilian labor force:

$$\frac{Unemployment}{rate} = \frac{Number\ of\ unemployed}{Civilian\ labor\ force} \times 100$$

In February 2010, the number of civilians unemployed in the United States was 14.87 million, and the civilian labor force totaled 153.5 million. Using these data, we can calculate that the unemployment rate in February 2010 was 9.7 percent:

$$Unemployment\ rate = \frac{14.87\ million}{153.5\ million} \times 100$$

$$= 0.097 \times 100 = 9.7\ percent$$

THE WORST CASE OF U.S. UNEMPLOYMENT

By far, the worst employment downturn in U.S. history occurred during the Great Depression, which began in late 1929 and continued until 1941. Unemployment rose from only 3.2 percent of the labor force in 1929 to more than 20 percent in the early 1930s, and double-digit unemployment persisted through 1941. The debilitating impact of having millions of productive people out of work led Americans (and people in other countries as well) to say, "Never again." Some economists would argue that modern macroeconomics, with its emphasis on the determinants of unemployment and its elimination, truly began in the 1930s.

VARIATIONS IN THE UNEMPLOYMENT RATE

Exhibit 11.2 on the next page shows U.S. unemployment rates over the last 50 years. Unemployment since 1960 ranged from a low of 3.5 percent in 1969 to a high of 10.8 percent in 1982. The

unemployment rate the percentage of the population aged 16 and older who are willing and able to work but are unable to obtain a job

labor force the number of people aged 16 and older who are available for employment

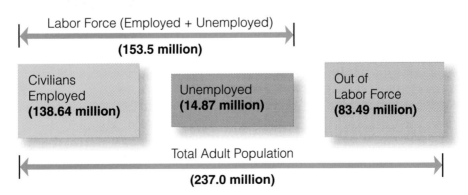

EXHIBIT 11.1 The U.S. Labor Force, 2010

Labor Force (Employed + Unemployed)
(153.5 million)

Civilians Employed **(138.64 million)**   Unemployed **(14.87 million)**   Out of Labor Force **(83.49 million)**

Total Adult Population
(237.0 million)

SOURCE: Bureau of Labor Statistics, *Current Population Survey,* Employment Situation Summary Table A. Washington D.C., March 5, 2010. Available at http://www.bls.gov/news.release/empsit.a.htm (accessed March 25, 2010).

discouraged worker an individual who has left the labor force because he or she could not find a job

financial crisis of 2008 led to unemployment rates of 9.7 percent by early 2010. Unemployment in the worst years is two or more times what it is in good years. Before 1960, variations in unemployment were more pronounced.

ARE UNEMPLOYMENT STATISTICS ACCURATE REFLECTIONS OF THE LABOR MARKET?

In periods of prolonged recession, some individuals think that the chances of landing a job are so bleak that they quit looking. These people are called **discouraged workers.** Individuals who have not actively sought work for four weeks are not counted as unemployed; instead, they fall out of the labor force. Also, people looking for full-time work who grudgingly settle for part-time jobs are counted as "fully" employed, even though they are only "partly" employed. At least partially balancing these two biases in government employment statistics, however, is the number of people who are overemployed—that is, working overtime or at more than one job. Also, a number of jobs in the underground economy (e.g., drug dealing, prostitution, gambling, and so on) are not reported. In addition, many people may claim they are seeking work when, in fact, they may just be going through the motions so they can continue to collect unemployment compensation or receive other government benefits.

WHO ARE THE UNEMPLOYED?

Unemployment usually varies greatly across different segments of the population and over time.

Education as a Factor in Unemployment

According to the Bureau of Labor Statistics, the unemployment rate across the sexes and races among college graduates is significantly lower than for those who do not complete high school. In July 2009, the unemployment rate for individuals without high school diplomas was 15.4 percent, compared with 4.7 percent for those with bachelor's degrees and higher. Further, college graduates have lower unemployment rates than people who have some college education but did not complete their bachelor's degrees (7.9 percent).

Age, Sex, and Race as Factors in Unemployment

The incidence of unemployment varies widely among the population. Unemployment tends to be greater among the very young, among blacks and other minorities, and among workers with few skills. The unemployment rate for adult females tends to be higher than that for adult males.

EXHIBIT 11.2 U.S. Unemployment Rates, 1960–2009

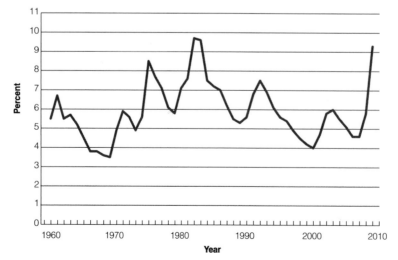

SOURCE: Bureau of Labor Statistics, *CPS Tables*, Annual Averages—Household Data, Employment status of the civilian noninstitutional population, 1940s to date. Washington, D.C. Available at http://www.bls.gov/cps/tables.htm#empstat (accessed March 25, 2010).

Considering the great variations in unemployment for different groups in the population, we calculate separate unemployment rates for groups classified by sex, age, race, family status, and type of occupation. Exhibit 11.3 shows unemployment rates for various groups. Note that the variation around the average unemployment rate for the total population of 9.7 percent was considerable. The unemployment rate for blacks was much higher than the rate for whites, a phenomenon that has persisted throughout the post–World War II period. Unemployment among teenagers was much higher than adult unemployment, at 25 percent. Some would regard teenage unemployment a lesser evil than unemployment among adults, because most teenagers have parents or guardians on whom they can rely for subsistence.

CATEGORIES OF UNEMPLOYED WORKERS

According to the Bureau of Labor Statistics, the four main categories of unemployed workers are **job losers** (those who have been temporarily laid off or fired), **job leavers** (those who have quit their jobs), **reentrants** (those who worked before and are reentering the labor force), and **new entrants** (those entering the labor force for the first time—primarily teenagers). It is a common misconception that most workers are unemployed because they have lost their jobs. Although job losers may typically account for 63 percent of the unemployed, a sizable fraction is due to job leavers, new entrants, and reentrants, as seen in Exhibit 11.4 on the next page.

job loser an individual who has been temporarily laid off or fired

job leaver a person who quits his or her job

reentrant an individual who worked before and is now reentering the labor force

new entrant an individual who has not held a job before but is now seeking employment

HOW MUCH UNEMPLOYMENT?

Even though unemployment is painful to those who have no source of income, reducing unemployment is not costless. In the short run, a reduction in unemployment may come at the expense of a higher rate

---

EXHIBIT 11.3 Unemployment in the United States by Age, Sex, and Race

a. U.S. Unemployment, by Sex and Age

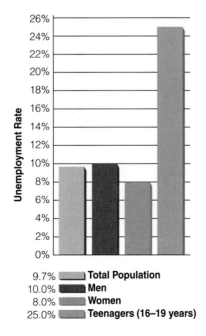

9.7%	Total Population
10.0%	Men
8.0%	Women
25.0%	Teenagers (16–19 years)

b. U.S. Unemployment, by Race or Ethnic Group

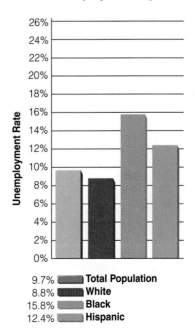

9.7%	Total Population
8.8%	White
15.8%	Black
12.4%	Hispanic

SOURCE: Bureau of Labor Statistics, *Current Population Survey*, Employment Situation Summary Table A. Washington, D.C., March 5, 2010. Available at http://www.bls.gov/news.release/empsit.a.htm (accessed March 25, 2010).

underemployment a situation in which a worker's skill level is higher than necessary for a job

labor force participation rate the percentage of the working age population in the labor force

of inflation, especially if the economy is close to full capacity, where resources are almost fully employed. Moreover, trying to match employees with jobs can quickly lead to significant inefficiencies because of mismatches between a worker's skill level and the level of skill required for a job. For example, the economy would be wasting resources subsidizing education if people with PhDs in biochemistry were driving taxis or tending bars. That is, the skills of the employee may be higher than those necessary for the job, resulting in what economists call **underemployment**. Another source of inefficiencies is placing employees in jobs beyond their abilities.

HOW LONG ARE PEOPLE USUALLY UNEMPLOYED?

The duration of unemployment is equally as important as the amount of unemployment. The financial consequences of a head of household's being unemployed for four or five weeks are usually not extremely serious, particularly if the individual is covered by an unemployment compensation system. The impact becomes much more serious if that person is unemployed for several months. Therefore, it is useful to look at the average duration of unemployment to discover what

EXHIBIT 11.5 Duration of Unemployment

Duration	Percent Unemployed
Less than 5 weeks	18
5 to 14 weeks	23
15 to 26 weeks	18
27 weeks and over	41

SOURCE: Bureau of Labor Statistics, Current Population Survey, Employment Situation Summary Table A. Washington, D.C., March 5, 2010. Available at http://www.bls.gov/news.release/empsit.a.htm (accessed March 25, 2010).

percentage of the labor force is unemployed longer than a certain period, say 15 weeks. Exhibit 11.5 presents data on the duration of unemployment. As you can see in this table, 18 percent of the unemployed were out of work less than five weeks, and 41 percent of the total unemployed were out of work for more than six months. The duration of unemployment tends to be greater when the amount of unemployment is high and smaller when the amount of unemployment is low. Unemployment of any duration, of course, means a potential loss of output. This loss of current output is permanent; it is not made up when unemployment starts falling again.

LABOR FORCE PARTICIPATION RATE

The percentage of the working age (aged 16 and older) population that is in the labor force is what economists call the **labor force participation rate**. Since 1950, the labor force participation rate increased from 59.2 percent to slightly under 64.8 percent today. During this time, the gender makeup of the labor force participation rate has changed significantly. For example, the number of women working shifted dramatically, reflecting the changing role of women in the workforce. Some factors contributing to this dramatic change are technological advances in household appliances and the decline in average household size. In Exhibit 11.6, we see that in 1950, less than 34 percent of women were working or looking for work. At the start of 2010 that figure was roughly 59 percent. In 1950, more than 85 percent of men were working or looking for work. In 2010 the labor force participation rate for men fell to 71 percent, as many men stay in school longer and opt to retire earlier.

EXHIBIT 11.4 Reasons for Unemployment

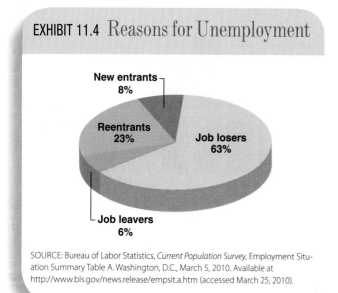

New entrants 8%

Reentrants 23%

Job losers 63%

Job leavers 6%

SOURCE: Bureau of Labor Statistics, *Current Population Survey*, Employment Situation Summary Table A. Washington, D.C., March 5, 2010. Available at http://www.bls.gov/news.release/empsit.a.htm (accessed March 25, 2010).

EXHIBIT 11.6 Labor Force Participation Rates for Men and Women

	1950	1960	1970	1980	1990	2000	2010
Total	59.2%	59.4%	60.4%	63.8%	66.4%	67.1%	64.8%
Men	86.4%	83.3%	79.7%	77.4%	76.1%	64.8%	71.0%
Women	33.9%	37.7%	43.3%	51.5%	57.5%	59.9%	58.9%

SOURCE: Bureau of Labor Statistics, *Current Population Survey*, Table A-1. Employment status of the civilian population by sex and age. Washington, D.C., March 5, 2010. Available at http://www.bls.gov/news.release/empsit.a.htm (accessed March 25, 2010).

SECTION CHECK 2

2.1 The consequences of unemployment for society include a reduction in potential output and consumption—a decrease in efficiency.

2.2 The unemployment rate is found by taking the number of people officially unemployed and dividing by the number in the civilian labor force.

2.3 Unemployment rates are highest for minorities, the young, and less-skilled workers.

2.4 The duration of unemployment tends to be greater (smaller) when the amount of unemployment is high (low).

ⓢ3 Types of Unemployment

Keep the following questions in mind as you read through this section. You'll find the answers in Section Check 3.

3.1 What is frictional unemployment?

3.2 What is structural unemployment?

3.3 What is cyclical unemployment?

3.4 What is the natural rate of unemployment?

In examining the status of and changes in the unemployment rate, it is important to recognize that un-employment can take several forms. In this section, we will examine the three types of unemployment—frictional, structural, and cyclical—and evaluate the relative effects of each on the overall unemployment rate.

FRICTIONAL UNEMPLOYMENT

In a dynamic economy in which people are constantly losing or leaving their jobs, some frictional unemployment is always present. **Frictional unemployment** is the temporary unemployment that results from the search time that occurs when people are searching for suitable jobs and firms are looking for suitable workers. People seeking work do not usually take the first job offered to them. Likewise, firms do not usually take the first person they interview. People and firms engage in a search to match up skills and interests. While the unemployed are looking, they are frictionally unemployed. Frictional unemployment occurs when people are searching for jobs. They might be laid off from a current job, changing jobs, or searching for the "right" job after finishing school. Economists expect many people to fall into this category.

For example, consider an advertising executive who was fired in Chicago and is now actively looking for similar work in San Francisco. Of course, not all unemployed workers were fired; some may have voluntarily quit their jobs. In either case, frictional unemployment is short term and results from normal turnover in the labor market, as when people change from one job to another.

Some unemployment occurs because certain types of jobs are seasonal in nature. This type of unemployment is called *seasonal unemployment*. For example, a ski instructor in Aspen might become seasonally unemployed at the end of April when ski season is over. Or a roofer in Minnesota may become

frictional unemployment
the unemployment that results from workers searching for suitable jobs and firms looking for suitable workers

seasonally unemployed during the harsh winter months. In agricultural areas, employment increases during harvest season and falls after the season is over. Even a forest firefighter in a national park might only be employed during the summer and fall, when forest fires peak. Occupations that experience either sharp seasonal shifts in demand or are subject to changing weather conditions may lead to seasonal unemployment—like in agriculture where employment increases during harvest season. Because this type of unemployment can make the unemployment rate higher in the off-season and lower during the in-season, the Bureau of Labor Statistics (BLS) publishes a seasonally adjusted unemployment rate as well. These figures are more accurate because they take into account the effects of seasonal unemployment.

SHOULD WE WORRY ABOUT FRICTIONAL UNEMPLOYMENT?

Geographic and occupational mobility are considered good for the economy because they generally lead

human resources to go from activities of relatively low productivity or value to areas of higher productivity, increasing output in society as well as the wage income of the mover. Indeed, some of this frictional unemployment involving searches by firms and workers to find *more* suitable matchups is obviously beneficial to the economy. Even though the amount of frictional unemployment varies somewhat over time, it is unusual for it to be much less than 2 percent of the labor force. Actually, frictional unemployment tends to be somewhat greater in periods of low unemployment, when job opportunities are plentiful. This high level of job opportunity stimulates mobility, which, in turn, creates some frictional unemployment.

STRUCTURAL UNEMPLOYMENT

A second type of unemployment is structural unemployment. Like frictional unemployment, **structural unemployment** is related to occupational movement or mobility—in this case, to a lack of mobility. Structural unemployment occurs when workers lack the necessary skills for jobs that are available or have particular skills that are no longer in demand. For example, if a machine operator in a manufacturing plant loses his job, he could still remain unemployed despite the openings for computer programmers in his community. The quantity of unemployed workers conceivably could equal the number of job vacancies, with the unemployment persisting because the unemployed lack the appropriate skills. Given the existence of structural unemployment, it is wise to look at both unemployment and job vacancy statistics in assessing labor market conditions. Structural unemployment, like frictional unemployment, reflects the dynamic dimension of a changing economy. Over time, new jobs open up that require new skills, while old jobs that required different skills disappear. It is not surprising, then, that many people advocate government-subsidized

What type of unemployment would occur if these coal miners lost their jobs as a result of a permanent reduction in demand for coal and needed retraining to find other employment?

retraining programs as a means of reducing structural unemployment.

Another reason for structural unemployment is that low-skilled workers are frequently unable to find desirable long-term employment. Some of these low-skilled jobs do not last long and involve little job training, so a worker may soon be looking for a new job. Because they acquired no new skill from the old job, they may be stuck without long-term secure work. That is, structural workers cannot be said to be "in-between jobs" like those who are frictionally unemployed. Structural unemployment is more long term and serious than frictional unemployment because these workers do not have marketable skills.

The dimensions of structural unemployment are debatable, in part because of the difficulty in precisely defining the term in an operational sense. Structural unemployment varies considerably—sometimes it is low and at other times, as in the 1970s and early 1980s, it is high. To some extent, in the latter period, jobs in the traditional sectors, such as automobile manufacturing and oil production, were giving way to jobs in the computer and biotechnology sectors. Consequently, structural unemployment was higher.

SOME UNEMPLOYMENT IS UNAVOIDABLE

Some unemployment is actually normal and important to the economy. Frictional and structural unemployment are simply unavoidable in a vibrant economy. To a considerable extent, we can view both frictional and structural unemployment as phenomena resulting from imperfections in the labor market. For example, if individuals seeking jobs and employers seeking workers had better information about each other, the amount of frictional unemployment would be considerably less. It takes time for suppliers of labor to find the demanders of labor services, and it takes time and money for labor resources to acquire the necessary skills. But because information and job searches are costly, bringing together demanders and suppliers of labor services does not occur instantaneously.

CYCLICAL UNEMPLOYMENT

Often, unemployment is composed of more than just frictional and structural unemployment. In years of relatively high unemployment, some joblessness may result from short-term cyclical fluctuations in the economy. We call this **cyclical unemployment**. Whenever the unemployment rate is greater than normal, such as during a recession, it is due to cyclical unemployment. Most attempts to solve the cyclical unemployment problem emphasized increasing aggregate demand to counter recession.

cyclical unemployment unemployment due to short-term cyclical fluctuations in the economy

natural rate of unemployment the median, or "typical," unemployment rate, equal to the sum of frictional and structural unemployment when they are at a maximum

The Cost of Cyclical Unemployment

When the unemployment rate is high, numerous economic and social hardships result. The economic costs are the forgone output when the economy is not producing at its potential level. According to Okun's Law (really, a rule of thumb), a 1 percent increase in cyclical unemployment reduces output by 2 percentage points. Thus, we can actually estimate the economic costs of not producing at our potential output. The costs are particularly high for those groups with the least skills—the poorly educated and teenagers with little work experience.

THE NATURAL RATE OF UNEMPLOYMENT

It is interesting to observe that over the period in which annual unemployment data are available, the median, or "typical," annual unemployment rate has been at or slightly above 5 percent. Some economists call this typical unemployment rate the **natural rate of unemployment**. When unemployment rises well above 5 percent, we have abnormally high unemployment; when it falls well below 5 percent, we have abnormally low unemployment. The natural rate of unemployment of approximately 5 percent roughly equals the sum of frictional and structural unemployment when they are at their maximums. Thus, we can view unemployment rates below the natural rate as reflecting the existence of below-average levels of frictional and structural unemployment. When unemployment rises above the natural rate, however, it reflects the existence of cyclical unemployment. In short, the natural rate of unemployment is the unemployment rate that occurs when the economy is experiencing neither a recession nor a boom. The natural rate of unemployment is also called the *full employment rate of unemployment*.

The natural rate of unemployment can change over time as technological, demographic, institutional, and

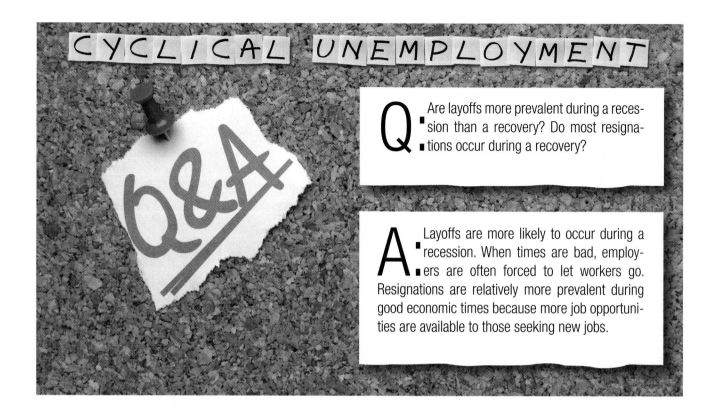

CYCLICAL UNEMPLOYMENT

Q: Are layoffs more prevalent during a recession than a recovery? Do most resignations occur during a recovery?

A: Layoffs are more likely to occur during a recession. When times are bad, employers are often forced to let workers go. Resignations are relatively more prevalent during good economic times because more job opportunities are available to those seeking new jobs.

other conditions vary. For example, as baby boomers age, the natural rate falls because middle-aged workers generally experience lower unemployment rates than do younger workers. In addition, the Internet and job placement agencies have improved access to employment information and allowed workers to find jobs more quickly. Also, the new work requirements of the welfare laws increased the number of people with jobs. Thus, the natural rate is not fixed, because it can change with demographic changes over time.

Full Employment and Potential Output

When all the resources of an economy—labor, land, and capital—are fully employed, the economy is said to be producing its **potential output**. Literally, *full employment of labor* means that the economy is providing employment for all who are willing and able to work with no cyclical unemployment. It also means that capital and land are fully employed. That is, at the natural rate of unemployment, all resources are fully employed, the economy is producing its potential output, and no cyclical unemployment is present. It does not mean the economy will always be producing at its potential

potential output the amount of real output the economy would produce if its labor and other resources were fully employed, that is, at the natural rate of unemployment

output of resources. For example, when the economy is experiencing cyclical unemployment, the unemployment rate is greater than the natural rate. It is also possible for the economy to temporarily exceed the natural rate, as workers put in overtime or moonlight by taking on extra employment.

SECTION CHECK 3

3.1 Frictional unemployment results when workers move from one job to another as workers search for suitable jobs and firms look for suitable workers.

3.2 Structural unemployment results when people who are looking for jobs lack the required skills for the jobs that are available if a long-term change in demand occurs.

3.3 Cyclical unemployment is caused by recession.

3.4 The natural rate of unemployment is achieved when cyclical unemployment is almost completely eliminated.

⑤4 Reasons for Unemployment

Keep the following questions in mind as you read through this section. You'll find the answers in Section Check 4.

4.1 How does a higher minimum wage lead to greater unemployment among the young and unskilled?

4.2 How does an efficiency wage cause a higher rate of unemployment?

4.3 Does unemployment insurance increase the unemployment rate?

In this section, we will look at the causes of frictional and structural unemployment. In later chapters, we will discuss the causes of cyclical unemployment.

WHY DOES UNEMPLOYMENT EXIST?

In many markets, prices adjust to the market equilibrium price and quantity, and no prolonged periods of shortage or surplus occur. However, in labor markets, obstacles prevent wages from adjusting and balancing the quantity of labor supplied and the quantity of labor demanded. In Exhibit 11.7, we see that W_1 is higher than the market equilibrium wage that equates the quantity demanded of labor with the quantity supplied of labor. At W_1, the quantity of labor supplied is greater than the quantity of labor demanded, resulting in an excess quantity supplied of labor—unemployment. That is, more people want to work at the going (non-equilibrium) wage than employers want to hire, and those who are not able to find work are "unemployed." Why? Economists cite three reasons for the failure of wages to balance the labor demand and labor supply equilibrium—minimum wages, unions, and the efficiency wage theory.

MINIMUM WAGES AND UNEMPLOYMENT

Many different types of labor markets exist for different types of workers. The labor market for workers with little experience and job skills is called the unskilled labor market. Suppose the government decided to establish a **minimum wage rate** (an hourly wage floor) for unskilled workers above the equilibrium wage, W_E.

At the minimum wage, the quantity of labor supplied grows because more people are willing to work at a higher wage.

minimum wage rate an hourly wage floor set above the equilibrium wage

However, the quantity of labor demanded falls because some employers would find it unprofitable to hire low-skilled workers at the higher wage. At W_1, a gap exists between the quantity of labor demanded and the quantity supplied, representing a surplus of unskilled workers—unemployment, as seen in Exhibit 11.7.

Because minimum wage earners, a majority of whom are 25 years or younger, are a small portion of the labor force, most economists believe the effect of minimum wage on unemployment is small.

THE IMPACT OF UNIONS ON THE UNEMPLOYMENT RATE

Unions negotiate their wages and benefits collectively through their union officials, a process called collective bargaining. If, through this process of collective bargaining, union officials are able to increase wages, then unemployment will rise in the union sector. If the bargaining raises the union wage above the equilibrium level, the quantity of union labor demanded will decrease, and the quantity of union labor supplied will increase—that is, union workers will be unemployed. The union workers who still have their jobs will be better off, but some who are equally skilled will be unemployed and will either seek nonunion work or wait to be recalled in the union sector. Many economists believe that is

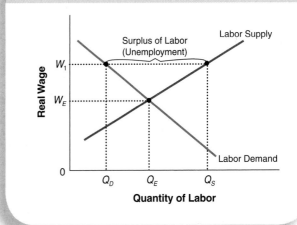

EXHIBIT 11.7 Wages above Equilibrium Lead to Greater Unemployment

why wages are approximately 15 percent higher in union jobs, even when nonunion workers have comparable skills. On the other hand, even though wages in the union sector are typically higher than the market wage, the presence of unions does not necessarily lead to greater unemployment, because workers can find jobs in the nonunion sector. Less than 10 percent of private sector jobs are unionized.

EFFICIENCY WAGE

In economics, it is generally assumed that as productivity rises, wages rise, and workers can raise their productivity through investments in human capital such as education and on-the-job training. However, some economists follow the **efficiency wage model**, which is based on the belief that *higher wages lead to greater productivity.*

In the efficiency wage model, employers pay their employees more than the equilibrium wage to be more efficient. Proponents of this theory suggest that it may lead to attracting the most productive workers, fewer job turnovers, and higher morale, which in turn can lead to lower hiring and training costs. In addition, higher-paid workers may be healthier (better diets) and therefore more productive. This is particularly true in developing countries. In Exhibit 11.7, suppose workers are paid W_E. Why wouldn't they shirk at their current job if someone else will hire them almost immediately at the same wage? In short, there are few adverse consequences to shirking. One option for firms is to pay an efficiency wage. However, if all firms pay an efficiency wage, like W_1 in Exhibit 11.7, then why can't they just shirk and if fired, find another firm that will pay them W_1? The reason is because at W_1, firms are paying higher than the equilibrium wage reducing the number of jobs, so fired workers might face a prolonged period of unemployment.

In 1914, Henry Ford increased his workers' wages from $3 to $5 per day—roughly twice the going wage rate for unskilled workers. This wage rate led to long lines of workers seeking jobs at the Ford plant—that is, quantity supplied greatly exceeded quantity demanded at the efficiency wage rate. Ford knew that assembly-line work was boring, and to overcome the problem he was having with morale and absenteeism, he decided to increase daily wages to $5 a day. At the time, many business leaders were skeptical because this put Ford's

By raising his workers' wages from $3 to $5 per day, Henry Ford was able to reduce turnover and absenteeism and generally improve worker productivity.

labor costs at nearly twice that of his rivals. However, Ford's profits continued to mount. Historical records suggest that the efficiency wage led to lower turnover, less absenteeism, better hires, and less shirking—in short, greater worker productivity. Even though the higher wages led to higher labor costs, the costs were more than offset by the increase in worker productivity.

Some scholars have argued that the positive effects of the efficiency wage are unique to assembly-line production and its high degree of worker interdependence. However, it is costly for firms to pay an efficiency wage. Consequently, firms must monitor their workers' efforts. If enough firms resort to paying the efficiency wage rate, it leads to a surplus of workers who want jobs and cannot find them. This, like a binding minimum wage, leads to unemployment.

JOB SEARCH

Another reason for unemployment has to do with the nature of labor markets. Because of frictional unemployment, some unemployment would exist even if labor supply and labor demand were balanced. Different firms offer different compensation packages (i.e., salary, fringe benefits, and working conditions), and workers are sometimes unaware of these packages when they seek the "best" job available. It takes time and money to locate the best available opportunities. Also, not all job seekers are the same: They have different tastes and preferences about types of jobs and job locations. Sometimes it is difficult to get the information about particular jobs to the right job candidate. These search activities prolong the duration of unemployment. However, the search goes on because the job seeker hopes to find a better offer.

The labor demand and supply curves are constantly shifting. That is, labor markets are constantly in flux—there are always people losing jobs, leaving jobs, and reentering jobs. In a growing and dynamic economy, jobs are constantly being destroyed and created, leading to temporary unemployment as workers search for the best jobs for their skills.

UNEMPLOYMENT INSURANCE

Losing a job can lead to considerable hardships, and unemployment insurance is designed to partially offset the severity of the unemployment problem. The program does not cover those who were fired or quit their jobs. To qualify, recipients must have worked a certain length of time and lost their jobs because the employer no longer needed their skills. The typical compensation is half salary for 26 weeks. Although the program is intended to ease the pain of unemployment, it also leads to prolonged periods of unemployment, as job seekers stay unemployed for longer periods searching for new jobs.

For example, some unemployed people may show little drive in seeking new employment, because unemployment insurance lowers the opportunity cost of being unemployed. Say a worker making $400 a week when employed receives $220 in compensation when unemployed; as a result, the cost of losing the job is not $400 a week in forgone income but only $180. It has been estimated that the existence of unemployment compensation programs may raise overall unemployment rates by as much as 1 percent.

Without unemployment insurance, a job seeker would be more likely to take the first job offered, even if the job did not match the job seeker's preferences or skill levels. A longer job search might mean a better match, but it comes at the expense of lost production and greater amounts of tax dollars.

DOES NEW TECHNOLOGY LEAD TO GREATER UNEMPLOYMENT?

The widespread belief that technological advances inevitably result in the displacement of workers is not necessarily true. Generally, new inventions are cost saving, and these cost savings usually generate higher incomes for producers and lower prices and better products for consumers—benefits that ultimately result in the growth of other industries. If the new equipment is a substitute for labor, it might displace workers. For example, many fast-food restaurants installed self-service beverage bars to replace workers. However, new capital equipment requires new workers to manufacture and repair the new equipment. The most famous example of this trade-off is the computer, which was supposed to displace thousands of workers. Instead, the computer generated a whole new growth industry that created jobs. The problem is that it is easy to see only the initial effect of technological advances (displaced workers) but difficult to recognize the implications of that invention throughout the whole economy over time.

Some economists believe that some of the real-wage differentials between skilled and unskilled workers in the last couple of decades are due to technical changes that are biased toward skilled workers. New machines, with highly sophisticated computerization, require highly skilled workers. Consequently, the new machines make these workers more productive and therefore they receive higher real wages. In Exhibit 11.8(a), we graph the labor market for skilled workers. Because of the increase in demand for skilled labor—skilled workers can produce more with the new machines—their real wages and employment are higher. At the same time, the demand is lower for workers who do not have the technical training to work with specialized machinery, and the demand for unskilled workers falls, as seen in Exhibit 11.8(b). As a result of the decrease in demand for unskilled workers, real wages and employment fall.

It has been estimated that the existence of unemployment compensation programs may raise overall unemployment rates by as much as 1 percent.

EXHIBIT 11.8 Skill-Biased Technical Change and Wage Inequality

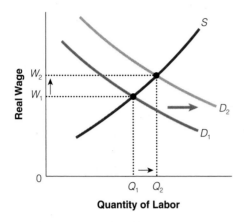

a. Skilled Workers

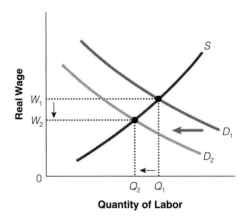

b. Unskilled Workers

Thus, skill-biased technical change tends to create even greater disparities between the wages of skilled and unskilled workers. The message: stay in school (vocational or traditional).

SECTION CHECK 4

4.1 At the minimum wage, the quantity of labor supplied grows. However, the quantity of labor demanded falls because some employers would find it unprofitable to hire low-skilled workers at the higher wage. Thus a higher minimum wage can lead to higher unemployment—particularly among unskilled teenage workers.

4.2 If the efficiency wage rate is greater than the equilibrium wage rate, the quantity of labor supplied is greater than the quantity of labor demanded, resulting in greater amounts of unemployment.

4.3 Some unemployed persons may show little drive in seeking new employment, given the existence of unemployment compensation. Unemployment compensation lowers the opportunity cost of being unemployed.

⑤5 Inflation

Keep the following questions in mind as you read through this section. You'll find the answers in Section Check 5.

5.1 What is the purpose of a price-level index?

5.2 Who are the winners and losers during inflation?

5.3 Can wage earners avoid the consequences of inflation?

Just as full employment brings about one kind of economic security, an overall stable **price level** increases another form of economic security.

STABLE PRICE LEVEL AS A DESIRABLE GOAL

Most prices in the U.S. economy tend to rise over time. The continuing rise in the *overall* price level is called **inflation**. Even when the level of prices is stable, some prices will be rising while others are falling. However, when inflation is present, the goods and services with rising prices will outweigh the goods and services with lower prices. Without stability in the price level, consumers and producers will experience more difficulty in coordinating their plans and decisions. When the *overall* price level is falling, it is called **deflation**. The average price level in the U.S. economy fell throughout the late nineteenth century.

In general, the only thing that can cause a *sustained* increase in the rate of inflation is a high rate of growth in money, a topic we will discuss further in upcoming chapters.

MEASURING INFLATION

We often use the term *purchasing power* when we discuss how much a dollar can buy of goods and services. In times of inflation, a dollar cannot buy as many goods and services. Thus, the higher the inflation rate, the greater the rate of decline in purchasing power.

In periods of high and variable inflation, households and firms have a difficult time distinguishing between changes in the **relative price** of individual goods and services (the price of a specific good compared to the prices of other goods) and changes in the general price level of all goods and services. Suppose the price of milk rises by 5 percent between 2010 and 2011, but the overall price level (inflation rate) increases by only 2 percent during that period. Then we could say that between 2010 and 2011, the relative price of milk rose only 3 percent (5 − 2 percent). The next year, the price of milk might increase 5 percent again, but the general inflation rate might be 6 percent. That is, between 2011 and 2012, the relative price of milk might actually fall by 1 percent (5 − 6 percent). Remember, the relative price is the price of a good relative to all other goods and services. Because of this difficulty in establishing relative prices, inflation distorts the information that flows from price signals. Does the good have a higher price because it has become relatively more scarce and therefore more valuable relative to other goods, or did the price rise along with all other prices because of inflation? This muddying of price information undermines good decision making.

Thus, we need a method to measure inflation. We adjust for the changing purchasing power of the dollar by constructing a price index. Essentially, a **price index** attempts to provide a measure of the prices paid for a certain bundle of goods and services over time.

THE CONSUMER PRICE INDEX AND THE GDP DEFLATOR

There are many different types of price indices. The most well-known index, the **consumer price index (CPI)**, measures the trend in the prices of certain goods and services purchased for consumption purposes—see Exhibit 11.9. The CPI may be most relevant to households trying to evaluate their changing financial positions over time.

The **GDP deflator** corrects for changing prices in even broader terms. The GDP deflator measures the average level of prices of all final goods and services produced in the economy.

HOW IS A PRICE INDEX CREATED?

Constructing a price index is complicated. First, literally thousands of goods and services are in our economy; attempting to include all of them in an index would be cumbersome and make the index expensive to compute, and it would take a long time to gather the necessary data. Therefore, a "bundle" or "basket" of representative goods and services is selected by the index calculators (the Bureau of Labor Statistics of the U.S. Department of Labor for consumer and wholesale price indices and the Office of Business Economics of the Department of Commerce for the GDP deflator).

Calculating a Simple Price Index

Suppose a consumer typically buys 24 loaves of bread and 12 gallons of milk in a year. The table that follows on the next page lists the prices of bread and milk and the cost of the consumer's typical market basket in the years 2010–2012.

relative price the price of a specific good compared to the price of other goods

price index a measure of the trend in prices paid for a certain bundle of goods and services over a given period

consumer price index (CPI) a measure of the cost of a market basket that represents the consumption of a typical household

GDP deflator a price index that helps measure the average price level of all final consumer goods and services produced

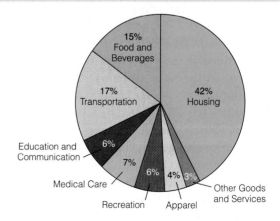

EXHIBIT 11.9 The Typical CPI Shopping Basket of Goods and Services

SOURCE: Bureau of Labor Statistics, *Consumer Price Index - February 2010*, Table 1. Consumer Price Index for All Urban Consumers. Washington, D.C., March 18, 2010. Available at http://www.bls.gov/news.release/cpi.t01.htm (accessed March 25, 2010).

Year	Price of Bread	Price of Milk	Cost of Market Basket
2010	$1.00	$2.00	(24 × $1.00) + (12 × $2.00) = $48.00
2011	$1.15	$2.10	(24 × $1.15) + (12 × $2.10) = $52.80
2012	$1.40	$2.20	(24 × $1.40) + (12 × $2.20) = $60.00

Using the numbers from the table above and the following formula, we can calculate a price index to measure the inflation rate.

$$\text{Price index} = \frac{\text{Cost of market basket in current year}}{\text{Cost of market basket in base year}} \times 100$$

The year 2010 is designated as the base year, so its value is set equal to 100.

Year	Price Index
2010	$48/$48 × 100 = 100
2011	$52.80/$48 × 100 = 110
2012	$60/$48 × 100 = 125

A comparison of the price indices shows that between 2010 and 2011, prices increased an average of 10 percent. In addition, between 2010 and 2012, 25 percent inflation occurred.

$$\text{Price index} = \frac{\text{Cost of market basket in 2012}}{\text{Cost of market basket in 2010}} \times 100$$

$$= \frac{\$60}{\$48} \times 100 = 125$$

That is, the price index for 2012 compared with 2010 is 125. Therefore, using the price index formula, we can say that prices are 25 percent higher in 2012 than they were in 2010, the base year.

Unfortunately, not all prices move by the same amount or in the same direction. Consequently, we need to calculate an average of the many price changes. This calculation is complicated by several factors. First, goods and services change in quality over time, so the observed price change may, in reality, reflect a quality change in the product rather than the purchasing power of the dollar. A $300 television set today is dramatically better than a television set in 1950. Second, new products come on the market and old products occasionally disappear. For example, color TV sets did not exist in 1950 but are a major consumer item now. How can we calculate changes in prices over time when some products did not even exist in the earlier period? Clearly, calculating a price index is not a simple, direct process, and many factors can potentially distort the CPI.

GDP DEFLATOR VERSUS CPI

Is the CPI or the GDP deflator a better indicator of inflation? Or does it not really matter which one we use? In Exhibit 11.10, we see that the two measures tend to move in the same direction but that the CPI tends to be much more volatile—it bounces around more than the GDP deflator. However, both measures probably overstate the inflation rate. One important difference between them that can yield different results is that the GDP deflator measures the price of all goods and services that are *produced domestically*, while the CPI measures the goods and services *bought by consumers*. For example, a Porsche produced in Stuttgart, Germany, will show up in the CPI, but it will not show up in the GDP deflator because it was not produced in the U.S. economy. More important, the same is true for the price of oil, because much of U.S. oil is imported. Consequently, oil price increases are fully captured in the CPI but only partially captured in the GDP deflator—partially captured because those increases do add to the cost of production.

However, suppose the price of an airplane or aircraft carrier being produced domestically for the military increases. Because it is produced domestically, its price will show up in the GDP deflator but not in the typical consumer basket—the CPI.

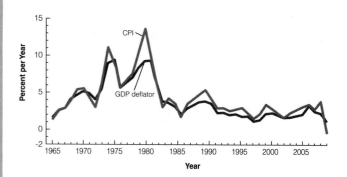

EXHIBIT 11.10 The CPI and the GDP Deflator

SOURCES: Bureau of Labor Statistics, *Consumer Price Index*, Table Containing History of CPI-U U.S. All Items Indexes and Annual Percent Changes From 1913 to Present. Washington, D.C., March 18, 2010. Available at ftp://ftp.bls.gov/pub/special.requests/cpi/cpiai.txt (accessed March 25, 2010). Bureau of Economic Analysis, National Economic Accounts, Current-dollar and "real" GDP. Washington, D.C., February 26, 2010. Available at http://bea.gov/national/index.htm#gdp (accessed March 25, 2010).

THE PRICE LEVEL OVER THE YEARS

Unanticipated and sharp changes in the price level are almost universally considered to be "bad" and to require a policy remedy. What is the historical record of changes in the overall U.S. price level? Exhibit 11.11 shows changes in the consumer price index (CPI), the standard measure of inflation, from 1913 to 2009. Can you believe that in 1940, stamps were 3 cents per letter, postcards were a penny, the median price of a house was $2,900, and the price of a new car was $650? However, the problem with comparing prices today with prices in the past is that it focuses on the number of dollars it takes to buy something, rather than the purchasing power of the dollar. For example, if prices and wages both doubled overnight, raising the price of a quart of milk from $1 to $2, you would be no worse off because you would still work the same number of minutes to buy a quart of milk.

WHO LOSES WITH INFLATION?

Inflation brings about changes in peoples' purchasing power, and these changes may be either desirable or undesirable. Suppose you retire on a fixed pension of $2,000 per month. Over time, that $2,000 will buy less and less if prices generally rise. Your real income—your income adjusted to reflect changes in purchasing power—falls. Inflation lowers income in real terms for people on fixed-dollar incomes. Likewise, inflation can hurt creditors. For example, suppose a bank loaned someone money for a house at a 4 percent fixed rate for 20 years, in the early 1960s (a period of low inflation). However, the 1970s was a period of high inflation rates (roughly 10 percent per year). Under this scenario, because the lender did not correctly anticipate the higher rate of inflation, the lender is the victim of unanticipated inflation. That is, the borrower is paying back with dollars that have much less purchasing power than those dollars they borrowed in the early 1960s. Another group that sometimes loses from inflation, at least temporarily, comprises people whose incomes are tied to long-term contracts. If inflation begins shortly after a labor union signs a three-year wage agreement, it may completely eat up the wage gains provided by the contract. The same applies to businesses that agree to sell quantities of one thing, say coal, for a fixed price for a given number of years.

If some people lose because of changing prices, others must gain. Debtors pay back dollars worth less in purchasing power than those borrowed. Corporations that can quickly raise the prices on their goods may have revenue gains greater than their increases in costs, providing additional profits. Wage earners sometimes lose from inflation because wages may rise at a slower rate than the price level. The redistributional impact of inflation is not the result of conscious public policy; it just happens.

The uncertainty that inflation creates can also discourage investment and economic growth. When inflation rates are high, they also tend to vary considerably, which creates a lot of uncertainty. This uncertainty

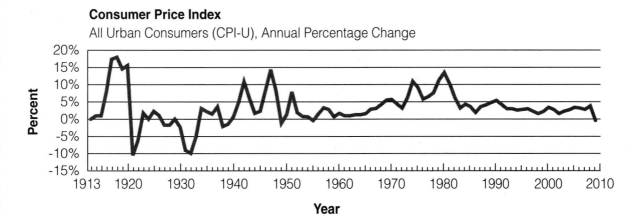

EXHIBIT 11.11 Inflation in the United States, 1913–2009

Consumer Price Index

All Urban Consumers (CPI-U), Annual Percentage Change

SOURCE: Bureau of Labor Statistics, *Consumer Price Index*, Table Containing History of CPI-U U.S. All Items Indexes and Annual Percent Changes From 1913 to Present. Washington, D.C., March 18, 2010. Available at ftp://ftp.bls.gov/pub/special.requests/cpi/cpiai.txt (accessed March 25, 2010).

hyperinflation extremely high rates of inflation for sustained periods of time

menu costs the costs imposed on a firm from changing listed prices

shoe-leather cost the cost incurred when individuals reduce their money holdings because of inflation

complicates planning for businesses and households, which is vital to capital formation, as well as adding an inflation risk premium to long-term interest rates.

Moreover, inflation can raise one nation's price level relative to price levels in other countries. In turn, this shift can make financing the purchase of foreign goods difficult, or it can decrease the value of the national currency relative to that of other countries.

Costs of High Inflation

Predictably low rates of inflation, while still a problem, are considerably better than high and variable inflation rates. A slow predictable rate of inflation makes predicting future price increases relatively easy. Consequently, setting interest rates will be an easier task and the redistribution effects of inflation will be minimized. In addition, high and variable inflation rates make it almost impossible to set long-term contracts because prices and interest rates may be changing by the day, or even by the hour in the case of **hyperinflation**—extremely high rates of inflation for sustained periods of time.

In its extreme form, inflation can lead to a complete erosion of faith in the value of the pieces of paper we commonly call money. In Germany, after both world wars, prices rose so fast that people in some cases finally refused to take paper money, insisting instead on payment in goods or metals, whose prices tend to move predictably with inflation. Unchecked inflation can feed on itself and may ultimately lead to hyperinflation of 300 percent or more per year. We saw these rapid rates of inflation in Argentina in the 1980s and Brazil in the 1990s. Most economists believe we can live quite well in an environment of low, steady inflation, but no economist believes we can prosper with high, variable inflation.

OTHER COSTS OF INFLATION

Another cost of inflation is the cost incurred by firms as a result of being forced to change prices more frequently. For example, a restaurant might have to print new menus, or a department or mail-order store may have to print new catalogs, to reflect changing prices. These costs are called **menu costs**; they are the costs of changing posted prices. In some South American economies in the 1980s, inflation increased at more than 300 percent per year, with prices changing on a daily, or even hourly, basis in some cases. Imagine how large the menu costs could be in an economy such as that!

The **shoe-leather cost** of inflation is the cost of going to and from the bank to check on your assets (so often that you wear out the leather on your shoes). Specifically, high rates of inflation erode the value of a currency, which means that people will want to hold less currency—perhaps going to the ATM once a week rather than twice a month. That is, the higher inflation rates lead to higher nominal interest rates, which may induce more individuals to put money in the bank rather than allowing it to depreciate in their pockets. So, the cost is really the time and convenience sacrificed to keep less money on hand than you would if inflation were not a factor. The effects of shoe-leather costs of inflation, like those of

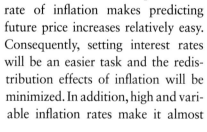

INFLATION AND CAPITAL GAINS TAXES

In an environment of inflation, the tax code can distort market signals and may lead to a reduction in saving, lending, and investment. To many economists, the problem stems from capital gains tax (a tax on a person's assets) being taxed in nominal terms rather than in real terms (adjusted for inflation). For example, suppose you sold a stock in 1980 for $50,000 that you bought in 1970 for $40,000. In real terms, adjusted for inflation, you would have lost money because the 25 percent increase in the stock price would be less than the percentage change in the inflation rate (over 100%). In fact, inflation was so high in the 1970s you would have lost money on your stock in real terms and then have to pay capital gains tax on the nominal gains— $10,000 ($50,000 − $40,000)—ouch! Thus, many economists believe capital gains should be taxed on real gains. In this case, you could write off capital losses because you actually lost money on your investment in real terms. These costs are not just a redistribution cost but can impact economic growth if the taxes are discouraging saving and investment.

(CPI) increases. With these clauses, laborers automatically get wage increases that reflect rising prices. The same is true of many pensioners, including those on Social Security. Personal income taxes likewise are now indexed (adjusted) for inflation. However, some of the tax code is still not indexed for inflation. These factors affect the incentives to work, save, and invest.

Some economists argue that we should go one step further and index everything, meaning that all contractual arrangements would be adjusted frequently to take account of changing prices. Such an arrangement might reduce the impact of inflation, but it would also entail additional contracting costs (and not every good—most notably, currency—can be indexed). An alternative approach has been to try to stop inflation through various policies relating to the amount of government spending, tax rates, and the amount of money created. **Wage and price controls**—legislation limiting wage and price increases— offer still another approach to the inflation problem.

menu costs, are modest in countries with low inflation rates but can be quite large in countries where inflation is substantial.

DO CREDITORS ALWAYS LOSE DURING INFLATION?

Usually, lenders are able to anticipate inflation with reasonable accuracy. For example, in the late 1970s, when the inflation rate was more than 10 percent a year, nominal interest rates on a 90-day Treasury bill were relatively high. In 2002, with low inflation rates, the nominal interest rate was relatively low. If the inflation rate is anticipated accurately, new creditors will not lose nor will debtors gain from a change in the inflation rate. However, nominal interest rates and real interest rates do not always run together. For example, in periods of high *unexpected* inflation, the nominal interest rates can be high when the real interest rates are low or even negative.

PROTECTING OURSELVES FROM INFLATION

Increasingly, groups try to protect themselves from inflation by means of cost-of-living clauses in contracts. Many long-term contracts between firms and unions include a cost of living allowance (COLA) that automatically increases when the consumer price index

SECTION CHECK 5

5.1 A price-level index allows us to compare prices paid for goods and services over time by creating a measure of how many dollars it would take to maintain a constant purchasing power over time.

5.2 Inflation generally hurts creditors and those on fixed incomes and pensions; debtors generally benefit from inflation.

5.3 Wage earners attempt to keep pace with inflation by demanding higher wages each year or by indexing their annual wage to inflation.

© ROEL SMART/ISTOCKPHOTO.COM / © STEFAN KLEIN/ISTOCKPHOTO.COM

Ⓢ6 Economic Fluctuations

Keep the following questions in mind as you read through this section. You'll find the answers in Section Check 6.

6.1 What are short-term economic fluctuations?

6.2 What are the four stages of a business cycle?

6.3 What is the difference between a recession and a depression?

The aggregate amount of economic activity in the United States and most other nations has increased markedly over time, even on a per capita basis, indicating economic growth. Short-term fluctuations in the level of economic activity also occur.

SHORT-TERM FLUCTUATIONS IN ECONOMIC GROWTH

We sometimes call the short-term fluctuations in economic activity **business cycles**. Exhibit 11.12 illustrates the distinction between long-term economic growth and short-term economic fluctuations. Over a long period, the line representing economic activity slopes upward, indicating increasing real output. Over short periods, however, both upward and downward output changes occur. Business cycles refer to the short-term ups and downs in economic activity, not to the long-term trend in output, which in modern times has been upward.

THE PHASES OF A BUSINESS CYCLE

A business cycle has four phases—expansion, peak, contraction, and trough—as illustrated in Exhibit 11.13. The period of **expansion** is when output (real GDP) is rising

business cycles short-term fluctuations in the economy relative to the long-term trend in output

expansion when output (real GDP) is rising significantly—the period between the trough of a recession and the next peak

peak the point in time when expansion comes to an end, that is, when output is at the highest point in the cycle

contraction when the economy is slowing down—measured from the peak to the trough

trough the point in time when output stops declining, that is, when business activity is at its lowest point in the cycle

EXHIBIT 11.12 Business Cycles and Economic Growth

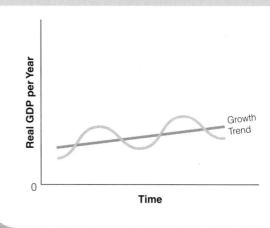

significantly. Usually, during the expansion phase, unemployment is falling and both consumer and business confidence are high. Thus, investment is rising, as are expenditures for expensive durable consumer goods, such as automobiles and household appliances. The **peak** is the point in time when the expansion comes to an end, when output is at the highest point in the cycle. The **contraction** is a period of falling real output and is usually accompanied by rising unemployment and declining business and consumer confidence. The contraction phase is measured from the peak to the **trough**—the point in time when output stops declining and business activity is at its lowest point in the cycle. Investment spending and expenditures on consumer durable goods fall sharply in a typical contraction. The

EXHIBIT 11.13 Four Phases of a Business Cycle

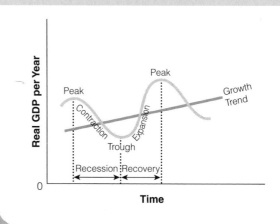

contraction phase is also called **recession**, a period of significant decline in output and employment (lasting more than a few months). Unemployment is relatively high at the trough, although the actual maximum amount of unemployment may not occur exactly at the trough. Often, unemployment remains fairly high well into the expansion phase. The expansion phase is measured from the trough to the peak.

HOW LONG DOES A BUSINESS CYCLE LAST?

The length of any given business cycle is not uniform. Because it does not have the regularity that the term *cycle* implies, economists often use the term *economic fluctuation* rather than *business cycle*. In addition, economic fluctuations are almost impossible to predict. In both the 1980s and the 1990s, expansions were quite long by historical standards. The contraction phase is one of recession, a decline in business activity. A severe recession is called a **depression**. Likewise, a prolonged expansion in economic activity is sometimes called a **boom**. Exhibit 11.14 shows the record of U.S. business cycles since 1920. Notice that contractions seem to be getting shorter over time. The National Bureau of Economic Research (NBER) Business Cycle Dating Committee determined that a recession began in March 2001, ending an expansion that lasted from March 1991 to March 2001. The attacks of September 11, 2001, clearly deepened the contraction and may have been instrumental in turning a contraction into a recession. The committee met in November of 2008 and determined that the economy peaked in December 2007, marking the end of a 73-month expansion and the beginning of a recession. There is a delay before the NBER announces the beginning or end of a recession, because of the complexities involved in gathering and evaluating the data. So the official beginning and end dates of a recession are not known until many months later.

recession a period of significant decline in output and employment

depression severe recession or contraction in output

boom period of prolonged economic expansion

EXHIBIT 11.14 A Historical Record of U.S. Recessions, 1920–2009

Peak	Trough	Length of Recession (months)
January 1920	July 1921	18
May 1923	July 1924	14
October 1926	November 1927	13
August 1929	March 1933	43
May 1937	June 1938	13
February 1945	October 1945	8
November 1948	October 1949	11
July 1953	May 1954	10
August 1957	April 1958	8
April 1960	February 1961	10
December 1969	November 1970	11
November 1973	March 1975	16
January 1980	July 1980	6
July 1981	November 1982	16
July 1990	March 1991	8
March 2001	November 2001	8
December 2007	—	—

SOURCES: National Bureau of Economic Research, Inc., *Business Cycle Expansions and Contractions*, U.S. Department of Commerce. Washington, D.C., December 1, 2008. Available at http://www.nber.org/cycles.html (accessed March 18, 2010).

SEASONAL FLUCTUATIONS AFFECT ECONOMIC ACTIVITY

The determinants of cyclical fluctuations in the economy are the major thrust of the next several chapters, and some fluctuation in economic activity reflects seasonal patterns. Business activity, whether measured by

production or by the sale of goods, tends to be high in the two months before the winter holidays and somewhat lower in summertime, when many families are on vacation. Within individual industries, of course, seasonal fluctuations in output often are extremely pronounced, agriculture being the best example. Often, key economic statistics, such as unemployment rates, are seasonally adjusted, meaning the numbers are modified to account for normal seasonal fluctuations. Thus, seasonally adjusted unemployment rates in summer months are below actual unemployment rates, because employment is normally high in summertime due to the inflow of school-age workers into the labor force.

FORECASTING CYCLICAL CHANGES

The farmer and the aviator rely heavily on weather forecasters for information on climatic conditions in planning their activities. Similarly, businesses, government agencies, and, to a lesser extent, consumers rely on economic forecasts to learn of forthcoming developments in the business cycle. If it looks as if the economy will continue in an expansionary phase, businesses may expand production to meet a perceived forthcoming need; if it looks as if contraction is coming, businesses may decide to be more cautious.

Forecasting Models

Using theoretical models, which will be discussed in later chapters, economists gather statistics on economic activity in the immediate past, including, for example, consumer expenditures, business inventories, the supply of money, governmental expenditures, tax revenues, and so on. Using past historical relationships between these factors and the overall level of economic activity (which form the basis of the economic theories), they formulate *econometric models*. Statistics from the immediate past are plugged into the model, and forecasts are made. Because human behavior changes, and our assumptions about certain future developments may not be correct, our numbers are imperfect, and our econometric models are not always accurate. But like the weather forecasts, although the econometric models are not perfect, they are helpful.

Leading Economic Indicators

One less sophisticated but useful forecasting tool is watching trends in **leading economic indicators**. Some types of economic activity change before the economy as a whole changes. If in March these activities show an increase after having declined for several months, past experience suggests that the entire output will start rising after a few months, perhaps in July or August. About a dozen such leading indicators exist, including the lengths of the average workweek, the size of the nation's money supply, prices of stocks, the number of new businesses formed, and new orders for plants and equipment. The Department of Commerce combines all these into an index of leading indicators. If the index rises sharply for two or three months, it is likely (but not certain) that increases in the overall level of activity will follow.

Since the development of the leading economic indicators, the composite index of leading economic indicators has never failed to give some warning of an economic downturn. Unfortunately, the lead time has varied widely. The composite index turned down 23 months prior to the 1957–1958 recession but gave only a three-month warning before the 1981–1982 slump. This variance in lead time can cause particular policy problems. Specifically, the use of leading economic indicators to predict future trends can make policy decisions less accurate. For example, if the federal government responds with policies to combat the recession as soon as the leading economic indicators begin predicting a recession, then the recession that would have occurred may fail to materialize. On the other hand, a self-fulfilling prophecy may result if businesses respond with cutbacks in orders for plants and equipment as soon as the leading economic indicators begin predicting a recession.

The economic indicators do provide a warning of a likely downturn, but they do not provide accurate information on the depth or duration of the downturn.

SECTION CHECK 6

6.1 Business cycles (or economic fluctuations) are short-term fluctuations in the amount of economic activity, relative to the long-term growth trend in output.

6.2 The four stages of a business cycle are expansion, peak, contraction, and trough.

6.3 Recessions occur during the contraction phase of a business cycle. Severe long-term recessions are called depressions.

Chapter 11: Self-Review

Now that you're finished reading the chapter, review the questions below. You can write your answers in the space provided, then go online to see the answers at www.cengagebrain.com.

S1—MACROECONOMIC GOALS

1. What is the Employment Act of 1946?

S2—EMPLOYMENT AND UNEMPLOYMENT

2. Fill-in-the-Blanks: The unemployment rate _____ as the number of unemployed people increases and it _____ when the labor force grows, *ceteris paribus*.

3. Why might the fraction of the unemployed who are job leavers be higher in a period of strong labor demand?

4. Suppose you live in a community of 100 people. If 80 people are aged 16 and older and 72 people are willing and able to work, what is the unemployment rate in this community?

S3—TYPES OF UNEMPLOYMENT

5. True or False: Frictional unemployment occurs when the unemployment rate is greater than normal.

6. What is the traditional government policy "cure" for cyclical unemployment?

7. True or False: At full employment (at the natural rate of unemployment), only frictional unemployment is present.

S4—REASONS FOR UNEMPLOYMENT

8. What is an efficiency wage?

9. True or False: New technology increases unemployment.

10. In a severe recession, what would tend to happen to the people in the following categories:
    a. job losers
    b. job leavers
    c. reentrants
    d. new entrants

S5—INFLATION

11. Say you owe money to Big River Bank. Will you gain or lose from an unanticipated decrease in inflation?

12. How could inflation make people turn to exchange by barter?

S6—ECONOMIC FLUCTUATIONS

13. True or False: Unemployment will fall during an economy's expansionary phase and rise during a contractionary phase.

Are you richer than Andrew Carnegie?

Carnegie, a steel magnate at the turn of the 20th century, was one of the wealthiest Americans ever to live, with a net worth valued at $100 billion in today's dollars. However, despite all his wealth, Carnegie could not buy many of the things you can today. When his business was at its height, he could not travel by air or by car, he had no AC for hot and humid days, and he could not watch television in high definition, surf the Internet, call or text friends on his cell phone, or listen to music from iTunes. The medical care he had access to was nowhere near as advanced as what you can find. All of these things have been made possible for you because of the increases in productivity and economic growth that America has experienced since Carnegie's day.

12

Economic Growth

J ohn Maynard Keynes, one of the most influential economic thinkers of all time, once said that "in the long run, we are all dead." He made this statement because he was primarily concerned with explaining and reducing short-term fluctuations in the level of business activity. He wanted to smooth out the business cycle, largely because of the implications that cyclical fluctuations had for buyers and sellers in terms of unemployment and price instability. No one would deny that Keynes's concerns were important and legitimate.

At the same time, however, Keynes's flippant remark about the long run discounts the fact that human welfare is greatly influenced by long-term changes in a nation's capacity to produce goods and services. Emphasis on short-run economic fluctuations ignores the longer-term dynamic changes that affect output, leisure, real income, and lifestyle.

What are the determinants of long-run economic change in our ability to produce goods and services? What are some of the consequences of rapid economic change? Why are some nations rich, whereas others are poor? Does growth in output improve our economic welfare? We will explore these questions in this chapter.

Sections in Chapter 12

Ⓢ1 Economic Growth

Keep the following questions in mind as you read through this section. You'll find the answers in Section Check 1.

1.1 What is economic growth?

1.2 What is the Rule of 70?

1.3 What is productivity?

Economic growth is usually measured by the annual percentage change in real output of goods and services per capita (real GDP per capita), reflecting the expansion of the economy over time. We focus on per capita because

> **economic growth** an upward trend in the real per capita output of goods and services

we want to isolate the effect of increased population on economic growth. That is, an increase in population, *ceteris paribus,* will lower the standard of living because more people will be sharing a fixed real GDP. It is also important to note that our economic growth rate does not say anything about the distribution of output and income. For example, a country could have extraordinary growth in per capita output and yet the poor might make little or no improvement in their standard of living. That is, it is possible that income group made little or no gain.

In Chapter 2, we introduced the production possibilities curve. Along the production possibilities curve, the economy is producing at its potential output. How much the economy will produce at its potential output, sometimes called its *natural rate of output*, depends on the quantity and quality of its resources, including labor, capital (factories, machinery, tools, productive skills, etc.), and natural resources (land, coal, timber, oil, iron, etc.). In addition, technology can increase the economy's production capabilities. As shown in Exhibit 12.1, improvements in and greater stocks of land, labor, capital, and entrepreneurial activity will shift the production possibilities curve outward. Another way of saying that economic growth has shifted the production possibilities curve outward is to say that it has increased potential output.

THE RULE OF 70

If Nation A and Nation B start off with the same population and the same level of real GDP, will a slight difference in their growth rates over a long period of time make much of a difference? Yes. In the first year or two, the difference will be small; but even over a decade the difference will be large, and after 50 to 100 years it will be huge. The final effect will be a much higher standard of living in the nation with the greater economic growth, *ceteris paribus.*

A simple formula called the Rule of 70 shows how long it will take a nation to double its output at various growth rates. If you take a nation's growth rate and divide it into 70, you will have the approximate time it will take to double the income level. For example, if a nation grows at 3.5 percent per year, then the economy will double every 20 years (70/3.5). However, if an economy only grows at 2 percent per year, the economy will double every 35 years (70/2); and at a 1 percent annual growth rate, it will take 70 years to double income (70/1). So even a small change in the growth rate of a nation will have a large impact over a lengthy period.

In Exhibit 12.2, we see the growth rates in real GDP for the United States since 1790. The exhibit shows U.S. real GDP per capita (measured in year 2005 dollars) grew from $1,025 in 1790 to $42,247 in 2009. Compared to in the depth of the Great Depression in 1932, Americans today, on average, can purchase almost 7 times the amount of goods and services.

In Exhibit 12.3, we see a comparison of selected industrial countries. Because of differences in growth rates, some countries will become richer than others over time. With relatively slower economic growth, today's richest countries will not be the richest for very long. On the other hand, with even slight improvements in economic growth, today's poorest countries will not remain poor for long. China and India have both experienced spectacular economic growth over the past 20 years. Because of this economic growth, much of the world is now poorer than these two heavily populated countries. Other countries, such as Ireland, once one of the poorest countries in Western Europe, is now one of the richest. Disappointing growth rates over the past 30 years have left Argentina's economy and standard of living unchanged for a quarter of a century.

Because of past economic growth, the "richest" or "most-developed" countries today have many times the market output of the "poorest" or "least-developed" countries. Put differently, the most-developed countries produce and market more output in a day than the least-developed countries do in a year. The international differences in income, output, and wealth are indeed striking and have caused a great deal of friction between developed and less-developed countries. The United States and the nations of the European

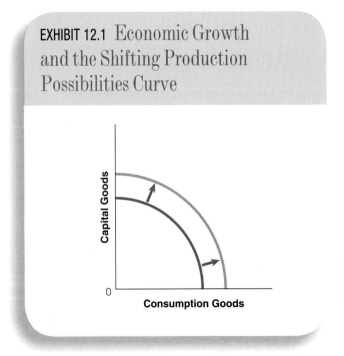

EXHIBIT 12.1 Economic Growth and the Shifting Production Possibilities Curve

EXHIBIT 12.2 U.S. Real GDP per Capita (year 2005 dollars)

SOURCE: Bureau of Economic Analysis, National Economic Accounts, Current-dollar and "real" GDP. Washington, D.C., February 26, 2010. Available at http://bea.gov/national/index.htm#gdp (accessed March 25, 2010).

Union experienced sizable increases in real output over the past two centuries; but even in 1800, most of these nations were better off in terms of market output than many impoverished present-day countries such as Ethiopia, India, and Nepal. See the U.S. real GDP per capita growth from 1790–1860 in Exhibit 12.2.

China and India

Both China and India have per capita real GDP levels that are far less than the United States. The power of compound interest could well change this ranking in the future. As Nobel laureate Robert Lucas once said, "Once one starts to think about differences in growth rates among countries, it is hard to think about anything else." But the current rate of economic growth in these two countries will change things in the future. India experienced an average annual growth rate of almost 9 percent per year from 2003–2008. The economic growth rate slowed in 2008–2009 as India felt the effect of the global financial crisis. India has a highly educated English-speaking population and is a major exporter of software services and software workers.

China is growing at about 10 percent per year. Foreign investment in China has helped spur output of both domestic and export goods. China only grew at 9

EXHIBIT 12.3 Growth in Real GDP per Capita in Selected Industrial Countries

	1979–2008
United States	1.8%
Japan	1.9
Germany	1.6
France	1.5
Italy	1.5
United Kingdom	2.1
Canada	1.6

SOURCE: Bureau of Labor Statistics, *International Comparisons of GDP per Capita and per Employed Person*, Table 2. Washington, D.C. July 28, 2009. pg13. Available at http://www.bls.gov/fls/flsgdp.pdf (accessed March 25, 2010).

percent annually in 2008, its slowest growth rate since 2001. The global financial crisis had a larger impact on China than India because China's economy is more heavily reliant on exports. Exports account for about one-third of China's GDP. Since economic liberalization began in 1978, China's investment and export-led economy has grown 70 times bigger and is the fastest-growing major economy in the world. China has the world's third largest nominal GDP, although its per capita income is still low, behind roughly a hundred countries.

The rapid economic growth in both countries has pulled millions out of poverty.

PRODUCTIVITY: THE KEY TO A HIGHER STANDARD OF LIVING

Will the standard of living in the United States rise, level off, or decline over time? For a large part, the answer depends on productivity growth. **Productivity** is the amount of goods and services a worker can produce per hour. Productivity is especially important because it determines a country's standard of living. That is, sustained economic growth occurs when workers'

productivity rises. For example, slow growth of capital investment can lead to lower labor productivity and, consequently, lower wages. On the other hand, increases in productivity and higher wages can occur as a result of carefully crafted economic policies, such as tax policies that stimulate investment or programs that encourage research and development.

The link between productivity and the standard of living may be understood most easily by recalling the circular flow model where we show that aggregate expenditures are equal to aggregate income. In other words, the aggregate value of all goods and services produced in the economy must equal the payments made to the factors of production—the wages and salaries paid to workers, the rental payment to capital, the profits, and so on. That is, the only way an economy can increase its rate of consumption in the long run is by increasing the amount it produces. But why are some countries so much better than others at producing goods and services? We will answer this question in the next section, as we examine the determinants of productivity—physical capital, human capital, natural resources, and technology.

© MIKE BLANK/GETTY IMAGES

How could these workers increase their productivity? New plant equipment, additional training, and advancements in technology could all increase the productivity of each worker. Greater productivity could then lead to higher wages and in turn a higher standard of living.

⑤2 Determinants of Long-Run Economic Growth

Keep the following questions in mind as you read through this section. You'll find the answers in Section Check 2.

2.1 What factors contribute to long-run economic growth?

2.2 What is human capital?

Why are there vastly different standards of living around the world? The answer can be found in a single concept: labor productivity. Real GDP per capita depends on increases in labor productivity. **Labor productivity** is defined as output per unit of worker. Sustained economic growth can only occur if the amount of output by the average worker increases. As we explained earlier, a nation's standard of living ultimately depends on its ability to produce goods and services.

Can putting a greater percentage of the work force to work contribute to higher real GDP per capita? In the short run, perhaps, but not in the long run. We know that labor is needed in all forms of productive activity. But other things being equal, an increase in the quantity of labor inputs does not necessarily increase output per capita. For example, if the increase in the quantity of labor inputs is due to an increase in population, per capita growth might not occur, because the increase in output could be offset by the increase in population. It is also true that the rate of employment growth and the rate of population growth are similar. So, while real GDP could rise as a result of population growth, it is not likely to lead to large increases in real GDP output per worker, which must come from increases in productivity.

labor productivity output per unit of worker

FACTORS THAT CONTRIBUTE TO ECONOMIC GROWTH

We will look at four major factors that contribute to growth in productivity. These include physical capital, human capital, natural resources, and technology. Today's workers generally produce more output than workers in the past. Of today's workers, those in some countries, like the United States, generally produce more output than do workers in most other countries. Workers with higher productivity usually have more physical capital like buildings and computers, are more educated than their counterparts, and have benefited from tremendous technological advancements.

Four factors in productivity growth
1) Physical capital
2) Human capital
3) Natural resources
4) Technology

Now that we know how productivity leads to long-run economic growth, let's look at the factors that lead to greater productivity.

Physical Capital

Recall that physical capital includes goods such as tools, machinery, and factories that have already been produced and are now producing other goods and services. Combining workers with more capital makes workers more productive. Thus, capital investment can lead to increases in labor productivity.

Even in primitive economies, workers usually have some rudimentary tools to further their productive activity. Consider the farmer who needs to dig a ditch to improve drainage in his fields. If he used just his bare hands, it might take a lifetime to complete the job. If he used a shovel, he could dig the ditch in hours or days. But with a big earth-moving machine, he could do it in minutes. Most economists agree that capital formation has played a significant role in the economic development of nations. Physical capital, like human capital, increases labor productivity.

Per-Worker Production Function

In Chapter 2, we found that by increasing the rate of saving, we can produce a greater amount of new capital goods and increase the stock of productive capital for the future. Because resources are scarce, in order to invest in new capital, society must sacrifice some current consumption. To save more now, we need to consume less now. Ultimately, this will allow society to consume more in the future.

In Exhibit 12.4, we see how the amount of capital per worker influences the amount of output per worker. This positively sloped curve is called the per-worker production function. Holding the other determinants of output constant (human capital, natural resources and technology), we see that, moving up along the production function, when the quantity of capital per worker rises, so does the amount of output per worker, but at a diminishing rate—the curve eventually becomes flatter as more capital per worker is added. That is, capital is subject to diminishing marginal returns. If the economy has a very low level of capital, an extra unit of capital leads to a relatively large increase in output—a movement from point A to point B in Exhibit 12.4. If the economy already has a great deal of capital, an extra unit of capital leads to a relatively smaller increase in output—a movement from point C to point D in Exhibit 12.4. Imagine that you owned a small store and you had 10 employees and one computer. As you added more computers, output per worker rose, but only up to a point. What if you added 20 computers to your work force of 10? Adding more computers (capital) still adds to output but by smaller and smaller additional amounts. This is what is called diminishing marginal returns to capital. Thus, in the long run, other things equal, the benefits of a higher saving rate and additional capital stock become smaller and the rate of growth slows.

Some economists believe diminishing marginal returns to capital can help explain the variation in growth rates between rich and poor countries. In poor countries, where there is little capital, small increases in capital investment can lead to relatively large increases in productivity. In rich countries, where workers already have large amounts of capital, increases in capital

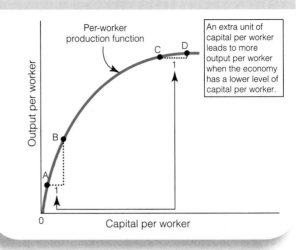

EXHIBIT 12.4 Per-Worker Production Function

An extra unit of capital per worker leads to more output per worker when the economy has a lower level of capital per worker.

investment may have a very small additional effect on productivity. Economists call this the catch up effect.

Human Capital

When workers acquire qualitative improvements (learning new skills, for example), output increases. Workers with a large stock of human capital are more productive than those with small stocks of human capital. Indeed, it has become popular to view labor skills as human capital that can be augmented or improved by education and on-the-job training. Like physical capital, human capital must be produced, usually by means of teachers, schoolrooms, libraries, computer labs, and time devoted to studying. Human capital may be more important than physical capital as a determinant of labor productivity. Human capital also includes improvements in health. Better health conditions allow workers to be more productive. In fact, University of Chicago economist and Nobel laureate Robert Fogel has shown that improved health from better nutrition has a significant impact on long-run economic growth.

Natural Resources

An abundance of natural resources, such as fertile soil, and other raw materials, such as timber and oil, can enhance output. Many scholars cite the abundance of natural resources in the United States as one reason for its historical success. Canada and Australia are endowed with a large natural resource base and high per capita incomes. Resources are, however, not the whole story; for example, Japan and Hong Kong have had tremendous economic success despite having relatively few natural resources. In addition, Kuwait and Saudi Arabia are rich because they sit on top of large pools of oil. On the other hand, Brazil has a large and varied natural resource base, yet its income per capita is relatively low compared with that of many developed countries. It appears that a natural resource base can affect the initial development process, but sustained growth is influenced by other factors. However, most economists would agree that a limited resource base does pose an important obstacle to economic growth.

Technology

Most economists believe that it is the progress in technology that drives productivity. It is technology that allows workers to produce more even with the same amount of physical and human capital. Technological change can lead to better machinery and equipment, increases in capital, and better organization and production methods. Technological advances stem from human ingenuity and creativity in developing new ways of combining the factors of production to enhance the amount of output from a given quantity of resources. The process of technological advance involves invention and innovation. **Innovation** is the adoption of the product or process. For example, in the United States, the invention and innovation of the cotton gin, the Bessemer steel-making process, and the railroad were important stimuli to economic growth. New technology, however, must be introduced into productive use by managers or entrepreneurs who

weigh the perceived estimates of benefits of the new technology against estimates of costs. Thus, the entrepreneur is also an important economic factor in the growth process.

innovation applications of new knowledge that create new products or improve existing products

Technological advances permit us to economize on one or more inputs used in the production process. They can permit savings of labor. For example, when a new machine does the work of many workers, technology is said to be embodied in capital and to be labor saving. Technology, however, can also be land (natural resource) saving or even capital saving. For example, nuclear fission has permitted us to build power plants that economize on the use of coal, a natural resource. The reduction in transportation time that accompanied the invention and innovation of the railroad allowed businesses to reduce the capital they needed in the form of inventories. Because goods could be obtained more quickly, businesses could reduce the stock kept on their shelves.

And inventions can come in all sizes. Obviously, the semiconductor chip made a huge impact on productivity and growth, but so did the Post-it note that was introduced in the early 1980s, the laptop computer, and barcode scanners that were first introduced in Wal-Mart stores. We have also seen huge advances in communication (the Internet) and medicines.

In short, better methods of organization and production can lead to increases in labor productivity. When fewer workers are needed in a grocery store or a department store due to better methods of organization or new machinery and equipment, labor productivity rises.

How much more output would we get if we add more workers?

In Exhibit 12.5 on the next page, we see that technological change can shift the per-worker production curve upward, producing more output per worker with the same amount of capital per worker.

Technological change allows the economy to escape the full impact of diminishing marginal returns to capital. Thus, in the long run, *ceteris paribus*, an economy must experience technological advance in order to improve its standard of living and overcome the diminishing marginal returns to capital.

NEW GROWTH THEORY

The greater the reward for new technology, the more research and technology will occur. According to Paul

EXHIBIT 12.5 Technological Change and the Per-Worker Production Function

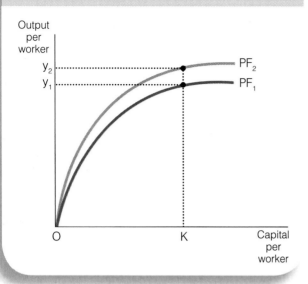

Output per worker

y_2
y_1

PF$_2$
PF$_1$

O   K   Capital per worker

© MAXP/SHUTTERSTOCK

Romer, a new growth economist, economic growth can continue unimpeded, as long as we keep coming up with new ideas. And there is a role for government, too—encouraging the creation of new ideas. While the market is a great engine for economic growth, it can be "turbocharged" with strong institutional support for education and science. Romer believes that it is ideas that drive economic growth. To Romer, economic growth comes from increases in value—rearranging fixed amounts of matter and making new combinations that are more valuable. "There are zillions of combinations that we can use to make new goods and services we value."

SECTION CHECK 2

2.1 The factors that contribute to economic growth are increased quantity and quality of labor, natural resources, physical capital, and technological advances.

2.2 Labor, or human capital, can be improved through investment in human capital—that is, education, on-the-job training, and experience can improve the quality of labor.

Ⓢ3 Public Policy and Economic Growth

Keep the following questions in mind as you read through this section. You'll find the answers in **Section Check 3**.

3.1 Why is the saving rate so important for increasing economic growth?

3.2 Why is research and development so important for economic growth?

3.3 Why are property rights so important for increasing economic growth?

3.4 Why is education so important for economic growth?

Economic growth means more than an increase in the real income (output) of the population. A number of other important changes accompany changes in output. Claims that economic growth stimulates political freedom or democracy have even been made, but evidence for that correlation is far from conclusive. Even though some democratic societies are rich and some authoritarian ones are poor, the opposite also holds. That is, some features of democracy, such as majority voting and special interest groups, may actually be growth retarding. For example, if the majority decides to vote for large land reforms and wealth transfers, the consequences will be higher taxes and market distortions that will reduce incentives for work, investment, and ultimately economic growth. However, a nation can pursue a number of policies that will increase economic growth.

© ROBYN MACKENZIE/ISTOCKPHOTO.COM

SAVING RATES, INVESTMENT, CAPITAL STOCK, AND ECONOMIC GROWTH

One of the most important determinants of economic growth is the saving rate. To consume more in the future, we must save more now. Generally, higher levels of saving will lead to higher rates of investment and capital formation and, therefore, greater economic growth. Individuals can either consume or save their income. If individuals choose to consume all their income, they will have nothing left for saving, which businesses could use for investment purposes to build new plants or replace worn-out or obsolete equipment. With little investment in capital stock, there will be little economic growth. Capital can also increase as a result of injections of capital from abroad (foreign direct investments), but the role of national saving rates in economic growth is of particular importance.

Exhibit 12.6 clearly shows that sustained rapid economic growth is associated with high rates of saving and investment around the world. However, investment alone does not guarantee economic growth. Economic growth hinges on the quality and type of investment as well as on investments in human capital and improvements in technology.

INFRASTRUCTURE

Infrastructure (e.g., highways, ports, bridges, power lines, airports, and information technology) is critical to economic coordination and activity. Some infrastructure is private and some is public. In the past several decades, the amount of government investment in

EXHIBIT 12.6 Saving Rates and GDP Growth during High-Growth Periods in Selected Economies

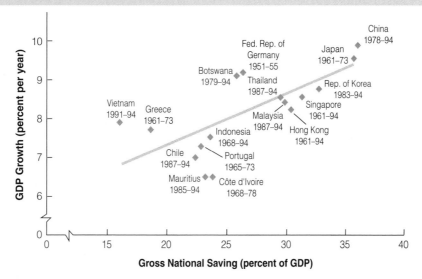

NOTE: Data are annual averages for the periods indicated.

SOURCE: World Bank, *World Development Report, 1996*, Oxford University Press, 1996. Republished with permission of the World Bank, from World Development Report 1996; permission conveyed through Copyright Clearance Center, Inc.

U.S. infrastructure has fallen. Some economists argue that improvements in infrastructure could lead to higher productivity. Others argue the causality runs in the other direction—that higher productivity leads to greater infrastructure. In addition, a special interest problem concerns favored districts with political clout that end up as the recipients of improved infrastructure, which may not be an efficient solution. Most would agree, however, that poor infrastructure is a major deterrent to economic growth.

RESEARCH AND DEVELOPMENT

Some scholars believe that the importance of **research and development (R&D)** is understated. Research and development consists of the activities undertaken to create new products and processes that will lead to technological progress. The concept of R&D is broad indeed—it can include new products, management improvements, production innovations, or simply learning by doing. However, it is clear that investing in R&D and rewarding innovators with patents have paid big dividends in the past 50 to 60 years. Some would argue that even larger rewards for research and development would spur even more rapid economic growth. Some types of scientific research may have far-reaching benefits that cannot be captured by a private firm. Such a case presents a compelling argument for government support of basic research. GPS satellite systems in cars, for example, were originally designed for military purposes. In addition, an important link exists between R&D and capital investment. As already noted, when capital depreciates over time, it is replaced with new equipment that embodies the latest technology. Consequently, R&D may work hand-in-hand with investment to improve growth and productivity. Lastly, R&D may benefit foreigners as they import goods from technologically advanced countries to make their firms more efficient.

THE PROTECTION OF PROPERTY RIGHTS IMPACTS ECONOMIC GROWTH

Economic growth rates tend to be higher in countries where the government enforces property rights. Property rights give owners the legal right to keep or sell their properties—land, labor, or capital. Without property rights, life would be a huge "free-for-all," where people could take whatever they wanted. Economists call the government's ability to protect private property rights and enforce contracts the *rule of law*.

In most developed countries, property rights are effectively protected by the government. However, in developing countries, such protection is not usually the case. If the government does not enforce property rights, the private sector must respond in costly ways that stifle economic growth. For example, an unreliable judiciary system means that entrepreneurs must often rely on informal agreements that are difficult to enforce. As a result, they may have to pay bribes to get things done, and even then, they may not get the promised services. Individuals may have to buy private security or pay "organized crime" for protection against crime and corruption. In addition, landowners and business owners may be fearful of coups or takeovers from a new government, which might confiscate their property altogether. In short, if government is not adequately protecting property rights, the incentive to invest will be hindered, and political instability, corruption, and lower rates of economic growth will be likely. However, it may well be a two-way street. In the words of former U.N. Secretary-General Kofi Annan, "There will be no development without security and no security without development."

FREE TRADE AND ECONOMIC GROWTH

Allowing free trade can also lead to greater output because of the principle of comparative advantage. Essentially, the principle of comparative advantage suggests that if two nations or individuals with different resource endowments and production capabilities specialize in producing a smaller number of goods and services and engage in trade, both parties will benefit. Total output will rise.

EDUCATION

Education, investment in human capital, may be just as important as improvements in physical capital. At any given time, an individual has a choice between current work and investment activities such as education that can increase future earning power. An individual will usually accept reduction in current income to devote effort to education and training. In turn, a certain return on the investment is expected because in later years, the individual will earn a higher wage rate (the amount of the increase depending on the nature of the education and training as well as natural ability). For example, in the United States, a person with a college education can be expected to earn almost twice as much per year as a high school graduate.

One argument for government subsidizing education is that the investment can increase the skill level of the population and raise the standard of living. However, even if the individual does not benefit financially from increased education, society may benefit culturally and in other respects from having its members highly educated. For example, more education can lead to lower crime rates, new ideas that may benefit society, and more informed voters.

With economic growth, illiteracy rates fall and formal education grows. The correlation between per capita output and the proportion of the population that is able to read or write is striking. Improvements in literacy stimulate economic growth by reducing barriers to the flow of information; when information costs are high, out of ignorance, many resources flow to or remain in uses that are unproductive. Moreover, education imparts skills that are directly useful in raising labor productivity, whether it is mathematics taught to a sales clerk, engineering techniques taught to a college graduate, or just good ideas that facilitate production and design.

Many economists believe that the tremendous growth in East Asia (South Korea, Taiwan, Hong Kong, and Singapore) in the last half of the twentieth century

Policy: Institutional Economics

Douglass C. North, an economic historian, was the recipient of the Nobel Prize in Economics in 1993. One of North's contributions is his analysis of the linkage between institutional changes and economic growth. According to North, "The sources of sustained economic growth and the determinants of income distribution are to be found in the institutional structure of a society. Economic historians can no longer write good economic history without explicitly taking into account the institutional structure of the system, both economic and political. We can't avoid the political aspect because decisions made outside the marketplace have had, and will continue to have, a fundamental influence upon growth and welfare."

Institutions matter because they affect the choices open to people, shape incentives, and are an important determinant of human action. The institutional structure of a society (or the "rules of the game," as Mr. North calls it) includes formal rules (such as constitutions, property rights, laws of contract), informal constraints (conventions, customs, codes of conduct), and the means of enforcing both formal and informal standards of behavior (courts, social ostracism, personal beliefs). As in sports, the way the game is played and its outcome depend on the nature of the rules, the character of the players, and the fairness (impartiality) of the referee. Moreover,

the choice of the rules and the enforcement mechanisms will be affected by prevailing ideology and culture.

According to North, rules must be credible if they are to be effective. That is, they must be enforced. Private enforcement is possible, but as economic life becomes more complex, political institutions become the major instrument for defining and enforcing property rights. The history of economic performance cannot be separated from the history of political performance. The New Institutional Economics studies both.

North has shown that those countries that (1) adopt a rule of law, one which limits the power of government over economic life and protects the rights of persons and property and (2) maintain open markets and freedom of contract are more likely to achieve long-run economic prosperity than those that do not.

According to North, economic change is "path dependent": The future depends on the past and present choices. History is not predetermined or based on some grand design; it is the sum of human actions. How we act will depend on the rules we inherit and formulate, as well as on our cultural and moral heritage. But ultimately, it is individuals who must choose.

SOURCES: Douglass C. North, *Growth and Welfare in the American Past*, 2nd ed. (Englewood Cliffs, NJ: Prentice Hall, 1974); and James Dorn, "North Wins Nobel for New Institutional Economics," *The Margin* (Spring 1994), 56.

gross domestic product (GDP) the measure of economic performance based on the value of all final goods and services produced within a country during a given period

was a result of good basic education for many of their citizens. This reason was one of many factors that contributed to growth, including high rates of saving and a large increase in labor force participation.

However, in poorer developing countries, the higher opportunity costs of education present an obstacle. Children in developing countries are an important part of the labor force starting at a young age. If they attend school, children cannot help in the fields—planting, harvesting, fence building, and participating in many other tasks—which many households depend on in the rural areas of developing countries. A child's labor contribution to the family is far less important in a developed country. Thus, the higher opportunity cost of education in developing countries is one of the reasons that school enrollments are lower.

Education may also be a consequence of economic growth, because as incomes rise, people's tendency to consume education increases. People increasingly look to education for more than the acquisition of immediately applicable skills. Education becomes a consumption good as well as a means of investing in human capital. There are also a number of factors that can lead to slower economic growth. Countries that fail to enforce the rule of law, experience wars and revolutions, and have poor education and health systems and low rates of saving and investment are not likely to grow very rapidly.

© DBIMAGES/ALAMY

Many economists believe that the recent growth in East Asian countries is a result of improved basic education.

SECTION CHECK 3

3.1 Generally, higher levels of saving will lead to higher rates of investment and capital formation and, therefore, to greater economic growth.

3.2 Innovations resulting from investments in research and development have the potential to accelerate economic growth even further.

3.3 Economic growth rates tend to be higher in countries where the government enforces property rights more vigorously.

3.4 Education, investment of human capital, is important to improving standards of living and economic growth.

⑤4 Measuring Economic Growth and Its Components

Keep the following questions in mind as you read through this section. You'll find the answers in **Section Check 4.**

4.1 What is gross domestic product?

4.2 Why must expenditures equal income?

Now let's take a look at how we measure economic growth.

WHAT IS GROSS DOMESTIC PRODUCT?

The measure of aggregate economic performance that gets the most attention in the popular media is **gross domestic product (GDP)**, which is defined as the value of all final goods and services produced within a country during a given period. By convention, that period is almost always one year. But let's examine the rest of this definition. What is meant by "final good or service" and "value"?

Measuring the Value of Goods and Services

Value is determined by the market prices at which goods and services sell. Underlying the calculations, then, are the various equilibrium prices and quantities for the multitude of goods and services produced.

What Is a Final Good or Service?

The word *final* means that the good is ready for its designated ultimate use. Many goods and services are intermediate goods or services—that is, used in the production of other goods. For example, suppose U.S. Steel Corporation produces some steel that it sells to Ford for use in making an automobile. If we counted the value of steel used in making the car as well as the full value of the finished auto in the GDP, we would be engaging in **double counting**—adding the value of the steel in twice, first in its raw form and second in its final form, the automobile.

PRODUCTION, INCOME, AND THE CIRCULAR FLOW MODEL

When we calculate GDP in the economy, we are measuring the value of total production—our total expenditures on the economy's output of goods and services. However, we are also measuring the value of total income. Why? It is because every dollar of spending by some buyer ends up being a dollar of income for some seller. In short, expenditures, (spending) must equal income. And this is true whether it is a household, firm, or the government that buys the good or service. The main point is that when we spend (the value of total expenditure), it ends up as someone's income (the value of total income). Buyers have sellers.

In Exhibit 12.7, we reintroduce the circular flow model to show the flow of money in the economy. For example, households use some of their income to buy domestic goods and services and some to buy foreign goods and services (imports). Households also use some of their income to pay taxes and invest in financial markets (stocks, bonds, saving accounts, and other financial assets). When income flows into the financial system as saving, it makes it possible for consumers, firms, and government to borrow. This market for saving and borrowing is vital to a well-functioning economy.

Firms sell their goods and services to domestic and foreign consumers and foreign firms and government. Firms use their factors of production (labor, land, capital,

double counting adding the value of a good or service twice by mistakenly counting the intermediate goods and services in GDP

EXHIBIT 12.7 The Expanded Circular Flow Model

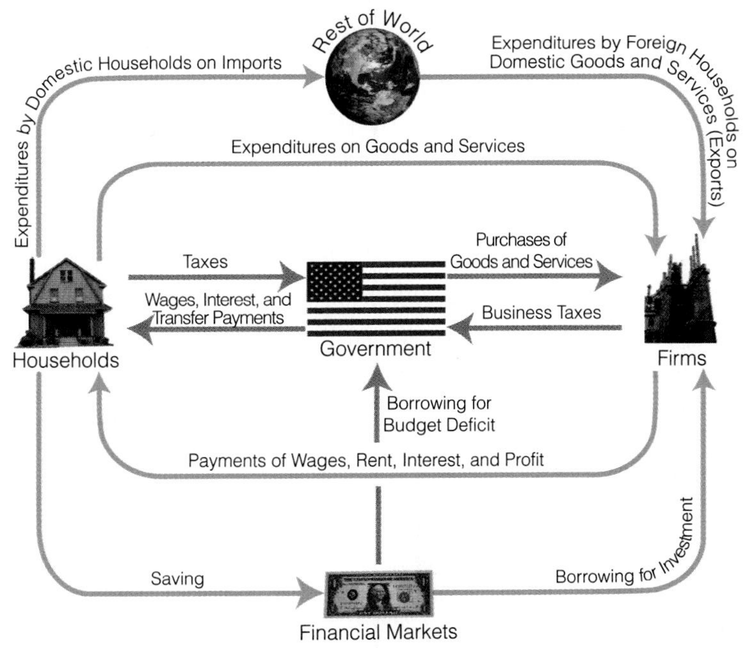

Rest of World

Expenditures by Domestic Households on Imports

Expenditures by Foreign Households on Domestic Goods and Services (Exports)

Expenditures on Goods and Services

Taxes

Purchases of Goods and Services

Wages, Interest, and Transfer Payments

Business Taxes

Households

Government

Firms

Borrowing for Budget Deficit

Payments of Wages, Rent, Interest, and Profit

Saving

Borrowing for Investment

Financial Markets

expenditure approach calculation of GDP by adding the expenditures by market participants on final goods and services over a given period

consumption purchases of final goods and services

investment the creation of capital goods to augment future production

and entrepreneurship) to produce goods and services. Firms pay wages to workers, interest for the use of capital, and rent for land. Profits are the return to entrepreneurs for taking the risk of producing the goods and services. Wages, rent, interest, and profit comprise aggregate income in the economy. Government provides transfer payments such as Social Security and unemployment insurance payments. Whether we add up the aggregate expenditure on final goods and services or the value of aggregate income (wages, rent, interest, and profit), we get the same GDP. For an economy as a whole, expenditures and income are the same. Actually, while the two should be exactly the same, there may be a slight variation because of data issues.

SECTION CHECK 4

4.1 Gross domestic product (GDP) is the value of all final goods and services produced within a country during a given time period.

4.2 All of our spending (the value of total expenditure) ends up as someone's income (the value of total income). Every buyer has a seller.

⑤5 Measuring Total Production

Keep the following questions in mind as you read through this section. You'll find the answers in **Section Check 5**.

5.1 What are the four categories of purchases included in the expenditure approach?

5.2 How are net exports calculated?

5.3 How is national income calculated?

5.4 What does personal income measure?

One approach to measuring GDP is the **expenditure approach**.

THE EXPENDITURE APPROACH TO MEASURING GDP

With the expenditure approach, GDP is calculated by adding how much market participants spend on final goods and services over a specific period of time. For convenience and for analytical purposes, economists usually group spending into four categories: consumption, designated by the letter C; investment, I; government purchases, G; and net exports, which equals exports (X) minus imports (M), or X − M. According to the expenditure method, then,

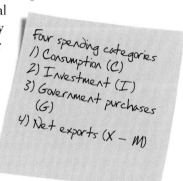

Four spending categories
1) Consumption (C)
2) Investment (I)
3) Government purchases (G)
4) Net exports (X − M)

$$GDP = C + I + G + (X - M)$$

Consumption (C)

Consumption refers to the purchase of consumer goods and services by households. For most of us, a large percentage of our income in a given year goes for consumer goods and services. The consumption category does not include purchases by business or government. As Exhibit 12.8 indicates, in 2008, U.S. consumption expenditures totaled more than $9 trillion ($10,130 billion). This figure was 70 percent of GDP. In this respect, the 2008 data were fairly typical. In every year since 1929, when GDP accounts began to be calculated annually, consumption has been more than half of total expenditures on goods and services (even during World War II).

Investment (I)

Investment, according to economists, refers to the creation of capital goods—inputs such as machines and tools whose purpose it is to produce other goods.

How Stable Are Investment Expenditures? In recent years, investment expenditures generally hovered around 15 percent of gross domestic product. Investment spending is the most volatile category of GDP, however, and tends to fluctuate considerably with changing business conditions. When the economy is booming, investment purchases tend to increase dramatically. In downturns, the reverse happens. In the first year of the Great Depression, investment purchases declined by 37 percent. In recent years, expenditures on capital goods have been a smaller proportion of GDP in the United States than in many other developed nations. This fact worries some people who are concerned about GDP growth in the United States compared to that in other countries, because investment in capital goods is directly tied to a nation's future production capabilities.

Government Purchases (*G*)

The portion of government purchases included in GDP is expenditures on goods and services. For example, a government must pay the salaries of its employees, and it must also make payments to the private firms with which it contracts to provide various goods and services, such as highway construction companies and weapons manufacturers. All these payments would be included in GDP. However, *transfer payments* (such as Social Security, farm subsidies, and welfare) are not included in government purchases, because this spending does not go to purchase newly produced goods or services but is merely a transfer of income among the country's citizens (which is why such expenditures are called transfer payments).

Exports (*X − M*)

Some of the goods and services produced in the United States are exported for use in other countries. The fact that these goods and services were made in the United States means that they should be included in a measure of U.S. production. Thus, we include the value of exports when calculating GDP. At the same time, however, some of our expenditures in other categories (consumption and investment, in particular) were for foreign-produced goods and services. These imports must be excluded from GDP to obtain an accurate measure of U.S. production.

Thus, GDP calculations measure net exports, which equals total exports (*X*) minus total imports (*M*). Net exports are a small proportion of GDP and are often negative for the United States.

> **factor payments** wages (salaries), rent, interest payments, and profits paid to the owners of productive resources

OTHER MEASURES OF TOTAL PRODUCTION AND TOTAL INCOME

In addition to computing the gross domestic product, the Bureau of Economic Analysis (BEA) also computes five additional measures of production and income: gross national product, net national product, national income, personal income, and disposable personal income.

Incomes received by people providing goods and services are actually payments to the owners of productive resources. These payments are sometimes called **factor payments**. Factor payments include wages for the use of labor services, rent for land, payments for the use of capital goods in the form of interest, and profits for entrepreneurs who put labor, land, and capital together. Before we can measure national income, we must make three adjustments to GDP. First, we must look at the net income of foreigners—that is, we add any income earned abroad by U.S. citizens or firms and we subtract any income earned in the United States by foreign firms and citizens. This difference between net income of foreigners

Five measures of production and income
- *Gross national product*
- *Net national product*
- *National income*
- *Personal income*
- *Disposable personal income*

EXHIBIT 12.8 GDP: The Expenditure Approach

Category	Amount (billions of current dollars)	Percent of GDP
Consumption (*C*)	$10,088	71%
Investment (*I*)	1,631	11
Government purchases (*G*)	2,931	21
Net exports of goods and services (*X − M*)	−392	−3
Gross domestic product	$14,258	100%

SOURCE: Bureau of Economic Analysis, National Economic Accounts, Gross Domestic Product News Release, Table 3. Washington, D.C., February 26, 2010. Available at http://bea.gov/national/index.htm#gdp (accessed March 25, 2010).

gross national product (GNP) the difference between net income of foreigners and GDP

depreciation annual allowance set aside to replace worn-out capital

net national product (NNP) GNP minus depreciation

indirect business taxes taxes, such as sales tax, levied on goods and services sold

national income (NI) a measure of income earned by owners of the factors of production

personal income (PI) the amount of income received by households before personal taxes

disposable personal income the personal income available after personal taxes

and GDP is called **gross national product (GNP)**. For example, we would add to GDP the profits sent back to the United States from Wal-Mart stores in Canada and Mexico. However, the profits Toyota earns in the United States are sent back to Japan and are subtracted from U.S. GDP, so GNP becomes the income earned worldwide by U.S. firms and residents. In the United States, the difference between GDP and GNP is small because net income of foreigners is a small percentage of GDP.

The second adjustment we make to find national income is to deduct depreciation from GNP. **Depreciation** payments are annual allowances set aside for the replacement of worn-out plant and equipment. After we subtract depreciation, we have **net national product (NNP)**.

The final adjustment is to subtract **indirect business taxes**. The best example of an indirect business tax is a sales tax. For example, a compact disc might cost $14.95 plus a tax of $1.20 for a total of $16.15. The retail distributor (record store), record producer, and others will share $14.95 in proceeds, even though the actual equilibrium price is $16.15. In other words, the output (compact disc) is valued at $16.15, even though recipients get only $14.95 in income. Besides sales taxes, other important indirect business taxes include excise taxes (e.g., taxes on cigarettes, automobiles, and liquor) and gasoline taxes.

Now we can measure **national income (NI)**, which is a measure of the income earned by owners of resources—factor payments. Accordingly, national income includes payments for labor services (wages, salaries, and fringe benefits), payments for use of land and buildings (rent), money lent to finance economic activity (interest), and payments for use of capital resources (profits). To obtain GDP, we add indirect business taxes, depreciation, and net income of foreigners.

We should keep in mind that not all income can be used by those who earn it. **Personal income (PI)** measures the amount of income received by households (including transfer payments) before income taxes. **Disposable personal income** is the personal income available to individuals after taxes.

WHICH OF THESE BUSINESSES WOULD CONTRIBUTE THEIR PROFITS TO THE U.S. GNP?

5.1 Four categories of spending are used in the GDP calculation: consumption (*C*), investment (*I*), government purchases (*G*), and net exports (*X* − *M*).

5.2 Net exports are calculated by subtracting total imports from total exports.

5.3 National income (NI) is measured by adding together the payments to the factors of production—wages, rent, interest, and profit.

5.4 Personal income (PI) measures the amount of income received by households (including transfer payments) before personal taxes.

⑤6 Problems in Calculating an Accurate GDP

Keep the following questions in mind as you read through this section. You'll find the answers in Section Check 6.

6.1 What are the problems with using GDP to measure output?

6.2 What is per capita GDP?

The primary problem in calculating accurate GDP statistics becomes evident when attempts are made to compare the GDP over time. Between 1970 and 1978, a period of relatively high inflation, GDP in the United States rose more than 100 percent. What great progress! Unfortunately, however, the "yardstick" used in adding the values of different products, the U.S. dollar, also changed in value over this period. A dollar in 1979, for example, would certainly not buy as much as a dollar in 1970, because the *overall* price level for goods and services increased.

HOW DO WE SOLVE THIS PROBLEM?

One solution to this problem would be to use physical units of output—which, unlike the dollar, do not change in value from year to year—as the measure of total economic activity. The major problem with this approach is that different products have different units of measurement. How can anyone add tons of steel to bushels of wheat, kilowatts of electricity, gallons of paint, cubic feet of natural gas, miles of air passenger travel, and number of magazines sold? To compare GDP values over time, the calculations must use a common, or standardized, unit of measure, which only money can provide.

A Price-Level Index

The dollar, then, is the yardstick of value we can use to correct the inflation-induced distortion of the GDP. We must adjust for the changing purchasing power of the dollar by using a price index. As we discussed in the last chapter, a price index attempts to provide a measure of the prices paid for a certain bundle of goods and services over time. The price index can be used to deflate the nominal or current dollar GDP values to a real GDP expressed in dollars of constant purchasing power.

REAL GDP

Once the price index has been calculated, the actual procedure for adjusting nominal, or current dollar, GDP to get real GDP is not complicated. For convenience, an index number of 100 is assigned to some base year. The base year is arbitrarily chosen—it can be any year.

The formula for converting any year's nominal GDP into real GDP (in base-year dollars) is as follows:

$$\text{Real GDP} = \frac{\text{Nominal GDP}}{\text{Price-level index}} \times 100$$

Suppose the GDP deflator (price-level index) was expressed in terms of 2005 prices (2005 = 100), and the price index figure for 2010 was 110. The increase in the figure means that prices were 10 percent higher in 2010 than they were in 2005. To correct the 2010 nominal GDP, we take the nominal GDP figure for 2010—say, $14,000 billion—and divide it by the price-level index (110), which results in a quotient of $127.27 billion. We then multiply this number by 100, giving us $12,727.00 billion, which would be the 2010 GDP in 2005 dollars (that is, 2010 real GDP, in terms of a 2005 base year).

In Exhibit 12.9 on the next page, notice that in years after the base year (2005), nominal GDP is greater than real GDP. This means the price level has risen since 2005, lowering the purchasing power of the dollar. Prior to 2005, nominal GDP was less than real GDP; the purchasing power of the dollar was higher relative to the base year (2005). Also, notice that nominal GDP rises more rapidly than real GDP because inflation is included in the nominal GDP figures.

Is Real GDP Always Less than Nominal GDP?

In modern times, inflation has been prevalent. For many readers of this book, the price level (as measured by the consumer price index and the GDP deflator) has risen in every year of their lifetime, because the last year with a declining price level was 1955. Therefore, the adjustment of nominal (money) GDP to real GDP will tend to reduce the growth in GDP suggested by nominal GDP figures. Given the distortions introduced by inflation, most news reports about GDP today speak of real GDP changes, although this distinction is not always made explicit.

REAL GDP PER CAPITA

The measure of economic well-being, or standard of living, most often used is **real gross domestic product per capita**. We use a measure of real GDP for reasons

already cited. To calculate real GDP per capita, we divide the real GDP by the total population to get the value of real output of final goods and services per person. *Ceteris paribus*, people prefer more goods to fewer, so a higher GDP per capita would seemingly make people better off, improving their standard of living. Economic growth, then, is usually considered to have occurred anytime the real GDP per capita has risen. In Exhibit 12.10, we see that in the United States the real gross domestic product per capita has grown sharply from 1958 to 2008. Real GDP per capita is almost three times larger in 2008 than it was in 1958. However, the growth in real GDP per capita is not steady, as seen by the shaded areas that represent recessions in Exhibit 12.10. Falling real GDP per capita can bring on many human hardships, such as rising unemployment, lower profits, stock market losses, and bankruptcies.

Why Is the Measure of per Capita GDP so Important?

Because one purpose of using GDP as a crude welfare measure is to relate output to human desires, we need to adjust for population change. If we do not take population growth into account, we can be misled by changes in real GDP values. For example, in some less-developed countries in some periods, real GDP has risen perhaps 2

EXHIBIT 12.9 Nominal and Real GDP 1950–2009 (2005 base year)

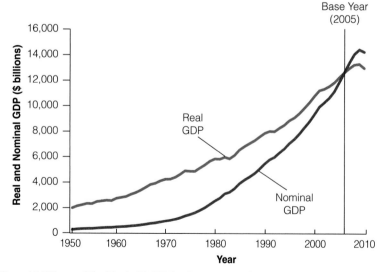

SOURCE: Louis D. Johnston and Samuel H. Williamson, "What Was the U.S. GDP Then?" *MeasuringWorth*, 2008. Available at http://www.measuringworth.org/usgdp/ (accessed March 17, 2010).

If we do not take **population growth** into account, we can be misled by changes in real GDP values.

percent a year, but the population has grown just as fast. In these cases, the real output of goods and services per person has remained virtually unchanged, but this would not be apparent in an examination of real GDP trends alone.

SECTION CHECK 6

6.1 It is difficult to compare real GDP over time because of the changing value of money over time.

6.2 Per capita real GDP is real output of goods and services per person. In some cases, real GDP may increase, but per capita real GDP may actually drop as a result of population growth.

EXHIBIT 12.10 Real GDP per Capita

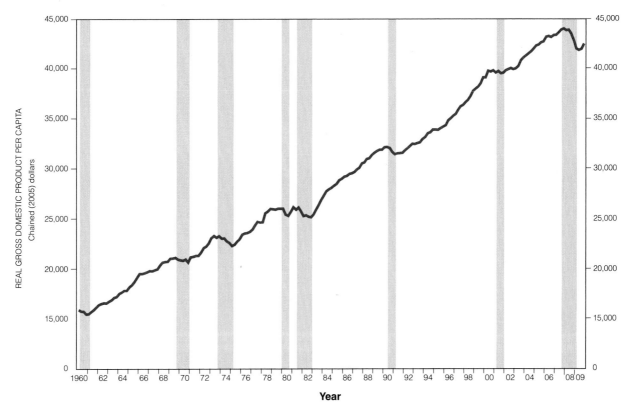

NOTE: Shaded areas represent recessions.

SOURCE: Bureau of Economic Analysis, *Survey of Current Business,* Selected NIPA Tables. 90(3) Washington, D.C., March 2010. D-53. Available at http://www.bea.gov/scb/ (accessed March 25, 2010).

⑤7 Problems with GDP as a Measure of Economic Welfare

Keep the following questions in mind as you read through this section. You'll find the answers in **Section Check 7**.

7.1 What are some of the deficiencies of GDP as a measure of economic welfare?

7.2 What are nonmarket transactions?

7.3 What is the underground economy?

Real GDP is often used as a measure of the economic welfare of a nation. The accuracy of this measure for that purpose is questionable, however, because several important factors are excluded from its calculation. These factors include nonmarket transactions, the underground economy, leisure, externalities, and the quality of the goods purchased.

NONMARKET TRANSACTIONS

Nonmarket transactions include the provision of goods and services outside traditional markets for which no money is exchanged. We simply do not have reliable enough information on this output to include it in the GDP. The most important single nonmarket transaction omitted from the GDP is the services of housewives (or househusbands). These services are not sold in any market, so they are not entered into the GDP; but they are none-theless performed. For example, if a single woman hires a tax accountant, those payments enter into the calculation of GDP. Suppose, though, that the woman marries her tax accountant. Now the woman no longer pays her husband for his accounting services. Reported GDP falls after the marriage, although output does not change.

In less-developed countries, where a significant amount of food and clothing output is produced in the home, the failure to include nonmarket economic activity in GDP is a serious deficiency. Even in the United States, homemade meals, housework, and the vegetables and flowers produced in home gardens are excluded, even though they clearly represent an output of goods and services.

THE UNDERGROUND ECONOMY

It is impossible to know for sure the magnitude of the underground economy, which includes unreported income from both legal and illegal sources. For example, illegal gambling and prostitution are not included in the GDP, leading to underreporting of an unknown magnitude. The reason these activities are excluded, however, has nothing to do with the morality of the services performed; rather, the cause of the exclusion is that most payments made for these services neither are reported to government authorities nor go through normal credit channels. Likewise, cash payments made to employees "under the table" slip through the GDP net. Estimates of the size of the underground economy vary from less than 4 percent to more than 20 percent of GDP. It also appears that a significant portion of this unreported income comes from legal sources, such as self-employment.

MEASURING THE VALUE OF LEISURE

The value that individuals place on leisure is omitted in calculating GDP. Most of us could probably get a part-time job if we wanted to, earning some additional money by working in the evening or on weekends. Yet we choose not to do so. Why? The opportunity cost is too high—we would have to forgo some leisure. If you work on Saturday nights, you cannot see your friends, go to parties, attend concerts, watch television, or go to the movies. The opportunity cost of leisure is the income for-gone by not working. For example, if people start taking more three-day weekends, GDP will surely fall, but can we necessarily say that the standard of living will fall? GDP will fall, but economic well-being may rise.

Leisure, then, has a positive value that does not show up in the GDP accounts. To put leisure in the proper perspective, ask yourself whether you would rather live in Country A, which has a per capita GDP of $25,000 a year and a 30-hour work week, or Country B, with a $25,000 per capita GDP and a 50-hour work week. Most people would choose Country A. The prob-lem posed by this omission in GDP can be fairly sig-nificant in international comparisons or observations of one nation over time.

GROWING UNDERGROUND

Underground economies are large and growing rapidly in most countries. High taxes and labor market regulations are the reasons why 17 percent of economic activity goes unreported in OECD [Organization for Economic Co-operation and Development] countries, while corruption explains the large black market in some developing ones.

By definition, national income statistics capture economic activity reported by individuals and corporations. A large and growing portion of economic activity, however, goes unrecorded in most countries. This "underground" economy consists of legal activities that are concealed, mainly for reasons of tax evasion. Underground activity grew during the 1970s, when government became pervasive in national economies. As tax rates were raised to finance public spending programs, an increasing number of individuals risked dodging taxes. It is only since the 1980s that economists have attempted to estimate the size of underground economies. This task is inherently difficult.

Nevertheless, it is important to estimate the size and growth of all economic activity, not only the reported kind. For one thing, cross-country comparisons of per capita income depend on it. By one account, Italy would be one of the richest European countries if its large black market were included alongside reported income. More importantly, GDP growth figures and unemployment rates may be severely distorted if a sudden increase in taxes pushes more people underground. Accurate statistics about overall economic activity and true unemployment are essential for effective economic policy decisions.

An article in the *Journal of Economic Literature* takes a closer look at the size, causes, and consequences of underground economies. Its authors, Friedrich Schneider of the University of Linz and Dominick Enste of the University of Cologne, claim that no cross-country comparison of underground economies has yet been undertaken. In their research, the authors compare the relative size of under-ground economies for 76 countries and track their growth over time. They point out that even though estimates of underground economies are naturally inexact, economists generally agree that they are growing in most countries. Moreover, underground economies vary significantly in size, from a small fraction of "official" GDP (Switzerland), to nearly three-quarters of economic output (Nigeria, Egypt, and Thailand).

But first, what drives people underground? The authors argue that underground activity grows when tax rates rise. This is most noticeable in Scandinavian countries where governments have created some of the most generous public programs over the past few decades, and have consequently witnessed a substantial rise in their underground economies. This unsurprising claim is substantiated by the data. Norway, for example, has seen its underground economy grow from a negligible 1.5 percent of GNP in 1960 to a staggering 18 percent in 1995 (based on the currency demand approach). The high fiscal burden in other Scandinavian countries has led to a similar growth in their underground economies. In contrast, countries with relatively small public sectors—such as Switzerland and the United States—have developed much smaller underground markets.

The study shows that underground economies have grown in all OECD countries over the past few decades, representing an alarming 17 percent of reported GDP by 1997. In countries such as Spain, Portugal, Italy, Belgium, and Greece, the estimated size of unreported economic activity stood at 22 to 30 percent. "In the European Union at least 20 million workers and in OECD countries about 35 million work in the unofficial economy. Moreover, the amount doubled within 20 years."

The authors find evidence that fewer regulations (that are properly enforced), lower tax rates, and a better rule of law lead to smaller underground economies, and consequently generate higher tax revenues. These factors are absent in many countries of Latin America, where underground economies amount to one-quarter to one-third of official GNP, and in the former Soviet Union, where underground economies stand at more than one-third of reported income.

SOURCE: Author's discussion of Friedrich Schneider and Dominick H. Enste, "Shadow Economies: Size, Causes and Consequences," *Journal of Economic Literature* (March 2000), and *Economic Intuition* (Summer 2000).

While the quality of automobiles has obviously improved, GDP may not reflect these changes.

© JEFF NAGY/ISTOCKPHOTO.COM / © WERNER STOFFBERG/ISTOCKPHOTO.

GDP AND EXTERNALITIES

As we have discussed in earlier chapters, positive and negative externalities may result from the production of some goods and services. As a result of these externalities, the equilibrium prices of these goods and services—the figures used in GDP calculations—do not reflect their true values to society (unless, of course, the externalities have been internalized). For example, if a steel mill produces 100,000 more tons of steel, GDP increases; GDP does not, however, decrease to reflect damages from the air pollution that results from the production of that additional steel. Likewise, additional production of a vaccine would be reflected in the GDP, but the positive benefit to members of society—other than the purchaser—would not be included in the calculation. In other words, while GDP measures the goods and services produced, it does not adequately measure the "goods" and "bads" that result from the production processes.

QUALITY OF GOODS

GDP can also miss important changes in the improvements in the *quality* of goods and services. For example, the quality of a computer bought today differs significantly from one that was bought 10 years ago, but it will not lead to an increase in measured GDP. The same is true of many other goods, from cellular phones to automobiles to medical care.

OTHER MEASURES OF ECONOMIC WELL-BEING

Even if we included some of these statistics that are difficult to measure, such as nonmarket transactions, the underground economy, leisure, externalities, and the quality of products, GDP would still not be a precise measure of economic well-being. Many other indices of well-being should be considered: life expectancies, infant mortality rates, education and environmental quality, levels of discrimination and fairness, health care, low crime rates, and minimum traffic congestion, just to name a few. GDP is a measure of economic production, not a measure of economic well-being. However, greater levels of GDP can lead to improvements in economic well-being, because society will now be able to afford better education and health care and a cleaner, safer environment.

SECTION CHECK 7

7.1 Factors making it difficult to use GDP as a welfare indicator include nonmarket transactions, the underground economy, leisure, externalities, and the quality of goods.

7.2 Nonmarket transactions are the exchanges of goods and services that do not occur in traditional markets and for which no money is exchanged.

7.3 The underground economy is the unreported production and income that come from legal and illegal activities.

Chapter 12: Self-Review

Now that you're finished reading the chapter, review the questions below. You can write your answers in the space provided, then go online to see the answers at www.cengagebrain.com.

S1–ECONOMIC GROWTH

1. Why does the production possibilities curve shift outward with economic growth?

2. Fill-in-the-Blank: When the Dutch "created" new land with their system of dikes, their production possibilities curve shifted _____.

S2–DETERMINANTS OF LONG-RUN ECONOMIC GROWTH

3. True or False: No single factor is capable of completely explaining economic growth patterns.

4. Fill-in-the-Blank: Countries with relatively _____ labor would be leaders in labor-saving innovations.

S3–PUBLIC POLICY AND ECONOMIC GROWTH

5. What impact will free trade have on economic growth?

6. True or False: Increasing the capital stock will lead to economic growth.

S4–MEASURING ECONOMIC GROWTH AND ITS COMPONENTS

7. True or False: GDP measures all goods or services produced.

S5–MEASURING TOTAL PRODUCTION

8. If Mary received a welfare check this year, would that transfer payment be included in this year's GDP? Why or why not?

9. True or False: Inventory investment and net exports can be negative.

S6–PROBLEMS IN CALCULATING AN ACCURATE GDP

10. Fill-in-the-Blank: If we overestimated inflation over time, our calculations of real GDP growth would be _____-estimated.

11. Why would the growth in real GDP overstate the growth of output per person in a country with a growing population?

S7–PROBLEMS WITH GDP AS A MEASURE OF ECONOMIC WELFARE

12. True or False: GDP measures include nonmarket transactions.

13. How do pollution and crime affect GDP? How do pollution- and crime-control expenditures impact GDP?

A whole host of changes

could alter consumption patterns: an increase in consumer confidence, an increase in wealth, an increase in population, or a tax cut.

© GETTY IMAGES

13

Aggregate Demand and Aggregate Supply

in this chapter, we develop the aggregate demand and aggregate supply model. The *AD/AS* model is a variable price model; that is, it allows us to see changes in the price level and changes in real GDP simultaneously.

We explain changes in the price level and real GDP in both the short run and long run. This model will help us understand such key macroeconomic variables as inflation, unemployment, and economic growth. In the following chapters, we will also use this model to help us understand how stabilization policies can help with problems that result from recession and inflationary expansion.

Ⓢ1 The Aggregate Demand Curve

Keep the following questions in mind as you read through this section. You'll find the answers in Section Check 1.

1.1 How is the aggregate demand curve different from the demand curve for a particular good?

1.2 Why is the aggregate demand curve downward sloping?

The **aggregate demand curve** reflects the total amount of real goods and services that all groups together want to purchase in a given period. In other words, it indicates the quantities of real gross domestic product demanded at different price levels. Note that this is different from the demand curve for a particular good presented in Chapter 3, which looked at the relationship between the relative price of a good and the quantity demanded.

Sections in Chapter 13

HOW IS THE QUANTITY OF REAL GDP DEMANDED AFFECTED BY THE PRICE LEVEL?

The aggregate demand curve slopes downward, which means an inverse

> **aggregate demand curve** graph that shows the inverse relationship between the price level and RGDP demanded

(or opposite) relationship exists between the price level and real gross domestic product (RGDP) demanded. Exhibit 13.1 illustrates this relationship, where the quantity of RGDP demanded is measured on the horizontal axis and the overall price level is measured on the vertical axis. As we move from point A to point B on the aggregate demand curve, we see that an increase in the price level causes RGDP demanded to fall. Conversely, if a reduction in the price level occurs—a movement from B to A—RGDP demanded increases. Why do purchasers in the economy demand less real output when the price level rises and more real output when the price level falls?

WHY IS THE AGGREGATE DEMAND CURVE NEGATIVELY SLOPED?

Three complementary explanations exist for the negative slope of the aggregate demand curve: the real wealth effect, the interest rate effect, and the open economy effect.

The Real Wealth Effect

If you had $1,000 in cash stashed under your bed while the economy suffered a serious bout of inflation, the purchasing power of your cash would be eroded by the extent of the inflation. That is, an increase in the price level reduces real wealth and would consequently decrease your planned purchases of goods and services, lowering the quantity of RGDP demanded.

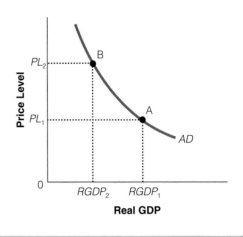

EXHIBIT 13.1 The Aggregate Demand Curve

In the event that the price level falls, the reverse would hold true. A falling price level would increase the real value of your cash assets, increasing your purchasing power and increasing RGDP demanded. The connection can be summarized as follows:

$\uparrow$*Price level* $\Rightarrow$ $\downarrow$*Real wealth* $\Rightarrow$ $\downarrow$*Purchasing power* $\Rightarrow$ $\downarrow$*RGDP demanded*

and

$\downarrow$*Price level* $\Rightarrow$ $\uparrow$*Real wealth* $\Rightarrow$ $\uparrow$*Purchasing power* $\Rightarrow$ $\uparrow$*RGDP demanded*

The Interest Rate Effect

If the price level falls, households and firms will need to hold less money to conduct their day-to-day activities. Firms will need to hold less money for such inputs as wages and taxes; households will need to hold less money for such purchases as food, rent, and clothing. At a lower price level, households and firms will shift their "excess" money into interest-earning assets such as bonds or savings accounts. This will increase the supply of funds to the loanable funds market, leading to lower interest rates. As interest rates fall, households and firms will borrow more and buy more goods and services—thus, the quantity of RGDP demanded will increase. In sum:

$\downarrow$*Price level* $\Rightarrow$ *Households and firms reduce their holdings of money and save more* $\Rightarrow$*Supply of loanable funds increases* $\Rightarrow$ *Interest rates fall* $\Rightarrow$ *Households and firms are encouraged to borrow and spend* $\Rightarrow$ *RGDP demanded increases*

If the price level rises, households and firms will need to hold more money to buy goods and services and conduct their daily activities. Households and firms will need to borrow money, and this increased demand for loanable funds will result in higher interest rates. At higher interest rates, consumers may give up plans to buy new cars or houses, and firms may delay investments in plants and equipment. In sum:

↑*Price level* ⇒ *Households and firms increase their holdings of money* ⇒ *Demand for loanable funds increases* ⇒ *Interest rates rise* ⇒ *Households and firms are discouraged from borrowing and spending* ⇒ *RGDP demanded decreases*

The Open Economy Effect

Many goods and services are bought and sold in global markets. If the price level in the United States rises relative to the price level in other countries, U.S. exports will become relatively more expensive and foreign imports will become relatively less expensive. Some U.S. consumers will shift from buying domestic goods to buying foreign goods (imports). Some foreign consumers will stop buying U.S. goods. U.S. exports will fall and U.S. imports will rise. Thus, net exports will fall, thereby reducing the amount of RGDP purchased in the United States. A lower price level makes U.S. exports less expensive and foreign imports more expensive. So U.S. consumers will buy more domestic goods, and foreign consumers will buy more U.S. goods. This will increase net exports, thereby increasing the amount of RGDP purchased in the United States.

SECTION CHECK 1

1.1 An aggregate demand curve shows the inverse relationship between the total amounts of real goods and services (RGDP) that are demanded at each possible price level.

1.2 The aggregate demand curve is downward sloping because of the real wealth effect, the interest rate effect, and the open economy effect.

⑤2 Shifts in the Aggregate Demand Curve

Keep the following questions in mind as you read through this section. You'll find the answers in Section Check 2.

2.1 What is the difference between a movement along and a shift in the aggregate demand curve?

2.2 What variables shift the aggregate demand curve to the right?

2.3 What variables shift the aggregate demand curve to the left?

Like the supply and demand curves described in Chapter 3, the aggregate demand curve may experience both shifts and movements.

SHIFTS VERSUS MOVEMENTS ALONG THE AGGREGATE DEMAND CURVE

In the previous section, we discussed three factors—the real wealth effect, the interest rate effect, and the open economy effect—that result in the downward slope of the aggregate demand curve. Each of these factors, then, generates a movement *along* the aggregate demand curve, in reaction to changes in the general price level. In this section, we will discuss some of the many factors that can cause the aggregate demand curve to shift to the right or left.

The whole aggregate demand curve can shift to the right or left, as shown in Exhibit 13.2 on the next page. Put simply, if some non-price level determinant causes total spending to increase, the aggregate demand curve will shift to the right. If a non-price level determinant causes the level of total spending to decline, the aggregate demand curve will shift to the left. Let's look at some specific factors that could cause the aggregate demand curve to shift.

AGGREGATE DEMAND CURVE SHIFTERS

Anything that changes the amount of total spending in the economy (holding price levels constant) will

EXHIBIT 13.2 Shifts in the Aggregate Demand Curve

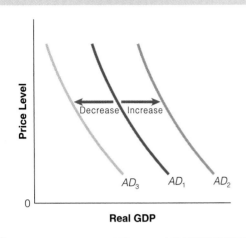

affect the aggregate demand curve. An increase in any component of GDP (C, I, G, or $X - M$) will cause the aggregate demand curve to shift rightward. Conversely, decreases in C, I, G, or $X - M$ will shift aggregate demand leftward.

Changing Consumption (*C*)

A whole host of changes could alter consumption patterns. For example, an increase in consumer confidence, an increase in wealth, or a tax cut can increase consumption and shift the aggregate demand curve to the right. An increase in population will also increase the aggregate demand because more consumers will be spending more money on goods and services.

Of course, the aggregate demand curve could shift to the left as a result of decreases in consumption demand. For example, if consumers sense that the economy is headed for a recession or if the government imposes a tax increase, the result will be a leftward shift of the aggregate demand curve. Because consuming less is saving more, an increase in saving, *ceteris paribus*, will shift aggregate demand to the left. Consumer debt may also cause some consumers to put off additional spending. In fact, some economists believe that part of the 1990–1992 recession was due to consumer debt that had built up during the 1980s. In addition to maxing out their credit cards, some individuals lost equity in their homes and, consequently, experienced reductions in their wealth and purchasing power—again shifting aggregate demand to the left.

Changing Investment (*I*)

Investment is also an important determinant of aggregate demand. Increases in the demand for investment goods occur for a variety of reasons. For example, if business confidence increases or real interest rates fall, business investment will increase and aggregate demand will shift to the right. A reduction in business taxes would also shift the aggregate demand curve to the right, because businesses would now retain more of their profits to invest. However, if interest rates or business taxes rise, we would expect to see a leftward shift in aggregate demand.

Changing Government Purchases (*G*)

Government purchases are another part of total spending and therefore must have an impact on aggregate demand. An increase in government purchases, *ceteris paribus*, shifts the aggregate demand curve to the right, whereas a reduction shifts aggregate demand to the left.

Changing Net Exports (*X − M*)

Global markets are also important in a domestic economy. For example, when major trading partners experience economic slowdowns (as did the Asian market in the late 1990s), they will demand fewer U.S. imports. This causes U.S. net exports ($X - M$) to fall, shifting aggregate demand to the left. Alternatively a boom in the economies of major trading partners may lead to an increase in our exports to them, causing net exports ($X - M$) to rise and aggregate demand to increase.

⑤3 The Aggregate Supply Curve

Keep the following questions in mind as you read through this section. You'll find the answers in Section Check 3.

3.1 What does the aggregate supply curve represent?

3.2 Why do producers supply more as the price level increases in the short run?

3.3 Why is the long-run aggregate supply curve vertical at the natural rate of output?

The **aggregate supply (AS)** curve is the relationship between the total quantity of final goods and services that suppliers are *willing* and *able* to produce and the overall price level. The aggregate supply curve represents how much RGDP suppliers are willing to produce at different price levels. In fact, the two aggregate supply curves are a **short-run aggregate supply (SRAS) curve** and a **long-run aggregate supply (LRAS) curve**. The short-run relationship refers to a period when output can change in response to supply and demand, but input prices have not yet been able to adjust. For example, nominal wages are assumed to adjust slowly in the short run. The long-run relationship refers to a period long enough for the prices of outputs and all inputs to fully adjust to changes in the economy.

WHY IS THE SHORT-RUN AGGREGATE SUPPLY CURVE POSITIVELY SLOPED?

In the short run, the aggregate supply curve is upward sloping, as shown in Exhibit 13.3. At a higher price level, then, producers are willing to supply more real output, and at lower price levels, they are willing to supply less real output. Why would producers be willing to supply more output just because the price level increases? Two possible explanations are the profit effect and the misperception effect.

The Profit Effect

For many firms, input costs—wages and rents, for example—are relatively constant in the short run. Workers and other material input suppliers often enter into long-term contracts with firms at prearranged prices. Thus, the slow adjustments of input prices are due to contracts that do not adjust quickly to output price level changes. So when the price level rises, output prices rise relative to input prices (costs), raising producers' short-run profit margins. With this short-run profit effect, the increased profit margins make it

> **aggregate supply (AS) curve** the total quantity of final goods and services suppliers are willing and able to supply at a given price level
>
> **short-run aggregate supply (SRAS) curve** the graphical relationship between RGDP and the price level when output prices can change but input prices are unable to adjust
>
> **long-run aggregate supply (LRAS) curve** the graphical relationship between RGDP and the price level when output prices and input prices can fully adjust to economic changes

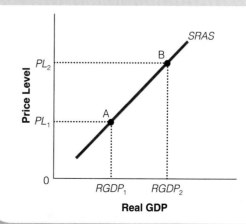

EXHIBIT 13.3 The Short-Run Aggregate Supply Curve

in producers' self-interest to expand production and sales at higher price levels. If the price level falls, output prices fall and producers' profits tend to fall. Again, this is because many input costs, such as wages and other contracted costs, are relatively constant in the short run. When output price levels fall, producers find it more difficult to cover their input costs and, consequently, reduce their levels of output.

The Misperception Effect

The second explanation for the upward-sloping short-run aggregate supply curve is that producers can be fooled by price changes in the short run. For example, suppose a cotton farmer sees the price of his cotton rising. Thinking that the *relative price* of his cotton is rising (i.e., that cotton is becoming more valuable in real terms), he supplies more. Suppose, however, that cotton was not the only thing for which prices were rising. What if the prices of many other goods and services were rising at the same time as a result of an increase in the price level? The relative price of cotton, then, was not actually rising, although it appeared so in the short run. In this case, the farmer was fooled into supplying more based on his *short-run misperception* of relative prices. In other words, producers can be fooled into thinking that the relative prices of the items they are producing are rising and mistakenly increase production.

WHY IS THE LONG-RUN AGGREGATE SUPPLY CURVE VERTICAL?

Along the short-run aggregate supply curve, we assume that wages and other input prices are constant. This assumption is not the case in the long run, which is a period long enough for the price of all inputs to fully adjust to changes in the economy. When we move along the long-run supply curve, we are looking at the relationship between RGDP produced and the price level, once input prices have been able to respond to changes in output prices. Along the long-run aggregate supply ($LRAS$) curve, two sets of prices are changing: the price of outputs and the price of inputs. That is, along the $LRAS$ curve, a 10 percent increase in the price of goods and services is matched by a 10 percent increase in the price of inputs. The long-run aggregate supply curve is thus insensitive to the price level. As we can see in Exhibit 13.4, the $LRAS$ curve is drawn as perfectly vertical, reflecting the fact that the level of RGDP producers are willing to supply is not affected by changes in the price level. Note that the vertical long-run aggregate supply curve will always be positioned at the natural rate of output, where all resources are fully employed ($RGDP_{NR}$).

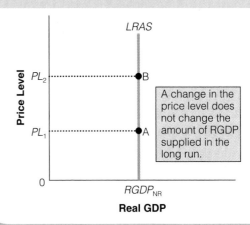

EXHIBIT 13.4 The Long-Run Aggregate Supply Curve

A change in the price level does not change the amount of RGDP supplied in the long run.

That is, in the long run, firms will always produce at the maximum level allowed by their capital, labor, and technological inputs, regardless of the price level.

The long-run equilibrium level is where the economy will settle when undisturbed and when all resources are fully employed. Remember that the economy will always be at the intersection of aggregate supply and aggregate demand; but that point will not always be at the natural rate of output, $RGDP_{NR}$. Long-run equilibrium will only occur where the aggregate supply and aggregate demand curves intersect along the long-run aggregate supply curve at the natural, or potential, rate of output.

SECTION CHECK 3

3.1 The short-run aggregate supply curve measures how much RGDP suppliers are willing to produce at different price levels.

3.2 In the short run, producers supply more as the price level increases because wages and other input prices tend to change more slowly than output prices. For this reason, producers can make a profit by expanding production when the price level rises.

3.3 In the long run, input prices change proportionally with output prices. The position of the $LRAS$ curve is determined by the level of capital, land, labor, and technology at the natural rate of output, $RGDP_{NR}$.

Ⓢ4 Shifts in the Aggregate Supply Curve

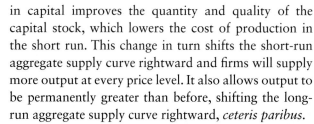

Keep the following questions in mind as you read through this section. You'll find the answers in **Section Check 4**.

4.1 Which factors of production affect the short-run and long-run aggregate supply curves?

4.2 What factors shift the short-run aggregate supply curve exclusively?

We will now examine the determinants that can shift the short-run and long-run aggregate supply curves, as shown in Exhibit 13.5.

SHIFTING SHORT-RUN AND LONG-RUN SUPPLY CURVES

Any change in the quantity of any factor of production available—capital, land, labor, or technology—can cause a shift in both the long-run and short-run aggregate supply curves. We will now see how these factors can change the positions of both types of aggregate supply curves.

How Capital Affects Aggregate Supply

Changes in the stock of capital will alter the amount of goods and services the economy can produce. Investing

in capital improves the quantity and quality of the capital stock, which lowers the cost of production in the short run. This change in turn shifts the short-run aggregate supply curve rightward and firms will supply more output at every price level. It also allows output to be permanently greater than before, shifting the long-run aggregate supply curve rightward, *ceteris paribus*.

Changes in human capital can also alter the aggregate supply curve. Investments in human capital include educational or vocational programs and on-the-job training. All these investments in human capital cause productivity to rise. As a result, the short-run aggregate supply curve shifts to the right, because a more skilled workforce lowers the cost of production. The *LRAS* curve also shifts to the right, because greater output is achievable on a permanent, or sustainable, basis, *ceteris paribus*.

Land (Natural Resources)

Remember that, in economics, *land* has an all-encompassing definition that includes all natural resources. An increase in natural resources, such as successful oil exploration, would presumably lower the costs of production and expand the economy's sustainable rate of output, shifting both the short-run and long-run aggregate supply curves to the right. Likewise, a decrease in available natural resources would result in a leftward shift of both the short-run and long-run aggregate supply curves. For example, in the 1970s and early 1980s, when the OPEC cartel was strong and effective at raising world oil prices, both short-run and long-run aggregate supply curves shifted to the left, as the members of the cartel deliberately reduced the production of oil.

The Labor Force

The addition of workers to the labor force, *ceteris paribus*, can increase aggregate supply. For example, during the 1960s, women and baby boomers entered the labor force in large numbers. This increase tended to depress wages and increase short-run aggregate supply, *ceteris paribus*. The expanded labor force also increased the economy's potential output, increasing long-run aggregate supply. Japan's aging population has been causing a decrease in the labor force in recent years—a leftward shift in the long-run aggregate supply curve, *ceteris paribus*.

Technology and Entrepreneurship

Bill Gates of Microsoft, Steve Jobs of Apple, and Larry Ellison of Oracle are just a few examples of entrepreneurs who, through inventive activity, developed innovative technology. Computers and specialized software—ATMs, bar-code scanners, and biotechnology—led to

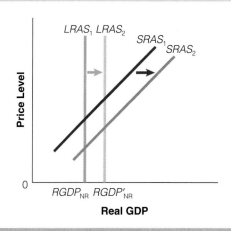

EXHIBIT 13.5 Shifts in Both Short-Run and Long-Run Aggregate Supply

Under CEO Larry Ellison's guidance, Oracle became a leading supplier in the market for database software. Oracle's software has helped many firms access, store, organize, and retrieve information in more efficient ways.

many cost savings and increased productivity across the board. These activities shifted both the short-run and long-run aggregate supply curves rightward by lowering costs and expanding real output possibilities.

Government Regulations

Increases in government regulations can make it more costly for producers. This increase in production costs results in a leftward shift of the short-run aggregate supply curve, and a reduction in society's potential output shifts the long-run aggregate supply curve to the left as well. Likewise, a reduction in government regulations

on businesses would lower the costs of production and expand potential real output, causing both the *SRAS* and *LRAS* curves to shift to the right.

WHAT FACTORS SHIFT SHORT-RUN AGGREGATE SUPPLY ONLY?

Some factors shift the short-run aggregate supply curve but do not change the long-run aggregate supply curve. The most important of these factors are wages and other input prices, productivity, and unexpected supply shocks. Exhibit 13.6 illustrates the effect of these factors on short-run aggregate supply.

EXHIBIT 13.6 Shifts in Short-Run Aggregate Supply but Not Long-Run Aggregate Supply

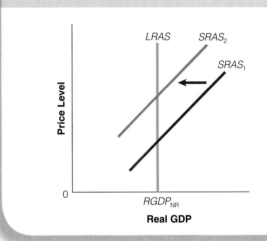

Q: Why do wage increases (and other input prices) affect the short-run aggregate supply but not the long-run aggregate supply?

You can find the answer on the next page.

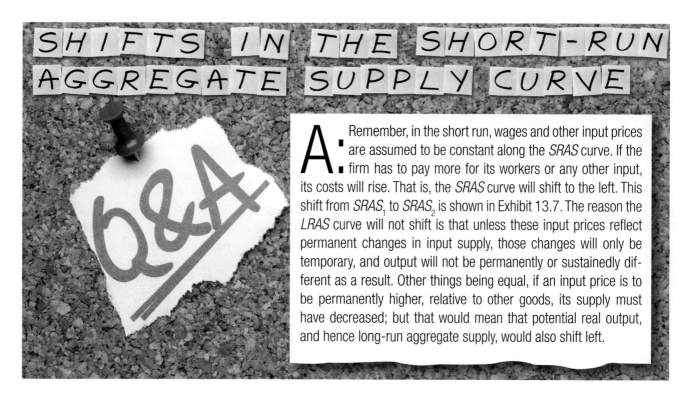

SHIFTS IN THE SHORT-RUN AGGREGATE SUPPLY CURVE

A: Remember, in the short run, wages and other input prices are assumed to be constant along the *SRAS* curve. If the firm has to pay more for its workers or any other input, its costs will rise. That is, the *SRAS* curve will shift to the left. This shift from *SRAS₁* to *SRAS₂* is shown in Exhibit 13.7. The reason the *LRAS* curve will not shift is that unless these input prices reflect permanent changes in input supply, those changes will only be temporary, and output will not be permanently or sustainedly different as a result. Other things being equal, if an input price is to be permanently higher, relative to other goods, its supply must have decreased; but that would mean that potential real output, and hence long-run aggregate supply, would also shift left.

Wages and Other Input Prices

The price of factors, or inputs, that go into producing outputs will affect only the short-run aggregate supply curve if they do not reflect permanent changes in the supplies of some factors of production. For example, if wages increase without a corresponding increase in labor productivity, it will become more costly for suppliers to produce goods and services at every price level, causing the *SRAS* curve to shift to the left. As Exhibit 13.7 shows, long-run aggregate supply will not shift because, with the same supply of labor as before, potential output does not change. For example, a decrease in an input price (such as oil) will shift the *SRAS* curve to the right. If the price of steel or oil rises, automobile producers will find it more expensive to do business because their production costs will rise, again resulting in a leftward shift in the short-run aggregate supply curve. The *LRAS* curve will not shift, however, as long as the capacity to make steel has not been reduced.

Temporary Supply Shocks

Supply shocks are unexpected temporary events that can either increase or decrease the short-run aggregate supply. For example, major widespread flooding, earthquakes, droughts, and other natural disasters can increase the costs of production, causing the short-run aggregate supply curve to shift to the left, *ceteris paribus*. However, once the temporary effects of these disasters have been felt, no appreciable change in the economy's productive capacity has occurred, so the long-run aggregate supply doesn't shift as a result. Other temporary supply shocks, such as disruptions in trade due to war or labor strikes, will have similar effects on short-run aggregate supply. However, favorable weather conditions or temporary price reductions of imported resources such as oil can shift the short-run aggregate supply curve rightward.

supply shocks unexpected temporary events that can either increase or decrease aggregate supply

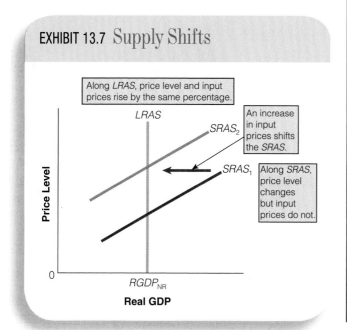

EXHIBIT 13.7 Supply Shifts

Along *LRAS*, price level and input prices rise by the same percentage.

An increase in input prices shifts the *SRAS*.

Along *SRAS*, price level changes but input prices do not.

Price Level

LRAS

SRAS₂

SRAS₁

0

*RGDP*ₙᵣ

Real GDP

Natural disasters such as droughts can temporarily increase the costs of production. This farmer would have to pay extra to bring water in from somewhere else.

© MASTERFILE / © PERRY KROLL/ISTOCKPHOTO.COM

SECTION CHECK 4

4.1 Any increase in the quantity of any of the factors of production—capital, land, labor, or technology—that are available will cause both the long-run and short-run aggregate supply curves to shift to the right. A decrease in any of these factors will shift both of the aggregate supply curves to the left.

4.2 Changes in the input price and temporary supply shocks will shift the short-run aggregate supply curve but will not affect the long-run aggregate supply curve.

Ⓢ5 Macroeconomic Equilibrium

Keep the following questions in mind as you read through this section. You'll find the answers in **Section Check 5**.

5.1 What is short-run macroeconomic equilibrium?

5.2 What is the long-run macroeconomic equilibrium?

5.3 What are recessionary and inflationary gaps?

5.4 What is wage and price inflexibility?

The short-run equilibrium level of real output and the price level are given by the intersection of the aggregate demand curve and the short-run aggregate supply curve. When this equilibrium occurs at the potential output level, the economy is operating at full employment on the long-run aggregate supply curve, as shown in Exhibit 13.8. Only a short-run equilibrium that is at potential output is also a long-run equilibrium. Short-run equilibrium can change when the aggregate demand curve or the short-run aggregate supply curve shifts rightward or leftward; but the long-run equilibrium level of RGDP only changes when the *LRAS* curve shifts. Sometimes, these supply or demand changes are anticipated; at other times, however, the shifts occur unexpectedly. Economists call these unexpected shifts *shocks*.

RECESSIONARY AND INFLATIONARY GAPS

As we have just seen, equilibrium will not always occur at full employment. In fact, equilibrium can occur at less than the potential output of the economy, $RGDP_{NR}$

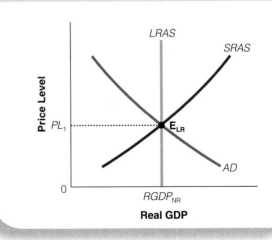

EXHIBIT 13.8 Long-Run Macroeconomic Equilibrium

(a **recessionary gap**), temporarily beyond $RGDP_{NR}$ (an **inflationary gap**), or at potential GDP. Exhibit 13.9 shows these three possibilities. In (a), we have a recessionary gap at the short-run equilibrium, ESR, at $RGDP_1$. When RGDP is less than $RGDP_{NR}$, the result is a recessionary gap—aggregate demand is insufficient to fully employ all of society's resources, so unemployment will be above the normal rate. In (c), we have an inflationary gap at the short-run equilibrium, E_{SR}, at $RGDP_3$, where aggregate demand is so high that the economy is temporarily operating beyond full capacity ($RGDP_{NR}$); this gap will lead to inflationary pressure, and unemployment will be below the normal rate. In (b), the economy is just right where AD_2 and $SRAS$ intersect at $RGDP_{NR}$—the long-run equilibrium position.

DEMAND-PULL INFLATION

Demand-pull inflation occurs when the price level rises as a result of an increase in aggregate demand. Consider the case in which an increase in consumer optimism results in a corresponding increase in aggregate demand. Exhibit 13.10 on the next page shows that an increase in aggregate demand causes an increase in the price level and an increase in real output. The movement is along the $SRAS$ curve from point E_1 to point E_2 and causes an inflationary gap. Recall that an increase in output occurs as a result of the increase in the price level in the short run, because firms have an incentive to increase real output when the prices of the goods they are selling are rising faster than the costs of the inputs they use in production.

Note that E_2 in Exhibit 13.10 is positioned beyond $RGDP_{NR}$—an inflationary gap. It seems strange that the economy can operate beyond its potential, but it is possible—temporarily—as firms encourage workers to work overtime, extend the hours of part-time workers, hire recently retired employees, reduce frictional unemployment through more extensive searches for employees, and so on. However, this level of output and employment *cannot* be sustained in the long run.

COST-PUSH INFLATION

The 1970s and early 1980s witnessed a phenomenon known as **stagflation**, where lower growth and higher prices occurred together. Some economists believe that this situation was caused by a leftward shift in the short-run aggregate supply curve, as shown in Exhibit 13.11 on the next page. If the aggregate demand curve did not increase significantly but the price level did, then the inflation was caused by supply-side forces, which is called **cost-push inflation**.

recessionary gap the output gap that occurs when the actual output is less than the potential output

inflationary gap the output gap that occurs when the actual output is greater than the potential output

demand-pull inflation a price-level increase due to an increase in aggregate demand

stagflation a situation in which lower growth and higher prices occur together

cost-push inflation a price-level increase due to a negative supply shock or increases in input prices

---

EXHIBIT 13.9 Recessionary and Inflationary Gaps

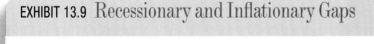

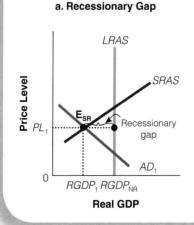

a. Recessionary Gap

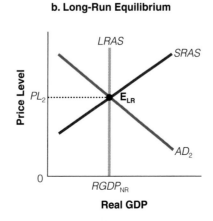

b. Long-Run Equilibrium

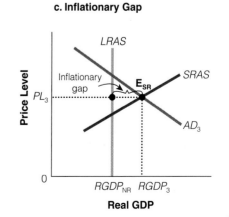

c. Inflationary Gap

EXHIBIT 13.10 Demand-Pull Inflation

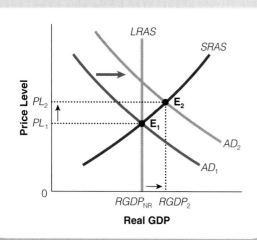

The increase in oil prices was the primary culprit responsible for the leftward shift in the aggregate supply curve. As we discussed in the previous section, an increase in input prices can cause the short-run aggregate supply curve to shift to the left; and this spelled big trouble for the U.S. economy—higher price levels, lower output, and higher rates of unemployment. The impact of cost-push inflation is illustrated in Exhibit 13.11.

In Exhibit 13.11, we see that the economy is initially at full-employment equilibrium at point E_1. A sudden increase in input prices, such as an increase in the price of oil, shifts the *SRAS* curve to the left—from $SRAS_1$ to $SRAS_2$. As a result of the shift in short-run aggregate supply, the price level rises to PL_2, and real output falls from $RGDP_{NR}$ to $RGDP_2$ (point E_2). Firms demand fewer workers as a result of higher input costs

EXHIBIT 13.11 Cost-Push Inflation

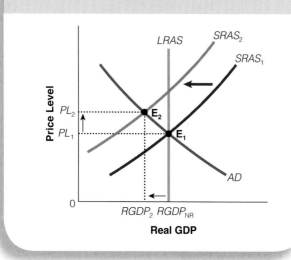

that cannot be passed on to consumers. This lower demand, in turn, leads to higher prices, lower real output, and more unemployment—and a recessionary gap. In the United States, these negative supply shocks occurred in 1974, 1979, 1990, 2005, and 2007–2008. These supply shocks can change real GDP significantly, but temporarily, away from potential aggregate output at $RGDP_{NR}$. In 2007, the price of many raw materials shot up globally—a global negative supply shock. Many countries around the world felt the effects of the negative supply shock.

However, recessions are not all bad—they can at least slow the rate of inflation. Two periods of serious inflation, 1974–1975 and 1979–1981, were followed by recessions and a slower rate of inflation.

What Helped the United States Recover in the 1980s?

As far as energy prices are concerned, oil prices fell during the 1980s when OPEC lost some of its clout because of internal problems. In addition, many non-OPEC oil producers increased production. The net result in the short run was a rightward shift in the aggregate supply curve. Holding aggregate demand constant, this rightward shift in the aggregate supply curve leads to a lower price level, greater output, and lower rates of unemployment—moving the economy back toward E_1 in Exhibit 13.11.

A DECREASE IN AGGREGATE DEMAND AND RECESSIONS

Just as cost-push inflation may cause a recessionary gap, so may a decrease in aggregate demand. For example, consider the case in which consumer confidence plunges and the stock market "tanks." As a result, aggregate demand falls, shown in Exhibit 13.12 as the shift from AD_1 to AD_2, leaving the economy in a new short-run equilibrium at point E_2. Households, firms, and governments buy fewer goods and services at every price level. In response to this drop in demand, output falls from $RGDP_{NR}$ to $RGDP_2$, and the price level falls from PL_1 to PL_2. Therefore, in the short run, this fall in aggregate demand causes higher unemployment and a reduction in output—and it, too, can lead to a recessionary gap.

The recession of 2001 and the slow recovery that followed can be attributed to three shocks that affected aggregate demand: the end of the stock market boom, the terrorist attacks of September 11 (this event had an impact on both stock market wealth and consumer

EXHIBIT 13.12 Short-Run Decrease in Aggregate Demand

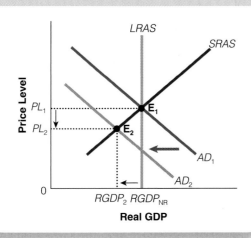

confidence), and a series of corporate scandals that rocked the stock market. Corrective stabilizing measures were taken following these events to prevent even further damage. For example, the Federal Reserve continued to lower interest rates. Lower interest rates stimulate the economy by encouraging investment and consumption spending. Other stabilizing measures included a tax cut passed by Congress in 2001 and increased government spending to help rebuild New York City and provide financial assistance to the ailing airline industry. Both the 2001 tax cut and the war on terrorism led to an increase in government spending. Both of these policies shifted the aggregate demand curve to the right, reducing the

Both the 2001 tax cut and the war on terrorism lead to increased government spending, which helped reduce the depth of the 2001 recession.

magnitude of the 2001 recession. The recovery did not pick up steam until 2003.

Most of the post-war recessions have been caused by negative demand shocks. Negative supply shocks have been relatively few, but quite severe, in terms of unemployment rates. The 2007–2009 recession appears to be the product of both negative demand and supply shocks.

ADJUSTING TO A RECESSIONARY GAP

Many recoveries from a recessionary gap occur because of increases in aggregate demand—perhaps consumer and business confidence picks up, or the government lowers taxes and/or lowers interest rates to stimulate the economy. That is, an eventual rightward shift in the aggregate demand curve takes the economy back to potential output—$RGDP_{NR}$.

However, it is possible for the economy to *self-correct* through declining wages and prices. In Exhibit 13.13, at point E_2, the intersection of PL_2 and $RGDP_2$, the economy is in a recessionary gap—that is, the economy is producing less than its potential output. At this lower level of output, firms lay off workers to avoid inventory accumulation. In addition, firms may cut prices to increase demand for their products. Unemployed workers and other input suppliers may also bid down wages and prices. That is, laborers and other input suppliers are now willing to accept lower wages and prices for the use of their resources, and the resulting reduction in production costs shifts the short-run supply curve from $SRAS_1$ to $SRAS_2$. Eventually, the economy returns to a long-run equilibrium at point E_3, the intersection of $RGDP_{NR}$ and a lower price level, PL_3.

EXHIBIT 13.13 Adjusting to a Recessionary Gap

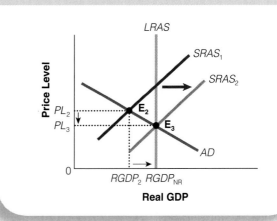

SLOW ADJUSTMENTS TO A RECESSIONARY GAP

Many economists believe that wages and prices may be slow to adjust, especially downward. This downward **wage and price inflexibility** may prolong the duration of a recessionary gap.

For example, in Exhibit 13.13 we see that the economy is in a recession at E_2 and $RGDP_2$. The economy will eventually self-correct to $RGDP_{NR}$ at E_3, as workers and other input owners accept lower wages and prices for their inputs, shifting the $SRAS$ curve to the right from $SRAS_1$ to $SRAS_2$. However, if wages and other input prices are sticky, the economy's adjustment mechanism might take many months to totally self-correct.

Japan witnessed several recessionary gaps in the 1990s and even experienced deflation as the self-adjustment mechanism predicts. However, the adjustment out of the recessionary gap was slow and painful.

WHAT CAUSES WAGES AND PRICES TO BE STICKY DOWNWARD?

Empirical evidence supports several explanations for the downward stickiness of wages and prices. Firms may not be able to legally cut wages because of long-term labor contracts (particularly with union workers) or a legal minimum wage. Efficiency wages may also limit a firm's ability to lower wage rates. Menu costs may cause price inflexibility as well.

Efficiency Wages

In economics, it is generally assumed that as productivity rises, wages will rise, and that workers can raise their productivity through investments in human capital such as education and on-the-job training. However, some economists believe that in some cases, *higher wages will lead to greater productivity*.

In the efficiency wage model, employers pay their employees more than the equilibrium wage as a means to increase efficiency. Proponents of this theory suggest that higher-than-equilibrium wages might attract the most productive workers, lower job turnover and training costs,

wage and price inflexibility the tendency for prices and wages to only adjust slowly downward to changes in the economy

and improve morale. Because the efficiency wage rate is greater than the equilibrium wage rate, the quantity of labor that would be willingly supplied is greater than the quantity of labor demanded, resulting in greater amounts of unemployment.

However, aside from creating some additional unemployment, the efficiency wage could also cause wages to be inflexible downward. For example, if aggregate demand decreases, firms that pay efficiency wages may be reluctant to cut wages, fearing that cuts could lead to lower morale, greater absenteeism, and general productivity losses. In short, if firms are paying efficiency wages, they may be reluctant to lower wages in a recession, leading to downward wage inflexibility.

Menu Costs

Some costs are associated with changing prices in an inflationary environment. Thus, the higher price level in an inflationary environment is often reflected slowly, as restaurants, mail-order houses, and department stores change their prices gradually so as to incur fewer *menu costs* (the costs of changing posted prices) in printing new catalogs, new mailers, new advertisements, and so on. Because businesses are not likely to change all their prices immediately, we can say that some prices are sticky, or slow to change. For example, many outputs, such as steel, are inputs in the production of other products, such as automobiles. As a result, these prices are slow to change.

Suppose aggregate demand unexpectedly decreases. This change could lower the price level. Some firms may adjust to the change quickly. Others, however, may move more slowly because of menu costs, causing their prices to become too high (above equilibrium). Ultimately, the sales and outputs will fall, potentially causing a recession.

Firms not responding quickly to changes in demand fail to do so for a reason; and to some economists, menu costs are at least part of that reason.

Today's Special — higher menu costs

ADJUSTING TO AN INFLATIONARY GAP

In Exhibit 13.14, the economy is in an inflationary gap at E_2, where $RGDP_2$ is greater than $RGDP_{NR}$. Because the price level, PL_2, is higher than the one workers anticipated, PL_1, workers become disgruntled with wages that have not adjusted to the new price level (if prices have risen but wages have not risen as much, real wages have fallen). Recall that along the SRAS curve, wages and other input prices are assumed to be constant. Therefore, workers' and input suppliers' purchasing power falls as output prices rise. Real (adjusted for inflation) wages have fallen. Consequently, workers and other suppliers demand higher prices if they are to be willing to supply their inputs. As input prices respond to the higher level of output prices, the short-run aggregate supply curve shifts to the left, from $SRAS_1$ to $SRAS_2$. Suppliers will continue to seek higher prices for their inputs until they reach the long-run equilibrium, at point E_3 in Exhibit 13.14. At point E_3, input suppliers' purchasing power is restored at the long-run equilibrium, at $RGDP_{NR}$ and a new higher price level, PL_3.

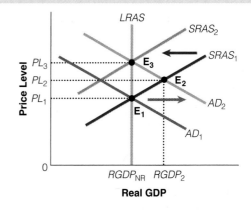

EXHIBIT 13.14 Adjusting to an Inflationary Gap

PRICE LEVEL AND RGDP OVER TIME

In Exhibit 13.15, we traced out the pattern of RGDP versus the price level. According to the Bureau of Economic Analysis, both the price level and RGDP have been rising over the last 36 years. So what is responsible for

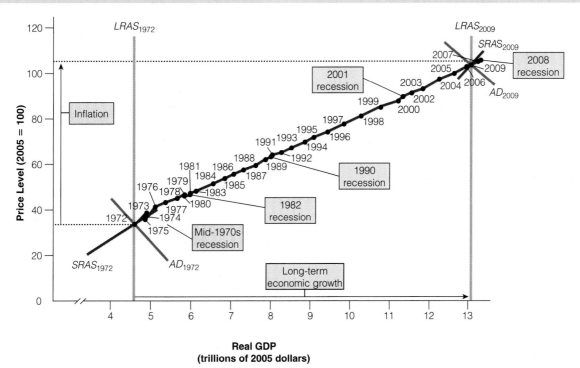

EXHIBIT 13.15 U.S. Price Level and RGDP

NOTE: In 2009 both the price level and real GDP declined from those figures of the previous year.

SOURCE: Bureau of Economic Analysis, National Economic Accounts, Current-dollar and "real" GDP. Washington, D.C., February 26, 2010. Available at http://bea.gov/national/index.htm#gdp (accessed February 26, 2010).

the changes? The answer is both aggregate demand and aggregate supply. Aggregate demand has risen because of growing population (which impacts consumption and investment spending), rising income, increases in government purchases, and increases in the money supply. Aggregate supply has been generally increasing as well, including increases in the labor force and improvements in labor productivity and technology.

SECTION CHECK 5

5.1 Short-run macroeconomic equilibrium occurs at the intersection of the aggregate demand curve and the short-run aggregate supply curve.

5.2 A short-run equilibrium is also a long-run equilibrium only if it is at potential output on the long-run aggregate supply curve.

5.3 If short-run equilibrium occurs at less than the potential output of the economy, $RGDP_{NR}$, the result is a recessionary gap. If the short-run equilibrium temporarily occurs beyond $RGDP_{NR}$, the result is an inflationary gap.

5.4 Wages and other input prices may be slow to adjust, especially downward. This downward wage and price inflexibility may lead to prolonged periods of recession.

⑤6 The Classical and the Keynesian Macroeconomic Models

Keep the following questions in mind as you read through this section. You'll find the answers in **Section Check 6**.

6.1 What is Say's law?

6.2 What was Keynes's criticism of the classical school?

6.3 What is the full-employment classical school model?

Historically, the two primary approaches to macroeconomics have been the classical school and the Keynesian school. Let's begin with the classical school. The classical school of thought believed that wages and prices adjust quickly to changes in supply and demand.

THE CLASSICAL SCHOOL AND SAY'S LAW

Writing at the beginning of the nineteenth century, the French economist Jean Baptiste Say formulated a notion, since dubbed Say's law, which in its simplest form states that "supply creates its own demand." More precisely, the production of goods and services creates income for owners of inputs (land, labor, capital, and entrepreneurship) used in production, which in turn creates a demand for goods. According to Say's law, we need not worry about output not being utilized; production creates income, which creates demand for goods, which leads to still more production. That is, Say's law establishes that full employment can be maintained because total spending will be great enough for firms to sell all the output a fully employed economy can produce. Say's ideas were incorporated into the teachings of classical economists of the late nineteenth century.

JEAN BAPTISTE SAY

Before the 1930s, the problem of unemployment was considered one that could be analyzed using micro-economic analysis; indeed, macroeconomics as we know it today did not exist. The theory that evolved to analyze unemployment suggested that joblessness could be eliminated by market forces, in the same way that shortages and surpluses of goods and services are eliminated by movement in the relative prices of those goods.

The Full-Employment Classical School Model

The macroeconomic models presented in this text draw from both schools of thought and emphasize the commonality between the two schools. The classical school focuses on the economy at full employment, because both schools agree that in the long run both wages and prices adjust freely to changes in demand and supply and the economy moves back naturally to its potential, full-employment output level. That is, eventually (in the long run) all markets adjust to their equilibrium values. Recall that full employment does not mean zero unemployment; rather, it refers to zero cyclical unemployment. Some structural and frictional unemployment occurs naturally in a dynamic and vibrant economy.

The actual output that the economy produces need not be the same as potential output—what the economy can produce without leading to inflation. If the economy is producing at less than its potential output, unemployment is greater than the natural rate; if the economy is producing at greater than its potential output, unemployment is less than the natural rate, causing

inflationary pressures. That is, it is possible on the peak of a business cycle that actual real GDP can exceed potential real GDP, but only for a short period of time. The problem is that the causal observer often confuses potential and actual output. When the economy is accelerating at a fast clip, some observers believe we are on a new growth trajectory. And when the economy slows, some observers confuse this change with doom and gloom.

Earlier in this chapter we discussed monetary and fiscal policy, using the *AS/AD* model to examine business cycles and short-run policy prescriptions that involve government intervention to help the economy get back to its long-run growth trajectory.

Changes in Aggregate Demand in the Classical Model

In Exhibit 13.16, we see the impact of either an increase or a decrease in aggregate demand in the classical model. According to Say's law, prolonged unemployment is impossible in the long-run classical model. Prices, wages, and interest rates all adjust quickly, which keeps workers and resources fully employed at the natural rate of real output, $RGDP_{NR}$. The classical school made very little distinction between the short run and the long run, so the only aggregate supply curve is the vertical long-run aggregate supply curve, *LRAS* in Exhibit 13.16. That is, there is no separate short-run aggregate supply curve in the classical model. Prices and wages adjust so quickly that the economy seldom remains far from $RGDP_{NR}$.

EXHIBIT 13.16 Changes in Aggregate Demand in the Classical Model

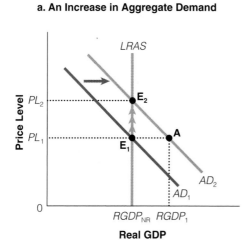

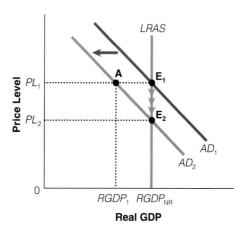

In Exhibit 13.16(a), if prices, wages, and interest rates were not completely and quickly flexible, an increase in aggregate demand from AD_1 to AD_2 might cause the economy to move toward point A beyond $RGDP_{AD}$. However, when the price level rises, input suppliers bid up input prices and the economy quickly adjusts to the new price level at PL_2, moving along the $LRAS$.

In Exhibit 13.16(b), there is a decrease in aggregate demand that could cause the economy to move toward point A, where resources (labor, factories, and other inputs) would be unemployed. However, because input suppliers will compete against each other, it will drive input prices down. If this occurs quickly, as predicted in the classical model, the economy will not experience prolonged unemployment and will adjust to the new price level, PL_2, along the $LRAS$.

KEYNES'S CRITICISM OF THE CLASSICAL SCHOOL

In 1936, John Maynard Keynes's book, *The General Theory of Employment, Interest and Money*, was published. Along with Adam Smith's *The Wealth of Nations* in the eighteenth century, *The General Theory of Employment, Interest and Money* was one of the most influential books in economics. In his book, Keynes attacked the classical economic theory. He pointed out the naiveté of Say's law: Not all income generated from output need be used to buy goods and services; it can also be saved, hoarded, or taxed away. Supply does not automatically create an adequate demand. Keynes's severest attacks were against classical ideas about unemployment. With unemployment rates at that time in the double digits, where did the classicists go wrong?

To begin with, when a recession begins, wages rarely fall quickly to a new equilibrium level consistent with full employment. Long-term labor contracts with unions, minimum wage laws, and other factors often prevent wages from falling as quickly as the classical model suggests. Thus, wage inflexibility prevents the market solution from working rapidly enough to avert a prolonged recession.

The Keynesian Short-Run Aggregate Supply Curve—Sticky Prices and Wages

Keynes and his followers argued that wages and prices are inflexible downward. As we just discussed, wage stickiness can arise as a result of long-term labor and raw material contracts, unions, and minimum wage laws. If wages and prices are sticky and the economy has sufficient excess capacity, then the short-run aggregate supply curve is flat, because full employment of all resources is not reached until $RGDP_{NR}$. That is, with so many resources idle, producers will not have to compete with each other for machinery or labor, and input prices will tend to stay flat.

In Exhibit 13.17(a), we see that in the flat portion of the $SRAS$ curve an increase in AD from AD_1 to AD_2 has little impact on the price level but considerable impact on real GDP and employment. When AD_1 increases to AD_2, we see an increase in real gross domestic product from $RGDP_1$ to $RGDP_2$—a new equilibrium where resources are more fully utilized. Similarly, a reduction in AD in this region will also leave the price level unchanged. Specifically, it means that the price level does not rise or fall in this situation, but RGDP does. This price and wage inflexibility when AD is falling played a significant part in the Keynesian theory. With stickiness of wages and other input costs, a reduction in aggregate demand will not lead to

When a recession begins, wages rarely fall quickly to a new equilibrium level consistent with full employment.

EXHIBIT 13.17 The Keynesian Aggregate Supply Curve

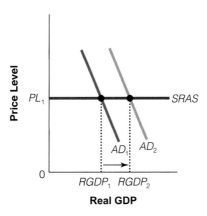

a. Keynesian Short-Run Aggregate Supply Curve

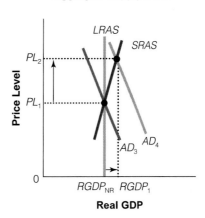

b. Modern Keynesian Short-Run Aggregate Supply Curve

a lower price level if the economy has sufficient excess capacity—say at $RGDP_1$. Historically, the mid- to late 1930s seems to fit the Keynesian model quite well, as the economy experienced increases in RGDP without simultaneous increases in the price level. It was a period of high unemployment of resources and double-digit unemployment—that is, sufficient level of excess capacity and little competition to bid up input prices.

Most macroeconomists now believe that price and wages are not completely inflexible downward. However, wages and prices do tend to be less flexible when excess capacity is available—the slope of the $SRAS$ is flatter the further it is below full employment. However, when the economy is temporarily operating beyond $RGDP_{NR}$, the $SRAS$ is steep because higher output prices are necessary if firms are expanding output in this unsustainable region beyond full employment. This is seen in Exhibit 13.17(b). That is, the firm can increase output by working labor and capital more intensively.

When resources are idle, output will be more responsive to changes in AD, and the price level will not be as responsive—the $SRAS$ is flatter—as it moves from AD_1 to AD_2. And when resources are at full capacity, output is less responsive to changes in AD and the price level is highly responsive—the $SRAS$ is steeper—as it moves from AD_3 to AD_4.

However, economists continue to debate about the actual shape of the aggregate supply curve.

Wage inflexibility prevents the market solution from working rapidly enough to avert a prolonged recession.

SECTION CHECK 6

6.1 Say's law stated that "supply creates its own demand." It also argued that full employment could be maintained in an economy.

6.2 Keynes rejected Say's law because, in addition to spending income from production of goods and services, it can go toward saving, hoarding, or taxes.

6.3 Potential real output is the level of real output the economy can produce without leading to inflation. If the economy is producing less than potential output, unemployment is greater than its natural rate. If the economy is temporarily producing more than potential output, unemployment is less than its natural rate.

Chapter 13: Self-Review

Now that you're finished reading the chapter, review the questions below. You can write your answers in the space provided, then go online to see the answers at www.cengagebrain.com.

S1—THE AGGREGATE DEMAND CURVE

1. **True or False:** An increased price level reduces the quantities of investment goods and consumer durables demanded.

2. **What is the open economy effect?**

S2—SHIFTS IN THE AGGREGATE DEMAND CURVE

3. **Fill-in-the-Blank:** An increase in the demand for consumption goods results in a(n) _____ in aggregate demand.

4. **Fill-in-the-Blank:** A falling demand for investment goods results in a(n) _____ in aggregate demand.

5. **True or False:** An increase in the money supply tends to decrease expenditures on consumption and investment, *ceteris paribus*.

S3—THE AGGREGATE SUPPLY CURVE

6. **What relationship does the short-run aggregate supply curve represent?**

S4—SHIFTS IN THE AGGREGATE SUPPLY CURVE

7. **Fill-in-the-Blank:** Lower input costs _____ the level of RGDP supplied at any given price level.

8. **What would happen to short- and long-run aggregate supply if unusually good weather led to bumper crops of most agricultural produce?**

S5—MACROECONOMIC EQUILIBRIUM

9. **What is demand-pull inflation?**

10. **True or False:** Cost-push inflation is caused by a rightward shift in the short-run aggregate supply curve.

11. **Fill-in-the-Blank:** The economy self-corrects for a short-run recession through _____ wages and prices.

S6—THE CLASSICAL AND KEYNESIAN MACROECONOMIC MODELS

12. **Fill-in-the-Blank:** The _____ school of thought emphasized that markets can rapidly adjust to changes.

13. **What would keep wages from falling quickly in a recession?**

14. **Fill-in-the-Blank:** If wages are sticky downward, a decrease in aggregate demand will primarily _____ real output.

SPEAK UP! THEY DID

Survey of ECON was built on a simple principle: to create a new teaching and learning solution that reflects the way today's faculty teach and the way you learn.

Through conversations, focus groups, surveys, and interviews, we collected data that drove the creation of the current version of Survey of ECON that you are using today. But it doesn't stop there—in order to make Survey of ECON an even better learning experience, we'd like you to SPEAK UP and tell us how Survey of ECON worked for you.

What did you like about it? What would you change? Are there additional ideas you have that would help us build a better product for next semester's students?

At **www.cengagebrain.com** you'll find all of the resources you need to succeed—**videos, flash cards, interactive quizzes,** and more!

Speak Up! Go to **www.cengagebrain.com**.

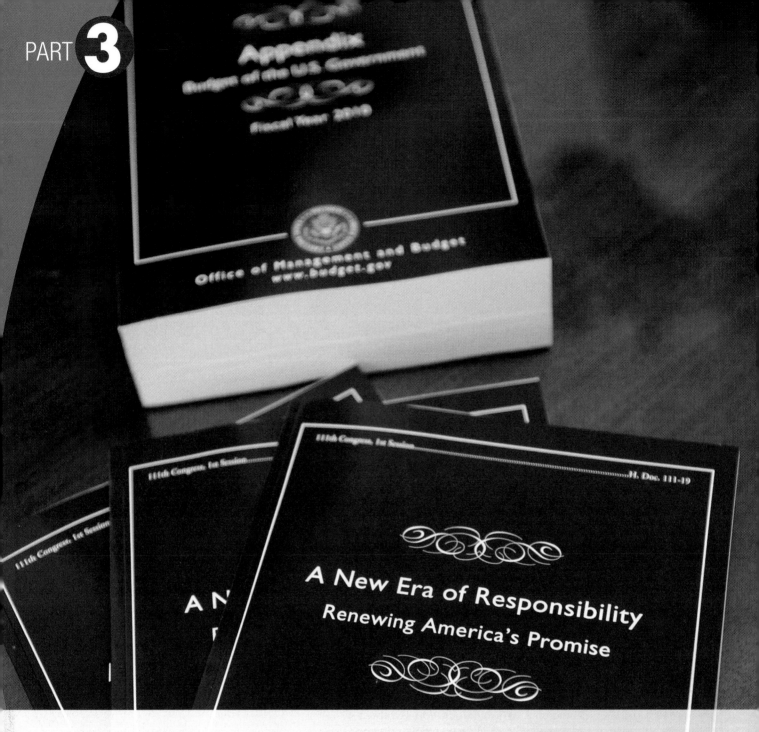

A New Era of Responsibility
Renewing America's Promise

Every year, the President delivers

a budget proposal like this one, the proposed budget for 2010, for approval by congress. The President's budget details proposed government spending for the coming fiscal year, which begins on October 1. The Congressional budget committees will then begin drafting budget resolutions to pass along to the House and Senate.

14

Fiscal Policy

in earlier chapters, we discussed how an economy can face a recessionary gap when aggregate demand is deficient or an inflationary gap when there is excessive aggregate demand.

In this chapter, we will see how the government can employ fiscal policy—the use of government purchases, transfers, and/or taxes—to combat recessions or curb inflationary pressures. We will see how the government obtains revenues through taxation and examine the different types of taxation. We will also see that a number of problems are associated with successfully enacting and applying fiscal policy to stabilize an economy. Finally, we will examine the supply-side effects of taxes.

⑤1 Fiscal Policy

Keep the following questions in mind as you read through this section. You'll find the answers in **Section Check 1**.

1.1 What is fiscal policy?

1.2 How does expansionary fiscal policy affect the government's budget?

1.3 How does contractionary fiscal policy affect the government's budget?

Fiscal policy is the use of government purchases, taxes, and transfer payments to alter RGDP and the price level. Sometimes it is necessary for the government to use fiscal policy to stimulate the economy during a contraction (or recession) or to try to curb an expansion in order to bring inflation under control. In the early 1980s, large tax cuts helped the U.S. economy out of a recession. In the 1990s, Japan used large government spending programs to try to spend itself out of a recessionary slump. In 2001, a large tax cut was implemented to combat an economic slowdown and to promote long-term economic growth in the United States. And the fiscal stimulus package that the Obama administration enacted in 2009 to combat the recession was the largest fiscal stimulus since World War II. But that was small compared to the $2.5 trillion spent

> **fiscal policy** use of government purchases, taxes, and transfer payments to alter equilibrium output and prices

Sections in Chapter 14

on the financial system. When should the government use such policies and how well do they work are just a couple of the questions we will answer in this chapter.

FISCAL STIMULUS AFFECTS THE BUDGET

Government spending (for purchases of goods and services and transfer payments) that exceeds tax revenues causes a **budget deficit**. When tax revenues are greater than government spending, a **budget surplus** exists. A balanced budget, where government expenditures equal tax revenues, seldom occurs unless efforts are made to deliberately balance the budget as a matter of public policy.

When the government wishes to stimulate the economy by increasing aggregate demand, it will increase government purchases of goods and services, increase transfer payments, lower taxes, or use some combination of these approaches. Any of these options will increase a budget deficit (or reduce a budget surplus). Thus, **expansionary fiscal policy** is associated with increased government budget deficits. Likewise, if the government wishes to dampen a boom in the economy by reducing aggregate demand, it will reduce its purchases of goods and services, increase taxes, reduce transfer payments, or use some combination of these approaches. Thus, **contractionary fiscal policy** will tend to create or expand a budget surplus or reduce an existing budget deficit.

budget deficit occurs when government spending exceeds tax revenues for a given fiscal year

budget surplus occurs when tax revenues are greater than government expenditures for a given fiscal year

expansionary fiscal policy use of fiscal policy tools to foster increased output by increasing government purchases, lowering taxes, and/or increasing transfer payments

contractionary fiscal policy use of fiscal policy tools to reduce output by decreasing government purchases, increasing taxes, and/or reducing transfer payments

JAPAN'S FISCAL POLICY EXPERIMENT

Prior to the 1990s, Japan experienced several decades of rapid economic growth with only a mild recession in 1974. However, the 1990s were a different story—the exuberant bubble burst, as the stock market made a major correction and land values plunged. Consequently, consumption and investment spending—two major components of aggregate demand—fell.

In the decade of the 1990s, Japan grew at an unusually slow rate—1.2 percent per year—almost 3 percentage points below the average growth rate of the previous decade. In order to combat the recession, the Japanese launched a fiscal policy stimulus package of unprecedented tax cuts and spending increases. Government expenditures rose from slightly over 30 percent of GDP to almost 40 percent of GDP. The Japanese government spent well over a trillion dollars during the decade to heal their ailing economy. Because of the tax cuts, government tax revenues fell from 34 percent to 31 percent of GDP. And the continued fiscal efforts, financed with lower taxes and higher government spending, led to a growing debt problem. (The debt-to-GDP ratio almost doubled in the decade of the 1990s—from 0.58 in 1991 to 1.1 in 2000.)

The results of the fiscal policy are mixed. The fiscal policy clearly did not bring about a full recovery. However, some economists argue that without the spending and tax cuts, the Japanese would have suffered a depression rather than a sustained period of slow economic growth. Other economists argue that the wasteful nature of government spending was the reason that fiscal policy was not more successful. The Japanese built bridges, railroad lines, tunnels, and highways to sparsely populated areas. It is safe to say that none of these projects would have been undertaken by the private sector. Thus, a better-designed fiscal policy might have been more effective.

SOURCE: John H. Makin, "Japan's lost decade: Lessons for America," *American Enterprise Institute for Public Policy Research,* February 2001. Available at http://www.aei.org/outlook/12375 (accessed July 8, 2010).

THE GOVERNMENT AND TOTAL SPENDING

In a previous chapter, we learned that the aggregate demand is equal to consumer spending, investment spending, government purchases, and net exports: $AD = C + I + G + (X - M)$. The government directly controls government purchases, but government can also indirectly affect aggregate demand through taxes and transfer programs. For example, an increase in taxes and/or a reduction in transfer payments can reduce disposable income and decrease consumer spending. Similarly, a decrease in taxes and/or an increase in transfer payment can increase disposable income and lead to an increase in consumer spending. The government can also influence investment spending through business taxes. For example, a tax cut for firms may increase investment spending and shift the aggregate demand curve to the right. Thus, the government can change aggregate demand in a number of ways.

Ⓢ2 Government Spending and Taxation

Keep the following questions in mind as you read through this section. You'll find the answers in **Section Check 2**.

2.1 On what does the public sector spend its money?

2.2 What are progressive and regressive taxes?

2.3 What is a flat tax?

2.4 What is the ability to pay principle?

2.5 What is the benefits received principle?

In this section, we'll see how the government obtains revenues through taxation to provide public goods and services, and we'll examine the different types of taxes the government can enforce.

GROWTH IN GOVERNMENT

The government's role in the economy increased markedly between 1930 and 1975, as may be seen in Exhibit 14.1. Although it is true that federal spending has changed little since 1960, the composition of government spending has changed considerably. National defense spending fell from roughly 10 percent of GDP in 1960 to 3.6 percent in 2000. However, the aftermath of the terrorist attacks of September 11, 2001, and the wars in Iraq and Afghanistan, led to increases in defense spending. It rose to 5.6 percent of GDP in 2009. Areas of government growth can be identified at least in part by looking at statistics on the types of government spending.

The share of GDP devoted to Social Security and Medicare rose from about 2.5 percent in 1960 to more than 7 percent today. Exhibit 14.2(a) shows that 34 percent of federal government spending in 2009 went to Social Security and income security programs. Another 22 percent was spent on health care and Medicare (for the elderly). The remaining federal expenditures were national defense, 19 percent; interest on the national debt, 5 percent; and miscellaneous items such as foreign aid, agriculture, transportation, and housing, 20 percent.

Exhibit 14.2(b) shows that state and local spending differs greatly from federal spending. Education and public welfare account for 41 percent of state and local expenditures. Other significant areas of state and local spending include highways, utilities, and police and fire protection.

GENERATING GOVERNMENT REVENUE

Governments have to pay their bills like any person or institution that spends money. But how do they obtain revenue? In most years, a large majority of government activity is financed by taxation. What kinds of taxes are levied on the American population?

At the federal level, most taxes or levies are on income. Exhibit 14.3 shows that 50 percent of tax revenues come in the form of income taxes on individuals and corporations, called personal income taxes and corporate income taxes, respectively. Most of the remaining revenues come from payroll taxes, which are levied on work-related income, that is, payrolls. These taxes are used to pay for Social Security and compulsory insurance plans such as Medicare. Payroll taxes are split between employees and employers. The Social Security share of federal taxes has steadily risen as the proportion of the population over age 65 has grown and as Social Security benefits have been increased. Consequently, payroll taxes have risen significantly in recent years. Other taxes on such items as gasoline, liquor, and tobacco products, provide for a small proportion of government revenues, as do customs duties, estate and gift taxes, and some minor miscellaneous taxes and user charges.

The U.S. federal government relies more heavily on income-based taxes than nearly any other government in the world. Most other governments rely more heavily on sales taxes, excise taxes, and customs duties.

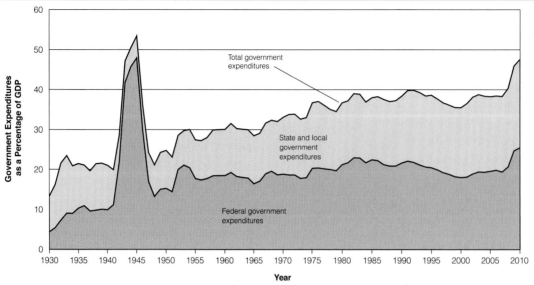

SOURCES: *Economic Report of the President*, 2010. Statistical Tables. Tables B-79 and B-86. Washington, D.C. February, 2010. Available at http://www.gpoaccess.gov/eop/tables10.html (accessed March 25, 2010); Christopher Chantril, "Time Series Chart of U.S. Government Spending," usgovernmentspending.com. Available at http://www.usgovernmentspending.com/downchart_gs.php?year=1930_2010&view=1&expand=&units=p&fy=fy11&chart=F0-fed_F0-statelocal&bar=0&stack=1&size=m&title=&state=US&color=c&local=c (accessed April 20, 2010).

A Progressive Tax

progressive tax a tax designed so that those with higher incomes pay a greater proportion of their income in taxes

One effect of substantial taxes on income is that the "take home" income of Americans is significantly altered by the tax system. **Progressive taxes**, of which the federal income tax is one example, are designed so that those with higher incomes pay a greater proportion of their income in taxes. A progressive tax is one tool that the government can use to redistribute income. It should be noted, however, that certain types of income are excluded from income for taxation purposes, such

EXHIBIT 14.2 Government Expenditures

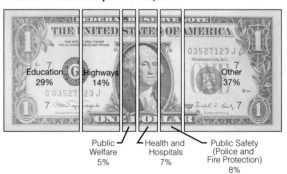

a. Federal Expenditures, 2009

National Defense 19%
Social Security 19%
Medicare 12%
Health 10%
Other 20%
Income Security 15%
Net Interest on the National Debt 5%

b. State and Local Expenditures, 2007

Education 29%
Highways 14%
Other 37%
Public Welfare 5%
Health and Hospitals 7%
Public Safety (Police and Fire Protection) 8%

SOURCES: *Economic Report of the President, 2010*. Statistical Tables. Table B-80. Washington, D.C. February, 2010. Available at http://www.gpoaccess.gov/eop/tables10.html (accessed March 25, 2010); U.S. Census Bureau, State & Local Government Finance 2007, U.S. Summary. Washington, D.C. December 11, 2009. Available at http://www.census.gov/govs/estimate/ (accessed April 6, 2010).

EXHIBIT 14.3 Tax Revenues

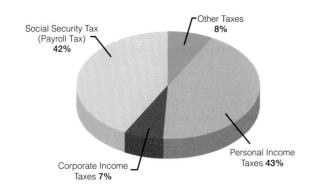

a. Tax Revenues, Federal Government, 2009

Social Security Tax (Payroll Tax) **42%**

Other Taxes **8%**

Personal Income Taxes **43%**

Corporate Income Taxes **7%**

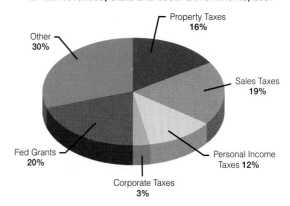

b. Tax Revenues, State and Local Governments, 2007

Property Taxes **16%**

Other **30%**

Sales Taxes **19%**

Fed Grants **20%**

Personal Income Taxes **12%**

Corporate Taxes **3%**

SOURCE: *Economic Report of the President, 2010.* Statistical Tables. Table B-80 and Table B-86. Washington, D.C. February, 2010. Available at http://www.gpoaccess.gov/eop/tables10.html (accessed March 25, 2010).

as interest on municipal bonds and income in kind—food stamps or Medicare, for example.

A Regressive Tax

Payroll taxes, the second most important source of income for the federal government, are actually **regressive taxes**; that is, they take a greater proportion of the income of lower-income groups than of higher-income groups. The reasons for this are simple. Social Security, for example, is imposed as a fixed proportion (now 6.2 percent on employees and an equal amount on employers) of wage and salary income up to $106,800 as of 2009. Also, wealthy persons have relatively more income from sources such as dividends and interest that are not subject to payroll taxes, and earnings above a certain level are not subject to some payroll taxes.

At first glance it appears that employers and employees split the burden of Social Security tax (called the Federal Insurance Contribution Act, or FICA).

However, recall our discussion of elasticity and its burden of taxation. Most labor economists believe the labor supply curve is relatively inelastic compared to the demand curve for labor, so employers will pass on most of the tax in the form of lower wages to employees. So, if workers are relatively unresponsive to a decrease in the wage rate (they have a relatively inelastic labor supply curve), then employers can pass most of the tax on in the form of lower wages, as seen in Exhibit 14.4. Congress may have intended a 50-50 split on the payroll tax between workers and firms. However,

regressive tax as a person's income rises, the amount his or her tax as a proportion of income falls

© JOSH RANDALL/SHUTTERSTOCK

	Current	M /02
gs Information		
Gross	4,389.30	
ns	0.00	
s	0.00	
	0.00	Year to Date
EARNINGS TOTAL	4,389.30	5,277.30
ble Gross	351.14	418.18
Gross	3,971.12	4,859.12

ory & Other Deductions	Current	Year to Date
Withholding	311.17	311.17
nal Federal Withholding	0.00	*****
	135.96	135.96
ithholding	0.00	*****
nal State Withholding	0.00	55.06
	62.67	75.55
	0.00	0.00
e Buyout	0.00	0.00
isability Insurance	351.14	351.14

EXHIBIT 14.4 Payroll Tax

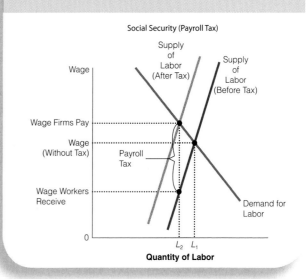

Social Security (Payroll Tax)

Wage

Supply of Labor (After Tax)

Supply of Labor (Before Tax)

Wage Firms Pay

Wage (Without Tax)

Payroll Tax

Wage Workers Receive

Demand for Labor

L_2 L_1

Quantity of Labor

we have learned that the burden of the tax does not depend on whether it is levied on the buyer or the seller but rather it depends on the price elasticity of supply and demand.

An Excise Tax

Some consider an **excise tax**—a sales tax on individual products such as alcohol, tobacco, and gasoline—to be the most unfair type of tax because it is generally the most regressive. Excise taxes on specific items impose a far greater burden, as a percentage of income, on the poor and middle classes than on the wealthy, because low-income families generally spend a greater proportion of their income on these items than do high-income families.

In addition, excise taxes may lead to economic inefficiencies. By isolating a few products and subjecting them to discriminatory taxation, excise taxes subject economic choices to political manipulation, which leads to inefficiency.

FINANCING STATE AND LOCAL GOVERNMENT ACTIVITIES

Historically, the primary source of state and local revenue has been property taxes. In recent decades, state and local governments have relied increasingly on sales and income taxes for revenues (see Exhibit 14.3). Today, sales taxes account for roughly 19 percent of revenues, property taxes account for 16 percent, and personal and corporate income taxes account for another 15 percent. Approximately 20 percent of state and local revenues come from the federal government as grants. The remaining share of revenues comes from license fees and user charges (e.g., payment for utilities, occupational license fees, tuition fees) and other taxes.

SHOULD WE HAVE A FLAT TAX?

Some politicians and individuals believe that we should scrap the current progressive income tax and replace it with a **flat tax**. A flat tax, also called a proportional tax, is designed so that everybody would be charged the same percentage of their income. How would a flat tax work? What do you think would be the advantages and disadvantages of a flat tax?

With a flat tax, a household could simply report its income, multiply it by the tax rate, and send in the money. Because no deductions are involved, the form could be a

single page! But most flat tax proposals call for exempting income to a certain level—say, the poverty line.

Actually, if the flat tax plan allowed individuals to deduct a standard allowance of, say, $20,000 from their wages, the tax would still be progressive. Here's how it would work: If you were earning less than $20,000 a year, you would not have to pay any income taxes. However, if you earned $50,000 a year, and the flat tax rate was 15 percent, after subtracting your $20,000 allowance you would be paying taxes on $30,000. In this system, you would have to pay $4,500 in taxes ($0.15 \times $30,000$) and your average tax rate would be 9 percent ($4,500/$50,000 = 0.09$). Now, say you made $100,000 a year. After taking your $20,000 allowance, you would have to pay a 15 percent tax on $80,000, and you would owe the government $12,000. Notice, however, that your average tax rate would be higher: 12 percent ($12,000/$100,000 = 0.12$) as opposed to 9 percent. So if the flat tax system allows individual taxpayers to take a standard allowance, like most flat tax proposals, then the tax is actually progressive. That is, lower- and middle-income families will pay, on average, a smaller average tax rate, even though everyone has the same tax rate over the stipulated allowance.

The advantages of the flat tax are that all of the traditional exemptions, such as entertainment deductions, mortgage interest deductions, business travel expenses, and charitable contribution deductions, would be out the door, along with the possibilities of abuses and misrepresentations that go with tax deductions. Taxpayers could fill out tax returns in the way they did in the old days, in a space about the size of a postcard. Advocates argue that the government could collect the same amount of tax revenues, but the tax would be much more efficient, as many productive resources would be released from looking for tax loopholes to doing something productive from society's standpoint.

Of course, some versions of the flat tax will hurt certain groups. Not surprisingly, realtors and home owners, who like the mortgage interest deductions, and tax accountants, who make billions every year preparing tax returns, will not be supportive of a flat tax with no deductions. And, of course, many legitimate questions would inevitably arise, such as: What would happen to the size of charitable contributions if the charitable contribution deduction was eliminated? And how much will the housing sector be hurt if the mortgage interest deduction was eliminated or phased out? After all, the government's intent of the tax break was to increase home ownership. And the deductions for hybrid cars are intended to get drivers into cleaner, more fuel-efficient cars. These deductions could be gone in most flat tax proposals. In addition, the critics of

40% of the low-income taxpayers pay about **3%**, and the top **20%** of income earners pay slightly less than **70%**.

the flat tax believe that the tax is not progressive enough to eliminate the inequities in income and are skeptical of the tax-revenue–raising capabilities of a flat tax.

TAXES: EFFICIENCY AND EQUITY

In Part 1 of this textbook, we talked about efficiency—getting the most out of our scarce resources. However, taxes for the most part are not efficient (except for internalizing externalities and providing public goods) because they change incentives and distort the values that buyers and sellers place on goods and services. That is, decisions made by buyers and sellers are different from what they would be without the tax. Taxes can be inefficient because they may lead to less work, less saving, less investment, and lower output.

Economists spend a lot of time on issues of efficiency, but policymakers (and economists) are also concerned about other goals, such as fairness. Income redistribution through taxation may also lead to greater productivity

Tax Deductions

Would people be more inclined to buy hybrid cars if tax deductions were eliminated?

for low-income workers through improvements in health and education. Even though what is fair to one person may not be fair to another, most people would agree that we should have a fair tax system based on either ability to pay or benefits received.

Ability to Pay Principle and Vertical Equity

The **ability to pay principle** is simply that those with the greatest ability to pay taxes (richer people) should pay more than those with the least ability to pay taxes (poorer people). This concept is known as **vertical equity**—people with different levels of income should be treated differently. The federal income tax is a good example of the ability to pay principle, because the rich pay a larger percentage of their income in taxes. That is, high-income individuals will pay a higher percentage of their income in taxes than low-income individuals. The richest 20 percent of households in the United States make slightly more than 60 percent of the income but pay roughly 85 percent of the federal income tax; the poorest 40 percent actually have a negative tax (many in the group receive tax credits). When you add payroll taxes (Social Security) and Medicare, the tax system becomes less progressive than the federal income tax: 40 percent of the low-income taxpayers pay about 3 percent and the top 20 percent of income earners pay slightly less than 70 percent. Sales taxes are not a good example of the ability to pay principle, because low-income individuals pay a larger percentage of their income in such taxes.

Benefits Received Principle

The **benefits received principle** means that the individuals receiving the benefits are those who pay for them. Take the gasoline tax: the more miles one drives on the highway, the more gasoline used and the more taxes

ability to pay principle
belief that those with the greatest ability to pay taxes should pay more than those with less ability to pay

vertical equity different treatment based on level of income and the ability to pay principle

benefits received principle the belief that those receiving the benefits from taxes are those who should pay for them

collected. The tax revenues are then used to maintain the highways. Or those who benefit from a new airport or an opera house should be the ones who pay for such public spending. Although this principle may work for some private goods, it does not work well for public goods such as national defense and the judicial system. Because we collectively consume national defense, it is not possible to find out who benefits and by exactly how much.

Administration Burden of Taxation

The administration burden of the income tax also leads to another deadweight loss. Imagine if everyone filled out a one-page tax form that took no more than 5 minutes. Instead the opportunity cost of the hours of time and services used in tax preparation is in the billions of dollars. The government also spends a great deal to enforce these taxes. A simplified tax system would reduce the deadweight loss.

Social Policy of Taxes

Taxes and subsidies can be efficiency enhancing when used to correct for externalities. For example, the government may view it as good social policy to subsidize cleaner, more efficient hybrid vehicles. Or they may want to put a high tax on cigarettes in an attempt to reduce teen smoking. In other words, taxes on alcohol and cigarettes may be used to discourage these activities—sometimes we call these "sin taxes."

SECTION CHECK 2

2.1 Over a third of federal spending goes toward pensions and income security programs.

2.2 A progressive tax takes a greater proportion of the income of higher-income groups than of lower-income groups. A regressive tax takes a greater proportion of the income of lower-income groups than of higher-income groups.

2.3 A flat tax charges all income earners the same percentage of their income.

2.4 The ability to pay principle is the belief that those with the greatest ability to pay taxes should pay more than those with less ability.

2.5 The benefits received principle means that individuals receiving the benefits are those who pay for them.

ⓢ3 Fiscal Policy and the *AD/AS* Model

Keep the following questions in mind as you read through this section. You'll find the answers in **Section Check 3**.

3.1 How can government stimulus of aggregate demand reduce unemployment?

3.2 How can government reduction of aggregate demand reduce inflation?

The primary tools of fiscal policy, government purchases, taxes, and transfer payments, can be presented in the context of the aggregate supply and demand model. In Exhibit 14.5, we have used the *AD/AS* model to show how the government can use fiscal policy as either an expansionary or contractionary tool to help close a recessionary or an inflationary gap.

As we discussed earlier, when the government purchases more, taxes less, and/or increases transfer payments, the size of the government's budget deficit will grow. Although budget deficits are often thought to be bad, a case can be made for using budget deficits to stimulate the economy when it is operating at less than full capacity. Such expansionary fiscal policy may have the potential to move an economy out of a contraction (or a recession) and closer to full employment.

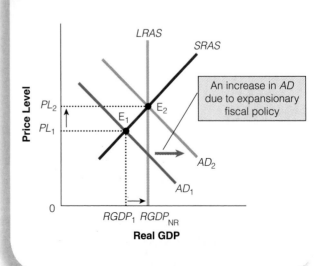

EXHIBIT 14.5 Expansionary Fiscal Policy to Close a Recessionary Gap

EXPANSIONARY FISCAL POLICY TO CLOSE A RECESSIONARY GAP

If the government decides to purchase more, cut taxes, and/or increase transfer payments, *ceteris paribus*, total purchases will rise. That is, increased government purchases, tax cuts, or transfer payment increases can increase consumption, investment, and government purchases, shifting the aggregate demand curve to the right. The effect of this increase in aggregate demand depends on the position of the macroeconomic equilibrium before the government stimulus. For example, in Exhibit 14.5, the initial equilibrium is at E_1, a recession scenario, with real output below potential RGDP. Starting at this point and moving along the short-run aggregate supply curve, an increase in government purchases, a tax cut, and/or an increase in transfer payments would increase the size of the budget deficit and lead to an increase in aggregate demand, ideally from AD_1 to AD_2. The result of such a change would be an increase in the price level, from PL_1 to PL_2, and an increase in RGDP, from $RGDP_1$ to $RGDP_{NR}$. If the policy change is of the right magnitude and timed appropriately, the expansionary fiscal policy might stimulate the economy, pull it out of the contraction and/or recession, and result in full employment at $RGDP_{NR}$. The recessionary gap is then closed.

CONTRACTIONARY FISCAL POLICY TO CLOSE AN INFLATIONARY GAP

Suppose that the price level is at PL_1 and that short-run equilibrium is at E_1, as shown in Exhibit 14.6. Say that the government decides to reduce its purchases, increase taxes, or reduce transfer payments. A government purchase change may directly affect aggregate demand.

A tax increase on consumers or a decrease in transfer payments will reduce households' disposable incomes, reducing purchases of consumption goods and services, and higher business taxes will reduce investment purchases. The reductions in consumption, investment, and/or government purchases will shift the aggregate demand curve leftward, ideally from AD_1 to AD_2. This lowers the price level from PL_1 to PL_2 and brings RGDP back to the full-employment level at $RGDP_{NR}$, resulting in a new short- and long-run equilibrium at E_2, and the inflationary gap is closed.

SECTION CHECK 3

3.1 If the government decided to purchase more, cut taxes, and/or increase transfer payments, that would increase total purchases and shift the aggregate demand curve to the right.

3.2 The government could reduce purchases, raise taxes, or increase transfer payments to shift the aggregate demand curve to the left.

Ⓢ4 The Multiplier Effect

Keep the following questions in mind as you read through this section. You'll find the answers in Section Check 4.

4.1 What is the multiplier effect?

4.2 How does the marginal propensity to consume affect the multiplier effect?

4.3 How does investment interact with the multiplier effect?

Any one of the major spending components of aggregate demand (C, I, G, or $X - M$) can initiate changes in aggregate demand, thereby producing a new short-run equilibrium. If policymakers are unhappy with the present short-run equilibrium GDP, perhaps t...

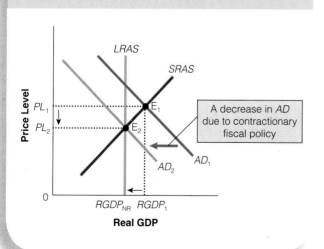

EXHIBIT 14.6 Contractionary Fiscal Policy to Close an Inflationary Gap

LRAS

SRAS

Price Level

PL_1

PL_2

E_1

E_2

A decrease in *AD* due to contractionary fiscal policy

AD_2

AD_1

0

$RGDP_{NR}$ $RGDP_1$

Real GDP

consider unemployment too high because of a current aggregate demand shortfall. If government were to increase its purchases of jet fighters, highways, and schools, this increased spending would lead to an increase in aggregate demand. That is, they can deliberately manipulate the level of government purchases to obtain a new short-run equilibrium value. But how much new additional government purchasing is necessary?

Save

Consume

What's your marginal propensity to save?

WHAT IS THE MULTIPLIER EFFECT?

Usually, when an increase in purchases of goods or services occurs, the ultimate increase in total purchases tends to be greater than the initial increase, which is known as the **multiplier effect**. But how does this effect work? Suppose the government increases its defense budget by $10 billion to buy aircraft carriers. When the government purchases the aircraft carriers, not only does it add to the total demand for goods and services directly, but it also provides $10 billion in added income to the companies that actually construct the aircraft carriers. These companies will then hire more workers and buy more capital equipment and other inputs to produce the new output. The owners of these inputs therefore receive more income because of the increase in government purchases. What will they do with this additional income? Although behavior will vary somewhat among individuals, collectively they will probably spend a substantial part of the additional income on additional consumption purchases, pay some additional taxes incurred because of the income, and save a bit of it as well. The **marginal propensity to consume (MPC)** is the fraction of additional disposable (after-tax) income that a household consumes rather than saves. That is, MPC is equal to the *change* in consumption spending (ΔC) divided by the change in disposable income (ΔDY).

$$MPC = \Delta C/\Delta DY$$

For example, suppose you won a lottery prize of $1,000. You might decide to spend $750 of your winnings today and save $250. In this example, your marginal propensity to consume is 0.75 (or 75 percent), because out of the extra $1,000, you decided to spend 75 percent of it ($0.75 \times \$1,000 = \$750$). The term *marginal propensity to consume* has two parts: (1) *marginal* refers to the fact that you received an *extra* amount of disposable income—an addition to your income, not your total income; and (2) *propensity to consume* refers to how much you tend to spend on consumer goods and services out of your additional income.

The flip side of the marginal propensity to consume is the **marginal propensity to save (MPS)**, which is the proportion of an addition to your income that you would save, or not spend on goods and services today. That is, MPS is equal to the change in savings (ΔS) divided by the change in disposable income (ΔDY).

$$MPS = \Delta S/\Delta DY$$

In the lottery example, your marginal propensity to save is 0.25, or 25 percent, because you decided to save 25 percent of your additional disposable income ($0.25 \times \$1,000 = \$250$). Because your additional disposable income must be either consumed or saved, the marginal propensity to consume plus the marginal propensity to save must add up to 1, or 100 percent.

THE MULTIPLIER EFFECT AT WORK

Suppose that out of every dollar in *added* disposable income generated by increased investment purchases, individuals collectively spend two-thirds, or 67 cents, on consumption purchases. In other words, the MPC is 2/3. The initial $10 billion increase in government purchases causes both a $10 billion increase in aggregate demand and an income increase of $10 billion to suppliers of the inputs used to produce aircraft carriers; the owners of those inputs, in turn, will spend an additional $6.67 billion (2/3 of $10 billion) on additional consumption purchases. A chain reaction has been started. The added $6.67 billion in consumption purchases by those deriving income from the initial investment brings a $6.67 billion increase in aggregate demand and in new income to suppliers of the inputs that produced the goods and services. These persons, in turn, will spend some two-thirds of their additional $6.67 billion in income, or $4.44 billion, on consumption purchases. This $4.44 billion becomes aggregate demand and income to still another group of people, who will then proceed to spend two-thirds of that amount, or $2.96 billion, on consumption purchases.

The chain reaction continues, with each new round of purchases providing income to a new group of people who in turn increase their purchases. As successive changes in consumption purchases occur, the feedback becomes smaller and smaller. The added income generated and the number of resulting consumer purchases get smaller because some of the increase in income goes to savings and tax payments that do not immediately flow into greater investment or government spending. As indicated in Exhibit 14.7, the fifth change in consumption is indeed much smaller than the first change in consumption.

What is the total impact of the initial increase in government purchases on additional consumption and income? We can find the answer by using the multiplier formula, calculated as follows:

$$Multiplier = 1/(1 - MPC)$$

In this case,

$$Multiplier = 1/(1 - 2/3) = 1/(1/3) = 3$$

An initial increase in government purchases of $10 billion will increase total purchases by $30 billion ($10 billion × 3), as the initial $10 billion in government purchases also generates an additional $20 billion in consumption.

CHANGES IN THE MPC AFFECT THE MULTIPLIER PROCESS

Note that the larger the marginal propensity to consume, the larger the multiplier effect, because relatively more additional consumption purchases out of any given income increase generates relatively larger secondary and tertiary income effects in successive rounds of the process. For example, if the MPC is 3/4, the multiplier is 4:

$$Multiplier = 1/(1 - 3/4) = 1/(1/4) = 4$$

If the MPC is only 1/2, however, the multiplier is 2:

$$Multiplier = 1/(1 - 1/2) = 1/(1/2) = 2$$

THE MULTIPLIER AND THE AGGREGATE DEMAND CURVE

As we discussed earlier, when the federal Department of Defense decides to buy additional aircraft carriers, it affects aggregate demand. It increases the incomes

EXHIBIT 14.7 The Multiplier Process

Change in government purchases	$10.00 billion—direct effect on *AD*	
First change in consumption purchases	6.67 billion (2/3 of 10)	
Second change in consumption purchases	4.44 billion (2/3 of 6.67)	
Third change in consumption purchases	2.96 billion (2/3 of 4.44)	The sum of the indirect effect on *AD*, through induced additional consumption purchases, is equal to $20 billion.
Fourth change in consumption purchases	1.98 billion (2/3 of 2.96)	
Fifth change in consumption purchases	1.32 billion (2/3 of 1.98)	

$30 billion = Total change in aggregate demand

of owners of inputs used to make the aircraft carriers, including profits that go to the owners of the firms involved. That is the initial effect. The secondary effect—the greater income that results—will lead to increased consumer purchases. In addition, the higher profits for the firms involved in carrier construction may lead them to increase their investment purchases. So the initial effect of the government's purchases will tend to have a multiplied effect on the economy. In Exhibit 14.8, we can see that the initial impact of a $10 billion additional purchase by the government directly shifts the aggregate demand curve from AD_1 to AD_2. The multiplier effect then causes the aggregate demand to shift out $20 billion further, to AD_3. If MPC is 2/3, the total effect on aggregate demand of a $10 billion increase in government purchases is therefore $30 billion.

TAX CUTS AND THE MULTIPLIER

If the government finds that it needs to use fiscal stimulus to move the economy to the natural rate, increased government spending is only one alternative. The government can also stimulate business and consumer spending through tax cuts. Both Japan (1999) and the United States (2001 and 2003) have recently employed tax cuts to stimulate their economies.

How much of an *AD* shift do we get from a change in taxes? As in the case of government spending, it depends on the marginal propensity to consume. However, the tax multiplier is smaller than the government spending multiplier because government spending has a direct impact on aggregate demand, whereas a tax cut has only an indirect impact on aggregate demand. Why? Because consumers will save some of their income from the tax cut. So if the MPC is 3/4, then when their disposable income rises by

$1,000, households will increase their consumption by $750 while saving $250 of the added income.

To compare the multiplier effect of a tax cut with an increase in government purchases, suppose there were a $10 billion tax cut and that the MPC is 2/3. The initial increase in consumption spending from the tax cut would be 2/3 × $10 billion (MPC × tax cut) = $6.67 billion. Because in this case people would save one-third of their tax cut income, the effect on aggregate demand of the change in taxes would be smaller than that of a change of equal size in government purchases. The cumulative change in spending (the increase in *AD*) due to the $10 billion tax cut is found by plugging the initial effect of the changed consumption spending into our earlier formula: 1/(1 − MPC) × $6.67 billion, which is 3 × $6.67 = $20 billion. So the initial tax cut of $10 billion leads to a stimulus of $20 billion in consumer spending. Although this amount is less than the $30 billion from government purchases, it is easy to see why tax cuts and government purchases are both attractive policy prescriptions for a slow economy.

TAXES AND INVESTMENT SPENDING

Taxes can also stimulate investment spending. For example, if a cut in corporate-profit taxes leads to expectations of greater after-tax profits, it could fuel additional investment spending. That is, tax cuts designed for consumers and investors can stimulate both the *C* and *I* components of aggregate demand. A number of administrations have used this strategy to stimulate aggregate spending and shift the aggregate demand curve to the right, including Kennedy (1963), Reagan (1981), and Bush (2001 and 2003).

A REDUCTION IN GOVERNMENT PURCHASES AND TAX INCREASES

A reduction in government purchases and tax increases are magnified by the multiplier effect, too. Suppose the government made cutbacks in the space program. Not only would it decrease government purchases directly, but aerospace workers would be laid off and unemployed workers would cut back on their consumption spending; this initial cutback would have a multiplying effect through the economy, leading to an even greater reduction in aggregate demand. Similarly, tax hikes would leave consumers with less disposable income, so they would cut back on their consumption, which would lower aggregate demand and set off the multiplier process, leading to an even larger cumulative effect on aggregate demand.

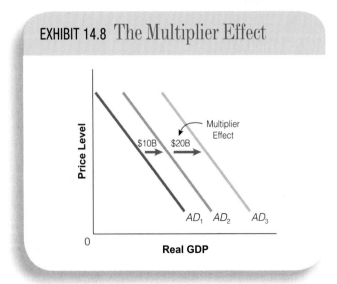

EXHIBIT 14.8 The Multiplier Effect

The Kennedy, Reagan, and Bush administrations used tax cuts to stimulate aggregate spending.

TIME LAGS, SAVING, AND IMPORTS REDUCE THE SIZE OF THE MULTIPLIER

The multiplier process is not instantaneous. If you get an additional $100 in income today, you may spend two-thirds of that on consumption purchases eventually, but you may wait six months or even longer to do it. Such time lags mean that the ultimate increase in purchases resulting from an initial increase in purchases may not be achieved for a year or more. The extent of the multiplier effect visible within a short time will be less than the total effect indicated by the multiplier formula. In addition, saving and money spent on import goods (which are not part of aggregate demand for domestically produced goods and services) will reduce the size of the multiplier, because each of them reduces the fraction of a given increase in income that will go to additional purchases of domestically produced consumption goods.

It is also important to note that the multiplier effect is not restricted to changes in government purchases and taxes. The multiplier effect can apply to changes that alter spending in any of the components of aggregate demand: consumption, investment, government purchases, or net exports.

Some have argued that the multiplier effect of a new sports stadium, for example, will lead to additional local spending that will be three or four times the amount of the initial investment. However, this outcome is unlikely. It is important to remember that money spent on the stadium (taxpayer dollars) could also have been spent on food, clothing, entertainment, recreation, and many other goods and services. So the expenditures on the stadium come at the expense of other consumer expenditures. In addition, the multiplier

is most effective when it brings idle resources into production. If all resources are fully employed, the expansion in demand and the multiplier effect will lead to a higher price level, not increases in employment and RGDP.

THE 2007–2009 RECESSION

The 2007–2009 recession will probably end up being the worst recession since the Great Depression. It has lead to the largest peacetime fiscal expansion in history. Many countries around the world have been increasing the size of their budget deficits by cutting taxes and increasing government spending. There is debate among economists on the effectiveness of fiscal policy to stimulate the economy and much of that debate depends on the size of the multiplier. A multiplier of 1 means that an increase in government purchases of $1 billion would increase aggregate demand and lead to an increase of $1 billion of RGDP. The economy could now have new highways, bridges, fighter jets, and aircraft carriers without sacrificing other components of aggregate demand such as private consumption and investment. How is this possible? The answer is that these are idle resources that are now being put to use. If the multiplier is greater than 1 it is even more magical; RGDP rises by more than the increase in government purchases.

The Obama economists believe the multiplier for government purchases is close to 1.6 (a $1 billion increase in government spending will increase a country's GDP by $1.6 billion) and the multiplier for taxes is closer to 1. Other economists believe that the multiplier is much smaller and will boost the economy by about 20 percent of what the Obama team expects.

However, economists do agree that the multiplier is very small—close to zero—when the economy is at or near full employment and that the effectiveness of fiscal policy depends on the type of action that is taken. For example, the short-run effect of government spending on infrastructure such as highways and bridges tends to be greater than, say, that of a tax cut by which individuals will save a large portion of their tax windfall. Tax cuts for poorer people may be more effective than those for richer, because the poor tend to spend a larger proportion of their additional (marginal) income. Economists also agree that tax multipliers are much higher when taxes are permanent than when they are temporary and that fiscal multipliers will be lower in heavily indebted economies than in prudent ones.

In the words of macroeconomist Robert Barro, "Do not use the cover of fiscal policy to undertake massive

The short-run effect of government spending on infrastructure such as highways and bridges tends to be greater than, say, that of a tax cut by which individuals will save a large portion of their tax windfall.

public works programs that do not pass muster from the perspective of cost-benefit analysis . . . it is wrong now to think that added government spending is free."[1]

1. Robert J. Barro, "Voodoo multipliers," *Economists' Voice*, February 2009, available at www.bepress.com/ev (accessed July 13, 2010).

SECTION CHECK 4

4.1 The multiplier effect is a chain reaction of additional income and purchases that results in a final increase in total purchases that is greater than the initial increase in purchases.

4.2 An increase in the marginal propensity to consume leads to an increase in the multiplier effect.

4.3 Because of a time lag, the full impact of the multiplier effect on GDP may not be felt until a year or more after an initial increase in investment.

Ⓢ5 Supply-Side Effects of Tax Cuts

Keep the following questions in mind as you read through this section. You'll find the answers in **Section Check 5**.

5.1 What is supply-side fiscal policy?

5.2 How do supply-side policies affect long-run aggregate supply?

5.3 What do its critics say about supply-side ideas?

The debate over short-run stabilization policies has been going on for some time, with no sign that it is close to being settled. When policymakers discuss methods of stabilizing the economy, the focus since the 1930s has been on managing the economy through demand-side policies. But one group of economists believes that we should be focusing on the supply side of the economy as well, especially in the long run, rather than just on the demand side. In particular, they believe that individuals will save less, work less, and provide less capital when taxes, government transfer payments (such as welfare), and regulations are too burdensome on productive activities. In other words, they believe that fiscal policy can work on the supply side of the economy as well as the demand side.

IMPACT OF SUPPLY-SIDE POLICIES

Supply-siders would encourage the government to reduce individual and business taxes, deregulate, and increase spending on research and development. Supply-siders believe that these types of government policies could generate greater long-term economic growth by stimulating personal income, savings, and capital formation.

Research and Development and the Supply Side of the Economy

Some economists believe that investment in research and development will have long-run benefits for the economy. In particular, greater research and development will lead to new technology and knowledge, which will permanently shift the short- and long-run aggregate supply curves to the right. The government could encourage investments in research and development by giving tax breaks or subsidies to firms. The challenge, of course, is to produce *productive* research and development.

How Do Supply-Side Policies Affect Long-Run Aggregate Supply?

We see in Exhibit 14.9 that rather than being primarily concerned with short-run economic stabilization, supply-side policies are aimed at increasing both the short-run and long-run aggregate supply curves. If these policies are successful and maintained, output and employment will increase in the long run, as reflected in the shift from $RGDP_{NR}$ to $RGDP'_{NR}$. Both short- and long-run aggregate supply will increase over time, as the effects of deregulation and major structural changes in plants and equipment work their way through the economy. It takes workers some time to fully respond to improved work incentives.

CRITICS OF SUPPLY-SIDE ECONOMICS

Of course, those who believe in supply-side economics have their critics. These critics are skeptical about the magnitude of the impact of lower taxes on work effort and the impact of deregulation on productivity. Critics claim that the tax cuts of the 1980s led to moderate real output growth but only through a reduction in real tax revenues, inflation, and large budget deficits.

Although real economic growth followed the tax cuts, supply-side critics say that it came as a result of a large budget deficit. The critics raise several questions: What will happen to the distribution of income if most supply-side policies focus on benefits to those with capital? Will people save and invest much more if capital gains taxes are reduced (capital gains are increases in the value of an asset)? It may be more likely that saving and investment is driven by changes in income and expectations of profitability. How much more work effort will we see if marginal tax rates are lowered? The increase in the quantity of labor supplied following a tax cut is likely to be limited since most workers are already working 40 hour weeks and do not have opportunities to work more hours. Will the new production that occurs from deregulation be enough to offset the benefits thought by many to come from regulation?

THE SUPPLY-SIDE AND DEMAND-SIDE EFFECTS OF A TAX CUT

A tax cut can lead to greater incentives to work and save—an increase in aggregate supply (short-run and long-run)—and to demand-side stimulus from the increased disposable income (income after taxes) and an increase in aggregate demand. But how much will the tax rate affect aggregate demand and aggregate supply? We do not know for sure, but let's look at two possible outcomes of the supply-side effects of a tax cut. We will focus on the aggregate demand curve and the *SRAS* curve. Suppose the tax cut leads to a large increase in *AD* but only a small increase in *SRAS*. What happens to the price level and RGDP? The more traditional view of a fiscal policy tax cut is shown in Exhibit 14.10(a) on the next page. We can see that RGDP increases from $RGDP_1$ to $RGDP_2$ and price level increases from PL_1 to PL_2. The good news is that the price level rises less than it would if there were no supply-side effect to the tax cut. Without the supply-side effect from the tax cut, the price level would rise to PL_3. But what if the supply-side effect were much larger, as shown in Exhibit 14.10(b)? It could completely offset the higher price-level effect of an expansionary fiscal policy, as RGDP rises from $RGDP_1$ to $RGDP_2$ and the price level stays constant at PL_1.

Both the Kennedy tax cut (1964) and the Reagan tax cut of the early 1980s, which lowered marginal tax rates and helped the economy recover from the 1980–1981 recession, likely raised the growth rate of potential GDP—shifting the *LRAS* rightward.

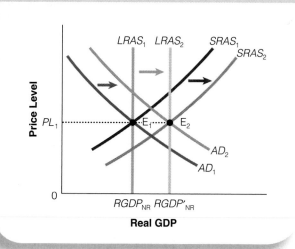

fiscal policy and the financial crisis

This [financial] crisis is rubbing salt in old wounds. It is reopening debates about one of the most contentious questions in macro, namely, the ability of government deficit spending (i.e., fiscal policy) to stimulate demand and get people back to work.

In January the fight over fiscal policy broke out in public after then-President-elect Barack Obama made what probably seemed to him a safe claim, saying: "There is no disagreement that we need action by our government, a recovery plan that will help to jump-start the economy." Not long after, some 250 conservative economists, in an open letter published in major newspapers, wrote: "With all due respect, Mr. President, that is not true."

. . . Believing in the power of the Fed, economists mostly stopped researching the use of fiscal policy to fight recessions or depressions. What's more, recessions had become rarer and milder—the so-called Great Moderation. So who needed stimulus? Says New York University economist Xavier Gabaix: "Up until a year ago, you would look very old-fashioned if you were talking about optimal fiscal policy."

Mainstream economists' adherence to orthodoxy was also apparent in their casual dismissal of worries about bubbles in housing and stocks. Former Fed Chairman Alan Greenspan denied that a national housing bubble was even possible, since housing was not a single national market. He also brushed off the dangers of Wall Street concoctions such as derivatives. Only last year did he concede he was wrong. In Senate testimony, he said he was shocked to have found a "flaw" in his ideology, adding: "I have been going for 40 years or more with very considerable evidence that it was working exceptionally well."

Politics compounded the trouble. As a rough first cut, you can divide macroeconomists based on how concerned they are about economic instability. One group, in the tradition of Keynes, worries about self-perpetuating economic declines that leave the economy in a deep trough it can't

escape. Members of this group say government needs to break downward spirals with the kinds of aggressive policies the U.S. is following now—cutting interest rates and raising government spending. The group includes Paul R. Krugman, the Princeton University economist and Nobel laureate; NYU's Nouriel Roubini, who was early in predicting a severe recession; and Yale University's Robert J. Shiller, who predicted the housing bust and the tech-stock bust.

Other economists have more confidence that the economy is self-equilibrating. They believe low interest rates and heavy deficit spending will be ineffective while leaving the U.S. with a mountain of debt. Count Harvard's Robert Barro in this camp, along with Chicago's Robert E. Lucas Jr., Arizona State University's Edward C. Prescott, and the University of Minnesota's Patrick J. Kehoe and V. V. Chari. No surprise, the equilibrium school mainly leans Republican, and the interventionist school seems to be crawling with Democrats.

Before this crisis, it seemed that economists might resolve their differences. The oft-combative Krugman, in the first edition of his textbook

> I have been going for 40 years or more with very considerable evidence that it was working exceptionally well.

Macroeconomics in 2006, wrote that "the clean little secret of modern macroeconomics is how much consensus economists have reached over the past 70 years."

The mood now is uglier. On the left, Krugman says: "This is really fairly shameful, that we should be wasting precious months as a profession retracing debates that were settled 70 years ago." On the right, John H. Cochrane of the University of Chicago dismisses those who advocate Keynesian stimulus, saying: "Professional economists, the guys I hang out with, are not reverting to ancient Keynesianism any more than physicists are going back to Aristotle when they can't understand how fast the universe is expanding." There are some middle-of-the-roaders, such as Columbia University's Michael Woodford, who argue that macroeconomists are converging on a methodology for asking questions. But even Woodford agrees that "recent debates don't particularly make the field look unified."

The easiest criticism of macroeconomists is that nearly all failed to foresee the recession despite plenty of warning signs. In early September 2008, the median growth forecast for the fourth quarter was 0.2%, according to a survey by Blue Chip Economic Indicators. The actual outcome was a 6.3% annualized decline. The Fed didn't do any better. In July 2008, Fed officials projected unemployment in the fourth quarter of 2008 would end up between 5.5% and 5.8%. The actual number was 6.9%. Their projection for the fourth quarter of 2009, done at the same time, was for a range of 5.2% to 6.1%. Today, with unemployment at 8.5%, most forecasters expect the rate to be nearing double digits by the end of 2009.

Now that fiscal policy is back on the table, economists are fighting over the size of the ripple effect—or "multiplier"—of increased government spending. Interventionist economists think multipliers are large when the economy is operating below capacity—and it certainly is now. According to a Fed report on April 15, one-third of manufacturing's productive capacity is going unused, the biggest share on record back to 1948.

6.1%

Difference between the fourth quarter 2008 consensus median growth forecast and the actual outcome.

33%

U.S. manufacturing productive capacity going unused in April 2009.

Obama Administration officials believe that their fiscal policy is on the right track. The stimulus program "is putting a little more energy into the consumer," National Economic Council Director [Larry] Summers [said]. "Two months ago you couldn't find anything positive." Christina D. Romer, Obama's chief economic adviser and a historian of the Depression, said in March that "at some point, recovery will take on a life of its own." Until then, she said, government should watch closely "to make sure the private sector is back in the saddle" before easing off.

Other economists say increased government spending may actually depress private employment. At a Council on Foreign Relations event on March 30, Chicago's Lucas called the Administration's multiplier math "kind of schlock economics."

The truth is, even backers of stimulus can't be sure it will work. As World War II ended, many economists worried that growth would lapse as military spending fell. Sewell Avery, the CEO of Montgomery Ward, was so anxious about a postwar depression that he refused to open new stores. Economists still aren't sure why he was wrong, so they can't say reliably whether fiscal stimulus will end this recession or just interrupt it. "Is it possible to engineer a durable recovery with fiscal expansion, or are you just buying time?" asks Krugman, who favors coupling stimulus with drastic action to fix the banks.

What, then, is the way forward? Once this crisis is past, the next agenda for macroeconomists will be to help make the economy far more robust—enough to survive the blunders of politicians, bankers, and economists of the future.

SOURCE: Excerpt from P. Coy, "What Good Are Economists Anyway?", *BusinessWeek*, April 27, 2009. pp. 26–31.

EXHIBIT 14.10 Two Possible Supply-Side Effects of a Tax Cut

a. Small Supply-Side Effect

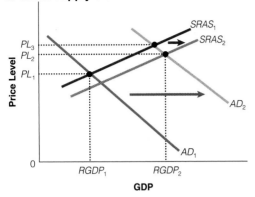

b. Large Supply-Side Effect

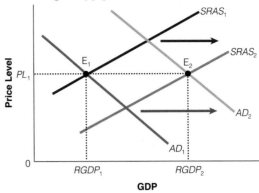

automatic stabilizers
changes in government transfer payments or tax collections that automatically help counter business cycle fluctuations

Fiscal policy was used infrequently in the United States and Europe from the 1980s to the late 1990s because of concerns over large budget deficits. However, the budget surplus that emerged in the latter half of the 1990s opened the gate for increased government spending and the Bush tax cut in 2001. Most economists agree that taxes alter incentives and distort market outcomes, as we learned in Chapter 5. Taxes clearly change people's behavior; and the tax cuts that lead to the strongest incentives to work, save, and invest will lead to the greatest economic growth and will be the least inflationary.

SECTION CHECK 5

5.1 Supply-side fiscal policy advocates believe that people will save less, work less, and provide less capital when taxes, government transfers, and regulations are too burdensome.

5.2 Supply-side policies are designed to increase output and employment in the long run, causing the long-run and short-run aggregate supply curves to shift to the right.

5.3 Critics of supply-side economics question the magnitude of the impact of lower taxes on work effort, saving, and investment, as well as the impact of deregulation on productivity.

⑤6 Automatic Stabilizers

Keep the following questions in mind as you read through this section. You'll find the answers in Section Check 6.

6.1 What are automatic stabilizers?

6.2 Which automatic stabilizers are the most important?

Some changes in government transfer payments and taxes take place automatically as business cycle conditions change, without deliberations in Congress or the executive branch of the government. Changes in government transfer payments or tax collections that automatically tend to counter business cycle fluctuations are called **automatic stabilizers**.

HOW DO THE TAX SYSTEM AND TRANSFER PAYMENTS STABILIZE THE ECONOMY?

The most important automatic stabilizer is the tax system. Personal income taxes vary directly in amount with income and, in fact, rise or fall by greater percentages than income itself. Big increases and big decreases in GDP are both lessened by automatic changes in income tax receipts. Because incomes, earnings, and profits all fall during a recession, the government collects less in taxes. When you work less, you are paid less and therefore pay less in taxes. It's like an automatic tax cut that acts to reduce the severity of a recession. This is also true

Automatic stabilizers act kind of like shock absorbers when the environment gets rough. They kick in without legislation and act quickly, reducing the severity when the business cycle changes.

© WESTEND61 GmbH/ALAMY

for payroll taxes, which depend on a worker's earnings, and corporate income taxes, which depend on a firm's profits. When earnings and profits fall during a recession, so do government revenues. So, like the personal income tax, the corporate income tax and payroll taxes are automatic stabilizers, too. This reduced tax burden partially offsets the magnitude of the recession. Beyond this factor, the unemployment compensation program is another source of automatic stabilization. During recessions, unemployment is usually high and unemployment compensation payments increase, providing income that will be consumed by recipients. During boom periods, such payments will fall as the number of unemployed decreases. The system of public assistance (payments such as food stamps, Temporary Assistance for Needy Families, and Medicaid) tends to be another important automatic stabilizer because the number of low-income persons eligible for some form of assistance grows during recessions (stimulating aggregate demand) and declines during booms (reducing aggregate demand). Perhaps the Great Depression would not have been so "great" if automatic stabilizers had been in place. Many had to dig into their savings and cut back on their spending, which made matters worse.

Automatic stabilizers are not strong enough to completely offset a serious recession. However, they certainly reduce the severity of a recession, without the problems associated with lags that were discussed in the last section.

SECTION CHECK 6

6.1 Automatic stabilizers are changes in government transfer payments or tax collections that happen automatically and with effects that vary inversely with business cycles.

6.2 The tax system is the most important automatic stabilizer; it has the greatest ability to smooth out swings in GDP during business cycles. Other automatic stabilizers are unemployment compensation and welfare payments.

⑤7 The National Debt

Keep the following questions in mind as you read through this section. You'll find the answers in **Section Check 7**.

7.1 How is a budget deficit financed?

7.2 What impact does a budget deficit have on the interest rate?

7.3 What impact does a budget surplus have on the interest rate?

As discussed earlier in the chapter, when government spending exceeds tax revenues, a budget deficit results. When tax revenues are greater than government spending, a budget surplus exists. A balanced budget occurs through deliberate efforts that are a matter of public policy.

© ISTOCKPHOTO.COM

Budget Deficit:
Government Spending > Tax Revenues

Budget Surplus:
Tax Revenues > Government Spending

HOW GOVERNMENT FINANCES THE DEBT

For many years, the U.S. government ran budget deficits and built up a large federal debt. How did it pay for those budget deficits? After all, it has to have some means of paying out the funds necessary to support government expenditures that are in excess of the funds derived from tax payments. One thing the government can do is simply print money—dollar bills. This approach was used to finance much of the Civil War budget deficit, both in the North and in the Confederate states. However, printing money to finance activities is highly inflationary and also undermines confidence in the government. Typically, the budget deficit is financed by issuing debt. The federal government in effect borrows an amount necessary to cover the deficit by issuing bonds, or IOUs, payable typically at some maturity date. The total of the values of all bonds outstanding constitutes the federal debt. Exhibit 14.11 on the next page shows the improvement in the federal budget balance since the early 1990s as a result of economic growth and the efforts of the president and Congress to control the growth of government spending.

EXHIBIT 14.11 Federal Budget (Percentage of GDP)

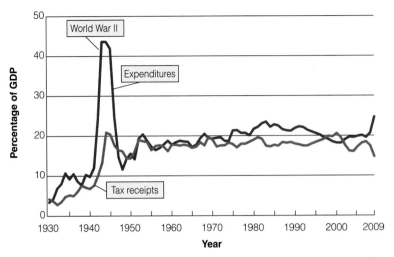

SOURCE: Office of Management and Budget, *Historical Tables,* Table 1.2, Budget of the United States Government, Fiscal Year 2011. Washington, D.C., 2010. Available at http://www.gpoaccess.gov/usbudget/fy11/hist.html (accessed March 27, 2010).

WHY RUN A BUDGET DEFICIT?

From 1960 through 1997, the federal budget was in deficit every year except one—in 1969, the government ran a small budget surplus. Budget deficits can be important because they provide the federal government with the flexibility to respond appropriately to changing economic circumstances. For example, the government may run deficits during special emergencies such as military involvements, earthquakes, fires, or floods. The government may also use a budget deficit to avert an economic downturn.

Historically, the largest budget deficits and a growing government debt occur during war years, when defense spending escalates and taxes typically do not rise as rapidly as spending. The federal government will also typically run budget deficits during recessions, as taxes are cut and government spending increases. However, in the 1980s, deficits and debt soared in a relatively peaceful and prosperous time. In 1980, President Reagan ran a platform of lowering taxes and reducing the size of government. Although the tax cuts occurred, the reduction in the growth of government spending did not. The result was huge peacetime budget deficits and a growing national debt that continued through the early 1990s, as shown in Exhibit 14.11.

However, when President Clinton took office in 1993, he set a goal to reduce the budget deficit. This goal was a high priority for both Democrats and Republicans. And after nearly a decade of uninterrupted economic growth, the deficit eventually turned into a budget surplus. In 2001 the budget surplus slipped into a deficit for three primary reasons: (1) the 2001 tax cut that President Bush promised in his presidential campaign; (2) the war on terrorism and wars in Iraq and Afghanistan; and (3) the 2001 recession that led to less tax revenue and greater government spending. In looking at the future projections shown in Exhibit 14.12, it appears the United States will face large deficits for the next decade.

AN INCREASE IN THE BUDGET DEFICIT: SHORT-RUN AND LONG-RUN EFFECTS

Recall that when the government borrows to finance a budget deficit, it causes the interest rate to rise. The higher interest rate will crowd out private investment by households and firms. Higher private investment and increases in capital formation are critical in a growing economy. However, what if the government runs a budget deficit reduction (or surplus)?

In the short run, deficit reduction is the same as running contractionary fiscal policy; either tax increases and/or a reduction in government purchases will shift the aggregate demand curve to the left, from AD_1 to AD_2, as seen in Exhibit 14.13. Unless this shift is offset by expansionary monetary policy (a topic we discuss in Chapter 16), a lower price level and lower RGDP will

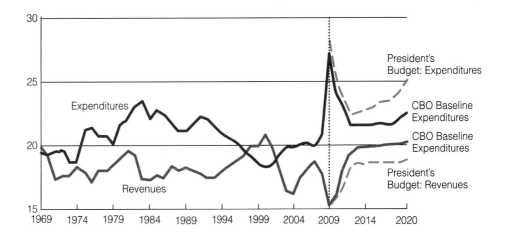

SOURCES: Office of Management and Budget, *Historical Tables*, Table 1.2, Budget of the United States Government, Fiscal Year 2011. Washington, D.C., 2010. Available at http://www.gpoaccess.gov/usbudget/fy11/hist.html (accessed March 27, 2010); Congressional Budget Office, *An Analysis of the President's Budgetary Proposals for Fiscal Year 2011*, Tables 1-1 and 1-2, Washington, D.C., March 2010. Available at http://www.cbo.gov/ftpdocs/112xx/doc11280/03-24-apb.pdf (accessed March 31, 2010).

result. That is, in the short run, an aggressive program of deficit reduction can lead to a recession.

In the long run, however, the story is different. Lowering the budget deficit, or running a larger budget surplus, leads to a lower real interest rate, which increases private investment and stimulates higher growth in capital formation and economic growth. In fact, this situation happened in the 1990s as the budget deficit was reduced and finally turned into a budget surplus. The reduction in the deficit increased the potential rate of output, shifting the *SRAS* and *LRAS* curves rightward in Exhibit 14.14. The final effect was a higher RGDP and a lower price level than would have otherwise prevailed. Both investment and RGDP grew as the budget deficit shrank. The long-run effects of a deficit

EXHIBIT 14.13 Reducing a Budget Deficit—The Short-Run Effects

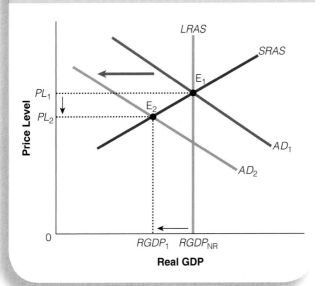

EXHIBIT 14.14 Reducing a Budget Deficit—The Long-Run Effects

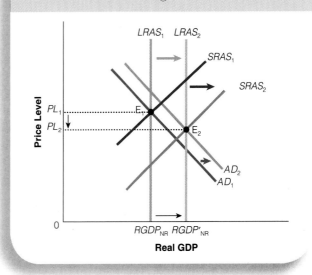

EXHIBIT 14.15 Public Debt Trends

Fiscal Year	Public Debt (billions of dollars)	Public Debt as a Percentage of GDP
1943	$ 142.6	79.1%
1945	260.1	117.5
1950	256.9	94.1
1955	274.4	69.3
1960	290.5	56.0
1965	322.3	46.9
1970	380.9	37.6
1975	541.9	34.7
1980	909.0	33.4
1985	1,817.4	43.8
1990	3,206.3	55.9
1995	4,920.6	67.0
2000	5,628.7	57.3
2005	7,905.3	63.5
2009	11,875.9	83.4

SOURCE: *Economic Report of the President, 2010*. Statistical Tables. Table B-78 and Table B-79. Washington, D.C. February, 2010. Available at http://www.gpoaccess.gov/eop/tables10.html (accessed March 25, 2010).

reduction are greater economic growth and a lower price level, *ceteris paribus*. The short-run recessionary effects of a budget deficit reduction can be avoided through the appropriate monetary policy, as we will explore in Chapter 16.

THE BURDEN OF PUBLIC DEBT

The "burden" of the debt is a topic that has long interested economists, particularly whether it falls on present or future generations. Exhibit 14.15 shows the burden as a percentage of GDP from 1943 to 2009. Arguments can be made that the generation of taxpayers living at the time that the debt is issued shoulders the true cost of the debt, because the debt permits the government to take command of resources that might be available for other, private uses. In a sense, the resources it takes to purchase government bonds might take away from private activities, such as private investment financed by private debt. No economist can deny, however, that the issuance of debt does involve some intergenerational transfer of incomes. Long after federal debt is issued, a new generation of taxpayers is making interest payments to people of the generation that bought the bonds issued to finance that debt.

If public debt is created intelligently, however, the "burden" of the debt should be less than the benefits derived from the resources acquired as a result,

particularly when the debt allows for an expansion in real economic activity or for the development of vital infrastructure for the future. The opportunity cost of expanded public activity may be small in terms of private activity that must be forgone to finance the public activity if unemployed resources are put to work. The real issue of importance is whether the government's activities have benefits that are greater than their costs; whether it is done through raising taxes, printing money, or running deficits, it is, for the most part, a "financing issue." It is also possible that parents can offset some of the intergenerational debt by leaving larger bequests.

SECTION CHECK 7

7.1 A budget deficit is financed by issuing debt.

7.2 When the government borrows to finance a budget deficit, it causes the interest rate to rise.

7.3 When the government runs a budget surplus, it adds to national saving, lowers the interest rate, and stimulates private investment and capital formation.

Chapter 14: Self-Review

Now that you're finished reading the chapter, review the questions below. You can write your answers in the space provided, then go online to see the answers at www.cengagebrain.com.

S1–FISCAL POLICY

1. **Fill-in-the-Blank: If the federal government decreases its purchases of goods and services, the budget deficit _____.**

2. **True or False: If the federal government increases taxes and/or decreases transfer payments, it is employing a contractionary fiscal policy.**

S2–GOVERNMENT SPENDING AND TAXATION

3. **What finances the majority of federal government spending?**

4. **True or False: Excise taxes on items such as alcohol, tobacco, and gasoline are considered flat taxes.**

5. **Fill-in-the-Blank: The federal income tax is an example of the _____ principle.**

S3–FISCAL POLICY AND THE *AD/AS* MODEL

6. **What is a recessionary gap?**

7. **Fill-in-the-Blank: The appropriate fiscal policy to combat a recessionary gap is _____.**

S4–THE MULTIPLIER EFFECT

8. **What would the multiplier be if the marginal propensity to consume was:**
   a. **1/3**
   b. **1/2**
   c. **3/4**

9. **True or False: The marginal propensity to consume is always less than one.**

S5–SUPPLY-SIDE EFFECTS OF TAX CUTS

10. **True or False: Supply-side economics is more concerned with short-run economic stabilization than long-run economic growth.**

11. **Why could you say that supply-side economics is really more about after-tax wages and after-tax returns on investment than it is about tax rates?**

S6–AUTOMATIC STABILIZERS

12. **True or False: Automatic stabilizers are affected by a time lag.**

13. **How do automatic stabilizers affect budget deficits and surpluses?**

S7–THE NATIONAL DEBT

14. **What will happen to the interest rate when a budget surplus occurs?**

What is money?

When we talk about money, we usually think of bills and coins, like these pennies that are about to be stamped at the mint. Hard currency, however, is not the only form of money that we use. While mints will create money by printing and stamping coins and bills, there is another way that money can be created, namely through banks creating loans. We'll discuss this money creation process in Section 3.

15

Monetary Institutions

Sections in Chapter 15

money is very important to the economy. Recall the circular flow model in which households trade money for the goods and services they buy in product markets, and firms exchange money for inputs they buy to produce the goods and services they sell in factor markets. In this chapter, we will discuss the different forms of money, the different functions of money, and how banks create money. We will learn how the Federal Reserve works to keep banks safe. At the end of the chapter, we will examine some periods of bank failure in the twentieth century.

(S)1 What Is Money?

Keep the following questions in mind as you read through this section. You'll find the answers in **Section Check 1**.

1.1 What is money?

1.2 How does money lower the costs of making transactions?

1.3 How does money serve as a store of value?

Money is anything that is generally accepted in exchange for goods and services. In colonial times, commodities such as tobacco and wampum (Native American beads made from shells) were sometimes used as money. At some times and in some places, even cigarettes and whiskey have been used as money. Using commodities as money has several disadvantages, however, the most important of which is that many commodities deteriorate easily after a few trades. Precious metal coins have been used for money for millennia, partly because of their durability.

THE FUNCTIONS OF MONEY

Money has four important functions in the economy: as a medium of exchange, a unit of account, a store of value, and a means of deferred payment.

money anything generally accepted in exchange for goods or services

Four functions of money
1) Medium of exchange
2) Unit of account
3) Store of value
4) Means of deferred payment

Let's examine the four important functions of money and see how they are different than other assets in the economy such as stocks, bonds, art, real estate, and a comic book collection.

Money as a Medium of Exchange

The primary function of money is to serve as a **medium of exchange**, to facilitate transactions, and to lower transaction costs. That is, sellers will accept it as payment in a transaction. However, money is not the only medium of exchange; rather, it is the only medium that is generally accepted for most transactions. How would people trade with one another in the absence of money? They would **barter** for goods and services that they desire.

The Barter System Is Inefficient Under a barter system, individuals pay for goods or services by offering other goods and services in exchange. Suppose you are a farmer who needs some salt. You go to the merchant selling salt and offer her 30 pounds of wheat for 2 pounds of salt. The wheat that you use to buy the

Tobacco was once used as money in colonial America—in particular, in Virginia and Maryland. Tobacco was used rather than other commodities because it was resistant to spoilage.

salt is not money, because the salt merchant may not want wheat and therefore may not accept it as payment. This issue is one of the major disadvantages of barter: The buyer may not have appropriate items of value to the seller. The salt merchant may reluctantly take the wheat that she does not want, later bartering it away to another customer for something that she does want. In any case, barter is inefficient because several trades may be necessary to receive the desired goods. That is, the problem with barter is that it requires a double coincidence of wants—both traders must be willing to trade their products with each other. Money solves the problem of double coincidence of wants because people will accept money for the items they sell.

Moreover, barter is extremely expensive over long distances. What would it cost me, living in California, to send wheat to Maine in return for an item in the L.L. Bean catalog? It is much cheaper to mail a check. Finally, barter is time-consuming because of difficulties in determining the value of the product that is being offered for barter. For example, the person selling the salt may wish to inspect the wheat first to make sure that it is pure and not contaminated with dirt or insects. Barter, in short, is expensive and inefficient, and it generally prevails only where limited trade is carried out over short distances, which generally means in relatively primitive economies. The more complex the economy (e.g., the higher the real GDP per capita), the greater the economic interactions between people, and consequently, the greater the need for one or more universally accepted assets serving as money. Only in a Robinson Crusoe economy, where people live in isolated settlements and are generally self-sufficient, is the use of money unnecessary.

Money as a Unit of Account

Besides serving as a medium of exchange, money is also a unit of account. With a barter system, one does not know precisely what 30 pounds of wheat are worth relative to 2 pounds of salt. With money, a common "yardstick" exists, so people can precisely compare the values of diverse goods and services. Thus, if wheat costs 50 cents a pound and salt costs $1 a pound, we can say that a pound of salt is valued at precisely two times as much as a pound of wheat ($1/$0.50 = 2). By providing a universally understood unit of account, money serves to lower the information costs involved in making transactions. Without money, a person might not know what a good price for salt is, because so many different commodities can be bartered for it. With money, only one price for salt is necessary, and that price is readily

By providing a universally understood unit of account, money serves to lower the information costs involved in making transactions.

available as information to the potential consumer. We use money as a unit of account when we measure and record economic value.

Money as a Store of Value

Money also serves as a store of value. It can provide a means of saving or "storing" things of value in an efficient manner. A farmer in a barter society who wants to save for retirement might accumulate enormous inventories of wheat, which he would then gradually trade away for other goods in his old age. This approach is a terribly inefficient way to save. The farmer would have to construct storage buildings to hold all his wheat; and the interest payments he would earn on the wheat would actually be negative, because it is quite likely that rats would eat part of it or it would otherwise deteriorate. Most important, physical goods of value would be tied up in unproductive use for many years. With money, the farmer saves pieces of paper that can be used to purchase goods and services in his old age. It is both cheaper and safer to store paper rather than wheat.

Money as a Means of Deferred Payment

Finally, money is a **means of deferred payment**. Money makes it much easier to borrow and to repay loans. With barter, lending is cumbersome and subject to an added problem. What if a wheat farmer borrows some wheat and agrees to pay it back in wheat next year, but the value of wheat soars because of a poor crop resulting from drought? The debt will be paid back in wheat that is far more valuable than that borrowed, creating a problem for the borrower. Of course, fluctuations in the value of money can also occur; indeed, inflation has been a major problem in our recent past and continues to be a problem in many countries. But the value of money fluctuates far less than the value of many individual commodities, so lending in money imposes fewer risks on buyers and sellers than lending in commodities.

SECTION CHECK 1

1.1 Money is anything that is generally accepted in exchange for goods and services.

1.2 By providing a universally understood unit of account, money serves to lower the information costs involved in making transactions.

1.3 Money is both cheaper and easier to store than other goods.

⑤2 Measuring Money

Keep the following questions in mind as you read through this section. You'll find the answers in **Section Check 2**.

2.1 What is currency?

2.2 What is liquidity?

2.3 What is included in the money supply?

Currency consists of coins and/or paper that some institution or government has created to be used in the trading of goods and services and the payment of debts. Currency in the form of metal coins is still used as money throughout the world today. But metal currency has a disadvantage: It is bulky. Also, certain types of metals traditionally used in coins, such as gold and silver, are not available in sufficient quantities to meet our demands for a monetary instrument. For these reasons, metal coins have for centuries been supplemented by paper currency, often in the form of bank notes. In the United States, the Federal Reserve System (the Fed) issues Federal Reserve notes in various denominations, and this paper currency, along with coins, provides the basis for most transactions of relatively modest size in the United States today. (The Federal Reserve System will be discussed further in the next chapter.)

> **means of deferred payment** the attribute of money that makes it easier to borrow and to repay loans

> **currency** coins and/or paper created to facilitate the trade of goods and services and the payment of debts

CURRENCY AS LEGAL TENDER

legal tender coins and paper officially declared to be acceptable for the settlement of financial debts

fiat money a means of exchange established by government declaration

demand deposits balances in bank accounts that depositors can access on demand

transaction deposits deposits that can be easily converted to currency or used to buy goods and services directly

traveler's checks transaction instruments easily converted into currency

In the United States and most other nations of the world, metallic coins and paper currency are the only forms of **legal tender**. In other words, coins and paper money have been officially declared to be money—to be acceptable for the settlement of debts incurred in financial transactions. In effect, the government says, "We declare these instruments to be money, and citizens are expected to accept them as a medium of exchange." Legal tender is **fiat money**—a means of exchange that has been established not by custom and tradition or because of the value of the metal in a coin but by government fiat, or declaration.

DEMAND DEPOSITS AND OTHER CHECKABLE DEPOSITS

Most of the money that we use for day-to-day transactions, however, is not official legal tender. Rather, it is a monetary instrument that has become "generally accepted" in exchange over the years and has now, by custom and tradition, become money. What is this instrument? It is balances in checking accounts in banks, more formally called **demand deposits**.

Demand deposits are defined as balances in bank accounts that depositors can access on demand by simply writing checks. Some other forms of accounts in financial institutions also have virtually all the attributes of demand deposits. For example, other checkable deposits earn interest but have some restrictions, such as higher monthly fees or minimum balance requirements. These interest-earning checking accounts effectively permit the depositors to write "orders" similar to checks and assign the rights to the deposit to other persons, just as we write checks to other parties. Practically speaking, funds in these accounts are the equivalent of demand deposits and have become an important component in the supply of money. Both these types of accounts are forms of **transaction deposits** because they can be easily converted into currency or used to buy goods and services directly. **Traveler's checks**, like currency and demand deposits, are also easily converted into currency or used directly as a means of payment.

THE POPULARITY OF DEMAND DEPOSITS AND OTHER CHECKABLE DEPOSITS

Demand deposits and other checkable deposits have replaced paper and metallic currency as the major source of money used for larger transactions in the United States and in most other relatively well-developed nations for several reasons, including the ease and safety of transactions, lower transaction costs, and transaction records.

Ease and Safety of Transactions

Paying for goods and services with checks is easier (meaning cheaper) and less risky than paying with paper money. Paper money is readily transferable: If someone takes a $20 bill from you, it is gone, and the thief can use it to buy goods with no difficulty. If, however, someone steals a check that you have written to the telephone company to pay a monthly bill, that person will probably have great difficulty using it to buy goods and services because he has to be able to identify himself as a representative of the telephone company. If someone steals your checkbook, the thief can use your checks as money only if he can successfully forge your signature and provide some identification. Hence, transacting business by check is much less risky than using legal tender; an element of insurance or safety exists in the use of transaction deposits instead of currency.

© JWOHLFEIL/SHUTTERSTOCK

> *Economists are not completely in agreement on what constitutes money for all purposes.*

Lower Transaction Costs

Suppose you decide that you want to buy a sweater that costs $81.28 from the current Urban Outfitters mail-order catalog. It is much cheaper, easier, and safer for you to send a check for $81.28 rather than four $20 bills, a $1 bill, a quarter, and three pennies. Transaction deposits are popular precisely because they lower transaction costs compared with the use of metal or paper currency. In small transactions, the gains in safety and convenience of checks are outweighed by the time and cost required to write and process them; in these cases, transaction costs are lower with paper and metallic currency. Therefore, it is unlikely that the use of paper or metallic currency will disappear entirely.

Transaction Records

Another useful feature of transaction deposits is that they provide a record of financial transactions. Each month, the bank sends the depositor canceled checks and/or a statement recording the deposit and withdrawal of funds. In an age when detailed records are often necessary for tax purposes, this feature is useful. Of course, it can work the other way, too. Paper currency transactions are also popular in business activities in which participants prefer no records for tax collectors to review.

CREDIT CARDS

A credit card is "generally acceptable in exchange for goods and services." At the same time, however, a credit card payment is actually a guaranteed loan available on demand to the cardholder, which merely defers the cardholder's payment for a transaction using a demand deposit. Ultimately, an item purchased with a credit card must be paid for with a check; monthly payments on credit card accounts are required to continue using the card. A credit card, then, is not money but rather a convenient tool for carrying out transactions that minimizes the physical transfer of checks or currency. In this sense, it is a substitute for the use of money in exchange and allows the cardholder to use any given amount of money in future exchanges.

> **nontransaction deposits** funds that cannot be used for payment directly but must be converted into currency for general use
>
> **near money** nontransaction deposits that are not money but can be quickly converted into money

SAVINGS ACCOUNTS

Economists are not completely in agreement on what constitutes money for all purposes. They agree, nearly universally, that coins, paper currency, demand and other checkable deposits, and traveler's checks are certainly forms of money, because all are accepted as direct means of payment for goods and services. Some economists, however, argue that for some purposes *money* should be more broadly defined to include **nontransaction deposits**. Nontransaction deposits are fund accounts against which the depositor *cannot* directly write checks, hence the name. If these funds cannot be used directly as a means of payment but must first be converted into money, why do people hold such accounts? People use these accounts primarily because they generally pay higher interest rates than transaction deposits.

The two primary types of nontransaction deposits that exist are savings accounts and time deposits (sometimes referred to as certificates of deposit, or CDs). Most purists would argue that nontransaction deposits are **near money** assets but not money itself. Why? Savings accounts and time deposits cannot be used directly to purchase a good or service. They are not a direct medium of exchange. For example, you cannot go into a supermarket, pick out groceries, and give the clerk the passbook to your savings account. You must convert funds from your savings account into currency or demand deposits before you can buy goods and services. Thus, strictly speaking, nontransaction deposits do not satisfy the formal definition of money. At the same time, however, savings accounts are assets that can be quickly converted into money at the face value of the account. In the jargon of finance, savings accounts are highly liquid assets. True, under federal law commercial banks legally can require depositors to request withdrawal of funds in writing and then defer making payment for several weeks. But in practice no bank prohibits immediate withdrawal, although early withdrawal from some time deposits, especially certificates of deposit, may require the depositor to forgo some interest income as a penalty.

MONEY MARKET MUTUAL FUNDS

Money market mutual funds are interest-earning accounts provided by brokers who pool funds into investments such as Treasury bills. These funds are invested in short-term securities, and depositors are allowed to write checks against their accounts subject to certain limitations. This type of fund experienced tremendous growth over the last 20 years. Money market mutual funds are highly liquid assets. They are considered to be near money because they are relatively easy to convert into money for the purchases of goods and services.

STOCKS AND BONDS

Virtually everyone agrees that many other forms of financial assets, such as stocks and bonds, are not money. Suppose you buy 1,000 shares of common stock in Microsoft at $30 per share, for a total of $30,000. The stock is traded daily on the New York Stock Exchange and elsewhere; you can readily sell the stock and get paid in legal tender or a demand deposit. Why, then, is this stock not considered money? First, it will take a few days for you to receive payment for the sale of stock; you cannot turn the asset into cash as quickly as you can a savings deposit in a financial institution. Second, and more importantly, the value of the stock fluctuates over time, and as the owner of the asset, you have no guarantee that you will be able to obtain its original nominal value at any time. Thus, stocks and bonds are not generally considered to be money.

LIQUIDITY

Money is an asset that we generally use to buy goods or services. In fact, it is so easy to convert money into goods and services that we say it is the most liquid of assets. When we speak of **liquidity**, we are referring to the ease with which one asset can be converted into another asset or goods and services. For example, to convert a stock into goods and services would prove to be somewhat more difficult—contacting your broker or going online, determining at what price to sell your stock, paying the commission for the service, and waiting for the completion of the transaction. Clearly, stocks are not as liquid an asset as money. But other assets are even less liquid—for example, converting your painting collection or your baseball cards or Barbie dolls into other goods and services.

THE MONEY SUPPLY

Because a good case can be made either for including or for excluding savings accounts, certificates of deposit (CDs), and money market mutual funds from an operational definition of the money supply depending on its intended purpose, we will compromise and do both. Economists call the narrow definition of money—currency, checkable deposits, and traveler's checks—**M1**. The broader definition of money, encompassing M1 plus savings deposits, time deposits (except for some large-denomination certificates of deposit), and noninstitutional money market mutual fund shares, is called **M2**.

The difference between M1 and M2 is striking, as evidenced by the different sizes of the total stock of money depending on which definition is used. As Exhibit 15.1 shows, M2 is more than four times the

---

money market mutual funds interest-earning accounts provided by brokers who pool funds into such investments as Treasury bills

liquidity the ease with which one asset can be converted into another asset or into goods and services

M1 the narrowest definition of money; includes currency, checkable deposits, and traveler's checks

M2 a broader definition of money that includes M1 plus savings deposits, time deposits, and noninstitutional money market mutual fund shares

---

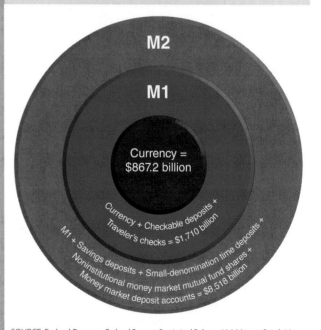

EXHIBIT 15.1 Two Definitions of the Money Supply: M1 and M2

M2

M1

Currency = $867.2 billion

Currency + Checkable deposits + Traveler's checks = $1,710 billion

M1 + Savings deposits + Small-denomination time deposits + Noninstitutional money market mutual fund shares + Money market deposit accounts = $8,518 billion

SOURCE: Federal Reserve, *Federal Reserve Statistical Release,* H.6 Money Stock Measures, Tables 1 and 3. Washington, D.C., March 25, 2010. Available at http://www.federalreserve.gov/releases/h6/Current/ (accessed March 31, 2010).

magnitude of M1. In other words, people strongly prefer to keep the bulk of their liquid assets in the form of savings accounts of various kinds.

HOW WAS MONEY "BACKED"?

Until fairly recently, coins in most nations were largely made from precious metals, usually gold or silver. These metals had a considerable intrinsic worth: If the coins were melted down, the metal would be valuable for use in jewelry, industrial applications, dentistry, and so forth. Until 1933, the United States was on an internal **gold standard**, meaning that the dollar was defined as equivalent in value to a certain amount of gold, and paper currency or demand deposits could be freely converted to gold coin. The United States abandoned the gold standard, however, eventually phasing out gold currency. Some silver coins and paper money convertible into silver remained; but by the end of the 1960s, even this tie between the monetary system and precious metals was gone—in part because the price of silver soared so high that the metal in coins had an intrinsic worth greater than its face value, leading people to hoard coins or even melt them down. When two forms of money are available, people prefer to spend the form of money that is less valuable. This tendency is a manifestation of **Gresham's Law**: "Cheap money drives out dear money."

WHAT REALLY BACKS OUR MONEY NOW?

Consequently, today no meaningful precious metal "backing" gives our money value. Why, then, do people accept dollar bills in exchange for goods? After all, a dollar bill is

PAWN SHOPS AND LIQUIDITY

Q&A

$PAWN SHOP$
BUY-SELL-LOAN

Q: What do pawn shops sell?
You can find the answer on the next page.

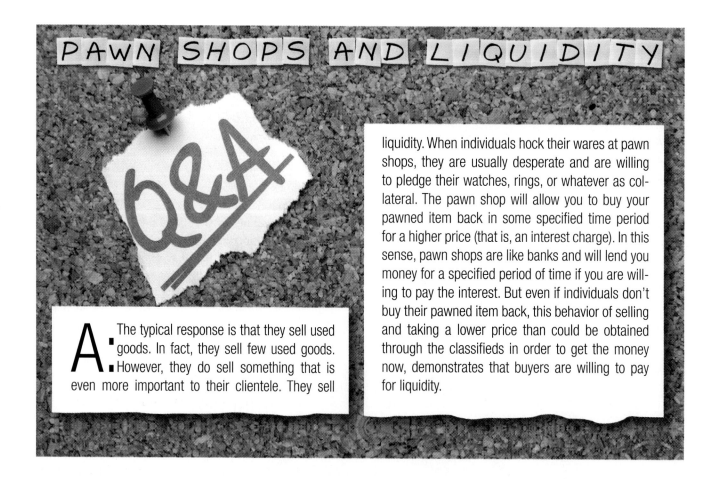

A: The typical response is that they sell used goods. In fact, they sell few used goods. However, they do sell something that is even more important to their clientele. They sell

liquidity. When individuals hock their wares at pawn shops, they are usually desperate and are willing to pledge their watches, rings, or whatever as collateral. The pawn shop will allow you to buy your pawned item back in some specified time period for a higher price (that is, an interest charge). In this sense, pawn shops are like banks and will lend you money for a specified period of time if you are willing to pay the interest. But even if individuals don't buy their pawned item back, this behavior of selling and taking a lower price than could be obtained through the classifieds in order to get the money now, demonstrates that buyers are willing to pay for liquidity.

a piece of generally wrinkled paper about 6 inches by 2.5 inches in size, with virtually no inherent utility or worth. Do we accept these bills because it states on the front of the bills, "This note is legal tender for all debts, public and private"? Perhaps, but we accept some forms of currency and money in the form of demand deposits without that statement.

The true backing behind money in the United States is faith that people will take it in exchange for goods and services. People accept with great eagerness these small pieces of green paper with pictures of long-deceased people with funny-looking hair simply because we believe that they will be exchangeable for goods and services with an intrinsic value. If you were to drop two pieces of paper of equal size on the floor in front of 100 students, one a blank piece of paper and the other a $100 bill, and then leave the room, most of the group would probably start scrambling for the $100 bill, while the blank piece of paper would be ignored. Such is our faith in the green paper's practical value that some will even fight over it. As long as people have confidence in something's convertibility into goods and services, "money" will exist and no further backing is necessary.

Because governments represent the collective will of the people, they are the institutional force that traditionally defines money in the legal sense. People are willing to accept pieces of paper as money only because of their faith in the government. When people lose faith in the exchangeability of pieces of paper that the government decrees as money, even legal tender loses its status as meaningful money. Something is money only if people will generally accept it. Governments play a key role in defining money, but much of its value is actually created by private businesses in the pursuit of profit. A majority of U.S. money, whether M1 or M2, is in the form of deposits at privately owned financial institutions.

People who hold money, then, must have faith not only in their government but also in banks and other financial institutions. If you accept a check drawn on a regional bank, you believe that bank or, for that matter, any bank will be willing to convert that check into legal tender (currency), enabling you to buy goods or services that you want to have. Thus, you have faith in the bank as well. In short, our money is money because of the confidence we have in private financial institutions and our government.

ⓢ3 How Banks Create Money

Keep the following questions in mind as you read through this section. You'll find the answers in **Section Check 3**.

3.1 How is money created?

3.2 What is a reserve requirement?

3.3 How do reserve requirements affect how much money can be created?

Financial intermediaries are financial institutions that accept funds from households and make them available to firms. They are the intermediary between savers and borrowers. The most important financial intermediaries in the process of money creation are commercial banks and savings and loans.

The biggest players in the banking industry are **commercial banks**. Commercial banks are financial institutions organized to handle the everyday financial transactions of businesses and households through demand deposit accounts and savings accounts and by making short-term commercial and consumer loans.

Another financial intermediary is the savings and loan. Savings and loans accept deposits in savings accounts and pay interest for these funds. The most important purpose of these institutions is to make mortgage loans on residential property.

THE FUNCTIONS OF FINANCIAL INSTITUTIONS

Financial institutions offer a large number of financial functions. For example, they often will pay an individual's monthly bills by automatic withdrawals, administer estates, and rent safe-deposit boxes, among other things. Most important, though, they are depositories for savings and liquid assets that are used by individuals and firms for transaction purposes. They can create money by making loans. In making loans, financial institutions act as intermediaries (the middle persons) between savers who supply funds and borrowers seeking funds to invest.

commercial banks financial institutions organized to handle everyday financial transactions of businesses and households through demand deposit accounts and savings accounts and by making short-term commercial and consumer loans

HOW DO BANKS CREATE MONEY?

As we have already learned, most money, narrowly defined, is in the form of transaction deposits assets that can be directly used to buy goods and services. But how did the balance in, say, a checking account get there in the first place? Perhaps it was through a loan made by a commercial bank. When a bank lends to a person, it does not typically give the borrower cash (paper and metallic currency). Rather, it gives the borrower the funds by issuing a check or by adding funds to an existing checking account. If you go into a bank and borrow $1,000, the bank probably will add $1,000 to your checking account at the bank, creating a new checkable deposit money.

HOW DO BANKS MAKE PROFITS?

Banks make loans and create checkable deposits to make profits. How do they make their profits? By collecting higher interest payments on the loans they make than they pay their depositors for those funds. If you borrow $1,000 from Bank One, the interest payment you make, less the expenses the bank incurs in making the loan, including their costs of acquiring the funds, represents profit to the bank.

RESERVE REQUIREMENTS

Because the way to make more profit is to make more loans, banks want to make a large volume of loans.

Stockholders of banks want the largest profits possible; so what keeps banks from making nearly infinite quantities of loans? Primarily, government regulatory authorities limit the loan issuance of banks by imposing **reserve requirements**. Banks are required to keep on hand a quantity of cash or reserve accounts with the Federal Reserve equal to a prescribed proportion of their checkable deposits.

FRACTIONAL RESERVE SYSTEM

Even in the absence of regulations restricting the creation of checkable deposits, a prudent bank would put some limit on their loan (and therefore deposit) volume. Why? For people to accept checkable deposits as money, the checks written must be generally accepted in exchange for goods and services. People will accept checks only if they know that they are quickly convertible at par (face value) into legal tender. For this reason, banks must have adequate cash reserves on hand (including reserves at the Fed that can be almost immediately converted to currency, if necessary) to meet the needs of customers who wish to convert their checkable deposits into currency or spend them on goods or services.

Our banking system is sometimes called a **fractional reserve system**, because banks, by law as well as by choice, find it necessary to keep cash on hand and reserves at the Federal Reserve equal to some fraction of their checkable deposits. If a bank were to create $100 in demand deposits for every $1 in cash reserves that it had, the bank might well find itself in difficulty before too long. Why? Consider a bank with $10,000,000 in demand and time deposits and $100,000 in cash reserves. Suppose a couple of large companies with big accounts decide to withdraw $120,000 in cash on the same day. The bank would be unable to convert into legal tender all the funds requested. The word would then spread that the bank's checks are not convertible into lawful money, possibly causing a "run on the bank." The bank would have to quickly convert some of its other assets into currency, or it would be unable to meet its obligations to convert its deposits into currency and it would have to close.

Therefore, even in the absence of reserve regulations, few banks would risk maintaining fewer reserves on hand than they thought prudent for their amount of deposits (particularly demand deposits). Reserve requirements exist primarily to control the amount of demand and time deposits and thus the size of the money supply; they do not exist simply to prevent bank failures.

While banks must meet their reserve requirements, they do not want to keep any more of their funds as additional reserves than necessary for safety, because cash assets do not earn any interest. To protect themselves but also earn some interest income, banks usually keep some of their assets in highly liquid investments, such as U.S. government bonds. These types of highly liquid, interest-paying assets are often called **secondary reserves**.

A BALANCE SHEET

Earlier in this chapter, we learned that money is created when banks make loans. We will now look more closely at the process of bank lending and its impact on the stock of money. In doing so, we will examine the structure and behavior of our hypothetical bank, Bank One. To get a good picture of the size of the bank, what it owns, and what it owes, we look at its **balance sheet**, which is like

This scene from It's a Wonderful Life shows a run on a savings and loan that demonstrates the power of the fractional reserve banking system. George's bank almost had to close because it did not have enough cash on hand to cover the high volume of withdrawals.

© NICHOLAS BELTON/ISTOCKPHOTO.COM / © HULTON ARCHIVE/GETTY IMAGES a financial "photograph" of the bank at a single moment. Exhibit 15.2 presents a balance sheet for Bank One.

Assets

The assets of a bank are the items of value that the bank owns (e.g., cash, reserves at the Federal Reserve, bonds, and its buildings), including contractual obligations of individuals and firms to pay funds to the bank (loans). The largest asset item for most banks is loans. Banks maintain most of their assets in the form of loans because interest payments on loans are the primary means by which they earn revenue. Some assets are kept in the form of non-interest-bearing cash and reserve accounts at the Federal Reserve to meet legal reserve requirements (and to meet the cash demands of customers). Typically, relatively little of a bank's reserves, or cash assets, is physically kept in the form of paper currency in the bank's vault or at tellers' windows. Most banks keep the majority of their reserves as reserve accounts at the Federal Reserve. As previously indicated, banks usually also keep some assets in the form of bonds that are quickly convertible into cash if necessary (secondary reserves).

Liabilities

All banks have substantial liabilities, which are financial obligations that the bank has to other people. The predominant liability of virtually all banks is deposits. If you have money in a demand deposit account, you have the right to demand cash for that deposit at any time. Basically, the bank owes you the amount in your checking account. Time deposits similarly constitute a liability of banks.

Capital Stock

For a bank to be healthy and solvent, its assets, or what it owns, must exceed its liabilities, or what it owes others. In other words, if the bank were liquidated and all the assets converted into cash and all the obligations to others (liabilities) paid off, some cash would still be left to distribute to the owners of the bank, that is, its stockholders. This difference between a bank's assets and its liabilities constitutes the bank's capital. Note that this definition of capital differs from the earlier definition, which described capital as goods used to further production of other goods (machines, structures, tools, etc.). In this case, the capital stock is the equity owned by shareholders both in and out of the community. As you can see in Exhibit 15.2, capital is included on the right side of the balance sheet, so that both sides (assets and liabilities plus capital) are equal in amount. Any time the aggregate amount of bank assets changes, the aggregate amount of liabilities and capital must also change by the same amount, by definition.

required reserve ratio the percentage of deposits that a bank must hold at the Federal Reserve Bank or in bank vaults

excess reserves reserve levels held above that required by the Fed

THE REQUIRED RESERVE RATIO

Suppose for simplicity that Bank One faces a reserve requirement of 10 percent on all deposits. This percentage is often called the required reserve ratio. But what does a **required reserve ratio** of 10 percent mean? It means that the bank must keep cash on hand or at the Federal Reserve Bank equal to one-tenth (10 percent) of its deposits. For example, if the required reserve ratio is 10 percent, banks are required to hold $100,000 in required reserves for every $1 million in deposits. The remaining 90 percent of cash is called **excess reserves**.

Reserves in the form of cash and reserves at the Federal Reserve earn no revenue for the bank; no profit is made from holding cash. Whenever excess reserves

EXHIBIT 15.2 Balance Sheet, Bank One

Assets		Liabilities and Capital	
Cash (reserves)	$ 2,000,000	Transaction deposits (checking deposits)	$ 5,000,000
Loans	6,100,000	Savings and time deposits	4,000,000
Bonds (U.S. government and municipal)	1,500,000	Total liabilities	$ 9,000,000
Bank building, equipment, fixtures	400,000	Capital	1,000,000
Total Assets	**$10,000,000**	**Total Liabilities and Capital**	**$10,000,000**

appear, banks will invest the excess reserves in interest-earning assets—sometimes bonds, but usually loans.

LOANING EXCESS RESERVES

Let's see what happens when someone deposits $100,000 at Bank One. We will continue to assume that the required reserve ratio is 10 percent. That is, the bank is required to hold $10,000 in required reserves for this new deposit of $100,000. The remaining 90 percent, or $90,000, becomes excess reserves, most of which will likely become available for loans for individuals and businesses.

However, the story doesn't end here. Let's say that the bank loans all its new excess reserves of $90,000 to an individual who is remodeling her home. At the time the bank makes the loan, its money supply increases by $90,000. Specifically, no one has less money— the original depositor still has $100,000, and the bank adds $90,000 to the borrower's checking account (demand

People do not usually borrow money and sit on it. They take out loans to make purchases.

deposit). A new demand deposit, or checking account, of $90,000 has been created. *Because demand deposits are money, the issuers of the new loan have created money.*

Furthermore, borrowers are not likely to keep borrowed money in their checking accounts for long, because they usually take out loans to make purchases. If a loan is used for remodeling, the borrower pays the construction company; the owner of the construction company, in turn, will likely deposit the money into his account at another bank to add even more funds for additional money expansion. This whole process is summarized in Exhibit 15.3.

Now suppose that Bank One faces a reserve requirement of 20 percent. The bank must keep cash on hand or at the Federal Reserve Bank equal to one-fifth (20%) of its deposits. If the bank's deposits (demand

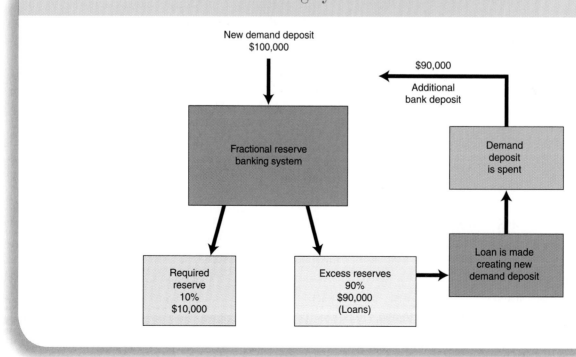

EXHIBIT 15.3 Fractional Reserve Banking System

New demand deposit
$100,000

Fractional reserve banking system

Required reserve
10%
$10,000

Excess reserves
90%
$90,000
(Loans)

Loan is made creating new demand deposit

Demand deposit is spent

$90,000
Additional bank deposit

and time) sum to $9,000,000, required reserves are calculated as follows:

$$Deposits \times Reserve\ ratio = \$9,000,000 \times 0.20$$
$$= \$1,800,000$$

The bank then is required to maintain $1,800,000 in cash. Bank One, however, actually has $2 million in cash, meaning that it has excess reserves, or $200,000.

$$Excess\ reserves = Actual\ reserves - Required\ reserves$$
$$= \$2,000,000 - \$1,800,000$$
$$= \$200,000$$

Suppose Bank One decided to make loans with its $200,000 in excess reserves. For simplicity's sake, let us suppose it makes one loan of $200,000 to a manufacturer for an addition to its chocolate factory. What will be the bank's balance sheet after it makes the loan? As Exhibit 15.4 indicates, both assets and liabilities rise by $200,000. The bank simply gives the borrower a checking account with $200,000 in it, a new deposit liability of the bank. In return, the borrower gives the bank an IOU agreeing to pay back the $200,000 plus interest at some future date. Thus, loans rise by $200,000 over the level on the initial balance sheet.

Note that in making the loan, Bank One did not have to reduce its cash reserves. It did not give the borrower cash; it simply created new money by giving the borrower $200,000 in a checking account. Therefore, even after making a loan equal to its initial excess reserves of $200,000, the bank still has some excess reserves. The bank's deposits rose to $9,200,000; 20 percent of that is $1,840,000. Yet the bank has $2,000,000 in actual reserves. Excess reserves are still $160,000 ($2,000,000 − $1,840,000 = $160,000).

If it still has some excess reserves, should the bank make still more loans? No. Why? Because when the chocolate manufacturer borrowed $200,000, it did so in order to expand the factory. Few people borrow money

and simply let the money sit in a checking account while they pay interest on the loan. It is reasonable to assume that the chocolate maker will shortly take all or part of the $200,000 out of the checking account, probably in the form of a check to a construction company for $200,000. What will the construction company do with the check? Put it in its bank. With many different banks in the United States, it is likely that the construction company has its checking account in another bank. Suppose its account is in Bank Two. Bank Two credits the account of the construction company with $200,000 in demand deposits, then takes the check and uses the facilities of the Federal Reserve System or a bank clearinghouse to present the check to Bank One for payment. Bank One will then have to pay Bank Two $200,000 in cash.

Therefore, Bank One will eventually (depending on how long it takes the chocolate manufacturer to spend the $200,000 it borrowed) face losing cash reserves equal to the loan. After Bank Two presents the check that was written by the chocolate manufacturer to Bank One for payment, Bank One's balance sheet changes again, as indicated in Exhibit 15.5 on the next page.

As the chocolate maker spends the $200,000, demand deposits fall by that amount, so that the bank's liabilities also decline by $200,000. The bank transfers $200,000 in cash to Bank Two. Incidentally, rarely is cash actually physically moved, given the expense and risk. Typically, the local Federal Reserve Bank simply reduces the cash reserves of Bank One by $200,000 and increases Bank Two's by $200,000.

When the smoke clears, the chocolate manufacturer has its factory addition, and Bank One has an interest-paying IOU equal to $200,000. Bank One's cash reserves have fallen, however, to an amount ($1,800,000) exactly equal to its required reserves. Had the bank initially loaned out more than its $200,000 in

EXHIBIT 15.4 Balance Sheet for Bank One after Loan

Assets		Liabilities and Capital	
Cash (reserves)	$ 2,000,000	Demand deposits	$ 5,200,000
Loans	6,300,000	Time deposits	4,000,000
Bonds (U.S. government and municipal)	1,500,000	Total liabilities	$ 9,200,000
Bank building, equipment, fixtures	400,000	Capital	1,000,000
Total Assets	**$10,200,000**	**Total Liabilities and Capital**	**$10,200,000**

EXHIBIT 15.5 Balance Sheet for Bank One after Loan Funds Are Spent

Assets		Liabilities and Capital	
Cash (reserves)	$ 1,800,000	Demand deposits	$ 5,000,000
Loans	6,300,000	Time deposits	4,000,000
Bonds (U.S. government and municipal)	1,500,000	Total liabilities	$ 9,000,000
Bank building, equipment, fixtures	400,000	Capital	1,000,000
Total Assets	**$10,000,000**	**Total Liabilities and Capital**	**$10,000,000**

excess reserves, the bank would have found its reserves below the required level as soon as the borrower spent the loan, assuming that the receiver of the funds had his or her bank account in another bank. Therefore, one important rule of thumb in banking is that a single bank in a banking system of many banks can safely make loans only equal to the amount of its excess reserves.

IS MORE MONEY MORE WEALTH?

When banks create more money by putting their excess reserves to work, they make the economy more liquid. Clearly, more money is in the economy after the loan, but is the borrower any wealthier? The answer is no. Even though borrowers have more money to buy goods and services, they are not any richer, because the new liability, the loan, has to be repaid.

In short, banks create money when they increase demand deposits through the process of creating loans. However, the process does not stop here. In the next section, we will see how the process of loans and deposits has a multiplying effect throughout the banking industry.

One important **rule of thumb** in banking is that a single bank in a banking system of many banks can safely make loans only equal to the amount of its excess reserves.

SECTION CHECK 3

3.1 Money is created when banks make loans. Borrowers receive newly created demand deposits.

3.2 Required reserves are the amount of cash or reserves—equal to a prescribed proportion of their deposits—that banks are required to keep on hand or in reserve accounts with the Federal Reserve.

3.3 A single bank in a banking system of many banks can safely make loans only equal to the amount of its excess reserves. The reserve requirement determines the point at which the bank has reached the limit of its excess reserves.

Ⓢ4 The Money Multiplier

Keep the following questions in mind as you read through this section. You'll find the answers in **Section Check 4**.

4.1 How does the process of multiple expansions of the money supply work?

4.2 What is the money multiplier?

We just learned that banks can create money (demand deposits) by making loans and that the monetary expansion of an individual bank is limited to its excess reserves. Let's now take a look at the multiple expansion effect created by these loans.

THE MULTIPLE EXPANSION EFFECT

The individual bank's limits in making loans ignores the further effects of a new loan and the accompanying expansion in the money supply. New loans create new money directly, but they also create excess reserves in other banks, which leads to still further increases in both loans and the money supply. With this multiple expansion effect, a given volume of bank reserves creates a multiplied amount of money.

New Loans and Multiple Expansions

To see how the process of multiple expansion works, consider what happens when Bank One receives a new cash deposit of $100,000. For convenience, say the bank is only required to keep new cash reserves equal to one-tenth (10 percent) of new deposits. Thus, Bank One is only required to hold $10,000 of the $100,000 deposit for required reserves. The bank therefore has $90,000 in excess reserves as a consequence of the new cash deposit.

Bank One will probably put its newly acquired excess reserves to work in some fashion earning income in the form of interest. Most likely, it will make one or more new loans totaling $90,000.

When the borrowers from Bank One get their loans, the borrowed money will almost certainly be spent on something new—machinery, a new house, a new car, or greater store inventories. The new money will lead to new spending.

The $90,000 spent by people borrowing from Bank One will likely end up in bank accounts in still other banks, such as Bank Two in Exhibit 15.6 on the next page. Bank Two now has a new deposit of $90,000 with which to make more loans and create still more money. So Bank Two's statement of changes in assets and liabilities, called a *T-account*, now looks like this:

Bank Two

	Assets	Liabilities	
Reserves	$ 9,000	Checking	
Loans	$81,000	deposits	$90,000

After the deposits, Bank Two has liabilities of $90,000. Thus, Bank Two creates $81,000 of money. Now if the money deposited in Bank Two is made available for a loan and is then deposited in Bank Three, the T-account for Bank Three will be:

Bank Three

	Assets	Liabilities	
Reserves	$ 8,100	Checking	
Loans	$72,900	deposits	$81,000

This process continues with Bank Three, Bank Four, Bank Five, and others. The initial cash deposit made by Bank One thus has a chain-reaction effect that ultimately involves many banks and a total monetary impact that is far greater than would be suggested by the size of the original deposit of $100,000. That is, every new loan gives rise to excess reserves, which lead to still further lending and deposit creation. Of course, each round of lending is smaller than the preceding one, because some (we are assuming 10 percent) of the new money created must be kept as required reserves.

THE MONEY MULTIPLIER

The **money multiplier** measures the potential amount of money that the banking system generates with each dollar of reserves. The following formula can be used to measure the total maximum potential impact on the supply of money:

Potential money creation = Initial deposit × Money multiplier

To find the size of the money multiplier, we simply divide 1 by the reserve requirement ($1/R$). The larger the reserve requirement, the smaller the money multiplier. Thus, a reserve requirement of 25 percent, or one-fourth, means a money multiplier of 4. Likewise, a reserve requirement of 10 percent, or one-tenth, means a money multiplier of 10.

In the example given in Exhibit 15.6, where Bank One (facing a 10% reserve requirement) receives a new $100,000 cash deposit, the initial deposit equals $100,000. Potential money creation, then, equals $100,000 (initial deposit) multiplied by 10 (the money multiplier), or $1,000,000. Using the money multiplier, we can calculate that the total potential impact of the initial $100,000 deposit is some $1,000,000 in money being created. In other words, the final monetary impact is 10 times as great as the initial deposit. Most of this increase, $900,000, has been created by the increase in demand

money multiplier measures the potential amount of money that the banking system generates with each dollar of reserves

EXHIBIT 15.6 The Multiple Expansion Process

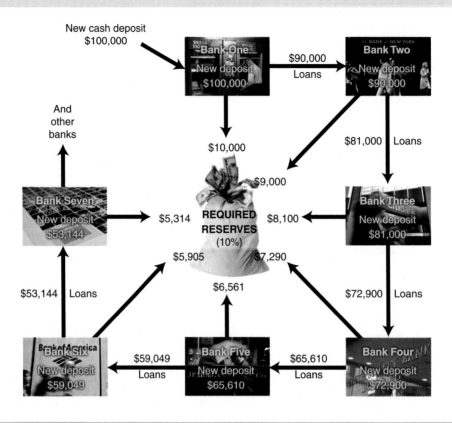

New cash deposit $100,000

Bank One
New deposit $100,000

$90,000 Loans

Bank Two
New deposit $90,000

And other banks

$10,000

$81,000 Loans

$9,000

REQUIRED RESERVES (10%)

Bank Three
New deposit $81,000

Bank Seven
New deposit $53,144

$5,314

$8,100

$5,905

$7,290

$53,144 Loans

$6,561

$72,900 Loans

Bank Six
New deposit $59,049

$59,049 Loans

Bank Five
New deposit $65,610

$65,610 Loans

Bank Four
New deposit $72,900

© BLOOMBERG VIA GETTY IMAGES / © JAMES BLINN/ISTOCKPHOTO.COM

deposits generated when banks make loans; the remaining $100,000 is from the initial deposit.

Why Is it Only "Potential" Money Creation?

Note that the expression "potential money creation" was used in describing the impact of creating loans and deposits out of excess reserves. Why "potential"? Some banks could choose not to lend all their excess reserves. Some banks might be extremely conservative and keep some extra newly acquired cash assets in that form. When they do, the chain reaction effect is reduced by the amount of excess reserves not loaned out.

Moreover, some borrowers may not spend all their newly acquired bank deposits, or they may wait a considerable period before doing so. Others may put their borrowed funds into time deposits rather than checkable deposits, which would reduce the M1 expansion process but not the M2 expansion process. Still others may choose to keep some of their loans as currency in their pockets. Such leakages and time lags in the bank money expansion process usually mean that the actual monetary impact of an initial deposit created out of

excess reserves within a short time is less than that indicated by the money multiplier. Still, the multiplier principle does work, and a multiple expansion of deposits will generally occur in a banking system that is characterized by fractional reserve requirements.

SECTION CHECK 4

4.1 New loans mean new money (demand deposits), which can increase spending as well as the money supply.

4.2 The banking system as a whole can potentially create money equal to several times the amount of total reserves or new money equal to several times the amount of excess reserves; the exact amount may be determined by the money multiplier, which is equal to one divided by the reserve requirement.

⑤5 The Collapse of America's Banking System, 1920–1933

Keep the following questions in mind as you read through this section. You'll find the answers in **Section Check 5**.

5.1 What caused the collapse of the banking system between 1920 and 1933?

5.2 How are bank failures avoided today?

Perhaps the most famous utterance from Franklin D. Roosevelt, the president of the United States from 1933 to 1945, was made on the day he assumed office, when he declared, "The only thing we have to fear is fear itself." These 10 words succinctly summarize the problems that led the world's leading economic power to a near total collapse in its system of commercial banking and, with that, to an abrupt and unprecedented decline in the money supply. The decline in the money supply, in turn, contributed to an economic downturn that had dire consequences for many, especially for the one-fourth of the labor force unemployed at the time of Roosevelt's first inaugural address.

WHAT HAPPENED TO THE BANKING INDUSTRY?

In 1920, 30,000 banks were operating in the United States; by 1933, the number declined to about 15,000. What happened? In some cases, bank failure reflected imprudent management or even criminal activity on the part of bank officers (stealing from the bank). More often, though, banks in rural areas closed as a consequence of having large sums of assets tied up in loans to farmers who, because of low farm prices, were not in a position to pay off the loans when they came due. Rumors spread that a bank was in trouble, and those rumors, even if false, became self-fulfilling prophecies. Bank "runs" developed, and even conservatively managed banks with cash equal to 15 percent or 20 percent of their deposit liabilities found themselves with insufficient cash reserves to meet the withdrawal requests of panicky depositors.

The bank failures of the 1920s, while numerous, were generally scattered around small towns in the country. In general, confidence in banks actually increased during that decade; and by the fall of 1929, there were $11 in bank deposits for every $1 of currency in circulation.

The first year following the stock market crash of 1929 saw little dramatic change in the banking system; but in late 1930, a bank with the unfortunately awesome-sounding name of the Bank of the United States failed—the largest bank failure in the country up to that time. This failure had a ripple effect. More runs on banks occurred as depositors became jittery. Banks, fearing runs, stopped lending their excess reserves, thereby aggravating a fall in the money supply and reducing business investment.

As depositors converted their deposits to currency, bank reserves fell, as did the ability of banks to support deposits. The situation improved a bit in 1932, when a newly created government agency, the Reconstruction Finance Corporation (RFC), made loans to distressed banks. By early 1933, however, the decline in depositor confidence had reached the point that the entire banking system was in jeopardy. On March 4, newly inaugurated President Roosevelt declared a national bank holiday, closing every bank in the country for nearly two weeks. Then, only the "good" banks were allowed to reopen, an action that increased confidence. By this time, the deposit-currency ratio had fallen from 11 to 1 (in 1929) to 4 to 1. Passage of federal deposit insurance in mid-1933 greatly strengthened depositor confidence and led to money reentering the banks. The recovery process began.

WHAT CAUSED THE COLLAPSE?

The collapse occurred for several reasons. First, the nation had thousands of relatively small banks. Customers believed that depositor withdrawals could force a bank to close, and the mere fear of bank runs made them a reality. Canada, with relatively few banks, most of them large with many branches, had no bank runs. Second, governmental attempts to stem the growing distress were weak and too late. Financial aid to banks was nonexistent; the Federal Reserve System and other governmental efforts began only in 1932—well into the decline. Third, deposit insurance, which would have bolstered customer confidence, did not exist. The financial consequences of bank failures were correctly perceived by the public to be dire. Fourth, growing depositor fear was enhanced by the fact that the economy was in a continuous downward spiral, eroding the basis for any optimism that bank loans would be safely repaid.

BANK FAILURES TODAY

The combination of the Federal Deposit Insurance Corporation (FDIC) and the government's greater willingness to assist distressed banks has reduced the number of bank failures in recent times. Now, when a bank runs into financial difficulty, the FDIC may assist another bank in taking over the assets and liabilities of the troubled bank so that no depositor loses a cent. We do not see depositors run on banks because the FDIC will make good on deposits. There are costs and benefits of insuring deposits. On the cost side is that bankers whose deposits are insured may take greater risks. On the benefit side, deposit insurance means that, changes in the money supply due to a loss of deposits from failed banks are no longer a big problem. Better bank stability means a greater stability in the money supply, which means, as will be more explicitly demonstrated in the next chapter, a greater level of economic stability.

However, in the 1980s, a savings and loan crisis occurred, one of the worst financial crises since the Great Depression. The inflation of the 1970s had created a problem for many savings and loans. They had made a large number of real estate loans in the early 1970s, when the inflation rate was relatively low at about 5 percent. Then, during most of the rest of that decade, inflation rates rose rapidly and nominal interest rates soared. The savings and loans were in a squeeze—they had to pay high interest rates to attract depositors but were earning low interest rates on their real estate loans from the early 1970s. This disastrous combination for the savings and loans caused many of them to go belly up.

Unfortunately, interest rates were not the only problem. The government eased regulations to make it easier for savings and loans to compete for deposits with other financial institutions in the national market. Deregulation, coupled with deposit insurance, put savings and loans in a gambling mood. Many savings and loans poured money into high-risk real estate projects and other risky ventures. Depositors had little incentive to monitor their banks because they knew they would be protected up to $100,000 on their accounts by the government. Eventually, more than a thousand thrift institutions went bankrupt. Depositors were saved, but taxpayers were not. Taxpayers ended up paying the bill for much of the savings and loan debacle—the bailout for the financial losses has been estimated to be more than $150 billion. The Thrift Bailout Bill of 1989 provided funds for the bailout and new, stricter provisions for banks.

Financial crises are a little like earthquakes. We know that they will happen but we don't know exactly when and with what magnitude. For example, not many economists forecasted the financial crisis of 2008–2009.

Sheila Bair was appointed as Chairwoman of the FDIC in 2006. Bair oversaw numerous measures to combat the financial crisis in 2008, raising depositor insurance levels and helping facilitate the sale of failed banks such as Washington Mutual.

SECTION CHECK 5

5.1 The banking collapse of 1920–1933 occurred because of customers' fears and the weakness of the government's attempts to correct the problem.

5.2 The creation of the Federal Deposit Insurance Corporation has largely eliminated bank runs in recent times.

Chapter 15: Self-Review

Now that you're finished reading the chapter, review the questions below. You can write your answers in the space provided, then go online to see the answers at www.cengagebrain.com.

S1–WHAT IS MONEY?

1. True or False: Using money is better than barter.

2. Why do virtually all societies create something to function as money?

S2–MEASURING MONEY

3. True or False: Our money is currently backed by gold.

4. Which one of each of the following pairs of assets is most liquid?
   a. Microsoft stock or a traveler's check
   b. a 30-year bond or a six-month Treasury bill
   c. a certificate of deposit or a demand deposit
   d. a savings account or 10 acres of real estate

5. True are False: Credit cards are a form of money.

6. Fill-in-the-Blank: M2 is a _____ definition of money than M1.

S3–HOW BANKS CREATE MONEY

7. If a bank had reserves of $30,000 and demand deposits of $200,000 (and no other deposits), how much could it lend out if it faced a required reserve ratio of:
   a. 10 percent?
   b. 15 percent?
   c. 20 percent?

8. Is a demand deposit an asset or a liability?

9. Fill-in-the-Blank: Legal reserve deposit regulations _____ bank profits.

S4–THE MONEY MULTIPLIER

10. Calculate the magnitude of the money multiplier if banks were to hold 100 percent of deposits in reserve.

11. True or False: The supply of money and the volume of bank loans both increase or decrease at the same time.

S5–THE COLLAPSE OF AMERICA'S BANKING SYSTEM, 1920–1933

12. How did the combination of increased holding of excess reserves by banks and currency by the public lead to bank failures in the 1930s?

13. What are the four reasons cited in the text for the collapse of the U.S. banking system in this period?

14. True or False: The creation of the FDIC increased bank stability.

The Federal Reserve

has been chaired by three men over the last 30 years. Paul Volker (top middle) served as chair from 1979–1987. He was succeeded by Alan Greenspan (bottom left), who chaired the Fed until 2006. Greenspan was then followed by the current chairman, Ben Bernanke (bottom right).

PART 3

© ROGER L. WOLLENBERG/UPI/LANDOV / © ALEX GRIMM/REUTERS/LANDOV

16

The Federal Reserve and Monetary Policy

t he chairperson of the Federal Reserve System is one of the most important policymakers in the country. The importance of the Federal Reserve System and monetary policy cannot be overestimated. In this chapter, we will see how deliberate changes in the money supply can affect aggregate demand and lead to short-run changes in the output of goods and services as well as the price level. That is, monetary policy can be an effective tool for helping to achieve and maintain price stability, full employment, and economic growth. We will also see that monetary-policy tools, just like fiscal-policy tools, have problems of implementation.

(S)1 The Federal Reserve System

Keep the following questions in mind as you read through this section. You'll find the answers in **Section Check 1**.

1.1 What is the most important function of a central bank?

1.2 Who controls the Federal Reserve System?

1.3 How is the Fed tied to Congress and the executive branch?

In most countries of the world, the job of manipulating the supply of money belongs to the "central bank."

THE FUNCTIONS OF A CENTRAL BANK

A central bank performs many functions. First, the central bank is a "banker's bank." It is the bank where commercial banks maintain their own cash deposits—their reserves. Second, the central bank performs a number of service functions for commercial banks, such as transferring funds and checks between various commercial banks in the banking system. Third, the central bank typically serves as the primary bank for the central government, handling, for example, its payroll accounts.

Sections in Chapter 16

Fourth, the central bank buys and sells foreign currencies and generally assists in the completion of financial transactions with other countries. Fifth, it serves as the "lender of last resort," helping banking institutions in financial distress. Sixth, the central bank is concerned with the stability of the banking system and the money supply, which, as we have already seen, results from the loan decisions of banks. The central bank can and does impose regulations on private commercial banks; it thereby regulates the size of the money supply and influences the level of economic activity. The central bank also implements monetary policy, which, along with fiscal policy, forms the basis of efforts to direct the economy to perform in accordance with macroeconomic goals.

LOCATION OF THE FEDERAL RESERVE SYSTEM

In most countries, the central bank is a single bank; for example, the central bank of Great Britain, the Bank of England, is a single institution located in London. In the United States, however, the central bank is 12 institutions, closely tied together and collectively called the Federal Reserve System. The Federal Reserve System, or Fed, as it is nicknamed, comprises separate banks in Boston, New York, Philadelphia, Richmond, Atlanta, Dallas, Cleveland, Chicago, St. Louis, Minneapolis–St. Paul, Kansas City, and San Francisco. As Exhibit 16.1 shows, these banks and their branches are spread all over the country, but they are most heavily concentrated in the eastern states.

Each of the 12 banks has branches in key cities in its district. For example, the Federal Reserve Bank of Cleveland serves the fourth Federal Reserve district and has branches in Pittsburgh, Cincinnati, and Columbus. Each Federal Reserve Bank has its own board of directors and, to a limited extent, can set its own policies. Effectively, however, the 12 banks act in unison on major policy issues, with control of major policy decisions resting with the Board of Governors and the

The Six Functions of the Fed

1) Banker's bank
2) Service functions for commercial banks
3) Bank for the government
4) Manages transactions with other countries
5) Lender of last resort
6) Maintains banking system stability

Federal Open Market Committee, headquartered in Washington, D.C. The Chairman of the Federal Reserve Board of Governors (currently Ben Bernanke) is generally regarded as one of the most important and powerful economic policymakers in the country.

THE FED'S RELATIONSHIP TO THE FEDERAL GOVERNMENT

The Federal Reserve System was created in 1913 because the U.S. banking system had so little stability and no central direction. Technically, the Fed is privately owned by the banks that "belong" to it. Banks

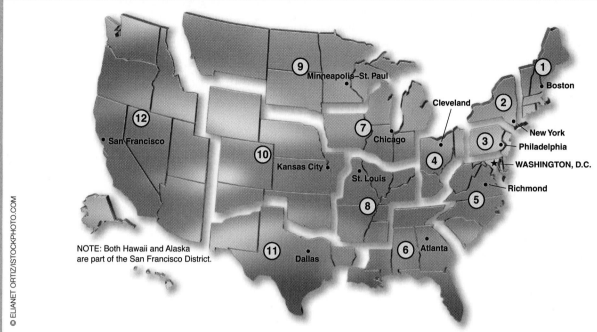

NOTE: Both Hawaii and Alaska are part of the San Francisco District.

SOURCE: Board of Governors of the Federal Reserve System, *95th Annual Report,* 2008, Maps of the Federal Reserve System. Federal Reserve. Washington, D.C. June 2009. Available at http://federalreserve.gov/boarddocs/rptcongress/annual08/default.htm (accessed March 27, 2010).

are not required to belong to the Fed; however, since the passage of new legislation in 1980, virtually no difference exists between the requirements for member and nonmember banks.

The private ownership of the Fed is essentially meaningless, because the Federal Reserve Board of Governors, which controls major policy decisions, is appointed by the president of the United States, not by the stockholders. The owners of the Fed have relatively little control over its operations and receive only small fixed dividends on their modest financial stake in the system. Again, the feature of private ownership but public control was a compromise made to appease commercial banks opposed to direct public (government) regulation.

The Fed's Ties to the Executive Branch

An important aspect of the Fed's operation is that, historically, it has enjoyed a considerable amount of independence from both the executive and legislative branches of government. In fact, central banks with greater degrees of independence appear to have a lower annual inflation rate, as seen in Exhibit 16.2. True, the president appoints the seven members of the Board of Governors, subject to Senate approval; but the term of appointment is 14 years. No member of the Federal Reserve Board will face reappointment from the president who initially made the

appointment, because presidential tenure is limited to two four-year terms. Moreover, the terms of board members are staggered, so a new appointment is made only every

EXHIBIT 16.2 Central Bank Independence and Inflation, 1960–1992

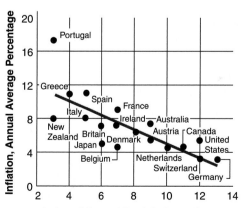

Index of Central-Bank Independence*
zero = least independent
*Calculated by V Grilli, D Masciandaro & G Tabellini

SOURCE: "Monetary Metamorphosis," *The Economist,* September 23, 1999. © The Economist Newspaper Limited, London 1999. Reprinted with permission.

two years. It is practically impossible for a single president to appoint a majority of the members of the board; and even if it were possible, members have little fear of losing their jobs as a result of presidential wrath. The chair of the Federal Reserve Board is a member of the Board of Governors and serves a four-year term. The chair is truly the chief executive officer of the system and effectively runs it, with considerable help from the presidents of the 12 regional banks.

FED OPERATIONS

Many of the key policy decisions of the Federal Reserve are actually made by its Federal Open Market Committee (FOMC), which consists of the seven members of the Board of Governors; the president of the New York Federal Reserve Bank; and four other presidents of Federal Reserve Banks, who serve on the committee on a rotating basis. The FOMC makes most of the key decisions influencing the direction and size of changes in the money supply; and their regular, closed meetings are accordingly considered important by the business community, news media, and government.

SECTION CHECK 1

1.1 Of the six major functions of a central bank, the most important is its role in regulating the money supply.

1.2 The Federal Reserve System consists of 12 Federal Reserve banks. Although these banks are independent institutions, they act largely in unison on major policy decisions. The Federal Reserve Board of Governors and the Federal Open Market Committee are the prime decision makers for U.S. monetary policy.

1.3 The President of the United States appoints members of the Federal Reserve Board of Governors to a 14-year term, with only one appointment made every two years. The president also selects the Chair of the Federal Reserve Board, who serves a four-year term. The only other government intervention in the Fed can come from legislation passed in congress.

⑤2 How Does the Federal Reserve Change the Money Supply?

Keep the following questions in mind as you read through this section. You'll find the answers in Section Check 2.

2.1 What are the three major tools of the Fed?

2.2 How can the Fed stimulate the economy?

2.3 How can the Fed restrain the economy?

As noted previously, the Federal Reserve Board of Governors and the FOMC are the prime decision makers for U.S. monetary policy. They decide whether to expand the money supply and, it is hoped, the real level of economic activity, or to contract the money supply, hoping to cool inflationary pressures. How does the Fed control the money supply, particularly when it is the privately owned commercial banks that actually create and destroy money by making loans, as we discussed earlier?

The Fed has three major methods by which to control the supply of money: It can engage in open market operations, change reserve requirements, or change its discount rate. Of these three, by far the most important is open market operations.

> Fed tools for controlling the money supply
> • Open market operations
> • Change reserve requirements
> • Change the discount rate

OPEN MARKET OPERATIONS

Open market operations involve the purchase and sale of government bonds by the Federal Reserve System. At its regular meetings, the FOMC decides to buy or sell government bonds. Open market operations are the most important method the Fed uses to influence the money supply for several reasons. First, it is a device that can be implemented quickly and cheaply—the Fed merely calls an agent who buys or sells bonds. Second, it can be done quietly, without a lot of political debate or a public announcement. Third, it is a rather powerful tool, as any given purchase or sale of bonds has an ultimate impact several times the amount of the initial transaction. Fourth, the Fed can use this tool to change the money supply by a small or large amount on any given day.

When the Fed buys bonds, it pays the seller of the bonds by a check written on one of the 12 Federal Reserve banks. The person receiving the check will likely deposit it in his or her bank account, increasing the money supply in the form of added transaction deposits. More important, the commercial bank, in return for crediting the account of the bond seller with a new deposit, gets cash reserves or a higher balance in its reserve account at the Federal Reserve Bank in its district.

For example, suppose our example bank, Bank One, has no excess reserves and that one of its customers sells a bond for $10,000 through a broker to the Federal Reserve System. The customer deposits the check from the Fed for $10,000 in his or her account, and the Fed credits Bank One with $10,000 in reserves. Suppose the reserve requirement is 10 percent. Bank One, then, needs new reserves of only $1,000 ($10,000 × 0.10) to support its $10,000, meaning that it has acquired $9,000 in new excess reserves ($10,000 new actual reserves minus $1,000 in new required reserves). Bank One can, and probably will, lend out its excess reserves of $9,000, creating $9,000 in new deposits in the process. The recipients of the loans, in turn, will likely spend the money, leading to still more new deposits and excess reserves in other banks.

In other words, the Fed's purchase of the bond directly creates $10,000 in money in the form of bank deposits and indirectly permits up to $90,000 in additional money to be created through the multiple expansion in bank deposits. (The money multiplier is 1/.10, or 10; 10 × $9,000 = $90,000.) Thus, if the reserve requirement is 10 percent, a potential total of up to $100,000 in new money is created by the purchase of one $10,000 bond by the Fed.

The process works in reverse when the Fed sells a bond. The individual purchasing the bond will pay the Fed by check, lowering demand deposits in the banking system. Reserves of the bank where the bond purchaser has a bank account will likewise fall. If the bank had zero excess reserves at the beginning of the process, it now has a reserve deficiency. The bank must sell secondary reserves or reduce loan volume, either of which leads to further destruction of deposits. Thus, a multiple contraction of deposits begins.

In short, if the Fed believes the economy needs to be stimulated, it will buy bonds from the private sector with open market purchases. If the Fed wishes to slow the economy down, it will sell bonds to the private sector with open market sales.

THE RESERVE REQUIREMENT

Even though open market operations are the most important and widely utilized tool for achieving monetary objectives that the Fed has at its disposal, they are not its potentially most powerful tool. The Fed possesses the power to change the reserve requirements of member banks by altering the reserve ratio. It can have an immediate and significant impact on the ability of member banks to create money. Suppose the banking system as a whole has $500 billion in deposits and $60 billion in reserves, with a reserve ratio of 12 percent. Because $60 billion is 12 percent of $500 billion, the system has no excess reserves. Suppose now that the Fed lowers reserve requirements by changing the reserve ratio to 10 percent. Banks then are required to keep only $50 billion in reserves ($500 billion × 0.10), but they still have $60 billion. Thus, the lowering of the reserve requirement gives banks $10 billion in excess reserves. The banking system as a whole can expand deposits and the money stock by a multiple of this amount, in this case 10 (10% equals 1/10; the banking multiplier is the reciprocal of this, or 10). The lowering of the reserve requirement in this case, then, would permit an expansion in deposits of $100 billion, which represents a 20 percent increase in the stock of money, from $500 to $600 billion.

When Does the Fed Use This Tool?

Relatively small reserve requirement changes can thus have a big impact on the potential supply of money. This tool is so potent, in fact, that it is seldom used. In other words, the power of the reserve requirement is not only its advantage but also its disadvantage, because a small reduction in the reserve requirement can make a huge change in the number of dollars that are in excess reserves in banks all over the country. Such huge changes in required reserves and excess reserves have the potential to disrupt the economy.

Frequent changes in the reserve requirement would make it difficult for banks to plan. For example, a banker might worry that if she makes loans now and then the Fed raises the reserve requirement, she would not have enough reserves to meet the new reserve requirements. However, if she does not make loans and the Fed leaves the reserve requirement alone, she loses the opportunity to earn income on those loans.

Carpenters don't use sledgehammers to hammer small nails or tacks; the tool is too big and powerful to

discount rate interest rate that the Fed charges commercial banks for the loans it extends to them

federal funds market market in which banks provide short-term loans to other banks that need cash to meet reserve requirements

use effectively. For the same reason, the Fed changes reserve requirements rather infrequently. In short, changing the reserve requirement is a blunt tool for controlling the money supply and is rarely used as a monetary tool.

THE DISCOUNT RATE

Banks having trouble meeting their reserve requirement can borrow funds directly from the Fed at its discount window. A bank might borrow from the Fed when it has too few reserves to meet the reserve requirement or has recently experienced an unexpectedly high amount of withdrawals. The interest rate the Fed charges on these borrowed reserves is called the **discount rate**. The Fed can control the money supply by altering the discount rate. If the Fed raises the discount rate, it discourages banks from borrowing reserves from the Fed. This reduces the quantity of reserves in the banking system, which leads to a reduction in the money supply. That is, if the Fed wants to contract the money supply, it will raise the discount rate, making it more costly for banks to borrow reserves.

If the Fed is promoting an expansion of money and credit, it will lower the discount rate, making it cheaper for banks to borrow reserves. Thus, a lower

> A lower discount rate will encourage banks to borrow from the Fed, increasing the quantity of reserves and the money supply.

discount rate will encourage banks to borrow from the Fed, increasing the quantity of reserves and the money supply.

The discount rate sometimes changes fairly frequently, often several times a year. Sometimes the rate will be moved several times in the same direction within a single year, which has a substantial cumulative effect.

The Significance of the Discount Rate

The discount rate is a relatively unimportant tool, mainly because member banks do not rely heavily on the Fed for borrowed funds and often the Fed would not lend them all they want to borrow. It is something most of them believe should be reserved for real emergencies. In October of 1987, when the stock market crashed, Fed chair Alan Greenspan used discount lending to help financial institutions that were in trouble. Many Wall Street brokerage firms needed temporary funds to finance the high volume of stock trades. The Fed was there to help. Also, in the financial crisis of 2008, the collapse of the housing market coupled with mortgage defaults meant that many financial institutions were in trouble. The Fed provided loans to many of these financial institutions that were in trouble.

When banks have short-term needs for cash to meet reserve requirements, they are more likely to take a short-term (often overnight) loan from another bank in the **federal funds market**. For that reason, many people pay a lot of attention to the interest rate on federal funds.

In recent years, the Federal Reserve has increased its focus on the federal funds rate as the primary indicator of its stance on monetary policy. The Fed announces a federal funds rate target at each FOMC meeting. This rate is watched closely, because it affects all the interest rates throughout the economy—auto loans, mortgages, and so on. Since January 2003, the discount rate has been set between 0.5 and 1.0 percentage points above the federal funds rate target. Setting the discount rate above the fund rate is designed to keep banks from turning to this source. Thus, most of discount lending is small.

The Fed could use the discount rate by altering the discount rate relative to the federal funds rate. However, the discount rate's main significance is that changes in the rate are commonly viewed as a signal of the Fed's intentions with respect to monetary policy. Discount rate changes are widely publicized, unlike open market operations, which are carried out in private and announced several weeks later in the minutes of the FOMC.

HOW THE FED REDUCES THE MONEY SUPPLY

The Fed can do three things to reduce the money supply or reduce the rate of growth in the money supply: (1) sell bonds, (2) raise reserve requirements, or (3) raise the discount rate. Of course, the Fed could also opt to use a combination of these three tools in its approach. These moves tend to decrease aggregate demand.

Tools for reducing the money supply
1) Sell bonds
2) Raise reserve requirements
3) Raise the discount rate

HOW THE FED INCREASES THE MONEY SUPPLY

If the Fed is concerned about underutilizing resources (e.g., unemployment), it can engage in precisely the opposite policies: (1) buy bonds, (2) lower reserve requirements, or (3) lower the discount rate. The Fed can also use a combination of these three approaches. These moves tend to increase aggregate demand.

DIFFICULTIES IN CONTROLLING THE MONEY SUPPLY

In a fractional reserve banking system, the Fed cannot precisely control the money supply because of two problems: people and banks.

The Fed cannot precisely control the amount of money that people want to hold as currency in circulation versus as deposits in their financial institutions. The more cash people put in the bank, the more excess reserves the bank has for lending purposes and the more money created. Alternatively, if people are concerned about the health of the financial system and choose to take money out of the bank in order to hold more currency, it would reduce banks' excess reserves, reducing lending and the supply of money. Either change can alter the money supply without any action from the Fed.

Banks can also choose to not lend out all of their excess reserves. When banks keep more excess reserves, the Fed has less control over the money supply because banks rather than Fed policy dictates how much will be lent out. If banks make money by making loans, why would they keep excess reserves? Banks may choose to become more cautious because of the current economic climate; to avoid risk they may choose to hold on to more excess reserves. Consequently, the banking system would create less money with a given level of reserves than it normally would and the money supply would fall.

This may not be a huge problem because the Fed keeps massive amounts of data on the behavior of banks and their depositors. As a result, changes in currency circulation or excess reserve holdings by banks can be remedied with offsetting policies the Fed can control.

Tools for increasing the money supply
1) Buy bonds
2) Lower reserve requirements
3) Lower the discount rate

SECTION CHECK 2

2.1 The three major tools of the Fed are open market operations, changing reserve requirements, and changing the discount rate.

2.2 If the Fed wants to stimulate the economy (increase aggregate demand), it will increase the money supply by buying government bonds, lowering the reserve ratio, and/or raising the discount rate.

2.3 If the Fed wants to restrain the economy (decrease aggregate demand), it will lower the money supply by selling government bonds, increasing the reserve ratio, and/or raising the discount rate.

ⓢ3 Money, Interest Rates, and Aggregate Demand

Keep the following questions in mind as you read through this section. You'll find the answers in Section Check 3.

3.1 How do changes in income change the money market equilibrium?

3.2 How does the Fed's buying and selling of bonds affect RGDP in the short run?

3.3 How are the real and nominal interest rates connected in the short run?

The Federal Reserve's policies with respect to the money supply have a direct effect on short-run nominal interest rates and, accordingly, on the components of aggregate demand.

THE MONEY MARKET

The **money market** is the market in which money demand and money supply determine the equilibrium *nominal* interest rate. When the Fed acts to change the money supply by changing one of its policy variables, it alters the money market equilibrium.

Money has several functions, but why would people hold money instead of other financial assets? That is, what is responsible for the demand for money? Transaction purposes, precautionary reasons, and asset purposes are at least some of the determinants of the demand for money.

Transactions Demand for Money

First, the primary reason that money is demanded is for transaction purposes—to facilitate exchange. Workers are generally paid by the week or month. However, most people want to hold on to money so they can buy goods and services on a continual basis, not just on payday. They want to keep money for everyday predictable expenses. For example, nobody would want to buy pizza with stocks and bonds. How costly would it be to convert less liquid assets like stocks or bonds into goods and services? Those costs would include the loss of interest and possible withdrawal

money market market in which money demand and money supply determine the equilibrium interest rate

penalties. In addition, the higher a person's income, the more transactions that person is likely to make (because consumption is income related); the greater will be GDP; and the greater will be the demand for money for transaction purposes, *ceteris paribus*.

Precautionary Demand for Money

Second, people like to have money on hand for precautionary reasons—so called "mattress money." If unexpected medical or other expenses require an unusual outlay of cash, people want to be prepared. The extent to which an individual holds cash for precautionary reasons depends partly on that person's income and partly on the opportunity cost of holding money, which is determined by market rates of interest. The higher the market interest rates, the higher the opportunity cost of holding money; and so people will hold less of their financial wealth as money.

Asset Demand for Money

Third, money has a trait—liquidity—that makes it a desirable asset. Other things being equal, people prefer assets that are more liquid to those that are less liquid. That is, people want to be able to easily convert some of their money into goods and services. For this reason, most people wish to have some of their portfolio in the form of money. At higher interest rates on other assets, the amount of money desired for this purpose will be smaller, because the opportunity cost of holding money will have risen.

© EMILIA SZYMANEK/ISTOCKPHOTO.COM

THE DEMAND FOR MONEY AND THE NOMINAL INTEREST RATE

The quantity of money demanded varies inversely with the nominal interest rate. When interest rates are higher, the opportunity cost—in terms of the interest income on alternative assets—of holding monetary assets is higher, and persons will want to hold less money. At the same time, the demand for money, particularly for transaction purposes, is highly dependent on income levels, because the transaction volume varies directly with income. Finally, the demand for money depends on the price level. If the price level increases, buyers will need more money to purchase their goods and services. If the price level falls, buyers will need less money to purchase their goods and services.

The demand curve for money is presented in Exhibit 16.3. At lower interest rates, the quantity of money demanded is greater, illustrated by a movement from A to B. That is, the lower the interest rate, the lower the opportunity cost of holding money. An increase in income will lead to an increase in the demand for money, depicted by a rightward shift in the money demand (*MD*) curve, a movement from A to C.

WHY IS THE SUPPLY OF MONEY RELATIVELY INELASTIC?

The supply of money is largely governed by the regulatory policies of the central bank. Whether interest rates are 4 percent or 14 percent, banks seeking to maximize profits will increase lending as long as they have reserves above their desired level. Even a 4 percent return on loans provides more profit than maintaining those assets in non-interest-bearing cash or reserve accounts at the Fed, which currently earn very low interest rate from the Fed. Given this fact, the money supply is effectively almost perfectly inelastic with respect to interest rates over their plausible range. Therefore, we draw the money supply (*MS*) curve as vertical, *ceteris paribus*, in Exhibit 16.4, with changes in Federal Reserve policies acting to shift the money supply curve.

THE MONEY MARKET

Equilibrium in the money market is found by combining the money demand and money supply curves, as shown in Exhibit 16.4. Money market equilibrium occurs at that *nominal* interest rate where the quantity of money demanded equals the quantity of money supplied. Initially, the money market is in equilibrium at *i** in Exhibit 16.4.

Money Market Equilibrium

In Exhibit 16.4, we see that equilibrium occurs at point E, where the quantity of money demanded by the public is equal to the quantity of the money supplied by the banking system, given the policies adopted by the Fed. At i_2, below the equilibrium interest rate, the quantity of money that people want to hold is greater than the quantity that is available from the banking system—there is a shortage at i_2. Consequently, people will try to increase their holdings of money by reducing their holdings of bonds or other interest-bearing assets. Because many people are trying to rid themselves of bonds, bond sellers realize they must increase interest on bonds to attract buyers. Thus, the interest rate rises to the equilibrium level, *i**.

At i_1, the interest rate is above the equilibrium level, the quantity of money people want to hold is less than the quantity that is available from the banking system; there is a surplus of money at i_1. Those that are holding the surplus of money (cash and checkable deposits) will try to exchange money for other assets such as bonds. As the demand for bonds rises, bond sellers can pay less

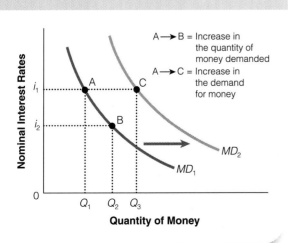

EXHIBIT 16.3 Money Demand, Interest Rates, and Income

A → B = Increase in the quantity of money demanded

A → C = Increase in the demand for money

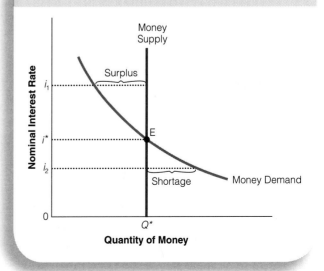

EXHIBIT 16.4 Money Market Equilibrium

interest but still attract enough buyers. As the interest rate falls, people become more willing to hold money, until the interest rate reaches equilibrium at i^*, where people are content holding the money the banking system has supplied.

The Money Market and the Aggregate Demand Curve

Recall the interest rate effect that moved us along the aggregate demand curve when the price level changed. We now look at that relationship in more detail. Specifically, when the price level rises from PL_1 to PL_2 in Exhibit 16.5, people demand more money and the money demand curve shifts from MD_1 to MD_2. That is, at the new higher price level, PL_2, many goods and services will have higher prices, so people will want to hold more money, MD_2 rather than MD_1.

How does an increase in the demand for money affect the money market? The increase in the demand for money, coupled with a fixed money supply (controlled by the Fed), will cause the interest rate to increase from i_1 to i_2. At the higher interest rate, the cost of borrowing and the return to saving are higher. In short, fewer households will be borrowing for houses and cars, and fewer firms will be investing in new factories and equipment. Thus, the quantity at RGDP demanded falls from $RGDP_1$ to $RGDP_2$.

Of course, the reverse is true as well. A lower price level leads to a decrease in the demand for money because, on average, goods and services have lower price tags. The reduction in the demand for money causes a reduction in the interest rate, which encourages consumption and investment that increases RGDP demanded. Hence, this leads to the downward sloping aggregate demand curve—a lower price level leads to an increase in RGDP demanded.

How Do Income Changes Affect the Equilibrium Position?

Rising national income increases the demand for money, shifting the money demand curve to the right from MD_1 to MD_2 and leading to a new higher equilibrium interest rate.

How Would an Increase in the Money Supply Affect Equilibrium Interest Rates and Aggregate Demand?

A Federal Reserve policy change that increased the money supply would be depicted by a shift in the money supply curve to the right. As a result of this shift, the equilibrium quantity of money demanded increases as equilibrium interest rates fall. The immediate impact of expansionary monetary policy is to decrease the interest rate. Because the money demand curve has not changed, the interest rate falls to the new equilibrium at E_2. The interest rate falls to induce people to hold the additional money supplied by the banking system, MS_2. The lower interest rate, or the fall in the cost of borrowing money, then leads to an increase in aggregate demand for goods and

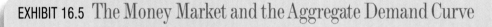

EXHIBIT 16.5 The Money Market and the Aggregate Demand Curve

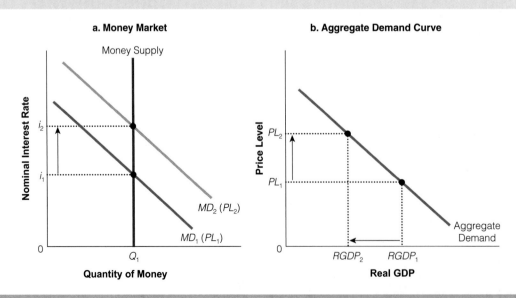

EXHIBIT 16.6 The Impact of an Increase in the Supply of Money

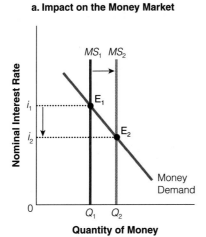

a. Impact on the Money Market

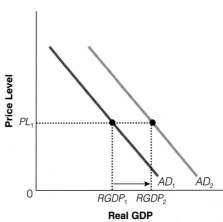

b. Impact on Aggregate Demand

services at the current price level. The lower interest rate will increase home sales, car sales, business investments, and so on. That is, an increase in the money supply will lead to lower interest rates and an increase in aggregate demand, as seen in Exhibit 16.6. Thus, when the Fed changes policy to increase the money supply, the interest rate falls. This increases RGDP demanded at each and every price level. If the Fed changes policy to reduce the money supply, the interest rate would rise, which would lower RGDP demanded at each and every price level.

DOES THE FED TARGET THE MONEY SUPPLY OR INTEREST RATES?

Most economists believe that the Fed should try to control interest rates. But other economists believe that the Fed should try to control the money supply. Unfortunately, the Fed cannot do both—it must pick one or the other.

Recall that the Fed controls the money supply but not the money demand. The demand for money is determined by households and firms. In Exhibit 16.7, the economy is initially at point A, where the interest rate is i_1 and the quantity of money is at Q_1. Now, suppose the demand for money were to increase because of an increase in national income, an increase in the price level, or because people desire to hold more money. As a result, the demand curve for money shifts to the right, from MD_1 to MD_2. If the Fed decides it does not want the money supply to increase, it can pursue a policy of no monetary growth, which leads to an increase in the interest rate to i_2 at point C. The Fed could also

try to keep the interest rate stable at i_1, but it can only do so by increasing the growth in the money supply through expansionary monetary policy. The Fed cannot simultaneously pursue policies of no monetary growth and monetary expansion; it must choose a higher interest rate, a greater money supply, or some combination of both. The Fed cannot completely control both the growth in the money supply and the interest rate. If it attempts to keep the interest rate steady in the face of increased money demand, it must increase the growth

EXHIBIT 16.7 Fed Targeting Money Supply versus the Interest Rate

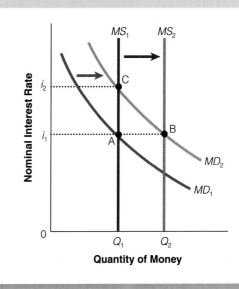

in the money supply. If it tries to keep the growth of the money supply in check in the face of increased money demand, the interest rate will rise.

In short, monetary policy can be applied in terms of the money supply or the interest rate (the federal funds rate). When FOMC sets a federal funds rate target, the Fed's bond traders are told to do whatever is necessary to get the equilibrium interest rate to the target level. To lower the federal funds rate, Fed bond traders buy government bonds. This increases the money supply and lowers the interest rate. If FOMC raises the target for the federal funds rate, its bond traders sell government bonds. This decreases the money supply and raises the interest rate.

The Problem

The problem with targeting the money supply is that the demand for money fluctuates considerably in the short run. Focusing on the growth in the money supply when the demand for money is changing unpredictably leads to large fluctuations in interest rates, as occurred in the U.S. economy during the late 1970s and early 1980s. These erratic changes in interest rates could seriously disrupt the investment climate.

Keeping interest rates in check also creates problems. For example, when the economy grows, the demand for money also grows, so the Fed has to increase the money supply to keep interest rates from rising. If the economy is in a recession, the demand for money falls, and the Fed has to contract the money supply to keep interest rates from falling. This approach leads to the wrong policy prescription—expanding the money supply during a boom eventually leads to inflation, and contracting the money supply during a recession makes the recession even worse.

WHICH INTEREST RATE DOES THE FED TARGET?

The Fed targets the federal funds rate. Remember the federal funds rate is the interest rate that banks charge each other for short-term loans. A bank that may be short of reserves might borrow from another bank that has excess reserves. The Fed has been targeting the federal funds rate since about 1965. At the close of the meetings of the FOMC, the Fed usually announces whether the federal funds rate target will be increased, decreased, or left alone as shown in Exhibit 16.8.

Monetary policy decisions may be enacted either through the money supply or through the interest rate. That is, if the Fed wants to pursue a contractionary monetary policy (a reduction in aggregate demand), this policy can take the form of a reduction in the money supply or a higher interest rate. If the Fed wants to pursue an expansionary monetary policy (an increase in aggregate demand), this policy can take the form of an increase in the money supply or a lower interest rate. So why is the interest rate used? First, many economists believe that the primary effects of monetary policy are felt through the interest rate. Second, the money supply is difficult to measure accurately. Third, as we mentioned earlier, changes in the demand for money may complicate money supply targets. Last, people are more familiar with changes in the interest rate than with changes in the money supply.

DOES THE FED INFLUENCE THE REAL INTEREST RATE IN THE SHORT RUN?

Most economists believe that in the short run the Fed can control the nominal interest rate and the real interest rate. Recall that the real interest rate is equal to the nominal interest rate minus the expected inflation rate. Therefore, a change in the nominal interest rate tends to change the real interest rate by the same amount, because the expected inflation rate is slow to change in the short run. That is, if the expected inflation rate does not change, the relationship between the nominal and real interest rates is a direct relationship: A 1 percent reduction in the nominal interest rate will generally lead to a 1 percent reduction in the real interest rate in the short run. However, for the long run—several years after the inflation rate has adjusted—the equilibrium real interest rate will be given by the intersection of the demand and supply of loanable funds curves.

EXHIBIT 16.8 Federal Funds Rate

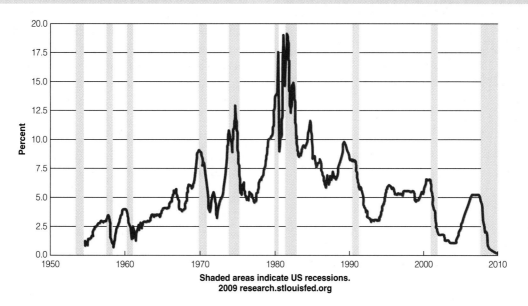

Shaded areas indicate US recessions.
2009 research.stlouisfed.org

SOURCES: Federal Reserve, *Federal Reserve Statistical Release*, Historical Data: Federal Funds (effective) Annual, Washington, D. C. March 26, 2010. Available at http://www.federalreserve.gov/releases/h15/data.htm (accessed March 27, 2010); National Bureau of Economic Research, Inc., Business Cycle Expansions and Contractions, U.S. Department of Commerce. Washington, D.C., December 1, 2008. Available at http://www.nber.org/cycles.html (accessed March 18, 2010).

SECTION CHECK 3

3.1 Rising incomes increase the demand for money and lead to a new, higher equilibrium interest rate, *ceteris paribus.*

3.2 When the Fed sells bonds to the private sector, bond purchasers take the money out of their checking accounts to pay for the bonds, and those banks' reserves are reduced by the size of the check. This reduction in bank reserves leads to a reduction in the money supply, which in turn leads to a higher interest rate and a reduction in aggregate demand, at least in the short run.

3.3 A change in the nominal interest rate tends to change the real interest rate by the same amount in the short run.

Ⓢ4 Expansionary and Contractionary Monetary Policy

Keep the following questions in mind as you read through this section. You'll find the answers in **Section Check 4**.

4.1 What is expansionary monetary policy?

4.2 What is contractionary monetary policy?

4.3 How does monetary policy impact real GDP and the price level?

Let's take a look at how the Fed might use its monetary policy to regulate economic growth.

EXPANSIONARY MONETARY POLICY IN A RECESSIONARY GAP

If the Fed engages in expansionary monetary policy to combat a recessionary gap, the increase in the money

EXHIBIT 16.9 Expansionary Monetary Policy in a Recessionary Gap

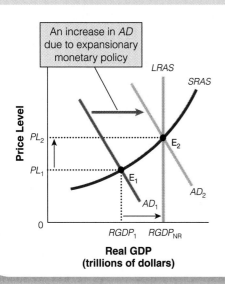

An increase in *AD* due to expansionary monetary policy

Real GDP (trillions of dollars)

supply will lower the interest rate. The lower interest rate reduces the cost of borrowing and the return to saving. Therefore, firms invest in new plants and equipment, while households increase their investment in housing at the lower interest rate. In short, when the Fed increases the money supply, interest rates fall, and the quantity demanded of goods and services increases at each and every price level. The aggregate demand curve shifts from AD_1 to AD_2, as seen in Exhibit 16.9. The result is greater RGDP growth at a higher price level at E_2. In this case, the Fed has eliminated the recession, and RGDP is equal to the potential level of output at $RGDP_{NR}$. During the recession of 2001, the Fed aggressively lowered the federal funds rate to stimulate aggregate demand when it was faced with a recessionary gap.

For example, in the first half of 2001, the Fed slashed interest rates to their lowest levels since August 1994. Between January 2001 and August 2001, the Fed cut the federal funds rate target by 3 percentage points, clearly demonstrating that it was concerned that the economy was dangerously close to falling into a recession. Then came the events of September 11 and the corporate scandals. By the end of the year, the federal funds rate, which began at 6.5 percent, was at 1.75 percent, the lowest it had been since 1961. With the slow recovery, the Fed pushed the rate down further, to 1.25 percent in November 2002. The Fed's actions were aimed at increasing consumer confidence, restoring stock market wealth, and stimulating investment. That is, the Fed's move was designed to increase aggregate demand in an effort to increase output and employment to long-run equilibrium at E_2.

CONTRACTIONARY MONETARY POLICY IN AN INFLATIONARY GAP

The Fed may engage in contractionary monetary policy if the economy faces an inflationary gap. Suppose the economy is at initial short-run equilibrium, E_1, in Exhibit 16.10. In order to combat inflation, suppose the Fed engages in an open market sale of bonds. This would lead to a decrease in the money supply, causing the interest rate to rise. The higher interest rate means that borrowing is more expensive, and the return to saving is higher. Consequently, firms find it more costly to invest in plants and equipment, and households find it more costly to finance new homes. In short, when the Fed decreases the money supply, it raises the interest rate and decreases the quantity of goods and services demanded at every price level. That is, the aggregate demand curve shifts leftward from AD_1 to AD_2 in Exhibit 16.10. The result is a lower RGDP and a lower price level, at E_2. The economy is now at $RGDP_{NR}$ where RGDP equals the potential level of output.

Corporate scandals and the September 11 terrorist attacks exacerbated the economic downturn of 2001. In its efforts to fight off a recession, the Fed cut rates from a high of 6.5 percent all the way down to 1.75 percent.

1400 Smith Street

EXHIBIT 16.10 Contractionary Monetary Policy in an Inflationary Gap

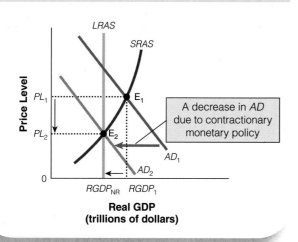

MONETARY POLICY IN THE OPEN ECONOMY

For simplicity, we have assumed that the global economy does not affect domestic monetary policy. This assumption is incorrect. Suppose the Fed decides to pursue an expansionary policy by buying bonds on the open market. As we have seen, when the Fed buys bonds on the open market, the immediate effect is that the money supply increases and interest rates fall. With lower domestic interest rates, some domestic investors will invest funds in foreign markets, exchanging dollars for foreign currency, which leads to a depreciation of the dollar (a decrease in the value of the dollar). The depreciation of the dollar makes the U.S. market more attractive to foreign buyers and foreign markets relatively less attractive to domestic buyers. That is, this shift means an increase in net exports—fewer imports and greater exports—and an increase in RGDP in the short run.

Similarly, the Fed may pursue a contractionary monetary policy by selling bonds on the open market. When the Fed sells bonds on the open market, the immediate effect is it reduces the money supply and causes interest rates to rise; foreign investors will convert their currencies to dollars to take advantage of the relatively higher interest rates. These purchases will lead to an appreciation of the dollar (an increase in the value of a currency), which will make U.S. goods and services relatively more expensive—foreigners will import less and domestic consumers will buy more exports. The result is a decrease in net exports and a reduction in RGDP in the short run.

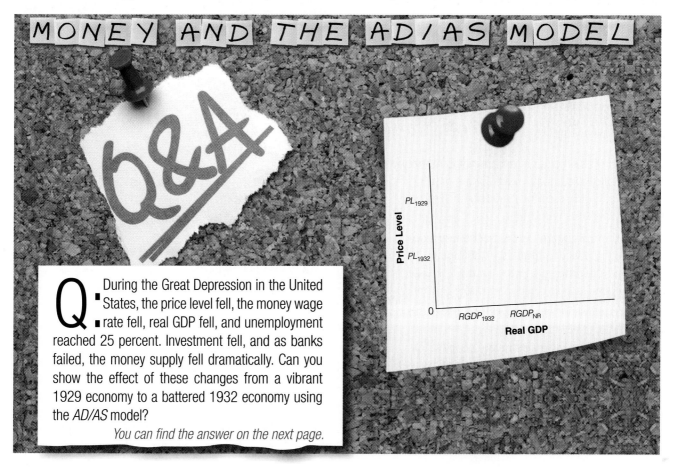

MONEY AND THE AD/AS MODEL

Q: During the Great Depression in the United States, the price level fell, the money wage rate fell, real GDP fell, and unemployment reached 25 percent. Investment fell, and as banks failed, the money supply fell dramatically. Can you show the effect of these changes from a vibrant 1929 economy to a battered 1932 economy using the AD/AS model?

You can find the answer on the next page.

A: The 1929 economy was at PL_{1929} and $RGDP_{NR}$, as you can see in the accompanying exhibit. The lack of consumer confidence coupled with the large reduction in the money supply, wealth lost in the stock market crash, and falling investment sent the aggregate demand curve reeling. As a result, the aggregate demand curve fell from AD_{1929} to AD_{1932}, real GDP fell to $RGDP_{1932}$, and the price level fell to PL_{1932}.

SECTION CHECK 4

4.1 The Fed engages in expansionary monetary policy to combat a recessionary gap. By increasing the money supply, the Fed can lower the interest rate.

4.2 The Fed engages in contractionary monetary policy to combat an inflationary gap. In order to combat inflation, the Fed engages in an open market sale of bonds, decreasing the money supply and raising the interest rate.

4.3 An expansionary monetary policy at full employment can temporarily increase real GDP, but in the long run, only the price level will rise.

⑤5 Money and Inflation

Keep the following questions in mind as you read through this section. You'll find the answers in Section Check 5.

5.1 What is the equation of exchange?

5.2 What is the velocity of money?

5.3 What is the quantity theory of money and prices?

For many centuries, scholars have known that there is a positive relationship between the money supply, the price level, the growth in the money supply, and the inflation rate. In the 1500s, there was a huge influx of gold and silver that flowed into Europe following the Spanish conquest in the New World. The influx of precious metals almost tripled the money supply of Europe.

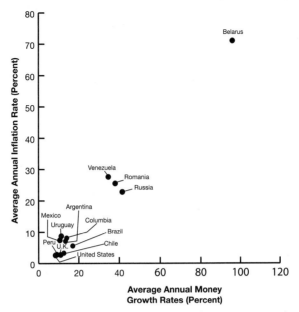

SOURCE: *International Financial Statistics*, International Monetary Fund, Washington, D.C., 2008, Volume LXI, pp. 51–53 and pp. 79–81.

Too many coins were chasing what goods were available, and prices rose steadily in the sixteenth century.

THE INFLATION RATE AND THE GROWTH IN THE MONEY SUPPLY

One of the major reasons that the control of the money supply is so important is that, in the long run, the amount of money in circulation and the overall price level are closely linked. It is virtually impossible for a country to have sustained inflation without a rapid growth in the money supply. The inflation rate tends to be greater in periods of rapid monetary expansion than in periods of slower growth in the money supply. In Exhibit 16.11, we see that international data supports the relationship between higher money growth and a higher inflation rate.

THE EQUATION OF EXCHANGE

In the early twentieth century, Yale economist Irving Fisher formalized the relationship between money and the price level with the equation of exchange. The equation of exchange (or quantity equation) can be written as:

$$M \times V = P \times Q$$

V represents the average number of times that each dollar is used in purchasing final goods or services in a one-year period.

where M is the money supply, however defined (usually M_1 or M_2), V is the velocity of money, P is the price level, and Q is real output (RGDP).

The **velocity of money** refers to its "turnover" rate, or the intensity with which money is used. Specifically, V represents the average number of times that each dollar is used in purchasing final goods or services in a one-year period. For example, a $20 bill may travel from you to the delicatessen owner, who passes it on to a doctor for the co-payment on medical services, who passes it on to a car dealership as part of a down payment for a new car. The faster money circulates, the higher the velocity. Velocity is defined as the nominal or current dollar value of output divided by the money supply, or:

$$V = Nominal\ GDP\ /\ M$$

Suppose we have a simple economy that only produces frozen yogurt. The economy produces 200 quarts of frozen yogurt per year. The frozen yogurt sells for $5 a quart and the quantity of money in the economy is $100. Plugging the numbers into our equation, we get:

$$V = Nominal\ GDP\ /\ M$$
$$= (P \times Q)\ /\ M$$
$$= (\$5 \times 200)\ /\ \$100 = 10$$

That is, the people in the economy spend $1,000 per year on frozen yogurt. If there is only $100 of money in the economy, each dollar must change hands on average 10 times per year. Thus, the velocity is 10.

velocity of money a measure of how frequently money is turned over

quantity theory of money and prices a theory of the connection between the money supply and the price level when the velocity of money is constant

The Quantity Theory of Money and Prices

If we make certain assumptions about the variables in the equation of exchange, we can clearly see the relationship between the money supply and the price level. This relationship is called the **quantity theory of money and prices**. If velocity (V) and real GDP (Q) both remain constant, then a 10 percent increase in the money supply will lead to a 10 percent increase in the price level—that is, the money supply and the price level change by the same proportion. We can then extend this equation to link the growth rates of these four variables. Using the *growth version of the quantity equation*, we can transform $M \times V = P \times Q$ into:

Growth rate of the money supply +
Growth rate of velocity = Growth rate of the price
level (inflation rate) + Growth rate of real output

This makes it easier to see the effects of the money supply on the inflation rate. Suppose money growth is 5 percent per year, the growth of real output is 3 percent per year, and velocity has not changed at all—its growth rate is 0 percent. What is the inflation rate? The growth rate of M (5 percent) + the growth rate of V (0 percent) = the growth rate of prices ___ + the growth rate of Q (3 percent). In this situation, the growth rate of prices (the inflation rate) is equal to 2 percent. We can also extend the analysis to predict the inflation rate when real GDP and velocity also vary. For example, if velocity grew at 1 percent annually rather than at zero percent in our example, the inflation rate would be 3 percent rather than 2 percent.

If velocity remains constant, then the growth rate of velocity (the percentage change from one year to the next) will be zero. Then we can simplify our equation once more:

Inflation rate = Growth rate of the money supply – Growth rate of real GDP

If this is the case, there are three possible scenarios:

1. If money supply grows at a faster rate than real GDP, then there will be inflation.

2. If money supply grows at a slower rate than real GDP, then there will be deflation.

3. If money supply grows at the same rate as real GDP, the price level will be stable.

Economists once expected they could treat the velocity of money as a given, because the determinants of velocity they focused on would change only very slowly. We now know that velocity is not constant, but often moves in a fairly predictable pattern. Historically, the velocity of money has been quite stable over a long period of time, particularly when using the M2 definition of money. Thus, the connection between money supply and the price level is still fairly predictable, especially during periods of high inflation.

If an increase in the money supply leads to inflation in the long run, why do countries allow the growth rate of their money supply to increase so rapidly? There are several possible reasons. For instance, due to war or political instability, countries' spending may exceed what they can raise through borrowing from the public or taxation, so they create more money to pay their bills. The more money they create, the larger amount of inflation they will experience.

Hyperinflation

The relationship between the growth rate of the money supply and the inflation rate is particularly strong when there is very rapid inflation, called hyperinflation. One of the most famous cases of hyperinflation was in Germany in the 1920s—inflation rose to roughly 300 percent *per month* for over a year. The German government had incurred large amounts of debt as a result of World War I and could not raise enough money to pay its expenses, so it printed huge amounts of money. The inflation rate increased so quickly that store owners would change their prices in the middle of the day, firms had to pay workers several times a week, and

During the 1920s, hyperinflation in Germany got so bad that workers, such as those pictured, used laundry baskets to carry out their pay packets.

© POPPERFOTO/GETTY IMAGES

many resorted to barter. Recently, Zimbabwe, Brazil, Argentina, and Russia have all experienced hyperinflation. The cause of hyperinflation is simply excessive money growth.

SECTION CHECK 5

5.1 The equation of exchange is expressed as $M \times V = P \times Q$, where M is the money supply, V is the velocity of money, P is the average level of prices of final goods and services, and Q is real GDP in a given year.

5.2 The velocity of money (V) represents the average number of times that a dollar is used in purchasing final goods or services in a one-year period.

5.3 The equation of exchange is a particularly useful tool when analyzing the effects of a change in the money supply on the price level or inflation rate in the aggregate economy.

Chapter 16: Self-Review

Now that you're finished reading the chapter, review the questions below. You can write your answers in the space provided, then go online to see the answers at www.cengagebrain.com.

S1—THE FEDERAL RESERVE SYSTEM

1. What are the six primary functions of a central bank?
   1)
   2)
   3)
   4)
   5)
   6)

S2—HOW DOES THE FEDERAL RESERVE CHANGE THE MONEY SUPPLY?

2. True or False: An open market sale of government securities (bonds) would be a tactic of expansionary monetary policy.

3. True or False: An increase in the discount rate would be a tactic of contractionary policy.

4. Fill-in-the-Blank: The money supply _____ if the Fed made an open market purchase of government bonds, *ceteris paribus*.

S3—MONEY, INTEREST RATES, AND AGGREGATE DEMAND

5. What are the three primary reasons for the demand for money?

6. Fill-in-the-Blank: An _____ relationship exists between the interest rate and the price of bonds.

7. True or False: The Fed signals its intended monetary policy through the federal funds rate target it sets.

8. True or False: If the earnings available on other financial assets rose, you would want to hold less money.

S4—EXPANSIONARY AND CONTRACTIONARY MONETARY POLICY

9. In which direction would the money supply change if:
   a. the Fed raised the reserve requirement?
   b. the Fed conducted an open market sale of government bonds?
   c. the Fed raised the discount rate?
   d. the Fed conducted an open market sale of government bonds and raised the discount rate?
   e. the Fed conducted an open market purchase of government bonds and raised reserve requirements?

S5—MONEY AND INFLATION

10. If nominal GDP is $200 billion and the money supply is $50 billion, what must velocity be?

11. True or False: If the money supply increases and velocity does not change, nominal GDP will increase.

12. Fill-in-the-Blank: The equation of exchange is _____.

13. True or False: In the equation of exchange, if *V* doubled, nominal GDP would triple.

The passing of the Reinvestment

and Recovery Act of 2009 was not without controversy. In an effort to bolster the economy in the face of the financial crisis, the $787-billion bill offered a wide range of provisions, including tax cuts, spending on welfare programs, and various infrastructure projects. Many questions arose, however, at the time of its passing: How much money should be spent, and on what? When will these initiatives come into effect? Should the government even be getting involved? Beyond the bill itself, further questions arose as to how the fiscal policy of the government fit in with the monetary policy of the Fed. As you can see, fiscal and monetary policy are not easy to implement. We'll discuss many of these issues in this chapter.

17

Issues in Macroeconomic Theory and Policy

Sections in Chapter 17

We begin this chapter by discussing the problems that exist in implementing fiscal and monetary policy. We discuss the problems with crowding out, time lags, imperfect information, and coordination. Can human behavior counteract government policy? What if the expansionary policy is anticipated? What if it is unanticipated? Or what if the anticipated expansionary policy is greater than the actual policy? Should policy makers even use expansionary and contractionary monetary and fiscal policies? Are they effective? Or should policy makers allow the economy to self-correct? What are the policy difficulties of dealing with supply shocks? Should the Fed use inflation targeting? And if so, should they target inflation at zero? Macroeconomists do not completely agree on the preceding questions. These are topics we will discuss throughout this chapter. In the final section, we will discuss the financial crisis of 2007–2009.

Ⓢ1 Problems in Implementing Fiscal and Monetary Policy

Keep the following questions in mind as you read through this section. You'll find the answers in **Section Check 1**.

1.1 What problems exist in implementing fiscal policy?

1.2 What problems exist in implementing monetary policy?

1.3 What problems exist in coordinating monetary and fiscal policies?

In this section we'll examine the problems that policy makers encounter when implementing fiscal and monetary policy. First, we'll look at fiscal policy and monetary policy. Then we'll discuss coordination issues and step back to get a look at the overall difficulties of macroeconomic policymaking.

crowding-out effect
theory that government borrowing drives up the interest rate, lowering consumption by households and investment spending by firms

POSSIBLE OBSTACLES TO EFFECTIVE FISCAL POLICY

Let's begin our discussion with the problems that fiscal policy makers must consider.

The Crowding-Out Effect

The multiplier effect of an increase in government purchases implies that the increase in aggregate demand will tend to be greater than the initial fiscal stimulus, other things being equal. However, because all other things will not tend to stay equal in this case, the multiplier effect may not hold true. For example, when an increase in government purchases stimulates aggregate demand, it also drives up the interest rate. In particular, when the government borrows money to finance the deficit, it increases the overall demand for money in the money market. The increase in the demand for money increases the price paid for borrowing money—the interest rate. As a result of the higher interest rate, consumers may decide against buying a car, a home, or other interest-sensitive goods, and businesses may cancel or scale back plans to expand or buy new capital equipment. In short, the higher interest rate will choke off private spending on goods and services; and, as a result, the impact of the increase in government purchases may

© MINDEN PICTURES/MASTERFILE

With the crowding-out effect, the increase in government spending can drive away private spending on goods and services.

be smaller than first assumed. Economists call this the **crowding-out effect**.

In Exhibit 17.1, suppose government purchases initially increased by $10 billion. This change by itself would shift aggregate demand to the right by $10 billion times the multiplier, from AD_1 to AD_2. However, when the government borrows in the money market to pay for increases in government purchases, the interest rate increases. The higher interest rate crowds out investment spending, causing the aggregate demand curve to shift left, from AD_2 to AD_3. Because both these processes are taking place at the same time, the net effect is an increase in aggregate demand from AD_1 to AD_3 rather than to AD_2.

Critics of the Crowding-Out Effect Critics of the crowding-out effect argue that the increase in government spending, particularly if the economy is in a severe recession, may actually improve consumer and business expectations and encourage private investment spending. It is also possible for the monetary authorities to increase the money supply in order to offset the higher interest rate, resulting from the crowding-out effect.

The Crowding-Out Effect in the Open Economy Another form of crowding out can take place in international markets. For example, say the government increases spending, which leads to an increase in the demand for money to pay for the spending and drives up the interest rate (assuming the money supply is unchanged). The higher U.S. interest rate will attract funds from abroad. To invest in the U.S. economy, foreigners will first have to convert their currencies into

EXHIBIT 17.1 The Crowding-Out Effect

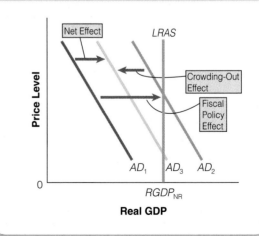

dollars. The increase in the demand for dollars relative to other currencies will cause the dollar to appreciate in value, making foreign imports relatively cheaper in the United States and U.S. exports relatively more expensive in other countries. This change will cause net exports $(X - M)$ to fall for two reasons. One, because of the higher relative price of the dollar, foreign imports will become cheaper for those in the United States, and imports will increase. Two, because of the higher relative price of the dollar, U.S.-made goods will become more expensive to foreigners, and exports will decrease. The increase in imports and the decrease in exports will cause a reduction in net exports and a fall in aggregate demand. The net effect will be that fiscal policy will have a smaller effect on aggregate demand than it would otherwise.

Time Lags in Fiscal Policy Implementation

It is important to recognize that in a democratic country, fiscal policy is implemented through the political process, and that process takes time. Often, the lag between the time that a fiscal response is desired, the time an appropriate policy is implemented, and the time its effects are felt is considerable. Sometimes a fiscal policy designed to deal with a contracting economy may actually take effect during a period of economic expansion, or vice versa, resulting in a stabilization policy that actually destabilizes the economy.

The Recognition Lag Government tax or spending changes require both congressional and presidential approval. Suppose the economy is beginning a downturn. It may take two or three months before enough data are gathered to indicate the actual presence of a downturn. This time span is called the *recognition lag*. Sometimes a future downturn can be forecast through econometric models or by looking at the index of leading indicators, but usually decision makers are hesitant to plan policy on the basis of forecasts that are not always accurate.

The Implementation Lag At some point, however, policy makers may decide that some policy change is necessary. At this point, experts are consulted, and congressional committees hold hearings and listen to testimony on possible policy approaches. During the consultation phase, many decisions have to be made. If, for example, a tax cut is recommended, what form should the cut take, and how large should it be? Across-the-board income tax reductions? Reductions in corporate taxes? More generous exemptions and deductions

from the income tax (e.g., for child care, casualty losses, education of children)? In other words, who should get the benefits of lower taxes? Likewise, if the decision is made to increase government expenditures, which programs should be expanded or initiated, and by how much? Because these questions have profound political consequences, reaching decisions is seldom easy and usually involves substantial compromise and a great deal of time.

Finally, once the House and Senate have completed their separate deliberations and have arrived at a final version of the fiscal policy bill, it is presented to Congress for approval. After congressional approval is secured, the bill then goes to the president for approval or veto. These steps are all part of what is called the *implementation lag*.

From 1990 to 1991, the actual output of the economy was less than the potential output of the economy—a recessionary gap. Because automatic stabilizers resulted in lower taxes and larger transfer payments, consumption did not fall as far as it might have.

However, before President Clinton began his term in 1993, he believed that more was needed, so he put together a stimulus package of additional government spending and tax cuts. But by the time the bill reached the floor of Congress, the recession was over, illustrating how difficult it is to time fiscal stimulus. When the economy went into recession in March of 2001, it was not until a year later that the stimulus package was signed into law. Another example is when President John F. Kennedy thought the economy was operating below its potential in 1962; Congress finally passed a tax cut in 1964.

The Impact Lag Even after legislation is signed into law, it takes time to bring about the actual fiscal stimulus desired. If the legislation provides for a reduction in withholding taxes, for example, it might take a few months before the changes show up in workers' paychecks. With respect to changes in government purchases, the delay is usually much longer. If the government increases spending for public works projects such as sewer systems, new highways, or urban renewal, it takes time to draw up plans and get permissions, to advertise for bids from contractors, to get contracts, and then to begin work. Further delays might occur because of government regulations. For example, an environmental impact statement must be completed before most public works projects can begin, a process that often takes many months or even years, called the *impact lag*.

PROBLEMS IN CONDUCTING MONETARY POLICY

The lag problem inherent in adopting fiscal policy changes is less acute for monetary policy, largely because the decisions are not slowed by the same budgetary process. That is, the implementation lag is longer for fiscal policy. The FOMC of the Federal Reserve, for example, can act quickly (in emergencies almost instantly, by conference call) and even secretly to buy or sell government bonds, the key day-to-day operating tool of monetary policy. However, the length and variability of the lag before its effects on output and employment are felt are still significant, and the time before the full price-level effects are felt is even longer and more variable. According to the Federal Reserve Bank of San Francisco, the major effects of a change in policy on growth in the overall production of goods and services usually are felt within three months to two years; the effects on inflation tend to involve even longer lags, one to three years or more.

How Do Commercial Banks Implement the Fed's Monetary Policies?

One limitation of monetary policy is that it ultimately must be carried out through the commercial banking system. The central bank (the Federal Reserve System in the United States) can change the environment in which banks act, but the banks themselves must take the steps necessary to increase or decrease the money supply. Usually, when the Fed is trying to constrain monetary expansion, it has no difficulty in getting banks to make appropriate responses. Banks must meet their reserve requirements; and if the Fed raises bank reserve requirements, sells bonds, and/or raises the discount rate, banks must obtain the necessary cash or reserve deposits at the Fed to meet their reserve requirements. In response, banks will call in loans that are due for collection, sell secondary reserves, and so on in order to obtain the necessary reserves. In the process of collecting loans, the banks decrease the money supply.

When the Federal Reserve wants to induce monetary expansion, however, it can provide banks with excess reserves (e.g., by lowering reserve requirements or buying government bonds), but it cannot force the banks to make loans, thereby creating new money. Ordinarily, of course, banks want to convert their excess reserves to interest-earning income by making loans. But in a deep recession or depression, banks might be hesitant to make enough loans to put all those reserves to work,

fearing that they will not be repaid. Their pessimism might lead them to perceive that the risks of making loans to many normally creditworthy borrowers outweigh any potential interest earnings (particularly at the low real interest rates that are characteristic of depressed times). Some have argued that banks maintaining excess reserves rather than loaning them out was, in fact, one of the monetary policy problems that arose in the Great Depression.

Banks that Are Not Part of the Federal Reserve System and Policy Implementation

A second problem with monetary policy relates to the fact that the Fed can control deposit expansion at member banks, but it has no control over global and nonbank institutions that also issue credit (loan money) but are not subject to reserve requirement limitations; examples are pension funds and insurance companies. Therefore, while the Fed may be able to predict the impact of its monetary policies on loans issued by member banks, global and nonbanking institutions can alter the impact of monetary policies adopted by the Fed. Hence, the real question is how precisely the Fed can control the short-run real interest rates and the money supply through its monetary policy instruments.

FISCAL AND MONETARY COORDINATION PROBLEMS

Another problem that may arise out of existing institutional policy-making arrangements is the coordination of fiscal and monetary policy. Congress and the president make fiscal policy decisions, whereas monetary policy making is in the hands of the Federal Reserve System. A macroeconomic problem arises if the federal government's fiscal decision makers differ with the Fed's monetary decision makers on policy objectives or targets. For example, the Fed may be more concerned about keeping inflation low, while fiscal policy makers may be more concerned about keeping unemployment low.

Alleviating Coordination Problems

In recognition of potential macroeconomic policy coordination problems, the chairman of the Federal Reserve Board has participated for several years in meetings with top economic advisers of the president. An attempt is made in these meetings to reach a consensus on the appropriate policy responses, both monetary and fiscal. Still, they sometimes disagree, and the Fed occasionally works to partly offset or even

> **The government and the Federal Reserve must coordinate their policy decisions if they want to be effective.**

neutralize the effects of fiscal policies that it views as inappropriate. Some people believe that monetary policy should be more directly controlled by the president and Congress, so that all macroeconomic policy will be determined more directly by the political process. Also, it is argued that such a move would enhance coordination considerably. Others, however, argue that it is dangerous to turn over control of the nation's money supply to politicians, rather than allowing decisions to be made by technically competent administrators who are more focused on price stability and more insulated from political pressures applied by the public and special interest groups.

Timing Is Critical

The timing of fiscal policy and monetary policy is crucial. Because of the significant lags before the fiscal and monetary policy has its impact, the increase in aggregate demand may occur at the wrong time. For example, imagine that we are initially at AD_1 in Exhibit 17.2. The economy is currently suffering from low levels of output and high rates of unemployment. In response, policy makers decide to increase government purchases and implement a tax cut, or alternatively they could have increased the money supply. But from the time when the policy makers recognize the problem to the time when the policies have a chance to work themselves through the economy, business and consumer confidence both increase, shifting the aggregate demand curve rightward from AD_1 to AD_2—increasing RGDP and employment. When the fiscal policy takes hold, the policies will have the undesired effect of causing inflation, with little permanent effect on output and employment. This effect may be seen in Exhibit 17.2, as the aggregate demand curve shifts from AD_2 to AD_3. At E_3, input owners will require higher input prices, shifting the $SRAS$ leftward from $SRAS_1$ to $SRAS_2$ and to the new long-run equilibrium at E_4.

Imperfect Information

In addition, the problem of imperfect information enters the picture. For example, in order to know how much to stimulate the economy, policy makers must know the size of the multiplier and by how much RGDP should increase. But some economists disagree on the natural rate of real output ($RGDP_{NR}$), and it may be difficult to know where RGDP is at any given moment in time; government estimates are approximations and are often corrected at a later period. The government must also know the exact MPC. If the estimate is too low, the multiplier will be less than expected and the stimulus will be too small. If the estimate of MPC is too high, the multiplier will be more than expected and the stimulus will be too large.

OVERALL PROBLEMS WITH MONETARY AND FISCAL POLICY

Much of macroeconomic policy in this country is driven by the idea that the federal government can counteract economic fluctuations: stimulating the economy (with increased government spending, tax cuts, and easy money) when it is weak and restraining it when it is overheating. However, policy makers must adopt the right policies in the right amounts at the right time for such "stabilization" to do more good than harm; and to do

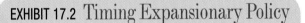

EXHIBIT 17.2 Timing Expansionary Policy

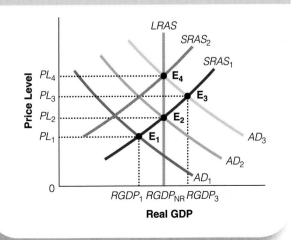

© MASTERFILE

Some economists believe that fine-tuning the economy is like driving a car with an unpredictable steering lag on a winding road, or driving while looking only through the sideview mirror.

this, government policy makers need far more accurate and timely information than experts can give them.

First, economists must know not only which way the economy is heading but also how rapidly it is changing. Even the most current data on key variables such as employment, growth, productivity, and so on, reflect conditions in the past, not the present. The unvarnished truth is that in our incredibly complicated world, no one knows exactly what the economy will do, no matter how sophisticated the econometric models used; our models are only approximations. It has often been said, and not completely in jest, that the purpose of economic forecasting is to make astrology look respectable.

But let's assume that economists can outperform astrologers at forecasting. Indeed, let's be completely unrealistic and assume that economists can provide completely accurate economic forecasts of what will happen if macroeconomic policies are unchanged. Even then, they cannot be certain of how best to promote stable economic growth.

If economists knew, for example, that the economy was going to dip into another recession in six months, they would then need to know exactly how much each possible policy would spur activity to keep the economy stable. But such precision is unattainable, given the complexity of economic forecasting. Furthermore, despite assurances to the contrary, economists aren't always certain what effect a policy will have on the economy. Will an increase in government purchases quicken economic growth? It is widely assumed so; but how much? Moreover, increasing government purchases increases the budget deficit, which could send a frightening signal to the bond markets. The result might be to drive up interest rates and choke off economic activity. Thus, even when policymakers know in which

direction to nudge the economy, they cannot be sure which policy levers to pull, or how hard to pull them, in order to fine-tune the economy to stable economic growth.

But let's further assume that policy makers know when the economy will need a boost and which policy will provide the right boost. A third crucial consideration is how long it will take a policy before it has its effect on the economy. The trouble is that, even when increased government purchases or an expansionary monetary policy does give the economy a boost, no one knows precisely how long it will take to do so. The boost may come quickly or it may come many months (even years) in the future, when it may add inflationary pressures to an economy already overheating rather than help the economy to recover from a recession.

Macroeconomic policymaking is rather like driving down a twisting road in a car with an unpredictable lag and degree of response in the steering mechanism. If you turn the wheel to the right; the car will eventually veer to the right, but you don't know exactly when or how much. In short, severe practical difficulties are inherent in trying to fine-tune the economy. Even the best forecasting models and methods are far from perfect. Economists are not exactly sure where the economy is or where or how fast it is going, making it difficult to prescribe an effective policy. Even if we do know where the economy is headed, we cannot be sure how large a policy's effect will be or when it will take effect.

SECTION CHECK 1

1.1 Problems with implementing fiscal policy include the crowding-out effect and time lags, such as the recognition, implementation, and impact lags.

1.2 Both monetary and fiscal policy face difficult forecasting and lag problems; however, the Fed can take action much more quickly. But its effectiveness depends largely on the reaction of the private banking system to its policy changes, and its intended effects can be offset by global and nonbank financial institutions, over which the Fed lacks jurisdiction.

1.3 In the United States, monetary and fiscal policy are carried out by different decision makers, thus requiring cooperation and coordination for effective policy implementation.

⑤2 Rational Expectations and Real Business Cycles

Keep the following questions in mind as you read through this section. You'll find the answers in Section Check 2.

2.1 What is the rational expectations theory?

2.2 What do critics say about the rational expectations theory?

2.3 What is the real business cycle theory?

2.4 What do the critics say about the real business cycle theory?

Can human behavior counteract government policy? Is it possible that people can anticipate the plans of policy makers and alter their behavior quickly to neutralize the intended impact of government action? For example, if workers see that the government is allowing the money supply to expand rapidly, they may quickly demand higher money wages to offset the anticipated inflation. In the extreme form, if people could instantly recognize and respond to government policy changes, it might be impossible to alter real output or unemployment levels through policy actions, because government policy makers could no longer surprise households and firms. An increasing number of economists believe that there is at least some truth to this point of view. At a minimum, most economists accept the notion that real output and the unemployment rate cannot be altered with the ease that was earlier believed; some believe that the unemployment rate can seldom be influenced by fiscal and monetary policies.

THE RATIONAL EXPECTATIONS THEORY

The relatively new extension of economic theory that leads to this rather pessimistic conclusion regarding macroeconomic policy's ability to achieve our economic goals is called the **theory of rational expectations**. The notion that expectations or anticipations of future events are relevant to economic theory is not new; for decades, economists have incorporated expectations into models analyzing many forms of economic behavior. Only in the recent past, however, has a theory evolved that tries to incorporate expectations as a central factor in the analysis of the entire economy.

The interest in rational expectations has grown rapidly in the last decade. Acknowledged pioneers in the development of the theory include Professor Robert Lucas of the University of Chicago and Professor Thomas Sargent of the University of Minnesota. In 1995, Professor Lucas won the Nobel Prize for his work in rational expectations.

Rational expectations economists believe that wages and prices are flexible and that households and firms incorporate the likely consequences of government policy changes quickly into their expectations. In addition, rational expectations economists believe that the economy is inherently stable after macroeconomic shocks and that tinkering with fiscal and monetary policy cannot have the desired effect unless households and firms are caught "off guard" (and catching them off guard gets harder the more you try to do it).

> **theory of rational expectations** belief that workers and consumers incorporate the likely consequences of government policy changes into their expectations by quickly adjusting wages and prices

Rational Expectations and the Consequences of Government Macroeconomic Policies

Rational expectations theory, then, suggests that government economic policies designed to alter aggregate demand to meet macroeconomic goals are of limited effectiveness. When policy targets become public, it is argued, people will alter their own behavior from what it would otherwise have been to maximize their own utility, and in so doing, they largely negate the intended impact of policy changes. If government policy seems tilted toward permitting more inflation to try to reduce unemployment, people start spending their money faster than before, become more adamant in their demands for wages and other input prices, and so on. In the process of quickly altering their behavior to reflect the likely consequences of policy changes, they make it more difficult (costly) for government authorities to meet their macroeconomic objectives. Rather than fooling people into changing real wages, and therefore unemployment, with inflation "surprises," changes in inflation are quickly reflected into expectations with little or no effect on unemployment or real output even in the short run. As a consequence, policies intended to reduce unemployment through stimulating aggregate demand will often fail to have the intended effect. Fiscal and monetary policy, according to this view, will work only if the people are caught off guard or are fooled by policies and thus do not modify their behavior in a way that reduces policy effectiveness.

Anticipation of an Expansionary Monetary Policy

Consider the case in which an increase in aggregate demand is a result of an expansionary monetary policy. This increase is reflected in Exhibit 17.3 in the shift from AD_1 to AD_2. Because of the predictable inflationary consequences of that expansionary policy, prices immediately adjust to a new level at PL_2. Consumers, producers, workers, and lenders who *anticipated* the effects of the expansionary policy simply build the higher inflation rates into their product prices, wages, and interest rates. That is, households and firms realize that expansionary monetary policy can cause inflation if the economy is working close to capacity. Consequently, in an effort to protect themselves from the higher anticipated inflation, workers ask for higher wages, suppliers increase input prices, and producers raise their product prices. Because wages, prices, and interest rates are assumed to be flexible, the adjustments take place immediately. This increase in input costs for wages, interest, and raw materials causes the aggregate supply curve to shift up or leftward, shown as the movement from $SRAS_1$ to $SRAS_2$ in Exhibit 17.3. So the desired policy effect of greater real output and reduced unemployment from a shift in the aggregate demand curve is offset by an upward or leftward shift in the aggregate supply curve caused by an increase in input costs.

Unanticipated Expansionary Policy

Again, consider the case of an increase in aggregate demand that results from an expansionary monetary policy. However, this time it is *unanticipated*. The increase in the money supply is reflected in Exhibit 17.4 in the shift from AD_1 to AD_2. This unanticipated change in monetary policy stimulates output and employment in the short run, as the equilibrium moves from point A to point B. At the new short-run equilibrium, the output is at $RGDP_2$ and the price level is at PL_2. This output is beyond $RGDP_{NR}$, so it is not sustainable in the long run. Because it is unanticipated, workers and other input owners are expecting the price level to remain at PL_1, rather than PL_2. However, when input owners eventually realize that the actual price level has changed, they will require higher input prices, shifting the $SRAS$ from $SRAS_1$ to $SRAS_2$. At point C, we see that output has returned to $RGDP_{NR}$ but at a higher price level, PL_3.

Therefore, when the expansionary policy is unanticipated, it leads to a short-run expansion in output and employment. But in the long run, the only impact of the change in monetary policy is a higher price level—inflation. In short, when the change is correctly anticipated, expansionary monetary (or fiscal) policy does not result in a change in real output. However, if the expansionary monetary (fiscal) policy is unanticipated, the result is a short-run increase in RGDP and employment, but in the long run, it just means a higher price level.

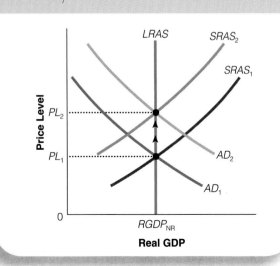

EXHIBIT 17.3 Rational Expectations and the *AD/AS* Model

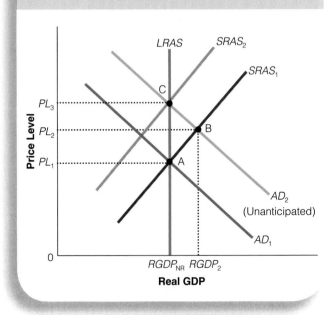

EXHIBIT 17.4 An Expansionary Policy that Is Unanticipated

In fact, the only way that monetary or fiscal policy can change output in the rational expectations model is with a surprise—an unanticipated change. For example, on April 18, 2001, between regularly scheduled meetings of the Federal Open Market Committee, the Fed surprised financial markets with an aggressive half-point cut in the interest rate. The Fed was trying to boost consumer confidence and impact falling stock market wealth. The surprise reduction in the interest rate sent the stock market soaring as the Dow posted one of its largest single-day point gains, and the NASDAQ had its fourth largest percentage gain. Former Fed Chairman Greenspan hoped that this move would shift the AD curve rightward, leading to higher levels of output.

When an Anticipated Expansionary Policy Change Is Less than the Actual Policy Change

In the context of the rational expectations model (wages and prices are flexible), suppose people are expecting a large increase in the money supply as a result of expansionary monetary policy. Then, the *anticipated* price level increases from PL_1 to PL_3 when the anticipated aggregate demand increases from AD_1 to AD_3, as seen in Exhibit 17.5. If people anticipate the new price level PL_3, wages and other input prices adjust quickly, and the $SRAS$ shifts leftward from $SRAS_1$ to $SRAS_2$. But what if the increase in the money supply ends up being

less than people anticipated? Say the *actual* increase in the money supply only shifts AD from AD_1 to AD_2. The economy moves from point A to point B rather than to point C as many had expected, which leads to a higher price level but a lower level of RGDP—a recession.

That is, a policy designed to increase output may actually reduce output if prices and wages are flexible and the expansionary effect is less than people anticipated.

Critics of Rational Expectations Theory

Of course, rational expectations theory does have its critics. Critics want to know whether households and firms are completely informed about the impact that, say, an increase in money supply will have on the economy. In general, all citizens will not be completely informed, but key players such as corporations, financial institutions, and labor organizations may well be informed about the impact of these policy changes. But other problems arise. For example, are wages and other input prices really that flexible? That is, even if decision makers could anticipate the eventual effect of policy changes on prices, those prices may still be slow to adapt (e.g., what if you had just signed a three-year labor or supply contract when the new policy was implemented?).

Most economists reject the extreme rational expectations model of complete wage and price flexibility. In fact, most economists still believe a short-run trade-off between inflation and unemployment results because some input prices are slow to adjust to changes in the price level. However, in the long run, the expected inflation rate adjusts to changes in the actual inflation rate at the natural rate of unemployment, $RGDP_{NR}$.

New Keynesians and Rational Expectations

Recall that in the Keynesian model, wages and prices are assumed to be inflexible. For example, workers who work under contracts that fix their wages for several years may be aware of price increases, but cannot renegotiate their labor contracts. The same may be true for other input suppliers. That is, firms may have negotiated fixed-price contracts with their suppliers for substantial periods of time.

Suppose that many people anticipate an increase in aggregate demand from AD_1 to AD_2 in Exhibit 17.6 on the next page. In the rational expectations model, where wages and prices

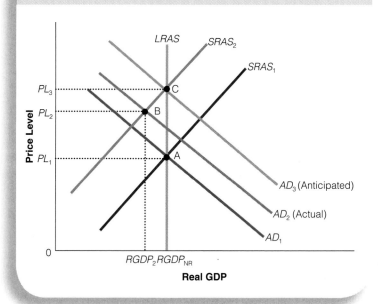

EXHIBIT 17.5 An Actual Expansionary Policy that Is Less than the Anticipated Policy

are completely flexible, that means that SRAS will quickly move from $SRAS_1$ to $SRAS_3$ when AD_1 moves to AD_2, so RGDP does not change.

However, if some wages and other input supply prices are fixed, when aggregate demand shifts from AD_1 to AD_2, then the $SRAS$ curve does not shift from $SRAS_1$ to $SRAS_3$. It may shift from $SRAS_1$ to $SRAS_2$ instead, leading to an increase in real aggregate output to $RGDP_2$ in the short run.

THE REAL BUSINESS CYCLE THEORY

The **real business cycle theory** shares some of the same assumptions as the rational expectations theory: Households and firms form their expectations rationally, and wages and prices adjust quickly. However, instead of unexpected changes in the money supply causing fluctuations in real GDP, the real business cycle theorists believe that technological changes lead to changes in the growth rate of productivity. In short, they believe that positive and negative productivity shocks are the cause of the business cycle. That is, these economists believe real shocks such as new technology (new products or production methods), resource prices (such as oil), changes in government regulation, unusually good or bad weather, international disturbances, or any other factor that can change productivity can cause fluctuations in the economy. In short, negative shocks cause recessions, and positive shocks cause expansions.

For example, real business cycle theorists believe that significant changes in technology can lead to stronger productivity growth and therefore greater economic expansion. For example, productivity (output per worker) could fall as a result of large increases in oil prices, similar to what occurred in the 1970s.

With a negative productivity shock, the marginal productivity of labor falls, leading to a fall in real wages and a subsequent reduction in the quantity of labor supplied as people choose to work less. Lower profit expectations cause firms to cut back on new capital purchases (new or remodeled plants and equipment) and lay off workers. In short, several quarters of below-average productivity output lead to declines in investment and average hours worked as well as an economy that finds itself in a recession. This event may have been the case in the 2001 recession.

Of course, the reverse could happen after large, and perhaps unexpected, productivity improvements. This scenario characterized the second half of the 1990s and resulted in an increase in the marginal productivity of labor, higher real wages, and people choosing to work more. In addition, firms with expectations of higher profits will invest in new capital and equipment. Together, these factors will lead to an increase in output consumption and investment—an economic expansion.

In the real business cycle theory, it is the potential output that fluctuates (the *LRAS*); not the output deviating from potential output—as is the case with recessionary or inflationary gaps. According to real business cycle theorists, prices and wages are sufficiently flexible that they adjust quickly. Because the economy is always operating close to full employment, the Fed just needs to keep an eye on inflation and intervention should be unnecessary.

The empirical evidence shows a strong correlation between declining productivity and the business cycle. However, some economists argue that the causality could go in the opposite direction—the recession causes the declining productivity. Other critics argue that the model assumes that wages and prices are completely flexible, a claim that is at odds with the facts. And others believe that technology shocks are incapable of explaining *all* of the swings in productivity; they claim that some of the changes must come from aggregate demand. However, the real business cycle theorists do force economists to think more about the supply side.

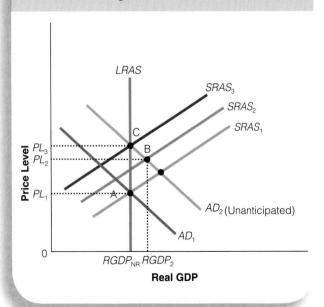

EXHIBIT 17.6 New Keynesians and Rational Expectations

2.1 Rational expectations economists believe that wages and prices are flexible and thus should be left alone. They also believe that households and firms form rational expectations that essentially negate the desired effect of a policy change.

2.2 Critics of rational expectations theory question whether wages and prices are flexible. They also believe that most people are not truly informed about the effects of policy changes and therefore won't adjust their behavior.

2.3 Real business cycle theorists believe that technological change leads to changes in the growth of productivity and that positive and negative productivity shocks are the cause of the business cycle.

2.4 Some critics argue that the recession causes declines in productivity, not the other way around. Real business cycle theory also assumes wage and price flexibility, which critics question. Other critics believe that technology shocks are incapable of explaining *all* of the swings in productivity.

⑤3 Controversies in Macroeconomic Policy

Keep the following questions in mind as you read through this section. You'll find the answers in Section Check 3.

3.1 Are fiscal and monetary policies effective?

3.2 Should central banks target inflation?

3.3 Could indexing reduce the costs of inflation?

Economies tend to fluctuate. Consumer or business pessimism leads to a reduction in aggregate demand.

As aggregate demand falls, so does output and employment. The rising unemployment and the fall in income cause additional damage to the economy. The economy is now operating to the left of the *LRAS* (or inside its production possibilities curve); resources are not being used efficiently when actual output is less than potential output. Many economists believe that in the short run, policy makers have the ability to alter aggregate demand. If the aggregate demand is insufficient, policy makers can stimulate aggregate demand by increasing government spending, cutting taxes, and increasing the growth rate of the money supply. If aggregate demand is excessive, policy makers can reduce aggregate demand by decreasing government spending, increasing taxes, and reducing the growth rate of the money supply.

These macroeconomists are called *activists*, and they believe that in the short run, discretionary monetary and fiscal policy can stimulate the economy that is in a recessionary gap or dampen the economy that is in an inflationary boom with aggregate demand management. However, other economists believe that aggregate demand stimulus cannot *keep* the rate of unemployment below the natural rate. Most economists accept the basic notion of the natural rate hypothesis that suggests the unemployment rate will be close to the natural rate in the long run. Other economists, *rational expectations theorists*, believe that government economic policies designed to alter aggregate demand are not all that effective because households and firms form expectations to economic policy causing prices and wages to adjust quickly, leaving the output roughly the same but at a higher price level. To these economists, monetary and fiscal policy will only work if it comes as a surprise to the public.

The *real business cycle theorists* believe that economic fluctuations are the result of external shocks to the economy. The shocks change productivity, which shifts the *LRAS*. The real business cycle theorist, like economists of the new classical school (rational expectations), believes that prices and wages are flexible and that the market adjusts quickly and restores full employment at the new level of output. That is, fiscal or monetary policies are not needed except to keep inflation in check.

However, most economists do not accept the notion that households and firms have rational expectations and that wages and prices adjust quickly because of wage and other input contracts. Even if households and firms formed rational expectations, if prices and wages adjusted slowly, expansionary monetary policy could lead to a lower unemployment level.

Most macroeconomists believe both that monetary and fiscal policy can shift the aggregate demand and that the intervention can be counterproductive. Recall our discussion in the previous chapter about the lags associated with both fiscal and monetary policies. The long and uncertain lags may lead to policies that are counterproductive. In other words, the policies aimed at closing a recessionary gap may cause an inflationary gap if the stimulus occurs at the wrong time. Or policies aimed at closing an inflationary gap may overshoot the goal and cause a recessionary gap. The problem is that we do not operate with a clear crystal ball. For policy makers, timing and the exact size of the stimulus are essential for effective stabilization policies.

Other economists believe that the potency of expansionary fiscal policy will be diminished by the crowding-out effect. That is, expansionary fiscal policy increases the real interest rate when it borrows money to finance its deficit, which crowds out private investment. It is also possible that the economy is stimulated with fiscal or monetary policy in the short run for political gains that will only be inflationary in the long run. Recall that expansionary monetary policy lowers the real interest rate and stimulates private investment.

Other questions the policy makers will have to answer are: What are the output effects of the fiscal or monetary policy? What is the marginal propensity to consume (MPC) of the tax cut? How much will the central bank have to change the real interest rate to get the desired change in residential and commercial spending?

For most economists, monetary policy is the preferred tool for stabilization because the inside lags (the time from when a policy is needed to the time it is implemented) are much shorter. Recall that the federal open market committee (FOMC) meets eight times a year. Fiscal policy requires Congress to convene and debate the tax cuts or expenditure increases. However, fiscal policy may be used in special circumstances when monetary policy alone cannot do the job. Automatic stabilizers (e.g., taxes that impact disposable income and unemployment compensation) are an important part of fiscal policy and have a much smaller lag because they are implemented automatically.

POLICY DIFFICULTIES WITH SUPPLY SHOCKS

Recall that a negative supply shock, like those the United States experienced in the 1970s and 2007–2009, leads to an increase in the price level and a reduction in real aggregate output (RGDP), as seen in Exhibit 17.7.

After a negative demand shock (not shown but a leftward shift in the AD curve from, say, point A), policy makers can employ expansionary fiscal and/or monetary policy which can help shift the economy back to its original position. However, this is not the case with a negative supply shock. For example, suppose policy makers choose to use expansionary fiscal and/or monetary policy as a response to the recession caused by the supply shock; this increase in aggregate demand causes an increase in aggregate output (RGDP) but leads to even greater inflation, as seen in Exhibit 17.8(a). Or if policy makers choose to use contractionary fiscal and/or monetary policy to control inflation, this decrease in aggregate demand leads to a lower price level but causes an even lower level of aggregate output with higher rates of unemployment, as seen in Exhibit 17.8(b). In short, stagflation caused by a supply shock makes economic policy making very difficult.

WHAT SHOULD THE CENTRAL BANK DO?

Most economists believe that monetary policy should take the lead in stabilization policy and that the central bank should be independent and insulated from political pressure to avoid political business cycles. Political business cycles may occur if central banks ally themselves with an incumbent party and pursue expansionary monetary policy prior to an election. Even though the short-run

Without proper timing or the right stimulus, it is easy for policy makers to miss their target.

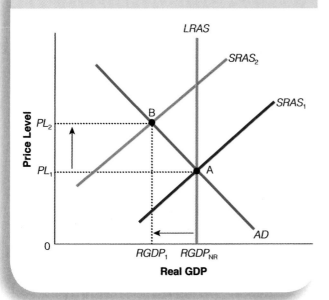

EXHIBIT 17.7 A Negative Supply Shock

if the money supply were only allowed to increase by, say, 3–5 percent per year (enough to accommodate new economic growth), the result would be less uncertainty and greater economic stability. In other words, if the fixed rule is followed and the growth rate is 3 percent per year and the monetary growth rate is 3 percent per year, the average rate of inflation is zero. This situation seldom occurs, but the point here is that it would add credibility to the Federal Reserve as being tough on inflation. It would make it clear that what the Fed says it's going to do is consistent with what it actually does.

INFLATION TARGETING

Some macroeconomists believe that we can do better than targeting the growth rate of monetary aggregates. These economists believe we should target the inflation rate. Targeting the inflation rate would require the central bank to attempt to stay in a certain band of inflation for a specified period of time—say 2–3 percent. The key to targeting is that it enhances credibility and could help to "anchor" inflationary expectations and lead to greater price stability. After all, successful monetary policy hinges critically on the ability to manage expectations. Several countries have inflation targets in place: The Bank of England is at 2 percent, the Bank of Canada is at 2 percent, Brazil is at 4.5 percent, and Chile is at the range between 2 percent and 4 percent. Empirical studies show a tendency for

impact may be increased output, employment, and a victory for the incumbent party in the election, the long-run impact will be inflation. So, faced with these potential problems, how should the central bank set its monetary policy?

Some macroeconomists believe that the central bank should adopt rules, such as a constant growth rate in the money supply. According to the rule advocates,

EXHIBIT 17.8 Policy Response to a Supply Shock

a. Expansionary Monetary and/or Fiscal Policy

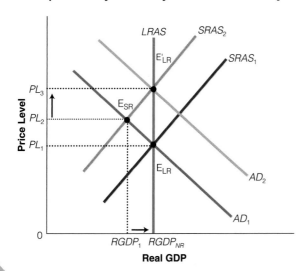

b. Contractionary Monetary and/or Fiscal Policy

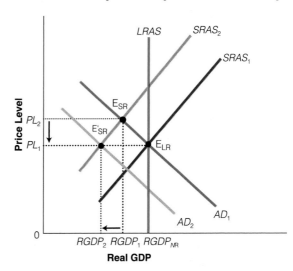

inflation rates to fall in countries that use inflation targeting.

Critics of inflation targeting will argue that central banks need flexibility. Good leaders, like Volker and Greenspan, proved that they can handle the job without set rules or targets. In other words, the United States has kept inflation low without rules or targeting, so those opposed to targets say, "If it ain't broke, don't fix it." Others argue that it may cause banks to focus too much attention on inflation at the expense of other goals such as output and employment. For example, a recessionary gap will normally cause the central bank to lower the interest rate to stimulate spending, output, and employment rather than just focus on inflation. Some might ask: If the Fed is going to put a target band on inflation, why not put one on unemployment and long-term interest rates too?

Targeting Inflation at Zero

So, if central banks are targeting low inflation rates of 2 percent, why not target inflation rates at 0 percent? After all, we have seen the costs to inflation: shoe leather costs, menu costs, changes in tax liabilities, changes in the distribution of income—and it leads to a distortion of the price system. However, these costs are probably small if inflation rates are low and expected to stay low. The other problem associated with a zero inflation rate is that it would be difficult to precisely hit the target all the time, and it could lead to deflation (the average price level of goods and services are falling), as it did in Japan in the 1990s. Also, some macroeconomists worry that if the inflation rate is targeted at zero the interest rate may fall to zero in a recession and render expansionary macroeconomic policy powerless. Other problems are unanticipated shocks and unanticipated financial crises. Monetary authorities need the flexibility to respond to these shocks by temporarily going outside the target range. For instance, the Federal Reserve was there to respond to the stock market crash of October 19, 1987—when stock prices fell by more than 20 percent in a single day (the biggest ever one-day decline)—and to the shock created by the terrorist attacks on September 11, 2001, when the Federal Reserve made massive discount loans to banks to avoid a financial crisis.

Why not target inflation rates at 0%?

Reducing the inflation rate by 1% may reduce output by as much as 5%. Disinflation is not painless.

Critics of targeting a zero inflation rate believe that achieving zero inflation is almost impossible and the costs are too high. The costs of disinflation (lowering the rate of inflation) can be high. Reducing the inflation rate by 1 percent may reduce output by as much as 5 percent. Disinflation is not painless.

The Taylor Rule

A variant of monetary rules and inflation targeting is the Taylor rule. It is a hybrid—part rule, part discretion. Taylor's formula uses a rule to decide when to use discretionary decisions. According to John Taylor, "The federal funds rate is increased or decreased according to what is happening to both real GDP and inflation. In particular, if real GDP rises 1 percent above potential GDP the federal funds rate should be raised, relative to the current inflation rate, by .5 percent. And if inflation rises by 1 percent above its target of 2 percent, then the federal funds rate should be raised by .5 percent relative to the inflation rate. When real GDP is equal to potential GDP and inflation is equal to its target of 2 percent, then the federal funds rate should remain at about 4 percent, which would imply a real interest rate of 2 percent on average. The policy rule was purposely chosen to be simple. Clearly, the equal weights on inflation and the GDP gap are an approximation reflecting the finding that neither variable should be given a negligible weight." If the central bank used this rule, market participants could easily predict central bank behavior, creating greater stability and certainty.

Asset Price Inflation

Some economists believe that the Fed should be concerned about asset pricing—especially housing and stock market prices. The period of 1999–2004 saw inflation at a low rate of about 2.5 percent per year, yet housing prices were rising 25 percent and higher in some markets. In some countries, such as Australia and Great Britain, the central banks are paying closer attention to the growth in asset prices even when consumer price inflation is low. Others believe that the central bank should not concern itself with the value that consumers place on stocks and housing. If the bubble bursts, the Fed can lower interest rates to bolster the economy.

Of course, as we found out during the financial crisis of 2007–2009, there are several questions that must be answered. One of the most important is: Can you identify housing or stock bubbles when they are appearing? The extent of monetary policy intervention may depend on the bubble. In the recession of 2007–2009, the housing bubble spread throughout the economy quickly and violently, before interest rate policy could be used to offset the damaging effects.

INDEXING AND REDUCING THE COSTS OF INFLATION

Another approach to some of the problems posed by inflation is **indexing**. As you recall, inflation poses substantial equity and distributional problems only when it is unanticipated or unexpected. One means of protecting parties against unanticipated price increases is to write contracts that automatically change the prices of goods or services whenever the overall price level changes, effectively rewriting agreements in terms of dollars of constant purchasing power. Wages, loans, and mortgage payments—everything possible—would be changed every month or so by an amount equal to the percentage change in some broad-based price index. Thus, if prices rose by 1.2 percent this month and your last month's wage was $1,000, your wage this month would be $1,012 ($1,000 × 1.012). By making as many contracts as possible payable in dollars of constant purchasing power, those involved could protect themselves against unanticipated changes in inflation.

Why Isn't Indexing Used More Extensively?

Indexing seems to eliminate most of the wealth transfers associated with unexpected inflation. Why then is it not more commonly used? One main argument against indexing is that it can worsen inflation. As prices go up, wages and certain

other contractual obligations (e.g., rents) also automatically increase. This immediate and comprehensive reaction to price increases leads to greater inflationary pressures. One price increase leads to a second, which in turn leads to a third, and so on.

Other Problems Associated with Indexing

We might ask, so what? If prices rise rapidly, but wages, rents, and so forth move up with prices, real wages and rents remain constant. However, if inflation gets bad enough, it could become almost impossible administratively to maintain the indexing scheme. The index, to be effective, might have to be changed every few days, but the information to make such frequent changes is not currently available. To get the necessary information quickly, then, might be quite expensive, involving a small army of price-checking bureaucrats and a massive electronic communications system. Other inefficiencies occur as well. During the German hyperinflation of the early 1920s, prices at one point rose so rapidly that workers demanded to be paid twice a day, at noon and at the end of the workday. During their lunch hour, workers would rush money to their wives, who would then run out and buy real goods before prices increased further.

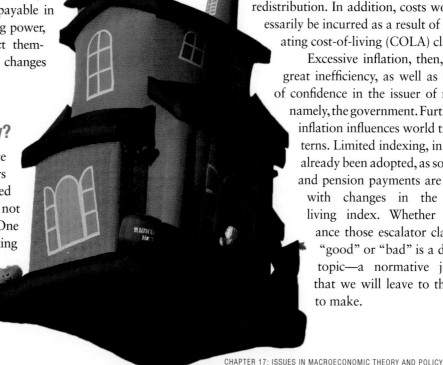

Other big problems include the fact that indexing reduces the ability for relative price changes to allocate resources where they are more valuable. Not everything can be indexed, so indexing would cause wealth redistribution. In addition, costs would necessarily be incurred as a result of renegotiating cost-of-living (COLA) clauses.

Excessive inflation, then, leads to great inefficiency, as well as to a loss of confidence in the issuer of money—namely, the government. Furthermore, inflation influences world trade patterns. Limited indexing, in fact, has already been adopted, as some wage and pension payments are changed with changes in the cost-of-living index. Whether on balance those escalator clauses are "good" or "bad" is a debatable topic—a normative judgment that we will leave to the reader to make.

Ⓢ4 The Financial Crisis of 2007–2009

Keep the following questions in mind as you read through this section. You'll find the answers in **Section Check 4.**

4.1 What impact did low short-term interest rates have on the housing market?

4.2 What role did relaxed standards for mortgage loans have on the housing market?

4.3 What impact did the higher interest rate of 2005 have on the housing market?

The best word to sum up the financial crisis of 2007–2009 is *debt*. In technical terms, it is called excessive leverage. In short, too many homeowners and financial firms had assumed too much debt and taken on too much risk. Why did this happen? There is plenty of blame to go around—poorly informed borrowers, predatory mortgage lenders, incompetent rating agencies, lax regulators, misguided government policies, and outright fraud.

Many economists believe the crisis started in the housing market with declining housing prices caused by overbuilding, excessive appreciation, and aggressive (i.e., risky) mortgages—a formula that only works when housing prices are rising.

Housing prices were rising at an extraordinary rate from 2000–2006. Housing prices peaked in 2006 and fell sharply in 2007; with the worst of the housing decline concentrated in California, Florida, Arizona, and Nevada.

LOW INTEREST RATES (2002–2004) LED TO AGGRESSIVE BORROWING

After the 2001 recession, the Fed pursued an expansionary monetary policy that pushed interest rates down to historically low levels. The federal funds rate was maintained at 2 percent or lower for almost three years. Economists disagree on whether this was the correct government policy. Some argue that the Fed pursued the appropriate policy to stimulate economic growth and employment after the 2001 recession and terrorist attacks in order to head off potential deflation. Once deflation sets in, it is very difficult to successfully use expansionary monetary policy. In addition, worldwide interest rates were very low at this time due to the large amount of savings in emerging markets. Because the U.S. financial markets appeared relatively safe, many of these global funds flowed into the United States, lowering the interest rate and eventually helping to fuel the housing bubble.

Critics of the Fed argue that it lowered interest rates too much for too long in a growing economy. Most

The housing market in Nevada was one of the hardest hit during the financial crisis. In October 2008, nearly 1 in every 74 Nevada homes had received foreclosure filings.

would agree that monetary policy was "too loose for too long" in the United States and around the world.

But whatever the reason for the low interest rates, there is common agreement that the low interest rates increased aggressive borrowing that encouraged less qualified buyers to purchase houses. The low interest rates set off a housing boom, especially in California, Florida, and the Northeast.

DEREGULATION IN THE HOUSING MARKET AND SUBPRIME MORTGAGES

In the last several decades, the federal government encouraged the mortgage industry, especially Fannie Mae and Freddie Mac, to lower lending standards for low-income families in an effort to increase home ownership. Fannie Mae and Freddie Mac are the government-sponsored enterprises that fund or guarantee the majority of mortgage loans in the United States.

Specifically, lenders devised innovative adjustable rate mortgages with extremely low "teaser" rates, making it possible for many new higher-risk buyers to purchase houses, often with little or no money as a down payment and, in some cases, no documentation of income. Most of these loans ended up in the hands of high-risk borrowers. These loans were called subprime loans because the borrower had less than a prime credit rating and many would not have qualified for a conventional loan.

In 2006, almost 70 percent of the subprime loans were in the form of a new innovative product called a hybrid. These loans started at a very low fixed rate for the initial period, say three to seven years, and then reset to a much higher rate for the remainder of the loan. Many subprime borrowers just expected to refinance later—thinking their property would continue to appreciate and interest rates would remain low. In retrospect, borrowers and lenders focused too much on the borrower's ability to cover the low initial payment and not enough on risk.

Speculators flipped (quickly bought and sold) properties with inflated appraisals and outright lying on loan applications. In addition, excessive credit provided to subprime borrowers (individuals who may not have qualified for conventional loans) fueled the housing bubble. Mortgage originators were not worried about making risky loans because they could pass on the risk to others (particularly Fannie Mae and Freddie Mac, who were aggressively buying such loans). Because origination fees on loans were due up front, and others

would buy the loans, lenders were less concerned if the loan was ever repaid. It is safe to say that if mortgage companies had given loans only to safe investors, the United States would not have had a financial crisis.

Subprime mortgages jumped from 8 percent of the total in 2001 to 13.5 percent in 2005, as shown in Exhibit 17.9 on the next page. These new buyers pushed housing prices higher. The increase in the lending to "subprime" borrowers helped inflate the housing bubble. The rising housing prices then led to overly optimistic expectations with both borrowers and lenders thinking that with housing prices increasing, the risks were minimal. (After all, housing prices jumped almost 10 percent a year nationally from 2000–2006, as shown in Exhibit 17.10 on the next page.)

Lenders were eager to make loans to anyone because they thought the prices for housing would continue to rise and, if borrowers defaulted, lenders would be left with an asset worth more than they were owed.

In short, the relaxed lending standards, backed by the government, put many low-income families into homes they could not afford. Unscrupulous mortgage brokers even falsified loan application forms so clients could qualify for larger loans. Many borrowers also did not completely understand the terms of their loans.

WHO BOUGHT THESE RISKY SUBPRIME MORTGAGES?

Many of these risky subprime mortgages were sold to investment banks such as Bear Stearns and Merrill Lynch. They pooled them with other securities into packages and sold them all over the world. Part of the impetus for them was the great demand for mortgage-backed securities in the global market. A mortgage-backed security (MBS) is a package of mortgages bundled together and then sold to an investor, like a bond. Foreign investors were hungry to invest in these securities because the U.S. housing market traditionally has been strong and stable. These mortgage-backed securities were also thought to have minimal risk because of the diversity of mortgages in each portfolio and because they had high security ratings. Security rating agencies gave their highest ratings to these securities—AAA (Standard's and Poor) and Aaa (Moody's). High ratings encouraged investors to buy securities backed by subprime mortgages, helping finance the housing boom. The rating agencies clearly underestimated the risk of these securities. The risk was spread among many different investment institutions, but no one knew exactly where the bad loans had ended up.

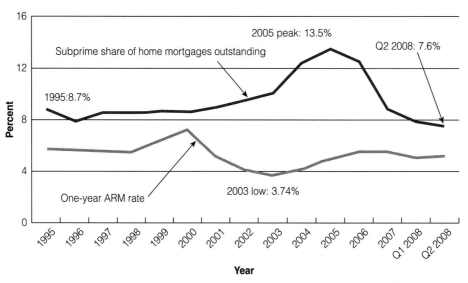

Consumers Borrowing against Their Equity

To complicate matters further, consumers borrowed hundreds of billions of dollars against the equity from the appreciation in their homes, fueling consumption spending and an increase in household debt, combined with a fall in personal saving. The low interest rates subsidized massive borrowing, and credit market debt soared as well.

EXHIBIT 17.10 The Recent Run-Up of Nominal Home Prices Was Extraordinary (1890–Q2 2008)

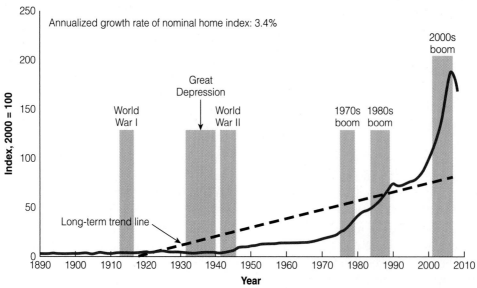

NOTE: The annualized growth rate is the geometric mean.

FED INTEREST RATE INCREASES AND THE HOUSING BUST

The low interest rates of the 2002–2004 period and other factors led to the Fed becoming concerned about rising prices. In 2005–2006, therefore, the Fed reversed course and pushed short-term interest rates up. For those holding new adjustable rate mortgages (ARMs), it meant their monthly payments rose. Higher interest rates and falling housing prices were a recipe for disaster. Consequently, many homes went into default and foreclosure—both subprime borrowers and prime borrowers lost their homes. (The default rate was much lower on those holding fixed mortgage rates.)

When housing prices crashed, not only did too many homeowners find themselves over their heads, but there was also a huge excess inventory of new homes. From 2006–2008, housing construction fell by a whopping $350 billion—a huge hit on the economy. And by December of 2007, the United States was officially in a recession.

As housing prices fell and interest rates rose, foreclosures jumped. Once home prices fell below loan values, borrowers could not qualify to refinance and many were forced into foreclosure. When houses turn "upside down"—people owe more on their loan than the house is worth—many walk away from their houses. If a homeowner had put 20 percent down and had an appreciable amount of equity, she would have a greater incentive to make it work. Zero-down mortgages meant more defaults, especially when given to someone with a poor credit rating and little documentation of income. There was a major mispricing of risk in the mortgage markets.

When housing prices fell and mortgage delinquencies soared, the securities-backed subprime mortgages lost most of their value. When subprime borrowers defaulted, the investors that took the hit started demanding their money back by surrendering these securities to the banks. The result was a large decline in the capital of many banks and financial institutions, tightening credit around the world. One investment bank went bankrupt (Lehman Brothers in September 2008) and two were sold at fire-sale prices to other banks (Bear Stearns in March 2008 and Merrill Lynch in September 2008). The failures of three of the five largest investment banks augmented the instability in the global financial system. The remaining two investment banks, Morgan Stanley and Goldman Sachs, opted to become commercial banks, thereby subjecting themselves to more stringent regulation.

Banks ended up receiving a double hit. Their securities investors started demanding money and their borrowers were failing to pay their loans. And troubled banks were not able to raise more money, because other banks and investors sensed that they were in trouble and refused to lend to them.

It is also easy to see why the government-sponsored financial intermediaries, Freddie Mac and Fannie Mae, collapsed. Many economists believe it had to do with moral hazard, when individuals take additional risks because they are insured. Investors knew that the government supported Freddie and Fannie mortgage-backed securities, so they considered them very low risk. With the government behind them, Freddie and Fannie had an incentive to issue risky securities and buy risky mortgages from banks. Banks knew that Freddie and Fannie would buy almost any mortgage they created. However, when people stopped paying their mortgages, the two giant intermediaries lost billions of dollars. Their stocks became worthless and the government had to take control of both Fannie Mae and Freddie Mac.

Financial markets depend on lenders making funds available to borrowers. However, when lenders become reluctant to make loans, it becomes difficult to assess credit risk. This happened in 2008, which led the Federal Reserve and other central banks around the world to pour hundreds of billions of dollars (euros, pounds, etc.) into credit markets to ease the pain of the financial crisis. In addition, the government has enacted large fiscal stimulus packages of close to $1 trillion. The borrowing and spending is intended to offset the reduction in private sector demand caused by the crisis.

SECTION CHECK 4

4.1 Maintaining very low interest rates for a substantial period of time contributed to the housing price run-up. The rapid increase in housing prices during the housing bubble made both borrowers and lenders expect that the risks of subprime lending were not great.

4.2 The standards for low-income families to qualify for home loans were reduced, increasing the number of high-risk borrowers.

4.3 After several years of maintaining low real interest rates, the Fed began pushing short-term interest rates up in 2005. The higher interest rates and falling housing prices pushed many homeowners into default and foreclosure.

DEVELOPMENTS IN INTRODUCTORY ECONOMICS COURSES

When you look at the current economic crisis, you are probably most aware of how much things have changed and how the future of the economy in many ways may seem uncertain. So what does this mean for you, as you might be taking your first economics course? Has economics changed too?

N. Gregory Mankiw, who teaches introductory economics at Harvard, has often been asked these same questions. His answer is two-fold. On the one hand fundamental economic principles, such as market efficiency and supply and demand, are still relevant and need to be discussed.

However, Mankiw does offer four particular issues that may bear closer examination. As you consider these issues, here are some things you might want to be aware of.

1) The Role of Financial Institutions

When financial institutions are doing their jobs, redirecting the resources of savers to investors, it's easy to forget about them. However, with the role of financial institutions right in the middle of the current economic crisis, you may want to take a closer look at what happens when these institutions aren't fulfilling their role properly. As Mankiw says, "The process of financial intermediation is most noteworthy when it fails."

2) The Effects of Leverage

How does a 20 percent drop in housing prices result in banks losing 100 percent of their money? Many financial institutions made big investments in the housing market, but the use of leverage (essentially borrowing money to increase their principle investments) jeopardized bank solvency. Leverage can dramatically increase both gains and losses, and you'll want to pay attention to how both of these situations fit in the broader economic landscape.

3) The Limits of Monetary Policy

What would happen if the central bank cut interest rates to zero and it was not enough to get the economy going again? At the time this book was written, the Federal Reserve had been targeting the interest rate between zero and 0.25 percent since December 2008. On the one hand, it is good to be aware of the Fed's other monetary policy tools such as broadening the types of financial assets it purchases; however, you should also know that the effectiveness of these tools is difficult to determine.

> The Fed is acting with the conviction that it has other tools to put the economy back on track.
> —N. Gregory Mankiw

4) The Challenge of Forecasting

While the crisis caught many economists by surprise, this is not atypical of most economic slumps. Fluctuations in economic activity are very difficult to predict. And as Mankiw points out, economics is not the only discipline in which forecasting is difficult. So while economics won't magically allow you to predict the future, it will help in assessing risks and preparing for surprises.

SOURCE: N. Gregory Mankiw, "That Freshman Course Won't Be Quite the Same", *The New York Times*, May 24, 2009. Available at http://www.nytimes.com/2009/05/24/business/economy/24view.html?_r=1&scp=8&sq=n+gregory+mankiw&st=nyt (accessed April 8, 2010).

Chapter 17: Self-Review

Now that you're finished reading the chapter, review the questions below. You can write your answers in the space provided, then go online to see the answers at www.cengagebrain.com.

S1—PROBLEMS IN IMPLEMENTING FISCAL AND MONETARY POLICY

1. What is the crowding-out effect?

2. True or False: The lag time for adopting policy changes is shorter for fiscal policy than for monetary policy.

3. True or False: The activities of global and nonbank institutions weaken the Fed's influence on the money market.

S2—RATIONAL EXPECTATIONS AND REAL BUSINESS CYCLES

4. Fill-in-the-Blanks: In a world of rational expectations, it is _____ to reduce unemployment below its natural rate but potentially _____ to reduce inflation rates.

5. True or False: According to rational expectations theory, both expected and unexpected changes in inflation can affect real wages and unemployment.

6. Give an example of a positive productivity shock.

7. Fill-in-the-Blanks: Real business cycle theorists as well as rational expectations economists believe that wages and prices are _____ and that markets adjust _____.

S3—CONTROVERSIES IN MACROECONOMIC POLICY

8. What is a political business cycle?

9. What are the arguments against inflation targeting?

10. True or False: If each possible good were indexed to changes in the general price level, it would be easy for relative price changes to signal changing relative scarcities.

S4—THE FINANCIAL CRISIS OF 2007–2009

11. Why were those who took out hybrid loans at far greater risk of foreclosure when the Fed began raising interest rates?

12. Why was home building such an important factor in the crisis?

13. Fill-in-the-Blanks: After several years of maintaining _____ real interest rates, the Fed reversed course and pushed short-term interest rates _____.

UNITED STATES / **ÉTAS-UNIS**			1.1998
EUROPEAN UNION / **UNION EUROPÉENNE**			1.4996
ENGLAND / **ANGLETERRE**			2.1998
JAPAN / **JAPON**			0.0109
SWITZERLAND / **SUISSE**			0.9895
AUSTRALIA / **AUSTRALIE**			0.9596
DENMARK / **DANEMARK**			.2084
HONG KONG / **HONG KONG**			00.166
ISRAEL / **ISRAËL**			.2594

If you lived in Canada

and you were leaving the country, you would need to convert your money into the currency of the country you were going to so that you could make purchases there. Why do the rates matter, though? And what makes them different? Where would you get the most advantageous deal when exchanging currencies? If you were a firm doing business, how would these different exchange rates affect the profitability of your business in other countries?

NEW ZEALAND / **NOUVELLE-ZÉLANDE**			0.8597
NORWAY / **NORVÈGE**			0.1997
SINGAPORE / **SINGAPOUR**			0.8420

18

International Economics

conomics is largely about exchange. But up to this point we have focused on trade between individuals within the domestic economy. In this chapter, we extend our coverage to international trade. Why do countries trade? Hong Kong has no oil—how are they going to get it? Bananas could be grown in the most tropical parts of the United States or in expensive greenhouses, but wouldn't it be easier to import bananas from Honduras?

Stop for a moment and imagine a world without international trade. Chocolate is derived from cocoa beans that are imported from South America and Africa. There are imported cars from Germany and Japan, shoes and sweaters from Italy, shirts from India, and watches and clocks from Switzerland. Consumers love trade because it provides us with more choices. It is good for producers, too; and the speed of transportation and communication has opened up world markets. In addition, lower costs are sometimes the result of economies of scale. Free trade gives firms access to large world markets. It also fosters more competition, which helps to keep prices down.

In the first half of this chapter we will study the reasons for the importance of trade. We will also look at the arguments for and against trade protection. In the second half of this chapter we'll discuss international finance.

Sections in Chapter 18

Ⓢ1 The Growth in World Trade

Keep the following questions in mind as you read through this section. You'll find the answers in Section Check 1.

1.1 What does the United States export and import?

1.2 Who trades with the United States?

In a typical year, about 15 percent of the world's output is traded in international markets. Of course, the importance of the international sector varies enormously

EXHIBIT 18.1 Major U.S. Trading Partners

Top Trading Partners—Exports of Goods in 2008			Top Trading Partners—Imports of Goods in 2008		
Rank	Country	Percent of Total	Rank	Country	Percent of Total
1	Canada	20.1	1	China	16.4
2	Mexico	11.7	2	Canada	15.7
3	China	5.5	3	Mexico	10.1
4	Japan	5.1	4	Japan	6.6
5	Germany	4.2	5	Germany	4.6
6	United Kingdom	4.1			

SOURCE: Central Intelligence Agency, *North America: United States, The World Factbook.* Updated March 24, 2010. Available at https://www.cia.gov/library/publications/the-world-factbook/geos/us.html (accessed April 8, 2010).

from place to place across the world. Some nations are virtually closed economies (no interaction with other economies), with foreign trade equaling only a small proportion (perhaps 5 percent) of total output, while in other countries trade is much more important.

THE IMPORTANCE OF INTERNATIONAL TRADE

In the last three decades, the sum of U.S. imports and exports has increased from 11 percent of GDP to roughly 30 percent. In addition, incoming and outgoing investments (capital flows) have risen from less than 1 percent to roughly 3 percent of GDP. In Germany, roughly 30 percent of all output produced is exported, while Ireland and Belgium each export more than 70 percent of GDP.

U.S. exports include capital goods, automobiles, industrial supplies, raw materials, consumer goods, and agricultural products. U.S. imports include crude oil and refined petroleum products, machinery, automobiles, consumer goods, industrial raw materials, food, and beverages.

TRADING PARTNERS

In the early history of the United States, international trade largely took place with Europe and with Great Britain in particular. Now the United States trades with a number of countries, the most important of which are Canada, Mexico, China, Japan, Germany, and the United Kingdom, as seen in Exhibit 18.1.

SECTION CHECK 1

1.1 U.S. exports include capital goods, automobiles, industrial supplies, raw materials, consumer goods, and agricultural products. U.S. imports include crude oil and refined petroleum products, machinery, automobiles, consumer goods, industrial raw materials, food, and beverages.

1.2 Some of the United States' most important trade partners include Canada, Japan, Mexico, China, Germany, and the United Kingdom.

⑤2 Comparative Advantage and Gains from Trade

Keep the following questions in mind as you read through this section. You'll find the answers in **Section Check 2.**

2.1 Does voluntary trade lead to an improvement in economic welfare?

2.2 What benefits can a nation derive from specialization?

Using simple logic, we conclude that the very existence of trade suggests that trade is economically beneficial. Our conclusion is true if we assume that people are utility maximizers and are rational, are intelligent, and engage in trade on a voluntary basis. Because almost all trade is voluntary, it would seem that trade occurs because the participants feel that they are better off because of the trade. Both participants in an exchange of goods and services anticipate an improvement in their economic welfare. Sometimes, of course, anticipations are not realized (because the world is uncertain); but the motive behind trade remains an expectation of some enhancement in utility or satisfaction by both parties.

Granted, "trade must be good because people do it" is a rather simplistic explanation. The classical economist David Ricardo is usually given most of the credit for developing the economic theory that more precisely explains how trade can be mutually beneficial to both parties, raising output and income levels in the entire trading area.

THE PRINCIPLE OF COMPARATIVE ADVANTAGE

Ricardo's theory of international trade centers on the concept of comparative advantage. As we discussed in Chapter 2, persons, regions, or countries can gain by specializing in the production of the good in which they have a comparative advantage. That is, if they can produce a good or service at a lower opportunity cost than others can, we say that they have a *comparative advantage* in the production of that good or service. In other words, a country or a region should specialize in producing and selling those items that it can produce at a lower opportunity cost than other regions or countries.

COMPARATIVE ADVANTAGE AND ABSOLUTE ADVANTAGE

Q: Renee Saunts is a successful artist who can complete one painting in each 40-hour workweek. Each painting sells for $4,000. As a result of her enormous success, however, Renee is swamped in paperwork. To solve the problem, Renee hires Drake to handle all the bookkeeping and typing associated with buying supplies, answering inquiries from prospective buyers and dealers, writing art galleries, and so forth. Renee pays Drake $300 per week for his work. After a couple of weeks in this arrangement, Renee realizes that she can handle Drake's chores more quickly than Drake does. In fact, she estimates that she is twice as fast as Drake, completing in 20 hours what it takes Drake 40 hours to complete. Should Renee fire Drake?

You can find the answer on the next page.

Q&A

A: Clearly Renee has an absolute advantage over Drake in both painting and paperwork, because she can do twice as much paperwork in 40 hours as Drake can, and Drake can't paint well at all. Still, it would be foolish for Renee to do both jobs. If Renee did her own paperwork, it would take her 20 hours per week, leaving her only 20 hours to paint. Because each watercolor takes 40 hours to paint, Renee's output would fall from one painting per week to one painting per two weeks.

When Drake works for her, Renee's net income is $3,700 per week ($4,000 per painting minus $300 in Drake's wages); when Drake does not work for her, it is only $2,000 per week (one painting every two weeks). Even though Renee is both a better painter and better at Drake's chores than Drake, it pays for her to specialize in painting, in which she has a comparative advantage, and allow Drake to do the paperwork. The opportunity cost to Renee of paperwork is high. For Drake, who lacks skills as a painter, the opportunity cost of doing the paperwork is much less.

Comparative advantage analysis does not mean that nations or areas that export goods will necessarily be able to produce those goods or services more cheaply than can other nations in an absolute sense. What is important is *comparative* advantage, not *absolute* advantage. For example, the United States may be able to produce more cotton cloth per worker than India can, but this capability does not mean that the United States should necessarily sell cotton cloth to India. For a highly productive nation to produce goods in which it is only marginally more productive than other nations, the nation must take resources from the production of other goods in which its productive abilities are markedly superior. As a result, the opportunity costs in India of making cotton cloth may be less than in the United States. With that, both can gain from trade, despite potential absolute advantages for every good in the United States.

COMPARATIVE ADVANTAGE, SPECIALIZATION, AND THE PRODUCTION POSSIBILITIES CURVES

Wendy and Calvin live on opposite ends of a small town. Wendy can produce either food or cloth. On a daily basis, she can produce 10 pounds of food, 5 yards of cloth, or any linear combination of the two goods along her production possibilities curve in Exhibit 18.2 (to simplify the calculations, we have drawn linear production possibilities curves). If Wendy spends the whole day producing food, she can produce 10 pounds. If she spends the whole day producing cloth, she can produce 5 yards. Recall that the production possibilities curve represents the maximum possible combinations of food and cloth she can produce, given her fixed set of resources and technology. The negatively sloped production possibilities curve means that when she produces one good, with her fixed resources, she gives up the opportunity to produce another good.

What is Wendy's opportunity cost of producing cloth? It is what Wendy gives up in food production for each unit of cloth production, which is 2 pounds of food per yard of cloth. Therefore, her opportunity cost of producing a yard of cloth is 2 pounds of food. What is the opportunity cost of Wendy producing food? It is what she gives up in cloth production for each unit increase in food production—1 yard of cloth per 2 pounds of food. That is, for each pound of food Wendy produces, she gives up producing 1/2 yard of cloth.

Calvin, who lives on the other side of town, can also produce food or cloth. On a daily basis, he could produce 3 pounds of food, 4 yards of cloth, or any linear combination of the two along his production possibilities curve in Exhibit 18.3. When he spends the day

EXHIBIT 18.2 *Wendy's Production Possibilities Curve*

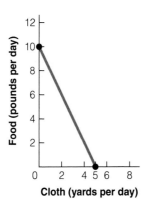

$$OC_{CLOTH} = \frac{\text{loss in food}}{\text{gain in cloth}} = \frac{10}{5} = \frac{2 \text{ pounds of food}}{1 \text{ yard of cloth}}$$

$$OC_{FOOD} = \frac{\text{loss in cloth}}{\text{gain in food}} = \frac{5}{10} = \frac{1 \text{ yard of cloth}}{2 \text{ pounds of food}}$$

or

1 yard of cloth costs 2 pounds of food.
1 pound of food costs 1/2 yard of cloth.

EXHIBIT 18.3 Calvin's Production Possibilities Curve

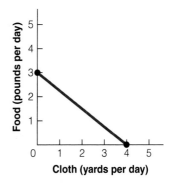

$$OC_{CLOTH} = \frac{\text{loss in food}}{\text{gain in cloth}} = \frac{3 \text{ pounds of food}}{4 \text{ yards of cloth}}$$

$$OC_{FOOD} = \frac{\text{loss in cloth}}{\text{gain in food}} = \frac{4 \text{ yards of cloth}}{3 \text{ pounds of food}}$$

or

1 yard of cloth costs 3/4 pounds of food.
1 pound of food costs 4/3 yards of cloth.

producing cloth, he can produce 4 yards. When he spends the day producing food, he can produce 3 pounds. To produce cloth, Calvin must decrease his production of food. What is Calvin's opportunity cost of producing cloth? It is what he gives up in producing food for each unit of cloth production, which is 3 pounds of food per 4 pounds of cloth. Therefore, his opportunity cost of producing cloth is 3/4 pound of food. What is Calvin's opportunity cost of producing food? It is what he gives up in cloth production for each unit of food production, which is 4 yards of cloth per 3 pounds of food. Therefore, the opportunity cost of producing a pound of food is 4/3 yards of cloth per day.

Absolute and Comparative Advantage

Now let's compare Wendy's production possibilities curve to Calvin's production possibilities curve to see who has an absolute advantage in producing cloth and who has an absolute advantage in producing food. An absolute advantage occurs when one producer can perform a task using fewer inputs than the other producer. In Exhibit 18.4 on the next page, we see that Wendy is more productive than Calvin at producing food. Along the vertical axis, we can see that if Wendy uses all of her resources to produce food, she can produce 10 pounds

of food per day. If Calvin devotes all of his resources to producing food, he can only produce 3 pounds of food per day. We say that Wendy has an absolute advantage over Calvin in the production of food.

Along the horizontal axis in Exhibit 18.4, we can see that Wendy is also more productive than Calvin at producing cloth. If Wendy devotes all of her resources to producing cloth, she can produce 5 yards of cloth per day. If Calvin devotes all of his resources to producing cloth, he can only produce 4 yards of cloth per day. We say that Wendy also has an absolute advantage over Calvin in the production of cloth. She has an absolute advantage in producing both food and cloth. Therefore, should Wendy produce both food and cloth and Calvin produce nothing? No!

Recall from Chapter 2 that a comparative advantage exists when one person can produce a good at a lower opportunity cost than can another person. So who has the comparative advantage (lowest opportunity cost) in producing food? In this case, Wendy's opportunity cost of producing food is less than Calvin's. Wendy's opportunity cost of producing a pound of food is 1/2 yard of cloth, whereas Calvin's opportunity cost of producing 1 pound of food is 4/3 yards of cloth. Therefore, Wendy is the more efficient producer of food—she gives up less in cloth when she produces food, compared to Calvin.

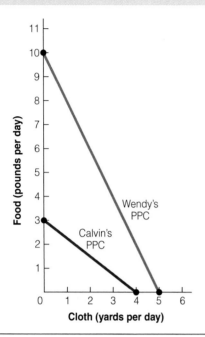

EXHIBIT 18.4 Absolute and Comparative Advantage

	Cloth (yds/day)	Food (lbs/day)	OC of Cloth	OC of Food
Wendy	5	10	2 lb of food	1/2 yd of cloth
Calvin	4	3	3/4 lbs of food	4/3 yds of cloth

Remember, comparative advantage is always a relative concept.

Who has the comparative advantage in producing cloth? That is, who can produce cloth at the lowest opportunity cost? That would be Calvin, because he gives up only 3/4 pound of food to produce 1 yard of cloth. If Wendy were to produce a yard of cloth, she would have to give up 2 pounds of food. The lowest opportunity cost producer of cloth is Calvin. In other words, to produce one more yard of cloth, Calvin gives up fewer pounds of food than does Wendy. Therefore, Calvin is the more efficient producer of cloth—he gives up less in food when he produces cloth, compared to Wendy. Calvin has a comparative advantage in producing cloth.

Gains from Specialization and Exchange

Suppose Wendy and Calvin meet and decide to specialize in those activities in which they have a comparative advantage. Wendy would specialize in the production of food and Calvin would specialize in the production of cloth. By specializing, Wendy can produce 10 pounds of food per day (point B' in Exhibit 18.5) and Calvin can produce 4 yards of cloth per day (point B in Exhibit 18.5). *However, to achieve any of the gains from comparative advantage and specialization, there must be trade.*

After specializing in the good in which they have a comparative advantage, suppose Wendy and Calvin agree to trade at the exchange "price" of 1 pound of food for 1 yard of cloth. If Wendy trades 3 yards of cloth for 3 pounds of food, she can obtain a position along the new production possibilities curve which is beyond her original production possibilities curve, point C' in Exhibit 18.5. Wendy can now have 7 pounds of food and 3 yards of cloth—a combination she could not have obtained without specialization and trade.

Calvin also benefits from specialization and trade. In the trade, he receives 3 pounds of food for 3 yards of cloth and now can enjoy 3 pounds of food and 1 yard of cloth a combination, at point C in Exhibit 18.5, he could not have obtained without specialization and trade. In sum, the exchange has allowed both Wendy and Calvin to produce and consume a combination of the two goods beyond what would have been attainable if it were not for specialization and trade.

Individuals and Nations Gain from Specialization and Trade

Just as Calvin and Wendy benefit from specialization and trade, so do the people of different nations. Because of specialization, according to comparative advantage, both nations can be better off, even if one nation has an absolute advantage in both goods over the other. Furthermore, the greater the difference in opportunity cost between the two trading partners, the greater the benefits from specialization and exchange.

Note that when we say nations trade with nations, we really mean that the people of a nation trade with people of other nations. When China trades clothes to the United States for Boeing 787 jetliners, they both benefit from the exchange, because they are able to obtain them at a lower cost than if they produced those goods themselves. Free trade does not guarantee that each individual will be better off or that everyone will receive the same benefits, but it does mean that collectively, the population of each nation will benefit from the trade. Indeed, unskilled workers in high wage countries may temporarily lose jobs. Recall that when NAFTA was passed, its critics argued that low skilled workers would lose jobs because of U.S. trade with Mexico. However, that does not appear to have happened to any large extent. Instead, consumers have been enjoying lower priced goods because of the trade.

EXHIBIT 18.5 The Gains from Specialization and Trade

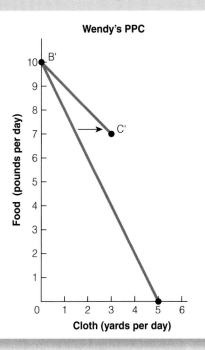

Wendy's PPC

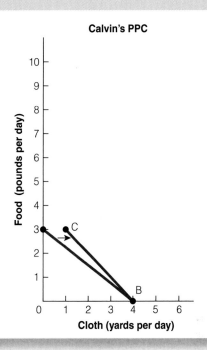

Calvin's PPC

SECTION CHECK 2

2.1 Voluntary trade occurs because participants feel that they are better off as a result of the trade. Through trade and specialization in products in which it has a comparative advantage, a country can enjoy a greater array of goods and services at a lower cost.

2.2 A nation can gain from trade if it can produce the good or service relatively more cheaply than can anyone else. That is, a country should specialize in producing and selling those items that it can produce at a lower opportunity cost than can other countries.

⑤3 Supply and Demand in International Trade

Keep the following questions in mind as you read through this section. You'll find the answers in **Section Check 3**.

3.1 Who benefits and who loses when a country becomes an exporter?

3.2 Who benefits and who loses when a country becomes an importer?

Recall from Chapter 4 that the difference between the most a consumer would be willing to pay for a quantity of a good and what a consumer actually has to pay is called *consumer surplus*. The difference between the lowest price for which a supplier would be willing to supply a quantity of a good or service and the revenues a supplier actually receives for selling it is called *producer surplus*. With the tools of consumer and producer surplus, we can better analyze the impact of trade. Who gains? Who loses? What happens to net welfare?

FREE TRADE AND EXPORTS— DOMESTIC PRODUCERS GAIN MORE THAN DOMESTIC CONSUMERS LOSE

Using the concepts of consumer and producer surplus, we can graphically show the net benefits of free trade. Imagine an economy with no trade, where the equilibrium price, P_{BT}, and equilibrium quantity, Q_{BT}, of wheat are determined exclusively in the domestic economy, as shown in Exhibit 18.6 on the next page. Suppose that this imaginary economy decides to engage in free trade.

EXHIBIT 18.6 Free Trade and Exports

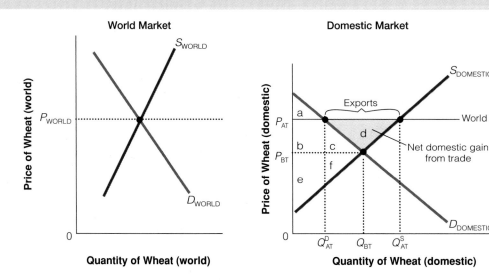

Domestic Gains and Losses from Free Trade (exports)			
Area	Before	After	Change
Consumer Surplus (*CS*)	a + b + c	a	−b − c
Producer Surplus (*PS*)	e + f	b + c + d + e + f	+b + c + d
Total Welfare from Trade (*CS* + *PS*)	a + b + c + e + f	a + b + c + d + e + f	+d

You can see that the world price (established in the world market for wheat), P_{AT}, is higher than the domestic price before trade, P_{BT}. In other words, the domestic economy has a comparative advantage in wheat, because it can produce wheat at a lower relative price than the rest of the world can. So this wheat-producing country sells some wheat to the domestic market and some wheat to the world market, all at the going world price.

The price after trade (P_{AT}) is higher than the price before trade (P_{BT}). Because the world market is huge, the demand from the rest of the world at the world price (P_{AT}) is assumed to be perfectly elastic. That is, domestic wheat farmers can sell all the wheat they want at the world price. If you were a wheat farmer in Nebraska, would you rather sell all your bushels of wheat at the higher world price or the lower domestic price? As a wheat farmer, you would surely prefer the higher world price. But this preference is not good news for domestic cereal and bread eaters, who now have to pay more for products made with wheat because P_{AT} is greater than P_{BT}.

Graphically, we can see how free trade and exports affect both domestic consumers and domestic producers.

At the higher world price, P_{AT}, domestic wheat producers are receiving larger amounts of producer surplus. Before trade, they received a surplus equal to area e + f; after trade, they received surplus b + c + d + e + f, for a net gain of area b + c + d. However, part of the domestic producers' gain comes at domestic consumers' expense. Specifically, consumers had a consumer surplus equal to area a + b + c before the trade (at P_{BT}), but they now have only area a (at P_{AT})—a loss of area b + c.

Area b reflects a redistribution of income, because producers are gaining exactly what consumers are losing. Is that good or bad? We can't say objectively whether consumers or producers are more deserving. However, the net benefits from allowing free trade and exports are clearly visible in area d. Without free trade, no one gets area d. That is, on net, members of the domestic society gain when domestic wheat producers are able to sell their wheat at the higher world price. Although domestic wheat consumers lose from the free trade, those negative effects are more than offset by the positive gains captured by producers. Area d is the net increase in domestic wealth (the welfare gain) from free trade and exports.

EXHIBIT 18.7 Free Trade and Imports

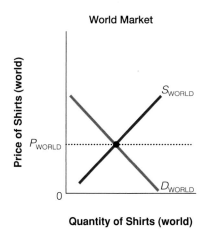

World Market

Price of Shirts (world)

S_{WORLD}

P_{WORLD}

D_{WORLD}

0

Quantity of Shirts (world)

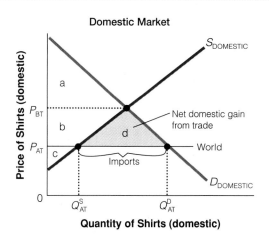

Domestic Market

Price of Shirts (domestic)

$S_{DOMESTIC}$

a

P_{BT}

b

d

Net domestic gain from trade

P_{AT}

c

World

Imports

$D_{DOMESTIC}$

0

Q^S_{AT}

Q^D_{AT}

Quantity of Shirts (domestic)

Domestic Gains and Losses from Free Trade (imports)			
Area	Before Trade	After Trade	Change
Consumer Surplus (CS)	a	a + b + d	b + d
Producer Surplus (PS)	b + c	c	−b
Total Welfare from Trade (CS + PS)	a + b + c	a + b + c + d	+d

FREE TRADE AND IMPORTS— DOMESTIC CONSUMERS GAIN MORE THAN DOMESTIC PRODUCERS LOSE

Now suppose that our economy does not produce shirts as well as other countries of the world. In other words, other countries have a comparative advantage in producing shirts, and the domestic price for shirts is above the world price. This scenario is illustrated in Exhibit 18.7 above. At the new, lower world price, the domestic producer will supply quantity Q^S_{AT}. However, at the lower world price, the domestic producers will not produce the entire amount demanded by domestic consumers, Q^D_{AT}. At the world price, reflecting the world supply and demand for shirts, the difference between what is domestically supplied and what is domestically demanded is supplied by imports.

At the world price (established in the world market for shirts), we assume that the world supply to the domestic market curve is perfectly elastic—that the producers of the world can supply all that domestic consumers are willing to buy at the going price. At the world price, Q^S_{AT} is supplied by domestic producers, and

the difference between Q^D_{AT} and Q^S_{AT} is imported from other countries.

Who wins and who loses from free trade and imports? Domestic consumers benefit from paying a lower price for shirts. In Exhibit 18.7, before trade, consumers only received area a in consumer surplus.

After trade, the price fell and quantity purchased increased, causing the area of consumer surplus to increase from area a to area a + b + d, a gain of b + d. Domestic producers lose because they are now selling their shirts at the lower world price, P_{AT}. The producer surplus before trade was b + c. After trade, the producer surplus falls to area c, reducing producer surplus by area b. Area b, then, represents a redistribution from producers to consumers; but area d is the net increase in domestic wealth (the welfare gain) from free trade and imports.

SECTION CHECK 3

3.1 With free trade and exports, domestic producers gain more than domestic consumers lose.

3.2 With free trade and imports, domestic consumers gain more than domestic producers lose.

⑤4 Tariffs, Import Quotas, and Subsidies

Keep the following questions in mind as you read through this section. You'll find the answers in Section Check 4.

4.1 What are the effects of a tariff?

4.2 What are the effects of an import quota?

4.3 What is the economic impact of subsidies?

In this section we'll discuss three mechanisms of trade protection: tariffs, import quotas, and subsidies.

TARIFFS

A **tariff** is a tax on imported goods. Tariffs are usually relatively small revenue producers that retard the

Tariffs lead to:
1) Smaller total quantity sold
2) Higher price for domestic consumers
3) More sales at higher prices for domestic producers
4) Lower foreign sales

expansion of trade. They bring about higher prices and revenues for domestic producers, and lower sales and revenues for foreign producers. Moreover, tariffs lead to higher prices for domestic consumers. In fact, the gains to producers are more than offset by the losses to consumers. With the aid of a graph we will see how the gains and losses from tariffs work.

THE DOMESTIC ECONOMIC IMPACT OF TARIFFS

The domestic economic impact of tariffs is presented in Exhibit 18.8, which illustrates the supply and demand curves for domestic consumers and producers of shoes. In a typical international supply and demand illustration, the intersection of the world supply and demand curves would determine the domestic market price. However, with import tariffs, the domestic price of shoes is greater than the world price, as in Exhibit 18.8. We consider the world supply curve (S_W) for domestic consumers to be perfectly elastic; that is, we can buy all we want at the world price (P_W). At the world price, domestic producers are only willing to provide quantity Q_S, but domestic consumers are willing to buy quantity Q_D—more than domestic producers are willing to supply. Imports make up the difference.

As you can see in Exhibit 18.8, the imposition of the tariff shifts the perfectly elastic supply curve from foreigners to domestic consumers upward from S_{WORLD} to $S_{WORLD+TARIFF}$, but it does not alter the domestic supply or demand curve. At the resulting higher domestic price (P_{W+T}), domestic suppliers are willing to supply more, Qi_S, but domestic consumers are willing to buy less, Q'_D. At the new equilibrium, the domestic price (P_{W+T}) is higher and the quantity of shoes demanded (Q'_D) is lower. But at the new price, the domestic quantity demanded is lower and the quantity supplied domestically is higher, reducing the quantity of imported shoes. Overall, then, tariffs lead to (1) a smaller total quantity sold, (2) a higher price for shoes for domestic consumers, (3) greater sales of shoes at higher prices for domestic producers, and (4) lower sales of foreign shoes.

Although domestic producers do gain more sales and higher earnings, consumers lose much more. The increase in price from the tariff results in a loss in consumer surplus, as shown in Exhibit 18.8. After the tariff, shoe prices rise to P_{W+T}, and, consequently, consumer surplus falls by area c + d + e + f, representing the welfare loss to consumers from the tariff.

Area c in Exhibit 18.8 shows the gain to domestic producers as a result of the tariff. That is, at the higher price, domestic producers are willing to supply more shoes, representing a welfare gain to producers resulting from the tariff. As a result of the tariff revenues, government gains area e. This is the import tariff—the revenue government collects from foreign countries on imports. However, we see from Exhibit 18.8 that consumers lose more than producers and government gain from the tariff. That is, on net, the deadweight loss associated with the tariff is represented by area d + f.

ARGUMENTS FOR TARIFFS

Despite the preceding arguments against trade restrictions, they continue to be levied. Some rationale for their existence is necessary. Three common arguments for the use of trade restrictions deserve our critical examination.

Temporary Trade Restrictions Help Infant Industries Grow

A country might argue that a protective tariff will allow a new industry to more quickly reach a scale of operation at which economies of scale and production efficiencies can be realized. That is, temporarily shielding the young industry from competition from foreign firms will allow the infant industry a chance to grow. With early protection, these firms will eventually be able to compete effectively in the global market. It is presumed that without this protection, the industry could never get on its feet. At first hearing, the argument sounds valid, but it involves many problems. How do you identify "infant industries" that genuinely have potential economies of scale and will quickly become efficient with protection? We do not know the long-run average total cost curves of industries, a necessary piece of information. Moreover, if firms and governments are truly convinced of the advantages of allowing an

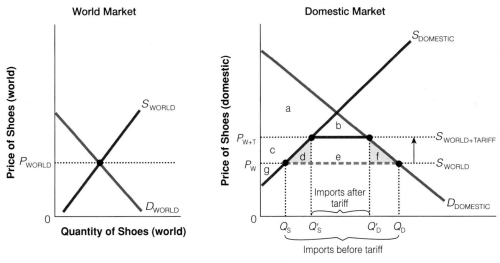

EXHIBIT 18.8 Free Trade and Tariffs

Gains and Losses from Tariffs			
Area	Before Tariffs	After Tariffs	Change
Consumer Surplus (CS)	a + b + c + d + e + f	a + b	−c − d − e − f
Producer Surplus (PS)	g	c + g	+c
Government Revenues (Tariff)	0	e	+e
Total Welfare from Tariff (CS + PS + Tariff Revenues)	a + b + c + d + e + f + g	a + b + c + e + g	−d − f

industry to reach a large scale, would it not be wise to make massive loans to the industry, allowing it to begin large-scale production all at once rather than slowly and at the expense of consumers? In other words, the goal of allowing the industry to reach its efficient size can be reached without protection. Finally, the history of infant industry tariffs suggests that the tariffs often linger long after the industry is mature and no longer in need of protection.

Tariffs Can Reduce Domestic Unemployment

Exhibit 18.8 shows how tariffs increase output by domestic producers, thus leading to increased employment and reduced unemployment in industries where tariffs have been imposed. Yet the overall employment effects of a tariff imposition are not likely to be positive; the argument is incorrect. Why? First, the imposition of a tariff by the United States on, say, foreign steel is going to be noticed in the countries adversely affected by the tariff. If a new tariff on steel lowers Japanese steel sales to the United States, the Japanese will likely retaliate by imposing tariffs on U.S. exports to Japan, say, on machinery exports. The retaliatory tariff will lower U.S. sales of machinery and thus employment in the U.S. machinery industries. As a result, the gain in employment in the steel industry will be offset by a loss of employment elsewhere.

Even if other countries did not retaliate, U.S. employment would likely suffer outside the industry gaining tariff protection. The way that other countries pay for U.S. goods is by getting dollars from sales to the United States—imports to us. If new tariffs lead to restrictions on imports, fewer dollars will be flowing overseas in payment for imports, which means that foreigners will have fewer dollars available to buy our exports. Other things being equal, this situation will tend to reduce our exports, thus creating unemployment in the export industries.

Tariffs Are Necessary for Reasons of National Security

Sometimes it is argued that tariffs are a means of preventing a nation from becoming too dependent on foreign suppliers of goods vital to national security. That is, by making foreign goods more expensive, we can protect domestic suppliers. For example, if oil is vital to operating planes and tanks, a cutoff of foreign

supplies of oil during wartime could cripple a nation's defenses.

The national security argument is usually not valid. If a nation's own resources are depletable, tariff-imposed reliance on domestic supplies will hasten depletion of domestic reserves, making the country even *more* dependent on imports in the future. If we impose a high tariff on foreign oil to protect domestic producers, we will increase domestic output of oil in the short run; but in the process, we will deplete the stockpile of available reserves. Thus, the defense argument is of questionable validity. From a defense standpoint, it makes more sense to use foreign oil in peacetime and perhaps stockpile "insurance" supplies so that larger domestic supplies would be available during wars.

Are Tariffs Necessary to Protect against Dumping?

Dumping occurs when a foreign country sells its products at prices below their costs or below the prices for which they are sold on the domestic market. For example, the Japanese government has been accused for years of subsidizing Japanese steel producers as they attempt to gain a greater share of the world steel market and greater market power. That is, the short-term losses from selling below cost may be offset by the long-term economic profits from employing this strategy. Some have argued that tariffs are needed to protect domestic producers against low-cost dumpers because they will raise the cost to foreign producers and offset their cost advantage.

The United States has antidumping laws; if a foreign country is found guilty of dumping, the United States can impose antidumping tariffs on that country's products, thereby raising the price of the foreign goods that are being dumped. In practice, however, it is often difficult to prove dumping; foreign countries may simply have lower steel production costs. So what may seem like dumping may in fact be comparative advantage.

IMPORT QUOTAS

Like tariffs, **import quotas** directly restrict imports, leading to reductions in trade and thus preventing nations from fully realizing their comparative advantage. The case for quotas is probably even weaker than the case for tariffs. Unlike what occurs with a tariff, the U.S. government does not collect any revenue as a result of the import quota. Despite the higher prices, the loss in consumer surplus, and the loss in government revenue, quotas come about because people often view them as being less protectionist than tariffs—the traditional, most-maligned form of protection.

Besides the rather blunt means of curtailing imports by using tariffs and quotas, nations have devised still other, more subtle means of restricting international trade. For example, nations sometimes impose product standards, ostensibly to protect consumers against inferior merchandise. Effectively, however, those standards may be simply a means of restricting foreign competition. For example, France might keep certain kinds of wine out of the country on the grounds that they are made with allegedly inferior grapes or have an inappropriate alcoholic content. Likewise, the United States might prohibit automobile imports that do not meet certain standards in terms of pollutants, safety, and gasoline mileage. Even if these standards are not intended to restrict foreign competition, the regulations may nonetheless have that impact, restricting consumer choice in the process.

THE DOMESTIC ECONOMIC IMPACT OF AN IMPORT QUOTA

import quota a legal limit on the imported quantity of a good that is produced abroad and can be sold in domestic markets

rent seeking efforts by producers to gain profits from government protections such as tariffs and import quotas

The domestic economic impact of an import quota on autos is presented in Exhibit 18.9 on the next page. The introduction of an import quota increases the price from the world price, P_W (established in the world market for autos) to P_{W+Q}. The quota causes the price to rise above the world price. The domestic quantity demanded falls and the domestic quantity supplied rises. Consequently, the number of imports is much smaller than it would be without the import quota. Compared with free trade, domestic producers are better off but domestic consumers are worse off. Specifically, the import quota results in a gain in producer surplus of area c and a loss in consumer surplus of area c + d + e + f. However, unlike the tariff case, where the government gains area e in revenues, the government does not gain any revenues with a quota. Consequently, the deadweight loss is even greater with quotas than with tariffs. That is, on net, the deadweight loss associated with the quota is represented by area d + e + f. Recall that the deadweight loss was only d + f for tariffs.

If tariffs and import quotas hurt importing countries, why do they exist? The reason they exist is that producers can make large profits or "rents" from tariffs and import quotas. Economists call these efforts to gain profits from government protection **rent seeking**.

Tariffs on foreign exports can lead to retaliatory tariffs on domestic exports.

EXHIBIT 18.9 Free Trade and Import Quotas

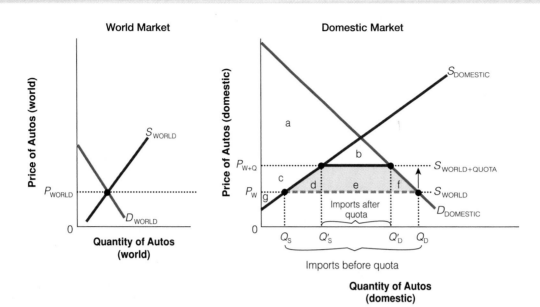

Gains and Losses from Import Quotas			
Area	**Before Quota**	**After Quota**	**Change**
Consumer Surplus (*CS*)	a + b + c + d + e + f	a + b	−c − d − e − f
Producer Surplus (*PS*)	g	c + g	+c
Total Welfare (*CS* + *PS*) from Quota	a + b + c + d + e + f + g	a + b + c + g	−d − e − f

Some countries might use methods other than tariffs and import quotes to restrict trade. For example, France might impose quality standards on certain products such as imported wine.

Because this money, time, and effort spent on lobbying could have been spent producing something else, the deadweight loss from tariffs and quotas will likely understate the true deadweight loss to society.

THE ECONOMIC IMPACT OF SUBSIDIES

Working in the opposite direction, governments sometimes try to encourage exports by subsidizing producers. With a subsidy, revenue is given to producers for each exported unit of output, which stimulates exports. Although not a barrier to trade like tariffs and quotas, subsidies can distort trade patterns and lead to inefficiencies. How do these distortions happen? With subsidies, producers will export goods not because their costs are lower than those of a foreign competitor but because their costs have been artificially reduced by government action, transferring income from taxpayers to the exporter. The subsidy does not reduce the amounts of actual labor, raw material, and capital costs of production—society has the same opportunity costs as before. The nation's taxpayers end up subsidizing the output of producers who, relative to producers in other countries, are inefficient. The nation, then, is exporting products in which it does not have a comparative advantage. Gains from trade in terms of world output are eliminated or reduced by such subsidies. Thus, while usually defended as a means of increasing exports and improving a nation's international financial position, subsidies are usually of dubious worth to the world economy and even to the economy doing the subsidizing.

According to the World Bank and the International Monetary Fund (IMF), world trade has benefited enormously from greater openness in trade since 1950. Tariffs on goods have fallen from a worldwide average of 26 percent to less than 9 percent today. On average, trade has grown more than twice as fast as world output.

SECTION CHECK 4

4.1 Tariffs bring about higher prices and revenues to domestic producers and lower sales and revenues to foreign producers. Tariffs lead to higher prices and reduce consumer surplus for domestic consumers. Tariffs result in a net loss in welfare because the loss in consumer surplus is greater than the gain to producers and the government.

4.2 Like tariffs, import quotas restrict imports, lowering consumer surplus and preventing countries from fully realizing their comparative advantage. The net loss in welfare from a quota is proportionally larger than for a tariff because it does not result in government revenues.

4.3 Sometimes government tries to encourage production of a certain good by subsidizing its production with taxpayer dollars. Because subsidies stimulate exports, they are not a barrier to trade like tariffs and import quotas. However, they do distort trade patterns and cause overall inefficiencies.

⑤5 The Balance of Payments

Keep the following questions in mind as you read through this section. You'll find the answers in **Section Check 5**.

5.1 What is the balance of payments?

5.2 What are the three main components of the balance of payments?

5.3 What is the balance of trade?

The record of all of the international financial transactions of a nation over a year is called the balance of payments. The **balance of payments** is a statement that records all the exchanges requiring an outflow of funds to foreign nations or an inflow of funds from other nations. Just as an examination of gross domestic product accounts gives us some idea of the economic health and vitality of a nation, the balance of payments provides information about a nation's world trade position. The balance of payments is divided into three main sections: the current account, the capital account, and an "error term" called the statistical discrepancy. These are highlighted in Exhibit 18.10 on the next page. Let's look at each of these components, beginning with the current account, which is made up of imports and exports of goods and services.

THE CURRENT ACCOUNT

A **current account** is a record of a country's imports and exports of goods and services, net investment income, and net transfers.

Export Goods and the Current Account

Any time a foreign buyer purchases a good from a U.S. producer, the foreign buyer must pay the U.S. producer for the good. Usually, the foreign buyer must pay for the good in U.S. dollars, because the producer wants to pay his workers' wages and other input costs with dollars. Making this payment requires the foreign buyer to exchange units of her currency at a foreign exchange dealer for U.S. dollars. Because the United States gains claims for foreign goods by obtaining foreign currency in exchange for the

balance of payments the record of international transactions in which a nation has engaged over a year

current account a record of a country's imports and exports of goods and services, net investment income, and net transfers

dollars needed to buy exports, all exports of U.S. goods abroad are considered a credit, or plus (+), item in the U.S. balance of payments. Those foreign currencies are later exchangeable for goods and services made in the country that purchased the U.S. exports.

Import Goods and the Current Account

When a U.S. consumer buys an imported good, however, the reverse is true: The U.S. importer must pay the foreign producer, usually in that nation's currency. Typically, the U.S. buyer will go to a foreign exchange dealer and exchange dollars for units of that foreign currency. Imports are thus a debit (−) item in the balance of payments, because the dollars sold to buy the foreign currency add to foreign claims for foreign goods, which are later exchangeable for U.S. goods and services. U.S. imports, then, provide the means by which foreigners can buy U.S. exports.

Services and the Current Account

Even though imports and exports of goods are the largest components of the balance of payments, they are not the only ones. Nations import and export services as well. A particularly important service is tourism. When U.S. tourists go abroad, they are buying foreign-produced services in addition to those purchased by citizens there. Those services include the use of hotels,

sightseeing tours, restaurants, and so forth. In the current account, these services are included in imports. On the other hand, foreign tourism in the United States provides us with foreign currencies and claims against foreigners, so they are included in exports. Airline and shipping services also affect the balance of payments. When someone from Italy flies American Airlines,

When foreigners purchase tourism services inside a country, these actually count as exports for that country. Tourism could provide the country with foreign currencies and claims against foreign consumers.

EXHIBIT 18.10 U.S. Balance of Payments, 2009 (billions of dollars)

Type of Transaction						
Current Account			**Capital Account**			
1. Exports of goods	$ 1,046		10. U.S.-owned assets abroad	$−237		
2. Imports of goods	−1,563		11. Foreign-owned assets in the United States	435		
3. Balance of trade (lines 1 + 2)		−517	12. Capital account balance (lines 10 + 11)			198
4. Service exports	509		13. Statistical discrepancy	222		
5. Service imports	−371		14. Net Balance (lines 9 + 12 + 13)			$0
6. Balance on goods and services (lines 3 + 4 + 5)		−379				
7. Unilateral transfers (net)	−130					
8. Investment income (net)	89					
9. Current account balance (lines 6 + 7 + 8)		−420				

SOURCE: Bureau of Economic Analysis, *U.S. International Transactions Account Data*, Table 1. Washington, D.C., March 18, 2010. Available at http://www.bea.gov/international/bp_web/simple.cfm?anon=71&table_id=1&area_id=3 (accessed April 9, 2010).

that person is making a payment to a U.S. company. Because the flow of international financial claims is the same, this payment is treated just like a U.S. export in the balance of payments. If an American flies on Alitalia, however, Italians acquire claims against the United States; and so it is included as a debit (import) item in the U.S. balance-of-payments accounts.

Net Transfer Payments and Net Investment Income

Other items that affect the current account are private and government grants and gifts to and from other countries. When the U.S. gives foreign aid to another country, a debit occurs in the U.S. balance of payments because the aid gives foreigners added claims against the United States in the form of dollars. Private gifts, such as individuals sending money to relatives or friends in foreign countries, show up in the current account as debit items as well. Because the United States usually sends more humanitarian and military aid to foreigners than it receives, net transfers are usually in deficit.

Net investment income is also included in the current account (line 8)—U.S. investors hold foreign assets and foreign investors hold U.S. assets. Payments received by U.S. residents are added to the current account and payments made by U.S. residents are subtracted from the current account. In 2008, a net flow of $2 billion came into the United States.

The Current Account Balance

The balance on the current account is the net amount of credits or debits after adding up all transactions of goods (merchandise imports and exports), services, and transfer payments (e.g., foreign aid and gifts). If the sum of credits exceeds the sum of debits, the nation is said to run a balance-of-payments surplus on the current account. If debits exceed credits, however, the nation is running a balance-of-payments deficit on the current account.

The Balance of Trade and the Balance of the Current Account

The balance of payments of the United States for 2009 is presented in Exhibit 18.10. Notice that exports and imports of goods and services are by far the largest credits and debits. Notice also that U.S. exports of goods were $517 billion less than imports of goods. The import/export goods relationship is often called the **balance of trade.** The United States, therefore, experienced a balance-of-trade deficit that year of $517 billion. However, some of the $517 billion trade deficit is offset by credits from a $138 billion surplus in services. This difference leads to a $379 billion deficit in the balance of goods and services. When $130 billion of net unilateral transfers (gifts and grants between the United States and foreigners) and $89 billion of investment income (net) from the United States are added (the foreigners gave more to the United States than the United States gave to the foreigners), the total deficit on the current account is $420 billion. Exhibit 18.11 on the next page shows the balance on the current account since 1975.

> **balance of trade** the net surplus or deficit resulting from the level of exportation and importation of merchandise

THE CAPITAL ACCOUNT

How was this deficit on the current account financed? Remember that U.S. credits give us the financial means to buy foreign goods and that our credits were $545

The capital account records foreign purchases or assets in the United States (a monetary inflow) and U.S. purchases of assets abroad (a monetary outflow).

EXHIBIT 18.11 U.S. Balance of Trade on Goods, 1975–2009

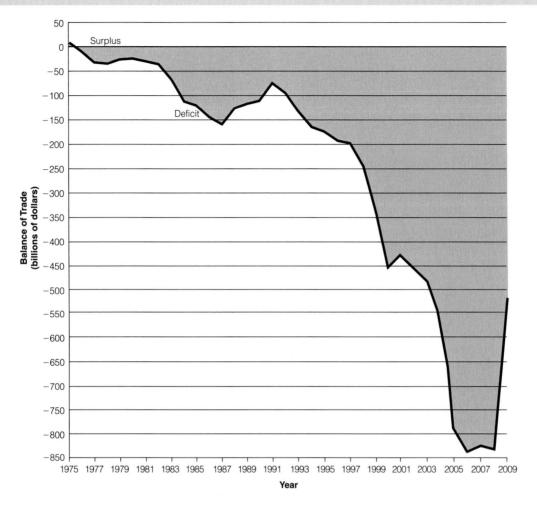

SOURCE: Bureau of Economic Analysis, *U.S. International Transactions Account Data*, Table 1. Washington, D.C., March 18, 2010. Available at http://www.bea.gov/international/bp_web/simple.cfm?anon=71&table_id=1&area_id=3 (accessed April 9, 2010).

capital account records the foreign purchases or assets in the domestic economy (a monetary inflow) and domestic purchases of assets abroad (a monetary outflow)

billion less than our debits from imports and net unilateral transfers to foreign countries. This deficit on the current account balance is settled by movements of financial, or capital, assets. These transactions are recorded in the *capital account*, so that a current account deficit is financed by a capital account surplus. In short, the **capital account** records the foreign purchases or assets in the United States (a monetary inflow) and U.S. purchases of assets abroad (a monetary outflow).

What Does the Capital Account Record?

Capital account transactions include such items as international bank loans, purchases of corporate securities, government bond purchases, and direct investments in foreign subsidiary companies. In 2009, the United States purchased foreign assets of $237 billion, which was a further debit because it provided foreigners with U.S. dollars. On the other hand, foreign investments in U.S. bonds, stocks, and other items totaled $435 billion. In addition, the United States and other governments buy and sell dollars. On net in 2009, foreign-owned assets in the United States made about $198 billion more than did U.S. assets abroad. On balance, then, a surplus (positive credit) in the capital account from capital movements amounted to $198 billion, offsetting the $420 billion deficit on the current account.

THE STATISTICAL DISCREPANCY

In the final analysis, it is true that the balance-of-payments account (current account minus capital account) must balance so that credits and debits are equal. Why? Due to the reciprocal aspect of trade, every credit eventually creates a debit of equal magnitude. These errors are sometimes large and are entered into the balance of payments as the *statistical discrepancy*. Including the errors and omissions recorded as the statistical discrepancy, the balance of payments does balance. That is, the number of U.S. dollars demanded equals the number of U.S. dollars supplied when the balance of payments is zero.

BALANCE OF PAYMENTS: A USEFUL ANALOGY

In concept, the international balance of payments is similar to the personal financial transactions of an individual. Each individual has a personal "balance of payments," reflecting that person's trading with other economic units: other individuals, corporations, and governments. People earn income or credits by "exporting" their labor service to other economic units or by receiving investment income (a return on capital services). Against that, they "import" goods from other economic units; we call these imports consumption. This debit item is sometimes augmented by payments made to outsiders (e.g., banks) on loans and so forth. Fund transfers, such as gifts to children or charities, are other debit items (or credit items for recipients of the assistance).

As individuals, if our spending on consumption exceeds our income from exporting our labor and capital services, we have a "deficit" that must be financed by borrowing or selling assets. If we "export" more than we "import," however, we can make new investments and/or increase our "reserves" (savings and investment holdings). Like nations, an individual who runs a deficit in daily transactions must make up for it through accommodating transactions (e.g., borrowing or reducing personal savings or investment holdings) to bring about an ultimate balance of credits and debits in his or her personal account.

SECTION CHECK 5

5.1 The balance of payments is the record of all the international financial transactions of a nation for any given year.

5.2 The balance of payments is made up of the current account, the capital account, and an "error term" called the statistical discrepancy.

5.3 The balance of trade refers strictly to the import and export of goods (merchandise) from/to other nations. If our imports of foreign goods are greater than our exports, we are said to have a balance-of-trade deficit.

⑤6 Exchange Rates

Keep the following questions in mind as you read through this section. You'll find the answers in **Section Check 6**.

6.1 What are exchange rates?

6.2 How are exchange rates determined?

6.3 How do exchange rates affect the demand for foreign goods?

When a U.S. consumer buys goods from a seller in another country—who naturally wants to be paid in her own domestic currency—the U.S. consumer must first exchange U.S. dollars for the seller's currency in order to pay for those goods. American importers must, therefore, constantly buy yen, euros, pesos, and other currencies in order to finance their purchases. Similarly, someone in another country buying U.S. goods must sell his domestic currency to obtain U.S. dollars to pay for those goods.

THE EXCHANGE RATE

The price of a unit of one foreign currency in terms of another is called the **exchange rate**. If a U.S. importer has agreed to

exchange rate the price of one unit of a country's currency in terms of another country's currency

derived demand the demand for an input derived from consumers' demand for the good or service produced with that input

pay euros (the currency of the European Union) to buy a cuckoo clock made in the Black Forest in Germany, she would then have to exchange U.S. dollars for euros. If it takes $1 to buy 1 euro, then the exchange rate is $1 per euro. From the German perspective, the exchange rate is 1 euro per U.S. dollar.

CHANGES IN EXCHANGE RATES AFFECT THE DOMESTIC DEMAND FOR FOREIGN GOODS

Prices of goods in their currencies combine with exchange rates to determine the domestic price of foreign goods. Suppose the cuckoo clock sells for 100 euros in Germany. What is the price to U.S. consumers? Let's assume that tariffs and other transaction costs are zero. If the exchange rate is $1 = 1 euro, then the equivalent U.S. dollar price of the cuckoo clock is 100 euros times $1 per euro, or $100. If the exchange rate were to change to $2 = 1 euro, fewer clocks would be demanded in the United States, because the effective U.S. dollar price of the clocks would rise to $200 (100 euros × $2 per euro). The higher relative value of a euro compared to the dollar (or, equivalently, the lower relative value of a dollar compared to the euro) would lead to a reduction in U.S. demand for German-made clocks.

THE DEMAND FOR A FOREIGN CURRENCY

The demand for foreign currencies is known as a **derived demand**, because the demand for a foreign currency derives directly from the demand for foreign goods and services or for foreign investment. The more that goods from a foreign country are demanded, the more of that country's currency is needed to pay for those goods. This increased demand for the currency will push up the exchange value of that currency relative to other currencies.

THE SUPPLY OF A FOREIGN CURRENCY

Similarly, the supply of foreign currency is provided by foreigners who want to buy the exports of a particular nation. For example, the more that foreigners demand U.S. products, the more of their currencies they will supply in exchange for U.S. dollars, which they use to buy our products.

DETERMINING EXCHANGE RATES

We know that the demand for foreign currencies is derived from the demand for foreign goods, but how does that affect the exchange rate? Just as in the product market, the answer lies with the forces of supply and demand. In this case, it is the supply of and demand for a foreign currency that determine the equilibrium price (exchange rate) of that currency.

THE DEMAND CURVE FOR A FOREIGN CURRENCY

As Exhibit 18.12 shows, the demand curve for a foreign currency—the euro, for example—is downward sloping, just as it is in product markets. In this case, however, the demand curve has a negative slope because as the price of the euro falls relative to the dollar, European products become relatively more inexpensive to U.S. consumers, who therefore buy more European goods. To do so, the quantity of euros demanded by U.S.

© COMSTOCK IMAGES/GETTY IMAGES

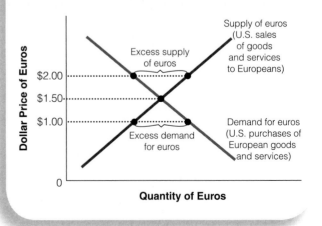

EXHIBIT 18.12 Equilibrium in the Foreign Exchange Market

consumers will increase as U.S. consumers buy more European goods as the price of the euro falls. For this reason, the demand for foreign currencies is considered to be a derived demand.

THE SUPPLY CURVE FOR FOREIGN CURRENCY

The supply curve for a foreign currency is upward sloping, just as it is in product markets. In this case, as the price, or value, of the euro increases relative to the dollar, U.S. products will become relatively less expensive to European buyers, who will thus increase the quantity of dollars they demand. Europeans will, therefore, increase the quantity of euros supplied to the United States by buying more U.S. products.

EQUILIBRIUM IN THE FOREIGN EXCHANGE MARKET

Equilibrium is reached where the demand and supply curves for a given currency intersect. In Exhibit 18.12, the equilibrium price of a euro is $1.50. As in the product market, if the dollar price of euros is higher than the equilibrium price, an excess quantity of euros will be supplied at that price; that is, a surplus of euros will exist. Competition among euro sellers will push the price of euros down toward equilibrium. Likewise, if the dollar price of euros is lower than the equilibrium price, an excess quantity of euros will be demanded at that price; that is, a shortage of euros will occur. Competition among euro buyers will push the price of euros up toward equilibrium.

SECTION CHECK 6

6.1 The price of a unit of one foreign currency in terms of another is called the exchange rate.

6.2 The exchange rate for a currency is determined by the supply of and demand for that currency in the foreign exchange market.

6.3 If the dollar appreciates in value relative to foreign currencies, foreign goods become more inexpensive to U.S. consumers, increasing U.S. demand for foreign goods.

(S)7 Equilibrium Changes in the Foreign Exchange Market

Keep the following questions in mind as you read through this section. You'll find the answers in **Section Check 7**.

7.1 What factors cause the exchange rate to change?

7.2 What factors cause the supply and demand curves for a currency to shift?

The equilibrium exchange rate of a currency changes many times daily. Sometimes, these changes can be quite significant. Any force that shifts either the demand for or supply of a currency will shift the equilibrium in the foreign exchange market, leading to a new exchange rate. Among such factors are changes in consumer tastes for goods, income levels, relative real interest rates, and relative inflation rates, as well as speculation.

INCREASED TASTES FOR FOREIGN GOODS

Because the demand for foreign currencies is derived from the demand for foreign goods, any change in the U.S. demand for foreign goods will shift the demand schedule for foreign currency in the same direction. For example, if a cuckoo clock revolution sweeps through the United States, German producers will have reason to celebrate, knowing that many U.S. buyers will turn to Germany for their cuckoo clocks. However, because Germans will only accept payment in the form of euros, U.S. consumers and retailers must convert their dollars into euros before they can purchase their clocks. The increased taste for European goods in the United States will, therefore, lead to an increased demand for euros. As shown in Exhibit 18.13 on the next page, this increased demand for euros shifts the demand curve to the right, resulting in a new, higher equilibrium dollar price of euros.

RELATIVE INCOME INCREASES OR REDUCTIONS IN U.S. TARIFFS

Any change in the average income of U.S. consumers will also change the equilibrium exchange rate, *ceteris paribus*. If on the whole incomes were to increase in the United States, Americans would buy more goods, including imported goods, hence more European goods would be bought. This increased demand for European goods would lead to an increased demand for euros, resulting in a higher exchange rate for the euro. A decrease in U.S. tariffs on European goods would tend to have the same effect as an increase in incomes, by making European goods more affordable. Exhibit 18.13 shows that it would again lead to an increased demand for European goods and a higher short-run equilibrium exchange rate for the euro.

INCREASES IN EUROPEAN INCOMES, REDUCTIONS IN EUROPEAN TARIFFS, OR CHANGES IN EUROPEAN TASTES

If European incomes rose, European tariffs on U.S. goods fell, or European tastes for American goods increased, the supply of euros in the euro foreign exchange market would increase. Any of these changes would cause Europeans to demand more U.S. goods and therefore more U.S. dollars to purchase those goods. To obtain these added dollars, Europeans would have to exchange more of their euros, increasing the supply of euros on the euro foreign exchange market. As Exhibit 18.14 demonstrates, the result would be a rightward shift in the euro supply curve, leading to a new equilibrium at a lower exchange rate for the euro.

HOW DO CHANGES IN RELATIVE REAL INTEREST RATES AFFECT EXCHANGE RATES?

If interest rates in the United States were to increase relative to, say, European interest rates, *ceteris paribus*, the rate of return on U.S. investments would increase relative to that on European investments. European investors would then increase their demand for U.S. investments and therefore offer euros for sale in order to buy dollars to buy U.S. investments, shifting the supply curve for euros to the right, from S_1 to S_2 in Exhibit 18.15.

In this scenario, U.S. investors would also shift their investments away from Europe by decreasing their demand for euros relative to their demand for dollars, from D_1 to D_2 in Exhibit 18.15. A subsequent, lower equilibrium price ($1.50) would result for the euro as a result of the increase in U.S. interest rates. That is, the euro would depreciate, because euros could now buy fewer units of dollars than before. In short, the higher U.S. interest rates would attract more investment to the United States, leading to a relative

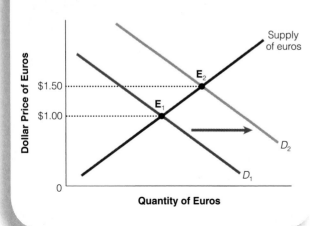

EXHIBIT 18.13 Impact on the Foreign Exchange Market of a U.S. Change in Taste, Income Increase, or Tariff Decrease

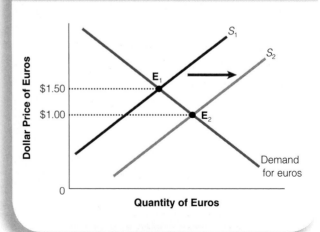

EXHIBIT 18.14 Impact on the Foreign Exchange Market of a European Change in Taste, Income Increase, or Tariff Decrease

EXHIBIT 18.15 Impact on the Foreign Exchange Market from an Increase in the U.S. Interest Rate

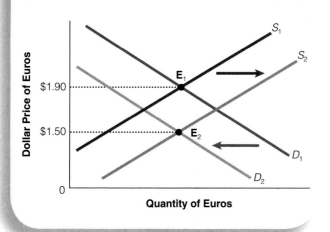

EXHIBIT 18.16 Impact on the Foreign Exchange Market from an Increase in the European Inflation Rate

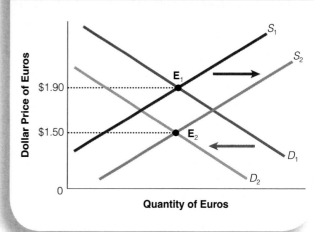

appreciation of the dollar and a relative depreciation of the euro.

CHANGES IN THE RELATIVE INFLATION RATE

If Europe experienced an inflation rate greater than that experienced in the United States, *ceteris paribus*, what would happen to the exchange rate? In this case, European products would become more expensive to U.S. consumers. Americans would then decrease the quantity of European goods demanded and thus decrease their demand for euros. The result would be a leftward shift of the demand curve for euros.

On the other side of the Atlantic, U.S. goods would become relatively cheaper to Europeans, leading Europeans to increase the quantity of U.S. goods demanded and thus to demand more U.S. dollars. This increased demand for dollars would translate into an increased supply of euros, shifting the supply curve for euros outward. Exhibit 18.16 shows the shifts of the supply and demand curves and the new lower equilibrium price for the euro resulting from the higher European rate.

EXPECTATIONS AND SPECULATION

Every trading day, roughly a trillion dollars in currency trades hands in the foreign exchange markets. Suppose

currency traders believe that in the future the United States will experience more rapid inflation than will Japan. If currency speculators believe that the value of the dollar will soon be falling because of the anticipated rise in the U.S. inflation rate, those who are holding dollars will convert them to yen. This move will lead to an increase in the demand for yen—the yen appreciates and the dollar depreciates relative to the yen, *ceteris paribus*. In short, if speculators believe that the price of a country's currency is going to rise, they will buy more of that currency, pushing up the price and causing the country's currency to appreciate.

SECTION CHECK 7

7.1 Any force that shifts either the demand or the supply curves for a foreign currency will shift the equilibrium in the foreign exchange market and lead to a new exchange rate.

7.2 Any changes in tastes, income levels, relative real interest rates, or relative inflation rates will cause the demand for and supply of a currency to shift.

WEAK DOLLAR CRIMPS STUDY ABROAD

—by Kelly Evans and Sara Murray

Wilmer Gutierrez, a 21-year-old junior at Goucher College in Baltimore, had hoped to go to Denmark next fall to study European politics. But the weak dollar has prompted a change of plan: Now, he will head to Argentina to study the Latin American political system.

With the greenback down 20% against the Danish krone and up 4% against the Argentine peso in the past two years, Mr. Gutierrez says he has little choice but to head south. "It's very frustrating," he says.

Many other college students, hit by sticker shock, also are steering clear of Western Europe, especially the United Kingdom, and opting for study-abroad programs in Asia, Africa, and Latin America. Many of those destinations are cheaper to begin with and have currencies that haven't been as rough on the dollar.

Over the past two years, the dollar, while up a bit from recent lows, has lost more than 20% of its value against the euro and about 6% against the pound. The result: While programs in places like Rome, Paris, Barcelona, and London are still at the top of students' lists, enrollment there is slowing. And interest in alternative destinations is surging.

Nearly a quarter of a million students from the U.S. studied abroad for academic credit during the 2005–2006 school year, according to the most recent data from the Institute of International Education, a New York-based nonprofit organization that administers study-abroad programs. Each college handles study-abroad programs differently—some directly host programs in other countries so students pay the same tuition as they would for a semester at home in the U.S. Others allow students to enroll in programs offered by other colleges or by third-party study-abroad providers that enroll them directly in foreign institutions. . . .

Language students often choose their location to become fluent speakers and learn about the culture of a chosen region; others, such as business students, may choose a program that enhances their résumé (such as China, India, or the Middle East).

Geoffrey Bannister, president and chief academic officer of Cultural Experiences Abroad, a company based in Tempe, Ariz., that runs study-abroad programs, says enrollment in the company's Western Europe programs grew just 8% for next fall, much less than the usual increase of 20% to 25%. Buenos Aires, meanwhile, is getting a lot of interest, he says. . . .

Nathan Bullock, a University of Richmond sophomore who is majoring in history and international studies, considered expenses carefully when deciding between Hong Kong and France for the current semester.

The university was going to charge him the same tuition regardless of where he went, so his decision came down to room and board—and he knew his dollars would go further in Hong Kong, where the currency is pegged to the dollar.

"Just getting an apartment or living with a family would be so expensive in France," he says. In Hong Kong, his room and board costs about HK$3,000, or about US$385 a semester. In addition, it's an easy jumping-off point for other parts of Asia, where traveling can be a bargain.

Even in Shanghai, the most expensive place he has visited, Mr. Bullock spent only 55 yuan a night—less than $8—for a room in a hostel. By comparison, in Paris, the cheapest hostels run 12 to 16 euros, or about $18 to $24.

American students in Europe understand the need to scale back. "Just to lead a normal student life here is so expensive," says Sarah Ott, a junior at Ohio's Kenyon College who is studying in Paris.

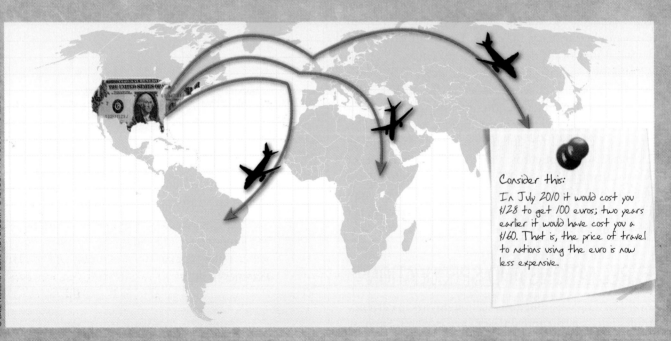

Consider this:

In July 2010 it would cost you $128 to get 100 euros; two years earlier it would have cost you a $160. That is, the price of travel to nations using the euro is now less expensive.

To save money, Ms. Ott says, she and other students avoid cozy cafes, which can easily charge $7 or $8 for a glass of soda. Instead, they get takeout sandwiches and carry around six-packs of Coca-Cola. They patronize bars offering cheap beer rather than nightclubs. And they pinch pennies during sightseeing jaunts to nearby cities.

"I went into it thinking traveling would be a cheap little weekend away," Ms. Ott says. "Not so much."

Daeya Malboeuf, a spokeswoman for Syracuse University's study-abroad programs, says the school urges students in its London program to save money by staying in the city on weekends. And it serves free coffee so students "don't have to go to Starbucks," where a medium-size latte runs about 2.40 pounds, or about $4.75.

"We used to be able to say the cost of a semester abroad was the same as a semester here," Ms. Malboeuf says, because a strong dollar made traveling overseas relatively cheap. "We don't say that anymore."

While London, Florence, and Madrid continue to be top destinations for Syracuse students, she says, Hong Kong, Beijing, and Santiago are growing quickly in popularity. . . .

SOURCE: From *The Wall Street Journal* May 14, 2008. Reprinted by permission of *The Wall Street Journal,* Copyright © 2008 Dow Jones & Company, Inc. All Rights Reserved Worldwide.

Ⓢ8 Flexible Exchange Rates

Keep the following questions in mind as you read through this section. You'll find the answers in Section Check 8.

8.1 How are exchange rate changes different under a flexible-rate system than in a fixed-rate system?

8.2 What major problems exist in a fixed-rate system?

8.3 What are the major arguments against flexible rates?

Since 1973, the world has essentially operated on a system of flexible exchange rates. Flexible exchange rates mean that currency prices are allowed to fluctuate with changes in supply and demand, without governments stepping in to prevent those changes. Before that, governments operated under what was called the *Bretton Woods fixed exchange rate system*, in which they would maintain a stable exchange rate by buying or selling currencies or reserves to bring demand and supply for their currencies together at the fixed exchange rate. The present system evolved out of the Bretton Woods fixed-rate system and occurred by accident, not design. Governments were unable to agree on an alternative fixed-rate approach when the Bretton Woods system collapsed, so nations simply let market forces determine currency values.

ARE EXCHANGE RATES MANAGED AT ALL?

To be sure, governments sensitive to sharp changes in the exchange value of their currencies do still intervene from time to time to prop up their currency's exchange rate if it is considered to be too low or falling too rapidly, or to depress its exchange rate if it is considered to be too high or rising too rapidly. Such was the case when the U.S. dollar declined in value in the late 1970s, but the U.S. government intervention appeared to have little if any effect in preventing the dollar's decline. However, present-day fluctuations in exchange rates are not determined solely by market forces. Economists sometimes say that the current exchange rate system is a **dirty float system**, meaning that fluctuations in currency values are partly determined by market forces and partly influenced by government intervention. Over the years, however, such governmental support attempts have been insufficient to dramatically alter exchange rates for long, and currency exchange rates have changed dramatically.

> **dirty float system** a description of the exchange rate system that means that fluctuations in currency values are partly determined by government intervention

WHEN EXCHANGE RATES CHANGE

When exchange rates change, they affect not only the currency market but the product markets as well. For example, if U.S. consumers were to receive fewer and fewer British pounds and Japanese yen per U.S. dollar, the effect would be an increasing price for foreign imports, *ceteris paribus*. It would now take a greater number of dollars to buy a given number of yen or pounds, which U.S. consumers use to purchase those foreign products. It would, however, lower the cost of U.S. exports to foreigners. If, however, the dollar increased in value relative to other currencies, then the relative price of foreign goods would decrease, *ceteris paribus*. But foreigners would find that U.S. goods were more expensive in terms of their own currency prices, and, as a result, would import fewer U.S. products.

THE ADVANTAGES OF FLEXIBLE RATES

As mentioned earlier, the present system of flexible exchange rates was not planned. Indeed, most central bankers thought that a system where rates were not fixed would lead to chaos. What in fact has happened? Since the advent of flexible exchange rates, world trade has not only continued but expanded.

The most important advantage of the flexible-rate system is that the recurrent crises that led to speculative rampages and major currency revaluations under the fixed Bretton Woods system have significantly diminished. Under the fixed-rate system, price changes in currencies came infrequently, but when they came, they were of a large magnitude: 20 percent or 30 percent changes overnight were fairly common. Today, price changes occur daily or even hourly, but each change is much smaller in magnitude, with major changes in exchange rates typically occurring only over periods of months or years.

Some governments work harder to manage the price of their currency. For example, in January 2010, the Chinese government put measures in place linking the value of the Chinese yuan to that of the dollar. But with the Chinese economy growing faster than the U.S. economy, many began to suggest that the yuan was undervalued, giving China certain advantages in trade.

© CHINAFOTOPRESS/GETTY IMAGES

FIXED EXCHANGE RATES CAN RESULT IN CURRENCY SHORTAGES

Perhaps the most significant problem with the fixed-rate system is that it can result in currency shortages, just as domestic price and wage controls lead to shortages. Suppose we had a fixed-rate system with the price of one euro set at $1.00, as shown in Exhibit 18.17. In this example, the original quantity of euros demanded and supplied is indicated by curves D_1 and S, so $1.00 is the equilibrium price. That is, at a price of $1.00, the quantity of euros demanded (by U.S. importers of European products and others wanting euros) equals the quantity supplied (by European importers of U.S. products and others).

Suppose that some event happens to increase U.S. demand for Dutch goods. For this example, let us assume that Royal Dutch Shell discovers new oil reserves in the North Sea and thus has a new product to export. As U.S. consumers begin to demand Royal Dutch Shell oil, the demand for euros increases. That is, at any given dollar price of euros, U.S. consumers want more euros, shifting the demand curve to the right, to D_2. Under a fixed exchange rate system, the dollar price of euros must remain at $1, where the quantity of euros demanded (Q_2) now exceeds the quantity supplied, Q_1. The result is a shortage of euros—a shortage that must be corrected in some way. As a solution to the shortage, the United States may borrow euros from the Netherlands, or perhaps ship the Netherlands some of its reserves of gold. The ability to continually make up the shortage (deficit) in this manner, however, is limited, particularly if the deficit persists for a substantial time.

EXHIBIT 18.17 How Flexible Exchange Rates Work

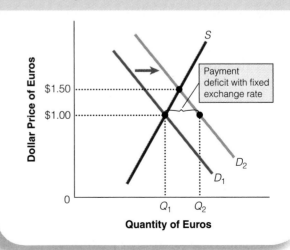

FLEXIBLE RATES SOLVE THE CURRENCY SHORTAGE PROBLEM

Under flexible exchange rates, a change in the supply or demand for euros does not pose a problem. Because rates are allowed to change, the rising U.S. demand for European goods (and thus for euros) would lead to a new equilibrium price for euros, say at $1.50. At this higher price, European goods are more costly to U.S. buyers. Some of the increase in demand for European imports, then, is offset by a decrease in quantity demanded resulting from higher import prices. Similarly, the change in the exchange rate will make U.S. goods cheaper to Europeans, thus increasing U.S. exports and, with that, the quantity of euros supplied. For example, a $40 software program that cost Europeans 40 euros when the exchange rate was $1 per euro costs less than 27 euros when the exchange rate increases to $1.50 per euro ($40 divided by $1.50).

FLEXIBLE RATES AFFECT MACROECONOMIC POLICIES

With flexible exchange rates, the imbalance between debits and credits arising from shifts in currency demand and/or supply is accommodated by changes in currency prices, rather than through the special financial borrowings or reserve movements necessary with fixed rates. In a pure flexible exchange rate system, deficits and surpluses in the balance of payments tend to disappear automatically. The market mechanism itself is able to address world trade imbalances, dispensing with the need for bureaucrats attempting to achieve some administratively determined price. Moreover, the need to use restrictive monetary and/or fiscal policy to end such an imbalance while maintaining a fixed exchange rate is alleviated. Nations are thus able to feel less constraint in carrying out internal macroeconomic policies under flexible exchange rates. For these reasons, many economists welcomed the collapse of the Bretton

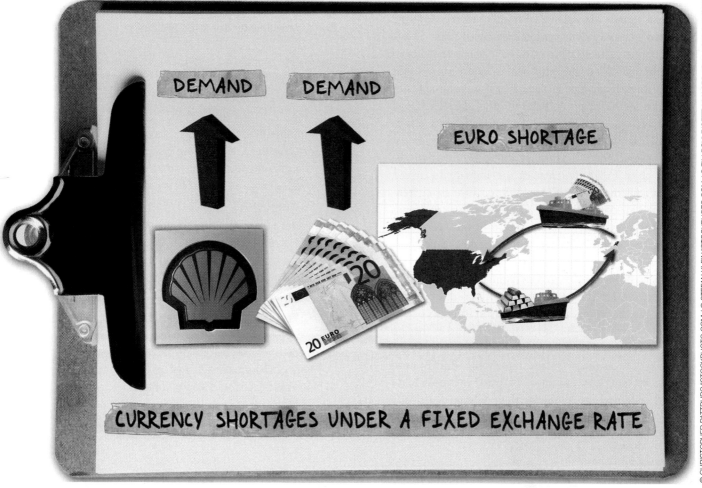

CURRENCY SHORTAGES UNDER A FIXED EXCHANGE RATE

Woods system and the failure to arrive at a new system of fixed or quasi-fixed exchange rates.

THE DISADVANTAGES OF FLEXIBLE RATES

Despite the fact that world trade has grown and dealing with balance-of-payments problems has become less difficult, flexible exchange rates have not been universally endorsed. Several disadvantages of this system have been cited.

Flexible Rates and World Trade

Traditionally, the major objection to flexible rates was that they introduce considerable uncertainty into international trade. For example, if you order some perfume from France with a commitment to pay 1,000 euros in three months, you are not certain what the dollar price of euros, and therefore of the perfume, will be three months from now, because the exchange rate is constantly fluctuating. Because people prefer certainty to uncertainty and are generally risk averse, this uncertainty raises the costs of international transactions. As a result, flexible exchange rates can reduce the volume of trade, thus reducing the potential gains from international specialization.

Proponents of flexible rates have three answers to this argument. First, the empirical evidence shows that international trade has, in fact, grown in volume faster since the introduction of flexible rates. The exchange rate risk of trade has not had any major adverse effect. Second, it is possible to, in effect, buy insurance against the proposed adverse effect of currency fluctuations. Rather than buying currencies for immediate use in what is called the "spot" market for foreign currencies, one can contract today to buy foreign currencies in the future at a set exchange rate in the "forward" or "futures" market. By using this market, a perfume importer can buy euros now for delivery to her in three months; in doing so, she can be certain of the dollar price she is paying for the perfume. Since floating exchange rates began, booming futures markets in foreign currencies have opened in Chicago, New York, and in foreign financial centers. The third argument is that the alleged certainty of currency prices under the old Bretton Woods system was fictitious, because the possibility existed that nations might, at their whim, drastically revalue their currencies to deal with their own fundamental balance-of-payments problems. Proponents of flexible rates, then, argue that they are therefore no less disruptive to trade than fixed rates.

Flexible Rates and Inflation

A second, more valid criticism of flexible exchange rates is that they can contribute to inflationary pressures. Under fixed rates, domestic monetary and fiscal authorities have an incentive to constrain their domestic prices, because lower domestic prices increase the attractiveness of exported goods. This discipline is not present to the same extent with flexible rates. The consequence of a sharp monetary or fiscal expansion under flexible rates would be a decline in the value of one's currency relative to those of other countries. Yet even that may not seem to be as serious a political consequence as the Bretton Woods solution of an abrupt devaluation of the currency in the face of a severe balance-of-payments problem.

Advocates of flexible rates would argue that inflation need not occur under flexible rates. Flexible rates do not cause inflation; rather, it is caused by the expansionary macroeconomic policies of governments and central banks. Actually, flexible rates give government decision makers greater freedom of action than fixed rates; whether they act responsibly is determined not by exchange rates but by domestic policies.

SECTION CHECK 8

8.1 Changes in exchange rates occur more often under a flexible-rate system, but the changes are much smaller than the drastic, overnight revaluations of currencies that occurred under the fixed-rate system.

8.2 Under a fixed-rate system, the supply and demand for currencies shift, but currency prices are not allowed to shift to the new equilibrium, leading to surpluses and shortages of currencies.

8.3 The main arguments presented against flexible exchange rates are that international trade levels will be diminished due to uncertainty of future currency prices and that the flexible rates would lead to inflation.

Chapter 18: Self-Review

Now that you're finished reading the chapter, review the questions below. You can write your answers in the space provided, then go online to see the answers at www.cengagebrain.com.

S1–THE GROWTH IN WORLD TRADE

1. **True or False:** U.S. producers and consumers should be more concerned about Canadian trade restrictions than Swedish trade restrictions.

S2–COMPARATIVE ADVANTAGE AND GAINS FROM TRADE

2. **True or False:** A country cannot have an absolute advantage in producing one good or service without also having a comparative advantage in its production.

S3–SUPPLY AND DEMAND IN INTERNATIONAL TRADE

3. **Fill-in-the-Blank:** If the world price of a good is greater than the domestic price prior to trade, it implies that the domestic economy has a _____ in producing that good.

4. **True or False:** When a country has a comparative advantage in the production of a good, domestic producers gain more than domestic consumers lose from free international trade.

S4–TARIFFS, IMPORT QUOTAS, AND SUBSIDIES

5. **Fill-in-the-Blanks:** Tariffs _____ domestic producer surplus but _____ domestic consumer surplus.

6. **True or False:** Subsidizing exports by industries without a comparative advantage tends to harm the domestic economy.

S5–THE BALANCE OF PAYMENTS

7. **True or False:** British purchasers of U.S. goods and services must first exchange pounds for dollars.

8. **True or False:** A Nigerian family visiting Chicago enjoys a Chicago Cubs baseball game at Wrigley Field. This expense should be recorded as an export of services on the balance-of-payments account.

S6–EXCHANGE RATES

9. **How are each of the following events likely to affect the value of the dollar relative to the euro?**
   a. Interest rates in the European Union increase relative to those in the United States.
   b. The European Union price level rises relative to the U.S. price level.
   c. The European central bank intervenes by selling dollars on currency markets.
   d. The price level in the United States falls relative to the price level in Europe.

S7–EQUILIBRIUM CHANGES IN THE FOREIGN EXCHANGE MARKET

10. **What will happen to the supply of dollars, the demand for dollars, and the equilibrium exchange rate of the dollar in each of the following cases? Fill in the table below.**

	Supply of Dollars	Demand for Dollars	Equilibrium Exchange Rate
Americans buy more European goods.			
Europeans invest in the U.S. stock market.			
European tourists flock to the United States.			
Europeans buy U.S. government bonds.			
American tourists flock to Europe.			

S8–FLEXIBLE EXCHANGE RATES

11. **True or False:** Flexible exchange rates cause higher rates of inflation.

LISTEN UP! SHE DID

Survey of ECON was designed for students just like you—busy people who want choices, flexibility, and multiple learning options.

Survey of ECON delivers concise, focused information in a fresh and contemporary format. And... **Survey of ECON** gives you a variety of online learning materials designed with you in mind.

At **www.cengagebrain.com,** you'll find electronic resources such as **videos,** and **interactive quizzes** for each chapter.

These resources will help supplement your understanding of core concepts in a format that fits your busy lifestyle. Visit **www.cengagebrain.com** to learn more about the multiple resources available to help you succeed!

INDEX

Note: Boldface indicates key terms.

Section Summaries

Ⓢ1 Economics: A Brief Introduction

Economics is the study of the choices we make among our many wants and desires given our limited resources. Scarcity forces us to ch... choices are costly beca... give up other opportun... we value—this is the e... problem. Our scarce re... grouped into four cate... land, capital, and entre... Entrepreneurship is the process of combining labor, land, and capital to produce goods and services. Goods are tangible items that we value or desire, and services are intangible acts for which people are willing to pay. Everyone faces scarcity, and it cannot be eliminated.

> Each Review Card contains summaries for each chapter section. These will provide an overview of the basic concepts from each chapter.

Ⓢ2 Economic Behavior

Economists assume that individuals act as if they are motivated by self-interest and respond in predictable ways to changing circumstances. Self-interest to an economist is not a narrow monetary self-interest. A person acting in self-interest might pursue personal gain, but that does not necessarily exclude helping others. Rational behavior ...le do the ...their values ...current and ...stances. ...ek ...e them better off, we can predict what will happen when incentives are changed.

> Some cards have images from the chapter which can be used as memory prompts to help you recall the information in the written summary.

Ⓢ3 Markets

A market is the process of buyers and sellers exchanging goods and services. In most countries, resources are allocated through a market economy. Efficiency is achieved when the economy gets the most out of its scarce resources. Voluntary exchange and the price system guide people's choices and help determine what ...re produced and how they're ...d. Market failure occurs ... economy fails to allocate ...s efficiently on its own. We ...ular flow model to illustrate ...of goods and services. ...ds and firms interact with each other in product markets (where households buy and firms sell) and factor markets (where households sell and firms buy).

Ⓢ4 Economic Theory

A theory is an established explanation that accounts for known facts or phenomena. Specifically, economic theories are statements or propositions about patterns of human behavior that occur expectedly under certain circumstances. Theories use abstraction to weed out relevant from irrelevant information. A theory begins with a hypothesis, which is tested through empirical analysis. If the data collected supports the hypothesis, it can be tentatively accepted as an economic theory.

Conventionally, we distinguish two main branches of economics: microeconomics, which deals with smaller units in the economy, and macroeconomics, which deals with the aggregate or total economy.

Ⓢ5 Pitfalls to Avoid in Scientific Thinking

The two major pitfalls to avoid are confusing correlation with causation

Key Terms

economics the study of choices we make among our many wants and desires given our limited re...

> Key Terms from the chapter's margins appear in this column (and continue on the back of the card) in the same order in which they appear in the chapter.

resource... ...and servi...

scarcity ...(material ...resources...

the eco... us to choose, and choices are costly because we must give up other opportunities that we value

labor the physical and human effort used in the production of goods and services

land the natural resources used in the production of goods and services

capital the equipment and structures used to produce goods and services

human capital the productive knowledge and skill people receive from education, on-the-job training, health, and other factors that increase productivity

entrepreneurship the process of combining labor, land, and capital to produce goods and services

goods items we value or desire

tangible goods items we value or desire that we can reach out and touch

intangible goods goods that we cannot reach out and touch, such as friendship and knowledge

services intangible items of value provided to consumers, such as education

economic goods scarce goods created from scarce resources—goods that are desirable but limited in supply

bads items that we do not desire or want, where less is preferred to more, such as terrorism, smog, or poison oak

rational behavior people do the best they can, based on their values and information, under current and anticipated future circumstances

market the process of buyers and sellers exchanging goods and services

efficiency when an economy gets the most out of its scarce resources

market failure when the economy fails to allocate resources efficiently on its own

· (continues)

Section Summaries—Continued

and the fallacy of composition. The fact that two events usually occur together (correlation) does not necessarily mean that the one caused the other to occur (causation). The fallacy of composition tells us that if a thing is true for an individual, it is not necessarily true on a group level.

(S)6 **Positive and Normativ**

Positive analysis deals with factua explain the world. Normative anal judgments trying to improve the distinction is that positive stateme normative statements cannot.

(S)7 **Why Study Economics?**

Perhaps the best reason for studying economics is that so many of the things of concern in the world around us are at least partly economic in character. The study of economics matic, disciplined way of thinking.

orking with Graphs

use of visual aids, such as graphs, greatly nderstanding of a theory. This textbook will ughout to enhance the understanding of omic relationships. This appendix provides to read and create your own graphs.

> **How to Use this Card:**
> 1. **Look over the card to preview new concepts you'll be introduced to in the chapter.**
> 2. **Read the chapter to fully understand the material.**
> 3. **Go to class (and pay attention).**
> 4. **Review the card one more time to make sure you've grasped the key concepts.**
> 5. **Don't forget, this card is only one of many ECON Survey learning tools available to help you succeed in your economics course.**

product markets markets in which holds are buyers and firms are sellers of g and services

factor (or input) markets markets which households sell the use of their inputs (capital, land, labor, and entrepreneurship) to firms

simple circular flow model an illustration of the continuous flow of goods, services, inputs, and payments between firms and households

theory a statement or proposition used to explain and predict behavior in the real world

hypothesis a testable proposition

empirical analysis the use of data to test a hypothesis

ceteris paribus holding all other things constant

microecono and firm behavio marketplace

> The list below offers a wide range of tools to help you review and sharpen your understanding of economic concepts from this chapter.

aggregate level of output

correlation when two events occur together

causation when one event brings about another event

fallacy of composition the incorrect view that what is true for the individual is always true for the group

positive statement an objective, testable statement that describes what happens and why it happens

normative statement a subjective, contestable statement that attempts to describe what should be done

axis the vertical axis on a graph

axis the horizontal axis on a graph

e chart visual display showing the lative size of various quantities that add to 100 percent

bar graph visual display showing the comparison of quantities

time-series graph visual tool to show changes in a variable's value over time

scatter diagram a graph showing the relationship of one variable to another

variable something that is measured by a number, such as your height

positive relationship when two variables change in the same direction

negative relationship when two variables change in opposite directions

slope the ratio of rise (change in the Y variable) over run (change in the X variable)

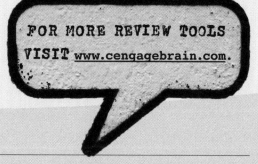

FOR MORE REVIEW TOOLS
VISIT www.cengagebrain.com.

Online Study Tools

At *www.cengagebrain.com*, you can

- ❑ Download printable Key Term Flash Cards
- ❑ Study online with interactive Key Term Flash Cards
- ❑ Complete Practice Quizzes with instant feedback
- ❑ Play "Beat the Clock" to master concepts
- ❑ Complete the Crossword Puzzle to review key terms
- ❑ Watch the ABC News video "The Unintended Consequences of Safety Precautions"

- ❑ Watch the Ask the Instructor video "Why do economists talk about money and wealth? Do they really believe that people are motivated only by money?"
- ❑ Download and review Exhibit Worksheets
- ❑ Access Economic Application "Economic Analysis"
- ❑ Access Graphing Workshop "Working with Graphs"
- ❑ Check your answers to the Chapter 1 Self-Review on page 21

CHAPTER 4

Price Elasticity of Demand

$$\text{Price elasticity of demand } (E_D) = \frac{\text{Percentage change in quantity demand}}{\text{Percentage change in price}}$$

Total Revenue (TR)

$TR = P \times Q$

Price Elasticity of Supply

$$\text{Price elasticity of supply } (E_S) = \frac{\% \, \Delta \text{ in the quantity supplied}}{\% \, \Delta \text{ in price}}$$

CHAPTER 6

Profits

profit = total revenue – total cost

Accounting Profits

accounting profits = total revenue – total explicit costs

Economic Profits

economic profits = total revenue – (explicit costs + implicit costs)

Marginal Product (MP)

marginal product = change in total output of a good that results from a one-unit change in input

$MP = \Delta Q / \Delta V$

Total Cost (TC)

total cost = total fixed cost + total variable cost

$TC = TFC + TVC$

Average Total Cost (ATC)

average total cost = total cost/output

$ATC = TC/Q$

Average Fixed Cost (AFC)

average fixed cost = total fixed cost/output

$AFC = TFC/Q$

Average Variable Cost (AVC)

average variable cost = total variable cost/output

$AVC = TVC/Q$

Marginal Cost (MC)

marginal cost = change in total cost resulting from a one-unit change in output

$MC = \Delta TC / \Delta Q$

CHAPTER 7

Average Revenue (AR)

average revenue = total revenue/number of units sold

$AR = TR/q$

Marginal Revenue (MR)

marginal revenue = increase in total revenue resulting from a one-unit increase in sales

$MR = \Delta TR / \Delta q$

Profit Maximizing Level of Output

$MR = MC$

CHAPTER 10

Marginal Revenue Product (MRP)

marginal revenue product = marginal product × price of the product

$MRP = MP \times P$

CHAPTER 11

Unemployment Rate

$$\text{unemployment rate} = \frac{\text{number of unemployed}}{\text{civilian labor force}}$$

Price Index

$$\text{price index} = \frac{\text{cost of market basket in current year} \times 100}{\text{cost of market basket in base year}}$$

CHAPTER 12

Gross Domestic Product (*GDP*)

gross domestic product = consumption + investment + government purchases + net exports

$GDP = C + I + G + (X - M)$

Real GDP

$Real\ GDP = \dfrac{Nominal\ GDP}{price\text{-}level\ index} \times 100$

CHAPTER 14

Aggregate Demand

aggregate demand = consumption + investment + government purchases + net exports

$AD = C + I + G + (X - M)$

Marginal Propensity to Consume (*MPC*)

marginal propensity to consume = change in consumption spending/change in disposable income

$MPC = \Delta C/\Delta DY$

Marginal Propensity to Save (*MPS*)

marginal propensity to consume = change in savings/change in disposable income

$MPS = \Delta S/\Delta DY$

Multiplier Formula

$Multiplier = 1/(1 - MPC)$

Budget Deficit and Budget Surplus

Budget Deficit: Government Spending > Tax Revenues
Budget Surplus: Tax Revenues > Government Spending

CHAPTER 15

M1

M1 = Currency + Checkable deposits + Traveler's checks

M2

M2 = M1 + Savings deposits + Small-denomination time deposits + Noninstitutional money market mutual fund shares + Money market deposit accounts

Required Reserves

required reserves = deposits × reserve ratio

Excess Reserves

excess reserves = actual reserves − required reserves

Money Multiplier

potential money creation = initial deposit × money multiplier

CHAPTER 16

Equation of Exchange

money supply × velocity of money = price level × real output

$M \times V = P \times Q$

Velocity of Money

velocity of money = nominal GDP/money supply

$V = Nominal\ GDP/M$

Growth Version of the Quantity Equation

Growth rate of the money supply + Growth rate of velocity = Growth rate of the price level (inflation rate) + Growth rate of real output

Inflation Rate

Inflation Rate = Growth rate of the money supply − Growth rate of real GDP

Section Summaries

Ⓢ1 Economics: A Brief Introduction

Economics is the study of the choices we make among our many wants and desires given our limited resources. Scarcity forces us to choose, and choices are costly because we must give up other opportunities that we value—this is the economic problem. Our scarce resources can be grouped into four categories: labor, land, capital, and entrepreneurship. Entrepreneurship is the process of combining labor, land, and capital to produce goods and services. Goods are tangible items that we value or desire, and services are intangible acts for which people are willing to pay. Everyone faces scarcity, and it cannot be eliminated.

Ⓢ2 Economic Behavior

Economists assume that individuals act as if they are motivated by self-interest and respond in predictable ways to changing circumstances. Self-interest to an economist is not a narrow monetary self-interest. A person acting in self-interest might pursue personal gain, but that does not necessarily exclude helping others. Rational behavior merely means that people do the best they can, based on their values and information, under current and anticipated future circumstances. Because most people seek opportunities that make them better off, we can predict what will happen when incentives are changed.

Ⓢ3 Markets

A market is the process of buyers and sellers exchanging goods and services. In most countries, resources are allocated through a market economy. Efficiency is achieved when the economy gets the most out of its scarce resources. Voluntary exchange and the price system guide people's choices and help determine what goods are produced and how they're produced. Market failure occurs when the economy fails to allocate resources efficiently on its own. We use a circular flow model to illustrate the flow of goods and services. Households and firms interact with each other in product markets (where households buy and firms sell) and factor markets (where households sell and firms buy).

Ⓢ4 Economic Theory

A theory is an established explanation that accounts for known facts or phenomena. Specifically, economic theories are statements or propositions about patterns of human behavior that occur expectedly under certain circumstances. Theories use abstraction to weed out relevant from irrelevant information. A theory begins with a hypothesis, which is tested through empirical analysis. If the data collected supports the hypothesis, it can be tentatively accepted as an economic theory.

Conventionally, we distinguish two main branches of economics: microeconomics, which deals with smaller units in the economy, and macroeconomics, which deals with the aggregate or total economy.

Ⓢ5 Pitfalls to Avoid in Scientific Thinking

The two major pitfalls to avoid are confusing correlation with causation

Key Terms

economics the study of choices we make among our many wants and desires given our limited resources

resources inputs used to produce goods and services

scarcity exists when human wants (material and nonmaterial) exceed available resources

the economic problem scarcity forces us to choose, and choices are costly because we must give up other opportunities that we value

labor the physical and human effort used in the production of goods and services

land the natural resources used in the production of goods and services

capital the equipment and structures used to produce goods and services

human capital the productive knowledge and skill people receive from education, on-the-job training, health, and other factors that increase productivity

entrepreneurship the process of combining labor, land, and capital to produce goods and services

goods items we value or desire

tangible goods items we value or desire that we can reach out and touch

intangible goods goods that we cannot reach out and touch, such as friendship and knowledge

services intangible items of value provided to consumers, such as education

economic goods scarce goods created from scarce resources—goods that are desirable but limited in supply

bads items that we do not desire or want, where less is preferred to more, such as terrorism, smog, or poison oak

rational behavior people do the best they can, based on their values and information, under current and anticipated future circumstances

market the process of buyers and sellers exchanging goods and services

efficiency when an economy gets the most out of its scarce resources

market failure when the economy fails to allocate resources efficiently on its own

(continues)

Section Summaries—Continued

and the fallacy of composition. The fact that two events usually occur together (correlation) does not necessarily mean that the one caused the other to occur (causation). The fallacy of composition tells us that if a thing is true for an individual, it is not necessarily true on a group level.

 6 Positive and Normative Economics

Positive analysis deals with factual statements trying to explain the world. Normative analysis deals with value judgments trying to improve the world. An important distinction is that positive statements can be tested but normative statements cannot.

 7 Why Study Economics?

Perhaps the best reason for studying economics is that so many of the things of concern in the world around us are at least partly economic in character. The study of economics provides a systematic, disciplined way of thinking.

APPENDIX: Working with Graphs

Sometimes the use of visual aids, such as graphs, greatly enhances our understanding of a theory. This textbook will use graphs throughout to enhance the understanding of important economic relationships. This appendix provides a guide on how to read and create your own graphs.

product markets markets in which households are buyers and firms are sellers of goods and services

factor (or input) markets markets in which households sell the use of their inputs (capital, land, labor, and entrepreneurship) to firms

simple circular flow model an illustration of the continuous flow of goods, services, inputs, and payments between firms and households

theory a statement or proposition used to explain and predict behavior in the real world

hypothesis a testable proposition

empirical analysis the use of data to test a hypothesis

ceteris paribus holding all other things constant

microeconomics the study of household and firm behavior and how they interact in the marketplace

macroeconomics the study of the whole economy, including the topics of inflation, unemployment, and economic growth

aggregate the total amount—such as the aggregate level of output

correlation when two events occur together

causation when one event brings about another event

fallacy of composition the incorrect view that what is true for the individual is always true for the group

positive statement an objective, testable statement that describes what happens and why it happens

normative statement a subjective, contestable statement that attempts to describe what should be done

Y-axis the vertical axis on a graph

X-axis the horizontal axis on a graph

pie chart visual display showing the relative size of various quantities that add up to 100 percent

bar graph visual display showing the comparison of quantities

time-series graph visual tool to show changes in a variable's value over time

scatter diagram a graph showing the relationship of one variable to another

variable something that is measured by a number, such as your height

positive relationship when two variables change in the same direction

negative relationship when two variables change in opposite directions

slope the ratio of rise (change in the Y variable) over run (change in the X variable)

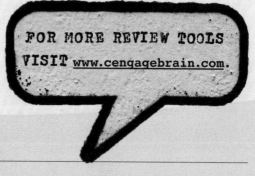

FOR MORE REVIEW TOOLS VISIT www.cengagebrain.com.

Online Study Tools

At *www.cengagebrain.com*, you can

- ❑ Download printable Key Term Flash Cards
- ❑ Study online with interactive Key Term Flash Cards
- ❑ Complete Practice Quizzes with instant feedback
- ❑ Play "Beat the Clock" to master concepts
- ❑ Complete the Crossword Puzzle to review key terms
- ❑ Watch the ABC News video "The Unintended Consequences of Safety Precautions"

- ❑ Watch the Ask the Instructor video "Why do economists talk about money and wealth? Do they really believe that people are motivated only by money?"
- ❑ Download and review Exhibit Worksheets
- ❑ Access Economic Application "Economic Analysis"
- ❑ Access Graphing Workshop "Working with Graphs"
- ❑ Check your answers to the Chapter 1 Self-Review on page 21

Section Summaries

1 Choices, Costs, and Trade-Offs

We all face scarcity, and as a consequence, we must make choices. Economics is about understanding the effects that scarcity has on our decision making. In a world of scarcity, we all face trade-offs; when we make choices, we forgo other valued alternatives. Society must make trade-offs as well. The highest or best forgone opportunity resulting from a decision is called the opportunity cost. Opportunity costs can include both monetary and nonmonetary costs, such as time. It is easy to mistake "free" for a zero monetary price. Many allegedly free goods may not cost consumers any money, but they still use society's scarce resources.

2 Marginal Thinking

Many choices we face involve *how much* of something to do rather than *whether* to do something or not. Marginal thinking is concerned with additional, or marginal, choices; marginal choices involve the effects of adding or subtracting, from the current situation, the small (or large) incremental changes to a plan of action. The rule of rational choice tells us that individuals will pursue an activity if the expected marginal benefits are greater than the expected marginal costs. The net benefit is the difference between the expected marginal benefits and the expected marginal costs.

3 Specialization and Trade

People generally specialize in what they produce because of opportunity costs. By concentrating their energies on only one, or a few, activities, individuals can make the best use of (and thus gain the most benefit from) their limited resources. If an individual can produce a good or service at a lower opportunity cost than others, we say that she has a comparative advantage in the production of that good or service.

The primary advantages of specialization are that employees acquire greater skill from repetition, they avoid wasted time in shifting from one task to another, and they do the types of work for which they are best suited. Specialization also promotes the use of specialized equipment for specialized tasks.

Trade, or voluntary exchange, directly increases wealth by making both parties better off. Standards of living can be increased through trade and exchange. The economy as a whole can create more wealth when each person specializes in the task that he or she does best. Through specialization and trade, a country can gain a greater variety of goods and services at a lower cost.

© LISA F. YOUNG/SHUTTERSTOCK

Key Terms

opportunity cost the value of the best forgone alternative that was not chosen

marginal thinking focusing on the additional, or marginal, choices; marginal choices involve the effects of adding or subtracting, from the current situation, the small (or large) incremental changes to a plan of action

rule of rational choice individuals will pursue an activity if the expected marginal benefits are greater than the expected marginal costs

net benefit the difference between the expected marginal benefits and the expected marginal costs

specializing concentrating on the production of one or a few goods

comparative advantage occurs when a person or country can produce a good or service at a lower opportunity cost than others

production possibilities curve the potential total output combinations of any two goods for an economy

increasing opportunity cost the opportunity cost of producing additional units of a good rises as society produces more of that good

consumer sovereignty consumers vote with their dollars in a market economy; this accounts for what is produced

command economy economy in which the government uses central planning to coordinate most economic activities

market economy an economy that allocates goods and services through the private decisions of consumers, input suppliers, and firms

mixed economy an economy in which government and the private sector determine the allocation of resources

labor intensive production that uses a large amount of labor

capital intensive production that uses a large amount of capital

Section Summaries—Continued

⑤4 The Production Possibilities of an Economy

The production possibilities curve represents the potential total output combinations of any two goods for an economy, given the inputs and technology available to the economy. It illustrates an economy's potential for allocating its limited resources in producing various combinations of goods in a given time period.

An economy cannot operate outside the production possibilities curve because in the given time period, it does not have sufficient resources to produce that level of output. If, however, the economy operates inside the production possibility curve, it is not producing at full capacity and is operating inefficiently. Efficiency requires society to use its resources to the fullest extent—getting the most from its scarce resources and wasting none.

The law of increasing opportunity cost tells us that the opportunity cost of producing additional units of a good rises as society produces more of that good. This is because some resources and skills cannot be easily adapted from their current uses to alternative uses.

The economy can only grow with qualitative or quantitative changes in the factors of production—for instance, advancement in technology or improvements in labor productivity. Growth, however, does not eliminate scarcity. An economy can also grow by increasing its capital stock.

⑤5 Economic Systems

Every economy must answer three fundamental questions: (1) What goods and services will be produced? (2) How will the goods and services be produced? (3) Who will get the goods and services produced? Consumer sovereignty explains how individual consumers in market economies determine what is to be produced. Economies can be organized as command economies, market economies, and mixed economies. When deciding how to produce goods and services, firms may face a trade-off between using more machines (capital) or more workers (labor). This decision will depend on relative factor prices. In a market economy, the goods and services an individual can obtain depend on her income.

FOR MORE REVIEW TOOLS VISIT www.cengagebrain.com.

© ISTOCKPHOTO.COM

Online Study Tools

At *www.cengagebrain.com,* you can

- ❑ Download printable Key Term Flash Cards
- ❑ Study online with interactive Key Term Flash Cards
- ❑ Complete Practice Quizzes with instant feedback
- ❑ Play "Beat the Clock" to master concepts
- ❑ Complete the Crossword Puzzle to review key terms
- ❑ Watch the ABC News videos "Incentives for Hand-washing" and "Specialization and Chinese Neckties"
- ❑ Watch the Ask the Instructor videos "Why is economics difficult for a lot of students?," "Why do economists emphasize marginal analysis?," and "How important is the rate of economic growth to you?"
- ❑ Download and review Exhibit Worksheets
- ❑ Access Economic Applications "Scarcity, Choice, and Opportunity Cost" and "Production Possibilities Frontiers"
- ❑ Access Graphing Workshop "Production Possibilities"
- ❑ Check your answers to the Chapter 2 Self-Review on page 45

Section Summaries

Ⓢ1 Competitive Markets

Buyers determine the demand side of the market. Buyers include the consumers who purchase the goods and services and the firms that buy inputs. Sellers determine the supply side of the market. Sellers include the firms that produce and sell goods and services and the resource owners who sell their inputs to firms—workers who "sell" their labor and resource owners who sell raw materials and capital.

A competitive market is one in which a number of buyers and sellers are offering similar products, and no single buyer or seller can influence the market price. Because many markets contain a large degree of competitiveness, the lessons of supply and demand can be applied to many different types of problems. The model of supply and demand is very good at predicting changes in prices and quantities in many markets, large and small.

Ⓢ2 Demand

The law of demand states that the quantity of a good or service demanded varies inversely (negatively) with its price, *ceteris paribus*. The horizontal summing of the demand curves of all the individuals in an economy is called the market demand curve. A change in a good's own price is said to lead to a change in quantity demanded. The other factors that influence the demand curve are called *determinants of demand*, and a change in these other factors shifts the entire demand curve. Important determinants of demand are the prices of related goods, income, number of buyers, consumers'

preferences and information, and expectations.

It is important to understand the difference between the change in the price of a good (a movement *along* a demand curve) and a change in one of the determinants of demand (a shift in the demand curve).

Ⓢ3 Supply

According to the law of supply, the quantity supplied will vary directly with the price of the good. The market supply curve may be thought of as the horizontal summation of the supply curves for individual firms. A change in the price of the good in question is shown as a movement along a given supply curve, leading to a change in quantity supplied. A change in any other factor that can affect supplier behavior results in a shift in the entire supply curve, leading to a change in supply. The determinants of supply are input prices, prices of related products, expectations, number of suppliers, technology, regulation, taxes and subsidies, and weather. Essentially, if there is a change in the good's own price, it leads to a change in the quantity supplied. If one of the other factors influences sellers' behavior, we say it results in a change in supply.

Ⓢ4 Market Equilibrium Price and Quantity

The market equilibrium is found at the point at which the market supply and market demand curves intersect. The price at the intersection of the market supply curve and the market demand curve is called the equilibrium price, and the quantity is called the equilibrium quantity. At the equilibrium price, the amount

Key Terms

competitive market a market in which the many buyers and sellers have little market power—each buyer's or seller's effect on market price is negligible

law of demand the quantity of a good or service demanded varies inversely (negatively) with its price, *ceteris paribus*

individual demand schedule a schedule that shows the relationship between price and quantity demanded

individual demand curve a graphical representation that shows the inverse relationship between price and quantity demanded

market demand curve the horizontal summation of individual demand curves

change in quantity demanded a change in a good's own price leads to a change in quantity demanded, a move along a given demand curve

change in demand the prices of related goods, income, number of buyers, tastes, and expectations can change the demand for a good; that is, a change in one of these factors shifts the entire demand curve

substitutes an increase (decrease) in the price of one good causes the demand curve for another good to shift to the right (left)

complements an increase (decrease) in the price of one good shifts the demand curve for another good to the left (right)

normal good a good for which demand increases if income increases and demand decreases if income decreases

inferior good a good for which demand decreases if income decreases and demand increases if income decreases

law of supply the quantity of a good or service supplied varies directly (positively) with its price, *ceteris paribus*

individual supply curve a graphical representation that shows the positive relationship between the price and quantity supplied

individual supply schedule a schedule that shows the relationship between price and quantity supplied

market supply curve a graphical representation of the amount of goods and services that suppliers are willing and able to supply at various prices

Section Summaries—Continued

that buyers are willing and able to buy is exactly equal to the amount that sellers are willing and able to produce.

If a surplus (or excess quantity supplied) exists, frustrated suppliers will cut their prices and cut back on production; as prices fall, consumers will buy more, eliminating the surplus. If a shortage (or excess quantity demanded) exists, frustrated buyers will be forced to compete for the existing supply, bidding up the price. In turn, the higher price will decrease the quantity demanded and also encourage producers to increase the quantity supplied until the equilibrium is reached.

Often both supply and demand shift in the same time period. When this happens we can predict the change in one variable (price or quantity), but we are unable to predict the direction of the effect on the other variable with any certainty. The change in the second variable, then, is said to be indeterminate.

As the foundations of the market system, supply and demand determine the prices of goods and services and how scarce resources are allocated. Within the market system, market prices are critical for communicating important information to both buyers and sellers. This communication results in a shifting of resources from those uses that are valued less to those that are valued more.

change in quantity supplied a change in a good's own price leads to a change in quantity supplied, a move along a given supply curve

change in supply input prices, prices of related products, expectations, number of suppliers, technology, regulation, taxes and subsidies, and weather can change the supply for a good; that is, a change in one of these factors shifts the entire supply curve

market equilibrium the point at which the market supply and market demand curves intersect

equilibrium price the price at the intersection of the market supply and demand curves; at this price, the quantity demanded equals the quantity supplied

equilibrium quantity the quantity at the intersection of the market supply and demand curves; at the equilibrium quantity, the quantity demanded equals the quantity supplied

surplus a situation in which quantity supplied exceeds quantity demanded

shortage a situation in which quantity demanded exceeds quantity supplied

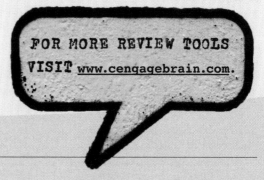

FOR MORE REVIEW TOOLS VISIT www.cengagebrain.com.

Online Study Tools

At *www.cengagebrain.com,* you can

- ❑ Download printable Key Term Flash Cards

- ❑ Study online with interactive Key Term Flash Cards

- ❑ Complete Practice Quizzes with instant feedback

- ❑ Play "Beat the Clock" to master concepts

- ❑ Complete the Crossword Puzzle to review key terms

- ❑ Watch the ABC News video "The Relationships between Markets"

- ❑ Watch the Ask the Instructor videos "What factors affect the auction price of your house?" and "Do

the terms 'shortage' and 'scarcity' mean the same thing?"

- ❑ Download and review Exhibit Worksheets

- ❑ Access Economic Applications "Supply and Demand" and "Equilibrium"

- ❑ Access Graphing Workshops "Demand," "Supply," and "Market Equilibrium"

- ❑ Check your answers to the Chapter 3 Self-Review on page 67

Section Summaries

Ⓢ1 Price Elasticity of Demand

The price elasticity of demand measures the responsiveness of quantity demanded to a change in price. Specifically, price elasticity is defined as the percentage change in quantity demanded divided by the percentage change in price. If the quantity demanded is responsive to even a small change in price, we call it elastic. On the other hand, if a huge change in price results in only a small change in quantity demanded, then the demand is said to be inelastic. A good is said to be unit elastic if the quantity demanded changes in direct proportion to the price.

For the most part, the price elasticity of demand depends on three factors: (1) the availability of close substitutes, (2) the proportion of income spent on the good, and (3) the amount of time that has elapsed since the price change.

Ⓢ2 Total Revenue and the Price Elasticity of Demand

Total revenue (*TR*) is the amount sellers receive for a good or service. Total revenue is simply the price of the good (*P*) times the quantity of the good sold (*Q*): $TR = P \times Q$. Total revenue varies inversely with price if

demand is relatively price elastic—if the demand curve is relatively inelastic, total revenue will vary directly with a price change.

We can see how the slopes of demand curves can be used to estimate their *relative* elasticities of demand: the steeper one demand curve is relative to another, the more inelastic it is relative to the other. Although the slope remains constant, the elasticity of a linear demand curve changes along the length of the curve—from relatively elastic at higher price ranges to relatively inelastic at lower price ranges.

Ⓢ3 Price Elasticity of Supply

The price elasticity of supply is the measure of the sensitivity of the quantity supplied to changes in price of a good. The price elasticity of supply is calculated in much the same manner as the price elasticity of demand. Goods with a supply elasticity that is greater than 1 ($E_s > 1$) are said to be relatively elastic in supply. Goods with a supply elasticity that is less than 1 ($E_s < 1$) are said to be inelastic in supply. In a condition of *perfectly inelastic supply*, an increase in price will not change the quantity supplied. At the other extreme is a perfectly elastic supply curve, where the elasticity equals infinity. Time is usually critical in supply elasticities, because it is more costly for sellers to bring forth and release products in a shorter period.

Ⓢ4 Supply, Demand, and Policies of Government

Price controls involve the use of the power of the state to establish prices different from the equilibrium prices

Key Terms

price elasticity of demand the measure of the responsiveness of quantity demanded to a change in price

elastic when the quantity demanded is greater than the percentage change in price ($E_D > 1$)

inelastic when the quantity demanded is less than the percentage change in price ($E_D < 1$)

unit elastic demand demand with a price elasticity of 1; the percentage change in quantity demanded is equal to the percentage change in price

total revenue (*TR*) the amount sellers receive for a good or service, calculated as the product price times the quantity sold

price elasticity of supply the measure of the sensitivity of the quantity supplied to changes in price of a good

price ceiling a legally established maximum price

price floor a legally established minimum price

unintended consequences the secondary effects of an action that may occur after the initial effects

consumer surplus the difference between the price a consumer is willing and able to pay for an additional unit of a good and the price the consumer actually pays; for the whole market, it is the sum of all the individual consumer surpluses

producer surplus the difference between what a producer is paid for a good and the cost of producing that unit of the good; for the market, it is the sum of all the individual sellers' producer surpluses—the area above the market supply curve and below the market price

marginal cost (*MC*) the change in total costs resulting from a one-unit change in output

total welfare gains the sum of consumer and producer surpluses

deadweight loss net loss of total surplus that results from an action that alters a market equilibrium

Section Summaries—Continued

that would otherwise prevail. A price ceiling is a legal maximum price; rent control is a common example of a price ceiling. A price floor is a legal minimum price; minimum wage laws are examples of price floors. Though well intentioned, these kinds of price controls can have unintended consequences. Policy makers must be aware of such effects.

The relative elasticity of supply and demand also determines the distribution of the tax burden for a good. If demand is relatively less elastic than supply in the relevant tax region, the largest portion of the tax is paid by the consumer. If demand is relatively more elastic, the largest portion of the tax is paid by the producer.

© MAURITIUS/PHOTOLIBRARY

⑤5   Consumer Surplus, Producer Surplus, and the Efficiency of Markets

Consumer surplus is the monetary difference between the amount a consumer is willing and able to pay for an additional unit of a good and what the consumer actually pays (market price). Marginal willingness to pay falls as more is consumed of a given good in a given period. Producer surplus is the difference between what a producer is paid for a good and the cost of producing one unit of that good. Producers would never knowingly sell a good that is worth more to them than the asking price. Marginal cost is the cost of producing one more unit of a good. The total welfare gains to the economy from trade in this good is the sum of the consumer and producer surpluses created. A deadweight loss is the net loss of total surplus that results from the misallocation of resources.

FOR MORE REVIEW TOOLS VISIT www.cengagebrain.com.

Online Study Tools

At *www.cengagebrain.com*, you can

- ❑ Download printable Key Term Flash Cards

- ❑ Study online with interactive Key Term Flash Cards

- ❑ Complete Practice Quizzes with instant feedback

- ❑ Play "Beat the Clock" to master concepts

- ❑ Complete the Crossword Puzzle to review key terms

- ❑ Watch the ABC News video "Elasticity of Demand for Gasoline"

- ❑ Watch the Ask the Instructor videos "Is price elasticity of demand the same thing as slope?" and "Why are taxes on cigarettes so high?"

- ❑ Download and review Exhibit Worksheets

- ❑ Access Economic Application "Elasticity"

- ❑ Access Graphing Workshops "Demand, Price Elasticity, and Total Revenue" and "Consumer/Producer Surplus"

- ❑ Check your answers to the Chapter 4 Self-Review on page 91

Section Summaries

⑤1 Externalities

Sometimes the market system fails to produce efficient outcomes because of side effects economists call externalities. In the case of negative externalities (such as pollution), the market supplies too much. With positive externalities (such as education), the private market supplies too little of the good in question.

With negative externalities, the government can use taxes or other forms of regulation to correct the underallocation problem.

With positive externalities, the government can provide subsidies or other forms of regulation to correct the underallocation problem. Individuals sometimes act independently, without government prompting, to reduce negative externalities or create more positive externalities.

⑤2 Public Goods

Public goods can be another source of market failure. Most goods in the economy are private goods, which means they are rival and excludable. Public goods are neither rival nor excludable—that is, anyone can enjoy their benefits and it would be too costly to prevent an individual from doing so. It would also be difficult to force individuals to pay for such goods. This can create a free-rider problem, in which people try to take advantage of benefits that they don't pay for. If everyone was a free rider, however, the ride would no longer exist. In these cases, the government must finance or provide the good or service, as no private company could profitably supply efficient levels of the goods.

Everything that the government produces, however, has an opportunity cost, and these must be considered by policy makers.

⑤3 Asymmetric Information

When the available information is initially distributed in favor of one party relative to another, asymmetric information is said to exist. This can reduce market efficiency, as lower-quality goods can drive higher-quality goods out of the market. A situation in which an informed party benefits in an exchange by taking advantage of knowing more than the other party is called adverse selection. Adverse selection can be reduced if the buyer can acquire more information. Ideally, the seller would reveal her superior information to the buyer; however, this would not be rational if the product is of inferior quality. The threat of punishment could provide adequate incentives for the seller to be truthful. Sellers can also use reputation and standardization to convince buyers that their products are high quality. Moral hazard is another potential problem, where individuals might take more risks if they know they won't have to shoulder the full consequences of their actions.

Key Terms

externality a benefit or cost from consumption or production that spills over onto those who are not consuming or producing the good

positive externality occurs when benefits spill over to an outside party who is not involved in producing or consuming the good

negative externality occurs when costs spill over to an outside party who is not involved in producing or consuming the good

public good a good that is nonrival in consumption and nonexcludable

private good a good that is rival in consumption and excludable

free rider a consumer who derives benefits from something he or she has not paid for

common resource a rival good that is nonexcludable

asymmetric information occurs when the available information is initially distributed in favor of one party relative to another in an exchange

adverse selection a situation in which an informed party benefits in an exchange by taking advantage of knowing more than the other party

moral hazard taking additional risks because you are insured

winner's curse a situation that arises in certain auctions in which the winner is worse off than the loser because of an overly optimistic value placed on the good

median voter model a model that predicts candidates will choose a position in the middle of the distribution

rational ignorance lack of incentive to be informed

special-interest groups groups with an intense interest in particular voting issues that may be different from that of the general public

© BRIAN BEHUNIN/ISTOCKPHOTO.COM

Section Summaries—Continued

Ⓢ4 Public Choice

When the market fails, as in the case of an externality or a public good, it may be necessary for the government to intervene. Government intervention, however, can make matters worse. Public choice theory is the application of economic principles to politics. It assumes that the behavior of individuals in politics will be guided by self-interest, just as it is in the marketplace. Scarcity and competition are present in the public sector as well as in the private sector. On the other hand, the individual consumption-payment link, which is present in the private sector, breaks down, as public choices are often made by majority rule. The median voter model predicts that politics will generally tend toward the middle of the political spectrum. One of the keys to an efficiently working democracy is a concerned and informed electorate, but this can be costly and the issues can be complicated. Public choice economists refer to the lack of incentive to become informed as rational ignorance. Special-interest groups may have intense feelings about and a degree of interest in particular issues that are at variance with those of the general public.

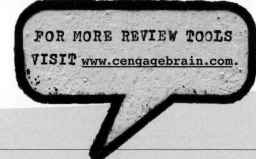

FOR MORE REVIEW TOOLS VISIT www.cengagebrain.com.

Online Study Tools

At *www.cengagebrain.com,* you can

- ❑ Download printable Key Term Flash Cards

- ❑ Study online with interactive Key Term Flash Cards

- ❑ Complete Practice Quizzes with instant feedback

- ❑ Play "Beat the Clock" to master concepts

- ❑ Complete the Crossword Puzzle to review key terms

- ❑ Watch the ABC News videos "Second-Hand Smoke," "The Tragedy of the Commons," and "Cell Phones and Hidden Taxes"

- ❑ Watch the Ask the Instructor videos "How does government affect the economy?," "What is the meaning of public goods?," and "How does 'adverse selection' affect markets?"

- ❑ Download and review Exhibit Worksheets

- ❑ Access Economic Applications "Taxes, Spending, and Deficits" and "Economics and the Environment"

- ❑ Access Graphing Workshop "Externalities"

- ❑ Check your answers to the Chapter 5 Self-Review on page 109

Section Summaries

Ⓢ1 Firms and Profits: Total Revenues Minus Total Costs

Explicit costs are the input costs that require a monetary payment. Implicit costs do not require an outlay of money. Accountants do not include implicit costs in the firm's total cost; economists do.

Economists generally assume that the ultimate goal of every firm is to maximize its profits, the difference between what they give up for their inputs and the amount they receive for their goods and services. A zero economic profit means that the firm is covering both explicit and implicit costs—the total opportunity costs of its resources. Sunk costs should be ignored when making economic decisions, because they have already been incurred and cannot be recovered.

Ⓢ2 Production in the Short Run

The short run is defined as a period too brief for some production inputs to be varied. The long run is a period in which a firm can adjust all production inputs. The production function illustrates the relationship between the quantity of inputs and the quantity of outputs.

The marginal product (MP) of any input is the increase in the quantity of output obtained from one additional unit of input used. The initial rise in the marginal product is the result of more effective use of fixed inputs as the number of workers increases. As additional workers are added, machines are brought into efficient operation and thus the marginal product of the workers rises. Adding more and more of a variable input to a fixed input, however, will eventually lead to diminishing marginal product. A point will ultimately be reached beyond which marginal product will decline.

Ⓢ3 Costs in the Short Run

The short-run total costs of a business fall into two distinct categories: fixed costs and variable costs. Fixed costs are those costs that do not vary with the level of output, such as insurance premiums or property taxes. The sum of the firm's fixed costs is called the total fixed cost (TFC). Variable costs, such as expenditures for wages and raw materials, vary with the level of output, increasing as output increases. The sum of the firm's variable costs is called the total variable cost (TVC). The sum of the total fixed costs and total variable costs is called the firm's total cost (TC).

Sometimes we find it convenient to discuss these costs on a per-unit-of-output or average basis. Average total cost (ATC) is the per-unit cost of operation; total cost divided by output. Average fixed cost (AFC) is

Key Terms

explicit costs the opportunity costs of production that require monetary payment

implicit costs the opportunity costs of production that do not require monetary payment

profits the difference between total revenues and total costs

accounting profits total revenues minus total explicit costs

economic profits total revenues minus explicit and implicit costs

sunk costs costs that have been incurred and cannot be recovered

short run a period too brief for some production inputs to be varied

long run a period over which all production inputs are variable

production function the relationship between the quantity of inputs and the quantity of outputs

total output (Q) the total amount of output of a good produced by the firm

marginal product (MP) the change in total output of a good that results from a one-unit change in input

diminishing marginal product as a variable input increases, with other inputs fixed, a point will be reached at which the additions to output will eventually decline

fixed costs costs that do not vary with the level of output

total fixed cost (TFC) the sum of the firm's fixed costs

variable costs costs that change with the level of output

total variable cost (TVC) the sum of the firm's variable costs

total cost (TC) the sum of the firm's total fixed costs and total variable costs

average total cost (ATC) a per-unit cost of operation; total cost divided by output

average fixed cost (AFC) a per-unit measure of fixed costs; fixed costs divided by output

average variable cost (AVC) a per-unit measure of variable costs; variable costs divided by output

marginal cost (MC) the change in total costs resulting from a one-unit change in output

© ISTOCKPHOTO.COM / © CHAPEL HOUSE PHOTOGRAPHY

Section Summaries—Continued

the per-unit measure of fixed costs; fixed costs divided by output. Average variable cost (AVC) is the per-unit measure of variable costs; variable costs divided by output. Marginal cost (MC) shows the change in total cost associated with a change in output by one unit.

⑤4 The Shape of the Short-Run Cost Curves

If an additional worker's marginal product is lower (higher) than that of previous workers, marginal costs increase (decrease). The relationship between the marginal and the average amount is simply a matter of arithmetic; when a number (the marginal cost) being added into a series is smaller than the previous average of the series, the new average will be lower than the previous one. Likewise, when the marginal number is larger than the average, the average will rise. A declining average fixed cost is the primary reason for the decline in the average total cost curve. The average total cost rises at high levels of output because of diminishing marginal product. When the average variable cost is falling, marginal costs must be

less than the average variable cost; and when the average variable cost is rising, marginal costs are greater than the average variable cost. The same relationship holds for the marginal cost curve and the average total cost curve.

⑤5 Cost Curves: Short-Run versus Long-Run

The main difference between short-run and long-run cost curves is that in the long run, firms can substitute lower-cost capital. In the short run, however, firms can only increase output by increasing variable inputs, such as workers and raw materials.

By examining the long-run average total cost curve for a firm, we can see three possible production patterns. Economies of scale occur in an output range where the long-run average total cost falls as output increases. Firms that expand beyond a certain point encounter diseconomies of scale; that is, they incur rising per-unit costs as their output grows. Firms experience constant returns to scale when their per-unit costs remain stable as output grows.

economies of scale occur in an output range where *LRATC* falls as output increases

minimum efficient scale the output level where economies of scale are exhausted and constant returns to scale begin

diseconomies of scale occur in an output range where *LRATC* rises as output expands

constant returns to scale occur in an output range where *LRATC* does not change as output varies

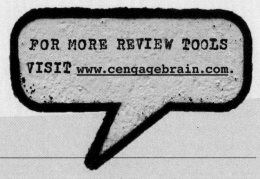

FOR MORE REVIEW TOOLS
VISIT www.cengagebrain.com.

Online Study Tools

At *www.cengagebrain.com*, you can

- ❑ Download printable Key Term Flash Cards
- ❑ Study online with interactive Key Term Flash Cards
- ❑ Complete Practice Quizzes with instant feedback
- ❑ Play "Beat the Clock" to master concepts
- ❑ Complete the Crossword Puzzle to review key terms
- ❑ Watch the ABC News video "Low-Cost Airlines"
- ❑ Watch the Ask the Instructor videos "What do we mean by fixed versus variable costs?," "Why can't

we feed the world from a flower pot?," and "Why do economists and accountants disagree?"

- ❑ Download and review Exhibit Worksheets
- ❑ Access Economic Application "Production and Costs"
- ❑ Access Graphing Workshop "Production and Cost"
- ❑ Check your answers to the Chapter 6 Self-Review on page 127

Section Summaries

$1 A Perfectly Competitive Market

A perfectly competitive market is characterized by (1) many buyers and sellers, (2) identical (homogeneous) products, and (3) easy market entry and exit. When there are many buyers and sellers, each firm is so small in relation to the industry that its production decisions have no impact on the market. Perfectly competitive firms are called price takers because they must accept the market price. In a perfectly competitive market, firms sell identical (homogeneous) products. Perfectly competitive markets have no significant barriers to entry or exit. Firms can enter or exit the market freely.

$2 An Individual Price Taker's Demand Curve

As price takers, perfectly competitive firms must sell at the market-determined price, where the market price and output are determined by the intersection of the market supply and demand curves. Likewise, individual sellers can change their outputs, and it will not alter the market price. When the market price for the given product increases, say as a result of an increase in market demand, the price-taking firm will receive a higher price for all its output. However, if the price decreases, the firm will receive a lower price. The perfectly competitive model does not assume any knowledge on the part of individual buyers and sellers about market demand and supply—they only have to know the price of the good they sell.

$3 Profit Maximization

The objective of the firm is to maximize profits. To maximize profits, the firm wants to produce the amount that maximizes the difference between its total revenues and total costs. Total revenue (TR) from a product equals the price of the good (P) times the quantity (q) of units sold. Average revenue (AR) equals total revenue divided by the number of units sold of the product. Marginal revenue (MR) is the additional revenue derived from the production of one more unit of the good. The firm will maximize its profits at the level of output that maximizes the difference between total revenue and total cost—that is, when marginal revenue equals marginal cost.

$4 Short-Run Profits and Losses

Determining whether the firm is generating economic profits can be done in three easy steps. First, find the profit-maximizing output level, where marginal revenue equals marginal cost. Second, identify the market price and find total revenue at the profit-maximizing output level. Third, multiply the average total cost by the output level to find the total cost. If total revenue is greater than total cost, the firm is generating economic profits, and if total revenue is less than total cost then the firm is generating economic losses. If total revenue and cost are equal, the firm has zero economic profit—a normal return.

Key Terms

perfect competition a market structure characterized by many buyers and sellers, identical (homogeneous) products, and easy market entry and exit

price taker a perfectly competitive firm that takes the price it is given by the intersection of the market demand and market supply curves

total revenue (TR) the product price times the quantity sold

average revenue (AR) the total revenue divided by the number of units sold

marginal revenue (MR) the increase in total revenue resulting from a one-unit increase in sales

profit-maximizing level of output a firm should always produce at the output level at which $MR = MC$

short-run supply curve the portion of the MC curve above the AVC curve

short-run market supply curve the horizontal summation of the individual firms' supply curves in the market

constant-cost industry an industry in which input prices (and cost curves) do not change as industry output changes

increasing-cost industry an industry in which input prices rise (and cost curves rise) as industry output rises

decreasing-cost industry an industry in which input prices fall (and cost curves fall) as industry output rises

productive efficiency where a good or service is produced at the lowest possible cost

allocative efficiency where $P = MC$ and production will be allocated to reflect consumer preferences

Section Summaries—Continued

A firm making an economic loss must decide whether to continue producing or shut down. If it cannot cover its average variable cost, the firm will shut down in the short run.

The short-run market supply curve is the summation of all the individual firms' supply curves (that is, the portion of the firms' *MC* above *AVC*) in the market.

Ⓢ5 Long-Run Equilibrium

If the firm is able to make economic profits with the goods it produces, it will increase the resources devoted to producing that good. These profits will draw other firms into the market and create a supply response, shifting the market supply curve to the right. This will cause the equilibrium market price to fall, returning the firm to zero economic profits.

The equilibrium condition in the long run in perfect competition is for each firm to produce at the output that minimizes average total cost—that is, the firm is operating at its minimum efficient scale. At this long-run equilibrium, all firms in the industry earn zero economic profit.

Ⓢ6 Long-Run Supply

Long run supply varies based on the type of industry. The three major types are constant-cost, increasing-cost, and decreasing-cost industries. In a constant-cost industry, the prices of inputs do not change as output is expanded. In an increasing-cost industry, the cost curves of individual firms rise as the total output of the industry increases. In decreasing-cost industries, an expansion in the output of an industry can lead to a reduction in input costs and shift the *MC* and *ATC* curves downward, and the market price falls because of external economies of scale. For markets to operate efficiently, they must achieve both productive efficiency, where firms produce goods and services in the least costly way, and allocative efficiency, where firms produce the goods that reflect society's preferences.

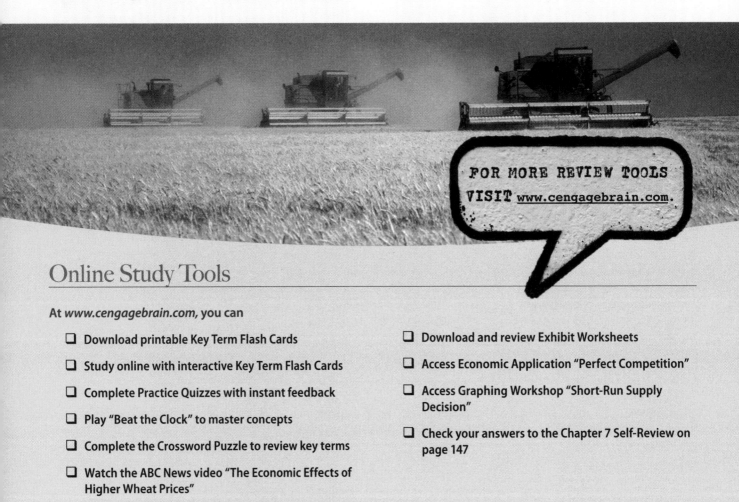

FOR MORE REVIEW TOOLS VISIT www.cengagebrain.com.

© BRAND X PICTURES/GETTY IMAGES

Online Study Tools

At *www.cengagebrain.com*, you can

- ❏ Download printable Key Term Flash Cards
- ❏ Study online with interactive Key Term Flash Cards
- ❏ Complete Practice Quizzes with instant feedback
- ❏ Play "Beat the Clock" to master concepts
- ❏ Complete the Crossword Puzzle to review key terms
- ❏ Watch the ABC News video "The Economic Effects of Higher Wheat Prices"
- ❏ Watch the Ask the Instructor videos "Is the used car market perfectly competitive?" and "Do competitive firms earn economic profit in the long run?"

- ❏ Download and review Exhibit Worksheets
- ❏ Access Economic Application "Perfect Competition"
- ❏ Access Graphing Workshop "Short-Run Supply Decision"
- ❏ Check your answers to the Chapter 7 Self-Review on page 147

Section Summaries

(S)1 Monopoly: The Price Maker

A true or pure monopoly exists when a market consists of only one seller of a product with no close substitute and natural or legal barriers to prevent entry competition. Monopolists are price makers that try to pick the price that will maximize their profits based on the market demand curve. Pure monopolies are rare. Some public utilities are provided by one producer. Governments are the sole suppliers of some goods as well.

A monopolist might create barriers to entry by establishing legal barriers, taking advantage of economies of scale, or controlling important inputs.

(S)2 Demand and Marginal Revenue in Monopoly

In monopoly, the demand curve is downward sloping—the firm cannot set both the price and the quantity it sells. Because a monopolist's marginal revenue is always less than the price, the marginal revenue curve will always lie below the demand curve. A monopolist will never knowingly operate on the inelastic portion of its demand curve, because increased output will lead to lower total revenue in this region and total costs will rise.

(S)3 The Monopolist's Equilibrium

The monopolist, like the perfect competitor, will maximize profits at the output where $MR = MC$. The same basic three-step method discussed in Chapter 7 can be used to determine whether the firm is generating an economic profit, an economic loss,

or zero economic profits at the profit-maximizing level of output. In monopoly, profits can persist in the long run, because barriers to entry will keep new firms out of the market.

If demand is insufficient to cover the monopolist's average total costs, the monopolist will incur a loss.

The government uses patents and copyrights to confer a form of monopoly. These provide producers incentives to incur the upfront costs of producing some goods, such as prescription drugs.

Key Terms

monopoly the single supplier of a product that has no close substitute

natural monopoly a firm that can produce at a lower cost than a number of smaller firms can

average cost pricing setting price equal to average total cost

price discrimination the practice of charging different consumers different prices for the same good or service

© HULTON ARCHIVE/GETTY IMAGES / © LISA F. YOUNG/SHUTTERSTOCK

The monopolist's three-step method
—find the profit-maximizing output level
—find total revenue at the profit-maximizing output level
—find total cost.

© ISTOCKPHOTO.COM

Section Summaries—Continued

Ⓢ4 Monopoly and Welfare Loss

To most economists, the most serious objection to monopoly is that monopolies result in market inefficiencies. Compared to the perfectly competitive market, monopolists charge higher prices and produce less output. This situation may also be viewed as "unfair," in that consumers are burdened more than under the alternative competitive arrangement. Since the monopolist produces at a level where price is greater than marginal cost, this means that the monopolist isn't producing enough from society's perspective. This is the welfare or deadweight loss.

Ⓢ5 Monopoly Policy

Antitrust policies and regulation are the two major approaches for dealing with monopoly situations. Through antitrust policies, the government can make monopolistic practices illegal and impose costs on monopolists that would decrease their profits. The Sherman Antitrust Act, the first important law regulating monopoly, prohibited practices such as price fixing and collusion.

Under government regulation, a company would not be allowed to charge any price it wants. This is common when the government doesn't want to break up a natural monopoly, such as in the water or power industries.

Monopolistic firms also cannot perform at the optimal output, because they would operate at a loss. Regulators might encourage an average cost pricing strategy. Costs can be difficult to calculate, however, and monopolists may have little incentive to keep costs down.

Ⓢ6 Price Discrimination

Price discrimination is the practice of charging different consumers different prices for the same good or service. For price discrimination to be possible, three conditions must be met: the firm must hold monopoly power, the demand curves for various groups within the market must differ, and the buyer must not be able to easily resell the product. Price discrimination results from the profit-maximization motive.

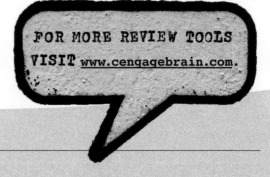

FOR MORE REVIEW TOOLS VISIT www.cengagebrain.com.

Online Study Tools

At *www.cengagebrain.com*, you can

- ❑ Download printable Key Term Flash Cards
- ❑ Study online with interactive Key Term Flash Cards
- ❑ Complete Practice Quizzes with instant feedback
- ❑ Play "Beat the Clock" to master concepts
- ❑ Complete the Crossword Puzzle to review key terms
- ❑ Watch the ABC News videos "The Country's Most Expensive Gasoline" and "Market Failure in Pharmaceuticals"

- ❑ Watch the Ask the Instructor videos "Why are cable rates so high?" and "Which antitrust cases have received a lot of attention?"
- ❑ Download and review Exhibit Worksheets
- ❑ Access Economic Application "Monopoly"
- ❑ Access Graphing Workshops "Monopoly Behavior in the Short Run," "Monopoly verses Perfect Competition," and "Price Discrimination"
- ❑ Check your answers to the Chapter 8 Self-Review on page 167

Section Summaries

 1 Monopolistic Competition

Monopolistic competition is a market structure in which many producers of somewhat different products compete with one another. Monopolistic competition is based on three characteristics: (1) product differentiation, (2) many sellers, and (3) free entry.

 2 Price and Output Determination in Monopolistic Competition

Monopolistically competitive sellers are price makers. We can use the same three-step method from Chapters 7 and 8 to determine if the firm is making an economic profit. Since entry is free in monopolistic competition, profits and losses probably will not last in the long run. Long-run equilibrium will occur when demand is equal to average total costs for each firm at a level of output at which each firm's demand curve is just tangent to its *ATC* curve.

3 Monopolistic Competition versus Perfect Competition

Both monopolistic competition and perfect competition have many buyers and sellers and relatively free entry. However, product differentiation enables a monopolistic competitor to have some influence over price. It also results in certain inefficiencies.

Firms in monopolistic competition do not produce at the minimum point of *ATC*, failing to meet productive efficiency, and they do not charge a price equal to marginal cost, failing to meet allocative efficiency. The inefficiency of monopolistic competition is a result of product differentiation. Because consumers value variety, the loss in efficiency must be weighed against the gain in increased variety.

 4 Oligopoly

Oligopolies exist, by definition, where relatively few firms control all or most of the production and sale of a product. Oligopoly is characterized by mutual interdependence among firms; each firm shapes its policy by constantly observing and anticipating the moves of rival firms. Substantial economies of scale are often present in oligopoly markets, creating a barrier to entry, as small scale production for new firms can be very unprofitable.

5 Collusion and Cartels

Because the actions and profits of oligopolists are dominated by mutual interdependence, the temptation is great for firms to collude—to agree to act jointly in pricing and other matters to increase profits. A cartel is a collection of firms making an agreement. Cartels lead to joint profit maximization, in which firms together will set optimum price and output levels according to mutually estimated demand and cost schedules.

Most strong collusive oligopolies are rather short lived for two reasons: First, in the United States and many other nations, collusive oligopolies are illegal. Second, for collusion to work, firms must cooperate in setting the price, but there is a great temptation for firms to cheat by slightly lowering their price.

Tacit collusion can occur when a single large firm in a market acts as a price leader; the price leader will publicly announce its pricing decisions

Key Terms

monopolistic competition a market structure with many firms selling differentiated products

product differentiation goods or services that are slightly different, or perceived to be different, from one another

excess capacity occurs when the firm produces below the level at which average total cost is minimized

oligopoly a market structure in which relatively few firms control all or most of the production and sale of a product

mutual interdependence when a firm shapes its policy with an eye to the policies of competing firms

collude when firms act together to restrict competition

cartel a collection of firms that agree on sales, pricing, and other decisions

joint profit maximization determination of price based on the marginal revenue derived from the market demand schedule and marginal cost schedule of the firms in the industry

price leader a large firm in an oligopoly that unilaterally makes changes in its product prices that competitors tend to follow

price follower a competitor in an oligopoly that goes along with the pricing decision of the price leader

price leadership when a dominant firm that produces a large portion of the industry's output sets a price that maximizes its profits, and other firms follow

predatory pricing setting a price deliberately low in order to drive out competitors

game theory firms attempt to maximize profits by acting in ways that minimize damage from competitors

cooperative game collusion by two firms in order to improve their profit maximizations

noncooperative game each firm sets its own price without consulting other firms

dominant strategy strategy that will be optimal regardless of opponents' actions

prisoners' dilemma the basic problem facing noncolluding oligopolists in maximizing their own profits

Section Summaries—Continued

and other firms in the market, called price followers, will match that pricing decision.

There are three types of mergers: horizontal, vertical, and conglomerate mergers. Most antitrust issues arise with horizontal mergers. Antitrust laws also forbid predatory pricing, price discrimination, and tying.

Ⓢ6 Game Theory and Strategic Behavior

Game theory analyzes oligopoly equilibrium price and output as a strategic game, in which firms in such circumstances act in a way that minimizes damage from competitors. Most games are noncooperative games, in which each firm sets its own price without consulting other firms. A famous game that has a dominant strategy and demonstrates the basic problem confronting noncolluding oligopolists is known as the prisoners' dilemma. At a Nash equilibrium, each firm is said to be doing as well as it can given the actions of its competitor. Most oligopolistic interactions are repeated games, which makes cooperation possible.

© BARIS SIMSEK/ISTOCKPHOTO.COM

payoff matrix a summary of the possible outcomes of various strategies

tit-for-tat strategy used in repeated games, the strategy in which one player follows the other player's move in the previous round; leads to greater cooperation

FOR MORE REVIEW TOOLS VISIT www.cengagebrain.com.

Online Study Tools

At *www.cengagebrain.com*, you can

☐ Download printable Key Term Flash Cards

☐ Study online with interactive Key Term Flash Cards

☐ Complete Practice Quizzes with instant feedback

☐ Play "Beat the Clock" to master concepts

☐ Complete the Crossword Puzzle to review key terms

☐ Watch the ABC News video "Airline Mergers"

☐ Watch the Ask the Instructor videos "Is the auto industry more competitive now than in the past?" and "What are the differences among the four market structures?"

☐ Download and review Exhibit Worksheets

☐ Access Economic Applications "Monopolistic Competition" and "Oligopoly"

☐ Access Graphing Workshops "Short-Run Equilibrium in Monopolistic Competition," "Long-Run Equilibrium in Monopolistic Competition," and "Game Theory"

☐ Check your answers to the Chapter 9 Self-Review on page 188

Section Summaries

⑤1 Input Markets

Input markets are the markets for the factors of production used to produce output. In input or factor markets, the demand for an input derived from consumers' demand for the good or service produced with that input is called a derived demand.

⑤2 Supply and Demand in the Labor Market

In a competitive labor market, the demand for labor is determined by its marginal revenue product (*MRP*), which is the additional revenue that a firm obtains from one more unit of input. The marginal resource cost (*MRC*) is the amount that an extra input adds to the firm's total costs.

The downward-sloping demand curve for labor indicates a negative relationship between wage and the quantity of labor demanded. Marginal revenue product is equal to marginal product (*MP*) multiplied by marginal revenue.

Profits are maximized if the firm hires only to the point at which the wage equals the expected marginal revenue product.

In the market supply curve, a positive relationship exists between the wage rate and the quantity of labor supplied.

⑤3 Labor Market Equilibrium

The equilibrium wage and quantity in competitive markets for labor is determined by the intersection of labor demand and labor supply. The demand curve for labor can be shifted by increases in labor productivity and changes in the output price of the good. The labor supply curve can be shifted by immigration and population growth, worker preferences, nonwage income, and amenities.

⑤4 Labor Unions

Labor unions were formed to increase their members' wages and to improve working conditions. The union negotiates with firms through a process called collective bargaining. Labor unions influence the quantity of union labor hired and the wages, primarily through their ability to alter the supply of labor services.

Key Terms

derived demand the demand for an input derived from consumers' demand for the good or service produced with that input

marginal revenue product (*MRP*) marginal product times the price of the output

marginal resource cost (*MRC*) the amount that an extra input adds to the firm's total cost

marginal product (*MP*) the change in total output of a good that results from a one-unit change in input

collective bargaining negotiations between representatives of employers and unions

in-kind transfers transfers in the form of goods and services instead of money, including food stamps, school lunch programs, housing subsidies, and Medicaid, among others

poverty rate the percentage of the population who fall below the poverty line

poverty line a set of money income thresholds, established by the federal government, that vary by family size and are used to detect who is poor; if a family's total income is less than the established family threshold, then that family, and every individual in it, is considered poor

progressive tax system tax system that imposes higher marginal tax rates on higher incomes; the federal income tax is designed to be a progressive tax system

cash transfers direct cash payments such as welfare, Social Security, and unemployment compensation

Supplemental Security Income (SSI) a welfare program designed for the most needy, elderly, disabled, and blind

Temporary Assistance for Needy Families (TANF) a welfare program designed to help families that have few financial resources

Earned Income Tax Credit (EITC) a welfare program that allows the working poor to receive income refunds that can be greater than the taxes they paid during the last year

Section Summaries—Continued

5 Income Distribution

In many economies, some individuals will have high income and others will have low income. Factors such as age, demographic factors, institutional factors, and governmental redistribution activities influence income distribution data. Studies indicate that income mobility is significant in the United States—there will always be high- and low-income earners, but the people in those segments are likely to change. Reasons for income differences include age, skill, human capital, and preferences toward risk and leisure. While income inequality within nations is substantial, it is far less than income inequality among nations.

6 Poverty

The federal government measures poverty by using a set of money income thresholds that vary by family size. The poverty rate is the percentage of the population that falls below income threshold set by the government, called the poverty line.

A variety of programs are designed to reduce poverty and redistribute income. These include taxes, transfer payments, welfare programs, and government subsidies.

© STEPHEN STRATHDEE/ISTOCKPHOTO.COM / © ANTON ZHUKOV/ISTOCKPHOTO.COM

means-tested income transfer program program in which eligibility is dependent on low income; food stamps, Medicaid, and housing subsidies are examples of means-tested income transfer programs

FOR MORE REVIEW TOOLS VISIT www.cengagebrain.com.

Online Study Tools

At *www.cengagebrain.com,* you can

- ❑ Download printable Key Term Flash Cards
- ❑ Study online with interactive Key Term Flash Cards
- ❑ Complete Practice Quizzes with instant feedback
- ❑ Play "Beat the Clock" to master concepts
- ❑ Complete the Crossword Puzzle to review key terms
- ❑ Watch the ABC News videos "A Shortage of Nurses," "Beauty and Wages," and "Subsidizing Profitable Farmers"
- ❑ Watch the Ask the Instructor videos "How would a zero-radius lawn mower affect your productivity?,"

"What's the best thing workers can do to increase their value?," "Why do language teachers earn less?," and "Should you have gone to college?"

- ❑ Download and review Exhibit Worksheets
- ❑ Access Economic Applications "Labor Markets" and "Income Distribution and Poverty"
- ❑ Access Graphing Workshops "Demand for Labor," "Union Effects on Wages," and "The Effects of a Wage Differential"
- ❑ Check your answers to the Chapter 10 Self-Review on page 210

Section Summaries

1 Macroeconomic Goals

Nearly every society has three major macroeconomic goals: (1) maintaining employment of human resources at relatively high levels, (2) maintaining prices at a relatively stable level, and (3) achieving a high rate of economic growth. We use the term *real gross domestic product* (RGDP) to measure output or production.

S2 Employment and Unemployment

Relatively high rates of unemployment are viewed almost universally as undesirable. To calculate the unemployment rate, divide the number of unemployed by the number in the civilian labor force. In periods of prolonged recession, some individuals think that the chances of landing a job are so bleak that they quit looking. These people are called discouraged workers.

Education, age, sex, and race can be factors in unemployment. Categories of unemployed workers include job losers, job leavers, reentrants, and new entrants. The duration of unemployment tends to be greater when the amount of unemployment is high and smaller when the amount of unemployment is low. The percentage of the working age (16 years and older) population that is in the labor force is what economists call the labor force participation rate.

S3 Types of Unemployment

The three types of unemployment are frictional, structural, and cyclical unemployment. Frictional and structural unemployment are unavoidable in a vibrant economy, resulting from imperfections in the labor market. In years of relatively high unemployment, some joblessness may result from short-term cyclical fluctuations in the economy. Most attempts to solve the cyclical unemployment problem emphasized increasing aggregate demand to counter recession. Many economists consider the natural rate of unemployment to be around 5 percent.

S4 Reasons for Unemployment

Economists cite three reasons for the failure of wages to balance the labor demand and labor supply equilibrium—minimum wages, unions, and the efficiency wage theory. Because minimum wage earners are a small portion of the labor force, most economists believe the effect of minimum wage on unemployment is small. If union officials are able to increase wages, then unemployment will rise in the union sector. Some economists follow the efficiency wage model, which is based on the belief that higher wages lead to greater productivity.

Although the unemployment insurance is intended to ease the pain of unemployment, it also leads to prolonged periods of unemployment. The widespread belief that technological advances inevitably result in the displacement of workers is not necessarily true.

S5 Inflation

The continuing rise in the overall price level is called inflation. When the overall price level is falling, it is called deflation. The higher the inflation rate, the greater the rate

Key Terms

real gross domestic product (RGDP) the total value of all final goods and services produced in a given period, such as a year or a quarter, adjusted for inflation

Employment Act of 1946 a commitment by the federal government to hold itself accountable for short-run economic fluctuations

unemployment rate the percentage of the population aged 16 and older who are willing and able to work but are unable to obtain a job

labor force the number of people aged 16 and older who are available for employment

discouraged worker an individual who has left the labor force because he or she could not find a job

job loser an individual who has been temporarily laid off or fired

job leaver a person who quits his or her job

reentrant an individual who worked before and is now reentering the labor force

new entrant an individual who has not held a job before but is now seeking employment

underemployment a situation in which a worker's skill level is higher than necessary for a job

labor force participation rate the percentage of the working age population in the labor force

frictional unemployment the unemployment that results from workers searching for suitable jobs and firms looking for suitable workers

structural unemployment the unemployment that results from workers not having the skills to obtain long-term employment

cyclical unemployment unemployment due to short-term cyclical fluctuations in the economy

natural rate of unemployment the median, or "typical," unemployment rate, equal to the sum of frictional and structural unemployment when they are at a maximum

Section Summaries—Continued

of decline in purchasing power. A price index attempts to provide a measure of the prices paid for a certain bundle of goods and services over time. The most well-known index is probably the consumer price index (CPI). We can calculate a price index by dividing the cost of the market basket in the current year by the cost in the base year and multiplying by 100. Unanticipated and sharp changes in the price level are almost universally considered to be "bad" and to require a policy remedy.

 **6 Economic Fluctuations**

We sometimes call the short-term fluctuations in economic activity business cycles. The period of expansion is when output (real GDP) is rising significantly. The contraction, also called a recession, is a period of falling real output and is usually accompanied by rising unemployment and declining business and consumer confidence. Some fluctuation in economic activity reflects seasonal patterns. Businesses, government agencies, and consumers rely on economic forecasts to learn of forthcoming developments in the business cycle.

potential output the amount of real output the economy would produce if its labor and other resources were fully employed, that is, at the natural rate of unemployment

minimum wage rate an hourly wage floor set above the equilibrium wage

efficiency wage model a theory stating that higher wages lead to greater productivity

price level the average level of prices in the economy

inflation a rise in the overall price level, which decreases the purchasing power of money

deflation a decrease in the overall price level, which increases the purchasing power of money

relative price the price of a specific good compared to the price of other goods

price index a measure of the trend in prices paid for a certain bundle of goods and services over a given period

consumer price index (CPI) a measure of the cost of a market basket that represents the consumption of a typical household

GDP deflator a price index that helps measure the average price level of all final consumer goods and services produced

hyperinflation extremely high rates of inflation for sustained periods of time

menu costs the costs imposed on a firm from changing listed prices

shoe-leather cost the cost incurred when individuals reduce their money holdings because of inflation

wage and price controls legislation used to combat inflation by limiting changes in wages and prices

business cycles short-term fluctuations in the economy relative to the long-term trend in output

expansion when output (real GDP) is rising significantly—the period between the trough of a recession and the next peak

peak the point in time when expansion comes to an end, that is, when output is at the highest point in the cycle

contraction when the economy is slowing down—measured from the peak to the trough

trough the point in time when output stops declining, that is, when business activity is at its lowest point in the cycle

recession a period of significant decline in output and employment

depression severe recession or contraction in output

boom period of prolonged economic expansion

leading economic indicators factors that economists at the Commerce Department have found typically change before changes in economic activity occur

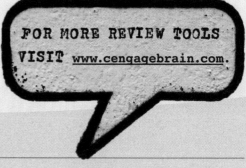

FOR MORE REVIEW TOOLS
VISIT www.cengagebrain.com.

Online Study Tools

At *www.cengagebrain.com*, you can

- ☐ Download printable Key Term Flash Cards

- ☐ Study online with interactive Key Term Flash Cards

- ☐ Complete Practice Quizzes with instant feedback

- ☐ Play "Beat the Clock" to master concepts

- ☐ Complete the Crossword Puzzle to review key terms

- ☐ Watch the ABC News videos "Looking for Work" and "Is There a Natural Rate of Unemployment?"

- ☐ Watch the Ask the Instructor videos "What is macroeconomics?," "What are the four types of

unemployment?," "Why was unemployment higher in the 1970s than in the 1990s?," and "Was there a recession in 1974?"

- ☐ Download and review Exhibit Worksheets

- ☐ Access Economic Applications "Employment, Unemployment, and Inflation;" "Output, Income, and the Price Level;" and "Recession"

- ☐ Check your answers to the Chapter 11 Self-Review on page 235

Section Summaries

ⓢ1 Economic Growth

Economic growth is usually measured by the annual percentage change in real output of goods and services per capita (real GDP per capita). The Rule of 70 shows how long it will take a nation to double its output at various growth rates. Growth rates vary widely across different countries. Productivity is the amount of good and services a worker can produce per hour. Sustained economic growth occurs when workers' productivity rises.

ⓢ2 Determinants of Long-Run Economic Growth

Labor productivity is the output per unit of worker. The four major factors that contribute to productivity growth include (1) physical capital, (2) human capital, (3) natural resources, and (4) technology. New Growth Theory argues that economic growth can continue unimpeded, as long as we keep coming up with new ideas.

ⓢ3 Public Policy and Economic Growth

One of the most important determinants of economic growth

© ROBYN MACKENZIE/ISTOCKPHOTO.COM

is the saving rate. To consume more in the future, we must save more now. Infrastructure is also critical to economic coordination and activity. Research and development consists of the activities undertaken to create new products and processes that will lead to technological progress. Economic growth rates tend to be higher in countries where the government enforces property rights. Allowing free trade can also lead to greater output because of the principle of comparative advantage. Education, investment in human capital, may be just as important as improvements in physical capital.

ⓢ4 Measuring Economic Growth and Its Components

Gross domestic product (GDP) is defined as the value of all final goods and services produced within a country during a given period. GDP also measures the value of total income, since every dollar of spending ends up being a dollar of income for a seller. We can use the circular flow model to show the flow of money in the economy.

ⓢ5 Measuring Total Production

With the expenditure approach, GDP is calculated by adding how much market participants spend on final goods and services over a specific period of time. Economists usually group spending into four categories: consumption (C), investment (I), government purchases (G), and net exports ($X - M$).

The Bureau of Economic Analysis (BEA) also

Key Terms

economic growth an upward trend in the real per capita output of goods and services

productivity the amount of goods and services a worker can produce per hour

labor productivity output per unit of worker

innovation applications of new knowledge that create new products or improve existing products

research and development (R&D) activities undertaken to create new products and processes that will lead to technological progress

gross domestic product (GDP) the measure of economic performance based on the value of all final goods and services produced within a country during a given period

double counting adding the value of a good or service twice by mistakenly counting the intermediate goods and services in GDP

expenditure approach calculation of GDP by adding the expenditures by market participants on final goods and services over a given period

consumption purchases of final goods and services

investment the creation of capital goods to augment future production

factor payments wages (salaries), rent, interest payments, and profits paid to the owners of productive resources

gross national product (GNP) the difference between net income of foreigners and GDP

depreciation annual allowance set aside to replace worn-out capital

net national product (NNP) GNP minus depreciation

indirect business taxes taxes, such as sales tax, levied on goods and services sold

national income (NI) a measure of income earned by owners of the factors of production

personal income (PI) the amount of income received by households before personal taxes

disposable personal income the personal income available after personal taxes

real gross domestic product per capita real output of goods and services per person

Section Summaries—Continued

computes five additional measures of production and income: gross national product, net national product, national income, personal income, and disposable personal income.

⑤6 Problems in Calculating an Accurate GDP

The primary problem in calculating accurate GDP statistics is changes in the overall price level for goods and services over time. To compare GDP values over time, the calculations must use a common, or standardized, unit of measure, which only money can provide.

Real GDP is equal to the nominal GDP divided by the price-level index times 100. To calculate real GDP per capita, we divide the real GDP by the total population to get the value of real output of final goods and services per person.

⑤7 Problems with GDP as a Measure of Economic Welfare

The accuracy of real GDP as a measure of economic welfare fails to account for certain factors, including nonmarket transactions, the underground economy, leisure, externalities, and the quality of the goods purchased.

FOR MORE REVIEW TOOLS
VISIT www.cengagebrain.com.

Online Study Tools

At *www.cengagebrain.com,* you can

- ❑ Download printable Key Term Flash Cards
- ❑ Study online with interactive Key Term Flash Cards
- ❑ Complete Practice Quizzes with instant feedback
- ❑ Play "Beat the Clock" to master concepts
- ❑ Complete the Crossword Puzzle to review key terms
- ❑ Watch the ABC News video "GDP and Happiness"
- ❑ Watch the Ask the Instructor videos "How important is the rate of economic growth to you?," "What's

the 'rule of 72' and why is it so important?," "Have computers affected worker productivity?," and "What is included in the calculation of GDP?"

- ❑ Download and review Exhibit Worksheets
- ❑ Access Economic Application "Productivity and Growth" and "National Income Accounts"
- ❑ Access Graphing Workshop "The Circular Flow Model"
- ❑ Check your answers to the Chapter 12 Self-Review on page 259

Section Summaries

Ⓢ1 The Aggregate Demand Curve

The aggregate demand curve reflects the total amount of real goods and services that all groups together want to purchase in a given period. Three complementary explanations exist for the negative slope of the aggregate demand curve: the real wealth effect, the interest rate effect, and the open economy effect.

Ⓢ2 Shifts in the Aggregate Demand Curve

Each of the three factors—real wealth, interest rate, and open economy effects—generates a movement along the aggregate demand curve, in reaction to changes in the general price level. Anything that changes the amount of total spending in the economy (holding price levels constant) will affect the aggregate demand curve. An increase in any component of GDP (C, I, G, or $X - M$) will cause the aggregate demand curve to shift rightward. Conversely, decreases in C, I, G, or $X - M$ will shift aggregate demand leftward.

Ⓢ3 The Aggregate Supply Curve

The aggregate supply (AS) curve is the relationship between the total quantity of final goods and services that suppliers are *willing* and *able* to produce and the overall price level. In the short run, the aggregate supply curve is upward sloping. Two possible explanations for this are the profit effect and the misperception effect. The long-run aggregate supply curve is vertical, reflecting the fact that the level of RGDP producers are willing to supply is not affected by changes in the price level.

Ⓢ4 Shifts in the Aggregate Supply Curve

Any change in the quantity of any factor of production available—capital, land, labor, or technology—can cause a shift in both the long-run and short-run aggregate supply curves. Some important factors that only shift the short-run aggregate supply curve are wages and other input prices, productivity, and unexpected supply shocks.

Ⓢ5 Macroeconomic Equilibrium

The short-run equilibrium level of real output and the price level are given by the intersection of the aggregate demand curve and the short-run aggregate supply curve. Equilibrium can occur at less than the potential

Key Terms

aggregate demand curve graph that shows the inverse relationship between the price level and RGDP demanded

aggregate supply (*AS*) curve the total quantity of final goods and services suppliers are willing and able to supply at a given price level

short-run aggregate supply (*SRAS*) curve the graphical relationship between RGDP and the price level when output prices can change but input prices are unable to adjust

long-run aggregate supply (*LRAS*) curve the graphical relationship between RGDP and the price level when output prices and input prices can fully adjust to economic changes

supply shocks unexpected temporary events that can either increase or decrease aggregate supply

recessionary gap the output gap that occurs when the actual output is less than the potential output

inflationary gap the output gap that occurs when the actual output is greater than the potential output

demand-pull inflation a price-level increase due to an increase in aggregate demand

stagflation a situation in which lower growth and higher prices occur together

cost-push inflation a price-level increase due to a negative supply shock or increases in input prices

wage and price inflexibility the tendency for prices and wages to only adjust slowly downward to changes in the economy

Today's Special — higher menu costs

© SCOTT STANLEY/ISTOCKPHOTO.COM

Section Summaries—Continued

output of the economy (a recessionary gap), beyond the potential output (an inflationary gap), or at potential GDP.

Demand-pull inflation occurs when the price level rises as a result of an increase in aggregate demand. If the aggregate demand curve did not increase significantly but the price level did, then the inflation was caused by supply-side forces, which is called cost-push inflation. A decrease in aggregate demand can also cause a recessionary gap. Eventual recoveries from a recessionary gap occur because of increases in aggregate demand. Downward wage and price inflexibility may prolong the duration of a recessionary gap. During an inflationary gap, suppliers will continue to seek higher prices for their inputs until they reach the long-run equilibrium.

⑤6 The Classical and the Keynesian Macroeconomic Models

The classical school of thought believed that wages and prices adjust quickly to changes in supply and demand. According to Say's law, "supply creates its own demand." The classical school focused on the economy at full employment; prolonged unemployment is impossible according to the long-run classical model.

According to Keynes, the problem with the classical model is that not all income generated from output need be used to buy goods and services; it can also be saved, hoarded, or taxed away. Supply does not automatically create an adequate demand. Keynes argued that wages and price are inflexible downward. Most macroeconomists now believe that wages and prices do tend to be less flexible when excess capacity is available.

© GRADTS/ISTOCKPHOTO.COM / © CHAPEL HOUSE PHOTOGRAPHY

FOR MORE REVIEW TOOLS VISIT www.cengagebrain.com.

Online Study Tools

At *www.cengagebrain.com,* you can

- ❑ Download printable Key Term Flash Cards
- ❑ Study online with interactive Key Term Flash Cards
- ❑ Complete Practice Quizzes with instant feedback
- ❑ Play "Beat the Clock" to master concepts
- ❑ Complete the Crossword Puzzle to review key terms
- ❑ Watch the ABC News video "Fears of Recession"
- ❑ Watch the Ask the Instructor videos "Do economists and the general public attach different meanings to the term investment?," "Can the aggregate supply

curve take on different shapes?," What circumstances can shift the aggregate supply curve?," and "Is one type of inflation worse than another?"

- ❑ Download and review Exhibit Worksheets
- ❑ Access Economic Application "Aggregate Demand/ Aggregate Supply"
- ❑ Access Graphing Workshops "Aggregate Demand," "Changes in Aggregate Demand," "Aggregate Supply," and "Types of Inflation"
- ❑ Check your answers to the Chapter 13 Self-Review on page 280

Section Summaries

Fiscal Policy

Fiscal policy is the use of government purchases, taxes, and transfer payments to alter RGDP and the price level. Sometimes it is necessary for the government to use fiscal policy to stimulate the economy during a contraction (or recession) or to try to curb an expansion in order to bring inflation under control.

Government spending that exceeds tax revenues causes a budget deficit. When tax revenues are greater than government spending, a budget surplus exists. Expansionary fiscal policy is associated with increased government budget deficits. Contractionary fiscal policy will tend to create or expand a budget surplus or reduce an existing budget deficit.

⑤2 Government Spending and Taxation

A large majority of government activity is financed by taxation. Fifty percent of tax revenues come in the form of income taxes. Progressive taxes are designed so that those with higher incomes pay a greater proportion of their income in taxes. With a regressive or payroll tax, a person's tax as a proportion of income falls as the person's income rises. An excise tax is a sales tax on individual products such as alcohol, tobacco, and gasoline. A flat tax is designed so that everybody would pay the same percentage of their income.

The ability to pay principle is simply that those with the greatest ability to pay taxes should pay more than those with the least ability to pay taxes. The benefits received principle means that the individuals receiving the benefits are those who pay for them.

⑤3 Fiscal Policy and the AD/AS Model

Increased government purchases, tax cuts, and/or increases in transfer payments, *ceteris paribus*, can shift the aggregate demand curve to the right. This would increase the price level. If this stimulus is of the right timing and magnitude, it can stimulate the economy and close the recessionary gap.

If the government decides to reduce its purchases, increase taxes, or reduce transfer payments, the aggregate demand curve will shift leftward. This will lower the price level and close the inflationary gap.

⑤4 The Multiplier Effect

When an increase in purchases of goods or services occurs, the ultimate increase in total purchases tends to be greater than the initial increase. This is known as the multiplier effect. The marginal propensity to consume (MPC) is the fraction of additional disposable (after-tax) income that a household consumes rather than saves. The marginal propensity to save (MPS) is the proportion of an addition to your income that you would save. The larger the MPC, the larger the multiplier effect.

⑤5 Supply-Side Effects of Tax Cuts

Supply-sider economists believe that if the government reduced individual and business taxes, deregulated,

Key Terms

fiscal policy use of government purchases, taxes, and transfer payments to alter equilibrium output and prices

budget deficit occurs when government spending exceeds tax revenues for a given fiscal year

budget surplus occurs when tax revenues are greater than government expenditures for a given fiscal year

expansionary fiscal policy use of fiscal policy tools to foster increased output by increasing government purchases, lowering taxes, and/or increasing transfer payments

contractionary fiscal policy use of fiscal policy tools to reduce output by decreasing government purchases, increasing taxes, and/or reducing transfer payments

progressive tax a tax designed so that those with higher incomes pay a greater proportion of their income in taxes

regressive tax as a person's income rises, the amount his or her tax as a proportion of income falls

excise tax a sales tax on individual products such as alcohol, tobacco, and gasoline

flat tax a tax that charges all income earners the same percentage of their income

ability to pay principle belief that those with the greatest ability to pay taxes should pay more than those with less ability to pay

vertical equity different treatment based on level of income and the ability to pay principle

benefits received principle the belief that those receiving the benefits from taxes are those who should pay for them

multiplier effect a chain reaction of additional income and purchases that results in total purchases that are greater than the initial increase in purchases

marginal propensity to consume (MPC) the additional consumption resulting from an additional dollar of disposable income

marginal propensity to save (MPS) the change in savings divided by the change in disposable income

automatic stabilizers changes in government transfer payments or tax collections that automatically help counter business cycle fluctuations

Section Summaries—Continued

and increased spending on research and development, these policies could generate greater long-term economic growth by stimulating personal income, savings, and capital formation.

Ⓢ6 Automatic Stabilizers

Changes in government transfer payments or tax collections that automatically tend to counter business cycle fluctuations are called automatic stabilizers. The most important automatic stabilizer is the tax system. Personal income taxes vary directly in amount with respect to income. Incomes, earnings, and profits all fall during a recession so the government collects less in taxes. When you work less, you are paid less and therefore pay less in taxes—an automatic tax cut. Automatic stabilizers are not strong enough to completely offset a serious recession, but they can reduce the severity.

Ⓢ7 The National Debt

One method the government can use to finance a budget deficit is to print money; however, this method is highly inflationary. Typically, the budget deficit is financed by issuing debt. Budget deficits can provide the federal government with the flexibility to respond appropriately to changing economic circumstances.

In the short run, deficit reduction is the same as running contractionary fiscal policy. In the long run, lowering the budget deficit, or running a larger budget surplus, leads to a lower real interest rate, which increases private investment and stimulates higher growth in capital formation and economic growth.

The real issue of importance regarding budget deficits is whether the government's activities have benefits that are greater than their costs.

© DWIGHT SMITH/SHUTTERSTOCK

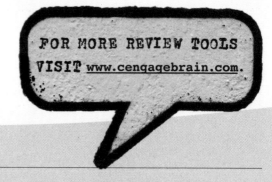
FOR MORE REVIEW TOOLS VISIT www.cengagebrain.com.

Online Study Tools

At *www.cengagebrain.com,* you can

- ❑ Download printable Key Term Flash Cards
- ❑ Study online with interactive Key Term Flash Cards
- ❑ Complete Practice Quizzes with instant feedback
- ❑ Play "Beat the Clock" to master concepts
- ❑ Complete the Crossword Puzzle to review key terms
- ❑ Watch the ABC News videos "Obama's New Deal," "When Should Taxes Be Raised?," and "National Debt"
- ❑ Watch the Ask the Instructor videos "What is fiscal policy all about?," "Should we amend the Constitution to require a balanced budget?,"

"What is 'crowding-out' and is it important?," and "What do economists mean by the term 'multiplier'?"

- ❑ Download and review Exhibit Worksheets
- ❑ Access Economic Applications "Fiscal Policy" and "Taxes, Spending, and Deficits"
- ❑ Access Graphing Workshops "Discretionary Policy and a Contractionary Gap," "Closing a Contractionary Gap," and "Responses to an Expansionary Gap"
- ❑ Check your answers to the Chapter 14 Self-Review on page 305

Section Summaries

 What Is Money?

Money is anything that is generally accepted in exchange for goods and services. Money has four important functions in the economy: as a medium of exchange, a unit of account, a store of value, and a means of deferred payment.

 Measuring Money

Currency consists of coins and/ or paper that some institution or government has created to be used in the trading of goods and services and the payment of debts. In the United States and most other nations of the world, metallic coins and paper currency are the only forms of legal tender. Legal tender is fiat money—a means of exchange that has been established by government fiat, or declaration.

Today, most money we use is not officially legal tender, but balances in checking accounts in banks, more formally called demand deposits. Transaction deposits can be easily converted into currency or used to buy goods and services directly. Other forms of payments and assets include credit cards, nontransaction deposits, money market mutual funds, stocks, and bonds. Liquidity refers to the ease with which one asset can be converted into another asset or goods and services.

M1 is the narrow definition of money, which includes currency, checkable deposits, and traveler's checks. M2, the broader definition of money, includes M1 plus savings deposits, time deposits (except for some large-denomination certificates of deposit), and noninstitutional money market mutual fund shares.

Until 1933, the currency of the United States operated on an internal gold standard. Today no precious metal is used to back or establish the value of our money.

 How Banks Create Money

Financial intermediaries serve many functions, the most important of which are creating loans and serving as depositories for savings and liquid assets that are used by individuals and firms for transaction purposes. When a bank lends to a person, it usually gives the borrower the funds by issuing a check or by adding funds to an existing checking account. Banks create money when they increase demand deposits through the process of creating loans. Because demand deposits are money, the issuers of new loans have created money.

 The Money Multiplier

New loans create new money directly, but they also create excess reserves in other banks, which leads to still further increases in both loans and the money supply. The money multiplier, calculated by dividing 1 by the reserve requirement, measures the potential amount of money that the banking system generates with each dollar of reserves. Potential money creation is equal to initial deposits times the money multiplier. This money creation is only potential because some banks might hold on to some of their excess reserves or some borrowers might not immediately spend all of their newly acquired deposits.

Key Terms

money anything generally accepted in exchange for goods or services

medium of exchange the primary function of money, which is to facilitate transactions and lower transaction costs

barter direct exchange of goods and services without the use of money

means of deferred payment the attribute of money that makes it easier to borrow and to repay loans

currency coins and/or paper created to facilitate the trade of goods and services and the payment of debts

legal tender coins and paper officially declared to be acceptable for the settlement of financial debts

fiat money a means of exchange established by government declaration

demand deposits balances in bank accounts that depositors can access on demand

transaction deposits deposits that can be easily converted to currency or used to buy goods and services directly

traveler's checks transaction instruments easily converted into currency

nontransaction deposits funds that cannot be used for payment directly but must be converted into currency for general use

near money nontransaction deposits that are not money but can be quickly converted into money

money market mutual funds interest-earning accounts provided by brokers who pool funds into such investments as Treasury bills

liquidity the ease with which one asset can be converted into another asset or into goods and services

M1 the narrowest definition of money; includes currency, checkable deposits, and traveler's checks

M2 a broader definition of money that includes M1 plus savings deposits, time deposits, and noninstitutional money market mutual fund shares

gold standard defining the dollar as equivalent to a set value of a quantity of gold, allowing direct convertibility from currency to gold

Section Summaries—Continued

Ⓢ5 The Collapse of America's Banking System, 1920–1933

In 1920, 30,000 banks were operating in the United States; by 1933, the number declined to about 15,000. By early 1933 the decline in depositor confidence had reached the point that the entire banking system was in jeopardy. President Roosevelt declared a two-week bank holiday, allowing only the healthy banks to reopen. The passing of federal deposit insurance also helped improve depositor confidence.

There were four major reasons for the collapse. First, the U.S. had lots of small banks, which were vulnerable to bank runs. Second, government aid was weak and too late. Third, deposit insurance did not exist. And fourth, the broader economic downturn further eroded depositor confidence.

The combination of the Federal Deposit Insurance Corporation (FDIC) and the government's greater willingness to assist distressed banks has reduced the number of bank failures in recent times.

Gresham's Law the principle that "cheap money drives out dear money"; given an alternative, people prefer to spend less valuable money

commercial banks financial institutions organized to handle everyday financial transactions of businesses and households through demand deposit accounts and savings accounts and by making short-term commercial and consumer loans

reserve requirements holdings of assets at the bank or at the Federal Reserve Bank as mandated by the Fed

fractional reserve system a system that requires banks to hold reserves equal to some fraction of their checkable deposits

secondary reserves highly liquid, interest-paying assets held by the bank

balance sheet a financial record that indicates the balance between a bank's assets and its liabilities plus capital

required reserve ratio the percentage of deposits that a bank must hold at the Federal Reserve Bank or in bank vaults

excess reserves reserve levels held above that required by the Fed

money multiplier measures the potential amount of money that the banking system generates with each dollar of reserves

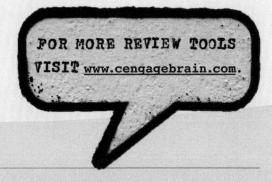

FOR MORE REVIEW TOOLS VISIT www.cengagebrain.com.

Online Study Tools

At *www.cengagebrain.com,* you can

- ❑ Download printable Key Term Flash Cards
- ❑ Study online with interactive Key Term Flash Cards
- ❑ Complete Practice Quizzes with instant feedback
- ❑ Play "Beat the Clock" to master concepts
- ❑ Complete the Crossword Puzzle to review key terms
- ❑ Watch the ABC News videos "Printing Your Own Money" and "Ithaca Hours"

- ❑ Watch the Ask the Instructor videos "What has been money in the past and what is money today?," "What are the principle functions of money?," and "How are banks different from other businesses?"
- ❑ Download and review Exhibit Worksheets
- ❑ Access Economic Application "Money and the Financial System"
- ❑ Check your answers to the Chapter 15 Self-Review on page 325

Section Summaries

Ⓢ1 The Federal Reserve System

A central bank performs many functions. First, the central bank is a "banker's bank." Second, the central bank performs a service function for commercial banks. Third, the central bank serves as the primary bank for the central government. Fourth, the central bank buys and sells foreign currencies and assists in financial transactions with other countries. Fifth, the central bank serves as the "lender of last resort." And sixth, the central bank monitors the stability of the banking system and the money supply.

In the United States, the central bank is composed of 12 banks, closely tied together and collectively called the Federal Reserve System. The Federal Reserve Board of Governors, which controls major policy decisions, is appointed by the president of the United States. Historically, the Fed has enjoyed a considerable amount of independence from both the executive and legislative branches of government.

Ⓢ2 How Does the Federal Reserve Change the Money Supply?

The Fed uses three major methods to control the supply of money: open market operations, changing reserve requirements, and/or changing the discount rate. Open market operations, the Fed's most important tool, involve the purchase and sale of government bonds. If the Fed wants to reduce the money supply or reduce the rate of growth in the money supply, it will sell bonds, raise reserve requirements, and/or raise the discount rate. If the Fed wants to increase the money supply, it will buy bonds, lower reserve requirements, and/or lower the discount rate.

Ⓢ3 Money, Interest Rates, and Aggregate Demand

The money market is the market in which money demand and money supply determine the equilibrium *nominal* interest rate. When the Fed acts to change the money supply by changing one of its policy variables, it alters the money market equilibrium.

Why do people hold money instead of other financial assets? Transaction purposes, precautionary reasons, and asset purposes are three of the major determinants of the demand for money.

The quantity of money demanded varies inversely with the nominal interest rate. The money supply is almost perfectly inelastic with respect to interest rates over their plausible range, as controlled by Federal Reserve policies. When the Fed changes policy to increase the money supply, the interest rate falls in the short run. At lower interest rates, households and businesses invest more and buy more goods and services, shifting

Key Terms

open market operations purchase and sale of government securities by the Federal Reserve System

discount rate interest rate that the Fed charges commercial banks for the loans it extends to them

federal funds market market in which banks provide short-term loans to other banks that need cash to meet reserve requirements

money market market in which money demand and money supply determine the equilibrium interest rate

velocity of money a measure of how frequently money is turned over

quantity theory of money and prices a theory of the connection between the money supply and the price level when the velocity of money is constant

Section Summaries—Continued

the aggregate demand curve to the right. The Fed cannot target both the money supply and interest rates at the same time.

(S)4 Expansionary and Contractionary Monetary Policy

When the Fed engages in expansionary monetary policy, it increases the money supply, interest rates fall, and the aggregate demand curve shifts to the right.

The Fed may engage in contractionary monetary policy if the economy faces an inflationary gap. When the Fed decreases the money supply, it increases the interest rate, and the aggregate demand curve shifts to the left.

(S)5 Money and Inflation

There is a positive relationship between the money supply, the price level, the growth in the money supply, and the inflation rate. The equation of exchange, $M \times V = P \times Q$, explains the relationship between money and the price level, where M is the money supply, P is the price level, Q is RGDP, and V is the velocity of money. The velocity of money refers to its "turnover" rate, or the intensity

with which money is used. The faster money circulates, the higher the velocity. The quantity theory of money explains the connection between the money supply and the price level when the velocity of money is constant.

© DIGITAL VISION/GETTY IMAGES

FOR MORE REVIEW TOOLS VISIT www.cengagebrain.com.

Online Study Tools

At *www.cengagebrain.com*, you can

- ❑ Download printable Key Term Flash Cards
- ❑ Study online with interactive Key Term Flash Cards
- ❑ Complete Practice Quizzes with instant feedback
- ❑ Play "Beat the Clock" to master concepts
- ❑ Complete the Crossword Puzzle to review key terms
- ❑ Watch the ABC News video "Financial Savior: September 11th Hero"

- ❑ Watch the Ask the Instructor videos "How does the Fed influence interest rates?" and "Why should we care how fast the money supply grows?"
- ❑ Download and review Exhibit Worksheets
- ❑ Access Economic Application "Monetary Policy"
- ❑ Access Graphing Workshops "The Money Market" and "Open Market Operations"
- ❑ Check your answers to the Chapter 16 Self-Review on page 346

Section Summaries

Ⓢ1 Problems in Implementing Fiscal and Monetary Policy

When implementing fiscal stimulus, the multiplier effect assumes all other things will remain equal; however, this may not always hold true. For example, when an increase in government purchases stimulates aggregate demand, it also drives up the interest rate. This in turn dampens private spending on goods and services, reducing the overall impact of the fiscal stimulus. This is known as the crowding-out effect.

Fiscal stimulus usually takes time before its effects are fully realized. Three types of time lags that occur are recognition lags, implementation lags, and impact lags.

The lag problem inherent in adopting fiscal policy changes is less acute for monetary policy because the decisions are not slowed by the budgetary process. The full effects of monetary policy changes on productivity, unemployment, and inflation, however, can take much longer. One limitation of monetary policy is that it ultimately must be carried out through the commercial banking system. Also, its ability to influence nonmember banks, international banks, and nonbank institutions is limited.

A further macroeconomic problem arises if the federal government's fiscal decision makers differ with the Fed's monetary decision makers on policy objectives or targets. The timing of fiscal policy and monetary policy is crucial.

Ⓢ2 Rational Expectations and Real Business Cycles

Rational expectations theory asserts that workers and consumers incorporate the likely consequences of government policy changes into their expectations by quickly adjusting wages and prices. Rational expectations economists believe that wages and prices are flexible and that government economic policies designed to alter aggregate demand to meet macroeconomic goals are of limited effectiveness. The only way that monetary or fiscal policy can change output in the rational expectations model is with a surprise—an unanticipated change. Critics of rational expectations theory suggest that households and firms may not be completely informed about the impact of monetary and fiscal policy.

The real business cycle theory also assumes that households and firms form their expectations rationally and wages and prices adjust quickly. However, they believe that positive and negative productivity shocks, such as new technology, resource price changes, government regulation, unusually bad weather, and international disturbances, are the cause of the business cycle. In the real business cycle theory, it is the potential output that fluctuates.

Ⓢ3 Controversies in Macroeconomic Policy

Many economists believe that in the short run, policy makers have the ability to alter aggregate demand. Other economists believe that aggregate demand stimulus cannot keep the rate of unemployment below the natural rate. Other economists, rational expectations theorists, believe that government economic policies designed to alter aggregate demand are not all that effective. The real business cycle

Key Terms

crowding-out effect theory that government borrowing drives up the interest rate, lowering consumption by households and investment spending by firms

theory of rational expectations belief that workers and consumers incorporate the likely consequences of government policy changes into their expectations by quickly adjusting wages and prices

real business cycle theory the belief that economic fluctuations are the result of external negative and positive productivity shocks to the economy

indexing use of payment contracts that automatically adjust for changes in inflation

Section Summaries—Continued

theorists believe that economic fluctuations are the result of external shocks to the economy. Most macroeconomists believe both that monetary and fiscal policy can shift the aggregate demand and that the intervention can be counterproductive. Other economists believe that the potency of expansionary fiscal policy will be diminished by the crowding-out effect.

Most economists believe that monetary policy should take the lead in stabilization policy and that the central bank should be independent and insulated from political pressure to avoid political business cycles. Some believe that the central bank should attempt to keep the inflation rate within a certain range for a specified period of time. One means of protecting parties against unanticipated price increases is to write contracts that automatically change the prices of goods or services whenever the overall price level changes, effectively rewriting agreements in terms of dollars of constant purchasing power. This method is known as indexing.

⑤4 The Financial Crisis of 2007–2009

One of the biggest factors in the financial crisis of 2007–2009 was debt, or excess leverage. After

the 2001 recession, the Fed pursued an expansionary monetary policy that pushed interest rates down to historically low levels, which persisted until 2004. This, accompanied by deregulation in the mortgage markets, resulted in low interest rates and aggressive borrowing that encouraged less qualified buyers to purchase houses. The Fed reversed its policy in 2005–2006, which pushed interest rates up. As homeowners found themselves caught between rising interest rates and falling housing prices, many mortgages began to default and homes went into foreclosure. Many of these mortgages were held by major investment banks, which began to lose a lot of money on these assets. Lehman Brothers eventually went bankrupt, and Bear Stearns and Merrill Lynch were bought out at fire-sale prices. As credit markets began to seize up, the Federal Reserve and other central banks around the world responded by pouring money into the ailing credit markets. The United States also enacted a stimulus package worth nearly $1 trillion.

© JAMIE FARRANT/ISTOCKPHOTO.COM

FOR MORE REVIEW TOOLS VISIT www.cengagebrain.com.

Online Study Tools

At *www.cengagebrain.com,* you can

- ☐ Download printable Key Term Flash Cards
- ☐ Study online with interactive Key Term Flash Cards
- ☐ Complete Practice Quizzes with instant feedback
- ☐ Play "Beat the Clock" to master concepts
- ☐ Complete the Crossword Puzzle to review key terms
- ☐ Watch the ABC News videos "Tumbling Home Values," "Lack of Confidence Leads to Collapse," and "Financial Meltdown on Wall Street"

- ☐ Watch the Ask the Instructor video "Can we count on monetary and fiscal policy to smooth out the business cycle?"
- ☐ Download and review Exhibit Worksheets
- ☐ Access Economic Application "Global Financial Crisis"
- ☐ Check your answers to the Chapter 17 Self-Review on page 369

Section Summaries

Ⓢ1 The Growth in World Trade

In a typical year, about 15 percent of the world's output is traded in international markets. In the last three decades, the sum of U.S. imports and exports has increased from 11 percent of GDP to roughly 30 percent.

Major U.S. trading partners include Canada, China, Japan, Mexico, Germany, and the United Kingdom.

Ⓢ2 Comparative Advantage and Gains from Trade

Both participants in an exchange of goods and services anticipate an improvement in their economic welfare. Persons, regions, or countries can gain by specializing in the production of the good in which they have a comparative advantage. What is important is comparative advantage, not absolute advantage.

The production possibilities curve illustrates how one partner in trade might have a comparative advantage in production of a good though they do not have an absolute advantage. To achieve any of the gains from comparative advantage and specialization, however, there must be trade. The greater the difference in opportunity cost between the two trading partners, the greater the benefits from specialization and exchange.

Ⓢ3 Supply and Demand in International Trade

Using the concepts of consumer and producer surplus, we can graphically show the net benefits of free trade.

With exports, domestic producers gain more than domestic consumers lose. With imports, domestic consumers gain more than domestic producers lose.

Ⓢ4 Tariffs, Import Quotas, and Subsidies

In this section, we discuss three mechanisms of trade protection: tariffs, import quotas, and subsidies. A tariff is a tax on imported goods. Tariffs lead to (1) a smaller total quantity sold, (2) a higher price for domestic consumers, (3) greater sales at higher prices for domestic producers, and (4) lower sales of foreign products.

Import quotas directly restrict imports, leading to reductions in trade and thus preventing nations from fully realizing their comparative advantage. Domestic producers are better off under quotas, but domestic consumers are worse off.

With a subsidy, revenue is given to producers for each exported unit of output, which stimulates exports. While usually defended as a means of

Key Terms

tariff a tax on imports

import quota a legal limit on the imported quantity of a good that is produced abroad and can be sold in domestic markets

rent seeking efforts by producers to gain profits from government protections such as tariffs and import quotas

balance of payments the record of international transactions in which a nation has engaged over a year

current account a record of a country's imports and exports of goods and services, net investment income, and net transfers

balance of trade the net surplus or deficit resulting from the level of exportation and importation of merchandise

capital account records the foreign purchases or assets in the domestic economy (a monetary inflow) and domestic purchases of assets abroad (a monetary outflow)

exchange rate the price of one unit of a country's currency in terms of another country's currency

derived demand the demand for an input derived from consumers' demand for the good or service produced with that input

dirty float system a description of the exchange rate system that means that fluctuations in currency values are partly determined by government intervention

© INSPIRESTOCK/GETTY IMAGES / © DIGITAL VISION/GETTY IMAGES

Section Summaries—Continued

increasing exports and improving a nation's international financial position, subsidies are usually of dubious worth to the world economy and even to the economy doing the subsidizing.

5 The Balance of Payments

The balance of payments is a statement that records all the exchanges requiring an outflow of funds to foreign nations or an inflow of funds from other nations. A current account is a record of a country's imports and exports of goods and services, net investment income, and net transfers. The import/export goods relationship is often called the balance of trade. The capital account records the foreign purchases or assets in the United States and U.S. purchases of assets abroad (a monetary outflow). Finally, the statistical discrepancy is included to account for any errors or omissions, and to make sure the balance of payments is balanced.

6 Exchange Rates

The price of a unit of one foreign currency in terms of another is called the exchange rate. Prices of goods in their currencies combine with exchange rates to determine the domestic price of foreign goods. The demand for foreign currencies is known as a derived demand. The equilibrium price (exchange rate) of a foreign currency is reached where the demand and supply curves of that currency intersect.

7 Equilibrium Changes in the Foreign Exchange Market

Any force that shifts either the demand for or supply of a currency will shift the equilibrium in the foreign exchange market, leading to a new exchange rate. Among such factors are changes in consumer tastes for goods, income levels, relative real interest rates, and relative inflation rates, as well as speculation.

8 Flexible Exchange Rates

Since 1973, the world has essentially operated on a system of flexible exchange rates. Flexible exchange rates mean that currency prices are allowed to fluctuate with changes in supply and demand, without governments stepping in to prevent those changes. The current exchange rate system is sometimes referred to as a dirty float system, meaning that fluctuations in currency values are partly determined by market forces and partly influenced by government intervention.

Since the advent of flexible exchange rates, world trade has not only continued but expanded. The most important advantage of the flexible-rate system is that the recurrent crises that led to speculative rampages and major currency revaluations under the fixed Bretton Woods system have significantly diminished. Furthermore, fixed exchange rates can result in currency shortages.

The major objection to flexible rates has been that they introduce considerable uncertainty into international trade, reducing trade volume and therefore potential gains from international specialization. Second, flexible exchange rates can contribute to inflationary pressures.

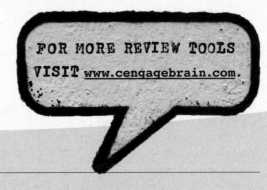

FOR MORE REVIEW TOOLS VISIT www.cengagebrain.com.

Online Study Tools

At *www.cengagebrain.com*, you can

- ❑ Download printable Key Term Flash Cards

- ❑ Study online with interactive Key Term Flash Cards

- ❑ Complete Practice Quizzes with instant feedback

- ❑ Play "Beat the Clock" to master concepts

- ❑ Complete the Crossword Puzzle to review key terms

- ❑ Watch the ABC News videos "Competition for Foreign Factories," "The Effects of Protectionism on the Candy Industry," "The Trade Deficit Hits Main Street," and "A Weak Dollar"

- ❑ Watch the Ask the Instructor videos "What are the arguments for trade restrictions?," "How is our economy related to the rest of the world?," "What causes the demand for foreign exchange to change?," and "Is a 'strong dollar' a good thing?"

- ❑ Download and review Exhibit Worksheets

- ❑ Access Economic Applications "International Trade" and "International Finance"

- ❑ Access Graphing Workshops "Foreign Exchange Market (euros)" and "Foreign Exchange Market (yen)"

- ❑ Check your answers to the Chapter 18 Self-Review on page 399